THE MIRROURE OF THE WORLDE

The allegories of the virtues and vices were common teaching tools in the Middle Ages for both religious and lay audiences to learn the basic tenets of the Christian faith. *The Mirroure of the Worlde* makes available for the first time the unique text in the fifteenthcentury British manuscript MS. Bodley 283, which is among the last and largest works in the tradition of lay religious instruction mandated by the Fourth Lateran Council.

The *Mirroure* is derived from conflations of *Le Miroir du Monde* and the *Somme le Roi,* both vernacular treatises on vices and virtues compiled in northeast France in the thirteenth century. Translated into Middle English by, it is believed, Stephen Scrope, the foremost English translator of the mid-fifteenth century, *The Mirroure of the Worlde* is one of the only books of virtues and vices that contains Latin text, an inclusion that points towards a more widespread knowledge of the language among laypeople than previously thought. Complete with explanatory notes and a glossary, this edition of *The Mirroure of the Worlde* widens the understanding of medieval moral instruction, religion, reading practices, and education.

ROBERT A. RAYMO is Emeritus Professor of English at New York University.

ELAINE E. WHITAKER is Associate Professor of English at the University of Alabama at Birmingham.

RUTH E. STERNGLANTZ has a PhD in English from New York University and is currently a James Wilson Fellow in Law and Philosophy at the University of Pennsylvania.

Medieval Academy Books, No. 106

THE MIRROURE OF THE WORLDE

A MIDDLE ENGLISH TRANSLATION OF *LE MIROIR DU MONDE*

Edited with Introduction, Notes, and Glossary by

Robert R. Raymo and Elaine E. Whitaker

with the assistance of Ruth E. Sternglantz

Published for the Medieval Academy of America by the
University of Toronto Press

University of Toronto Press Incorporated
Toronto Buffalo London

Reprinted in paperback 2014

ISBN 978-0-8020-3613-1 (cloth)
ISBN 978-1-4426-5736-6 (paper)

Printed on acid-free paper

National Library of Canada Cataloguing in Publication

Bodleian Library. Manuscript. Bodley 283
The mirroure of the worlde : a Middle English translation of Le miroir du monde / edited with introduction, notes, and glossary by Robert R. Raymo and Elaine E. Whitaker with the assistance of Ruth E. Sternglantz.

(Medieval Academy books ; no. 106)
Manucript held in the Bodleian Library, MS Bodley 283.
Includes bibliographical references and index.
ISBN 978-0-8020-3613-1 (bound) ISBN 978-1-4426-5736-6 (pbk.)

1. Virtues – Early works to 1800. 2. Vices – Early works to 1800. I. Raymo, Robert R. II. Whitaker, Elaine E. III. Sternglantz, Ruth E. IV. Medieval Academy of America. V. Title. VI. Series.

BJ1241.B62 2003 241 C2002-905104-5

Publication of this book has been aided by a grant from the Abraham and Rebecca Stein Faculty Fund of New York University, Department of English.

University of Toronto Press acknowledges the financial assistance to its publishing program of the Canada Council for the Arts and the Ontario Arts Council.

University of Toronto Press acknowledges the financial support for its publishing activities of the Government of Canada through the Book Publishing Industry Development Program (BPIDP).

Contents

Acknowledgments

In preparing this edition we have incurred many debts. We gratefully acknowledge the assistance of the librarians and staff of New York University Library, Rhodes College Library, University of Alabama at Birmingham Library, Folger Shakespeare Library, Library of Congress, Columbia University Library, Fordham University Library, Union Theological Seminary Library, New York Public Library, University of Maryland Library, the Index of Christian Art at Princeton and Dumbarton Oaks, and the Institut de Recherche et d'Histoire des Textes. Special thanks are due to our reference librarians, George Thompson and Tinker Dunbar, whose generous services have been invaluable to us. The Bodleian Library, British Library, Bibliothèque Nationale, Bibliothèque de l'Arsenal, Beinecke Library, Musée Condé, Bibliothèque Municipale d'Arras, Bibliothèque Municipale de Soissons, Bibliothèque Municipale de Tours, the library of St John's College, Cambridge, Koninklijke Bibliotheek, the library of Magdalen College, Oxford, and Pierpont Morgan Library graciously provided access to, or photographs of, rare books and manuscripts in their possession. Microfilm copies of manuscripts of *Le Miroir du Monde* in the Biblioteca Vaticana were obtained from the Knights of Columbus Library at St Louis University. Robert E. Lewis kindly allowed us to consult the then unpublished files of the *Middle English Dictionary*.

We received much helpful advice and assistance from distinguished scholars here and abroad. We are particularly indebted to Kathleen L. Scott for her exemplary codicological study of Bodley 283 as well as for her constant encouragement and support from the outset of the project; to Lister Matheson for his illuminating linguistic profile of Bodley 283; and to A.I. Doyle and Angus McIntosh for their expert views of its date and dialect. Jonathan Hughes shared with us his informative research (then unpublished) on Stephen Scrope and the Fastolf circle. For several other kinds of aid and guidance thanks are also due to Joop van Banning, Patricia Heath Barnum, Richard Beadle, Edith Brayer, Wilco van den Brink, Curt Bühler, Ann van Buren, Joseph Byrnes, Thomas Owen Clancy, Christopher Collins, Jamie Cottis, Martha W. Driver, Despina Gimbel, Pamela Gradon, Lila Graves, Kimball Higgs, David Howlett, Colin Jones, Margaret Laird, M. Laurent, Anne-Françoise Labie-Leurquin, Malcolm B. Parkes, Laurie Postlewate, Nancy F. Regalado, Edward Roesner, Sally Sanderlin, Lucy Freeman Sandler, Keith Val Sinclair, Evelyn Birge Vitz, David De Vries, Christina von Nolcken, and Roger S. Wieck. We greatly benefitted from the helpful criticism of A.S.G. Edwards, John Fisher, and Lister Matheson, who read the text in typescript and saved us from a number of errors. We owe a special debt of gratitude to Anthony Low for his scholarly advice and support. The technological skill, bibliographical knowledge, and scholarly acuity of Ruth E. Sternglantz have been indispensable to the completion of this project, and she is so acknowledged on the title page.

To C. Duncan Rice, former dean of arts and science at New York University and now vice-chancellor and principal of the University of Aberdeen, and to the Graduate School, Faculty Research Grants Committee, of the University of Alabama at Birmingham we wish to express our profound gratitude for subventions to defray the costs of travel, supplies, and research assistance.

The text is published with the kind permission of the Bodleian Library.

R.R.R.
E.E.W.

Abbreviations and Sigla

The following abbreviations are used for series and works cited in the introduction and explanatory notes. For fuller details see the bibliography.

AND	*Anglo-Norman Dictionary*
Ayen	*Ayenbite of Inwyt*
CC	*Corpus Christianorum*
Dicts	*The Dicts and Sayings of the Philosophers* (ed. Bühler)
Dives	*Dives and Pauper*
DNB	*Dictionary of National Biography*
EETS	Early English Text Society
LALME	*Linguistic Atlas of Late Mediaeval English*
MED	*Middle English Dictionary*
ODEP	*Oxford Dictionary of English Proverbs*
OED	*Oxford English Dictionary*
Othea	*The Epistle of Othea* (ed. Bühler)
PG	*Patrologia Graeca*
PL	*Patrologia Latina*
SND	*Scottish National Dictionary*
VV	*The Book of Vices and Virtues*

The following sigla are used for manuscripts of the *Mirroure of the Worlde* and *Le Miroir du Monde*.

A Bibliothèque Municipale, Arras, 183 (1057)
B Bodleian Library, Oxford, Bodley 283

C Musée Condé, Chantilly, 136
D Bibliothèque Nationale, Paris, 952
N Bibliothèque Nationale, Paris, 459
P Bibliothèque Nationale, Paris, 22934
Q Bibliothèque Nationale, Paris, 22935
R Bibliothèque de l'Arsenal, Paris, 2124
S Bibliothèque Municipale, Soissons, 221
U Biblioteca Apostolica Vaticana Fondo Reginense Latino 1448
V Biblioteca Apostolica Vaticana Fondo Reginense Latino 2055

THE MIRROURE OF THE WORLDE

Introduction

1. Description of the Manuscript

The Mirroure of the Worlde survives uniquely in the Bodleian Library, Oxford, MS Bodley 283 (S. C. 2338), a large, well-preserved volume of 186 leaves, collating i + A-$I^{20}K^{4}$ + i.[1] The leaves are mainly royal folio paper measuring 406 by 284 millimeters and bearing a watermark nearly identical to Piccard 163, a winged griffin rampant localized in Friuli in 1463.[2] The outer and middle leaves of each quire are parchment. Parchment bifolia also precede and follow the text, with one leaf attached to the binding and the other serving as an endleaf. The late-seventeenth-century foliation runs faultily from 1 on the fifth leaf to 181. Folio 155 has been misnumbered 156, and 74 has been used twice. Folio 136 originally bore the number 156 (later corrected).[3] Signatures consisting of capital letters and lower-case Roman numerals are preserved in whole or in part at the lower right-hand corner of the recto in the first half of each quire: A1–3, 5–10; B1–7, 9–10; C1–10; D2–10; E1–9; FGHI1–10; K1–2. Catchwords appear on 75 versos beginning with the eighth leaf. They are found at the lower margin near the gutter in the second half of each quire. Frame-ruling, in leadpoint, encloses a single column of text approximately 26 by 110 millimeters. The average number of lines to a full page is 42.

The manuscript was written by one scribe in a bastard secretary bookhand of the third quarter of the fifteenth century.[4] Kathleen L. Scott describes its general appearance as 'predominantly vertical, except for the beginning strokes of *v* and *w*, which sweep in a strong diagonal from left to right. The impression as a whole is of roundness and legibility, but in fact the letters are quite angular, being formed by several broken strokes rather than a single rounded one.'[5] The only distinctive feature of the hand is the addition of a circular stroke on final *g*.[6] Punctuation is carefully entered by point and virgule.[7] Marks of abbreviation are used sparingly. There is, however, a profusion of decorative flourishes – strokes through *h* and *ll*, a curved-back tail on final *p*, tags on final *d*, *f*, and *t*. Errors of transcription are corrected by a combination of expunction and cancellation, occasionally by erasure and dissolution.[8] Lacunae remain at folios 43ᵛ, 46ᵛ, 53ᵛ, 56ᵛ, 58ᵛ, 75ᵛ, 86, and 128. The scribe employs a dark brown ink (shading virtually to black at folio 137) for the text and a pale orange-red ink for rubrication of titles, authorities, and punctuation. Large initial letters of chapters and paragraphs are rendered in true red. They were entered by brush stroke, perhaps by a hand other than the scribe's, after the transcription of the text.[9] Marginalia are infrequent, the most common being '*notta*.'[10] The contemporary binding is of oak boards covered by whittawed leather stained red.[11] Tooled metal clasps survive on the back of the book and stubs of leather straps on the front.

Three artists were involved in the extensive decoration of Bodley 283.[12] Chief among them was a gifted Northern Netherlandish or Dutch artist called the Caxton Master, whose work is found in three other manuscripts – *Ovid Moralised*, *Writhe's Garter Book*, and *The Beauchamp Pageants* – produced in the 1480s.[13] Twenty-five of his naturalistic pen drawings accompany the text of the *Mirroure*. Their subjects and locations are as follows. 1: Moses receiving the Ten Commandments; Moses displaying the Tablets; Worship of the Golden Calf (f. 1). 2–13: Individual portraits of the Apostles (ff. 11–14). 14: Beast of the Apocalypse; Fall of the Rebel Angels (f. 16). 15: Pride, on a lion (f. 17). 16: Envy, on a dog (f. 38ᵛ). 17: Anger, on a lion (f. 42). 18: Sloth, on an ass (f. 48ᵛ). 19: Avarice, with a money box and coins (f. 59). 20: Lechery, on a goat and holding a mirror (f. 67ᵛ). 21: Gluttony, on a sow (f. 72ᵛ). 22: Last Judgment, with gates of Heaven and Hell (f. 87ᵛ). 23: The Garden of Virtues (f. 99ᵛ). 24: Pentecost (f. 111ᵛ). 25: A knight fighting the Beast of the Apocalypse (f. 137). The main sources of the Caxton Master's illustrations are the standard iconographic programs of *La Somme le Roi* and *Le Miroir du Monde* combined with conventional pictorial representations of vices in association with animals and emblems. The fusion of the Fall of the Rebel Angels with the Beast of the Apocalypse and the depiction of the knight battling the Beast are unique in fifteenth-century art and are probably his own creation.[14]

Two native artists were responsible for the painted and illuminated decoration of Bodley 283. The first, who worked in a traditional English style, produced the full-page floral border on folio i and the six-line initial *H* immediately within it. He may also have executed the eight-line initial *S* introducing the first sentence of the text.[15] For the second full-page border that frames the Caxton Master's drawing of Moses receiving the Ten Commandments and the opening lines of the text on folio 1, he collaborated with an illuminator trained in a foreign style, whose recurring trademark of an owl peering full face at the viewer is seen amid the ornamental pinks and sprays on the right. The two artists worked together on three other manuscripts between 1467 and 1480.[16]

Judging by the drawings of Pride (f. 17) and Lechery (f. 67^{v}), we can surmise that the manuscript was made between 1470 and 1475. Lechery has a distinctly English headdress with a butterfly veil and netting, and the low, rounded neck of her gown is filled by a velvet placard and a gorger of fine lawn. She wears a necklace with an elaborate pendant. The rounding of women's necklines began about 1470.[17] Pride is stylishly dressed in Flemish fashion. He wears a short gown with enormous shoulders and sleeves slashed at the elbows, 'piked' shoes, and a tall 'sugar loaf' hat. Such aristocratic finery reached the height of its popularity about 1470, but it appears to have fallen steadily out of favor thereafter. By 1475 men's shoulders had lost their grotesque padding and hats had been lowered.[18] A moralizing artist would scarcely have depicted the vice of Pride in anything other than ultramodish attire. High fashion in England reflected Flemish taste, and it is unlikely, in view of the strong courtly and commercial ties between the two countries, that major sartorial changes originating in Flanders would long have escaped the notice of English society. Assigning the manufacture of the manuscript to the 1470s, probably the mid-1470s, fits comfortably within the period of changing fashion and accords well with the *terminus ad quem* of the bookhand and the age of the paper.[19]

Bodley 283 was owned and perhaps commissioned by a prosperous London draper, Thomas Kippyng, whose name figures prominently in the Guildhall Records, Close Rolls, Plea and Memoranda Rolls, and Patent Rolls between 1462 and 1482.[20] His ownership is recorded in a note on a pastedown of the back cover: 'This boke oweth Thomas Kippyng of London draper.' As a member of the Drapers' Company, and a merchant of considerable substance, he belonged to the upper strata of London society and may well have been closely connected to the crown.[21] He was a principal founding member of the prestigious Luton Guild of the Holy Trinity, established in 1475 by Edward IV's chancellor, Bishop Thomas Rotherham, his brother John Rotherham and others. His is the sixth name to appear in the official register of the Guild's foundation and membership: 'Thomas kippyng draper de London.'[22] In 1480–1 he received appointment as 'an efficient man' to collect assessments in Langham Ward for Edward's 'benevolences.'[23] Bodley 283 provides the only evidence of his patronage of the luxury-book trade, and, since it shows very little wear or use, it may have been acquired more for display than for private study. De luxe books were an index of wealth and social standing, and great importance was attached to them as affirmations of status and power.[24]

The history of Bodley 283 after Kippyng's death remains obscure.[25] It was later owned by Robert Barker, printer to James I, who donated it together with four other books to the Bodleian Library in 1604.[26]

2. *The Mirroure of the Worlde*: Background and Sources

The Mirroure of the Worlde is a manual of moral instruction for laymen.[27] Its purpose is to prepare penitents for confession by means of the vices and virtues and to guide them in the path of godliness.[28] It belongs to a vast body of medieval prose religious literature owing its origin to the reforming zeal of the Fourth Lateran Council (1215), which in its twenty-first decree, known by its opening phrase *Omnis utriusque sexus*, made annual confession and Easter communion mandatory for all Christians and stimulated the production of treatises (for the clergy and later for the laity) expounding a system of moral constructs useful for the correct administering and receiving of the sacrament of penance.[29] This material was often combined with instruction in the essential dogmas of Christianity.[30] The tripartite structure of the *Mirroure* reflects its catechetical and penitential concerns. It begins with two brief expositions of the Commandments and the Creed designed to establish the foundations of the faith and to guarantee the orthodoxy of the moral teaching. This section (ll. 257–1250) occupies less than 10 per cent of the *Mirroure* and is followed by a long treatise on the vices and their remedies (ll. 1251–6299). The exposition of the vices is introduced by the allegory of the Beast of the Apocalypse. Each of the beast's seven heads represents one of the deadly sins and each of its ten horns a violation of one of the Commandments (ll. 1251–85). Biblical imagery, however, is soon abandoned for the symbolization of the trees of life and death, charity and concupiscence. The latter is rooted in pride, and its branches and shoots stand for the sins and their numerous species. The third and longest section of the *Mirroure* (ll. 6300–13005) consists of two independent treatises on virtue. The first depicts virtue in general as a mystical garden watered by the gifts of the Holy Ghost. In the center of the garden grows the Tree of Life, whose branches are the Beatitudes. The allegory is a portrayal of the progress of the human soul based on Canticles 4.12 and apparently is original to the *Miroir*. The second treatise deals with the individual virtues in relation to the petitions of the Pater Noster, the gifts of the Holy Ghost, and the Beatitudes. In this septimal scheme, possibly suggested by Hugh of St Victor's *De quinque septenis*,[31] the seven petitions produce the seven gifts that nourish the seven virtues opposed to the seven vices. The virtues in turn lead to the perfection of the eternal beatitudes. Thus is godliness rewarded with *a worshipful pees, a delitable pees, and an euerlastynge pees and a pees that surmounth and passeth alle wittes. It passeth alle oother woordes. For herte maye not thynke ne tonge devise what thynge Godde ordeyneth for his freendes* (ll. 12998–13001).

The *Mirroure* is derived from *Le Miroir du Monde* and *La Somme le Roi*, the two earliest vernacular treatises on vices and virtues, which are often confused and their titles interchanged in medieval manuscripts.[32] They are compilations inspired by, and to a large extent drawn from, William Peraldus's *Summa de vitiis* (1236) and *Summa de virtutibus* (1248).[33] Neither the *Miroir* nor the *Somme* is available in a modern critical edition.[34] The *Miroir* was written in northeast France after the *Summa de virtutibus* but before *La Somme le Roi* (March 1279, New Style 1280), which used it.[35] Its indebtedness for portions of the exposition of the commandments to Bonaventure's *Collationes De Decem Praeceptis* given at the University of Paris during the Lenten season of 1267 and to the *Tabula Exemplorum* (1270–77) would seem to narrow the date of composition – at least in its final form – to the 1270s.[36] The author is unknown. Dr Edith Brayer is of the opinion that he was a secular clerk.[37] He knew the classical Latin philosophers – particularly Cicero, Seneca, and Macrobius – and was familiar with French literature, citing *Garin le Loherenc* (l. 2586), quoting from Thibaut d'Amiens (ll. 1835–7, 1902) and Hélinand of Froidmont (ll. 2086–7, 5048, 8425–9), and naming the heroes of romance and epic: *Parceval, Rouland,* and *Olyver* (l. 2003). There is some evidence, however, to support the belief that he was a Cistercian (or became one before writing the *Miroir*). He had a strong regard for the Cistercian order, which is presented as a model of spirituality, and an intimate knowledge of the works of Bernard de Clairvaux.[38] With the authorship of the *Somme* we are on surer ground: it was composed by the Dominican, Lorens d'Orléans (? surnamed De Bois), at the request of Philip III of France, in whose honor it was named. Lorens was the king's personal confessor and tutor to his children. Before taking up his duties in the royal household he had been prior of Saint Jacques, the Dominican house, in Paris.[39] The *Somme* enjoyed a far greater vogue than the *Miroir*. Over 100 manuscripts are extant in Belgium, England, France, Germany, Italy, Netherlands, Russia, Spain, Switzerland, Vatican City, and the United States.[40] By the end of the Middle Ages it had been translated into Castilian, Catalan, English, Flemish, Italian, and Provençal.[41]

The precise relationship of the *Miroir* and the *Somme* must remain in the present state of research a matter of conjecture. It is clear, however, as Dr Brayer has demonstrated, that the *Somme* was deeply indebted to the *Miroir* for the discussion of the vices and the symbolization of the two trees. It also borrowed the *Ars Moriendi* (ll. 6478–6665) and adapted the account of virtue in general.[42] In its original form, the *Miroir* lacked the Commandments, Creed, sins of the tongue, and gifts of the Holy Ghost, but it included separate discussions of wisdom and confession. The treatment of vices in the *Miroir* is twice as long as it is in the *Somme*, the space devoted to the discussion of pride in the *Miroir* being more than four times that allotted to the discussion of pride in the *Somme*. The section of the *Somme* in which the gifts of the Holy Ghost are described consumes as much or more space in the manuscripts than is occupied by the complete *Miroir*.[43]

Toward the end of the fourteenth or the beginning of the fifteenth century, a process of scribal editing in French combined the *Miroir* and the *Somme*. Of the complex interaction of these two treatises during the late Middle Ages, Dr Brayer observes that 'il n'y a pas un *Miroir*, une *Somme* et une combinaison des deux; il y a des redactions du *Miroir*, des redactions de la *Somme*, et plusiers combinaisons differentes des deux textes.'[44] She distinguishes four characteristic combinations of the *Somme* and *Miroir* designated V, W, X, and Y.[45] The *Mirroure* is translated from the Y version, whose distinctive features are the incipit with alternate titles, commencing with *Le Miroir du Monde*; an extensive table of contents; an expanded exposition of the Commandments; minor additions to the Creed; the remedies inserted after each vice; and the date 1289 rather than 1279 in the colophon.[46] At least eleven French manuscripts of redaction Y survive, all dating from the fifteenth century:

1. Bibliothèque Municipale, Arras, 183 (1057) (A)[47]
2. Musée Condé, Chantilly, 136 (C)[48]
3. Bibliothèque de l'Arsenal, Paris, 2124 (R)[49]
4. Bibliothèque Nationale, Paris, Fonds Français 459 (N)[50]
5. Bibliothèque Nationale, Paris, Fonds Français 952 (D)[51]
6. Bibliothèque Nationale, Paris, Fonds Français 22934 (P)[52]
7. Bibliothèque Nationale, Paris, Fonds Français 22935 (Q)[53]
8. Bibliothèque Municipale, Soissons, 221 (S)[54]
9. Bibliothèque Municipale, Tours, 401 (T)[55]
10. Biblioteca Apostolica Vaticana Fondo Reginense Latino 1448 (U)[56]
11. Biblioteca Apostolica Vaticana Fondo Reginense Latino 2055 (V)[57]

None of these manuscripts can be considered the translator's exemplar, although it must have been closely related to V, which has six unique errors in common with the *Mirroure*.[58] The most complete and carefully executed witness of the Y redaction is P, which is the source of all quotations from the *Miroir* in this edition, unless otherwise indicated, with significant variants supplied from all the other witnesses except T, a partial and disarranged copy dispersed throughout a late miscellany of didactic and religious works.[59] Manuscripts P, R, S, and V append to the text a collection of French and Latin devotional pieces, mainly prayers, in prose and verse.[60] At the end of MSS C and N are seven stanzas entitled *Ce sont les sept degres pour monter en paradis*. The tables of contents vary considerably, and their chapter headings are far more extensive than those usually found within the texts. They were probably added to the Y redaction after its completion to improve reader access to its materials. Late medieval vernacular books of religion in England and on the continent were often provided with such apparatuses in order to facilitate their use.[61] Internally, meticulous cross-referencing provides a further practical guide to the contents of the *Miroir*, pointing readers to earlier or later discussions of particular topics.[62]

There are ten English translations, partial or complete, of *La Somme le Roi*, two from the fourteenth century (*Ayenbite of Inwyt* and *The Book of the Vices and Virtues*) and eight from the fifteenth century, including Caxton's *Ryal Book*.[63] All are in Midlands prose except the *Ayenbite of Inwyt.* Excerpts from a combined version of the *Miroir* and *Somme* appear in two fifteenth-century compendia of religious doctrine, *Disce Mori* and its derivative *Ignorancia Sacerdotum*, composed in the East Midlands and possibly a fifteenth-century devotional treatise on the seven deadly sins composed in south Herefordshire or northeast Monmouthshire.[64] The *Mirroure* is the only complete translation in English of the combined *Miroir* and *Somme.* Although it lacks the suppleness and fluidity characteristic of the best translation of the period, it is a substantial achievement all the same. It adheres closely to its source, rendering it intelligibly and for the most part accurately. As it proceeds, it becomes increasingly smooth and idiomatic. In the early stages it is not without slavishness and some looseness of syntactic structure, however, owing to the tendency of the translator, tentatively identified with Stephen Scrope below, to work sequentially with phrases and clauses rather than with whole sentences. Few liberties are taken with the French text. The translator regularly adapts it to a native audience by substituting English for French names.[65] Throughout the work, but particularly toward the end, he omits several narrative exempla.[66] Little is added to his source apart from occasional glosses of difficult or technical words or brief elucidatory phrases for the sake of clarity or emphasis and pleonasms involving synonyms and other forms of repetition as a means of rhetorical heightening and aural resonance.[67] There are passing allusions to contemporary political and religious issues.[68] Errors of translation occur, but they are few in proportion to the magnitude of the work and are due as often to misreading as to misunderstanding of the French.[69] Some faults lie with a corrupt exemplar.[70] Lacunae extending from a word to an entire paragraph mar the sense of several passages.[71] Whether these losses stem from a defective exemplar or from authorial or scribal carelessness is impossible to determine in most instances. Eight gaps are left for subsequent completion or glossing.[72]

The style of the *Mirroure* is influenced by its source. The *Somme* is marked by clarity and simplicity, whereas the *Miroir*, by contrast, is diffuse, allusive, and rhetorical in the ornate tradition of religious prose.[73] The *Mirroure* assimilates these influences and often reproduces them effectively. Its diction is heavily accented with French words, many of which enter the English language for the first time (e.g., *abusage, ardentnesse, botenettis, branchet, canonique, commaunderesse, engloute, envenimoures, esprove, glene, gurmantis, resoigne, redeavable*) or are employed in senses not previously recorded in English (e.g., *defauteth, degouted, deserueth, determined, feture, peintures, stablisseth, travayleth, tretyce, voyded*). Some are converted to English forms, for example, *drye* 'paid in cash' (*sec*), *fendesse* (*deableresse*), *giberisshe* (*patroullas*), *hynder* 'spoil' (*honnissent*), *ouerselle* (*survendent*), *springlyngis* (*getons*). The range of the translator's vocabulary is impressive. He was enamored of neologisms and used them freely to augment the English language. For the literate lay reader to whom it is addressed the *Mirroure* provided a standard orthodox guide to Christian spirituality in a language of refinement and grace.

3. Language

Judging from short specimens only, *A Linguistic Atlas of Late Medieval English* conjecturally assigns the language of Bodley 283 to the Soke of Peterborough or northeast Northamptonshire.[74] A subsequent analysis of the text by Lister M. Matheson employing the 'fit-technique' devised by Angus McIntosh and M.L. Samuels supports this attribution, merely extending the geographical area slightly to include northern Huntingdonshire.[75] Bodley 283 presents a profile of mixed usage whose dialect sources may be found largely in the productions of this linguistically diverse border region.[76] Precise evidence of its scribal provenance is provided by the regular occurrence of an innovatory subsystem of verbal inflections that characterize the late Middle English dialect of the North Midlands. Professor McIntosh has demonstrated that scribes working within a narrow belt stretching from northeast Leicester and Rutland to the Soke of Peterborough, northern Northamptonshire, and the extreme north of Huntingdonshire, and in parts of north Ely and northeast Norfolk, replaced the normal Midlands form of the present indicative third-person plural suffix with a new paradigm requiring an *-eth* ending for a verb in direct contact with a subject other than a personal pronoun and an *-en, -e*, or *-Ø* ending for a verb in direct contact with a personal pronoun subject. He exemplifies this phenomenon from the Middle English translation of the *Rosarium Theologie* in Gonville and Caius College, Cambridge, MS 354/581 (c. 1425–75).[77] The *Mirroure* follows the same paradigm. Of the nearly 1800 cases where plural personal pronouns directly precede or follow the verb all but a few have an *-e* ending (e.g., ll. 7763–4 *this aske wee whan that wee seye*, l. 5689 *ȝee knowe welle*, l. 3424 *þey make the* *herte to boyle*). There are two *-n* endings (ll. 4470–1 *theye longen*, l. 4502 *they doon*) and sporadic *-Ø* or *-e* endings (ll. 359, 365, 367 *we worshipp*, l. 369 *worshipp we*, l. 431 *theye set*, l. 8815 *þey ryn and lepe*, ll. 6877–8 *liff þeye*, ll. 4161, 4162 *we vnderstande*). Exceptions to the rule number a scant dozen (l. 461 *they werreþ*, l. 2247 *they seythe*, ll. 3884–5 *theye foryeteth*, l. 2850 *we ȝefeth*, l. 3500 *theye loueth*, ll. 3971–2 *they answerith*, ll. 4319–20 *theye hereth, seyeth, and pleyeth*, l. 4321 *theye speketh*, l. 5066 *theye stodieth*, ll. 6416–7 *theye maketh*, l. 6773 *theye avaunteth*, and, with a variant spelling of *-th*, l. 11767 *they liffed*). Verbs in direct contact with non-personal pronoun subjects take the *-th* ending (*-eth, -eþ, -ith, yth*, and a single instance of *-d* [l. 12018 *corromped*]) with two exceptions (l. 1414 *pepil love*, l. 4566 *men curse*). The paradigm applies with equal force to constructions in which the personal pronoun subject governs two verbs joined by a conjunction. The second of the two verbs normally has the *-th* ending, but occasionally has an *-e*. Examples of the former pattern in the *Mirroure* are *þey clense and maketh oother holy* (l. 12283), *they travayle the herte and distroyeth it* (l. 3422), *they commande and maketh* (l. 8205), and of the latter examples are *they blame and dispice* (l. 5866), *theye wexe, sprede, and multiplie* (ll. 1436–7), *they taxe and robbe* (l. 2273).[78] A closer localization within the geographical limits of the *-eth* plural is suggested by the combination of forms *shee* 93× beside *she* 25×; *siche* (spelled *sige* once) 318× beside *sich* 3×; invariable *iche* 15×; *any* 111× (*anyewhere* 1×, *anythyng* 1×, *anythynge* 13×); *hundreth* 7× (*hundrethfolde* 3×, *hunderethfolde* 1×, *hondrithes* 1×); *myche* 274× beside *mych* 2×, *mich* 1×, *miche* 18×, *moche* 9×, and *mooche* 2×; *hirre* 85× (*hirres* 5×) beside *her* 4×, *here* 5×, *herre* 1×, *hir* 25×, *hire* 2×, and *hyrre* 4×; *theym* 317× (*þeym* 2×, *theymselfe* 16×), *theyme* 455× (*þeyme* 1×, *theymeselfe* 12×), *theim* 1×, *theime* 1× beside *them* 1×, *theme* 1×, and *hem* 1×; and *theys* 'these' 2×.[79] These usages, together with the free variation of spelling that is a marked characteristic of the language (resulting in a bewilding profusion of forms, e.g., *vpon, uppon, apon, apone, open, opon, oppon; glootounye, glotonie, glotony, glotonye, glotounye, gloutony; loue, louf, loufe, loffe, louff, louffe, love, luff, luffe; neghborgh, neghborghe, neghborough, neghborugh, neghborughe, neghbourgh, neghbourghe, neyghborgh, neyghborghe, neyghborugh, neyȝghborghe*), point to a provenance at the boundaries of converging dialects, encompassing the Soke of Peterborough and northern Northamptonshire and Huntingdonshire, as previously mentioned, but also, in a westward direction, Rutland

and the contiguous areas of Leicestershire and Lincolnshire.[80] A number of northernisms, including the strong predominance of *-f(f)-* over *-u/v-* forms of 'love' (*n.* and *v.*) and 'live' in the ratio of about 7:1; *sen* 'since' 8× beside *sithen that* 2×, *sithyn that* 2×; *hynge* 'lean, incline' 2× (*hyngeth* 2×, *hinginge* 1×); the use of *is* with plural function; and occasional (mainly single) occurrences of *apon(e)* 'on, upon,' *behaldyng* 'seeing,' *bre(e)ther, brethre* 'brothers,' *dede* 'died,' *ȝone* 'that,' *halidayes, halydaye(s)* 'holy days,' *howghe* 'how,' *keste* 'cast,' *kyen* 'cows,' *kynnes* 'chilblains,' *nerhand(e)* 'close by,' *lange* 'long,' *os* 'as,' *poere* 'poor,' *sent* 'send,' *slokkenesse, slokynes* 'slothfulness,' *this* 'thus,' *those* 'those,' *waies* 'woes,' and *wars* 'worse,' may possibly reflect an earlier stage of transmission, although the majority of these forms had descended southward as far as the North and Northeast Midlands by the first half of the fifteenth century and are well attested to within the defined area of the *-eth* plural or in proximity to it.[81] Three lexical items belong to the same geographical region: *hoope* (l. 2424) in the northerly sense 'believe, think' (French *cuident*), *boltel* (l. 752) 'a garment of loosely woven cloth' (French *buletel*), and *harre* (l. 2531) 'chill, biting cold,' a rare word of Middle Dutch origin (*haar*).[82] The parenthetical clause *as who seye* is also northerly in character.[83]

East Anglian (mainly Norfolk) features also figure prominently in the language: *a* (*an*) as the reduced forms of 'have' in compound tenses; *yoven* as the past participle of 'give'; sporadic third-person singular indicative endings *-et* and *-it* for *-eth, -ith*, for example, *florisshet, prononcit*; *-ch-* for Old French [dʒ], for example, *langache, chanched* (*chaunched, chaunchyng*), and *charche(s)* (*charched, charcith*); *-th* for *-t* in final position, for example, *thath, magnificath*, and *with* 'wit'; *wh-* for *w-*, for example, *whanhoope* 'wanhope,' *whise* 'wise,' *whiffes* 'wives,' *whe* 'we,' *where* 'were,' *wherewhith* 'wherewith,' and *whas* 'was'; *tweyn(e)* 'two'; and minority forms of *hisse* 'his,' *weele* 'well,' *bvt* 'but,' *no* 'nor,' *wordly* 'worldly,' and *quom* 'whom.' The lowering of *i/y* to *e* is common: *besy, besines(se), cherche, dede, fellith, ferst, kende, levid, leve, mankendely, mende, pelir, pete, preve, previlage, theder, thredde, velayn, wete, wetyngly, worthenes*, and *wretyn*.[84] The word *caliones* (l. 8666) 'flints, pebbles' is recorded only from Norfolk and Suffolk.[85] The forms *hiere, hier-* 'hear' are generally regarded as southeastern from the region of lower Essex or Kent.[86]

Bodley 283 also preserves southwestern features in sufficient number and distribution to identify it as a reasonably accurate copy made by a

Devonshire scribe of a Northeast Midlands original: *ther, therre* 'dare,' *yeate, ȝeate, ȝeates, ȝeatis* 'gate(s),' and *ȝeaf, ȝeafe, ȝeaff* 'gave.' These forms are strongly characteristic of Devonshire, and their currency is narrowly confined to the areas of Cornwall, Devonshire, and Somerset.[87] In addition, there are occurrences of other features with southwestern, frequently Devonshire, associations: the development of initial *y-* in *yeien, yeyen* 'eyes'; the *hire, hir-* forms of 'hear'; the third-person singular present indicative *-ed* for *-eth* forms in *betokened, devised, envenimed, falsed, louffed, sufficed,* and *worshipped*; the unvoicing of initial *b* to *p* in *put* 'but' and 'butt'; the voicing of *ch* to *g* in *sige* 'such,' *legerie* 'lechery,' and *geffare* 'bargains'; the use of the suffix *-nys* in *hardenys*; and possibly the spellings *kyende* 'kind,' *myende* 'mind,' *moothe* 'mouth,' *strenght* 'strength,' and *wham* 'whom.'[88] The discussion of authorship will offer a possible explanation for the presence of these forms in an otherwise Midlands text.

Traces of Chancery English may perhaps be detected in the representation, almost without exception, of the Old English final velar *h* and palatal *h* before *t* as *gh*, whether it was actually pronounced or not: 'daughter,' 'draught,' 'drought,' 'enough,' 'fight (fought),' 'height,' 'knight,' 'laugh(ter),' 'light,' 'manslaughter,' 'might,' 'neighbor,' 'night,' 'nought,' 'ought,' 'right,' 'sought,' 'though,' 'through,' 'thought,' 'weight.' 'High (-er,-est),' however, is always *hye* 53×, *hie* 2× (*hyer* 8×, *hier* 1×, *heyer* 2×, *heyest* 1×, *hyest* 9×) and 'plight' *plite* 8×, *plyte* 3×. In French loan words *ig* is occasionally found, particularly *reigne* 2× (*reigned* 1×, *reigneth* 4×), possibly under Chancery influence. Each of *atteyn-* and *attaign-* occurs six times, and *ligne(e), lignie* 'lineage' occurs five times beside *linee* and *lyne* twice. There are single instances of *bareygne* and *barhaigne* (beside *barhayne*), *baigneth, coygne, montaigne, resoigne,* and *souereigne* (beside *souerayne* 3×, *souerein* 4×, *souereyn* 2×, and *souereyne* 6×). The *ig* is never found in *carayne* (*caroyne*), *certeyne* (*certoine*), *chevetaine, forein(e)* (*foreyn*), *germain* (*germayne*; French plural adjective *germeines*), *maintene, ordeyn(e), pleyne, restrayne* (*restreyn(e)*), *streynyd* (*streyningly*), *sustene* (*sustien, sustine, susteyned*).[89]

Finally, the graphetic profile shows a high degree of interchangeability of the written letter symbols without apparent phonetic value: *th/þ* (*the, þe*), *ȝ/y* (*ȝiftis, yiftis*), *c/s*, particularly in French loan words (*avice, avise*), *i/y* (*is/ys*), final *s/z* (*maners, manerz*), *e/a* (*aweye, awaye*), *u/w* (*aboute, abowte*), *u/v* (*understande, vnderstande*), final *s/ȝ* (*assemblees, assembleȝ*), *c/k* (*catte, katte*), medial *s/z/ȝ* (*philosophres, philozophres, philoȝophres*). It is of interest that the incidence of yoghs diminishes sharply between chapters 23 and 77 (ll. 2507–5173), a carryover, in all likelihood, from the different scribal stints of Bodley's exemplar.[90] They occasionally appear as hiatus markers (for example, *sighȝyng*, l. 9845). Thorns are used sparingly throughout the text, except for the last 800 lines, where over half of them (508 out of 998) occur. They are confined almost exclusively to initial positions, chiefly in the words *'the,' 'this,' 'that,'* and *'then,'* a phonologically conditioned practice of late Middle English scribes.[91]

4. Date

There is no external evidence to indicate when the *Mirroure* was made. Given the stages of transmission revealed by the linguistic profile, it is safe to assume that a substantial period of time must have elapsed between the original translation and the production of Bodley 283. Lexical evidence suggests a date of composition closer to mid-century. The *Mirroure* contains a large number of words and meanings that became current between c. 1425 and c. 1450, particularly between c. 1440 and c. 1450, when two-thirds of them occur, as the chart indicates. The dates of their initial appearance are as recorded in the MED.

Mirroure	*MED citation*	*First appearance*
abaieth	abaien	c. 1450
acostomed	accustomed	c. 1450
aduertised	advertisen	1426
attyce	atisen	c. 1450
autoriȝed 'given validity'	auctorisen	c. 1440
bailiship(p)	baillifship	c. 1425
baret *v.*	baraten	c. 1436
baretor *n.*	baratour	1439
beholdyng	biholdyng	c. 1443
boltel	bultel	1450
bountewousnes	bountevousnesse	1430
caliones	callioun	1430
chaufour	chaufour	1429–30
cloyster monk	cloistre	c. 1450
communion of seintes	communioun	c. 1440

consolacion 'satisfaction, pleasure'	consolacioun	c. 1439
contrariously	contrariousli	c. 1425
coustometh	customen	c. 1450
crompyng	crampen	c. 1450
curiosite 'elegance of workmanship'	curiosite	1450
defuse	diffuse	1448
delayeth 'obstruct (probate)'	delaien	c. 1436
derision	derisioun	c. 1432
dishoneste 'sexual indulgence'	dishoneste	c. 1439
disnaturel	disnatural	c. 1449
disordenat 'dissolute'	disordinate	c. 1441
dispiteth	despiten	c. 1440
disworshippe *n.*	disworshipe	c. 1425[92]
disworshipeth	disworshipen	c. 1450
employe 'apply, devote'	emploien	1425
emploie 'make use of'	emploien	1450
employe 'spend'	emploien	1429
enpride	empriden	1434
fervently 'gluttonously'	ferventli	c. 1450
fleer	fleer	1440
foliche	follich	c. 1440
frendlynes	frendlinesse	c. 1450
fructifie 'flourish'	fructifien	c. 1440
gurmantis 'drunkards'	gourmaunt	c. 1450
homly 'at home (with)'	homelye	1425
hounte	hounte	c. 1450
howte	howten	c. 1450
humaine lynage	humaine linage	c. 1450
iobbardis	jobard	c. 1440
iusticer	justicer	c. 1440
lewkenes	leukenesse	c. 1440
liein (?liem)	lien	c. 1440
mankyndely	mankindeli	c. 1440
mankyndelynes	mankindelines	c. 1440
mysbeleverris 'infidels'	misbilevere	c. 1440
mysbeleverris 'heretics'	misbilevere	c. 1438
mokke *v.*	mokken	c. 1450
moneye-makerys	moneie-makere	c. 1450
multiplyinge	multipliinge	c. 1450
negardshipp	nigardshipe	1439

noyseth 'hold, believe'	noisen	c. 1440
ouerthrowe *n.*	overthroue	c. 1440
outeragiousnes	outrageousnesse	1450
peitevines	Poitevin	c. 1430
recouere 'repeat'	recoveren	c. 1449
scusacions 'excuses'	skusacion	c. 1425
self-wille	self-wille	c. 1450
self-wit	self-witte	c. 1425
serteinte 'certainty of knowledge'	certeinte	c. 1443
singulerteis	singulerte	c. 1425
sloggyng	slugging	c. 1450
soulnesse	solnes	1443
soupleth	souplen	c. 1450
sperid 'fastened with a buckle'	speren	1440
standyng	stonden	c. 1440
sterveth	sterven	c. 1436
traictable	tractable	c. 1425
unncion (holy) ~	unctioun	1444
vaunce	vauncen	c. 1450
vaunt	vaunten	c. 1440
vauntour	vauntour	c. 1440
vauntying	vaunting	c. 1425
vigour *n.*	vigor	c. 1450
vigoure *v.*	vigoren	c. 1425
vigourousnes	vigorousnesse	1440
voided	voiden	c. 1440
without (this)	without (that)	1432
worthinessis	worthines	c. 1440[93]

The majority of these citations are to East Midlands texts (e.g., *The Pilgrimage of the Lyfe of Manhode, Jacob's Well, The Book of the Knight of La Tour Landry*) and in some cases, more restrictedly, to East Anglian texts (e.g., *Promptorium Parvulorum, Castle of Perseverance, Pilgrimage of the Life of Man*). Twenty-one are to the works of Stephen Scrope.[94]

A small number of words and meanings also lose their currency at this time. According to MED, *bountewousnes* 'generosity, beneficence' falls out of use c. 1440, *disordenat* 'dissolute' 1441, and *threteth* 'reviles' 1447. *Benignes(se)* 'good will, benevolence,' *bostously* 'rudely, harshly,' *caliones* 'pebbles,' *contrefete* 'misshapen, deformed,' *disgyssed* 'misshapen, monstrous,' *employe* 'spend,' *foliche* 'foolish,' *gader* 'accumulate wealth,' *muse* 'spend time idly,' *neghborughshipp* 'neighborliness,' *ouerhoope* 'arrogance, presumption,' *queynte* 'proud, haughty,' *talent* 'desire, inclination,' and *travaylyng* 'giving birth' are all last recorded c. 1450.[95] The invariable *y*- and *ȝ*- forms of 'give' and 'forgive' – the only *g*- form is in a corrector's hand – are not likely to belong to a period much later than c. 1450.[96]

In addition to the lexical evidence, the discussion of perjury among the Sins of the Tongue may provide another indication of a near mid-century date of composition.[97] Adhering to orthodox doctrine, the *Miroir* upholds the legitimacy of oaths, but cautions against their abuse: '*Et pource le deffend tant nostre seigneur non pas pource que on ne puisse en aucun point iurer san pechie sicome dient les docteurs mais pource que souvent iurer fait souvent pariurer et souvent pecher sen doit on garder.*'[98] The phrase '*sicome dient les docteurs*' 'as the canonists affirm' is replaced in the *Mirroure* by a reference to the Lollard opposition to all oaths: '*And therefore oure lorde defendeth it soo myche, not but that in some point a man maye swere withoute synne* ***aȝeins the opinion of lolleris*** *but because that ofte sweryng maketh often forsweryng and often to synne men sholde kepe theyme therfroo*' (ll. 5990–4). Although little is heard of the categorical rejection of oaths by the Lollards in the fifteenth century, it was clearly still a part of their reforming program in the late 1440s, when Reginald Pecock was engaged in the composition of *The Repressor of Over Much Blaming of the Clergy*. His catalogue of eleven Lollard heresies in the *Repressor* includes their objection to oaths, and he calls attention to his lengthy refutation of their position in an earlier (non-surviving) tract, *The Spreading or Filling of the Four Tables*, written before 1443.[99] The *Repressor* was completed in c. 1449 or 1450.[100]

5. Authorship

Although the *Mirroure* provides no external evidence of authorship, exact and extensive resemblances of language, vocabulary, phraseology, and style together with common errors of translation strongly suggest that it is the work of Stephen Scrope, who translated from the French *The Epistle of Othea* about 1440 and *The Dicts and Sayings of the Philosophers* in 1450, both initially dedicated to his stepfather, Sir John Fastolf, and, in the case of the *Othea*, commissioned by him.[101] Similarities of vocabulary are particularly striking. The *Othea*, *Dicts*, and *Mirroure* have in common several words, forms, and meanings that, judging from the MED, are never or rarely found elsewhere. In the following list an asterisk marks the entries that are exclusive to these works.

Mirroure	*Othea*	*Dicts*
abaieth 'barks at'		62/25
afore or (er(e))* *conj.* 'before'	55/9, 62/14, 77/6+	58/33, 108/23
anamly* *adv.* 'especially, particularly, chiefly'[102]	6/23, 11/28, 26/7+ (MS L)	
autoriȝed 'given validity'	39/21, 122/12	
barke 'superficial part or shell'	100/25	
bodyly 'deadly'	25/11 (MS L)	
bostously 'harshly, rudely'		120/30
clere seeris* 'clear-sighted persons'	42/13	
communion of seintes 'fellowship of the faithful'	44/8	
dispiteth 'scorns, belittles'	8/21, 10/3, 16/9	
disworshippe *n.* 'dishonor'		34/21, 94/33
disworshipeth 'treats with contempt'		70/21, 94/33
emploie 'make use of'	99/28	
ennoy 'annoyance, vexation'[103]		38/13
foliche *adj.* 'foolish'	108/28	
fructifieth 'prosper, flourish'	26/19, 37/1	
gurmantis* 'gluttons'[104]		260/8
iusticer* 'one who disciplines for sins or faults'[105]	13/4	
liein (?liem) 'fetter, bond'	69/13	
mankyndely *adj.* 'human'	8/4, 12/23, 53/15	
mankyndely* *adj.* 'humane, kindly'	17/12, 79/8	
mankyndelynes* 'manhood'	4/14	124/7
mysbeleverris 'infidels'	119/26	196/15
muse 'spend time idly'[106]	77/31, 81/23	
neghborughshipp 'neighborliness'		282/15
noyseth* 'hold, believe'	44/27	
ouerthrowe *n.*[107]	117/3	

soupleth* 'softens' (metal)		226/13
standyng *conj.* 'since, considering that'	8/6, 48/21, 88/9+	78/11, 156/13
to regard of 'with respect to'	8/9–10	150/25
vaunt	76/17, 78/22, 78/26+	
vauntour 'boaster'	78/29	
worthinessis 'acts of chivalry'	26/3	

Another verbal correspondence occurs in the dedication of the *Othea*, which speaks of Fastolf's '*good ffadyrhode*,' that is, his stepfatherhood, a sense not recorded in MED.[108] The phrase is repeated in the 'Schedule of Grievances,' which Scrope sent to Fastolf, complaining of his poverty, ill-use, and disinheritance, and in his angry '*Replycacions*' to Fastolf's reply.[109] Both the *Mirroure* (l. 6123) and the *Othea* (32/11) render *villains* as 'communes,' with the clear implication of 'rabble.'[110]

The *Dicts* and the *Mirroure* share errors of translation. Both confuse *chauve* 'bald' with *chanué* 'gray, hoary.' Thus Socrates is described as '*white hered*' rather than 'bald' in the *Dicts* (80/7), and the *Mirroure* mistakes a 'bat' (*chauve souris*) for a 'donne mouse' (l. 3161). Also, in the *Dicts* (166/8), *mousche* is, if not inaccurately, at least inappropriately, translated as '*flie*' instead of 'bee': *liche as a flie dothe that chesithe þe best of the floure*. There is a similar passage in the *Mirroure*, where *la petite mouchette* is rendered as '*litil flye*': *He farith as a litill flye þat maketh honye* (l. 8658). The secondary meaning of *mouchette* is *mouche à miel* or *abeille*. It is noteworthy that the *Mirroure* and all but two manuscripts of the *Dicts* have identical slips, which could have originated only with the author himself: '*come*' for '*ouercomme*' (l. 5165) and '*comen*' for '*ouercomen*' (106/24). British Library, London, MS Additional 34193 of the *Dicts* and the abbreviated version of it in the Bodleian Library, Oxford, MS Rawlinson Poetry 32 have '*ouercomen*' by scribal correction.[111] Errors of translation also are common to the *Othea* and the *Mirroure*. Both works confuse French *aboundant* 'abundant' with *abandone* 'lavish' (*Othea* 36/17–18 and *n*, *Mirroure* l. 12573) and, strangely, convert French *lien* 'bond, fetter' – a word that was obviously unfamiliar to Scrope – into English *liein* or possibly '*liem*' (*Othea* 69/19, *Mirroure* l. 11748). In the Longleat copy of the *Othea*, which at times represents Scrope's original draft, *bodely* (25/11) appears to have the meaning 'deadly.' The same sense is given to *bodyly* in the *Mirroure* (l. 4201).

Stylistic traits and phraseology also point to an identity of authorship. Scrope is fond of synonymization. He often pairs French and English words with an intervening *'or,' 'and,' 'that is to seye,'* or *'id est.'* The use of *id est* (expressed in the manuscript by the brevigraph ·*i*·) as a linking device occurs ten times in the *Dicts* and fifteen times in the *Mirroure*. When Scrope is unfamiliar with the French word, he leaves a blank space after *id est*, for example, *Dicts* 122/8 *sincerole id est* ———, and *Mirroure* l. 3410 *boterel id est* ———.[112] English words occasionally precede their French equivalents, a curious usage employed perhaps for elucidation or emphasis. Thus, we have, for example, *Othea* 27/7–8 *ouerwenyng or ouctrecuidez*; *Dicts* 28/24 (and 30/4) *oponly id est publiquement*; and *Mirroure* ll. 7520–1 *adopcion that is to seye avowerie*. Paired synonyms are sometimes placed side by side, that is, *Dicts* 114/22–3 *creator maker*, 290/15 *outragious too much*; *Mirroure* l. 4010 *besye diligent*, l. 5792 *feire polisshed*, l. 6656 *ientil sette*, ll. 11489–90 *putte depart from*, l. 12176 *above open*. This usage, along with *id est*, goes back to Middle French medical texts and is found in Middle English versions of Guy de Chauliac's *Chirurgia Magna* and John Arderne's *Fistula*, which belong dialectically to the same Northeast Midlands area as the *Mirroure*.[113] Scrope may have found these usages in those texts. He was interested in medical literature, as we have seen, and he has some vocabulary in common with Chauliac.[114] The repetition of the subject with a pronoun is a characteristic of style that the *Mirroure* shares with other didactic works of religious instruction.[115] It also occurs in the *Othea*, for example, 70/27–8 *Cirus ... he*, and in the *Dicts*, for example, 150/24–5 *þis prerogatiue ... it*, although, of course, with less frequency than in the *Mirroure* (e.g., ll. 290, 714–6, 831, 2652–3, 7039–40, 4998–9, 4194–5, 9619–20, 9711–2). Pleonasms generally are a peculiar feature of Scrope's style. The appositional 'this' in the phrase *'he this'* (*hym this/hym that*) 'this one' translating French *celui* (*Dicts* 110/14, *Mirroure* ll. 1545, 3129, 3510–1, 3518, 3573, 3636, 3863, 3912–13, 4187, 4299, 4829, 5024, 5956) is most uncommon before Scrope.[116] Similarly, the conjunctions *afore or* (*er(e)*) and *before or* 'before' (*Othea* 55/9, 62/14, 77/6, 87/29, *Dicts* 58/32, 108/33, *Mirroure* ll. 869, 5006–7) rarely or never appear elsewhere.[117] *Standyng* as a subordinate conjunction meaning 'considering, inasmuch as' is a Scropian signature. It is used in *Othea* 4×, *Dicts* 2×, and *Mirroure* 10×. The only other occurrence cited in MED is *Ludus Coventriae* 179/49.[118] The phrase *'us (me, him) must'* to express obligation or necessity is apparently unique to the *Dicts* (68/11–12 *him must obey*, 68/13 *him must suffre*, 260/23 *vs must think*) and *Mirroure* (ll. 2299–2300 *vs moste doo*, l. 8623, *vs moste ȝif acommpt*, l. 11627 *me moste put opon myn heede*).[119] Finally, two curious usages common to the *Dicts* and the *Mirroure* are perhaps also worthy of mention: the translation of *une meisme(s)* (*monnoie, semence*) as the emphatic numeral *on only* (*Dicts* 130/31, *Mirroure* l. 8979) and the metathesis of the generalizing pronoun *what that euer* 'whatever' (*Dicts* 76/5, 80/24, 90/17, *Mirroure* ll. 2231–2, 6818–19, 6851, 6969–70, 7155, 9154–5).[120]

The Scropes of Bolton and Masham were among the upper echelons of English nobility, and Stephen was extremely proud of his lineage.[121] His father, Sir Stephen Scrope, was the third son of Richard, the first lord of Bolton. The major portion of the family estates went to his eldest brother, William, and Sir Stephen himself received as a legacy only the Yorkshire manor of Wighton and other minor properties. His marriage to Dame Millicent Tiptoft, however, who was heiress to the Wiltshire manor of Castle Combe and the Oxfordshire manor of Oxenden, brought him substantial wealth and security. A strong supporter of Richard II, Sir Stephen was at the monarch's side when he surrendered to Bolingbroke at Flint Castle in 1399. Later, he took service with Thomas of Lancaster and acted as his deputy in Ireland, where he died in 1408. Within a few months, Dame Millicent made a hasty second marriage with John Fastolf, the former butler of Thomas of Lancaster and her late husband's servant, and almost immediately thereafter she entailed upon him all her estates, thereby effectively disinheriting her twelve-year-old son, Stephen. Fastolf soon sold his wardship to Sir William Gascoigne, then chief justice of England, for 500 marks, but Stephen was unhappy in Gascoigne's household, and after three years Fastolf was persuaded to take him back and to return the original sum. Some years later, Stephen bitterly complained that he had been bought and sold like a beast. It was at this time that he contracted an illness (possibly smallpox) that left him disfigured and unfit to pursue a military career. He held Fastolf responsible for his disability as well as for his disinheritance and the eventual deterioration of his family fortunes. Much of his life was spent in poverty and abject dependence upon his parsimonious stepfather for support. Between 1415 and 1420 and again in the mid-1420s he was on Fastolf's staff in France and Normandy as an accountant or supplier of herring to his troops. Fastolf returned from France in 1439, and in the 1440s and early 1450s Stephen was again in his employ, perhaps as a secretary. He married twice – in 1433 to Margaret Doreward, whose family on both sides had been speakers of the House of Commons, and in 1456 to Joan, the daughter of Sir Richard Bingham, a chief justice. The marriage to Joan was financially advantageous as well as socially acceptable, mitigating Stephen's straitened circumstances and enabling him to extricate himself somewhat from Fastolf's control. Despite Stephen's resentment of his stepfather's niggardly treatment, Fastolf was often solicitous of his stepson, and it was he who, perhaps in an effort to find a suitable occupation for Stephen's peculiar talents, directed him toward writing books. Both the *Othea* and the *Dicts* found a wide and appreciative audience, particularly among the nobility and gentry, in the last half of the fifteenth century. The *Othea* was reissued after 14 September 1444, with a new dedication to Humphrey Stafford, Duke of Buckingham, and a third time after 1460 to a 'hye princesse' who should almost certainly be identified with Buckingham's widow, Anne Neville, a known collector of English and French books.[122] The *Dicts* was revised by William Worcester in 1472 or 1473.[123] The major features of Stephen Scrope's dialect, as seen from his autographs and the surviving manuscript copies of his translations, will be shown in a separate study, as previously noted, to derive, like the *Mirroure*, from the Northeast Midlands.[124] Manuscripts of both the original and the revised versions of the *Dicts* also contain, to a greater or lesser degree, southwestern forms.[125] It is highly probable that their presence is due to William Worcester, a native of Bristol, who spent more than twenty years in Fastolf's service as secretary, steward, and surveyor of his geographically dispersed properties.[126] The frequent and extensive travel these duties entailed took him regularly to the West Country, to Castle Combe and Bristol in particular, as well as on visits to Somerset, Devonshire, and Gloucestershire.[127] In her edition of the *Dicts*, Schofield plausibly conjectured that Worcester, having obtained Fastolf's presentation copy after his death in 1459, carried it to Bristol, where he later revised it and either there or in 'the surrounding country' had copies of both versions made.[128] Worcester and Scrope were intimately associated in Fastolf's household, even occupying adjacent rooms at Caister Castle.[129] Scrope supplied Worcester (who was also Fastolf's physician) with medical recipes, and he is likely to have contributed material to the *Boke of Noblesse*.[130] Their works show a close community of interests and values grounded in chivalric ideals and classical philosophy and ethics.[131] Worcester apparently came into possession of Scrope's manuscripts after his death in 1472 and acted as his literary executor.[132] But he would surely have had access to Scrope's works on their completion, and copies of the *Dicts* incorporating southwestern forms could have been made much earlier than Schofield suggested. Worcester was particularly active as Fastolf's 'riding-servant' between 1448 and 1458.[133] The 'translation' of the *Mirroure* must have occurred in a manner similar to that of the *Dicts*. Its conduit to the Southwest could well have been Worcester, or Scrope himself, who finally came into his matrilinear inheritance, the lucrative manor of Castle Combe, in 1459.[134] He died there in 1472 and was probably buried in the parish church of St Andrew Apostle.[135] The reference in the *Mirroure* to St Andrew as an exemplification of martyrdom (1341) – a conspicuous addition to the French source, which mentions only St Laurence – may reflect his personal devotion to the patron saint of Castle Combe.[136]

Alterations from the French to the English text may also point to an association with the Scropes. In the midst of a discussion of heresy as a form of pride the *Miroir* alludes in a laudatory manner to the piety of the Cistercians (*les moines de Cisteaulx*) and the theological learning of the clerks of Paris (*les clers de Paris*). In the *Mirroure*, however, these references are removed and replaced with the '*monkes of the Chartirhous*' and the '*clerkys of Cambriche*': '*The grettest pride that is it is lollerie. Is not that a grete pride as when a veleine or an olde wicche, the whiche knoweth not aright the pater noster, wenyth to knowe more devynite than al the clerkys of Cambriche and wenyth to be better than al the monkes of the Chartirhous and wil not beleve that God maye doo nothynge in erthe but that theye maye vndirstonde and see, as that an hole man maye be in siche an oblie as that the preest holdeth at the auter, for the whiche he maye not beleve that it is verraye Goddys bodye!*' (ll. 1922–31). Although the text is regularly adapted to a native audience, these substitutions may have been suggested by the long relationship of the Scrope family with the Carthusians and Cambridge. The Charterhouse was esteemed for its austere piety in late medieval England.[137] It was popular throughout East Anglia, particularly in Norwich, although no house was ever founded there.[138] The Scropes were among its major patrons and supporters, lavishing their gifts upon the Hull Charterhouse.[139] There is no evidence that Stephen himself ever contributed to it – he would hardly have been in a position to do so given his limited means – but the exchange of '*Cisteaulx*' for '*Chartirhouse*' (even allowing for the marked decline in popularity of the Cistercians in England in the fifteenth century)[140] is a sign of the general admiration felt for the order as well as of its continued favor with the Scrope family. The reference to Cambridge is similarly indicative of the close ties of the Scropes with the university. Of the six members of the family who took university degrees in the late Middle Ages – for the aristocracy an exceptional number, exceeded only by the Nevilles, who could boast of eight university graduates[141] – five attended Cambridge. Three of them became chancellors of the university: Richard Scrope 1378–9, Stephen le Scrope (who took his bachelor's degree at Oxford before moving to Cambridge) 1414, and Richard Scroop 1461–2.[142] The latter, second son of Richard, third Lord Scrope of Bolton, was also warden of King's Hall, Cambridge, from 1457 to 1463.[143] Stephen is likely to have known him personally, having been reared with his father, Richard, and possibly having been with him when he fell at the siege of Rouen in 1420.[144] The Scropes maintained their connections with Cambridge throughout the fifteenth century, and it is not surprising that Stephen, although not an alumnus, seized the opportunity to pay tribute to its distinguished school of divinity.[145]

In a discussion of God's bounty to man, the *Miroir* refers to the pious practices of Cistercian converses (*ces convers de Cisteaulx*). This is replaced in the *Mirroure* by an allusion to the '*coventis of Celestinis*': '*Truly he is a velein and ful evil that forȝeteth siche bounte [or] whooso may do it and wil not seye his vii houres of the daye outher be nombre of pater nosteris, as the coventis of Celestinis doon, or othir weyes whoso can*' (ll. 1760–4). Here, too, is an association with the Scrope family. Henry V had endeavored without success to found an English branch of the continental order in atonement for the execution of Archbishop William Scrope in 1405. The *Mirroure* recalls this event and delicately draws attention to the unfulfilled obligation of the Lancastrian regime. An effort to canonize Archbishop Scrope, which began soon after his death, continued well into the reign of Henry VI.[146]

Bodley 283 lacks a dedication, and its colophon is taken unaltered from the French. Yet there is nothing in this fact to contradict the hypothesis of common authorship with the *Othea* and *Dicts*. Two of the three extant manuscripts of the *Othea* – those with dedications to Humphrey Stafford, Duke of Buckingham, and the '*hye princesse*' – give no evidence of authorship, nor do three of the six substantially complete extant manuscripts of the *Dicts* (a seventh is incomplete at the beginning and the end) and its abbreviated version in Rawlinson Poetry MS 32.[147] Ironically, in the preface to the Longleat version of the

Othea, Christine de Pisan is also denied credit for her work:' *And this seyde boke, at the instavnce & praer off a fulle wyse gentyl-woman of Frawnce called Dame Cristine, was compiled & grounded by the famous doctours of the most excellent in clerge the noble Vniuersyte off Paris.*'[148] It is well to remember that anonymity is a commonplace of medieval literature, and attributions of authorship are frequently lost or confused in transmission. Scrope translated the *Othea* at Fastolf's bidding in order that he might devote his retirement to '*gostly cheuallrie off dedes of armes spirituall, as in contemplacion of morall wysdome and exercisyng gostly werkyys.*'[149] He produced the philosophical *Dicts* for Fastolf's '*contemplacion and solace.*'[150] The *Mirroure* served a similar purpose. It offered him, a man of deep and genuine piety, and his circle of East Anglian gentry a comprehensive guide to Christian spirituality and salvation based in part on the moral teachings of the ancients and their medieval commentators that must have appealed to his love of classical learning, his taste for sententiae and exempla, his appetite for didactic religious literature, his dedication to prayer and other private devotions, and his profound concern with the four last things: Death, Judgment, Hell, and Heaven.[151] His familiarity with the *Miroir*, moreover, actually may have preceded Scrope's translation. A contemporary inventory of his library lists a *Vices et Vertus*, the alternate title of the *Miroir*.[152]

6. Editorial Procedure

Our aim in this edition is to present an accurate and readable text of Bodley 283. To achieve this purpose a number of interventions have been deemed necessary to supply omissions and correct scribal and authorial errors that confuse or obscure the meaning and are likely to check the reader. These are generally limited to a single word or a short phrase or an occasional transposition and are kept conservatively to a minimum. Errors of miscopying or mistranslation that require more extensive emendation or cannot be corrected with the substitution of a word or phrase are allowed to stand and are discussed in the annotations. To eliminate all the errors of the text would be, among other things, to misrepresent both what the translator saw and what he thought he saw in his exemplar, as well as to distort the nature of the translation. Apart from obvious mechanical errors, emendations are entirely based on the readings of the ten French manuscripts of the Y version of *Le Miroir du Monde* consulted for this edition. They follow the predominant forms of the scribe and together with all other additions and changes in the text are enclosed in square brackets and recorded in the textual notes. For the sake of clarity and for ease of reference, chapter titles absent from the text are supplied from the table of contents.

The spelling, which is highly inconsistent and is characterized by frequent doubling of vowels and consonants, has been retained; so, too, the orthography, including the letters *u* and *v*, *þ*, and *ȝ*. The only two exceptions to this practice are the treatment of initial *ff* which has been transcribed as *f* (*feith*, *firste*) or *F* (*Fraunce*) and the calligraphic variants *i*/*Ɨ* which have been transcribed as *i* or *I*. Lower case *j* is often used for the final minim of numerals (*iiij*). The personal pronoun is regularly written as *Ɨ* which also occurs as the initial letter of proper names (*Ɨnglond*, *Ɨsaye*).

Paragraphing, punctuation, word division, and capitalization are editorial. Quotations drawn from the Bible, the Church Fathers, and other sources are unmarked (although identified in the notes), since they are rarely precise and more often than not are absorbed into the body of the text. Lacunae affecting the sense of a passage are indicated by spaced periods enclosed in square brackets [...], and the French is provided in the explanatory notes. Common abbreviations, apart from those employed for numerals and money terms, are expanded to their usual values with due attention to normal scribal practice. *Ihū* is rendered as *Iesus* and *Ihrƚm* as *Ierusalem*. The brevigraph ·*i*· is expanded to *id est*. An otiose superscript *o* is sometimes appended to the final minim of cardinal numerals and is ignored in transcription. The most common mark of abbreviation is the bar, which takes the form of a horizontal stroke, a curved stroke, and, in one instance, a dotted circumflex. It normally represents a nasal in the *ion* suffix. At other times it seems to be meaningless, occurring in words that are complete, such as *m̄an*, *kyn̄n̄e*, *būt*, *Austyn̄*, *Galyen̄*, *Calden̄* beside *Calden* ll. 4415–16, *yēn̄*, *deken̄*, *hevyn̄*, *often̄*. In such cases it is ignored in transcription. The occasional idiosyncratic form *m̄e* is transcribed as *men*. Final *o(u)n* or *io(u)n* presents a problem of interpretation that is not unfamiliar to editors of fifteenth-century texts. Since *u* and *n* are virtually indistinguishable in the manuscript, the bar over the last two minims may be superfluous, as in the citations above, or a curtailment mark indicating suspension of *n* after *u*. The variable practice of the scribe results in the appearance of forms such as *adopcion̄*, *affeccion̄*, *ambicion̄*, *comparison̄*, *confession̄*, *reeson̄*, *religion̄*, *tribulacion̄*, *vppon̄* beside *adopcion, affeccion, ambicion, comparison, condicion, confession, reeson, religion, tribulacion, vppon*. The bars in these instances seem little more than otiose flourishes and are so regarded in this edition. Their lack of significance is confirmed by the fact that final *ioun* never occurs in words spelled out in full, nor does final *oun*, save in a single instance: *vppe soo doun* (l. 6692). Meaningless flourishes also appear as strokes through *h* and *ll*, a curl on *p*, a loop on final *g*, and tags on final *d*, *f*, and *t*.

The foliation of the text runs continuously from 1 to 180^{v}, rectifying the faulty enumeration to which attention has already been drawn. In consequence, folios 75 to 155 bear a numeral one greater than they do in the manuscript.

NOTES

1 Kathleen L. Scott has fully described Bodley 283 in *Mirroure of the Worlde*, 60–5, and in her earlier doctoral dissertation, 'Archeological Analysis,' 93–139. Additional details may be found in 'English Illuminating Shop,' 182–7; *Caxton Master*, 25–46; and *Later Gothic Manuscripts*, No. 136. There is a brief notice of the manuscript written by Dr Scott in Tudor-Craig, *Richard III*, No. 17. See also Madan and Craster, *Summary Catalogue* 316–17; *VV*, xxxviii–ix; and Kosmer, 'Style and Iconography,' Part 2, 40–2. Reviews of *The Mirroure of the Worlde* by Griffiths, Voigts, and Keen appeared in *The Book Collector*, *Speculum*, and *Burlington Magazine*, respectively; Jolliffe, *Check-List*, No. 62; Raymo, 'Works,' No. 10.

2 The watermark is reproduced in Scott, *Mirroure of the Worlde*, Fig. 14. Dr Paul Needham identified its source in a personal communication to Dr Scott (31 October 1989), noting also its similarity to Piccard 121, a winged griffin found on a smaller-sized paper produced in Venice between 1461 and 1463. The Bodley paper, he believes, came from the same mill as Piccard 123. Papers manufactured for manuscripts could be stored a long time before use. Cf. Stevenson, 'Paper as Bibliographical Evidence,' 201, and Spector, *Essays in Paper Analysis*, 18–21.

3 The mistaken foliation of the manuscript has been corrected in this edition.

4 The terminology is that formulated by Parkes, *English Cursive Book Hands*, xxi–iii. Brown, *Western Historical Scripts*, 110, notes that the hand was popularly employed for use in de luxe manuscripts of the

fifteenth and sixteenth centuries. The colophon is written in *textura semi-quadrata*.

5 Scott, *Mirroure of the Worlde*, 5 n.8.

6 The hand is not yet known elsewhere. It is similar, but apparently not identical, to the hand of the scribe who wrote Peter Idley's *Instructions to His Son* in Cambridge University Library, Cambridge, MS E.5.37 and John Lydgate's *Life of Our Lady* in the Bodleian Library, Oxford, MS Bodley 596. Cf. Scott, 'Archeological Analysis,' 220–1, 224.

7 For final pauses combinations of two virgules between two points occur with some frequency early in the manuscript. The use of two points seems unusual. Parkes, *English Cursive Book Hands*, 46, observes that the combination of a single point followed by two virgules became common in fifteenth-century manuscripts.

8 Folios 32^{v}, 33, and 33^{v} have been revised by expunction and cancellation with additions inserted by caret. Alterations have also been made to the text after erasure or washing at folio 24. All these changes are in later hands. A contemporary corrector has added *gevist* in the margin of folio 15.

9 Scott, *Mirroure of the Worlde*, 39.

10 Ibid., 62–3. A reference to Dame Anne (?Neville, Duchess of Buckingham, possibly the 'hye princesse' to whom the *Othea* was dedicated in the Pierpont Morgan Library MS, or more likely Anne, Warwick's daughter and the ill-fated wife of Richard III) appears in a later hand in the lower margin of folio 84 below line 6204.

11 Pollard, Fifteenth-Century Binders, 198. He believes such bindings to be rare after 1450.

12 The illustrations are fully reproduced and discussed in Scott, *Mirroure of the World*. See also Tuve, 'Virtues and Vices,' 53*n*, 64 pls 101$^{a\text{–}b}$, and *Allegorical Imagery*, 22, 88*n*, 103–5 figs. 7, 22–4; Pächt and Alexander, *Illuminated Manuscripts*, vol. 1, viii, 17 (No. 222), pl. XVI, figs. 222a–c, and vol. 3, 93 (No. 1082), pl. CI, figs. 1082a–b; Delaissé, *Dutch Manuscript Illustration*, 79–80, fig. 144; Scott, *Caxton Master*, 25–46; Hobson, *Great Libraries*, 167; Kosmer, 'Style and Iconography,' vol. 1, 46*n*, 275*n*, 276–7, 279*n*, vol. 2, 40–2, 188, and '"Noyous humoure,"' 3; Tudor-Craig, *Richard III*, pls 3, 7; Scott, *Gothic Manuscripts*, pls. 487–9, 494, and *Index of Images*, 59, where she notes that 'the artist apparently revised the order of the drawings for James the Less and Matthew, since the fuller's club is the conventional emblem for the former.'

13 Scott, *Caxton Master*, 3–24 (Magdalene College, Cambridge, MS F.4.34: *Ovid Moralised*), 47–54 (Duke of Buccleuch and Queensbury MS: *Writhe's*

Garter Book), 55–66 (British Library MS Cotton Julius E.iv: *Beauchamp Pageants*), and *Mirroure of the Worlde*, 31–2, and *Gothic Manuscripts*, Nos 96, 137; and Tudor-Craig, Nos 132, 133. Scholars differ on the precise dates of these manuscripts, but all assign them to the 1480s. On the basis of the paper Dr Paul Needham has redated the *Ovid Moralised* to 1483 or later (personal communication from Dr Scott). It should be added that Backhouse, 'Founders of the Royal Library,' 202, does not accept the identification of its illustrator as the Caxton Master.

14 Scott, *Caxton Master*, 27–45, *Mirroure of the Worlde*, 11–33, and *Gothic Manuscripts*, vol. 2, 353–4.

15 His work has been identified in twenty-five manuscripts dating from about 1461 to 1483. Scott, *Illuminating Shop*; *Mirroure of the Worlde*, 34–8, 40, 45–50, 56; and *Gothic Manuscripts*, vol. 2, 354.

16 Dr Scott considers the 'owl illuminator' to have been the pupil of the master artist who decorated the Chigi Caesar (written in England in 1450 by a Netherlandish scribe) and other humanistic manuscripts; see *Mirroure of the Worlde*, 38–44, and *Gothic Manuscripts*, vol. 2, 354. For a recent addition to the corpus of the Caesar Master – a Book of Hours of Sarum Use – see Griffiths, [Review], 236. The mobility of late medieval continental illuminators is discussed by Alexander, *Medieval Illuminators*, 124–5. On alien craftsmen in England see Meale, 'Patrons, Buyers and Owners,' 201–2 and nn. 2, 3.

17 For Lechery's headdress and neckline see M. Scott, *Late Gothic Europe*, 175, fig. 109; Bergmans, 'Marguerite d'York,' miniature, x, Convent of the Colettine Poor Clares, Ghent, MS 8, f. 40^{v} (portrait of Margaret of York, 1470), and Corstanje et al., *Vita Sanctae Coletae*, pl. 11; Pächt and Thoss, *Illuminierten Handschriften*, MS 2534, f. 17 (Jean de Wavrin, *Chroniques d'Angleterre*, 1470, showing both headdress and neckline in the person of the seated lady on the right); Arnould and Massing, *Splendours of Flanders*, 155, Cambridge University Library, Cambridge, MS Nn.3.2, f. 27^{v} (portrait of Lady Eloquence, c. 1470); Clayton, *Catalogue of Rubbings*, pl. 23, brass of Ralph St Leger and his wife Anne on their tomb in Ulcombe, Kent, 1470 (Buzza II, illustration 226); and Cunnington and Cunnington, *English Mediaeval Costume*, 162, fig. c. Cf. also Buzza, *English Female Costume*, vol. II, illus. 214, 220, 268 (*Robert Ingylton and Three Wives*, 1472; *Emma, Wife of John Wode*, 1471; *Lady with Flowing Hair*, c. 1470).

18 For the features of Pride's costume see M. Scott, *Late Gothic Europe*, 173–85, and the court scene from Jean de Wavrin's *Chroniques d'Angleterre* cited in the previous note. An outfit very similar to Pride's

dated c. 1470 is reproduced by Cunnington and Cunnington, *English Mediaeval Costume*, 138, fig. c. See also Van den Gheyn, pls 17, 35, 36, 37, Bibliothèque Nationale, Paris, MS f.fr.22547, f. 1 (*Geste d'Alexandre*, 1470); Arnould and Massing, *Splendours of Flanders*, 151, St John's College, Cambridge, MS H.13, f. 103 (Breviary of Margaret of York, c. 1470); Kren, *Renaissance Paintings*, fig. 1b, Österreichische Nationalbibliothek, Vienna, MS 2616, f. iv (*Charles the Bold Presenting An Ordinance to the First Master of the Livery*, 1469); *Siècle d'Or*, pl. 53, Bibliothèque Nationale, Paris, MS f.fr.201, f. 9^{v} (*Presentation of Book to Duke of Burgundy*, 1471); and Gaspar and Lyna, *Philippe le Bon*, pl. 22, Bibliothèque Royale, Brussels, MS 9967, f. 39 (*Ystoire de Helayne*, 1470). For the changes in fashion see Kren, *Renaissance Paintings*, 14, fig. 1a, British Library, London, MS Additional 36619, f. 1 (*Ordinance of Charles the Bold*, 1474–76); Hassall and Hassall, *Treasures*, pl. 33, and Pächt and Alexander, *Illuminated Manuscripts*, vol. 1, 352, pl. 27, Bodleian Library, Oxford, MS Douce 365 (S.C. 21940), f. 115 (a French miscellany illustrated by the Master of Mary of Burgundy, 1475), and vol. 1, 351, pl. 28, Bodleian Library, Oxford, MS Douce 208 (S.C. 21782), f. 1 (Caesar's *de Bello Gallico*, after 1474). Efforts to control immoderate dress through sumptuary legislation are discussed by F. Baldwin, *Sumptuary Legislation*, 101–10, and Scattergood 'Fashion and Morality,' 261–2. For additional descriptions of contemporary male and female dress, particularly the illustrations of *Cleriadus et Meliadice*, probably made for Edward IV or a member of his family c. 1470, see Sutton, 'Dress and Fashions,' especially 17–26.

19 In her earlier work, K.L. Scott dates the manuscript about 1465 ('Archeological Analysis,' 131 n. 34; 'Illuminating Shop,' 184, *n*80). In her later work she favors a date in the 1470s, 'probably c. 1475–80' (*Caxton Master*, 25–7; *Mirroure of the Worlde*, 31). In her most recent work the date is given as 'before 1485, probably 1470–1480' (*Gothic Manuscripts*, vol. 2, 352 and *Index of Images*, p. 59).

20 Scott, 'Archeological Analysis,' 131–7; 'Illuminating Shop,' 184–6; *Caxton Master*, 45–6; *Mirroure of the Worlde*, 8–10; and *Gothic Manuscripts*, vol. 2, 354.

21 On the exclusiveness and prominence of this company, see McCutchan, '"Solemne and a Greet Fraternitee,"' 314–15; Johnson, *History of the Drapers*, vol. 1, 356; Unwin, *Guilds and Companies*, 77–81; and Dyer, *Standards of Living*, 15–16.

22 Luton Guild Register, f. 13. For a description of the manuscript (now in the possession of the Luton Art Museum) and its illustrations and an

account of the social importance of the Guild see Gough, *Register of the Fraternity*; Knowles, *Religious Orders*, 207; Sotheby Park Bernet Sales Catalogue, 13 June 1983, Lot 19, 80–7; and Scott, 'Illustration and Decoration of the Register.' A frontispiece (f. 13^{v}) by a Bruges artist shows the king and queen kneeling before the throne of the Trinity; behind them are crowds of men and women among whom the Sotheby Cataloguer purports to identify Kippyng and his wife Agnes. Cf. also Hasler, *Royal Arms*, fig. 133, and Acworth, 'Misleading Brass,' 204.

23 Sharpe, *Calendar of Letter-Books*, 175–6. On 'benevolences' as a form of indirect taxation first imposed by Edward IV in 1473 see Jacob, *Fifteenth Century*, 584–5, and S.K. Fischer, *Econolingua*, 45.

24 Cf. Meale, 'Patrons, Buyers and Owners,' especially 212–13, 216–17, and Backhouse, 'Founders of the Royal Library,' 31–2.

25 Kippying had died by 12 May 1485 (K. Scott, 'English Illuminating Shops,' 185). Did this luxury book pass into the possession of the Staffords? See note 10, above.

26 Madan and Craster, *Summary Catalogue*, 317; K. Scott, 'Illuminating Shops,' 187. On Barker's career see Plomer, 'King's Printing House,' 353–69; DNB, vol. 1, 1127–8; and Handover, *Printing in London*, 81–5.

27 Cf. ll. 4471–3.

28 Cf. ll. 1450–9, 1634–6, 7406–15.

29 For the twenty-first decree see Tanner, *Church*, vol. 1, 245, and for the reforming program of the Council and the synodal legislation it inspired see Gibbs and Lang, *Bishops and Reform*, 94–182. Newhauser describes the generic characteristics of the treatise on the vices and virtues and presents a comprehensive account of its origin and development (*Vices and Virtues*, 55–152). For the place of the treatise within the larger cultural context of *pastoralia* see Boyle, 'Clerical Education,' 'Fourth Lateran Council,' 'Inter-Concilian Period'; Payen, 'La Pénitance'; Rusconi, 'La confessione dei peccatori,' 'De la Prédication'; and Gillespie, 'Vernacular Books,' and 'Thy Will Be Done.'

30 Newhauser, *Vices and Virtues*, 71–3, 85–9.

31 Hugh of St Victor, *De quinque septenis seu septenariis*, PL 175, cols 405–14. Cf. Bloomfield, 'Seven Deadly Sins,' 83–91, and Gillespie, 'Thy Will Be Done,' 97–8.

32 Brayer, '*La Somme le Roi*,' and 'Contenu,' 3–4; Carruthers, *La Somme le Roi*, 16–17.

33 Brayer, '*La Somme le Roi*,' 137–63; Carruthers, *La Somme le Roi*, 12–15. On the dates of Peraldus's works see Dondaine, 'Guillaume Peyraut,' 186–7. Wenzel would perhaps date them slightly earlier ('Peraldus's *Summa vitiorum*,' 136).

34 Brayer edited an early *Somme* manuscript, Bibliothèque Mazarine 870, in her unpublished dissertation, 'La Somme le Roi.' A defective and incomplete copy of the X redaction of the combined *Miroir* and *Somme* entitled *Le Mireour du Monde* was edited by Chavannes in 1845.
35 On the date of the *Somme* see Brayer, 'La Somme le Roi,' 34–8, and 'contenu,' 2. Brayer declines to date the *Miroir* precisely ('Contenu,' 445).
36 For the use of the *Tabula Exemplorum* and the *Collationes* see the explanatory notes to ll. 285–9, 378–88, 944–56, 967–87, 995–6, 1054–7, 1061–5.
37 Brayer, 'La somme le Roi,' 113–15.
38 Langlois, *La Vie en France*, 137. See the notes to ll. 1760–4, 1926–7.
39 Quétif and Échard, *Scriptores*, 386–8; Kaeppeli, *Scriptores*, 63–4; Brayer, 'La Somme le Roi,' 27–35; *VV*, xi–xix; Carruthers, *La Somme le Roi*, 5–7, and 'Lorens of Orléans,' 192–7.
40 We are grateful to Madame Labie-Leurquin of the Institut de Recherche et d'Histoire des Textes for providing us with a complete list of known extant manuscripts of the *Somme* and *Miroir*. Cf. *VV*, xix–xxi, and *Ayen* vol. 2, 112–14.
41 Kaeppeli, *Scriptores*, 63–4; *VV*, xxviii–xxxi; Carruthers, *La Somme le Roi*, 17–18.
42 Brayer, 'La Somme le Roi,' 80–133, and 'Contenu,' 7–38; Carruthers, *La Somme le Roi*, 9–10, 13–14.
43 Brayer, 'Contenu,' 433–48, 464–5.
44 Brayer, 'Contenu,' 7. The different redactions of the *Somme* are discussed on 461–4.
45 Ibid., 466–70.
46 Brayer, 'La Somme le Roi,' 129–33, and 'Contenu,' 468–9. The passage on the historical events commemorated on Sunday in the *Mirroure* (ll. 610–58) is taken from the *Manuale Sacerdotum Parochalium* or a closely related text, and it may or may not be exclusive to the Y redaction.
47 *Catalogue Général* (1872), 84; *Codices Manuscripti*, 14; Brayer, 'La Somme le Roi,' 271; Kosmer, 'Style and Iconography,' vol. 2, 122.
48 Chantilly, *Le Cabinet des Livres*, 124–6; *Catalogue Général* (1928), 28–9; Kosmer, 'Style and Iconography,' vol. 2, 133.
49 *Catalogue des Manuscrits*, 'La Somme le Roi,' Martin, 424–5; Brayer, 272; Kosmer, 'Style and Iconography,' vol. 2, 150.
50 Bibliothèque Imperiale, *Catalogue* (1868), 459; Brayer, 'La Somme le Roi,' 270; Kosmer, 'Style and Iconography,' vol. 2, 152.
51 Bibliothèque Imperiale, *Catalogue* (1868), 162; Brayer, 'La Somme le Roi,' 273–4; Kosmer, 'Style and Iconography,' vol. 2, 157.

52 Bibliothèque Nationale, *Catalogue* (1902), 14–15; Meyer, 'Notice sur le manuscrit 27,' 70; Brayer, 'La Somme le Roi,' 266–8; Kosmer, 'Style and Iconography,' 167.
53 Bibliothèque Nationale, *Catalogue* (1902), 15; Meyer, 'Notice sur le manuscrit 27,' 70–1; Brayer, 'La Somme le Roi,' 268–9; Kosmer, 'Style and Iconography,' vol. 2, 115.
54 *Catalogue Général* (1885), 137–8; Kosmer, 'Style and Iconography,' vol. 2, 180; Whitaker, 'Soissons MS 221,' 83, 86.
55 *Catalogue Général* (1900), 320–1; Kosmer, 'Style and Iconography,' vol. 2, 182.
56 *Manuscrits de la Reine*, No. 745; Langlois, 'Notice des manuscrits,' 152–3.
57 *Manuscrits de la Reine*, No. 776; Langlois, 'Notice des manuscrits,' 247–9; Kosmer, 'Style and Iconography,' vol. 2, 86–8.
58 See the explanatory notes to ll. 47–8, 212, 213–18, 2104, 7612, 12166. The *Mirroure* also shares unique readings with V at ll. 6456 and 8594–5.
59 A detailed description of MS T in typescript was kindly made available to us by the librarian, M. Laurent. Among the works in the miscellany are *Misère de la condition humaine, Enseignement d'un père à son fils*, and *Plainte de la Vierge au pied de la Croix*.
60 Sonet 493 (Langlois, 'Notice des manuscrits,' 249; Långfors, *Incipits de poèmes*, 104; Brayer, 'Livre d'heures,' 69; Sinclair, *Prières*, 57, and *Prières* (Supplément), 71; Rézeau, *Répertoire*, 44): *Doulce vierge Marie, royne de pitie*; 527 (Långfors, *Incipits de poèmes*, 104; Sinclair, Prières, 60; Naetebus, *Nicht-Lyrishen*, 182): *Doulz Ihesucrist nostre vray sire*; 704 (Langlois, 'Notice des manuscrits,' 249; Långfors, *Incipits de poèmes*, 148; Sinclair, *Prières*, 70): *Glorieux Dieu, souverain pere*; 1538 (Leroquais, *Livres d'heures*, 332 *n*16; Sinclair, *Prières*, 113–14, and *Prières* (Supplément), 126–8; Rézeau, *Répertoire*, 106–7): *O tres certaine esperance*; and possibly 617 (related to 527): *Et doulz Ihesu nostre vray sire*; Walther, Nos 2521 (*Cartula nostra tibi*) and 1996 (*Ave verum corpus*).
61 Parkes, 'Influence,' 132–5; Gillespie, 'Vernacular Books,' 329–31; Rouse and Rouse, *Authentic Witnesses*, 453–7.
62 See, for example, ll. 1326–30, 1378, 1468, 3461–2, 4108–9, 4766, 6206–8, 6622–3, 7039–41, 7415–19, 8391–3, 8684–5, 9313–16, 9489–94, 9799–9807, 11188–95, 12094–6, 12716–8, 12812–16.
63 Raymo, 'Works,' Nos. 4, 5, 6. Cf. Carruthers, *La Somme le Roi*, 19–22.
64 Raymo, 'Works,' Nos. 11, 12, 107. For the date, provenance, and authorship of *Disce Mori* and *Ignorancia Sacerdotum* see Doyle, '*Lectulus*,' 183–5. Diekstra, 'Fifteenth-Century Borrowings,' 82–3, identifies the sources of the treatise on the sins.

65 England, London, Cambridge, Chartirhouse regularly replace France, Paris, Citeaux.
66 See, for example, 500–1, 10515, 10690–1, 10770, 10799, 10904, 11025, 11256–61, 11310–12, 11345, 11418, 11676.
67 See text, below, 21. On pleonasm as an aspect of fifteenth-century prose style see Mueller, *Native Tongue*, 147–61.
68 See text, below, 24–5.
69 For misreading see, for example, 353, 388–9, 396–7, 667, 1138, 1281, 1575, 1649, 2119, 2134–5, 2766, 3174, 3250, 3381, 3750, 4187, 4906, 6692, 7575, 8626, 9757–8, 12749–50, and for mistranslation see, for example, ll. 285–9, 518–21, 664–5, 878, 1702–3, 1832, 1903, 1979–84, 2108, 2127–31, 3161, 3189–93, 3197, 3272, 3970, 4087–8, 4094–6, 4102, 4178, 5863, 5879, 5934, 6388, 6413.
70 See, for example, ll. 1146, 1875, 1899, 2004–5, 3992, 4431, 5156, 7555–64, 9378, 10344, 12737–9.
71 See, for example, ll. 1322, 2385, 2531, 3277, 3345, 12120.
72 See ll. 3410, 3605, 4074, 4257, 5579, 6334, 9111, 9724.
73 Brayer, 'Contents,' 6; Langlois, *La Vie en France*, 136.
74 LALME I.146. In an earlier private communication Professor Angus McIntosh had located the work in the vicinity of Oundle or Thrapston.
75 Professor Matheson presented his findings to a session on Stephen Scrope at the International Medieval Congress, Kalamazoo, Michigan, 6 May 1988. A comprehensive comparative linguistic analysis of Bodley 283, *Dicts*, *Othea*, and the Scrope autographs in British Library, London, MSS Additional 28209 and 28212, together with a Middle English translation of Jacques Legrand's *Livre des Bonnes Moeurs*, which may also be from his hand, will be published separately in a joint article by Professors Matheson and Raymo. For a description of the 'fit-technique' see McIntosh, 'Middle English Dialectology'; Samuels, *Linguistic Evolution*; and LALME I.10–12.
76 The main dialect sources cited by Professor Matheson are as follows: for Huntingdonshire, New College, Oxford, MS 95, Hand A (LP 541); for Soke of Peterborough, British Library, London, MS Harley 2415 (LP 556), Westminster School, London, MS 3, Hand A (LP 763), and Bodleian Library, Oxford, MS Tanner 1 (LP 766); and for Northamptonshire, Cambridge University Library, Cambridge, MS Kk.1.5, Part I (LP 736), Sidney Sussex College, Cambridge, MS 55, Hand B (LP 737), British Library, London, MSS Harley 6579, Hand E (LP 752), and Royal 18.B.ix, Hand A (LP 742), and Pennsylvania State University, University Park, MS V-3 (LP 738). The linguistic profiles are published in LALME III.187, 368–70, 373–5, 438–41.

77 McIntosh, 'Present Indicative Plural,' especially 237–44; Laing, 'Dialect Material,' vol. 1, 242–6. On the date of the Gonville MS see the *Rosarium*, 13 *n*13.

78 Constructions like 'they that say' may take either form of the verb. The *Mirroure* favors the reduced *e* or *Ø* forms, for example, *they that doo* (597), *theye that take* (4490), *wee that haue* (8340).

79 On the distribution of *siche, iche, any, hundreth, myche, theym,* and *theys* see LALME I.Dot Maps 6, 44, 68, 87, 97, 102, and 454; and on the distribution of *shee* and *hirre* see LALME II. Item Maps 4(5) and 5(5). For *hundreth* see also McIntosh, 'Word Geography,' 59 (Map 3).

80 The dialect sources most closely resembling the language of the *Mirroure* are, for example, for Rutland, British Library, London, MSS Harley 2371 (LP 554) and Cotton Vespasian E.XVI (LP 553), Bodleian Library, Oxford, MS Douce 114 (LP 99), and Cambridge University Library, Cambridge, MS Nn.III.10 (LP 540); for Leicestershire, British Library, London, MS Harley 4012 (LP 299), Trinity College, Dublin, MS 154 (LP 1), Bodleian Library, Oxford, MS Ashmole 61 (LP 71), Takimiya (Tokyo) 59 (*olim* Chetham 27092) (LP 767), and Leicestershire Record Office, Leicester, Indenture (LP 731). The linguistic profiles are published in LALME III.230, 233–4, 236–7, 251–2, 420–4.

81 For the distribution of *-f(f)-* forms of 'love' and 'live,' *sen, apon(e), dede, os, those, keste,* and *wars* see LALME I.Dot Maps 237, 393, 469, 593, 617, 717, 628, 823, 825, and 908. On *ȝone, nerhand(e),* and *kyen* see Kaiser, *Geographie*, 38, 84, 229; Burnley, 'Lexis and Semantics,' 461; and Glausser, *Linguistic Border*, 228–33.

82 Cf. MED, s.v. *bultel* n., c. For *harre* see the note to l. 2531; for *hoope* see Kaiser, *Geographie*, 28, 215–16, and Burnley, 'Lexis and Semantics,' 411, 460.

83 Cf. Nevanlinna, 'Background and History,' 588: 'In Northern and Northerly texts the predicate of the parenthetic phrase corresponding to *as who saith* in more Southernly regions seems to appear in the present subjunctive [*seie*] as a rule.' The relevant texts are cited on 588–97.

84 For the distribution of *a/an, yoven, -th* for *-t* forms, *weele, bvt, no, qwom, dede, felleth, ferst, kende, mende,* and *thredde*, see LALME I.Dot Maps 270, 272, 376, 399, 414, 432, 485, 913, 993, 1007, 1040, 1176; McIntosh, 'Written Middle English,' 46; and Beadle, 'Medieval Drama,' vol. 1, 64–5. For the distribution of *-et* and *-t* forms, *hisse, whas,* and *whe* see LALME IV.314, 322, 323; McIntosh, 'Written Middle English,' 38–9. Perhaps *qhoso* (1288) 'whoso' should be added to the list, but LALME IV.283 shows only the spelling *qwhso*. For the *-ch-* spellings of 'change'

and 'charge' see van Zutphen's comments in Lavynham, *A Litil Tretys*, lxxix.

85 Cf. MED, s.v. *callioun* n., a.

86 LALME I.Dot Map 1015 and Dobson, *English Pronunciation*, vol. 2, 996 *n*2.

87 For the distribution of *ther*, *yeate*, and *ȝeaf* see LALME I.Dot Maps 429, 1002, and 1120, and Kihlbom, *Fifteenth Century English*, 131, 132.

88 For the distribution of *yeyen*, *hire*, *kyende*, *myende*, *wham*, and the suffix *-nys* see LALME I.Dot Maps 611, 1014, 1041, 1106, and 1169; and for the spelling *moothe* and the forms in *-ed* see LALME IV.319, 323. For *hire*, *hir-* see Samuels, *Linguistic Evolution*, 108–9, and Davis, 'Scribal Variation,' 102. For *wham*, the unvoicing of initial *b*, and the voicing of *ch* see Matthews, 'South Western Dialect,' 201, 202, 205. The form *reculeth* 'retreats' (l. 5571) may also be southwestern (MED, s.v. *recoilen* v.).

89 On the Chancery forms see Fisher, Richardson, and Fisher, *Chancery English*, 29–30, and Richardson, 'Henry V,' 734. The minority form *mo(o)che* and the *-y-* spellings of 'again' and 'against' may also be characteristic of Chancery (Fisher, Richardson, and Fisher, *Chancery English*, 308, 314, 361). For the influence of 'metropolitan' spelling on provincial writers see Davis, 'Language,' and 'Scribal Variation.'

90 Only 70 yoghs in all positions – approximately 5 per cent of the total for the entire text – occur in these chapters, well below the average of 120 per 800 lines.

91 Jordan, *Mittelenglischen Grammatik*, sect. 203; Benskin, 'Local Archives,' 506 *n*9.

92 The earliest appearance of *disworshipe* as a noun occurs in a letter from Sir John Fastolf to Stephen Scrope that MED, following Poulett Scrope, *Castle Combe*, 271, misdates c. 1420. Its actual date is after 1424, probably 1425. Cf. Hughes, 'Stephen Scrope,' 111 and *n*13.

93 *Othea* 231 glosses *worthinesses* as 'worthy deeds.' MED, s.v. *worthines*, gives 'a chivalric act' or 'a feat of arms.'

94 The MED citations derive from the following sources: *Pilgrimage of the Lyfe of Manhode* 5×, *Proceedings and Ordinances of the Privy Council of England* 3×, *Promptorium Parvulorum* 5×, *Book of the Knight of La Tour Landry* 6×, *Gesta Romanorum* 1×, *Libel of English Policy* 1×, Ipswich Domesday 2×, *Perceval* 1×, *Merlin* 1×, *Alphabet of Tales* 2×, *Castle of Perseverance* 2×, *Jacob's Well* 1×, *Generides* 1×, *Memoriale Credencium* 1×, Account Rolls of the Abbey of Durham 1×, *A Myrour to Lewde Men and Wymmen* 2×, a later interpolation in Rolle's *Psalter* (s.v. *multi-*

pliinge) 1×, a late copy of Wyclif's sermons (s.v., *baillifship*) 1×, a letter by Fastolf (see *n*92) 1×, Idley (*Instructions to His Son*) 1×, Scrope (*Dicts, Othea*) 21×, Pecock (*Reule of Chrysten Religioun*) 3×, Chauliac (*Chirurgie*) 3×, Misyn (*Mending of Life*) 1×, Shillingford (*Letters*) 1×, Bishop (*Historical Notes*) 1×, Lydgate (*Fall of Princes, Pilgrimage of the Life of Man, A Mumming for the Mercers of London, Mumming at Bishopwood*) 9×, *Destruction of Troy* 1×, *St Cuthbert* 1×, *Prick of Conscience* 1×, *The Book of Margery Kempe* 1×, 'My ladyes' 1×, and The Constitution of Freemasons 1×. MED does not record the four occurrences of the word mankyndely (mankyndely lawe f. 3, mankyndely sciences, f. 4[r], mankyndeli creatures f. 17[r], and mankendli sciencis, f. 19[r]) in an anonymous English translation of *Le Livre des Bonnes Moeurs* which may also be by Scrope, as Denton Fox, 'Stephen Scrope,' has tentatively suggested.

95 MED, s.v. *countrefeten* v., 4 (last usage: *Merlin*, 1450); *bountewousnes* n. (last usage: Capgrave's *Life of St Norbert* and *Promptorium Parvulorum*, both 1440); *gaderen* v., 2c(a) (last usage: *Alphabet of Tales*, c. 1450); *overhope* n. (last usage: *Jacob's Well*, c. 1450); *queinte* adj. (last usage: *Pilgrimage of the Lyfe of Manhode*, c. 1450); *disordenat* adj. (last usage: *Proceedings and Ordinances of the Privy Council of England*, 1441); *emploien* v., 2b (last usage: *Merlin*, c. 1450); *follich* adj. (last usage: *Pilgrimage of the Lyfe of Manhode*, c. 1450); *talent* n. (last usage: *Merlin*, c. 1450); *beningnesse* n. (last usage: *Three Kings of Cologne*, c. 1450); *boistousli* adv. (last usage: Capgrave's *Life of St Augustine* and Scrope's *Dicts*, both c. 1450); *callioun* n. (last usage: *Pilgrimage of the Lyfe of Manhode* and *Merlin*, both c. 1450); *disgisen* v., 2c(a) (last usage: *Pilgrimage of the Lyfe of Manhode*, c. 1450); *musen* v., 4a (last usage: *Metrical Life of St Robert of Knaresborough*, c. 1450); and *neighborschipe* (last usage: Scrope's *Dicts*, c. 1450); *trauaylyng* (last usage: *Alphabet of Tales*, c. 1450); and *threten* (last usage: Bokenham, 1447).

96 Beadle, 'Medieval Drama,' vol. 1, 75.

97 Chap. 93, *Off Periurii*, ll. 5988–6055.

98 MS P, f. 81[v].

99 Pecock, *Repressor*, vol. 2, pt 5, chap. 15, 564. Cf. also Russell, 'Lolland Opposition,' 673. Green makes the point that 'His [Pecock's] replies to the Lollard attacks on the orthodox position give a remarkably good picture of the views which the mid-fifteenth century followers of Wyclif maintained' (*Reginald Pecock*, 168–9). Patrouch concurs: 'Pecock's list is valuable, for it tells us the main items to which the unorthodox laity were objecting in the mid-fifteenth century' (*Reginald Pecock*, 90). The *Four Tables* was written before 1443, since reference is made to it in

The Reule of Chrysten Religioun (Green, *Reginald Pecock*, 244). For Lollard activity in the 1440s see Nichols, *Seeable Signs*, 100–2; Harvey, *Jack Cade's Rebellion*, 29–30, 142–3; and Thomson, *Later Lollards*, 33–9, 63–7, 148–52, 178–81.

100 Green, *Reginald Pecock*, 89 and *n*1, and Hudson, *Lollards*, 167.

101 *Othea*, xviii, 121/5–10, and *Dicts* 2/1–10. On Fastolf as a patron of letters see Moore, 'Patrons of Letters,' 194–6. On the authorship and dates of these works see *Othea* (Warner, xxv–xxvi); *Othea* xviii–xxi, 121–2; *Dicts* xxvii–xxxix.

102 MED, s.v. *namely* adv.

103 MED, s.v. *anoi* n., citing the Auchinleck *Alexander* (c. 1300); OED, *ennoy* n., citing Caxton (1491).

104 MED, s.v. *gourmaunt* n.

105 MED, s.v. *justicer* n., 1b. It is also employed in the sense of 'ruler' (ll. 1593, 2517), a usage also found in the *Boke of Noblesse*, 499.

106 *Othea* 17/31, 81/23, misglossed as 'take amusement in.' MED, s.v. *musen* v., cites the correct meaning 'spend time idly' under section 4a. Cf. Godefroy, s.v. *amusen* v.; AND, *musen* v.

107 MED, s.v. *overthroue* n., cites only Scrope and the *Boke of Noblesse*, 18, for its use as a noun.

108. *Othea* 122/7.

109 Scrope, *Castle Combe*, 279, 282; Hughes, 'Stephen Scrope,' 115, 118–19. The original texts are in British Library, London, MSS Additional 28209, f. 21 (Schedule of Grievances) and Additional 28212, f. 22 (*Replycacions*).

110 *Vilain, vilenie,* and their adjectival and adverbial forms occur over seventy times in the *Miroir*. With the single exception of 'communes' they are translated by the forms of *velain, velains, velany* and *velansly* listed in the glossary.

111 *Dicts* 106/24 *n*1 and 296/2.

112 On the occurrences of *id est* in the *Mirroure* see Whitaker, 'Lacunae,' 192–7.

113 Stone, 'Loan Words,' 12; Wallner, 'The .i. Periphrasis,' 286; Jones, 'MS Sloane 76,' 27–8.

114 For example, *aduertised, contrariousli, conuersid, emploie, homelye, singulerteis*.

115 Mustanoja, 'Features of Syntax,' 73–4.

116 For this usage see Visser, *Historical Syntax*, 58; Einenkel, *Geschichte*, 137; Mustanoja, *Middle English Syntax*, 137; Lindström, 'Middle English Passage,' 153–7; *Myrour* 132/20 and *n*; MED, s.v. *he* pron., 1c.

117 MED, s.v. *bifore* conj., b, cites two instances of its use from Chaucer's *Legend of Good Women* and the Helmingham Hall version of the *Dicts*. No instances are cited of *afore or*.
118 MED, s.v. *stonden* v., 35b.
119 For an analogous form, *us is to donne*, see the note to l. 2299–2300.
120 See the notes to ll. 2231–2 and 8979.
121 For details of Scrope's life and family background see Scrope, 169–70, 264–88; *Dicts* (ed. Schofield), 1–22; Vale, 'Scropes,' 211–24; Rosenthal, *Patriarchy*, 77–91, 234–8; Hughes, 'Stephen Scrope.' He is also mentioned in the *Paston Letters*, vol. 1, 30, 86, 154–5, and vol. 2, 31–2, 134, 166, 181, 279, 284, 562. The household accounts he kept at Honfleur are preserved in British Library, London, Additional MS 28212, ff. 10–16^{v}.
122 *Othea*, xix–xxi, 3/1–34–4/1–25, appendix B, 125–7 (contributed by Dr A.I. Doyle); Bühler, 'Revisions,' 269–70; Hughes, 'Stephen Scrope,' 134. In addition to Buckingham's widow, his eldest daughter, Ann, and Gloucester's widow, Eleanor Cobham, have also been suggested.
123 *Dicts*, xxi–xxv, xli and *n*1, 292/17*n*, 20*n*. McFarlane, 'William Worcester,' 215 *n*2, dates the revision 1473; Sutton and Visser-Fuchs, 'Richard III's Books,' 156, c. 1475. For Worcester's annotations see Richmond, *Paston Family*, 259–61.
124 See above, *n*75.
125 *Dicts* (Schofield, 46–7). A few southern or southwestern forms are also to be found in the Longleat version of the *Othea*.
126 For Worcester's career see McFarlane, 'William Worcester'; Emden, *University of Oxford*, 2086–7; Worcester, *Itineraries* (ed. Harvey), ix–xviii; Kendrick, *British Antiquities*, 29–33; Gransden, *Historical Writing*, 327–41; Richmond, *Paston Family*, 248–51; Sutton and Visser-Fuchs, *Richard III's Books*, 154–65; Hughes, 'Stephen Scrope,' 120–1, 130–2. He figures prominently in the *Paston Letters*.
127 McFarlane, 'William Worcester,' especially 204–5. Worcester's account of his surveyorship of the manor of Castle Combe is in British Library, London, MS Additional 28208. His initial visit can be dated to 1436 (ibid., 199 *n*7). Davis 'Epistolary Usages,' has analyzed the characteristics of his language.
128 *Dicts* (ed. Schofield), 47.
129 Amyot, 'Transcript,' 263, 269; Scrope, *Castle Combe*, 278; Hughes, 'Stephen Scrope,' 133. Worcester had composed a lament on the death of Scrope's mother, Lady Millicent, in 1446 (British Library, London, MS Additional 38692, ff. 139–41, partially translated in Scrope, *Castle*

Combe, 262–3). Together, Scrope and Worcester opposed Fastolf's nuncupative will.

130 Worcester's medical compilations are in British Library, London, MS Sloane 4, with references to Scrope on ff. 38^v, 57^v. On the likelihood of Scrope's contribution to the *Boke of Noblesse* (and even possibly to *Tully of Old Age*) see *Dicts*, xxxix–xlvi, and Hughes, 'Stephen Scrope,' 132–3. For Scrope's and Worcester's shared interest in medicine see Hughes, 'Stephen Scrope,' 120, 125.

131 Hughes, 'Stephen Scrope,' 133–46. Sutton and Visser-Fuchs, emphasizing Worcester's humanistic interests, argue that he is the actual translator of Cicero's *De Senectute* and *De Amicitia* and Buonaccorso's *Controversia de nobilitate* printed by Caxton in 1481 (*Richard III's Books*, 160–1).

132 *Dicts*, xl–xli.

133 McFarlane, 'William Worcester,' 204 and *n*2.

134 *Dicts* (Schofield, 19–20); Hughes, 'Stephen Scrope,' 115–16. Fastolf had developed the estate into a highly profitable producer of fine, colored woolen cloth (Carus-Wilson, 'Industrial Growth,' 197–205).

135 Scrope, *Castle Combe*, 288.

136 See Worcester's *Itineraries* (ed. Harvey), 287, 381, for details of the church.

137 Knowles, *Religious Orders*, 129–38.

138 Tanner, *The Church*, 124; Gibson, *Theatre of Devotion*, 20.

139 Rosenthal, *Purchase of Paradise*, 59, 70, 156.

140 Knowles, *Religious Orders*, 361–2.

141 Rosenthal, 'Universities,' 417. Cf. Catto and Evans, *University of Oxford*, 512, for the interest of aristocratic families in university study.

142 Venn and Venn, *Alumni Cantabrigienses*, 35–6; Emden, *University of Cambridge*, 513–14; Vale, 'Scropes,' 143–97. The Scropes studied theology and civil and canon law and collected books (Cavanaugh, *Books*, 769–71). Leader, *University of Cambridge*, 170–91, and Hackett, *Original Statutes*, 131, comment on the high reputation of the Cambridge divinity school in the late Middle Ages.

143 Cobban, *King's Hall*, 286; Emden, *University of Cambridge*, 514–15; Vale, 'Scropes,' 213.

144 Hughes, 'Stephen Scrope,' 117.

145 Hackett pointedly observes: 'Whatever fame Cambridge achieved in the Middle Ages was due to its theology faculty' (*Original Statutes*, 131).

146 See the note to ll. 1760–4. The continuing efforts to canonize Scrope, which received the support of Edward IV in 1462, are described by

Wylie, *History of England*, 325–64; McKenna, 'Popular Canonization,' 618–23; Walker, 'Political Saints,' 84–5. For a missal dating from before 1445 which celebrates the cult of Saint Richard Scrope, see Mt., 'Early Missal,' 489.

147 Cf. *Dicts* (ed. Schofield), 40–5; (ed. Bühler), xix–xxix. The only attributions of authorship are, for the *Othea*, the Longleat MS and, for the *Dicts*, the Bodley, Emmanuel, and Harley MSS.

148 *Othea* 122/34–7. Christine was also denied authorship of *Les Faits d'Armes et de Chevalrie*, as noted by Driver, 'Mirrors,' 79 and *n9*. Gray, 'A Fulle Wyse Gentle-Woman of France,' 238, comments: 'Scrope adapted her [Christine's] dedication to Jean de Berry, and refers to him in this Preface. Possibly, taking her protestation of "the febilnesse/Of my smaller witte" literally, he was fitting her into a cultural pattern (of a "wise" lady ordering and sometimes organizing the making of a book of moral instruction) which would have been familiar to him: if so, it would suggest that he was not closely familiar with Christine's literary career. Speculations of a less charitable kind are also possible.'

149 *Othea* 121/17–19.

150 *Dicts* 2/8–9.

151 For Fastolf's piety and for his interests and tastes, and those of his circle, see Hughes, 'Stephen Scrope,' 129–46, and *Paston Letters*, vol. 1, 87–91.

152 *Fastolf Papers*, No. 43, f. 10.

THE MIRROURE OF THE WORLDE

[f. ii] HERE BEGYNNETH THE CHAPITRES OF THE BOOKE THAT IS CALLED THE MIRROURE OF THE WORLDE AND THAT SOME CALLETH VICE AND VERTU

[The Firste Chapitre Is of the X Commaundementis]

[f. 1] *Si vis ad vitam ingredi serua mandata.* Mathei xix. Men seye communly: Whoso seeth wel and lerneth eville o good right he moste repente. And this it is that Salamon seithe in a booke that we calle Ecclesiasticus: *Ante hominem vita et mors, bonum et malum; quod placuerit ei dabitur illi.* That is to seye that bothe man and woman hatthe before theime dethe and lif, good and eville; the whiche that pleseth theym shalle be ȝovyn to theym. For ȝif theye doo wel, that is to seye, if theye doo good dedys, theye shalle haue the liff that euer shalle laste, the whiche is the ioye of paradis. ȝif theye doo evil, theye shalle haue deethe of helle that neuer shalle ende. And this is the worde that men seye communly: Whoosoo dothe welle wel shalle haue. And the same seithe Seint Poule in his *Pistille ad Galathas: Bonum autem facientes, non deficiamus, in tempore enim suo metemus non deficientes*. [f. 1v] That is to seye, lete vs not faile to doo wel, and in due tyme we shalle fynde it. And because that the vnderstandyng of euery prince the whiche ȝifeth his commaundementis and setteth his lawes and his ordenaunsys and his stabilmentis to be kepte in his lande, he sholde be siche as to drawe and to lede the pepil to doo vertuous werkys. And therfore we see in citees and landes which be wel ordeyned that shrewys be ponysshid be diuerse peynes after that theye deserve to thentente that for the peyne wherein theye myght falle theye sholde restreyn theym from evil dedes and werkys and the good pepil be worshiped and for the worshipp that maye come to theym theye abide stille and dwelle in goode dedes and werkys. *Quia [honor] est [premium] virtutis pres[is]tens in bono*. Dere pepil, oure prince, oure lorde, oure kynge, whiche ȝaf vs his commandementis, his lawes, and his stabilmentis, that is to seye, oure lorde Crist Iesus, liche as Ysaye the prophete seithe: *Dominus legifer noster, Dominus rex noster*. For alle his entent alle the tyme that he was conuersant in this worlde it was to drawe the pepill to werkys of vertue be the whiche theye myght brynge aȝeyn good dessertes and good wagis, as Ysaye the prophet amonesteth vs wiche seithe thus: *Bonas facite vias vestras*. Make youre weyes good, seithe he. That weye is good whiche ledeth rightly and surely to a right terme and to a good ende. The terme and the ende to the whiche euery persone sholde take heede and desyre to come is to euerlastyng liff. And thereof speketh Seint Mathieu in his gospell ther where he seithe that ther was a yonge man whiche come to oure lorde Criste Iesus and askyd hym: Maister, what shalle I doo for to haue euerlastyng liff? And oure lord seide to hym the worde that I haue sette afore: *Si vis ad vitam ingredi, etc*. If thowe wilt entre into euerlastyng liff, thowe sholdest holde and kepe the commandementis of God. And in these wordis he seith ii thingys. For firste he techith and mevith vs to comen to grete profit in that he seith: *Si vis ad vitam ingredi, etc*, if thou wilt entre into the liff of paradis. Also he setteth a fulle light maner and a weye in this that he seith: *Serva mandata, etc.* Thowe sholdest holde and kepe the commandementis of God. And that the commandementis of God be light Seynt Iohn spekith therof in his firste Canonique, ther where he seithe: *Mandata eius grauia non sunt*. That is to seye, the commandementis of hym be not grevous. Of the whiche Dauid the prophete seithe in the Sauter: *Via[m] mandatorum tuorum cucurri*. That is [to] seye, sir, I haue ronne be the weye of thy commandementis, be a lyght weye men [f. 2] be wonte to rynne. And if thowe aske me howe many and whiche theye be, thowe shalt wite that ther be in the lawe x commandementis the whiche every Cristen man sholde beleve, for theye be the pointis of Cristendom, liche as a religious man that hatth ben a sufficiant tyme in his ordre sholde knowe the pointis of his religion. And ȝit it is no gret thyng to knowe theym, but it is gret shame not to knowe theym. And if thowe aske me why God ȝaf vs not euerlastyng lyff withowte wynyng it because that he is right curteys and right large. If I hadde labored in the vigneȝerde or in some worthy mannes werke and he ȝaf me myn hire therfore, it were no gret thyng. Soo it is of this if I kepe the commandementis of God and he ȝif me euerlastyng liff. Sir, it is not liche, but I seye that he ȝaf vs a grete thyng, for in ȝifyng vs theym to kepe he tooke heede to oure gret profit and worshipp. For in kepyng and fulfillyng theym he torneth it to oure worshipp more than if he hadde don other weys. If the kynge hadde ȝovyn to castelles to ii knyghtis and yif the ton had welle wonne it the tothir not, to whiche sholde it torne moste worshipp? Truly, it sholde torne gretter worship to hym that hadde wele wonne it than to the tothir. For if thow were wys, thowe haddest levyr vi pens to thy worshipp than v *s* to thy veleny and to thy confusion. Some myght aske me: Nowe, sire, sithen that God knewe that oure firste fadir trespassed o light commaundement, why ȝaf he vs x? Me semeth he keste a snare before vs for to overthrowe vs with into synne. I seye: He did not. Bot I seye: He vndidde the snare wherein we myght a fallen. For nature seithe and techith that a man sholde not doo to anothir but liche as he wolde men didde to hym, as to stele his goode or make hym to be noyed and soo forthe as of othir thyngys. Wherefore euery persone sholde knowe theym and fulfille theym the whiche alle creatures sholde worshipp.

The Firste Commandement

The firste commandement of the lawe is this: *Non habebis deos alienos*. That is to seye, thow shalt not haue ii goddes; thowe shalt haue no god but me; ne thowe shalt not worshipp ne beleve ne put thyn hope but alonly in me. For tho that put their hope principally in creatures syn dedly and don aȝeyns this commandement. Siche be tho that worshipp fals goddes and fals ymages and maketh theyr god of a creature what so it be. Therfor we worshipp not the [f. 2v] ymages, for theye be not made alonly but for to brynge to oure mynde the passion that God suffred for vs, the whiche alle creatures sholde worshipp, for whos luf seintes suffrede passion, and for to signifie to vs what lyf the seintis of paradis ledde in this world and for to ȝif vs ensample to folwe theym in weldede. And if any seye that we worshipp iii goddes, that is to seye, the fadir, the son, and the Holy Goste, I answer that in these iii thyngys we worship but o god whiche is maker of hevyn and of erthe. And I seye that þe fadir and the son and the Holy Goste is o god in iii persones. Than worship we not iii goddes but on alonly. And ȝif men seye that we worship a bodyly creature in the holy sacrement of the auter, I seye that we worshipp not the brede but veraly the body of Crist Iesus, the whiche is in forme of brede and in veray likenes therof; but it is consacrat be þe vertu that God ȝaf in wordes the whiche the preste prononcit ovir the brede whan he sacreth the precious body of Crist Iesus. And he maye doo that, the whiche made al thyng of nought, that is God of hevyn. Of whom men remembre that an enchantour of fendes made the fende for to comme in the middes of myche pepil, for he wolde an asked some grace of hym. And than it felle that a preste passed there forby, the whiche bare the precious body of oure lorde Crist Iesus. And than the fende felle on knees. And whan the prest torned, he bowed toward hym on the to knee. And than the enchantour asked hym: Why do ȝe that the whiche ȝe defended me to doo? The fende answerd and seide: It is writen that al the knees of hevyn, of erthe, and of helle boweth theym to the name of

Crist Iesus. Nowe than he seithe: Thowe shalt not love ii goddes. Aȝens this commandement syneth sorceres and devinours that derre vndirtake the thyngys that be for to comme and to telle of thyngys that be loste and hidde and desired, the whiche longeth alonly to God. This syn was founde of the fende longe agoon. This syn is like to the syn of Eve, oure first modir, whiche desired to be a goddesse. And she was a fendesse whan she ete of the frute that God forbade hirre, for the whiche she toke [the snare] of the fende, the whiche seide to theym: *Eritis sicut dii*. If ȝe eete of the fruit, ȝe shalle be evyn as God. The kynge wolde be fulle wrothe with that wolde desire his kyngedom in his owne reaume and with al tho that helde with hym. And therfore euery persone sholde thynke and beholde the peyne for the whiche al the worlde was ponysshed be that syn, that is to seye, sorwe, anguisshe, hungir, therst, colde, heete, angre, sekenes, and deeth and alle be this point. Beware now charmours and wycches and sorceris and al thoo that trauailleth to siche pepil. This is that the whiche is writen in a booke þat [f. 3] is called Leuitici xx: *Anima, qui declinauerit ad magos vel mario[los], et fornicata fuerit cum illis, ponam faciem meam contra eam, et interficiam eam [de medio populi mei]*. The soule that shall goo to enchantours and devinours and shalle haue syn with theym I shalle sette my face aȝeyns theym, as who seye, I shalle contrarie to theym and I shalle slee theym in the myddes of my pepil. And Seynt Iohn seithe in the Pocalipse: *Timidis et incredulis [et execratis] et homicidis et veneficiis et omnibus m[e]ndacibus pars illorum [erit] in stagno ignis ardentis et sulphuris quod est mors secunda*. That is to seye that to tho that hatthe reseyvid the feithe as is the feithe that a good Cristen man sholde kepe, the whiche theye haue forsakyn, and to tho that beleve it not wel and to corsed pepil and to mansleers and to envenimoures and to al lyerres, o part of their tourmentis is in the stang of helle of brennyng fire and of stinkyng bremston. This is the seconde deethe, for the first dethe is þe dethe of dedly syn. Wherfore Seynt Poule seithe: *Anima qui peccauerit ipsa morietur*. The thirde deeth is the dethe of helle, whiche lasteth alweye, wherfro God kepe vs. Of the whiche Holy Writ seithe: *Libera me de morte eterna*.

Feire lorde God, delyuere vs fro the dethe of helle. Aȝens this commandement syn tho that luf their tresore to myche, as golde or sylfer or other erthely thyngis. Whoso trespassith in siche thyngys, theye set their hertis and their hoope so that they forȝete and leve their creature whiche hatthe lente and ȝovyn theym al these goodes. And therfor theye sholde serve hym, luf hym, and thonke hym above alle thyngys [and] worshipp hym as this firste commandement techith vs. For whoso setteth his hert in creaturez more than in God, he maketh of creatures his god. As Seynt Austyn seithe: *Ab homine colitur quod pre [ce]teris diligitur*. On the same wise the gloton maketh his god of his bely, the lecherous of the folysshe womman, the covetouse of the richesse of this worlde, for theye doo and ofre to theym that the whiche theye sholde doo and ȝif to God. And therfore theye trespasse to this commandement.

The Seconde Commandement

The seconde commandement of the lawe is this: *Non assumes nomen Dei tui in vanum*. Thowe shalt not take the name of thy God in vayne. Aȝens this commandement synneth iii maner of pepil, that is to seye, tho the whiche seieth blames of God and myssewordes and velenies, blasphemyng hym as in sweryng velansly be his membres, [f. 3v] the whiche veleynly he spredde on the cros for oure synnes. And it semeth that siche pepil be wers than houndes, for houndes byte not ne at the leste desire not the handis of their maistris, the whiche thyng theye do specially whan theye blaspheme hym in tauernes whan theye haue dronke ynowe and not inoughe but to myche. O that mouthe with the whiche theye dranke the wyne anon theye mysseye Goddes creatures and biteth God, seying of hym velains wordes. Therfore siche pepil b[e] likenyd to wode houndes that biteth their maistres handes whan theye profre theym brede. And moreouere theye be traytoures, for theye werreþ oure lorde with his owne goodes. And this synne is contrarie aȝens owre fadir of hevyn. And it is to be punysshyd with an evil dethe, and þat it is thus Seynt Mathieu seithe in his gospell: *Qui maledixerit patri aut matri morte moriatur*. This is not seid alonly for tho that spekyth veleyns wordes but as wel for tho that suffreth theym to be seid in their houses, as in tauernes, and that theye myght lette theyme of the seyng. Vnethe any myght suffre men to mysseye his fadir in his owne house or to mysseye any good man. Howe maye men than suffre to here blame and veleny seid of oure fadir of hevyn? Wherefor siche pepil seme wers than Iuys whiche stopped their erys whan theye herde blaspheme seide of God. Of the whiche men rede þat a Iue pleied at the tablis with a knyght whom he herde blaspheme God, and than he lefte the pleye and wente his weye. In ancient tyme whan theye herde siche blasphemes they rente their clothis in signe of sorwe and displeser. And therby men myght knowe Goddes childe fro the fendes, for Goddes childir myght not suffre ne hire blaspheme of God their fadir, but the fendes childir suffreth it wel, the whiche men maye see be this example: Ther was a man hadde iii sones be his wyf as he suppoced. So as it befelle on a tyme þat theye chydde togedir, and his wyf come forthe and asked whiche of the iii childir was hisse. And he asked hir whiche it was, and she wolde not telle hym. After that the modir died, and the fader in the sekenes of his deeth left and ȝaf alle his good to his child. And because men wist not whiche it was, be the conseil of a iustice the fadir whan he was dede was set in a felde, and men toke to iche of his iii sones a bowe and an arwe, and it was seid to theyme that whoso shotte rightest to the herte of the dede body he sholde haue his goodes and sholde ben holden for right heire. And than ii of theym shotte as right as they coude. And whan men bade the thirde shote he answerd and seide that the sentence was to harde and that he had lever lese al his fadres goode than he sholde shoote atte hym or anythyng mysdo to the body. This worde herde it was than [iuged] that he was his natural sone and that o right the goodes sholde longe to [f. 4] hym. And evyn liche to this iugement and example we reede in the thirde Booke of Kynges of Salamon and of ii women. Also I seye that tho that be rightwosly Goddes childe maye not sustien blaspheme of God the fadir. Aȝens this commandement syn tho that wytyngly forswereth theym. And therfore seith Seynt Mathieu: *Dico vobis, non iurare omnino*. Thow shalt not swere for euery cause, as who seye, thowe shalt not swere for nought ne withoute a grete cause. This same oure lord defendeth in the gospell, seying that men shalle not swere be hevyn ne be erthe ne be noon othir creature. But men maye for a goode cause swere sauely withoutyn syn, as in iugement where men aske an hothe for trouthe or oute of iugement in othir goode, honest, and profitable causes. And but men sholde not swere in noon othir maner. And therfore whosoo swerith be the name of oure lorde withoute cause and for noght, if he swere fals wytyngly, he forswerith hym and dothe aȝens this commandement and synneth dedly, for he swerith aȝens his conscience, that is to seye, whan theye swere vesyly and with deliberacion. But tho that swereth trouthe to theire knowyng and notwithstandyng for noght or for some evil cause and it not maliciously but lightly and withoute blasfeme theye synne venyally, but the costome is perlious and maye happe to torne to dedly synne if theye take not goode heede therof. Bot tho that swereth horribly be God and be his seintis and that dispiseth theym in seying blasphemes the whiche be not to seye, theye synne dedly, for theye maye haue no cause to excuse theym by. And tho that moste vsith it moste greuously synneth. Also he that forswereth hym from the firste fals othe that he maketh, the gospell seithe that he byndeth the hande to the fende with the whiche he hatthe touchid the hande of hym to whom he sware. Vnto the tyme that he repente hym and confesse hym of that periurie, that hande is the fendes. And as ofte as he blisseth hym, he blesseth hym with the fendes hande. And al thynge that he blisseth it is blessed with the fendes hande. Wherfore men remembre that þer was a man the whiche wolde forswere hym for a galon of wyne. Soo it felle on a tyme that his felawes reprevyd and blamed hym therfore. But ȝit seyng his felawes that hande with the whiche he hadde made the fals othe was brent with the fire of helle. Also thoo that be necligent and doo no fruit of goode werkys, the whiche Seint Iohn seithe in the Pocalipse: *Nomen habes [quod] viuas et mortuus es*. Thowe haste a name of lif, and thowe art dede. It is of a man as of a tree, for than a man perseyvith that a tree hatthe lif whan it brancheth, floureth, and bereth branches and fruit. Evyn soo is it whan a man flowreth in goode wille to serve [f. 4v] God, if he make branchis of goode wordis, if he make fruit of goode werkys.

The Thirde Commandement

The thirde commandement is this: *Memento vt diem sabbati sanctifices*. Loke that thowe halowe the Satirdaye. That is to seye, on the Satirdaye thowe shalt not doo thye besyneses ne thy werkys as thowe doest on othir dayes but reste the the bettyr to take heede to praye to thye creature, whiche rested hym the vii daye of the werkys that he hadde don in vi dayes afore, in the which he ordeyned and made the worlde. This commaundement he fulfilleth gostely that to his power kepeth pees in his consciens the more holyly to serve God. Wherfore this worde Satirday whiche the Iuis calleth sabbat is as myche to seye as reste. This commandement maye noon kepe gostely that is in conscience of dedly synne, for siche a conscience maye not be in pees as longe as it is in that plite. And therfore seithe Eze iii: *Qui quiescit, quiescat*. That is to seye, whosoo resteth hym in his body, he resteth hym in thought and in conscience. This is aȝeyns many synerres that on the Sondaye and in the festes of God and of the blessed Virgine Marie and of the holy seyntes of hevyn which be not in pees but rather haunteth karolles and tauernes and bordelles and wasteth there the tyme that God hatthe ȝovyn theym for to serve hym and for to enploie in goode werkys, of the whiche theye moste ȝif acommpte atte the daye of doome. Aa, goode God, what scusacions shalle theye fynde in siche thynges? Also sumtyme theye waste there alle that theye haue wonne in their wokys labour and that wherwith theye sholde paye the whiche theye truly owe. Wherthurgh tho to whom they owe endureth and hatthe grete defaute of that these gurmantis spendeth thus folily. And than at evyn theye be dronken and wode and beteth bothe wyf and childe, the whiche perauenture be ȝit alle fastyng. And siche pepil disworshipeth God and his scintis that dothe siche werkys at their festes whan bodily theye sholde reste theym. Also theye sholde reste theym in thynkeyng, for theye sholde siche dayes thynke on their astate, that is to seye, howe theye haue dispent it and thynke what evilles theye haue doon and of the goodes that God hatthe sente theyme thanke hym therfore and for their evilles crye hym mercy and require hym of pardon and than repaire to verray [f. 5] confession be verray contricion. And this it is that Dauid the prophete seithe in the Sautier: *Preocupemus faciem eius in confessione.* Truly oure festes be not but a signifyng and a figure of the grete feste in hevyn and of the solempnitee whyder we tente to goo the whiche is for to come of the whiche al oure lyfe is the vigile the whiche is but as o daye to regard of the feste that we abide. And therfore God wil that in this vigile we make vs redy. But many oon dothe the contrarie, for theye make the feste before the vigile. And tho be theye that doo no penaunce here, but rather theye be in festes and in solaces and in wordly ioyes whiche shalle be ful soone paste. But aftirward theye shalle make the vigile in helle euerlastyngly with the fendes and their angell not only in brede and watyr bot in soo grete nede of watyr where the[y] shalle brenne in fyre and bremston and that theye shalle not inowe haue o drope of watyr to kele withalle their tonges. Hereof haue [we] an example in the gospell of Seynt Luke, of the evil riche man the whiche asked a drope of watyr so many ȝeris paste, but he hadde it not ȝit. And also we shalle knowe that in the stede of Satirdaye, which was streitly kept in the olde lawe, holy chirche ordeyned the Sondaye to be kept in oure newe lawe, for on the Sonday God made the worlde. *Beatus Augustinus dicit et ponit multa signa ad hoc: Dies Dominica est veneranda in qua visa fuit prima lux. [In genesi legitur fiat lux.] In hac autem die multa et magna miracula pro salute nostra fecit Dominus. In die Dominica recedit arcus post diluuium. In die Dominica pluit Dominus manna de celo in deserto filiis Israel. In die Dominica p[er]cussum est Mare Rubeum per manum Moysy et transierunt vii milia cum armentis et cetinerunt canticum nouum Domino. Et iterum percussit mare Moyses, et reuersum est mare in locum suum. Et mersus est Pharaon cum curribus et equitibus, et non est relictus ex eis vnus. In hac die percussit Moyses petram et fluxerunt quatuor flumina. In die Dominica natus est Iesus. In die Dominica baptisatus est Cristus, et venit spiritus sanctus super eum in specie columbe. In die Dominica fecit Dominus vinum ex aqua in Chana*

Galilee. In die Dominica saturauit Dominus quinque milia hominum ex quinque panibus etc. In die Dominica intrauit Dominus in ciuitatem Ierusalem et voluit vocari regem. In die Dominica resurrexit Dominus. In die Dominica venit Dominus ad apostolos ianuis clausis. In die Dominica committit Dominus pacem inter celum et terram, inter angelos et homines, inter Deum et hominem, inter corpus et animam, sicut apostolus dicit: Ipse est spes nostra qui fecit ex vtraque vnum. In hac die misit sanctum spiritum in die pentecostes in apostolos. In die Dominica dedit Dominus in Pathmos Insula Apocalipsi[m] Iohanni. In die Dominica raptus fuit Paulus et audiuit archana Dei qu[e] non licet homini loqui, [f. 5v] *vt ipsemet ait. In die Dominica Dominus noster Iesus Cristus venturus est in magestate sua cum angelis quando reddet vnicuique iuxta opera sua. Ante Domini passionem non appellabatur Dominica sed prima sabbati. Septem dies habet ebdomada: Sex dedit nobis ad operandum; vnam dedit nobis ad orandum, id est, remocionem malorum. Adueniente sancta die Dominica festinare deb[emus] ad ecclesiam, id est, orare Deum et nichil aliud facere debemus in sancta die Dominica sed recedentes ab opere in ecclesiis [proce]damus. Non enim ab opere recedendum est tantum sed a malis et a peccatis. Ingredere in plateam in altero die nec vnum inuenies. In die Dominica quosdam inuenies [ci]tharisantes, alios in armis plaudantes, alios rid[e]ntes et detrahentes proximo suo [et alia multa dicit que homines in festo faciunt]. Si [vero] ad ecclesiam veniunt, quid ibi vident? Ego dicam tibi. Vident Dominum super mensam, id est, Iesum Cristum super altare sacrificatum ad quem descendunt angeli. Ibidem assistit spiritus sanctus principaliter et alia multa dicit commenda[n]s illos qui vadunt ad ecclesiam et reprehendens facientes vanitates in tali tam sanctissimo die.* Seynt Austin setteth many tokenes why þe Sonday sholde be worshiped. For that daye God made first light, as it is writen in the Genesy, where God seid: *Fiat lux*. That is to seye, God commanded the light to be made, and it was made. On the holy Sondaye oure lorde didde many gret miraclis for oure sauacion. On the Sondaye the reynbowe departed hym after the flode. On the holy Sonday oure lorde reyned manna of hevyn in desert to the childir of Israel. On the Sondaye þe Rede See was s[mo]tte be the hande of Moyses. And ther passed with hym vii thousand men of armes, and they sange a newe songe to oure lorde. And Moyses smote the see aȝeyn and retorned vnto his place. And Pharaon with al his oste was drowned; ther [was] lefte not oon. On the holy Sondaye Moyses smote the stone in desert oute of the wiche sprange iiii flodis. On the holy Sondaye was borne oure lorde Criste Iesus. On the Sondaye Crist Iesus was baptised, and the Holy Goste descended on hym in likenesse of a doufe. On the Sondaye oure lorde chaunched water into wyne in a strete of Galalie whiche is called Chana. On the Sondaye oure lorde fedde v thousand men with v barly loffes and ii fisshes. On the Sondaye oure lorde entred into Ierusalem and wolde be called kynge. On the Sondaye oure lorde rose fro dethe to liff. On the Sondaye oure lorde entred to his apostlis the ȝatis shette. On the Sondaye he ioyned pees betwene hevyn and erthe, betwene man and angell, betwene God and man, betwene body and soule as the postel seithe: He is oure hope which hatthe made of ii thyngys on. On the Sondaye, the daye of Pente[f. 6]coste, oure lorde sente the Holy Goste into his apostlis. On the Sondaye oure lorde ȝaf the Pocalipse to Iohan in the Ile of Pathenos. And on the Sondaye Seynt Poule was ravisshed to the thridde hevyn and herde the secretis of God, the whiche he dorste not telle to no man, as he seithe. On the Sondaye oure lorde shalle come in his gret mageste with his angell and his seintis, whan he shalle ȝif euery man after that he hatthe wrought. Afore the passion of Criste Iesus, it was not called Sondaye but the first sabbat, that is to seye, the firste daye of the woke. The woke hatthe vii dayes, of the whiche God hatthe ȝovyn vs vi to werke, the viite to praye, that is to seye, to put aweye oure evilles. Whan the holy Sondaye cometh, we sholde haste vs to go to chirche, that is to seye, to praye to God and leve alle erthely werkys and doo non othir thynge on this holy Sondaye. And therto we sholde sesse of al eville and of al synne. Goo, seithe Seint Austyn, to that place anothir daye, and thowe shalt fynde there not one. On the holy Sondaye þou shalt fynde there somme that drawe aweye othir, some þat pleye with armys, somme that skorne, some that bakbite their neghborghis, and many othir harmys Seint Austin seithe that men doo on festful dayes. If theye come to the chirch, what se theye? I shalle telle the, seithe Seint Austin. Theye see oure lorde Criste Iesus sacred opon the auter to whom angelles descende. And ther principally [is] present the Holy Gooste, and many othir thyngis, as Seint Austin seith in recomendyng tho that goo to the chirche and in reprevyng tho that doo vaniteis in that daye whiche is so holy. And therfore men sholde kepe it holyly. For whoso breketh the Sondaye and other solempne festes that be stablisshed to be kepte in holy chirche, he synneth dedly, for he dothe aȝeyns the commandement of God and of holy chirche, if it be not for some necessite that holy chirche agreeth to. These iii commandementis setteth vs specially to Godde.

The Fourthe Commandement

We haue nowe spokyn of iii commandementis the whiche longeth to God. And the vii folwyng longeth to oure neyghbourghes, of the whiche the first is this: *Honora patrem tuum et matrem tuam, vt sis longeuus super terram*. Worshipp thy fadir and thy modir, and thowe [f. 6v] shalt life the lenger on erthe. This commandement amonestith vs to kepe vs from angryng fadir or modir willyngly. For he that disworshipeth his fadir or his modir willyngly with wronge or corseth theym or of malice dothe theym harme synneth dedly. And this worshipp is not alonly vndirstanden be wordys but be goodnes that men maye doo to theyme with worldly goodes, that is to seye, to doo theym goode. Of this we haue example of Criste Iesus whan he was put on the cros. He forȝate not his modir, but he betooke hir Seint Iohn to kepe. Of this same, bestis ȝifeth vs example the whiche hath no reson, for men seye of the crane that, whan the fadir and the modir be fedirles and olde so that their federes be fallen fro theym, their chekynys sekith for theym siche thyngys as that theye lakke vnto the tyme that their fediris be comen to theym aȝeyn or ellys that theye dye. Wherfore he is not greable to God that ȝeldeth not to his fadir in his age the goodnes that he hatthe doon to hym in his ȝougthe. And therfore seithe Seint Poule: *Filii, reddite vitam parentibus*. Childir, ȝelde to yowre fadires the goodnes that theye didde firste to ȝowe. Wherfore it happeth ofte of right iugement that tho that be harde to þe fadir and the modir in their age the same their childer dothe to theyme. Wherof men remembre that ther was a fo[l]ysshe man and an harde to his fadir, the whiche was auncient and olde, in so myche that he made hym lye in his stabill and ȝaf hym to clothe hym with olde clothis the wiche was called estamme ou flossoye, stamyne or boltel, with the whiche men were wonte to hille with hors, notwithstandyng the fadir had lefte al his heritage for to avaunce and to make riche his sone therwith and to sette hym in grete astate. It befelle thus that the sone of hym that was thus harde and felle was sory of his ayel that was so evil tretid, for the whiche he comme to his fadir and askyd hym a slavaine. And his fadir answerid and seide that he was clad welle inoughe, and he asked hym what he wolde doo withalle. And the childe answerid hym and seide: I shalle kepe it to þou be right olde, and than I shalle doo to the as thowe doest to myn ayel, whiche is thy fadir and that begate the and ȝaf the al that he had. And therfore seithe Salamon in Ecclesiastes iii: *Suscipe senectutem patris*. Faire sone, supporte the age of thy fadir. In this commandement also is conteyned the worshipp that we sholde doo to oure gostely faderis, that is to seye, to tho that hatthe the charches of oure soules and to teche vs and to chastie vs, as prelates of holy chirche be and tho that hatthe the charche of oure soules and for to kepe vs. And tho that wil not obeye to tho that hatthe the charche of theym, whan theye teche theyme the [f. 7] good whiche men be bounde to doo, synneth greuously, and the inobediens maye be siche that it maye be dedly synne. The thirde fadir is oure fadir of hevyn, whiche we sholde worshipp aboue alle othir and love above al thyng, of the whiche Seint Luke seith xi: *Pater noster qui es in celis etc.* And therfore we sholde kepe vs fro synne for the lufe of God and haue shame that þe fende deceyve vs not be synne, for we maye hyde nothyng fro oure lorde Criste Iesus. *Omnia nuda et apperta sunt oculis suis.*

The Fyfthe Commandement

The fyfthe commandement of the feithe is this: *Non occides*. That is to seye, thowe shalt slee no man neythir of vengeance ne for his good ne for noon othir evil cause. For it is dedly synne and aȝens the nature of man, the whiche techith to man that he sholde not doo to noon othir but siche as he wolde were doon to hymselfe, specially for iii causes: First, for alle we be brethir and of o condicion and of o nature and of o fadir and of o modir, that is to seye, of Adam and Eve, and gostely of o fadir the whiche is God and of o modir the whiche is holy chirche. Wherfor whoso sleith a Cristen man sleith his brothir, for the whiche Seint Iohn seithe: *Videte qualem caritatem Deus dedit nobis vt filii eius nominemur et sumus*. Beholde, seithe he, the gret loue that God shewith and ȝifeth to vs. That is to seye that we be called his childir, and soo we be. Therfore howe derre he that sleeth any Cristen man shewe hymselfe tofore God at the daye of dome? The seconde cause that sholde drawe vs from manslaughtir it is the loue and the charite of Criste Iesus whiche he shewid vs in oure redempcion. For though that God made man of noght, neuerthelesse he amended hym, for he bought hym not aȝen with nought bot with his propre blode, as Seint Petir seith. And because that God bought hym so dere, he is the principal chambir of Goddes hous. And to kepe this chambir is ordeyned be God the fadir the goode angellis of paradis. And liche as the constabil of a castel wolde be wrothe for a man that were take hym to kepe be the kynge if any persone bette hym or kylled hym, evyn soo whoso taketh the sowle fro the bodye of whom the angell is keper he angreth the [f. 7v] kynge of hevyn and his angell to whom he betoke hym. The iii cause that sholde drawe vs fro manslauwght is the foulnes and the horibilnes of the smytyng or of the entent therof, for ther is no dede thyng so horible as man, for the ymage of God is deseueryd fro hym whan the soule is passed. Therfore only for the orrour of the dede, men sholde restreyne theym fro manslaught. For it is on of the iii that crieth vengeance tofore God, for the whiche oure lorde seide to Caym that slowe his brothir Abel: *Ecce vox sangu[in]is fratris tui Abel clamat ad me de terra*. The vois of thi brothires blode Abel cryeth to me fro the erthe as askyng vengeance. In this commandement is defended the synne of ire, of hate, and of rancure. For as the scripture seithe: *Qui odit fratrem suum homicida est*. Whosoo hateth his brothir is a mansleer whan it is of his pure wille and thought afore, and he synneth dedly and dothe aȝeyns this commandement. And than synneth he more that dothe or purchasith shame or harme to any othir wrongefully or is in consell or in helpe to noye any othir wrongefully for to venge hym therwith. But indignacion to noye any the whiche passeth lightly withoute parfite wille and withoute consentyng of afore-thought is no dedly synne, but the costume therof it is fulle perlious.

The VI[te] Commandement

The vi commandement is this: *Non mechaberis*. That is to seye, thowe shalte doo none aduoutery, whiche is, thowe shalte not haue flesshely felechipp with non othir womman. In this commandement is forbedyn al flesshely synne that generally men calle lechery, the which is oon of the vii dedly synnes, althoughe it haue some branches that be noo dedly synnes, as lytil mevyng of the flesshe, the whiche man maye not eschewe in alle. And ȝit men sholde restrayne theyme and refreyne theym therfro as myche as theye myght and neythir norisshe theym ne cause theyme be outerage of mete ne drynke nor be evil thoughtys to longe kept nor be evil touchyngys, for in siche thyngys maye be gret peril. In this commandement is forbedyn v maner of synes of the flesshe. That is to seye, firste, symple fornicacion, the whiche is forbedyn for many causes and specially for iii causes: For peresshyng, for if it were grantid, alle the worlde sholde [f. 8] sprede into the lightnes of the flesshe, for ȝif one drowe not a womman to fornicacion anothir wolde, and in this maner the vertu of chastite and virginite the whiche is fulle plesant to God sholde perysshe. Also because that men sholde not be to flesshely, but that they sholde be gostely in forsakyng fornicacion, for be fornicacion man despiseth God and de-nyeth hym and forȝetith hym. Also it is forbedyn for raveyn and for thefte, the whiche folweth therof, for the women of fornicacion sholde not knowe howe longe theye sholde dwelle with their fornicatoures and therfore theye wolde stele fro their husbondes al that theye myght and soo theye sholde make theym pore and theye sholde make thefes and ribautis as it happeth fulle ofte. Also because that men wolde hate iche other and euery kylle othir whan on wolde take from anothir the lewde womman. And in this maner God didde werkys of mercy with men. The ii^{e} cause why fornicacion is forboden it is for the modir, for iiii causes: First, for oure lorde sawe that wommen hadde labour in the beryng, woo in þe childyng, and charche in the kepyng, hee therfore wolde that men before or that theye doo their flesshely dede were bounde with theyme for to norysshe their childer, because they sholde not haue al the birdeyn. Also because that in the tyme that theye be grete in childyng and maye not purveye for theymselfe that theye sholde purveye for theym. Also whan theye were viled and dispited men wolde leve theyme, an namly whan theye were olde and maye not laboure. Also theye sholde be fouled and disfigured soo that theye sholde inowe fynde noon husbondes. The iii cause is to multiplie for fruite be man, the whiche thyng sholde not be if women were comune, for v causes: Firste for theye sholde be barhaigne for the ofte beyng with man as we see be comune women and thus linee shulde perisshe and humaine lynage lessyn litil and litil. Also women wolde put aweye their childir whan men lefte the delyng with theym. Also by natural lawe the norisshyng longeth to the fadir, and that maye he not doo if he knowe not his ligne, and knowe it maye he not if he haue no propre wiff that be only soole to hym. Be this it sheweth if fornicacion were graunted it sholde be gretly aȝens naturel lawe, for it lettith that man maye not knowe his lignee. Also heritages sholde be confunded and loste whan men dyed and hadde no right heire. For these causes, God forbade simple fornicacion. But ther is but fewe in the worlde but that perysshith be this forbedyng and be this defens than be reson many sholde perisshe if fornicacion were graunted. Alsoo if it were soo that ther were lesse pepil it were no grete forse, for God setteth no store in fewe or in many men or be the[y] sonez, the whiche be neythir goode ne trewe ne profitable, opon þat [f. 8^{v}] the whiche Salamon seith that better it hadde been to shrewes that they hadde neuer be borne. And o goode man is bettir than m^{l} shrewes. And therfore oure lorde wolde that virginite and chastite were kepte in many statis. þer is o froward pepil that is displesed with that þe whiche God is plesed, as with theire propre wiff, and that pleseth theym the whiche displesith God, as evil possessions. Euery man wolde haue a hous propre, an hors propre. Why than pleseth it hym not to haue a wyf propre, sithyn that it pleseth God? The seconde synne of the flesshe whiche is forbedyn it is avoutree. The gret[nes] of this synne is shewyd be scripture in many thyngys, specially in iii as toward the womman: For first shee breketh the lawe that God set in mariage. Also shee lieth hir feith whan she levith hir husbond. Also shee dothe disceit, for she stablissheth othir childir than be hir goode mariage. The iii synne of the flesshe is desflourryng or the corrompyng of women that be virginis in ondue maner, whiche is called in Latyn *stuprum*. The gretnes of this synne maye be shewed be the vengeance that Iacobes childir tooke of Sichion, whiche hadde corromped their sistyr, whan he was kyllid and his fadir dede and alle the men of þat place and the women and the childir were ledde oute of the contre. Also to violens a woman ȝovyn and sacred to God, siche synne is sacrilege. And siche synnes be horrible and to grevous bothe to God and to the worlde. The iiii syn of the flesshe is called *incestus*, whiche is of a person flesshely to knowe of his flesshe or of his linage; and the nerer that theye be, the gretter is the synne. For the whiche Seint Poule commanded that he that hadde synned soo sholde be ȝovyn to the handes of the fende. Syn aȝens nature is the werst and ought to be fled of al other. For to venge this synne oure lorde made reyn from hevyn fyre and bremston opon the citees of Sodom and Gomor and on othir iii and al the londe aboute, and tho that dwelled there and that was borne in the lande sanke. Wherfor Lothes wif that than behelde it was changed into an ymage of salte. And this shewith vs howe myche the remembrance of this syn displesith God. Also vnnethe it was bot that þe sone of God ne had lefte to take the flesshe of mankynde for this syn, opon that the whiche Seynt Austyn seithe: Because of this synne is brokyn the feleshipp that we sholde haue with God. For as whan þat men hath evil enpeyred anothir mannes thynge, he is wonte to seye to hym that hatth enpeired it: Now ȝowres be it, evyn soo seithe God to hym that he hatth made man, [f. 9] and he wil be made a woman. He holdeth hym not for his creature, for bothe the ton and the tother putteth their sowles into helle into the fendes feleshipp. Of the whiche a wise man called Petrus Damianus telleth that ii men were in a wildirnesse whiche led hermitis lif and right sharpe penance. Of the whiche the ton was a foole and an idiot and charched with synne be the fende in so miche that the fende seide to hym that the synne aȝens nature was no gretter than thowe a man keste the pose oute of his nese, and than the synful caytif vsed to doo that syn. Wherfor the fende in his dethe bare his sowle into helle. Of the whiche his felawe merveyled gretly and was abasshed because that he hadde ben of ful labour of penaunce and of myche wachche. But than the angell tolde hym that he hadde shent and fouled al be siche a synne. Therfore in this commandement is forbedyn al maner of synne and of incontinence and of abusage [and] of lecherie of flesshe, be it of touchyngis with handes or othir weyes, the whiche is procured withoute the state of mariage.

The VII Commandement

The vii commandement is this: *Non furtum facies*. Thowe shalt doo no thefte. In this commandement is to vs forbodyn to take or withholde wrongefully anythynge from anothir, what so it be, aȝens the wille of hym that owith it. *Furtum est contraccio rei aliene [inu]ito domino ex cupiditate*, that is to seye, aȝeyns the wil of the principal lorde. But the childer of Israel that bare aweye the vessellis of golde and siluer of theym of Egipt didde no thefte, for it was be the commandement of oure lorde. And þe same he seithe be covetice. For whoso taketh the glaiue from another aȝeyns his wille because he sholde doo no harme, it is no thefte. In this commandement also is forbedyn opyn raveyn, as whan men takith a thyng opynly from an nothir, as these wyly baratu[r]s and covert theefes do, as a man selleth his thyng be condicion where theye ioyne a covent for to deceyve, as marchandis is to a terme, where men ȝefeth a thyng to hym that borweth it for c *s* the whiche he wolde ȝefe for l to hym that wolde paye. In siche wise and in siche thyngys is vsure, for therin that the which is comvne it is solde, that is, the tyme. Also in barat and in gyle as in besinesses and merchandises of weyght and of mesure, the whiche thyng fewe marchandes eschewe. Also in the hous and in the clothyng whiche is lente or in werke in the whiche thynge the value is not holden, bot for the coygne and for the moneye [f. 9^{v}] my thyng is made. And therfore in thy thyng be thy wit thowe wynyst but not of me. And therefore if men aske what it is, it is vsure and peruersion of right ordre, for of thy witt and of thy labour I aske wynnyng, and I wil appropre to me that whiche is comune, that is, the tyme, the whiche thyng longeth not to no man for to doo. But the vsurer wolde selle the light of the daye and the reste of the nyght. And of these ii thyngis he shalle haue default in helle, of the whiche Ieremie the prophete seithe: *Seruieritis diis alienis qui non dabunt vobis requiem*. And therfore the preest is a foole that syngeth for theym *requiem*, standyng that theye soilde it. Eze [v]ii: *Qui vendiderit aliquid quod vendiderit non reuertetur*. Moreouer, howe hatthe God mercy of theym or howe praye they to seintis for theym whan theye kepe not their festes? That is to seye, thoo that seke vsure be not alonly punisshed in helle, but with theym be punysshid tho that withholdeth siche thyngis evil getyn. For the whiche men remembre that ther was a man the whiche for to enriche his sones gate many thyngis shrewdely, the whiche thyngis he lefte to his sones and made never no restitucion. Of the whiche sones, on wente into religion, for he wiste wel that the heritage was evil getyn. The tothir sone abode in the worlde and folwed it and made no restitucion. Aftir that, whan the fadir and the sone was dede, theye discendid into the pit of helle, where theye were tormented, as oure lorde shewed to the sone that was in religion howe þat the fadir in the torment drewe the sone be the templis, seyng: Sone, cursed be thowe euerlastyngly, for because to make the riche I am dampned. And the same didde the sone to the fadir, seying: Naye, but thowe vnhappy fadir, for I am dampned because I folwed and kept after the that the whiche thow lefte me to kepe that thowe haddest evil and covetously getyn. And iche rente othir with their tethe and with theire nayles as ii woode houndes for the grete sorwe that theye felt. And therfore whooso withholdeth from anothir wrongefully synneth dedely ȝif he ȝelde it not aȝeyn there wher it sholde be yolden if he knewe it and maye doo it. And if he knowe it not he sholde doo be the counseile of his curat or of holy chirche.

The VIII Commandement

The viii commandement is this: *Non falsum testimonium dices*. Thowe shalt bere no fals witnes. In this commandement is defended alle maner of lyes that me shalle not lye, ne forswere theym, neythir in iugement ne owte of iugement, for to noye othir. For þo that lye make a fals witnes aȝeyns their verraye thought, for a lye is not ellys but a fals signifying of the vois or of the worde for an entent to deceyve. *Est enim mendacium* [f. 10] *falsa significacio vel probacio vocis cum intencione fallendi*. Whereof Seint Austin seithe he conseilleth no man to lye for no thyng, neythir for to save his bodily lif ne for non othir thy[n]ge, for he sholde not greve hymselfe for to ease anothir of the trowthe. He maye be stille if nede be. But God setteth not be oure lyes, for he wille no thynge but pure trouthe. This synne also shewith a man fals, for liche as a goode peny is better than x fals, evyn so a trewe man is better than x fals lyerres. Therfore it is merveille that a man wil vnethe take a fals peny wityngly and that he reckith not of hymselfe though he be fals and a lyer. Wherfore it shewith that he lofeth a peny bettir than hymselfe, and that is grete folye. Also this synne is liche the venym that fro it be entred into the mowthe it venymeth alle the man. This lye was the venym that the serpent of helle hadde in the mouthe whan he betrayed Eve, oure firste modir. And for this cause men seythe that the lye ȝeafe occasion to the serpent to haue venym in the mouthe. And therfore seithe Seynt Iohn: *Cum loquitur mendacium, ex propriis loquitur*. Whan the fende spekyth a lye, he spekyth of his owne condicion, for he is a lyer and the fadir of lyes. For the whiche a bisshopp seide that he hadde lever to haue is nevue lecherous than a lyer, for whan he sholde age, his lyes sholde encresse, and than the lechery sholde discrese. *Mendaces faciunt vt vera dicentes non credantur*. Lierres dothe so myche that men beliefe not trueseyrres. For he dothe iii harmes: He deceyveth the iuge, he hurteth and harmeth the innocent, and he sleieth hymselfe euerlastyngly. For the whiche it befelle that a lyer on a tyme was accused of a crime before a goode iuge, and at the laste whan he was ouercomyn, thowe shalt, quod he, be punysshid double for this crime, that thowe haste don it and because thowe haste denyed it. Also in þis commandement is contenyd that men shalle not myssey othir in entent to enpeire his goode name or the grace that he hath, for that is dedly synne. Aȝens this commandement do tho that seithe amysse of goode men and of goode women behynde theyme wityngly and be malice, whiche men calle bakbityng, and tho also that prayseth shrewis in their shrewdnes and of their folies knowen, seeyn, or herde, whiche is called syn of adulacion or of losengery, whan men seithe to theym in their presens outhir falsnes or lyes whan tho of whom theye speke be not present, for alle siche be false witnesses.

The IX^{te} Commandement

The ix^{te} commandement is this: *Non concupisces vxorem proximi tui*. Thowe shalt coveite not thy neyghborwes wyff, [f. 10^{v}] ne thowe shalt not desyre hirre in thyn herte. That is to seye, thowe shalt not consent to the synne of hir body. In this commandement is forbedyn þe desire or the consentyng to haue flesshely feleship with any woman oute of mariage and al evil signes outeward whiche be don to cause synne, as be evil wordis of that mater or al evil touchyngis of hymselfe or of anothir. And the differens of this commandement and of the vi aforeseide is this: The vi forbedith the dede outeward, but this forbedith the consentyng inward. For the consentyng to haue feleship with a woman whiche is not his be mariage is dedly synne, opon the sentence of the gospell of Seynt Mathieu, whiche seith: *Qui viderit mulierem ad concupiscendum eam, iam mechatus est in corde suo*. That is to seye, whoso seeth a woman and coveitith hirre in his herte synneth with the yee of his herte. This is to vndirstande if it be with a parfit consentyng and a full thought. For dedly synne is liche venym. Venym as longe as it touchith not the hert it is not perlious ne it sleithe not, but whan the delectacion descendith to the herte be consentyng, than it sleith it.

The X^{te} Commandement

The x^{te} commandement is this: *Non concupisces rem proximi tui*. Thowe shalt not coveite thy neȝborghes goode. This commandement forbedith wylle to haue any other manys goode wrongefully, whatsoeuer it be. In this commandement is forbedyn envie to anothir manes grace, for siche envie comyth of an evil covitice to haue the goodnes or the grace that men seeith in othir. And siche covetise whan the sertein consentyng and the ful thought is there it is dedly synne and aȝeins this commandement. Wherfore somtyme a persone lesith bothe his owne soule and the thynge that he coveyteth. For the whiche men remembre that ther was a man of the vilage whiche wente to an almesse that a brothirhode made of flesshe at a fastynggoyng where o man sawe hym whiche knewe wel that he hadde kyllid in his hous a fat swyne, and than he seide to hym: Lene me thy knyfe and I shalle kutte the a goode pece. And he toke it hym. And anone the tother sent it to his wiff for a tokyn and bade hir that she sholde sende the swyn that was in salt, for hir husbonde had soolde it to the brothirhoode. And shee didde soo anone. Than he that sent for the swyn cutte a goode pece therof and ȝeaf it to the tother and ȝeaf hym his knyfe aȝeyn, and the [f. 11] remenant he kepte stylle for the brethirhoode. Thus the envious loste that he coveited and ȝit more. But a light covetise to haue another mannys thyng be reson is no dedly synne. And if ther be any mevyng to hurte any othir withowte wille or consentyng it is no synne, and if it be it is venial.

Here endeth the x commandementis of oure lorde, of the whiche the iii first setteth vs to God; the tother ordeyneth vs to oure neȝghborghes. These x commandementis euery Cristyn creature that hatthe reson and age is bounde to kepe and to fulfille, for whoso wityngly dothe aȝeyns theym synneth dedly. For as ther be x wardis or mo on a lokke, whan on of the wardis is brokyn, it maye not opyn, in the same wise whoso kepith ix of the commandementis and wityngly brekith the x or on of theym he shalle never entre into paradis if he come not to amendement. And therfore seith Seint Iame: *Qui offenderit in vnum factus est omni[um] reus.*

Here Endeth þe X Commandementis of þe Feith

Here Begynneth the XII Articles of þe Feithe

Here begynneth the articlis of the Cristen feithe, the whiche euery Cristen man sholde beleve stedfastly, for elles he maye not be saved, standyng that he hatthe witte and reson. And theye be xii after the nombre of the xii apostlis, the whiche sette theym to be holden and to be kepte to alle tho that wille be saved. Of the whiche the firste longeth to the fadir, the tother [v]ii folwyng to the sone, the foure to the Holy Goste, for the grounde of the feithe is to beleve in the holy trinite, that is to seye, in the fadir and in the sone and in the Holy Goste, o god in iii persones. And these articles be contynned in the crede that the xii apostlis made of the whiche euery of theym set his.

[f. 11v] The Firste Article

The firste article of the feithe is this: I beleve in God the fadir almyghty, maker of hevyn and of erthe. In this men sholde vnderstande that he made the creatures that be in hevyn and in erthe. This article sette Seynt Petir in the crede.

The Seconde Article

The seconde longeth to the sone, as to his godhed or beyng, that is to seye, in that that he is on alonly with the fadir, and it is this: I beleve in oure lorde Crist Iesus, son of God the fadir. In this men sholde vndirstande and beleve that he is like and egal to the fadir in alle thyngys that longeth to the godheede, and it is alle o thynge with the fadir, save the persone of the sone, the whiche is an nothir thynge than the persone of the fadir. And this article sette Seynt Iohn the euuangeliste.

[f. 12] The III Article

The iii article and the tother fyfe that folweth aftir longeth to the sone opon the mankyndelynes, that is to seye, opon that that he is man and tooke veraye nature of dedly man. Wherfore in this article is conteyned that he was conceyved be the dede and the vertu of the Holy Goste and not only be the dede of man, for the Virgine Marie was ever hole virgine afore and after. This article set Seynt Iame, brothir to Seint Iohn.

The IIII Article

The iiii article longeth to the passion. That is to seye that he suffred dethe and passion vnder Pounce Pilate, the whiche was a paienyme and in that tyme iuge in Ierusalem be the Romaines. Vnder hym was Criste Iesus wrongefully iuged and crucified and dede and put in sepulcre. This article set Seint Andrewe.

[f. 12v] The V Article

The v article is that he descended into helle after his dethe for to drawe oute and to delyuere the sowles of holy faders and of tho that fro the begynnyng of the worlde deyed in gode feithe and in goode hoope that theye sholde be saved be hym, for because of the synne of the firste fadir moste nede be that al descended into helle and the goode pepil to abide ther in certeyn hoope that Criste Iesus, the sone of God, sholde comen to delyuere theym as he hadde promissed be the prophetes. And for this cause after his dethe he wolde descende into helle, this is to vnderstande, into that partie wher the holy faders were. But tho that were dede in theire synne and in theire mysbeleve tho drewe he not oute, for they be euerlastyngly dampned. This article set Seint Phelip.

The VIte Article

The vite article is of the resurreccion and seithe thus that the thirde daye of his dethe, for to fullefille the scriptures, he rose fro dethe to lyfe and apperid to his disciplis and proved to theym his resurreccion in many maneres. This article sette Seint Thomas.

[f. 13] The VII Article

The vii article is that the xl daye of his resurreccion, whan he had etyn with his disciplis, he styed into hevyn afore theym alle opynly, that is to saye, above alle hevines, the whiche is above alle creatures, to the right side of God the fadir where he sitteth. This article sette Seint Bertilmewe.

The VIII Article

The viii article is that he shalle come to the daye of dome for to iuge the quycke and the dede, the goode and the evyl, and he shalle ȝefe to euery persone after that he hatthe deservid in this worlde. These be the articlis longeyng to the son. And this article set Seint Mathieu.

The IX Article

The ix article and the remanant longeth to the Holy Goste. This article is that men sholde beleve that the Holy Gooste is the [f. 13v] ȝifte and the luff of the fadir and of the sone of whom commeth to vs alle grace and alle goodenes and that it is o god and o thyng with the fadir and the sonne. This article sette Seint Iame the lesse, brothir to Seint Simon.

The X Article

The x article is: I beleve in holy chirche general and in the communion of seintis and of goode men, the whiche be and shalle be togedir to the worldes ende in the feithe of Criste Iesus. In this article is vnderstanden the vii sacramentis of holy chirche: babteme, confirmacion, the sacrement of penance, ordre of mariage, ordre of prestehode, the sacrement of the auter, the laste holy vnccion. This article set Seint Simon.

The XI Article

The xi article is to beleve to haue remission of synnes that God ȝeveth be the vertu of the holy sacrementis of holy churche. This article sette Seint Iude, Seint Simones brother.

[f. 14] The XII Article

The xii article is to beleve the generall resurreccion of dede pepil and the euerlastyng liffe that is the ioye of paradis, the whiche God shall ȝif to tho that shalle serve hym be feithe and be goode dedis. This article ȝiffeth to vnderstande his contrarie, that is to seye, the euerlastyng peyne that God hatthe ordeyned to tho that shalle be dampned. This article is vnderstanden thus that euery persone, be he goode be he evill, at the daye of dome shalle be reysed fro dethe to lyff in his owne body that he wherein lyfed. And ȝif he levid wele, he shalle receyve his rewarde in body and in sowle in euerlastyng liffe, and evil pepil shal be dampned euerlastyngly bothe in body and in soule. And whoosoo belevith not this he is in peril of dampnacion of body and of sowle. This article set Seint Mathi.

Here Endeth the XII Articlis of the Feithe

Seint Iohn the wangelist in the Booke of Reuelaciones the

whiche is called the Pocalipse seithe that he sawe a beeste comme oute of the see, the whiche was gretely to drede and merveliously disgyssed, for the body of the beeste was of a leparde and the feete was of a bere, the throote was of a lyon, and it hadde vii heedes and x hornes and apone the x hornes x corounes. And Seynt Iohn sawe that the cruel bestee hadde power to fight with holy men and to conquere theym and to overcome theym. This diuerse beeste so contrefete and soo ferefulle betokeneth the feende that cometh fro the [f. 14v] see of helle, the whiche is fulle of alle sorwes and of alle bitternesses. The body of the beeste, as Seynt Iohn seith, was like a leparde, for liche as a leparde hatthe diuers coloure, so the feende hatthe diuers maneres of wyles and of disseitis to disceyve and to take and to tempte with the pepill. The feete were like to the feete of a bere, for liche as the bere hatthe strenght in the feete to defoule vnder his feete that the whiche he enbraseth and ouerthroweth evyn so doothe the feende with tho that he hatthe enbrassed and ouerthrowen be synne. The throte was of a lyon for his grete cruelnes that al wolde devoure. The vii heedes of the beeste of helle is the vii cheffe synnes be the whiche the feende [draweth] to hym nerehande al the worlde, that vnethe it happeth but that men falle in the throte of some of these vii heedes. And therefore seithe Seynt Iohn ful welle that it hadde power aȝeyns holy men, for in erthe is no man soo holy that parfytly maye eschewe al the maner of synnes that descendeth of these vii heedes withoute a specialle previlage of grace, as was in the Virgine Marie or in any other after the special grace that theye hadde of God. The x hornes of the beeste betokeneth the brekyng of the x commandementis of the feithe, the whiche the fende purchaseth as myche as he maye be the vii forseide synnes. The corounes above betokeneth the victorie that he hatthe ouer alle synneres because he maketh theym breke the commandementis of the lawe.

Of II Rootes Whens Al Evil and Alle Goode Commeth, III

Qhoso ȝifeth not that he luffeth taketh not that he desireth. Euery man wolde haue ioye, gladnesse, goode life, and his desire, and ȝit none wil leve evil lyffe. Ther is none so grete a foole but that he wolde gladly ȝiffe an evil gowne for a goode and also of alle other thyngys men wil gladly ȝif the evil for the goode, savyng an evil hert for a goode and an evil sowle for a goode. Foole, seithe the wise man, why ȝifest thowe not an evill luff for a goode? What hatthe thy sowle trespassed to the? Why hatest thowe it so cruelly? What is in thyn howse that thowe woldest not were goode? It is neyther women ne childer, ne cote ne shirte, no forsoothe it, ne hosyn ne shone. Why than wilt thowe not haue as wel a goode luffe and a goode liffe as thowe woldest haue the tother? Thowe praysest no [f. 15] more thi sowle than a curre as to regarde of thy dedis. Goode luffe maketh a goode hert, and a goode liffe maketh a goode soule. Therfore I seye to the and counsell the and praye the that [if] thowe wilt haue pees, ioye, and gladnes in this worlde and in the tother first take heede to qwom thowe gevist the luff of thyn hert, for that is the grettest tresor that þou haste. For whoso hatthe thy luff he hatthe thyn herte, and whoso hatthe thyn herte he hatthe al that thowe haste. As men be wonte to seye, whoso hatthe a karle he hatthe al that he hatthe. Therfore God asketh thy luffe.

The luffe is as the roote of a tree. For as Godde seithe in the gospelle: Of a goode tree commeth goode fruit. Evyn soo of goode luffe commeth good lyff, and of evil luffe evil liffe. Therfore seithe Seint Austyn that vertu is a luff welle set. The tone luffe is charite, the whiche is roote of alle goodnes; the toþer is covetice, the whiche is roote of alle evill. The ton filleth hevyn, where the chosyn hertis be; the tother filleth helle, where ther is neyther luff ne ordinance. Of these ii rootes groweth ii trees, of the whiche the ton is called the tree of liffe because that his fruit ȝifeth liffe withowte dethe; the tother is called the tree of dethe [...] the whiche maye not dye. This sheweth Adam and Eve ful wel to vs, the whiche wolde not taste of the trees, but theye ete of the defended tree, and dye theye moste therfore and theire heyres after theym. Of these ii trees, with the helpe of God, I wille shewe the the gret branches and the spryngis of the strengthe and the nature of these ii trees and of the fruitis because thowe maye chese the goode and flee and eschewe and hate the evil. And this is the firste thyng that moste be lerned and knowen to hym that wil lerne this konnyng. That is to seye, to kepe his hert and to haue ioye and to lede gode liff he moste knowe that the begynnyng of veraye ioye and of goode liff is pees of herte, as I haue tolde the, and surte [of] conscience. Thowe knowest wel that a grete kynge the whiche wil that his reaume be wel kept in pees and in ioye he moste haue iii thyngis: Firste he moste thynke to put vndir foote and to discomfit his enemys and to ouerthrow the evil lawes of his lande and also to strengthe his castell and to stuffe theym wel and also to doo right and to kepe rightwisnes. O, he hatthe a fulle grete reaume that kepeth his herte, the whiche is gretter than al the worlde, and he is a grete kynge that maye kepe it wel. Oure enemys be synes and evil lawes, as Seint Powle seithe, the [f. 15v] whiche be the vicis of the herte and of the bodye. Oure forteresses is vertues; the stuffe of the castell is goode dedes. Whoso wil than liff hily as a kynge first he moste distroye synnes and ouerthrowe vicis of the herte, the whiche be evil costomes, after that stedfast his hert with goode vertues so that he take heede of nothyng that maye trouble the herte, and to stuffe it with goode dedes, after þat to kepe iustice that theefes ne evil pepill rise not, an than liff in goode pees and in goode ioye as wise Salamon didde. And thus hatthe he the kyngdom of God in hym, that is to seye, the begynnyng of that the whiche ledith vs to the kyngedom of paradis. And Seint Poule seithe that this is neither drinke ne mete but it is iustice and pees and ioye with the Holy Gooste, that is to seye, to liff iustly and in feire pees and in right ioye, the whiche commeth of the Holy Gooste, and not of the worlde ne of the flesshe. For whosoo is takyn and hatthe pees because that the worlde wil it and that his flesshe desireth it that is a foule pees and a wooful [ioye], liche as it is of hym that hatthe pees with his enemys because that he is ȝolden to theym. But of a feire victorie commeth a feire pees. Howe sholde he ouercome his enemys that knoweth theym not, neyther theym ne theyre konyng? Whoso knowith not his aduersaries he gothe perliously to bataile. Therfore I seye that whoso wil come to a feire victorie and to a feire pees he sholde firste knowe his enemys and than doo his devoire to distroye theyme. Whoso wil make a feire gardine in a place fulle of nettlis, he moste firste put aweye the evil herbis and drawe oute the evill rootes and plant therin goode ympes. For a wel set man fareth as a delicious gardyn, but the hert of a synner, as Salamon seith, fareth as a wasted vyne and a deserte felde fulle of netlis and of brerys.

Of the Evil Roote Whens Al Synnes Groweth and of the VII Dedly Synnes General, IIII

The evil roote, as I haue seide vnto the, is a foule disordenat luffe. This roote casteth mo branches of synne than men can nombre, for evil gresse groweth faste. These be the brondes of the fire of helle whan theye be deedly and of the fire of purgatorie whan theye be veniall. Thus it [f. 16] happeth that the tree of synne hatthe mo spryngis oute than the tree of vertu, for in mo maneres men maye goo oute of the weye than goo aright and mysdrawe than to drawe aright. The vii principal branches that groweth of the evil roote be the vii chief vicis of the whiche cometh owte al the synnes that men doo. The firste vice is pride; the tother be envie, slouthe, wretthe, covetice, gloutony, lechery. Al these branches cometh oute of a disordenat luff and of an evil desire. Prowde men disordenatly desireth heynesse; the envious desireth the evil and the harme of other; the irous the whiche is a foole desireth to venge hym of other; the slowe, reste and idilnesse; the covetous, goode; the gloton, the delite of the throote; the lecherous, the delit of the reynes. Whan þis luff is so grete and this desire so fervent and so grete þat it passeth the luffe of God and maketh the commandementis to be brokyn, than is it called dedly synne, for it killeth the soule and taketh fro hym his liff, that is to seye, God, the whiche is the liff of the soule, liche as the soule is the liff of the bodye. Dedly synne is dedly werre, and whoso dothe it hatthe takyn a werre aȝeyns God. And therfore it is called dedly. These vii desires and these vii maneres of luff arn be that disordonat, because that a man luffeth that the whiche he sholde not luff more than that the whiche he sholde luffe.

[f. 16v] Pride was the firste synne that euer was, and therfore it is the begynnyng of alle synnes, for pride brake firste feleshipp and ordre as whan Lucifer for his grete beaute and wit wolde be aboue alle othir angellis [and] he was a feende and al his feleshipp. Ʒit into þis houre prowde pepil resembleth hym, whiche brekith and fordothe feleshipp and ordre whan theye wille be above al othir and more praysed and alowed than othir that be better than theye. Wherfore prowde and envious pepil love that theye sholde not love and desire that theye sholde not desire, that is to seye, the harme or the hyndryng of his neʒghborgh. The slowe man lovith litil that the whiche he sholde loue myche, that is, God, for whom that he wil do litil or noght, the whiche he sholde serve with alle his herte and with al his myght and love hym with alle his strengthe. The negarde and the likerous and the gloton of the throote and the lecherous bodye hatthe a disordenat luff, for theye luff to myche al that theye shulde luff lytill, that is, the delit of the flesshe and temporel goodes. But whan his desires and his lofes be not so grete that theye passe not the luff of God, os that it happeth whan men seke theire availe or their delit or worldely worshipp bot ʒit not so fervently that theye wille forfete the commandementis of God for it, this is called venial synne, that is to seye, pardonable, for men be not dampned for siche synnes, if the evil love cleme not the heier than the goode. But theye shalle be ful dere bought in this worlde or in the tother. And for to chastie and drawe vs fro these synnes and lofes God beteth vs and sendeth vs myshapes and sekenesses and withdraweth from vs temporell goodes. Iche of these vii branches whan þe feende maye plante theyme in oure hertis theye waxe, sprede, and multiplie oute of mesure and withoute nombre and becommeth as a [brere] or as a thorne or as a wasted vine whiche bereth venym in stede of wyne. Therfore whooso wil amend his liff and araye his hert first he moste cut aweye the breris, that is to seye, his synnes with the hoke of the tonge of confession and the evil rootes and the evil costumes and drawe oute al evil desires, and anone the goode gardne[r] Criste Iesus shalle sette there goode ympes, the whiche be goode vertues. Whoso knoweth not these vii branches and the smale springlyngis that groweth of theym he maye never confesse hym aright ne purge hym ne clense hym parfitly, ne he shalle not knowe whereof to crye God [f. 17] mercy ne werfore to thanke hym.

And therfore I wille shewe the this mirrour that thowe

maiste ofte see thyselfe therin and to avice the spottes of the face of thyn herte and to konne amende thy defautis and remembre thy synnes in beholdyng thy consience and to confesse the pleinly and to ordeyne and amende thy liff and thyn herte and that thowe maye so beholde thyselfe on al sides that thowe maye see thy deedis as pleinly as thowe maye see thy face in a mirrour. And therfore men sholde calle this booke the Mirrour of the Worlde, because that men seeith their synnes therin. Nowe I praye the for Goddys sake as derly as thowe lovest the helthe of thy sowle that thowe set wele thyn herte to vnderstande and to hire this and whan thowe herist any vice or any synne wherwith thy consience is mevid knowleche thy mysdede and crye God mercy and as of othir that I shalle reherce vnto the fro the whiche God kepeth the ȝelde graces to hym and thonke hym and prayse hym in thyn herte.

[Of Pride in Especiall], V

The firste roote of the evil branche wherof I haue spokyn it is pride, whiche is the eldeste doughter of the feende. Whooso haue this doughter hatthe grete parte in the feendis heritage. Pride hateth God and werreyeth hym for al the goodes that he hatthe ȝovyn hym, and ȝit God abateth pride and hateth it, and al seyntis [f. 17v] hateth it. Pride is the quene and modir and norice of vicis, for shee kepeth, defendeth, and norisshith al othir vicis. For ther is no synne holly withoute the synne of pride or withowte inreuerence or despit. Pride distroyeth al the goodenes that a man hatthe and alle his graces and goode werkys, for it maketh of almesse synne and of vertu vice. And with the goodes of God wherwith he sholde gete hevyn it maketh hym to gete helle. The sperit of pride is the firste vice that assauteth Goddis knyght and that laste levith hym, for whan he hatthe ouercomen al othir vicis than assaileth hym the pride of hymselfe. Pride blyndeth a man so that he nethir knoweth it ne seeth it, and it blyndeth hym so entierly that he shewith his pride over-alle and that al the worlde seeth it, and ȝit hymselfe nethir knowith it ne seeth it, for it soteth hym so holly that it exilleth and disceuith for noght bothe body and soule and for lesse than for noght, that is to seye, for the wynde of veinglorie. Pride is the stronge precious wyne of the feende with the whiche he maketh alle these grete men, these feire, these wise, and these riche men dronken. This is no wyne for boyes ne for chambereris ne for smalle pepil but for grete lordes whiche he maketh dronken of theire owne erroures, so that they knowe not theymselfe ne never confesseth theym aright. Howe sholde he confesse hym verily that knoweth not his owne deede ne seeth it not whan men telleth it hym? We see al daye that a persone whiche knoweth al his power and setteth his body to be praysed seyeth as thus: I am the man of the worlde, seithe he, that hatthe lefte pride. And whoso beholdeth wele his araye and his houshold and his dispens he sholde see but boste and vanite. Wherfore this is the perliouseste sekenes of al othir, for he is in fulle grete perille to whom al triacle torneth to venym. Thus dothe the chastisment of techyng to a proude man. The more men chastiseth hym and blameth hym, the more he defendeth hym. For he seith: I doo it not for evil, or: I wende not to a done it, or: I shalle never beleve that it is dedly synne, or: [if] that it is evil ȝit this is not so grete evil but that I wolde we didde never wers. Or he seithe: If I do evil ȝit dothe he wers, or: if this be true that ȝe telle me than is al the worlde loste, or: I knowe wel that I doo evil but that forthynkith me. God knoweth wel myn herte. But it is fulle harde; it moste nedis be don. Alas what here is an harde lorde þat moste [f. 18] be served with swete and with so grete labor and coste and with siche guerdon and to forsake his liege lorde and dothe vntrouthes and to hym traysone. This plante of pride whan it is roted in the herte it spredith hym ful strongely and casteth vii principall spryngis, of the whiche every of theym devideth hym in so many synnes that none maye nombre theym.

The Branches of Pride, VI

The firste plante is vntrouthe; the seconde, dispite; the thirde, overhope, the whiche we calle arrogans or presumpcion; the iiii, ambicion; the v, veinglorie; the vi, ypocrisie; the vii, shrewde fere. To these vii partes longeth vii synes wiche groweth of pride, and iche of these vii branches hatthe many smale branches.

The Firste Branche of Pride the Whiche Is Vntrouthe and Hatthe III Branches, VII

The firste branche of pride is vntrouthe and that hatthe iii branches, of the whiche on is veleny, anothir wodenes, the iii renoyng. Ther is none so grete veleny ne soo grete ingratitude as of this synne. Whereof I shalle telle the an example. Ther was a gret myghty kynge, wise, large, curteice, and a goode keper of iustice. He hadde a boye in his house [the whiche] was bothe pore and bonde. It befelle that the boye was takyn with thefte and condempned to the dethe. The kynge hadde grete pitee therof and ȝaf grete goode for to bye hym aȝein and brought hym aȝein and clad hym and made hym free and made hym knyght and bailie of a grete contre and was sworn to be true on peyne of his hede. Than he wente into his bailiship and sawe his lordshipp gret and wexe in pride. A grete baretor whiche hated his lorde become felawly with hym and with hym that a grete theef and many grete roveres, the whiche sawe that the balie was riche and nyce. Theye began than to prayse hym and to drawe hym to theire lyne. This bailie belevid theym and feleshipid hym with theyme and forgate al that euer his lorde dide to hym and holly torned the bakke to hym. Nowe telle me whoder he didde not gret veleny. Certis ȝis, and pride and vntrouthe and folie, for al the dayes of the worlde he sholde haue lofed hym with alle his herte for his grete frenesse and worship hym with alle his myght and doute hym with alle his witte for his grete myght and for his iustice and grete trouthe and taken heede of hym and thonke hym of his ientilles.

Ȝit this musart didde more, for of that the whiche was ȝovyn hym, of whiche he moste ȝif commpte, he ȝaf never noon ne sought after [f. 18v] the value of the londes ne of the rentes ne of issues ne of plees, but rather he entirmellid and wasted the goodes of his lorde with the tothir barettoures. Was not this grete folie? Ȝis truly, and ȝit he did a gretter woodenes, for he avoued to an nothir lorde the lande of his liege lorde and ȝit werreyed hym. Was not this a grete woodenes? What sholde men doo with siche a mystirman? Euery of vs is siche a rebaute. This grete kynge is almyghty God, whiche formed my body of myre and the soule of noght, for the whiche I sholde be his. For whan I was borne, I was prisoner to the fende and poore and bonde to synne and dampned to dethe, but þe swete kynge of hevyn, be his swetnes and bounte and not for the bounte that he had in me more than in the childe of a payenyme, of the whiche he hatthe no charge, he bought me aȝeyn with his owne blode and wasshed me in blode of baptesme and cladde me with the gowne of innocence and freed me from the foule seruage of synne and made me knyght whan he araied me with the grace of the Holy Gooste and [made me] with his householde and with his borde, that is to seye, with the holy sacrement of the auter, be the whiche al soules lifeth, and set in me v thyngys in my baliage, whiche the gospel calleth v besantis: first the body clene and innocent, the soule clere and shynyng, the worlde and temporel thyngys for to serve me, the tyme for to deserve his blisse, and his grace for to helpe me. These v besantis he ȝafe me to kepe and to wyn withal, and I delyuered and avoued and ȝafe to hym my godfaderes and godmoderes to plege that I sholde kepe feithe and trouthe to hym and doo to hym worship as to my liege lorde and louf hym above al thynge and that these thyngys sholde be multiplied that he hatth ȝovyn to me vnto my power not only in peyn of the lesyng of my hede but o peyn of euer-lastyng dethe. I ought wel to loufe soo swete a lorde and to worshipp so gret a kynge and to drede so gret a iusticer and to thanke so large a goodedoer. But what haue I doon? As soon as I come into my bailiship, that is to seye, as soon as I cowde knowe goode and evil, I ȝalde evil for goode, pride for debonnairte, veleni for curtesi. This is the grettest veleni that is, for þe gretter the bounte is, the gretter is the veleni, as whan a man knowith it not and forȝeteth it. If I hadde loste bothe myn handes, I wolde love hym ful myche that wolde gete me theym aȝeyn. Howe sholde I than louf hym that made me and ȝaf me my handes and my feete and body and soule and othir goodnes [that] noon maye preise it? But a grete [f. 19] many of rovers, that is to saye, the feleshipp of the iolynes of this worlde toke me to theym in my childehoode, and a maister barettour, a deciple of hym that firste deceyvid Eve, oure firste modir. Anoon theye drue oute of myn herte the rootes of holy fere and the plantes of naturelle louf that I sholde haue hadde to my creature, and aȝeynward theye planted the iolynes and the folie of the worlde and set me in so grete errour that theye made me al bestly and deceyved me and enchaunted me, so that whan I sawe the worlde so feire and so plesaunte anone I torned the backe to my right lorde and the visage to the worlde, and I set myn yen in the erthe as domme bestis doo. And so forȝat I my creature and toke no heede to my beyng no more than a beste ne whoo made me ne what I was ne whider I wente. Rathir I haue liffed to this daye thorogh my pride and my veleny that never I commpted ne thanked hym for his worshipes ne his curtesies. And in this synne of pride and veleny I haue synned of tymes [more] than I haue lifed dayes. And ther is no daye but that I reseyue bountees of hym more than m^{l} tymes, for the whiche I can hym neythir gree ne thanke ne take no more heede therof than the kynge dothe of calvys. Al the worlde is fulle of this synne of pride and of veleny. And, aboue alle othir, tho that be called curteis and gentil, thoo be theye that be moste veleynsce and vntrewe, for the more that theye reyseyue of oure lorde goodes and reseyve dayly, the more theye sholde thonke hym, loue hym, and worship hym. Nowe a litil I wil speke to siche pepil, because theye maye lerne to compt afore God and knoweleche his curtesies and amende their velenies. Nowe telle me, wil ȝe lerne curtesie? Beholde yowe in this mirrour, and see the visage of ȝour hert, and if ȝe fynde any spotis of vileny therin doo ȝoure devoir to waisshe theym wel, as ye wolde doo a spotte of youre body. For siche be called ientil vnder a feire visage that after is a stynkyng caroyne vnder a serkle of golde, liche as is a rotyn dungehille vndir a snowe. Ther is no vereye beaute to a ientil hert ne velany to a vileins hert. A veray velain is he that reseyuith gret bountewousnes and list not to sey grete mercy. ȝit is he more veleyns that forȝetith it and denyeth it, and in this part yit it is to gret, as whan men reseyvith it dayly and that never wil hire speke therof but alweye ȝeldeth evil for goode. Trowe ye not that it pleseth gretly to hye pepil whan ther bounte is wel besette?

Sertes yis, but fewe pepil setteth it wel, for theye ȝif it to bourdoures for a vers of a songe or for a iape that plesith theym for to be praysed that theye be large and curteise thurgh þe caytyvous pride of this worlde, but theye wil never doo it ne ȝif it to thoo that deserue it. But it pleseth God [f. 19v] that is kynge of curtesie, the whiche is so large, that he hatthe his handes alweye departed and streccheth forthe for to ȝif. It pleseth hym gretly whan men knowelecheth his goodnes and ȝeldeth hym thankes with goode herte. And wit wel, if thowe woldest compte to hym euery daye in on orison previly and remembre be smale parties al his goodnesses and his curtesies and aȝeynward thyn evilles and thy velenies and than ȝelde hym graces and thankes for his goodnesse and crye hym mercy for thy synnes, it were better to the than to were the hayre, for God is not plesed with oure tormentis but with oure goode wille and veray luff of hert. I shal nowe set the in the waye howe thowe sholdest compt to Godde and confesse the. Men seye that o bounte askith anothir; to hym that dothe myche, for the whiche myche moste be doon to hym. And thow wotest wel what thow haste reseyvid of Godde, for if thowe knewe it not thowe sholdest nevyr knowe howe myche thowe sholdest thonke hym and love hym and worship hym, and he asketh not ellys of the. Godde hatthe doon to the iii maner of bounteys: on comune with al othir men, on especial with alle thy senguler advises, and on senguler for the alonly.

For the firste, thowe howest hym as myche as the worlde is worthe; for the seconde, as myche as hymselfe is worthe; for the thirde, as myche as thowe art worthe and that thowe haste of value. Whan he made the, if he hadde wolde, he might a made the a boole or an hogge, but he made the to his liknes, lorde of the worlde and of hevyn, for al that thowe seyste with yee is made to serve the. For howe myche woldest thowe quyte the seruice of the son, of the mone, and of the sterres? Thowe sholdest see no sight, ne thowe myghtest not life withowte theym on houre of a daye. Erthe and water, daye and nyght sesse not to serve the. Ther where thowe slepest in thy bedde, they araye for the that with the whiche thowe sholdest liffe, for the whiche thowe sholdest loffe hym as myche as thowe he hadde ȝovyn the alle the worlde. That is trewe, seist thowe, if he hadde made it al for me alone. Oo fals and nyce hert, woldest thowe be lorde of alle the worlde on that condicion that ther were no moo but thowe alon? The kynge eteth not al his goodes be hymselfe; no more woldest thowe be alle alon in the reaume of Yngelond. Truly, if thowe were al alon in the worlde, thowe woldest desire ful sore to haue with the thy kyn and thy frendes and the feir feleshipp with whiche thowe haste hadde thy dispórtes. If thowe seye [f. 20] thowe woldest be be thyselfe, I preve that thowe liest. For why than folwist thowe the feleship of othir? Thowe goest to daunces; thowe goest to assemblees of pepil; thowe goest to bostes; thowe goest to feleshippes and to tormentis; thowe goest into othir veleins places. Sen that thowe doest thus, thowe liest if thowe seye that thowe wilte haue the worlde be thyselfe alone. Nowe take it to the aloon; thowe haste al these goodes in thy kepyng that I haue tolde the. Nowe goo; repent the; be al alone foreuer. Thowe sholdest nothyng [be] al alon, for thowe maiest nothyng doo so. Wherfore thowe oughtest the more to luff thy creature, because he hatthe ȝovyn the thee worlde and so many frendis and feir feleshipes than though he hadde made it aloonly for the. Knowe nowe thy gret lordeshipp, thy dignite, and thy richesse. Seye never nowe that thowe arte pore, as these covetouse pepil and these negardis doo, to whom it semeth that theye haue nought, standyng ther is an nothir feleship. Theye be veleyns and froward and that whiche theye haue is evil beset. For theye be liche a curre to whom men casten a morcel of brede. Anoon he swalweth it and forȝeth it and lokith after anothir; he hatthe no sauour in that whiche he taketh because he desireth so fervently anothir. Thus it farith be covetous pepil, the whiche breneth more than a leche fried, for theye haue no sauour in the goodnes that God hatthe ȝovyn theym, theye desire evir so myche othir. But thowe that haste vndirstandyng thynke with thyn hert that thowe woldest seye gremercy to hym that sholde ȝif the a feire thyng. Take heede than þat God hatthe ȝovyn the feir son, the moone, and the sterris, fruites, cornes, and al othir thyngis and sesseth never of sendyng to the. And, ȝif thowe were curteise, thowe sholdest than seye gremercy for iche of these, and thus thowe sholdest never sesse to seye gremercy and to thanke God, and so thowe shalt þan ever haue God in thyn herte, as Kynge Dauid had, the whiche seid: I shal euer preyse God in myn herte, and his praysyng shal never falle fro myn herte.

Of III Maner of Bount[e]z That God Hatthe Don to The, VIII

Ȝit owest thowe more for the iii special bountees that he hatthe doon to the with thoo that he hatthe chosen to his parte. For because of th[ee] he come into erthe and [f. 20v] was exiled xxxii ȝere, and he suffred more sorwe, shame, and veleny and many moo disseses than any othir man. He was solde, betyn, bounden, scorned, and scourged and iuged to the shamefulest deeth that was. And al that he suffred for the and for to haue thy luff, and lever he hadde to dye than to lese the. And nowe, sen he hatthe bought the, thowe owest hym as myche as thowe haste coste hym, that is to seye, as myche as hymselfe is worthe. And if thowe seye: Sir, that were true that ȝe telle me, if he had don this alonly for me. Oo veleyns and envious hert, if thowe were takyn with Torkys or with Sarrazins and al thy kyn and thy frendis with the, whedir woldest thowe cunne more thanke, whethir hym that deliuered the aloon or hym that delyuered the and thy frendes and thi childryn and thy wif? Why hatest thowe theyme so myche that thowe woldest a louffed þe more God if he had letyn theym be loste or goon to helle than because that he hatthe sauyd theym with the, forsoþe, because that thye ioye shal be the gretter whan thowe shalt see theyme in paradis with the? Nowe than thowe seist opynly that thowe sholdest the more feruently luff God for the feleship that thowe shalt haue for to fulfille thy ioye than though he hadde suffred dethe for the alonly. Therfore, for to ȝelde hym thankes for this bounte, wee seye to hym the vii houres of the daye and anamly because therfore is worshiped the sacrement of the auter and of the messe. Truly he is a velein and ful evil that forȝeteth siche bounte [or] whooso maye do it and wil not seye his vii houres of the daye outher be nombre of pater nosteris, as the coventis of Celestinis doon, or othir weyes whoso can. But he is a veleine and passyng evil that onys of the daye maye here that holy messe and wil not hire it. Certys he is gretely oute of his witte that liste not to reseyve soo grete a present as God is, the whiche ȝefeth hym to vs and liste alweye to come to visite, to solas, and to defende vs caitiffes and to forȝefe vs oure synnes and to feede oure soules with his flesshe and with his bloode. For the whiche bounte thowe owest hym ayenward as myche as hymselfe is worthe, for in paradis hymselfe shal be thy wages, as that he pr[om]yseth the. And if thowe wille deserve that wagis aright, thowe moste doo as miche for hym as the wagis be worthe that thowe reseyuyst of hym, because he ȝaf hym to the for to bye the aȝeyn. ȝit he ȝifeth hym dayly [f. 21] for to gouerne the, and ȝit he shal ȝif hym to the for to rewarde the iii tymes, for the whiche thowe oweste hym as miche as he is worthe. This maye not be ȝolden if thowe lifed m^{l} ȝere and euery daye suffred deethe for hym. Than art thowe a velein if thowe, as myche as thowe maist and as thowe art worthe, ȝif the not aȝeynward to hym.

Nowe lete vs come to the singuler goodes that he hatthe doon to the, for the whiche thowe sholdest louf hym gretely. We fynde here iii maner of goodes, that is to seye, bodyly, goostly, and temporell. Thowe that art a free man seest that God hatthe [made] to the a right compte and knowelechest of the goodnes that he hatthe doon to the vndeservid. Ther be many hondrithes and thousandes besyd the that hatthe not the bodily goodes that thowe haste. Some be velins, and thowe art ientyl. Some be febil, and thowe art hole and sounde. Some be crokyd, blynde, and lame; thowe art not soo. Some be pore and beggeris, and some be pore and laborerris that lifeth with sorowe, anguisshe, and ful grete travaile in this worlde. Thowe haste ben norisshed with the pappe withowte besynes or labour, and thowe haste hadde withowte disesse al that was nedeful to the bodye, thy rentes and thy lordshipis. Dayly thowe haste Seynt Martinis Feste. For to delite the with in thy v wittys God hatthe ȝovyn the more than thowe maiste thynke. Beholde howe thowe maiste opynly see that in this worlde thowe haste a lytyl paradis. And touchyng goostely goodis, take heede what God hatthe doon to the. Thowe seyste that al the worlde is fulle of shrewdenes; somme be nyce and foolles, othir be ribaudes, and some theefes and somme lechoures. From these synnes and many othir God hatthe kepte the be his grace. Telle me nowe what thowe haste doon for God. It is goon a m^{l} ȝere that ther was noon of thoo that I haue named to the. And hatthe he not doon al these bountees to the vndeservid? Truly, if thowe wilt compt to Godde and considre al the bountees that he hatthe ȝovyn to the and al the synnes that he hatthe forȝovyn the and al the perillis from whiche he hatthe kept the, thyn hert sholde telle the be right iugement that þou knowest noon liffyng in the worlde in whom God hatth doon so myche as in the, for thye cause thowe knowest wele but an nothir mannes cause thowe knowest not. And therfore thowe shalt seye: Lorde God, I am the mortel creature that is mooste holden to luff the, to thonke the, and to worship þe. [f. 21^{v}] I knowleche my pride and my veleny. I ȝalde never verily thankis for ȝour goodnes. I haue been as the hogge that eteth the glene; I loked not vpward to the oke from the whiche that come. The more that ȝe haue doon my wille, the more I haue forȝetyn ȝow. I am not worthy to seye the pater noster. I am not he that sholde calle ȝowe fadir, as he that holly is disheretid. Whooso sange siche a songe it wolde gretly plese God. And truly he were a grete caytif that wolde lese paradis for faute of seying of gremercy.

Swete Criste Iesus, whan I beholde ȝour grete curtesye than knowleche I my pride and my folie and my velenye. I am the evil bailie of the whiche I haue spokyn afore. Pride hatthe putte me in velenye, and also he hatthe shewid me lityl luff, for whoso wel luffeth seldom forȝeteth. If I were curteise, as wel as he sesseth not to kepe me and to thynke on me, on the same wise sholde I never sesse to prayse hym atte al tymes. Oo God, howe shal I doo at the grete daye of dome? Howe shal I compte to the verraye iuge and to the veray kynge of iustice? I made ii vowez in baptem, or my godfaderes for me. Theye be ful short, and also theye be ful hevy. Whan the preste askyd me: Wilt þou be a cristyned man? I answered: *Volo*. That is to seye, I wille. After that he askyd me: *Credis in Deum patrem omnipotentem?* I answered: *Credo*. That is, I beleve liche as ȝe haue seide to me. That is to seye, I vowe and promise here to God that I shalle kepe his feithe and his lawe and aboue al thynge I shal doo my deuoire to louff hym and to serve hym. This is the trouthe, and it saueth man. After that he asketh me: *Abrenuncias Sathane?* I answerid: *Abrenuncio.* That is to seye, I renoie and forswere the feende and al his werkys and al his techyngys and al his dedly synnes. Oo good lorde God, who is he that hatthe wel kepte ȝoure feith and ȝoure lawe? Ther is noon, for the worlde is so corrumped that vnnethe he ne shee, fader ne moder, godfadir ne godmodir that maketh son ne godson to vnderstande the feithe and the lawe that theye sholde beleve. But the firste thynge that moderis lerne their childe is to synge and to karol, as in dispyt of bapteme, and ȝeifeth this holy vessellis so miche drynke of foly and of vanite that vnethe shal euer entre there the lawe of God or of trouthe. This synne is liche as whosoo wolde put in the blessed chalis [f. 22] lekys or pese for despit. Oo good God, what ther be so many gret pepil in the worlde and berded carles that knoweth not ȝit their pater noster ne their crede ne what is dedly synne ne the x comandementis ne the xii articlis of the feithe. And hereof cometh al evillis, for because that thowe exhersisist not to God in thy childehoode as thowe promissed to God in thi bapteme ne to the goode techyng the whiche thy herte sholde haue whan thowe art fastyng, but thowe hauntist the foly of the worlde and the vanite of the worlde. And therfore it is thus myshapped to the for the othir iii goodes that God had ȝovyn to the, that is to seye, the bodye and the soule and the tyme of the worlde the whiche thowe hast employed in vanite and folie. And that is the folye of small pepil and the woodenes of grete pepil. Folie begunne is folie, and whan it is mayntenyd it is woodenes.

Of Vntrouthe, IXe

The secounde vntrouthe is woodenes. Be not theye veraye woode whiche knoweth wel that it is tyme to doo wel and to gedir in the goodes of hervest wherwith men shalle life in the tothir worlde and purveieth theym not therfore, liche the pismere whiche purveith hym in somer for the wynter? And also be þey not right woode that the goodes whiche be not theyris but theire lordis of the whiche theye moste ȝif acompte, that is to seye, of the precious tyme and of the temporel goodes that theye haue in kepyng, the vertues of the body and the thoughtys of the soule, theye waste theyme folilye in the sight of their lorde and purveieth nothynge for their compte? Also is not that grete folye that þou doest? If thowe sholdest goo for to dwelle ii ȝere beȝonde the see, thowe woldest purveye the to bere with the of thi goodes al that thowe myghtest. And thowe wotest wel and sothe it is that thowe goest to a longe viage wense noon retourneth, and thowe myghtest bere with the inoghe if thowe woldest, and thowe rekyst not ne thyn[f. 22[v]]kest not theron. Of these folies, al the worlde is fulle. If thowe haddest into this daye employed wel al thy goodes that God hatthe lente the and wysely dispent theyme, what thowe were nowe large and fre, and what thow sholdest abide the deethe gladly, and thowe sholdest bere with the ryche tresorres. Thowe myght surely compte to God and ȝelde to God goode reson of thy bataille, and þou sholdest abide grete wagys, where thowe abidest gret dampnacion, if thowe repente the and amende the not soone. Nowe haste thowe mused and thy tyme vsed, thye goodes hired, and al thy tyme wasted, and thowe hast noght conquerid. Therfore I counseile and praye the that thowe thynke to amende the and to compte to God be verray confession.

[Of Renoyng, the Whiche Is the Thirde], X[e]

The thirde vntrouthe the whiche that baily didde of whom I haue spokyn was whan he ȝalde to anothir lorde the lande that he hadde in his bailishipp and putte it vnder anothir lorde. This is the synne of reneying. As Seint Poule seithe, he that synneth dedly worshippeth the feende, and he cometh his seruaunt. And ȝit he seithe that he is a Cristen man. He reneyeth it be his werke and sheweth that he is noon. But specially he is called a man reneyed in iii maneres. He is called a man reneyed and a fals Cristen man because he belevith not that he sholde beleve, as lollerris doo, or because he trespasseth aȝeyns the feithe that he sholde beleve, as doo vntrwe forswererris and fals lierris, or because that theye beleve more than theye sholde, as doo sorsers, wicches, enchantures, and siche othir. Alle these be owte of the veraye feithe of Criste Iesus. The grettest pride that is it is lollerie. Is not that a grete pride as whan a veleine or an olde wicche, the whiche knoweth not aright the pater noster, wenyth to knowe more devynite than al the clerkys of Cambriche and wenyth to be better than al the monkes of the Chartirhous and wil not beleve that God maye doo nothynge in erthe but that theye maye vndirstande and see, as that an hole man maye be in siche an oblie as that the preest holdeth at the auter, for the whiche he maye [f. 23] not beleve that it is verraye Goddys bodye? Therfor [l]iche as it is right that he haue iugement as his maister Lucifer hadde, whiche prided hym anoon aȝeyns God and become a feende and felle into helle, on the same wyse it is right that he be set there anoon. The tothir maner of renoyinge is fals witnes and a feithe lied. A man that lyeth his feithe and forswerith hym wityngly he is no right Cristen man but as a fals peny amonge othir pens. Evyn as myche it availeth whan men seye: I promyse ȝowe opon my feithe, that is to seye, opon al that I holde of God. For whoso hatthe lied his feithe he hatthe it not, and whoso hatthe it not he is no Cristen man but a fals man; therfore his othe standeth to noon availe. The thirde maner is as whan men belevith othir weyes than the feithe techeth, as sorciers doo and tho that bel[e]ve theym, and beleveth in charmys and contrevith thyngis that wicches seithe. The feende peyneth hym alweye to corrumpe the verraye feithe and to make man beleve to litill, as lollerris doo, or to myche, as sorceris doo, to whom the feende techeth so many heresies sometyme gretter and more horrible than that is the whiche lollerris belevith. Of this renoynge al men and women be copable that doeth and beleveth that the whiche the feende techith that hatthe reneyed the Cristen feithe, and ȝit it falleth often liche as theye seye. But to this answerith Seynt Austyn and seithe that God suffreth it for ii causes: On is to prove the feithe of goode pepil, because it is veray meede to tho that beleve not in siche illusions. The tothir is because it is right iugement that the feende haue pouer to deseyve and to put in mysbelyve tho that levith the veraye feithe and betakith theym to hym and to his werkys. I haue nowe shewed the the maner of vntrouthe. Nowe loke and take heede that noon of these spottys be in the and peyne the to kepe trouthe aȝeynst thi lorde Criste Iesus that so miche goodnesse hatthe doon to the.

Of [Despite], XIe, the Whiche Is the IIe Branche of Pride

The secounde branche it is whan men liste not to doo worshipp when that men sholde doo it. Thowe shalte þan knowe that firste thowe sholdest doo [f. 23^{v}] worshipp to God and to his swete modir and after that to holy angellis and to seyntis; to God as to thy creature. And thow sholdest thynke that thowe art a pore page the whiche the kynge calleth to his service, and ȝit he wil that thowe be alweye tofore hym. Thowe moste thynke, if thowe be wise, to be liche a goode seruaunt that servith before the kynge at his boorde, the whiche alleweye hatthe the yee to his lorde, as Kynge Dauid didde that seyde: I haue alweye myn yen to the as a goode seruaunt to his lorde or a chamberier to the handis of hir ladye. And that is on of the grettest wites that is and that mooste withdraweth man fro synne, as whan a man thynketh that he is tofore the yen of oure lorde, the whiche seeth al and putteth al in writyng more deligently than any ialous man doothe of his wiff or than he thoughtis dothe of thoo that hatthe a clene herte. For theye be as shamefast if God see in their hertis any veleins thought as thowe woldest be if al the worlde sawe thy veleins membris. Thowe sholdest than kepe the soureinly to doo afore hym that the whiche thowe woldest not doo afore a man and anamly ther where his holy body resteth. And therfore whan thowe entrest into the chirche thowe sholdest thynke that thowe entrest into the kyngys chambir of hevyn tofore the baronage of paradis for to doo thye besynes. And therfore thowe sholdest be there with grete fere and in grete prayerris to avaunce with thyn owne cause and for to speke to the kynge and to the queen of paradis, for at a kyngys courte euery man is for hymselfe. And therfore euery creature maye knowe howe theye be foollis and synneth sore and grevously that lagȝheth and trifelith tofore þe body of Criste Iesus and tofore his swete modir and al the baronage of the grete courte of hevyn, ther where they sholde crye God mercy and shewe their besynes to his modir, tho that fonde nevir short messe ne longe fable, whiche gladlyer wil hire speke of Parceval or of Roulond or Olyver or pleye at tablis or at the dis or they goo to see a sot or an ape or a childe that maketh lesyngys or to disportys wherein lieth gret synne. For these pepil be in grete perille. Thynke nowe, for Goddis sake, is not this gret dispite to God whan thow wilte [f. 24] not goo to the chirche for to see hym that euery daye commeth from hevyn for to see the, ne thowe wilt not seye on oryson to hym? And ȝif thowe seye ought whan þou seyst thy pater noster, thow sellist hym the asse whan thowe seiest it, for in the seying thowe tornest hym thy backe, that is to seye, thy thought. Alas, swete Criste Iesus, in siche dispit art thowe this daye be thye suffrance and thy deboneirte that it plesith more to hire the feendis seruice in a karol fro myddaye to mydnyght than a messe or a sermon whiche lasteth but a while. Wel is fulfilled the worde of the prophete Ysaie, whiche seithe thus: My childir that I haue enhansed and norisshed ful softe haue me in dispite. Godde hateth gretely the man the whiche wil not hire speke hym of in goodnes, and theye recke litil though men seye shame befor hym. Thus is it of theym that maye not hire a sermon. If men swere velensly be God, they recke not. In this thowe sholdest worshippe Godde and shewe that thowe loufest hym in hyryng gladly to speke of hym and in hirynge his service. And if thowe maye whan thowe herist the messe, lete hym haue a present of the, an offrynge thowe it be litil and ȝit it profiteth more than thowe wenyst. And also God commandeth the in tholde lawe: Beware, seith he, that thow come not before me with voide handys. Also come not before hym in clothys that displesith hym with the whiche thowe doest hym shame as these ladyes dothe whiche araieth theyme as theye were to selle. For whan theye sholde speke with the kynge theye be cladde with the armes of his enemy. And that is o cause why no feste is aright kepte, for the hyer a feste is the more peyneth men to araye theym not only in the gyse the whiche sholde moste plese God but in maner that moste sholde please his enemy, that is to seye, to the worlde the whiche werreyeth hym ever.

Howe Men Sholde Kepe the Halidayes, XIIe

Thowe shalt knowe that on festful daies thowe sholdest doo iiii thyngys: Here Gods wourd and the sermon if men maye, visite the seeke, do almesse the more [f. 24^{v}] largely, and the lenger to be in prayeris. Also thowe sholdest worship God and prais hym and not make ioye and revel ne howte ne karol as Zarasinis doo afore ydoles. But tho be the dayes of alle the wooke whereopon men doo moste shame to God. Also thowe sholdest on the Sondaye hire the commandementis and the lawe pronunsed and hire the sermons preched because thowe maiste eschewe evill. And this is a grete dispite to God that for the defence of his seruauntis men list not eschewe a man to whom men sholde not speke o daye for a boffet if a man hadde ȝovyn it hym. This is a gret dispite whan he that is cursid be it right or wronge liste not to kepe hym fro comyng to the chirche afore God and the pepil but come as for to make the pepill acursed. He farith as he that were banysshed owte of Yngelond and wolde pleye hym in the halle at London afore the kynge, as who seye: Thus wil I doo in spite of the. Also thowe sholdest worship God for the goodes that he hatthe ȝovyn the ȝerely, of the whiche he hatth ȝovyn the ix partis, and the x he kepith to his vse. Alsoo, next God, thowe sholdest worshipp his blessed modir and seye hirre matines if thowe can theym and hire seruice, anamly on the Satirday, for that daye in especial is hirres. Also thowe sholdest worshipp angellis, anamly hym that kepeth the fro the enemy. Therfore Seynt Bernard seithe: In what place that thowe be, take heede that thowe doo worshipp to thyn angell and doo nothynge tofore hym whiche thowe woldest not doo tofore me. This is a thynge that gretely sholde drawe the fro synne, whan thowe haste so grete dignite as that God sendeth the his angellis for to serve the. Also Seynt Iame seythe: Thowe sholdest doo worshippe to alle men and despice noon, not a Sarazine, but thowe sholdest doo hym worship for the loufe of God to whos ymage he is made. A grete lorde sholde not dispice his page, for siche myght kepe his horse that o right sholde be more praysed than he. Though thowe be a knyght, thowe sholdest not dispice hym that geteth his bred with his hotte or with his barowe, but thowe sholdest thynke that he hatthe the beste parte of the game, for he moste labour with men in this worlde or with feendes in the tothir worlde. He wynneth alweye, and thowe lesest; he gederith togedir, and thowe dispendest; he purveieth hym, and thowe doest not. If thowe be a grete ladye clad in sylke or in othir riche clothis, thowe [f. 25] sholdest not dispice thy pore neghbourghe, for whan we shal al come to the grete feste whidirward we goo faster than a trot, men shalle not make ioye of the sarplere but of that the whiche is withinne it. Therfore I sholde dispice noon, for euery persone is my brothir germayne, not oonly of Adam and Eve, but he is the sone of God my fadir and seithe his pater noster as wele as I, and as wele he is the sone of holy chirche my moder as I am, and we abide al on heritage. Therfore I sholde dispice noon but louf hym and worship hym as he were my brothir germain twyse and beleve that euery persone is better than I.

Off Overhoope, XIIIe

The thirde principal branche of pride is arrogance, whiche we calle overhoopeyng, as whan a man wenyth more of hymselfe than he sholde. And this maye be in iii maneres: on, whan he wenyth to be better than he is; anothir, to kunne more than he can; the thirde, to maye more than he maye or ellis in othir wise, as whan he wenyth to be better, konnynger, myghtier than any othir. This synne is verily the [toure] of the feende wherwith he defendeth hym, soo that he rekkyth of no persone. And in this toure ho kepeth the tresor of al othir vicis, the whiche he hatthe conquerid of the soule. This is that þe whiche God seithe in the gospell: Whan the stronge soule kepeth his castell, he kepeth and holdeth in pees al that he hatthe within it. For the feende taketh aweye the mende from the proude ouerwenyng man, as whan þat he hatthe made hym thynke so myche in vertuz that he wenyth to haue more than he maye vniþe thynke hym of, but he thynketh not of hymselfe ne what he is ne whereto he shal becomme. Wherfore a man myght as wel speke to an asse as to hym or to consell siche a man. Therfore it is of harde if any siche confesse theyme aright.

Off Arrogans, XIIII

Off this branche isseth a plant of foly behaveyng, that is to seye, whan a man liste not to sitte on the rowe with othir [f. 25v] and often maketh somme disgesy thyng wereof menne spekyth.

Off Vauntyng, XV

After that cometh avauntyng, whiche is a foule synne bothe to God and to the worlde. The vauntour is he that can not synge but of hymselfe. He shewith al that he dothe as an henne that discrieth hirre egge be hirre kaklyng whan she hatthe leide it. This is a foule synne to hym that vanteth hym with his owne mouthe, but he doubleth it whan he prayseth losengeris. And some make their advocattes for to crye it, whiche lieth for theyme and also leseth theyre soules.

Off Derision, XVI

The thirde plante is derision, whiche hatthe skorne of othir of siche as fleeth synne for the louf of God. These be homly with the feende, the whiche kepeth hym his presoneris, and whan on ascapeth theye rynne after with grete crye and bryngeth theym aȝeyn into the prison of synne. These be felawes to Herode, the whiche for the hatered of God kylled innocentis, for theye sloughe soules that began to doo wel. These be wers to God than tho that put hym to the dethe opon the crosse whan theye take froo hym the soules that he wanne by his dethe, liche as he that wolde take aweye from a pore man of his wagis the whiche he hadde wonne with his labour in the felde. Truly, that sholde be wers to hym than al the labour that he hadde don al the daye. And shortly theye hate so God and louf the feende that theye maye not suffre God to wyn ne the feende to lese. These werreye the Holy Gooste and wolde steyne the grace of God. And God seithe that this synne shalle not be pardoned in this worlde ne in the tothir, but theye shalle answ[e]re for al the soules that theye haue leted from weledede.

Off Rebellion, XVII

[f. 26] The iiii plant is rebellion, that is whan a man is rebelle to thoo that wolde hym wele. If men repreve hym, he defendeth hym; if men chastie hym, he is wrothe; if men confesse hym, he levith no wit but his owne. Good God, what he hatthe a perlious sekenes that maye suffre noon to touche hym to whom medicinis tornyth to venym, for that whiche men seithe to hym for his availe he tornyth it to his harme. This synne doubleth othir and maketh it worthe ii; whan he ascuseth hym of his synne and defendeth hym, þe synne is nowe double confermyd. And therfor seye I þat this synne is the toure of the feende and the keper of his tresor and maketh it to be hidde in the herte. Oo God, seith Seynt Bernard, whan shalle he telle the synnes of his herte, the whiche men seeth not, whan he wil not knowleche thoo that he hatthe doon opynly but rather defendeth hym with his beeque and with his cleys?

Off Ambicion, XVIII

The iiii principal branche of pride is a foly desire, that is an evil desire to clyme hye, the whiche we calle ambicion. This vice is the feendis panne wherein he makyth his fritures and his delicious metes. For as God ioieth and deliteth in marteris the whiche su[f]frith martirdome for hym soo the feende is glad of tho that he maye torment. Oo goode God, what ther be many of tho in the worlde that the feende tormentith and fryeth as grees in a panne of iryn be ambicion, the whiche tormentith his scoleris that I see them geder togedir be grete rowtes, ambicion the whiche maketh theyme to wake so myche be the cresset that they be dryer than friture in the panne. Soo he tormentith his ypocrites and his knyghtis, the whiche hatthe so myche torment that theye seye: If we suffred as myche for God, we sholde be gretter martiris than Seynt Andrewe or Seynt Lauerens. Ambicion is the ouerthrowe of the feende, wherwith he ouerthroweth citeis, abbeis, bishopriches, anamly the toure of Seynt Petir of

Roome. Ambicion is the firste lesson that the feende lerneth his scoleris. At the begynnyng, he putteth owte their right yee, the whiche is their right entent, [f. 26v] and levith theyme the le[f]te, the whiche is covetice and ambicion. Man was made for to be in Goddes feleshipp. That is the hyest astate that a man maye coveite. To this hynesse sholde he drawe and tente be nature. And soo dothe he whan he hatth the right ye, the whiche is the right entent to come to perfeccion. But the feende putteth owte this yee, so that he may not looke so hye, and therfore he maketh hym coveite litil thyngys that he seeth with his lefte yee the [whiche] be worldly worshippis. For he putteth before hym the whele of fortune and shewith hym withowte more that side where he seeth tho that gothe vpward and tho that be above. And the tothir part of the whele he hideth soo that he seeth not thoo þat overthroweth and that be overthrowen. And therfore maketh he hym so myche to desire to goo vpward that to the comyng downe he maye not coveite ne thynke. Oo howe he deseyvith nowe and blyndith hym that neythir thynketh ne vnderstandeth howe slowely he shalle goo vp ne howe sodenly he shalle falle. A tree is in waxyng c wyntir, and in one houre it fallith or it is hewyn downe. Thus it fareth be the riches of this worlde; outhir it heyueth be grete leyser or it is in grete fere or it descendeth with grete sorwe. And this is doon in a litil houre of the daye. Oo goode God, howe ma[n]ye prikyng thornes be in this branche. What ther be many grete perilles and synnes or that a man be comyn vp. If we beholde these citees, these toures, cathedral chirches, stately abbeyes whe[r] Dame Fortune is, the whiche turneth faster than a mylle that the whiche was above vndir, what we sholde see stronge prikkyng thornes the [whiche] prikketh the pepil. Of this cometh losengery and lying, as thoo dothe whiche wolde please; than cometh detraccion to reyse blame of hym that men wille drawe abakke, because that it may noye hym; and after that envie and desyryng the dethe of othir that hatthe that the whiche he coveitethe.

Off Vainglorie, XIXe

The v branche of pride is vainglorie, that is a plesance in veine praysyng of any grace that he wenyth to haue in hymselfe. And whan a man wil be praysed of that for the whiche a man sholde prayse God, therin he shewith vainglorie, thefte, and vntrowthe, for it taketh from God that the whiche is his and that the whiche he wolde [f. 27] we sholde ȝelde to hym for al his goodnes, that is to seye, ioye and praysyng. Thus is the game depar[t]et that what that euer we seye or doo lete God haue his part that he maye haue the worship and we the availe and that he maye haue the preise and we the wages. And if we take from hym his parte anone we shalle lese oures. Othir vices causeth evilles to be doon, but this corrumpeth and distroyeth al goodenes. Vainglorie is a wynde that dothe grete merveilles, the whiche drowneth grete navies in the see and overthroweth grete toures and steplis and in the see of helle overthroweth tho that wenyth to be as sure as a towre on a roche. Vainglorie is the feendes peny, wherewith he byeth feir thyngys the whiche he fyndeth in the feyre of this worlde, as of these knyghtis that thynke of nothynge but to gete the praise and the vainglorie of this worlde. And lete noon dowte but that theye lese therfore the verray ioye that theye sholde haue. Neverthelesse theye seye that the ton ioye takyth not aweye the tothir. And forsothe in o maner they seythe sothe, for he were a grete fole and a nyce that wolde seye that alle knyghtes were dampned and loste the whiche in the worlde be soo gretly praysed, for that were grete pite.

Off Knyghthoode, XXe

Knyghthoode is a ful faire ordre and an hye in holy chirche, for he oweth his feithe to God and to kepe holy chirche, be the whiche pees is kept and iustice holden, werbye the pepil liffeth in pees, and clergie and religiouses to serve and worshippe God, and whoso hatthe verely his entent to this and dresseth hereto his peyne and his worthines he kepeth rightly his ordre and his religion. He his knyght and soudoier to God, as Seynt Iohn Baptest seithe, and his londes and his rentes be but his sowdes and his wagis that God ȝefeth hym to lif with as longe as he is in the oste of this worlde. After that he shalle ȝif hym his gret wagys, and he shal ȝeif hym his peny, that is to seye, the verray blisse of hevyn whan he shal come into his contre. And ȝit therfore it shal not leve but that he shal haue the prayse and the ioye of this worlde whan men noyseth hym [f. 27v] a goode knyght and a worthy man to God. Goode God, what this is a goode prayse whan men seye: See, there is a goode knyght, and anothir seithe: See, ther is a goode man to Godde. But tho doo shame to God and to al goode men and dampneth cheualry the whiche dothe outragiousnes and velanies and setteth al vpon their knyghthoode, the whiche despendeth mo than their knyghthoode and their londes is worthe. Also theye taxe and robbe the pore pepil and setteth theym to plegge and maketh theym to falle into vserers handes and putteth theyme to be cursed and causeth theym to lye and to be forsworne, as theye be theymselfe, the whiche doo but lye and holdeth no trowthe no lenger than theye maye fynde whereof to make their cheuysshans for to kepe and holde withal their outrages, their revellis, and theire feire housholdes and to feede their faucons and their menistrellis for to disgyse theym oftyner than vii tymes in the ȝere in robes and arayes that theye putte on their bakkes, so that be the commandementis theye set nothynge. Theye hire not matins thrise in the ȝere. And whan theye goo to here messe theye doo theire harme more than theire availe. Theye can not be stylle no more than an ape. Theye laugȝhe, iape, put, and drawe iche othir. Theye halsse ȝonge women. And for al that theye thynke the messe to longe. Theye maye not hire Goddes worde. And the hyer the feste is the more theye peyne theyme to greve God and to shewe their hynes and their pride. Also theye ryn xv myle for to see a feeste or games or karolles, but theye rekke not to breeke goode vigiles and ymbir dayes. Theye refreyne al daye the toon for the tothir. Theye ete oftyner than vii tymes o the daye, as ofte as þeye haue liste, as childir or sheepe; theye make god of their b[e]llies. Theye doo none almes, for theye maye not; ne theye seye no prayers, for theye wil not. And whan men blameth theyme of their folie theye ascuse theym be their knyghthoode and seye: Vs moste doo as other doo? Wil ȝe make vs to be cryed apon and to pleye the papelard? Lete al goo with a goode herte. God knoweth ful wel whoo is a goode pilgrime. Oo goode [f. 28] God, to what shame put theye that hye ordre of knyghthoode the whiche wil seye that noon maye be a goode knyght if he shewe owteward that he wil louf and serve God and if he be not a seruant to shrewes in whoos iugement he is holy sette, soo that theye derre neythir seye ne doo but as theye wolde seye, be it wel doon or wel seide, for to doo their pleser. Moreover, if his man myssetoke hym to hym, it were for noght to crye hym mercy, for he sholde neythir fynde in hym pete ne swetnesse no more than a lamme sholde doo in a wolfe. If thowe haue beaute of body, thowe haste grete nede to thonke and to louf God therfore. And specially as ofte as þou seest hym or hirre the whiche hatthe not siche beaute as thowe haste thowe sholdest be the meker and the ferefuler that thowe sholdest not lese the feire ȝifte that God hatthe made and ȝovyn to the. For if thowe make ioye as the pecok dothe of his taile whan he seeth it thowe synnest gretely or causeste othir to synne whan thowe vsest it shrewdely and tornest it to veinglorie and to the prayse of the worlde. Thy beaute is occasion of to myche synne whan thowe werreyeste God of so feire a iuel as he hatthe ȝovyn the. And sometyme thowe haste envie whan thowe art sory that othir passeth the in beaute; than sekyst thowe crafte or wiles wherebye thowe maiste deseyve othir and to make theym to suppose that thow art the feirest of al other. Of this cometh these faire arayes and disgysyngys and di[s]figuryngys in soo many maners that God shalle not knowe theyme at the daye of dome, as he seithe in the gospell: I knowe not what ye be. I made ȝowe not so fetis ne so iolye. And withowten faile these fooles putteth more besines to feede the yen of dotardes than to feede their owne bodyes, and theye doute more that the yen of the pepil sholde be evil served than theye doo of theymselfe that be in grete perille. And to seye shortly, men doo so myche synne for to pleyse the worlde be beaute of bodye and be siche araye owteward that noon maye nombre it, for alweye men contryve newe gyses, and al that is vanitee.

Off the Vanitee of the Tonge, XXI

The ȝifte of a goode tonge and of feire langage is ful presious. For to siche pepil [f. 28v] the feende seithe: Thowe haste spokyn ful wel; noon sholde a seide so as thowe haste seide. Or ellys he maketh it be seide to hym be his disciples that serueth hym of that crafte. Tho be losengeres the whiche be the kyngys bottelleris of helle that bryngeth in clarrie and piement to the kynge of helle, that is to seye, the whiche servith and maketh dronken with praysyngis these proude pepil that theye knowe not whens theye be. And al the goodnes that theye doo and seye theye ȝif it for the fals peny of veinglorie. And therfore the feende disporteth hym with al their spekyngys. O howe he herkenyth gladly and howe he hatthe this peny redy for to paye to the goode aduocat the whiche hatthe the tonge so plate and so flateryng that it is sharper than any sharpe rasour. Howe gladly on the Sonday he disporteth hym vndir lorell trees or amonge his gossepis atte their dorres. In siche places be luffed gretly plesant flatryng tonges for to glade feleshipes, and gret ioye haue tho that beste can serve of bourdes, of lies, and of lewde langage. Lytil thynke theye of that the whiche God seithe that of euery idil worde theye moste ȝif acompt at the daye of dome. God knoweth what theye go gladly to assemblees and festes and to these courtis that men kepe for too haue a prayse and a lose of the world. Alas theye take no heede of hym that is kynge and lorde as he that knoweth alle the assembleȝ. For ther euery persone peynyth theym but to obey to hym in siche wise as theye suppose beste to shewe vanite and to gete veinglorie, soo that atte the messe the whiche is but short God sometyme is more werreyed than worshiped, for ther be so many shewyngys of curtesies and halsyngis that noon maye thynke on their syn ne praye to God. Ther haue theye their ioye thoo that can helpe wele to flatre with the flaile of the tonge for to make othir laughe and playe. Theye wil not alonly speke there idil wordes but theye be moste shewed and praysed that iapyngly can beste lie and mysseye and scorne theyme that servith [f. 29] God and fleith siche iapes and vanitees. There these ministerell haue theire ioye, the whiche sessith not to werry God with the grace of feire speche the whiche he hatth ȝovyn theym. Theye be proprely the disciples of the sperit of vainglorie, in whos scole theye haue ben norisshed, that techith theym to seye these feire wordis and feire songes, the whiche theye haue so redily in their mouthes that liche as the Holy Gooste techith precheours and makith theyme for to speke, so the feende techith theym these iapes. And whan the feende hatthe alweye ben lord and maister of that tonge [...] that theye haue ȝovyn longe agon to the feende, the whiche he maketh his hors and it sholde be the nyȝghtyngale of the Holy Goost. Therfore I seye it is gret merveile that siche pepil lif to a goode ende. For to preyse in syngyng and in spekyng God hatth sette in the mouthe ii graces, to synge and to speke. As Seynt Bernard seith: Nothyng representeth so wel the state of the tothir worlde ne the office of angellis in erthe as tho doo that gladly and with goode herte syngeth and prayseth God. But vainglorie wolde haue al the feire songes. The ton of these be for to prayse God and his seyntis. The tothir be for to solace hymselfe with feire honeste wordis. Othir ther be that be of iolynes and of folie, the whiche be the herdis to kyndil with the fire of lecherie in the hertis of pepil. This veinglorie spredith ferre, for it is the wynde that bloweth overalle. Vnethe syngeth a man any tyme but that the feende ȝefeth hym of his sugre roset, the whiche is ful swete and sauory, and setteth al his labour and his entent to doo so myche at the begynnyng or in the middes or at the ende that the seruice of God becometh the seruice of the feende. Songes of holy chirche plese not God for the grete noyse that clerkys make ne for the wordys that be there but for the deuocion that the clerkys and othir haue therein. Wherfore Seynt Austyn seithe: As ofte, seithe he, as I delite me more in the swetnesse of the songe that I here than in the sentence of the wordes that men seye, I synne grevously. But in these songes the whiche be of foly louf that men synge in karolles men synne not only withoute more in veinglorie. But it is proprely the service of the chanones of helle, and tho that hireth theym [and] in siche songes and in siche karolles putteth theym theye doo proprely [f. 29v] the feendes seruice. And theye haue grete veinglorie that can beste serve in trifflis and in songes. Alas it is gret sorwe whan men doo the feendes seruice overalle so gladly and with so gret coste and with so gret distruccion of body and of soule, and ȝit it semith theym that it costeth noght. And men doo Goddis seruice so slowly and so lachely. Yit notwithstandyng theye wold be wel praysed, as it shewith in grete chirches. For vnethe ther is any that gothe thedir alonly for to seruice God, but whan that theye hoope to wynne moste than hastely and gladly theye ryn thedir or whan theye suppoce to be praysed for their beste singyng. Thus veinglorie ledith siche pepil the whiche hatthe reseyvid these feyre ȝiftis of God for to serve hym therwith and for to gete the grete coro[une] in hevyn, and yit theye vse it shrewdely and wolde haue the prayse of the worlde and bie veinglorie, wherwith theye myght have the veray blisse myche lightlyere and with lesse peyne.

Off Fortune, XXIIe

Whan the Lady Fortune hatthe reysed a man hye and torned here whele so þat he is commyn to worship and richesse, than is he hie sette as a wyndemylle is opon an hye hylle, whereas bloweth al the xii wyndes of vainglorie, the whiche assaileth the caytif and maketh hym to peyne hym to gete ioye and worship. Nowe theye make theyme feerse; nowe dispiseth he his neghborgh the which is better than he because he hatth more goode than he;, he peyneth hym nowe to kepe a feire howsholde and to make festes. Soo he ȝifeth his caytivouse hert to the worlde that it grefeth hym xl folde more to ȝif x *d* for God than to dispende dayly x *li* in pride and vainglorie, and he dispendeth more in outrage of mete than he myght dayly sustene with c pore pepill. A goode God, what this is gret peril to the soules of tho that thus ioyeth theyme in siche thyngys, anamly to clerkys that make siche thyngys and siche largesses of that the whiche is not theires. It is rathir of the patrimonie of Crist Iesus. For oure lorde seithe in the gospell: Whan thowe shalt make a feste, calle not therto riche pepil that maye feste the aȝeyn but pore pepil the whiche hatthe not whereof to feste the ne to guerdon [f. 30] the. These other doo al the contrarye, for the richer a man is and hatthe leste nede the gladlier theye feste theyme. Also it sufficeth theym not that men serve theym as a man, but theye moste be worshiped as God. And ther is so manye knellyngis and crompyng that the servauntis moste knelle more than the cloyster monke doothe to

God. A ȝonge ape maketh not so many knackes and mowes and games as moste be doon tofore theym. Also in these feire clothis wherein theye haue right grete ioye. Seynt Gregor seithe that if in precious gownes were no synne the riche man hadde not been blamed in the gospell of that he was clad in porple, the whiche was beried in helle, ne he hadde not praysed Seynt Iohn, the whiche was clad in a slavyne. Theye doo grete besynes to haue a faire sarplere, but of the fardel within theye rekke not, that is to seye, of the soule the whiche is within the bodye. Also theye haue soo many idil govnes the whiche dothe nothynge but hilleth perchis and felleth cofferis, and soo longe theye kepe theym that wormys eteth theym. Or theye kepe theyme for covetice or for pride or to be cladde in dyuerse gownes. And ȝit theye see the pore pepil tremble for colde, the whiche sholde haue th[e] relief of their gownes as wel as of their bordes, but theye haue neyther part ne lot, for pride bieth theyme and ȝifeth theym to mynystrelles for to gete with prayse and vaineglorie. Alas charitee wolde emploie it myche better, the whiche wolde by withalle hevyn and verray ioye. Also sommetyme theye make fyne marchandis, for theye ȝif theyme to their seruauntis and to their werkemen. But theye selle it theym derrer than theye sholde doo at market, for there where the werkeman sholde a getyn xx *s* he is ful glad whan he maye haue a garment of xv *s*. Also theye make so myche coriouste and disguysynges that it is merveile: gilt botonettis, redelid cootes, streit slevys with to wide mouthes, hosyn and shoone fetisly shapyn [and] sperid [with] boclis of sylfer. If ther were no grete syn in siche thyngys, wenyst thowe that God wolde take soo goode heede therto the whiche settith al in his scripture and noteth al that we doo and thynke c folde more than any ielous man dothe of his wyff? Wherefore he seithe be his prophete Ysaie, ther where he reprovith ladies and ientilwomen of their grete araie, he seithe: Ther shal come a daye that God shalle take fro theym their coiffes, their wymplis, their kevirchefes, their nouches, their chapelettis, and their ryngys, also the araye of their armes, handes, and feete, and of their shirtis [f. 30v] that be so fyne and thyne that men maye see their armes and the flesshe thorw it. If ther were no synne in these thyngis, why sholde God reherse theyme thus besily in his booke? But because that he spekyth in anothir place, where he spekyth of siche a soule the whiche had vsed his lif in siche dedis, as myche, seithe he, as she had ioye in hert and gladnes of bodye, ʒif hir the more sorwe to the body and to the soule the crueller and the horribler torment.

Off Losengeris, XXIII

After this cometh the prayse and the crye of foly tonges, the whiche syngeth al that these caitif hertis sekyth and desireth to hire and chaufeth theyme in the louf of the worlde and enchanteth theyme and blyndeth theyme, as the enchantour dothe the whiche maketh to be supposed of an eddir that it were a doufe. For theye make to be vnderstanden of hymselfe that it is not he, and he troweth theyme myche better than hymselfe and belevith that the swan is blacke and the ravyn white and that he is worthy and hardy, where he is as grete a coward as an hare. Whan he is a fleer of the pepill, than is he a goode iusticer; ʒif he be softe and negligent, than is he more deboneir than wyne. Theye make of evil wel and of synne almesse; al dremes torneth theym to goode; al is wel doon and seide, what that euer the sotted foole dothe or seithe. Thus þeye blynde theyme and robbe theyme of al goodes temporel and goostely, as the softe wynde the whiche robbed the pilgrym and tooke froo hym his mantel, of the whiche men telle an example. It befelle tha bise, *id est*, a storme, and a softe wynde made a waiour to take from a pilgryme his mantel. Bise began to blowe and he to tremble, and þe more he blewe the faster and the more he streynyd his mantel abowte hym. After that blewe the softe wynde, and he wexe warme and dispoiled hym and keste his mantel in his necke. And a stormy wynde rose and bare aweye his mantel. Bise, the whiche is a wynde [...] harre, sharpe, and harde, anamly in these grete courtes whan it bloweth. That is to seye, whan men seye trouthe, euery person restreynyth theym and trembleth and hideth their goodenes and is aferde and kepeth theyme in mekenes. But praysyng the whiche is the hye wynde of noone that [f. 31] gladeth and warmeth the herte and maketh it to desire and to shewe alle his goodes and rekkyth not to lese al his goodes, as Eȝechias didde the kynge of Ierusalem, not only he withoute moo but his heires and al his tresores that he hadde. For because that he shewid theym to losengeris the whiche come to hym fro the kynge of Babeloine hym moste nedes flee and was takyn and al his pepil and Ierusalem distroyed, liche as it is contenyd in the Lamentacion of Ieremie the prophete.

Howe Vainglorie Assaileth Vertues, XXIIII

It is goode to eschewe vainglorie, the whiche maketh hilles to qwake and overthroweth trees and toures, liche as we haue seide, for it temptith rightwis men and maketh [be] veniel syn to qwake or maketh theym overthrowe be dedly syn. The moo goode vertues that a man hatth the more the feende dieth be envie and the more assaileth hym be veinglorie. For the richer and the preciouser a tresor is the gladlier a goode marchant wil bye it and a theef the more desirously stele it. This maiste thowe see in al principal vertues and in the werkys that cometh of theym. Sobirnes is the firste. For whan a man is sobre and abstinent, if he faste or if he abstene hym fro flesshe or fro wyn, as ofte assauteth hym veinglorie because he doothe that the whiche othir dothe not. Chastite is the seconde. Whan a man is chaste, the clenner he kepith hym the ferventlier veinglorie assaileth hym. Largesse is the thirde, to strecche his hande to pore pepil or elles where that nede is. Thiiii is worthines to doo penaunce. The v is debonairenes lightly to forȝif. The vi is charite to louf his neghborgh. The vii is mekenes, that is to be softe and meke aȝens al thynge that maye come, anamly aȝens veinglorie. In al maneres that men wolde beste kepe theyme in these vii vertues veinglorie assaileth theym with pride. And the more men dothe to hate it the more it folwith and chaseth, liche as the shadewe dothe a man.

The Batail of Mekenes and of Veinglorie, XXV

[f. 31v] The ferst and the moste [noble] bataile that maye be is betwene mekenes and veinglorie. Mekenes seithe: Hide thi goode dedis that men see theym not that thowe lese theyme not be veinglorie. And veinglorie seithe aȝen to hym: Thowe art the mekest that is. Mekenes perseyvith that and seithe: Nowe haste thowe synned in veinglorie; goo nowe, goo and confesse the. Veinglorie assayleth hym aȝen and seithe: Nowe art thowe wel confessid; ther is fewe pepil the whiche dothe this synne that confessith theym. Than mekenes braieth and crieth and is wrothe. After that veinglorie commeth and seithe: Thow haste wele wept; nowe art thowe wele with Godde the whiche hatth ȝovyn the deuocion to wepe so grete plente of teres and to haue siche deuocion. Mekenes seeith this thought and is ful hevy. And in that same hevynes veinglorie assailleth hym ageyn. This is þe werre of Laurens Garin the whiche wil never haue ende.

An Noteable Example, XXVI

I wil telle the an example because I wil that thowe shalt knowe howe ofte that thowe synnest in veinglorie and whan it is dedly synne and whan is venial. A mayden entrid into a forest and felle into the handes of robboures, the whiche shent hirre and robbed hirre and drowe hirre to put hirre to the deethe. The kyngys son passed forthby and hadde pite, for the whiche he faught with thoo theefes, but ȝit he was gretely wounded. Neverthelesse he began to louf that ientilwoman soo that he bathed hirre, clothid hirre, and made hirre hoole and wedded hir and made hir quene. And he was as ielous of hirre as any man myght be of his wiff and made hirre to be kepte besily and tentifly with the grettest lordes that he hadde. And what that ever she didde or seide he noted it evyn as ielous men doo. It fortuned that ther was a fals and a malicious bacheler [f. 32] in the contre the whiche hated, werried, and grevid that princes son in al that he myght. The whiche bacheler whan he perceivid the grete louf that the kynge hadde to that lady and the worshipp that he didde to hirre he thought to aqueynte hym with the quene the more to greve the kynge withalle and shewid hirre contenance of louf. But at þe first it vailed hym not, for as a goode woman she torned the body from hym. And therin she didde as a goode woman. After that it felle that litil and litil she herkenyd to his feire wordys, but ʒit hirre herte was not there. And that was wel doon. Notwithstandyng, she was not alonly withowte default in as myche as shee toke hiede to the wordys of hym that hated hirre lorde. Ʒit after this that lady didde wers, for shee began to make grete ioie and to reseyve the seruauntes and the messangeris of this bacheler and araied hirre fresshely aʒeyns their comynge and shewid theym contenaunce of louf. Ʒit hirre herte was not there, for shee thought to kepe hirre and hirre feithe to hirre husbonde. Moreouer, it felle that tho seruauntis and messangeris went so ofte aboute that lady that shee sette hirre herte on theym and in their wordis and herde theyme gladly and ʒaf theym of hirre iuellis and didde grete coste to theym. Ʒitte shee loufed hirre lorde but not so truly as shee sholde a doon. Than after that it felle that shee loufed hym soo hertely that shee wexe wery of the feleship of hirre husbonde, bothe of hym and of hisse, soo that it grevid hirre sore whan shee was with hym. And the richesse of the whiche shee was lady shee dispent hit and sette it on the tothir and so ofte torned hirre backe to hirre lorde that it noyed hirre gretely whan she sholde atende to hym or to his seruice. And glad and besy was shee whan shee was with the bacheler or with thoo that come fro hym, soo that al hirre desirez was to be plesant to theyme. Nowe for my louf telle me: Didde shee not as an evil and an vntrewe woman? For Goddis sake, nowe beware that thy sowle be not this quene, the whiche loufeth so myche the ioye of this worlde. Thowe wotest wel that whan thow entredest into the forest of this worlde thowe were pore, foule, and hidouse and dispitful. And thowe felle into the feendes handes of helle, the whiche wolde a drawen the to the dethe of helle, but the kyngys son [f. 32v] of hevyn had pite therof and had lever die than lese the. He faught for the with thoo theefes to that he was wonded to the dethe. He rescewed the and wasshed the with his blode in bapteme and helyd the with the oynement of the Holy Goste and clothid the with the robe of innocens and made the lady and quene of hevyn and of erthe and ʒaf the of his iewellys in iii maneres, in goodes naturell, temporel, and spirituell, and made the to be servid with his angell and to be norisshed and kept lenger than any ielous man didde ever his wiff. This bacheler that hated so myche thi lorde Criste Iesus, it is the worlde that is so pore proude the whiche God hateth, Salamon seithe. And Seynt Iame seithe: Whoso wil be frende to the worlde he moste be enemy to God. And Seynte Iohn seithe: Whooso loufeth the worlde maye not haue the loufe of God. And God seithe in the gospell: Noon maye serve ii lordes. This hate is soo stedfasted that whan God at the dethe prayed for his apostles and for tho that crucified hym he seide: Feire fadir, I praye to the for theym, but I praye not to the for the worlde. This hate is ful stronge, anamly if men wil not forȝiff at the dethe. þynke nowe in thyn hert howe wel thowe louffest þis ennemy of God and his disportis and to wheder thowe emploiest the moste to plese hym or ellis God. And thus thowe maiest perceyve howe miche thowe synnest in vainglorie. Soo wolde God that it plesed nowe to thy blessed son that alle tho that shalle see this writyng knewe and vnderstoode welle the wordes that thowe seide [be] Ezechie the prophete to a soule that thowe louffed, þe whiche for the louff of the worlde had lefte þy louf, as the example sheweth that we haue set here afore. Howe thowe letest vs witte what thowe shalt doo to siche pepill at the dethe and at the daye of doome. Howe thowe remembrest to hym thye goodnesses and thy courtesies and reprovist hym egrely of his evilles and velenyes and the manasses that thowe makest to hym of the peines and the waies and of the tormentis that he hatthe deservid. Roote of evill nature, seithe oure lorde, engendred of Chaym, that is to seye, vntrewe seruauntis. Vnderstande me nowe, soule [f. 33] owte of the weye. Remembre the whan thow wer borne that thowe was pore, foule, and fyled with the bloode of synne, bothe vile, foule, and an outecaste. I had pite of the, I waysshed the, I helid the and clothed the forsoothe with presciouse clothis of diuerse coloures, and I ȝaf the al that longed to a woman, that is to seye, al the vii ȝiftis of the Holy Gooste, and I norisshed the with hony and with oyle and with brede of whete, and I ȝaf the richesse, worship, and beaute, and I louffed the, and I wedded the and kept the derely and worshipfully and in grete delites. And thowe ȝalde aȝeine to me evill aȝeyns goode. And for the grete beaute that I hadde ȝovyn the thowe didest folye and thowe louffed the childer of Egipte, that is to seye, the childer of the worlde; and as the comvne woman dothe thowe abaundoned the to al tho that come to the; thowe louffed theym and made theym ioye and feste with my goodes and with my richesses that I had ȝovyn the; and thowe ȝaf praysyng to tho that came with the in drawyng aȝeyns the costome of lyght women. O fole proved that dispendest so myche for the worlde, herkyn what the scripture seythe. Thowe were al tymes abaundoned to siche lecheries and in siche avouteries. Vnderstande wel that the louff of the worlde and of veinglorie is called avoutry and lechery, wherfore after he manaceth and seithe: Because that thowe haste doon these vntrowthes, I shalle deme the as men dothe a man that is a mordorere and a woman that is a bordolere, that is to seye, shamefully and cruelly; and I shalle brynge forthe al tho that thowe haste louffed and that thowe haste hated, that is to seye, men and angellis and feendes; and I shalle discouere al thy harlotries afore theyme; and I shalle delyuere the into the handes of þe feende the whiche had shame of thy dedes and of þine vntrouthes. For thowe haste passed the synne of Sodome and Gomorre, the whiche synned aȝeyns flesshely nature. Evyn soo thowe haste doon aȝeyns nature [gostely] whan a man whiche is made of myre synneth in pride and in vainglorie, for [f. 33v] pride is evyn aȝeyns gostely nature. I praye the nowe for Goddes sake to thynke on these wordes that God seiþe, the whiche be ful fereful and hevy. Avise the on myn example. And thowe shalt fynde v astates, of the whiche on was good and the tothir iiii evill, and be that thowe maye see what synnes commeth of vainglorie. And thowe shalt fynde also iiii degrees why that lady hated and fledde that seruaunte and his feleshipp. In this state be thoo that louffeth God truly and fleeth and hateth the bobans of the worlde and the veinglorie therof. Also shee herkenyd to theyme, but the hert was not there. In that state be tho that seketh not the prayse of the worlde whan theye be vnder and defouled but rather holdeth theym mekely and servith God. And whan they be with tho of the worlde, theye conforme theym to theyme and maketh contenaunce that siche liff plesith theyme, although that theye be hevy in herte that þey moste make that contenaunce. And theye synne in ii maneres, in that theye haue litil louff to God and in evill example that theye ȝif to other. For theye see the dede, and theye see not the hert. Also she ȝaf hym of hirre iewellis and reseyvid hym fulle gladly, boþe hym and hisse, though that aparte shee louffed hirre lorde. And in this state be thoo that gladly setteth the goodes and the graces that God hatthe ȝovyn theym to the service of the worlde and of the herte. Notwithstandyng theye serve God aparte, sometyme more for fere than for verry louff. Theye liff in perille. After that she torneth hirre bakke to hirre lorde, for shee was hevy to be with hym and his service grevid hirre myche. And glad and ioyouse she was with the tothir, for nothynge grevid hirre what that euere shee didde for hym. Of siche it is no doulte but that theye be in a sorowful state. Remembre wel nowe this example, and take hiede in whiche of the v statis thowe arte and howe ofte thowe synnest be vaineglorie.

Off Ypocrisie, XXVIIe

The vi^{te} branche of pride is ypocrisie, the whiche is as myche to seye as an [f. 34] gilte ypocrit the whiche is overgilte. Wherfor comunly to speke, euery persone that is feire outeward and foule inward is an ypocrite. And therfore seithe holy scripture that ther is no trowthe in the worlde. And proprely for this cause men calleth the worlde an ypocrite and ouergilte. This is a true thynge liche as it is writyn in the Booke of Iob, for the ypocritis ioye it is of the worlde, the whiche lasteth but a while. That the worlde is an ypocritt an ouergilt it is true, for we see in the worlde, that is to seye, in thoo the whiche louffeth owteward worldly riches and inward pouerte and many siche contirfet thyngis. And therfore holy scripture seithe that in the worlde is no trouthe. But proprely thoo be ypocritis that shewith to be as goode men and be not but enforceth theym more to haue the name of good men than to haue the trouthe of holynes. This ypocrisie is devised in iii branches. The firste be thoo that in secret places doo their arlotries and sheweth owteward as good men. God in the gospell calleth theyme double gilt, the whiche shewith outeward feire and inward theye be ful of harlotrie. And also he seithe: Outeward theye be like a lambe and inward like a wolfe. Vmbethinke the of the condicions of a lambe and of the hert of a wolfe, and thowe shalt lerne to knowe siche pepill. Liche as the wolfe is the strengest enemy that a lambe hathe, so the strengest enemys that holy men hatthe be papilardes and ypocrites, as it shewith wel be the veray lambe Criste Iesus, for þe strengest enemyes, the sotillest spies, the moste cruel accuserris that he hadde were ypocrites. But it longeth wel for the to knowe that al tho that seme ypocrites be noon ypocrites. But thoo that synneth secretly and pleyeth the papelard willyng to be holdyn for good men thoo be ypocrites. But whosoo coueryth and hiedeth hys synne because he wil not corrumpe his neyghbourys be evil example he dothe welle therein. The secounde braunche of ypocrisie is whan a man opynly and not only preuyly dothe goode dedis and gret penaunces [f. 34v] because the worlde sholde see it and for to haue the name of a goode man. Thoo be apys to the feende, the whiche maketh theym to laughe gretely with their iapes. And whan theye contirfete goode men theye make theyme proprely the feendes martires, the whiche he peyneth and tormenteth in many manerys, as be fastyng, be wakyng, be silence kepynge, be weryng the haire, be almes doyng. ȝit theye do not this but if it be in siche places when theye suppose tha men shal see it. Thoo be grete fooles that of goode metal maketh fals monoy. Therfor God seithe in the gospell: Why lese ȝe youre goode dedes? Ȝe myght selle theyme fulle dere. The thirde braunche of ypocrisie is in tho that wolde clymbe hye. Theye doo that goode men sholde doo soo that noon maye knowe theym. As God seithe in the gospell: Men knoweth not a tree of what nature it is but be the fruit. Evyn so, noon maye knowe theyme vnto the tyme that theye be waxen vp and þat theye be on heighte that theye maye bere fruit, for than shewe theye their vicis that theye haue hidde in the roote of pride, as covetise and malice and othir evil fruit be the whiche men knoweth that the tree was never goode and that al was ypocrisie and fantesie al that ever theye shewed afore. The scripture seithe to vs that ther is ii rootes of the whiche al synnes groweth, that is to seye, foly fere and evill louff. Of foly fere cometh foly shame, that is whan a man hatthe talent to doo welle and he derre not for the worlde. An ypocrit louffeth better the worlde than God and douteth more the wordis of the worlde than the iugement of God, for the whiche he is ashamed to doo welle. Wherfore the feende overthroweth o party on the right syde, anothir on the lefte syde. Oo goode God, what it is a gret vntrowthe and a lewde shame that any man hatthe shame to serve so noble and so hye a lorde as God is and hatth no shame to serve his seruaunt or also to haue shame to serve his noble and riche fadir of whom commeth alle the goodes that he hatthe and he hatthe no shame to serve his enemy and to doo hym worshipp, that is, the worlde, the whiche litil and litil taketh and shalle take al weye at þe laste. Butte God seithe in the gospell: Whoosoo [f. 35] hatthe shame of me afore men, I shalle haue shame of hym afore angellis. It is to grete pitee of blynde pepil the whiche the feende hatthe so enchaunted and blynded that theye vndirstande of worshipp that it were [h]ounte and of [h]ounte that it were worshipp. Oo goode lorde, ther is noon so grete worshipp as is to doo welle and to leve an onest lif and to haue goode lose and the name of a goode man. Ne ther is no verrey shame but to lede a shameful lif and to doo synne and to serve the feende and to plese shrewis, the whiche maye louff noon but thoo that be lyke to theyme.

Off Foly Fere and of Foly Shame, XXVIII[e]

The vii principall braunche of pride is devided in ii braunches, of the whiche groweth moo synnes and moo evilles than men maye noumbre. The too branche is to do evill; the tothir is to leve to doo wel. A goode God, howe many goode dedes men leve nowe-a-dayes for this fere and for this shame. Ther is in the worlde many oon that wolde lede and maintene al anothir lif than theye doo if they dorste. Myche more gladly theye wolde goo to the chirche and lenger abide there and hire sermones and ofter confesse theyme and were meke clothyng, and many othir maner of goodnes wolde theye doo ne were foly shame. And on the toþer side al the contrarie. Whan men aske theym: Whye doo ȝe soo, they answer: It forthynketh vs God knoweth. We knowe wel that we do evill, but we derre noon oþerweys doo for the worlde. Wil ȝe that we ȝefeth theym cause to crye oute on vs and to holde vs for iobbardis? Al the worlde sholde ryn on vs. For this cause, it is no merveille thoughe God hate the worlde. For the worlde hatith hym so cruelly that al tho that wolde serve hym at the chirche and wolde be of his meny the worlde hateth, dispiceth, and werrieth and putteth theyme from his service. And be his howteyng and his crye he turneth theym from the goode weye, and puttyth theym into the feendes preson, from the whiche theye wolde flee and ascape, liche as the theef wolde ascape from the wacche of the castell that ascryethe whan he ascapeth. Wherfore at this daye the worlde hatthe [f. 35v] the better of theym, for bothe clerkys and laymen be ȝolden to hym. And also the worlde hatthe drawen theym to hym with his lyne and made them monkes and nonnes of theire ordre truly soo that theye be alle in obediens to hym and werith his armes and his clothyng and hatthe forsakyn God their owne lorde, bothe clerkys and prestis, the whiche sholde be of his howsholde and liffe with his brede. Wherfor God is as acursed and in as grete sentence holden as ever was any man and soo enforced ayein that openly nowe is fulfilled the prophecye of Ieromye the prophete, the whiche seithe in the persone of Crist Iesus: Alas faire swete lady Marie, wherefore bare ye me euer betwene yowre precious sydes, man of strife, man of werre, and man acursed? Alle the worlde rynneth vpon me and curseth me. Noon therre shewe me frendeshipp, marchandyse, ne lene me to wynne with. The sentense thanne is fulle grevous, as whan a man is soo cursed that alle be acursed that fel[e]shippeth with hym and that sheweth contenaunce of love.

[Whye Pride Is to Flee, to Hate, and to Blame]

We haue spoken longe of the synne of pride and of the braunches that commeth therof and of the lytel braunches that commeth of the braunches. We wille nowe speke and telle som resones why pride is for to flee and wherefore men sholde parfitely hate it and whye it is soo souereynly to blame. For if ther be any goodnes in a persone and pride entre there, pride putteth owte alle his goodnes. For as Seynt Austyn seythe: Pride dothe his labour to distroye alle goodnes and al goode vertues. And therefore where pride is maye noo goodnes entre ne be, nor he maye ne wyl that any entre there. And Seynt Gregorie seithe: Like as mekenes feebleth and distroieth alle vices and assembleth and strengheth alle vertues, on thė same wyse pride distroyeth and febleth alle vertues. And liche as mekenes is not aloonly vertuous, but it is a vesselle to hide and to kepe in othir, on the same wyse, pride is not aloonly evyl, but it is the withlettyng of alle goodnesses. For the whiche a wise man seide to Alixander that he knewe welle that [f. 36] God was redye to a prowde man to yeve hym wisedom but he hatthe no place whereon to receyve it. That is to seye, he hadde noo mekenes in hym but rathir pride the whiche wille suffre noo wisedom to entre in hym, liche as holy scripture seithe in an nother place: The wisedom of God shalle never entre into a soule fulle of evil wille ne into a bodye ful of synne. Also pride is kynge and begynnyng of alle synnes and of al other vicys. For as Ecclesiastes seithe: Pride is the begynnyng of alle synnes, and whoosọo kepith it shalle be fulfilled with alle synnes, for of pride groweth heresies, detraccions, envie, stryfe, vauntyngis, and many other evilles. And Seynt Bernard seithe that pride is the begynny[n]g and the cause whye of dampnacion. Wherfore thowe that coveitest thyn helthe haue ever in thyn herte the corner of the cros ouer thyn heede that thowe reyse the not be pride, for pride is the firste synne that entreth into the soule and the laste that parteth therfroo. For whan a man hatthe overcome alle vicys and casteth theym awaye be vertue, aloonly pride abideth stylle and sesseth not to assaile man as longe as he lyveth. Alsoo pride is the feendes token be the whiche he knoweth his from other, for as men reede in the Booke of Ioob, the feende is open proude peple. And Seynt Austyn seithe that the moste certeyne tokyn that theye haue whiche shal be dampned is pride, and mekenes of thoo that shalle be saved. Wherfore he ought to be in grete sorwe that knoweth hymselfe proude. Also the proude man is anguisshous and contrarius to his neghborghes, for with hit he dispiseth them, as Ecclesiastes [seythe]: Lyche as mekenes is abhominable anamly to a proude man, soo poere despyte is abhominable to a riche man. He threteth hym be wordes in many maneres, in vauntyng hymselfe, in seying vylonie and despite of othir. And also he threteth hym in dede in many maneres and bodyly in betyng, in presonyng hym, and in takyng awaye his goodes, as men see nowe dayly in loordes, of whom the prophete seythe: Proude peple behaveth theym felly [f. 36v] and cruelly to meeke peple and to poore in alle maneres. And also he seithe: Thees proude peple shal be confounded, for theye haue don me velonye withoute cause. Also proude peple haten God and wolde be abowe hym and take from hym his glorye and his lordeshippe. It sheweth welle that theye hate God, for theye wolde haue no souereyne aboue theyme. And soo he wyl not haue God to his souereyne ne to his lord. And also he coveiteth to be like to hym whan he desireth too haue lordeshippe ouer ooþer peple and wil be sogget to noon other creature. And also he wolde take God hys lordeshippe. Also alle proude peple wolde resemble God as Lucyfer dydde. And Dauid seithe of thees proude peple that the pride of thoo the whiche haten the heyueth ever and enhuaunseth. For the proude man wolde withdrawe fro God that the whiche God wolde specially haue, that is to seye, glorye. And in that he disworshippeth oure lorde, not oonly to haue the veray glorye of paradys but the glorye of the goodes that he hath receyved of God or of the goodnes that God werketh in hym or be hym. For the whiche men seyen of Ioob: If I kysse, seithe Ioob, myn hande with myn owne mouthe, that is a gret vntrouthe. He kysseth his hande with his owne mouthe that prayseth thoo deedes the whiche he dothe or glorifyeth theym and setteth theym to hymselfe and knowelecheth not the grace of his maker be whom alle goodnes is doon and withowte whom noon maye be doon, as þat he seithe in the gospelle: Withowte me, ye maye nothynge doo welle. And the prophete seithe: Sire, thowe haste wrought in vs alle goode werkes. And because the proude man wil haue noo souereyne, neyther God ne noon other, therfor God holdeth hym vyle and hateth hym. For as Seynt Gregor seithe: The more glorious that a proude man is afore the peple the more foule and in despyte is he holden afore the angellis of hevyn. And Seynt Iohn seythe in the Pocalipse: The more that he is glorified in hymselfe and the more delytes that he hatthe hadde, the moo wepynges and tormentes be yoven vnto hym. And oure ladye seithe in the magnificath that oure lorde deposed and putte proude peple froo theyre seege and enhuaunsed the meeke and made theym sitte an hye. Also God hateth proude peple. And it is righte, for theye haten hym as we haue seide afoore. [f. 37] For the proude man wolde take from God that the whiche is his, that is to seye, glorye, as he seithe hymselfe: I wille not yeve my glorye to noon othir. And the proude man seithe: And I yeve it to myselfe. And also he wolde take fro hym hys lordshippe. For the proude man wil take vengeance of alle his wronges doon, and he oughte to leve theyme to God, the whiche shal yeve to euery man aftir that he hatth deserved. And therof he speketh by a prophete: I withhoold the vengeance to me. And because we haue spoken of glorye and that men sholde knowe whiche is veray and whiche is veinglorye, ye shalle knowe that ther is a veray glorye that goode men haue be goode [witnes] of theire consciens, the [whiche] wene not to be dedely synne, as Seynt Poule seithe. And yet in another place he seith: I am of noothynge soo certeyne that I sholde wene to be oute of dedely synne. And also I derre not iustyfye me in that point for God the whiche al seeith and knoweth siche thynge in me the whiche is doon and is for to doo that I knowe not meselfe. And therfore noon shulde iustifye hymselfe, for noon knoweth weder he is worthy to haue the love of oure lorde Godde or his hate. For noon may be certeyne in this worlde wheder he shalle be saved or dampned, for ther maye be siche that this daye is oute of synne the whiche maye soon fal into it, if God kepe hym not specially. And siche ther be that this daye maye be in synne and, whan it pleeseth Godde, maye soon be ryghtwysse. Alsoo ther is [a more] veray glorie. That is whan an hooly soule feleth in his herte the swetnes of the Hooly Gooste and that the Hooly Goost yeveth the wyttenes to his goost that we bee Goddis childer and that we shalle be parteneres in the herytage of hevyn, the whiche is the righte verray glorye. Vainglorye is likned too glorye fendely and mankendely. The firste is whan any gloryfieth hym in his malyce and of his evil deedes. Mankendely glorye is likned to glorye flesshely and goostelye. The flesshelye is the glorye of the worlde, the whiche is in feire cloothes and rycches and in worshippes. The goostely glorye is the glorye of ipocrites of whom we haue spoken afore. This flesshely and goostely vainglorye is moche to blame and lytyl to prayse. For the pride and the ricches of this worlde resembleth rotyn wode, the whiche shineth clere be nyght and not on the daye. Soo fare theye in this worlde; theye shyne outeward for theyre rychesse and for theyre noblesse, but atte the doome theyre derkenes shalle shewe [f. 37v] afore Godde and afore angellis. The glorye of proude peple is not ellys but doonge and wormes. This daye it shalle be reysed hye, and tomorwe a man shalle swette where to fynde it. The glorye of the synner is as a sakke that is fulle of stynkyng harlotrye and of wormes mete. Wherefore euery man oughte to dispyse vainglorye, anamely alle religious. As Seynt Ierom seithe: The firste vertu of the worlde is to despyse the iugement and the praysyng of men. And theye sholde not ioye theym therewith but be troubled [...] whan the angelle seide to hir that shee was fulle of grace and that shee was blissed above alle wommen.

[Of Remedies ayens Pride]

Nowe haue we spoken and shewed many resones whye the vice of pride is to blame and that a man oughte souereinly to hate it. Nowe wil we speke and set som remedye ayens this vice, to the whiche whoosoo wille wele and diligentlye take hiede maye the lyghtlyer eschewe it and kepe hym therfroo. The firste remedye ayeins pride and vainglorye is to hide secretelye any goodnes that a man dothe or wylle doo. For as Seynt Iohn seyth: Hiede secretelye the goodnes that thowe dooste. And if thowe maiste not al holely hyde it, haue wil in thyn herte to hiede it secretely. For liche as the tresor that many knoweth is soon lessed, soo the vertue that euery man seeith is soone loste. The seconde remedye is to considre and to discende to his owne sekenes. And if a man prayse hym and he knowe his defautes he sholde rathir haue shame than ioye, for he knoweth hym ooþerwise and seeth that siche praysyng is fals and þat it is not soo, of the whiche Boyce seithe: Thoo that men prayse and that be falsely praysed be ashamed and basshed of the praysyng. The thirde remedye is whan that men offren and yeven to a man glorye he sholde yeve it ayein to the kynge of glorye, to whom it longeth. As Dauid seithe: Sire, seithe he, the glorye be to the and nat to vs. And whoosoeuer vseth this vainglorie shalle not haue soo grete strenghthe as he hadde afore. Also ther is in general oothir remedies ayeins pride: First, Seynt Gregore seithe: Men sholde take heede to better than the[y] be, for liche as the beholdyng to wars than theye be is a tysyng and a reysyng of pride, on the same wise the takyng hiede to better than theye be causeth mekenes. [f. 38] Anothir remedye ther is, that is to be and to feleshippe with meeke peple. For as Ecclesiastes seithe: Lyche as he that feleshippeth with proude peple shalle becomme proude, on the same wise whoosoo feleshippeth with meeke peple shalle waxe meeke. And Dauid seithe in the Psalter: Thowe shalte be holy with holy peple and innocent with innocent peple, and with shrewes and evil peple thowe shalt waxe shrewed and evil. Also anothir remedye ther is, to consider and to take hiede to the fylthe and to the harlottrye of his owne bodye, firste to the fylthe of his concepcion, the whiche is the foulest harlotrye that is. Also he is as a sakke fulle of mire and of dunge, and at the laste he shalle be asshes and wormes mete. And howe, seithe Seint Ierome, sholde he enpryde hym that bereth euer syche harlottrye? And the prophete Mathias seithe: *Humiliacio tua in medio tui est*. That is to seye, thy meekenes is in the myddes of the. This harlotrye that thowe beryst yeveth the reson and cause to be meeke and that thowe sholdest not enpride the. Another remedye ther is be the example of the meekenes of Crist Iesus. Wherefore man ought to be ashamed to be proude, whan the creatour of al thyngis is meeke. For as Seint Austyn seithe: The medicyn ayeins pride for man is the meekenes of Crist Iesus, firste in his incarnacion, after in his meeke conuersacion. And vnto the dethe he wolde meeke hymselfe for oure redempcion. Also another remedie ther is, to consider the iugement of oure lorde, the whiche specially shalle be ayeins proude peple, lordes, and the myghty peple of this worlde. For as Dauid seithe: Oure lorde habondantly shalle yelde tormentis to proude peple. And hooly scripture seithe in another place that the grete peple of this worlde shalle be myghtely tormented. The laste remedye þat we sette is to consider oure wrecchednes. For be oure [f. 38v] spirit we be soo feeble and so [litil] vertuous that we maye not withstande ne resiste oo lighte temptacion ne a lighte thoughte ne sustene ne suffre mekely oo lytyl worde, and soo we leese soon al oure goodnes that we haue doon, if God haue not mercy on vs. Also of oure bodyes we be soo poore and soo feeble that we maye not resiste ne defende vs alloonly froo fleeys. Wherefore Seynt Austyn seithe: If a man blame the but a lytill, thowe angrest thyeselfe and haste despite therof. Fleeys letteth the to sleepe, and thowe maist not defend froo theym. And also oure caytifous bodies shalle becomme asshes and pouder. Me seemeth whoosoo thoughte weele on these thynges sholde haue goode cause to meeke hymselfe.

[Of the Synne of Envie]

Envye shalle never deye. Men seide soo longe agoon. And howe that it is trewe I shalle telle the. The firste synne that ever was made was pride, the whiche keste Lucyfer oute of hevyn and maade hym a feende. The seconde was envye that he hadde to man the whiche was maade for to [f. 39] haue the herytage of hevyn and the ioye of paradys that he lost. And thus envye maade man to synne. And be this synne deethe coom to the worlde, as Seynt Poule seithe. Envye is the moder of dethe. And therfore deethe loueth hym and he hym. Wherefore deethe hatthe no power ouer hym, for at the daye of doome when deethe shalle deye, as Seynt Poule seithe, than envye shalle begynne his lyfe and his lordeshipp withouten ende. But that shalle be in helle where envye shalle dwelle, for oon of the grettest tormentes that theye shalle haue there shalle be envye, for that shalle never fayle, the whiche theye shalle haue to Godde and to his seyntis and to thoo that theye knowe in this worlde and to poore peple whan theye knowe that theye be in hevyn. Here maiste thowe knowe in what plite an envyous man is whan that he is in helle, for he hatthe ever ernest to haue the prouendres of helle. There he hatthe euer his pensyon in ii maneres of tormentis: Oon is that hatthe woo of þe goodes that he seeyth oothir haue. Anothir is in a feer that he hatthe that better sholde comme to theym. Here maiste thowe see that of alle synnes this is the mooste vnhappy, for oother synners haue some ioye or some delite in this worlde, but he this hatthe helle here and abideth another in the toother worlde. Also it is mooste disfygured, for this is he that resembleth verily to the feende his fader, the whiche loveth but the evil of oother, and he hateth but the weele of other, as the feende doothe. And thowe knowest wel that love maketh a soule feire or foule. Also it is moost of dispeyre, for proprely it hateth and werreieth the Hooly Goost, the whiche is welle of alle goodenes. And God seythe that whoosoo synneth ageynste the Hooly Gooste shalle never haue [f. 39v] mercy in this worlde ne in the toother, for he synneth of his owne malyce. And men shoolde hooly vnderstand that ther is noon soo grete synne in this worlde but God pardoneth if he repente hym with goode herte. But vnnethe it happeth that any repenteth hym of siche synne as werreyeth the grace of the Hooly Gooste. And thowe shalt knowe that ther be vi synnes ayeinst the Hooly Goost: That is to seye, presumpcion, the whiche maketh the mercy of oure lorde to large, his iustyse to lytel praysed, and therfore myche peple synneth in hoope. The seconde is wannehope, the whiche taketh fro God his mercy lyche as presumpcion dooeth his rightwysnes. The thirde is hardenes of herte, that is whan a man hardeth soo in malyce that men maye not flytte hym ne he wil not amende hym. The iiii ys dispyte of penaunce, that is whan that a man thynketh in his herte that he wyl never repente hym of his synne. The v is to werreye the grace of the Hooly Gooste in another persone. The vi is to werreye trowthe wittyngly, specyally the trouthe of the Cristen feythe. Alle thees synnes be ayeins the grace of the Hooly Gooste. And theye be soo grete that vnnethes a man commeth to any goode repentaunce, and therfore vnnethe theye be foryeven. Also it is moost blynded, for it blyndeth alle goodnes, alle ioye, and alle clerenes, lyche as the clerenes of the sonne doothe the donne mouse. Also it is mooste vnnaturell. For as Seynt Denis seithe: It is good that of nature alle thyngys loveth and desyreth, but thees of nature hateth goodnes, and the envyous man is euer soorye whan he seeth goodnes. He hateth a man for the goodnes that is in hym, and he desyreth the evyll and loveth that the whiche he sholde hate of nature. But because that men be wonte to devyde alle maner of synnes in iii partees, men synne in herte be thoughte, men synne in the mouthe be speche, and men synne in dede. Therfore is this synne devyded in iii principal branches and to euery branche iii lytel branches, the whiche bereth soo myche venimous fruit that al the worlde is nerehand envenimed. Take hiede nowe howe in the [soule] be iii vertues, of the whiche oon is called reson that sheweth to man bothe goode and evyll. The ii vertu [f. 40] is called love, desyre, and covetyse. This vertu whan reson hatth shewed hym goodnes anoon he desyreth and coveyteth it and sekeith to haue it, and whanne he hatthe it he holdeth it and loveth it and enbraceth it. The iii vertu is called ire or rigoure in corage of the soule. This vertu as soon as reson sheweth hym [evyll] he dresseth hym ayeins it and rynneth vppon it and dryveth it aweye and distroyeth it. Wherefore man is called stronge, vigorous, and coragyous whan he overthroweth evyll ther where he seithe it. Also the herte of man be nature is ordeyned thertoo and myche the better be the grace of God whan that helpeth hym and enlumineth hym. But the herte of the envyous man is soo bestely and soo en[c]haun[t]ed with the feende that alle thees vertues be corromped in hym. Wherfore be reson, the whiche is the iye of the herte, alle that he seeth and vnderstandeth he mystorneth it and maketh it beestely and streccheth it into evylle wittys, and not God but the feende yeveth hym evyll entenciones. Of this roote groweth soo many evyl synnes of the herte that men maye not nombre theym, for theye sesse never to yeve evyl domes of oother. The deedys theye iuge and theye dampne the entente of the whiche the worlde is soo thikke that ther is no man soo weele sette ne soo goode but that the envyous man fyndeth inowe to seye and to lye. Alsoo this is the reson of the envyous man. Whan it sholde shewe to the reson of the soule that the whiche men calleth love and to desyre wele, it sheweth hym the evyl. And therof it happeth that in many where the herte of the envyous man seeyth evyl he rynneth thertoo and loveth it and maketh grete ioye. The envyous man hatthe noon ooþer ioye but this. Also this reson of the envyous man curseth because that the reson rynneth on hym and sheweth hym goodnes whan that he woolde that it sholde shewe to the corage of hys herte evyll. Anoon as a grehound he rynneth aftir the evyl be ire, be evil wylle, and be angre in al maner that he maye greve theym. And because þat [f. 40v] he maye not distroye al the goodnes that he seeyth, thereof groweth soo grete a sorowe to his herte that he is euer hevy withowte laughtyr. His herte trembleth. His body rotith. Here he begynneth helle, the whiche shalle never fayle hym. And that is righte, for whan that he gruccheth he wolde take from God hys bounte, his largesse, and his curtesye. For the whiche we fynde in scripture that God seide to syche a mysterman: Art thowe soory, seythe he, that I am good? Wilt thowe not suffre me to doo with myn what me luste? Theese be the iii envenimous branches oon the herte of the envyous man: fals iugement, evyl gladnes, and thykke sorowe. Trowest thowe that ther be any in the worlde? Trewely yea, oueralle inough, anamly amonge theese grete burgeses that desyren to haue the toune gouerned be theym there be grete envyes, grete malyseys, and grete sorowes that oon hath ayeins another. Whan oon encresceth, anoothir hath grete woo; whan he discreesceth, he hath grete ioye. Take heede nowe if þer be any grete charite with theym. Whan I thynke on the Ladye Envye, I con nought see in her but that gladly shee herboroweth in grete househoIdes and dwelleth euer in grete paleyses, where euery man tenteth to haue prys and to seke prayes and desyrously wayten to there lordes handes as a famylyer grehounde wayteth to see where any wyl caste hym any morselle either oon or other. There is Lady Envye hoole. There maketh shee here beeres for to tomble. There be anguisshes whan oon is avaunsed and anothir not. Nowe for Goddys sake take heede howe this man is vnhappy and a synner above al other in whom envye hath made his dwellyng place soo that euer what hee seeyth that any doothe wele he synneth, for he is soorye therof soo that alle the goodnes that is in the worlde to hym it is venym, sorowe, and synne. [f. 41] And thereto euer whan he seeyth or heeyrith that another synneth, he synneth with hym soo that euery tyme this caytyfe synneth and hurteth hymselfe whan he may see or hyre seye that any goodnes or any evil commeth to any that is in the worlde. Also aftir the haboundance of the herte the mouthe speketh, and therethorugh leepyth oute iii maner of venimous woordes. For as Dauid seyth: His bounte is fulle of malyce and of bittirnes. For to his power he lesseth the goodnes of oothir, and trewly with his boost he reyseth and encresceth the evilles of oothir. For al that he seyth and hiereth he torneth and peruerteth it into evylle. And theese be þe iii feendes of whom Seint Iohn speketh in the Pocalipse that he sawe comme owte of the mouthe of a dragon and of a beeste and of a false prophete in forme of froggys. The envyous man is the false prophete because he iugeth falsly, a dragon because he casteth fyre and flambe with his mouthe, a beeste because that he deuoureth goodnes and ouerthroweth goode peple as men doon a sheepe. The envyous man also hath iii maner of venymes: in dede, in herte, and in the mouthe. For to his powere al goodnes be they lytyl or grete, be they moyen or parfyte, he distroyeth outher be worde or dede. For, as God seithe in the gospel, goodnes is in iii degreys: First it is gresse, aftir it spyreth, and aftir that it is rype. On the same wise some goodenesses ther be that hatth a goode begynnyng to come forthe and to profyte. Siche goodnesses [far]eth as the gresse, oothir fareth as the spyre, the whiche profyteth wele, and oothir be parfyte, the whiche dooth myche goodnes. The envyous man hateth al and wolde shende and distroye al. For to steyne theese iii maner of goodnes there is no treson ne noon vntrouthe but that the envyous man wolde doo it and he maye. And that witnes I be an example of iii righte grete malyce: Oon was in Kynge Herode that kylled the innocentes, for thourgh the envye that he hadde to Criste Iesus [...] the whiche was in state [f. 41[v]] of perfeccion and dedde soo myche goodnes that he ferde as a tree fulle wexen with ripe fruite. If thowe wilt knowe what fruit a [tree] berith and what groweth of the stocke of envye, take hiede to the malyce of Herode, to the sotiltee of the feende, and to the vntrouthe of the Iewes, and thowe shalt see that ther is noon vntrowthe, morthre, trayson, ne synne soo horrible as thoo that growe of the stocke of envye.

[Of Remedies ayens the Synne of Envie]

Nowe haue we spoken of the synne of envye. Nowe wyl we speke of remedyes that ben ayeins that vice. The first is that a man sholde sette his love in syche goodnesses as be the goodnesses of Godde, the whiche many maye haue as wele and as lightely as oon aloon, for the whiche Seynt Gregor seythe: The iuste man because he coveyteth noothynge that is in erthe he con not haue envye to the goodenes ne to the profite that oothir hatthe. Also anothir remedye is to consider the loue that euery of vs sholde haue to oothir, for al creatures of kynde loveth his liknes. Wherfore euery of vs sholde loue oother, for we be al lyche and brether and alle of oo [n]ater, for we be descended of oo fader and of oo moder, the whiche is of Adam and of Eue. Oure lorde made al the angelles togeder, but he wolde that we sholde discende of oo fader and of oo moder because we sholde haue the gretter love togeder. Also we be brether goostely, for we be of oo fader of oure lorde Criste Iesus and of oon moder, that is, of holy chirche. And alle we tente to haue oon herytage, the whiche is the blys of hevyn, and goostely we be al felawes. And specyally alle iuste peple be parteneres and felawes in wynnynge or lesynge, of the whiche Dauid seythe: Syr, seythe he, I am partenere with alle thoo that loveth the and dredeth the. And that is reson, for we be alle membres of oon heede, the whiche is Criste Iesus. For as Seynt Poule seithe: Lyche, seithe he, as in oo body we haue many membres and yet al oure membres [f. 42] doothe not oo deed, for that the whiche the iye dooth the mouthe doeth not and soo of oothir, also we be many membres and oo bodye in Criste Iesus. And lyche as oure membres haue compascion oon of anothir soo that whan oon is hurte thoo other be soory and helpeth it, for whan the mouthe pleyneth the handes meven and feleth it ful softely and the iyen beholdeth pytousely and be compascion, on the same wise we sholde haue pyte euery of oother that be membres of Criste Iesus. For the whiche

Seynt Poule seythe: Whoo is, seithe he, in hooly chirche that is seke and I not seke with hym be compassion, and whoo is slaundred that I am not soory fore? Hee felt in hym alle the evilles that any oothir persone hadde, and soo sholde euery persone doo the whiche is a membre of Godde. The laste remedye that we wyl sette is the grete harme that commeth of envye. Oon harme is that the envious man leeseth his neghbourgh. Another harme is that the envyous man is disseuered froo the membres of hooly chirche, the whiche leveth goostely be the grace of the Holy Gooste. He is disseuered froo Godde. Lyche as the membre that is disseuered from a bodye the whiche is withowte lyfe and withoute soule, noo moore lyveth he goostely. And lyche as the envyous man wyl no[t] that noon haue noo goode ne noo parte of his goodes, on the same wise he is not worthy too haue parte of the goodes of owre lorde.

[Of the Synne of Ire and of Degrees That Descendeth Therof]

[f. 42v] The iii heede vice is angre. And yet thowe shalt knowe that ther is oon ire the whiche is vertu that holy men haue ayeins synne. For theye werrye it and hate it as theyre dedely enemye, the whiche putte to dethe Adam theire fader and alle theyre kynne that be come and shal comme of theym. Another ire ther is the whiche is vice, as whan a man is angrye withowte cause and withoute reson. And þou shalt knowe that this vice hatthe v degreeys [...] in diuers maneres of ire. For ther be som that be soon greved and that soon foryeteth angre. Theye be goode. Oother ther be that wyl soon be angred and wille not lyghtely forgete theyre angre. Theye be not goode. The iii be thoo that wyl be longe or theye be angry, but it is ful harde to peese theym ayein. Theye be not goode. The iiii there be som that wil be soon angry, and whan theye be angrye noon maye peese theym. Theye be evill. The v is that wil not lyghtely be angred, but whan theye be angred theyre fellenes wyl never owte of the herte. Theye be cruel, and men calle theyme cruel fellenes. In this vice of ire be v degreeys, the whiche thowe maiste knowe in v maneres that men knowen in an irous man.

Somtyme men seye: I see hym to myche tormented. That is to seye whan men greveth theym and troubleth theyme as the see doothe. For Isaye seithe that the herte of a felle man fareth as the blustrynge see, the whiche casteth hymselfe too and froo and foometh and maketh tormentis and noyse soo that men be basshed to see it. Somtyme men seye this fareth a man: I sawe hym soo enflamed that it seemed that fyre and flaume come oute of his visage. Nowe is fyre sette in the [f. 43] house. If it be not soon stanched, it shal waste alle the goodys that be therinne. Somtyme men seye: I sawe hym soo eegre that it seemed he was oute of his witte. For syche peple beteth women and childer lyche as a woode man that smyteth and kylleth alle thoo that kepeth hym, for he wote not whate he doothe ne whate he seithe. Somtyme men seye: I sawe hym soo woode that it semed that he had a feende in his bodye. And soo haue theye somtyme whan ire ouercometh theym. For whan theye knowe not where to wreke theyme, theye wreke theym on Godde or on his seintis. Theye swere and curse and renoyeth Godde. Somtyme men seye of a man that he is naturelly a foole and cruell. He is no man; hee is rathir a feende and hatthe [werre] on al partyes within and withowte, above and benethen. For iiii maner of werres that a man hatthe be the iiii principal branches that cometh oute of the nature of this [thorne].

[Of the Werre That the Ireous Man Hatth to Hymselfe]

The firste werre that the foole hatthe withinne, that is to seye, of hymselfe to his soule and to his bodye is whan ire bereth oppon hym. He casteth owte the Hooly Gooste, the whiche resteth not but in peesyble places, and receyveth the feende, the whiche luffeth noo loggeingis but fulle of noyse and of discorde. Wherfore of the Holy Goostes temple he maketh mawmentrie to the feende, for he casteth owte alle goodenes and putteth in al evil. The soule also hatthe ii maner of [f. 43v] goodes goostely, as meveable and vnmeveable. The meveable be the swetnes of the Holy Gooste. And þe feend robbeth the herte of thoo, for whan ire hatthe the yeate oopyn he taketh from hym the grace of contemplacion, the swetnes of deuocion, the so[o]tenes of holy meditacion, the sauour of prayer, the profyte of contricion, the gladnes to hyre speke of God, and alle the talent that he hatthe to doo wele. These be as meveable goodes of the soule, for nowe a man hatthe theyme and nowe a man hatthe theyme not, as it pleeseth the Hooly Gooste, the whiche departeth theym at his wylle where hym lyste. The tother vnmeveable goodes of the soule be the vertues that be rooted in the herte. The feende casteth his handes to thoo, as Ierom[ye] seithe. Firste, he casteth his hande to the feyrest, takyng aweye fro hym the vertue of charytee whan he putteth hym in hate. Also he taketh fro hym deboneyrte, pardon, mekenes, and pytee. Aftir that he taketh froo hym pees of herte, paciens, and mercy, soo that men fyndeth there neyther pardon ne mercy. For he is more bolned than a boterel, *id est*, [...]. Also he taketh froo hym the iiii cardinal vertuis: iustice, for he vengeth hymselfe; strenghthe, for in his corage he hatthe neyther vertu ne myghte but that hym moste doute; temperance, as whan that he maye neyther mesure his speche, hys dede, ne his thoughte; prudence, as whan he seeyth not for to gouerne hym, for he hatth loste bothe witte, mynde, and reson. And whan the Holy Goostes meni be goon oute the feendes meny entreth, that ys to seye, evyl thoughtes and evyl desyres, the whiche maketh bittyr woordes and noyous deedes to lepe oute of the herte. And thus vices entreth into the herte, the whiche aloonly tormenteth not the soule but they travayle the herte and distroyeth it, for theye take from it the reste of mete and of drynke. Men seeyth this al daye. And þey make the herte to boyle as a chaufour. And often it happeth that be ire men falleth into a sharpe frensye and somtyme dyeth therinne. As whan ire [f. 44] ouerleyeth a man, it putteth hym in siche hevynes and in syche dyspeyre that eyther he hongeth hym or drowneth hym. Alas howe moche werre hatthe this caytife.

[Of the Werre That He Hatth to God]

The ii werre and the ii branche that he hatthe it is above hym, that is to seye, to Godde. For there be som fooles, som woode peple, whan theye myshappe theye blame Godde therfore and dothe hym wronge and seythe of hym alle the shame that theye maye thynke and alle the foule plee that theye con make and casteth the peny vnder foote and treedeth in dispyte vppon the crosse and renoyeth Godde more than c tymes on the daye. If they thynke that he sendeth theyme to moche colde or to moche hete, to moche reyne or to moche drouthe, or if he sende theym sekenes or pouertee to chastice theym with, theye grucche and haue dysdeyne of God as of a boye.

[Of the Werre That He Hatth to Hys Meny]

The iii werre that the irous man hath is to thoo that be vnder hym: to his wife, to his meny, yea and yet to doumbe beestys. For whan ire bereth on hym he beteth women an childer, the whiche hatthe not trespassed to hym; his dogge and his catte he torneth vppe so downe; he breketh pottes and cuppes and al that euer he maye kacche in his handes. Is he not owte of his witte? It were grete almes to bynde hym.

[Oof the Werre That He Hatthe to His Neyghbors and Of the VII Branchettis That Groweth Therof]

The iiii branche is to his neghborghes outeward and to thoo that be nexte aboute hym. Of this branche groweth vii smale branches. For whan ire waxeth betwene ii, first groweth therof chydyng and dispyte and than rancoure, the whiche abydeth in the herte, aftyr that, hate, medlee, desyre of ven[f. 44^{v}]geance, manslaughte, and dedely werre.

[Of Euery Be Ordre, That Is to Seye, of Chidyng, of Rancure, of Hate, the Whiche Hatthe VII Degrez]

The firste lytel branche of this branche is chydyng. Of this wyl we speke amonge other synnes of the tonge. Aftir chydynge abideth rankoure in herte, the whiche maketh a man irous be hymselfe. For whan he sholde slepe or reste he chideth with his neghborgh or the wyfe with herre gossop. For the feende the whiche serveth for siche crafte seeyth to hym: Truly he seide soo to the. Good Godde, why answerest thowe noghte to hym this or that? Certys thowe shalte seye to hym yet: Is he not syche oon? He was to hardy whan he tooke ageyns the. Blame haue thow if thowe pleyne not to thy frendis that men maye see wheder thowe haue gretter power or he. And whan the caytif weneth to sleepe, he torneth on the toon side and on the tother. Be my [heede, s]eythe the feende, thow shalt not slepe yet and I maye. Thowe art vnhappye if thowe wilt suffre to be soo defouled. Truly thowe shalt tomorowe speke soo to thye neghborgh that þou shalt shewe whate thowe arte. In syche wyse the feende kyndeleth the fyre of rancure and than hate. And this hate hatthe vi degreeys. For whan I haue seide to whom that euer it be: Fayre freend, syche oon hatthe myssedoon to the; thowe moste foryeve hym and Godde shalle foryeve the thy myssedeedes, he answereth me somtyme: And I foryeve hym, but I shalle never love hym as I dedde afore. Or ellys he seyde to me: I wyl wele foryeve hym, but I wille no moore speke with hym. This is yet wers; in feythe this is a poore foryevenes. Feendis hateth togeder dedely, and notwithstandyng theye wylle speke togedder oon to anothir and ete togeder in oo loggyng. Thus in this wise thowe art wors than feendes. Or ellys he seythe: I wyl wel foryeve hym in soo myche that he shalle never haue harme for me, but though harme come to hym I shalle never wepe therfore. That is to seye, I shal [f. 45] be gladde for it. Or ellys he seythe: I hate hym not, but I maye not fayle my cosyn ne my nevewe to whom he hatthe doon vylonye. See here oon of the grettest perilles that longeth to soules that I knowe. For whan oon myssedooth to another men taketh not alleoonly ayeins [hym] but ayeins alle his kyn. And whan an harlot is beten, the whiche is of grete ligne, alle his kyn be in hate and in dedely synne. And that cometh because theye loueth better theyre kyn than Godde whan theye hadde leuer lese Godde and greve hym than fayle theyre kynne. What merveyle is it though that he lese his soule whan he is a mansleer for oon of his kyn to whom he woolde not leen v *s* of his pens? Or ellys he seythe oopynly to me: I hate hym so myche that I shalle never haue reste to I haue cleered myn herte, and if I may kacche hym or any that longeth to hym he shalle abeye, and I shal greve hym in al the maneres that I maye. Ferther maye not hate clyme. And this malyce passeth the malyce of shrewes that kylleth pylgremes for som maner of avayle that theye haue. But he this shal not doo but leese, for as sone as he hath kylled hym perauenture men shal seese alle that he hatthe and bete downe his howses, or men shal kylle hym if theye maye kacche hym. Also this malyce passeth the cruelnes of the feende, the whiche taketh noon but hym that doothe amysse. For if a man breke hym covenaunte and repente hym and goo to confession, he is ful soory and chargeth his felawes for to venge hym, as Godde seythe in the gospel. But he this repente hym neyther to fader ne to sonne that dothe thus. Soo he passeth the feende that for the defaute of an harlot sleeyth his nevewe.

[Of Medlee]

Aftir hate, medle commeth soon. For whoos lyppe that hangeth wepeith for lytel. And this synne is ayeins Godde and ayeins the nature of man, for of nature man ys a deboneyre creature. Wherfore men seye: He is no man; he is a lyon. And therfore theye be disnaturel that smyten togedir. If we vnderstande that al we be brethre and sustris of oo [f. 45v] fader and of oo mooder, it is gretelye ageyne nature for oon to fyghte with another. Also this syn is ageyne Godde, the whiche commaundeth vs that we shalle loue oure neghbourghes. The bodye of a seke man or of a meselle dooth hym but shame, torment, and woo. And notwithstandyng yet he loveth it, sussteyneth it, and dooth it al the goode that he maye. In this maist thowe lerne howe moche thowe sholdest loue thye neghbourghe. And though it greve the and noye the to loue hym, yet soffre hym and sokere hym and doo the best to hym that thowe maiste. For as Salamon seythe: Ther be iii thynges that pleeseth God greetelye: concorde and love of neghborughes in neghborughshipp, of brether and of felawes in an house, and of men and women in maryage. In þis iii, discorde is righte foule and displeysyng to Godde, that is for to seye, betwene nered-welleres and neghebourghes, betwene felawes and cosynes, and betwene husbandys and theyre wyves.

[Of Vengeance]

Aftir discorde men wylle venge theyme. And that is a fulle

grete synne. And this is the fyfthe smale branche of this stocke, for that is to take froo Godde that the whiche he kepeth to his owne vse. For iii thyngys he hatthe withholden proprely for hymselfe the whiche he wyl neyther yeve to man ne to angelle, that is, glorye, iugement, and vengeaunce. The proude man taketh from hym his glorye; the envyous man that d[e]emeth the herte, his iustice; the irous man, his vengeaunce lyche as the hye doome. This is mooste oon of the perlyous synnes of the worlde. For if a man slee his fader or the pope of Rome he maye sonner be foryoven than he that wylle be venged or hadde slayne his deedly enemye. For the toone maye repente hym and haue mercy, but howe shal he repente hym the thynge that he mooste desyred and of the whiche he was mooste gladde? And withowte verray repentaunce noon maye haue pardon therof no moore than a feende. This is a synne of the whiche commeth many evilles. For whanne [f. 46] a man venge hym of another he setteth alle his stodye to hurte hym be mysseyinges, be plee, be speche, and be alle that he maye. And a man taketh hym not alleoonly ayeins his myssedooer but ayeins his nevewe or his cosyn to brenne his hous or to distroye his fruit on the erthe. This is Herodes synne that for the hate the whiche he hadde to Criste Iesus he dedde slee alle the childer of that countree, for he doubted of euery of theym that it sholde ben he that sholde be kynge of Iewes and be whom he sholde leese his reaume. But he this assayleth the creatures of Godde, as cornys, vynes, houses, the whiche hatthe noothynge myssedoon ayeins hym ne myghte not noye hym. And therefore it is no merveyle thugh syche peple deye on eville deeth as the kynge dedde.

[Of Manslaught Bodyly and Gostely]

Off vengeance commeth manslaughte. And that falleth often. And this is the sixte smale branche of this stokke. Thowe shalt nowe wete that ther be ii maneres of manslaughtys, that is to seye, goostly and bodylye. Goostely, a man is a mansleer in iii maneres of hate, for he is a mansleer afore Godde that wy[t] al that his neghbourgh hateth deedly; also be bakkebytynge, the whiche is a[s] trayson behynde hym or be eville counsell to hurte oother; also to take from any hys lyveinge, as Salamon seithe: He that taketh the hyre from his werkeman and he that sleeth his neghbourgh brother it is to seye that theye be as evinly. Alsoo theye be mansleeres that seeth poore peple deye for hunger and fedeth theym not. Thoo be goostely mansleerrys that wittyngly maketh any to synne dedely. For he sleeth the soule the whiche is better than the bodye. Bodyly, man is a mansleer whan be his dede or be his tretyce man is treted to dethe. And this happeth outher be woorde or be dede; be woorde in ii maneres, be eville councell and be felle commaundement. Be dede, man is cause of anotheris deethe in iiii maneres, be iustice or be necessitee, [f. 46v] be myssehappe or be evil wille. Be iustyce as the provoost or the lorde that yeveth a iugement wherebye a man is distroyed. Whan he dooth it for to kepe pees and for to chastyce evyl peple, noothynge for hate ne for oothir evylle entente, he synneth not, rathir dooth almes for he kylleth hym not but the lawe kylleth hym and his myssedeedes. And neverthelesse though he doo it iustely, he is irreguler, *id est*, [...]. Be necessite or somtyme be fortune a man sleeyeth anoother as it happeth whan a man assayleth hym and he defendeth hym and sleeth hym. Than it is [not] manslaughte, standynge that he moste deye if he defende hym not. Also he is irreguler be myssehappe, as whan that men casteth a stone and kylleth a man be aventure soo that he haue taken goode hiede and seen noobodye. In that caas he is not to blame nor irrog[ular]ite if he dede wel as that he sholde doo and as that longeth to hym. Be this reeson, faderis, moderis, and norsces be mansleeris, the whiche kepyn not theyre childer as theye sholde doo. Man is a mansleer be wyl when he sleeth a Cristen man wyttyngly outhir be hymselfe or be his helpes. And thowe shalt witte that Godde allonly behooldeth not the dede but the herte and the wylle. For whan a man smyteth another or yeveth hym venym or peyneth hym on any oother wyse to slee hym, wheder he lyve or dye that he wolde slee, he is a mansleer [afore] Godde that seeyth the hertys. Yet it is a gretter synne whan the evyl is fulfylled. If thowe wilte knowe what synne this is, thynke whatte dignite man hatthe the whiche is the worthyest and the hyest creature that is and moost worthe and moost noble as he that is made to the lykenes of Godde and to the image, the whiche is the soon of the kynge of hevyn, brother to the seintis of hevyn, felawe to angellis, lorde of the worlde, heyre to the reaume of hevyn, boughte with soo precyous a tresor as with the bloode of the soon of God. And if the kynge of Inglond hadde a sonne that he loved as hys owne bodye or moore, howe myghtest thowe greve the kynge moore [f. 47] than to kylle hym? Thowe sholdest haue werre with hym and with alle his childer, with alle his freendis, with alle his courte, and with alle his reaume. On the same wise hatthe he this with Godde and with alle his reaume, with alle his seyntis, with alle his angellis, with alle his freendis, with alle the childer of holy chirche, with alle the creatures that be in hevyn and erthe. And alle cryeth ayeins hym, pleyneth of hym, and shalle pleyne atte the daye of doome as of theyre dedely enemye.

[Of Werre]

Off manslaughte groweth werres of the whiche waxeth soo many evilles and dedely synnes that men maye not nombre theym. For thowe knowest welle that as soon as a man is slayne alle his kyn wille venge hym. And theye be in hate and in peril, bothe theye and alle theyres and alle thoo that for loue or for hate, for ire or for dreede, wille helpe theym to doo it. And the hyer that thoo men be that werreth togedder more harmes ther be and gretter synnes. Thowe seeyst al daye falle that for oo werre that is betwene ii ryche men ther dyen moo than m^l men. Theye breke chirches; they brenne townes and abbeyes; theye distroye poore graunges; men, women, and childer exyled and disseheryted and broughte to begge theyre brede. This grete loorde that purchaceth alle this be his pride and be his malyce or be hate or be covetyce, whan shall he haue doon penaunce for alle thees evilles and for alle thees synnes that lyeth in his necke? Truly if he hadde taken a man in oon of thees townes that be distroyed be hym, if he hadde stolyn a cowe or slayne a man, brokyn a chirche or enforced a womman, he wolde haue hongen be the nekke. Howe many gallowes trowest thowe than that he hatthe deserved, the whiche abideth hym in helle for soo many causes of thefte, of sacrilege, and of dysseherytinge that he hatthe doon? Therfore scripture seythe [f. 47v] that grete loordes shalle haue grete tormentis and alsoo greete doomes.

[Howe Synnez Holdeth Togedir]

Nowe shalle we telle yowe howe synnes be knytte oon with another. The roote of synnes wherewith the synner is bounde holdeth togedder in siche wise þat thourgh pride he leveth Godde the fader because he wyl not be sogget to hym but rathir wyl be above alle other, and whan he seeyth that oother passeth hym he falleth in envye, and from envye into ire and into hate. Nowe thurgh pryde he hatthe loste the solas, ioye, and the love of his neghborughes. Be ire, he hatthe loste pees, gladnes of herte, and verraye hertis comforte and falleth into slouth and hevynes of herte and into noyance. And because that he hatthe loste alle verraye comfort inward, he setteth holy to purchace conforte and veinglorye outeward, firste be the iyen of temperal thyngys and soo falleth he into covetice. Than whan he hatthe ryches, he woolde haue the soolas of meetys and drynkes, wherethurgh he falleth into glotenye. And whan the bely is fulle and eschaufed, than asketh he the delite of the reynes, and the caytyf falleth in longa[i]g[n]e of lecherye. Thus maiste thowe see that thees vii vicys hoolde togedder as linkes doo in a cheyne. Woo is hym that with this cheyne is encheyned, for ther is noon that hatth power to vnbynde hym but Godde alloone.

[Of Remedies That Is Ayens the Synne of Ire]

It is righte, nowe that we haue spoken of this vice, to sette som remedye whereby men maye knowe to restreyne theyre owne ire. The firste is to thynke on the dethe of Criste Iesus. Wherefore Seynt Austyn seith: If we sette in oure mynde, seithe he, oure loordes passyon, that is to seye, the bitter deeth that he soffred for vs, we shoolde nothyng haue to soffre but that we shoolde gladly suffre it deboneyrly and eesyly for the love of hym. The secon[f. 48]de remedye for man is to be stylle and that he answere not to hym that doothe hym or seythe to hym any reproche or vilonye. For Salamon seythe in his Prouerbes: Whoosoo answereth not a felle foole he eeseth hym of his felnes. Of the whiche men rede in *Vitis Patr[u]m* of an hooly fader of whom men asked whye feendis hated hym soo mooche. He answered froo that he was made monke he purposed in his herte that never oo felle woorde shholde isse oute of his mouthe. The thirde remedye is to thynke and to considre that al that ever we haue to suffre is be the ordenaunce of God. For if a man thynke to doo evyl to another yet he maye not doo it but God yeve hym power. And somtyme he yeveth it, that is to the dampnacion of hym that dooth evil to oothir and to the saluacion of hym that suffreth it if he take it pacyently. And this oughte to be grete ioye to rightwis men. For al tribulacion fareth as a medycynable drynke that a ryghtwys leche yeveth to his freendis to drynke, as he ded to good Ioob, the whiche seyde in his thankyng: If we haue receyved goodes of Godde soo many as that we haue receyved oute of nombre, why receyve we not the evilles as welle? God yeveth theym to vs [...]. The iiii remedye is to considre his owne defaultis. And if he wylle that a man forbere hym in theyme, he sholde as gladly forbere oother in theyre defaultis. Wherefore Salamon seith: The [ne]dye is mercyfull. And for that som be lightly angry with oother defaultes because theye knowe not welle theyre owne in theymeselfe. Therefore seithe Seynt Austin: If thow angre the with thy seruaunte whan he doothe amysse, thowe sholdeste be angry with thyselfe; thowe dooest amysse. The fyfthe and the laste remedye that he shalle sette is to consyder to oure eende and too oure deethe and weretoo we shalle torne aftyr oure deethe. Of the whiche Ecclesiastes seithe: Remembre the of thy laste eende, and leve alle ire and alle hate, and vmbethynke the of oure loordes iugement, the whiche shalle be fulle ferefulle, and greve the not with thy neyghborugh. For whoosoo wil not foryeve alle ire and alle felounye in this worlde he shal never haue foryevenes of his synnes; he shalle rathir haue euerlastyng dampnacion with Iudas, Herode, and with the feendys.

[Of Synne of Slouthe and of the Branchettis]

[f. 48v] Nowe shalle we speke of the fourethe hede vice, the whiche is called slouthe and is as myche worthe as shrewdenes, hevynes, slouthe, langour, ennoy to doo welle, the whiche causeth a man that he loveth not but idelnes, rest, and to sleepe as an hogge for to confounde man and to doo hym shame. And ayenst thy[s] vice cryeth al that be in hevyn and in erthe: the sonne, the mone, and the sterrys, the whiche cesseth neythyr nyghte ne daye of rynnyng too and froo grete iorneys for to doo Goddis commaundement and for to serve man; also the erthe, the whiche sesseth not to bere fruite; and herbes the whiche euery of theyme serveth of his crafte to his [f. 49] power; also doome beestis, for the whiche Salamon seithe: Sent the slowe man to the pyssemer for to lerne witte; also worldely synneres, the which soffreth soo myche woo for to gete helle; also laborerys and pore peple, the whiche suffreth mych woo for to gete theyre lyvynge. These crye ayens slowe peple. Also good peple that soffreth soo myche penance for the love of God; also seyntis the whiche hatthe soffred soo many tormentis and angellis that cesseth not to prayse Godde, for the whiche Lucyfer that woolde sytte amonges theyme was put oute of hevyn; also Goddys sonne that soffred soo moche peyne whiles that he was in erthe yet for no nede that he hadde but for to shewe and to teche and to yeve example to vs for to travayle, for there is never oon idyll in Goddis hous. Aa goode loorde, whate man and womman oughte to haue grete shame that lyven in this wise the whiche waketh not with soo many cryes and is not quikned with soo many examples. This vice is an evyll roote the whiche casteth ful many evyl branches and fareth as erthe that bereth but nettelys. Take hiede nowe howe he gooeth whom love leedeth and the grace of God. It yeveth hym goode begynnyng, better amendyng, and right goode endyng. Ayeins these iii goodenesses be iii evilles that slouthe maketh. Slouthe maketh an evill begynnyng be vi vicis that groweth of hym and wors amendyng be oother vi vicys and ryght evyll eendyng be vi oother. It is noo mervel though he leese the game to whom the feende casteth thees xviii pointis, the whiche be xviii smale branches that groweth of this evyl stokke.

[Of Lewkenes]

The firste smal branche is lewkenes, of whom as it seemeth groweth al evilles, as whan a man loveth lytyl and wey[k]ly that the whiche he sholde love strongely and feruentlye. This is a disseordenat love the whiche feebleth and neantys-sheth and leueth alle goode deedys. [f. 49v] And hereof it commeth that an oolde felawe the whiche goothe with a potente is stronger to doo penaunce than is a fayre yonge man the whiche seemeth stronge as a champion or a knyghte that is worthe a torneye, for ther is noon that yeveth soo myche strenghthe as doothe love. And whan it fayleth strengthe [fayleth]. It fareth as lewke water doothe, the whiche doothe harme to the herte and maketh it to vomitte. And this lewkenes maketh a man abhominable and lewke anenst Godde for that he vomyteth hym and casteth hym owte of his house and from his servyce, as Seynt Iohn seithe in the Pocalipse. Whan a potte is lewke, flyes commeth the gladlyer thertoo than ootherwyse, and whan it boilleth, gladly theye eschewe it and flee it because it is to hoote. And whan the ovyn is lewke, gladly the harlot entreth into it. Oon the same wise, the feende is soon entred into a lewke herte.

[Of Tendirnesse]

The seconde lytyl branche is tendernes [...].

[Of Idelnesse]

[...] the whiche is a fulle grete synne, for it is ayeins the commaundement that Godde made to Adam. For he commaunded hym and seide to hym that he sholde labour and lyve with his swote. For as the gospell wittenesseth, whan the feende fyndeth man idell, he hatthe leve to tempte hym and to entre into hym as he dede into the hogges. For whan he fyndeth them idille he setteth theym awerke. Firste he maketh hem to [thynke] velonyes and than to desyre lecheries and malyses. Also idilnes is a fulle grete syn. For an idell man the whiche leeseth his tyme leeseth the mooste precyous thynge that he hatthe and that the whiche he shalle never recouere and the goodys that he myght doo and the wa[gi]z that he myghte gete.

Thowe shalt nowe knowe that ther be iiii maner of idelnesses. Som be idyl because that theye con not labour, oouther [f. 50] because theye maye not, the thridde because þat theye be ashamed, the fourthe because that theye wyl not. And al thees be to blame. For thoo that con not syn because theye lerne not. Thoo that seye theye maye not lyeth, for ther is noon so feble ne soo softely norryshed but that he maye wel praye and thanke Godde. And that is the beste and the moost honest labour that man maye doo. And whosoo doothe not that is idyll whatesooeuer he doo, if his dede be not vppon Godde. For whoosoo prayeth weele weele dooth: *Qui bene agit bene orat*. Thoo that haue shame to labour haue shame to doo welle. Theye oughte to haue shame to lyve, for theyr lyve is foule and shamefull. And it is noo lyfe for man but for an hogge, the whiche doothe noo goode whyle that he lyveth. Thoo that wyl not synneth moore than thoo oother, for theye be not worthye to eete brede, as Seint Poule seithe, because that theye labour not with men but rathir laboreth with feendys in places of sorowe.

[Of Hevynesse]

The fourthe smale branche is the vice of hevynes. For whan a man is hevye he loveth but lye and sleepe and the halfe of his lyfe leeseth and dispendith in sleepe. Oure loorde blameth myche that lyfe in the gospelle and biddeth that we shal wake and praye often, as he hym yaf vs example þe whiche spente the dayes in prechyng and the nyghtys in prayer. Of this vice groweth iiii maner of synnes. For fyrst theye synne in as myche as theye love soo myche reste that theye thynke theye haue never slepte inowe but compleyneth euer that theye maye not sleepe. Also siche tymys as that theye oughte best to wake than sleepe theye gladlyest, that is in the mornyng whan theye sholde prayse, speke, and praye, as the scripture wittenesseth vs and creatures as birdes that [f. 50v] syngeth in the mornynge and praysen God soo swetely. But theye hadde lever leese iii messys than oo swete whan hit commeth in the mornyng.

[Of Shrewdenesse]

The fyfthe lytil branche is shrewdenes, that is whan man lyeth in synnes þat greveth hym myche and agreeth to the feendis temptacions and seeth þat thorugh the whiche he leesith bothe Godde and his soule be fyne shrewdenes, that he wil not lifte vppe his hede be contricion ne crye oute be confession ne strecche forthe his hande be satisfaccion for to receyve the feyre cloothynge of vertu and the feire coroune of blysse of Goddis hande, the whiche prayeth hym swetely to repente hym. He this is like the shrewe the whiche had lever rote in a foule deepe preson than to haue the peyne to goo vppe a fewe greeys and goo his weye and to Naaman the whiche wolde not bathe hym in coolde water for to hele hym of his mesellerye and to thoo of whom Seint Poule seythe that for shrewdenes woolde not dyspoyle theym of an oolde lowsy rotyn gowne for a feyre riche gowne newe and clene and to thoo of whom hooly Isaye telleth that sawe feendis the which bare aweye al the goodes that theye haue as lyghtly as men sholde doo eggys from an hennes neest. And theye haue not soo myche strengthe to meve the wyngys for to defende theym as the henne doothe ayeins the puttokke ne to meve the mouthe for to crye as the curre doothe that abaieth the theef and dryveth hym aweye with his noyse. And ther is another shrewdenes in hym that hatthe a goode feelde and soffreth it fulle of netlys and fulle of thornys because he wil not ouercomme theyme, for he wyl neyther daunte his herte ne chastye his bodye. Dauid the prophet sheweth vs anoother shrewdenes of hym that kepeth breede, that is to seye, Goddys woorde dayly in his mouthe as theys clerkys and theys cloystererys doon, and theye dye for hunger and [sterveth] hooly because that theye foryeteth it atte evyn, that is to seye, to putte it in dede. Is it not [f. 51] nowe a grete shrewdenes that he wil not bowe his eerys withoute moore? But his herte the whiche is better had leuer leue mete than defende hym, that is to seye, from evyll thoughtis and desires, because theye maye not ne wyl not meve the to doo noo goode dede. And of hym that seythe the caste of the hous, thoo be worldis [charches] the whiche putteth oute his yee because he wil not torne the righte yee toward the walle, that is to seye, towarde Godde. And of hym that lyeth in his bedde, that is to seye, in delyte and letteth his feete brenne, thoo be his wylles the whiche bereth the sowle, as feete doothe the bodye, because he hatthe [not] soo myche strengthe to drawe theym to hym. Whan shalle syche a man wynne hevyn, the whiche be worthynes maye not defende hym froo flyes ne drawe his feete to hym ne torne hys heede to the walle ne chewe his brede?

[Of Pusillanimite]

The vi smale branche is pusillanimitee, that is to seye, feblenes of herte. In this vice be theye that be aferde of noughte the whiche ther not begynne to doo well for fere that good shulde fayle theym. And therfore it is righte that he fayle theyme. And soo he wylle, as Salamon seithe. This is liche the fere of theym that derre not goo be nyghte but dredeth and wote not whereof. This is lyche the fere of a dreme. A man dremeth that he moste passe over a brigge of glas or of isce and is soo soore aferde that he deyeth alle quykke. And yet he is not aferde of his de[d]ely enemye, the whiche o trouthe is ouer his heede with a swerde drawen. He this is liche to hym that derre not entre into the patthe of a goode weye for the snayle that sheweth hym his hornes and to a childe that ther not goo in the weye of hissyng of gees, the whiche maketh contenaunce as that theye woolde rynne on theym. For the feende hatth no power ayeins hym that is in grace but for to whistle as a goose and to shewe his hornes as a snayle, but when he hatthe a soule vnder hym he is cruelle and stronge as an vnycorne. Thees vi vycys hooldeth a man and taketh from hym goode begynnynge.

[Of the Secounde Evyl That Slouthe Dothe and of VI Tachis of Evil Delaye]

[f. 51v] Slouthe maye not haue goode begynnyng for oother vi vicys the whiche be vi tecches of an eville seruaunte, the whiche doon soo that noo worthy man wille withholde theym in his hous ne in his seruice, as whan he is vntrewe, negligent, foryetefull, sloggy, lache, and dysseyveable. Thees vi vicis taketh froo man goode understandyng. Whoosoo yeveth soon yeveth twiis, and whoosoo yeveth of his withdraweyngly leeseth his thanke, and yet it costeth hym as myche as hym that yeveth lyghtlye. That is trewe as the pater noster. Whan a man yeveth hym to serue Godde, the feende knoweth it welle. And because þat he woote welle that Godde yeveth to man good will to serue hym, if he maye not take froo hym that good wille, he maketh hym to leve it as myche as he maye, for the disputacion is grete betwene the goode angell and the badde. For thowe shalt knowe that euery man hatthe a goode angell to counselle hym, to kepe hym, and to teche hym to doo welle, and also hee hatthe an evil angell, the whiche doothe the contrarye and tysceth hym to leve goodnes be this vice þe whiche is called sloggyng or slouthe and techeth hym to doo eville be thoo oother cheef vicys. The good angell biddeth hym kepe his virginite and his innocence and begyn too doo welle whilest he is yonge and it shalle euer pleese hym moore and moore. And if thowe lyve hoolylye before angellis thowe shalt of God be loued and worshipped of the worlde, and alsoo thowe shalt lyve the meryer. For Salamon seithe: There is no ioye that maye compare to the ioye of a clene herte. And thowe shalt lyve the more surelye, for thow shalt neyther dowte dethe ne doome, helle, purgatorye, ne worldis blame, as thoo dowte that doothe eville. For the more goode that thowe doost, the more tresor thowe shalt haue in hevyn. He is a foole that hadde lever ii elles of clothe than xl. The evil angell [seyeth] to hym: Doo be witte siche as thowe wilt doo; thowe maiste yet lyve to goode age withowte ageinge. Alle goothe in the goode ende. Doo [f. 52] as oother doo. Wilt thowe nowe be cryed oon and holde for a dawe and for a papelard? The goode angell seythe to hym ayeinward: Of goode lyfe cometh goode ende. And Seint Poule seithe that God hooldeth theyme for fooles that in alle theyre lyfe cesseth not to sowe nettelys and that in hervest woolde gedder whete. Thowe haste a grete iorneye to doo. Ryse eerly, and thowe shalt doo as the wise. If thowe falle in the feendis prison, þou shalt not come owte whan that thowe wooldest; and the moore that thowe art bounde with synne and with evil costomes, the harder it shalle be to þe to ascape. It is to hardde to thynke to make a feyre seeme in an oolde pylche and for to lerne an oolde roile to amble and an oolde dogge to wepe and an oolde synner to serue God. They answerith: If thowe wilt doo soo, abide than vnto lenten, for þan is tyme to confesse the and to doo penaunce and not nowe. The goode angell answereth: Thowe hast noo mor[n]e. Men dyeth in oother tymes more than in lenten. Whoosoo wolde yeve the iii pounde worthe of land, thowe haddest leuer haue it todaye than tomorowe. Take todaye as gladly the kyngdom of hevin and the grace of God and vse the goode wylle that God hatthe yoven the, for peraventur thowe maiste leese it er noon in siche wise that thowe shalt never recouer it. That knoweth the feendys welle. And therfore seketh he soo many delayes: first to the yeris ende, than vnto aage, than vnto lenten, and than vnto that men haue doon theyre occupacions that theye haue in hande, and than vnto a wooke, and than vnto a daye, and vnto an houre when he maye noo ferther. And [knowe] withowte dowte of an houre of respyte that a man yeveth hym, men maye yeve it hym in siche plyte that he maye wel seye the terme of oo daye is worthe c *s*, for be siche respite he hatthe wonne moo than c ml soules and withdrawen frọo goode dede another c m[l] soules and from goode wille and ledde with hym into helle to p[e]rd[ici]on. Wherefore [f. 52v] there is noo perill soo greete as delaye of good begynnyng whan God yeveth the goode wylle.

[Of Negligence]

After delaye cometh negligence. For whoosoo begynneth goodnes delayinglye it is noo mervell though he doo it necligentlye. This is a vice with the whiche alle the worlde is spotted. Forsothe, I trowe that ther is noon that is quite of it, and that is because that he is to debonayre. Whoo is he that maye vaunt hym that withowte necgligence doothe his trewe power nyghte and daye to vse his tyme welle, to kepe his herte welle, to discipline his bodye welle, to helpe his neghbourgh with the graces that he hatthe for to multiplye, to prayse and to worshipp seintis, to desire, to praye, and to loue his maker? Whoo is he that is righte besy to employe welle the xxiiii houris the whiche be in the daye and in the nyghte, liche as the marchaunt doothe that is in the feyre with xxiiii marke of syluer? And whoo is hee that is soo besye, diligent, to kepe his herte and to desire it to serve God and to plese hym, as a ladye dooth too kemb her heede for to pleese her housbond? Of the whiche it is greete woo if men toke righte goode heede thertoo. And whoo is he that doothe siche peyne to discipline his bodye and to excite it to Goddis seruice as the kyngys favcouner doothe to dresse his bridde or as the laborer doothe to wynne vi *d* on the daye? And whoo is he that dooth soo trulye his deuoire to helpe his neghborgh as þe membres dooth of a mannes bodye oon to helpe anoother? And whoo is he that is soo besye to put in dede the graces that he hatthe and to multiplye theym as an vsurrere doothe his pens? And whoo is hee alsoo that coustometh and is tentif to kepe hym as God is to gouerne hym? And alsoo whoo thynketh on God as God dothe on hym? And whoo seithe [f. 53] gremercy for euery goodnes that God doothe to hym? For thes vi thynges to the whiche wee be bounden and in the whiche wee be necgligent, Salamon seithe to vs that the moste rightwisse man that is falleth vii tymes on the daye, truly xl. The debonaire Crist Iesus seide fulle welle to Seynt Petir whan he called hym and yafe hym power to binde and vnbinde if a man synned wheder he sholde foryeve hym vii tymes, and oure loorde seide to hym: I seye not to the vii tymes withoute more but be vii tymes lxx tymes.

[Of Forȝetilnesse]

Aftyr necgligens cometh foryetilnes. For whoosoo is necgligent often foryeteth. And whoo is he that is quyte of this synne and that is soo wise for to thynke to serve and to loue God, soo that alle his thoughtis be euer to hym and that alle his werkys be euer proprely for God and that in som of thees thynges [n]is ever foryetill? Truly noon. For, as Seynt Austin seythe, the commaundement that God biddeth vs, the whiche is þe firste and the grettest commaundement: Thowe shalt love thye God with alle thye wylle withowte any geynseyng, with alle thyn vnderstandyng withouten errour, with alle thy mynde withowte foryetyng, noon maye pleynelye fullefille it in this worlde. For the worlde and the bodye and the feende greveth the herte and the mynde soo myche that vnethe a man maye seye, if he be not righte parfite, oo verse or oo pater noster but that his herte thynketh ellyswhere. And this is the thynge that in the worlde moost greveth hooly soules and fyne hertis, the whiche wolde ever haue God in mynde, when theye see the herte that is soo fleeynge and ouerleyde with veyne thoughtis that ther where it herith the messe songyn as hye as men maye and hymselfe singeth therwith, he herith ne vnderstandeth hymselfe ne noon oother but maketh castellis in Spaygne and thynketh on idilnes. For [f. 53v] thees ii synnes of necgligence and foryetylnes wherein euery man falleth more than xl tymes on the daye theye be soo often confessed, thoo that loveth Godde wel and that knoweth wele theyre defautis and is ofter confessed in oo daye than oother be in an hole yere, the whiche seithe noo sighte where that þey doo noothynge vnethe wenynge to haue oo synne and theye mervelle that oother confesse theym soo often.

[Of Slokkenesse]

The tother tacche of an evil seruaunt is sloggynes, the whiche commeth for fault of herte and of evil costum, the whiche folweth a man soo that vnethe he yeveth hym too doo any good dede. And if the kynge of Ingland woolde haue a quycke seruaunte and a good, it is better right that the kynge of kyngys haue syche oon. And siche be angellis that serueth in hevyn. And siche shal we be whan we come thedder. And this require we whan we seye in the pater noster: [*Fiat voluntas tua sicut in celo et in terra*]. That is to seye, feyre fader of hevyn, make that thy wille be doon in vs as in angellis the whiche maye not be as longe as the soule bereth his bodye. Wherefore, though þat the sperit be iuste, lighte, and desyrous to flee be thought and be contemplacion, yette maye it not but whan it pleyseth the Hooly Goost, for it is bounden to the perche as a favcon the whiche maye not flee but whan his maister wille. Thowe shalt nowe knowe that ther be iii maner of lyeinys the whiche maketh man sloggy, that is to seye, synne and vsage of feblenes. It is noo merveyle though hee that lyeth in dedely synne be sloggy, yea forsoothe sloggy, to doo good. And though alle goodenes noye hym, yet it is mervel that he maye no goode doo, as he that hatth kynnes in his handys, dyggys in his feete, moules in his heelys, and morfewe in the necke. Wherefore with the dedely synne wherin he lyeth, he dooth more than ml oother synnes whan he maye not doo the goodnes that he sholde doo. Soo fa[f. 54]reth it be hym that is bounde be evil costum, for he maye not or he wille not doo the goodnes that he shold whan he is sette in siche plyte be evil lernyng. As Seint Bernard seythe: If he maye not eete his brede with the sauour of his bodye, let hym eete it with woo of herte. Therfore thoo be blyssed that in theyre yougthe lerneth good condicions, as the gentyl birde doothe. For Seint Bernard seithe that there [is] a ientille birde of siche nature that froo that his birdis begynne to flee he casteth theym oute of the nest and maketh theym to gete theyre lyvynge if theye wil eete because that theye sholde nat lerne evil [costum] and that theye sholde not becom sloggy in theire yough. And he wil not purveye for theym but rather maketh theym to serve. Whan that a man is bounde with feblenes of bodye and that this feebilnes commeth of nature than that feblenes is noo synne. It is rather a peyn and occasion to goo the sonner to God. And [if] it com of lewkenes, of tendernes, and of siche hevynes of the whiche we haue spokyn, than is that sloggynes synne. And if it com of fooly ferventnes or of vndiscrecion be the whiche it ouerledeth his bodye and putteth it in langour and in sloggynes, that sloggynes is not withowte dedely synne. For as Seint Bernard seith: Whoosoo travayleth his bodye and dismesureth it, he synneth in many maneres. For he taketh from his bodye his labour and his iorneyes, from his soule his deuocion, froo God his seruyce, from his neghbourgh his helpe and his goode example. And of alle thees thynges he is culpable to Godde because he wille not goo whan he maye goo be reson.

[Of Lachesse]

Aftir cometh that oother vice whan he is lache and empeyryng froo daye to daye. Thus doo many of the seruauntis of God, the whiche at the begynnyng be to worthye and to feruent, but theye goo empeyryng froo yere to yere, and thoo that were goostly atte the begynnyng becommeth more flesshelye [f. 54v] than oother, lyche as a lyonesse the whiche atte firste tyme hatthe v whelpes and atte the seconde iiii and at thirde iii and at fourthe ii and at the fyfte oon and euer aftir but bareygne. And therfor Salamon sent s[l]owe pepill to pyssemyres for to take example and to lerne witte, the whiche alle theyre lyfe encresceth and becometh more stronge and more [v]igorous. And soo doothe thoo that be ledde be the love of God into this natural place, that is, to [God]. Syche mevyng cresceth euer, the whiche is of nature, as it sheweth be hym that descendeth from heyghte. Froo the hyer he cometh, the moore he cometh froo the ayre. But whan it mounteth hye, because he doothe it vice, the moore he mounteth, the lachelyer he meveth. Lyche as a stoone of an engyne whan it mounteth soo hye that it maye noo ferther, though it touchid a man that were soo hye, it sholde haue noo power too hurte hym. Thus fareth it be worthy pepil and be slowe in the seruice of God. The toon mendeth euer in vigorousnesse; the toother fanteth euer in sorwes.

[Of Defaulte]

The vi vice of an evill seruaunt is whan he defauteth afore the ende of his terme. And men be wont to seye: Whoosoo serueth and not deserueth, his hire he leeseth; and whoosoo leveth the knotte, he leeseth the game. And Seint Poule seithe: Whoosoo sheweth the batayle hatthe not coroune of victorie. And whoosoo boweth beste he maye be nere to falle. And a man that is soo bowynge is nere to ouerthrowe and to falle in dedely syn and hooly to goo oute of Goddis seruice and if hee abide to praye he fareth as an hinginge walle, soo that hee the whiche sholde serue and bere moste be served and borne. And alsoo it fareth be hym as be the ymage that Nabugodonosor sawe in dreeme be a visyon the whiche hadde an hede of goolde, [f. 55] armes and feete of sylfer, belye and thyes of laton, and the breste halfe iryn and halfe myre. Thus slouthe ledeth a man: first as in feruentnesse and in charitee, the whiche we vnderstand be the goolde; than he goothe forthe be reson and trouthe, þe whiche we vnderstande be the sylver; aftir that he boweth be ipocrisye and be vauntyng, the whiche we vnderstande be laton the whiche resouneth and is liche goolde; aftir that he falleth into harlotrye and into hardenes of synne, the whiche we vnderstande be the iryn and the myre.

[Of the III Evil That Slowthe Dothe and VI Pointis That Be Therinne]

There be yet vi evil pointis wherewith slouthe putteth a man toward the ende, that is to seye, inobedience, impacience, grucchyng, hevynes, langoure, and wanhoope. Understande nowe howe that whan a man is sloggy, lache, and eville, if that a man charge hym to doo penaunce or any obedience that hym seemeth harde, first he excuseth hym that hee maye not doo it; and if he take [it] vppon hym, hee doothe but litel thereof or noughte and be his shrewdenes falleth into inobedience. Than Salamon seythe that a man shold stoon a sloggy felawe with myyry stoones and with the bowellys of a kowe. That is to seye that a man sholde repreve hym with harde shamefulle woordes. [f. 55v] Than falleth he into vnpacience. For lyche as he maye noothyng bere be obedience oon the same wise he maye noothynge suffre be pacience. He is nowe ever in ire and in eville wille, soo that noon derre speke to hym for his avayle. But the feende derre wel speke there for his avayle. Than he setteth hym in grucchynge. And Salamon seythe that his herte fareth as a whele, the whiche is charged with heye, that [slowly] gooth euer cryinge and brayinge. Soo he this compleyneth of alle his neghbourghes: of thoo that be above hym that theye be to cruelle, of thoo that be abowte hym that theye [...] con not serve hym ne doothe noothyng too hym aright. In siche wise he fyndeth abowte hym but sorwe. Than falleth he in hevynes and freteth his brydel be hymselfe and is euer hevy and moornyng and begynneth to take the er[res] of helle. And than this hevynes overledeth hym soo that whatsooeuer a man doothe to hym or seithe it noyeth hym and alle that ever he seithe or hereth. And thus than falleth he into langoure and is anoyed for to lyve in siche wise that he hymselfe desyreth the dethe, and somtyme hee purchaceth it. [f. 56] Aftir that whan that the fende hatthe putte hym into thees evill pointes [he] yeveth hym the bodyly strooke for he putteth hym into whanhoope and pleyeth with hym as with a man dispeyred, for he dowteth to doo noo synne whatesooeuer it be, and whan the feende hatthe caste hym into siche noyance and plyte and into siche langoure þan he resoneth hym and seithe to hym in his herte: Woofull caytif, whate doost thowe? Howe gooste thowe? Thowe maiste not endure thus. Sette alle atte alle and let this be. It were bettyr to dye than to lyve thus. The caytyf leveth hym and letteth it be and seithe the evill woorde: God shalle doo with me what he wylle, for I maye [ne] suffre thees sorwes [more]. Nowe is he recreant. Nowe the feende lepeth vppon hym as vppon his mare and ledeth hym hyder and thyder from oo synne to anoother. We see this oopynly in thees renogat monkes and in thees wanhooped mordererys that douteth not for to doo no malyce ne noon vntrowth. And it is noo merveyle. For God hatthe voyded theyme hys hous, and the feende hath receyved theym into his servys. And thoo that were sluggy and dulle to doo welle be nowe woorthy an vygorous to malyce and fareth as a woode hounde, the whiche knoweth neyther his maister ne noon oother but byteth bothe here and there and at laste dyeth in an evill dethe. Slouthe ledeth a man to syche an ende. Thees bee the xviii pointes that the feende hatthe vppon slowe pepyll. Therefore it is noo merveyle though theye lese the game.

[Of Remedies ayens the Synne of Slouthe]

Whan that we haue nowe spoken of the synne of slouthe and of sloggynes, we wil sette som remedyes ayeins this vice. The first reme[f. 56v]dye is that a man be euer besye in som goode besynes thorugh the whiche the feende fynde not a man idill, as that Seint Ierom seythe, for an idell man is in fulle greete perylle. And whan the feende seeith hym idyll, he tempteth hym in many maneres. He maketh hym to tente to oother thynges than he sholde doo whan he wille not tente too that the whiche he sholde. And of this we rede of Seint Antonye, the whiche was in his hermytage and was tempted with the synne of slouthe, and he seide to oure lorde: Syr, I desyre to be saved, but veyne thoughtis torment me and wille not lete me. Shewe me what I shalle doo and howe I sholde saue me. And he saugh an angell of oure lorde in lykenes of a man the whiche was lyke to hym, and he twyned a coorde. And than he roose and went to his prayers, and than hee sette hym ayein to his werke and ayein rose and went to his prayers. And he seide: Antonie, doo thus; soo shalt thowe be saved. Oure loorde hatthe therfore yoven diuers membres to man and many because he sholde serve hym withalle. Wherefore man sholde serve oure lorde somtyme in syngyng, in praysyng hym, in yevyng hym thankes with the mouthe, and with handes to labour in wrytynge. For as Seint Poule seithe: Whoosoo laboureth not sholde not ete. And Ecclesiastes seithe: Doo and werke al that thyn hande maye doo. The seconde remedye is to consydre the peynes of helle and the ioye of hevyn. And to this seithe Seint Austin: If thowe fere the, take heede to the hyre that thowe shalt haue. Wee haue example hereof in *Vitis Patrum* off a frere that come to his abbot and axed hym whye he was acciduell, *id est*, [...] in his chambyr. And the abbot answered to hym: Because thowe haste not seen the blysse that we abide ne the tormentis that we dowte. The thirde remedye is to be in feleshippe of goode pepill. For thoo that be slowe [f. 57] to doo welle, it is nede to theym to haue siche in theyre feleshipp that be theyre examples and there techynges maye shewe theym lyghte and attyce theym too doo welle and to helpe with theyre prayeres. The iiii remedye is to considre þe greete perylle that wee be in in this worlde. Thre tormentis and perilles there be that maketh men to wake and distorbed to slepe: peryl of watir, of fyre, and of thefys, in the whiche gostelye wee be atte alle tymes. There is noo daye but som wawe of evil thought walweth in owre hertys and that the fyre of evill desyre ne embrasceth oure conscience and but that oure v wittys the whiche sholde be oure seruauntis and owre keperes be theefes to vs and robbeth vs of oure goodes. Wherefore Ieremye seythe: My [ye] hatthe robbed my soule. The v remedye and the laste that we wil sette [i]s to beseche the grace of God. Therfore whan any feleth hym slowefulle or sloggy to doo welle he sholde be in prayere and aske of God his grace, withowte the whiche noon maye doo any goode deede, as oure lorde seithe in the gospelle: Withoute me, seithe he, that is to seye, withowte my grace, yee maye noothynge doo the whiche putteth oute alle slouthe. Cypion the Aufrycan, the whiche was oon of the wysest paynemys that euer was, he was gladly idyll and aloone, fulle of thoughtis and spake litill. Whan men asked hym whate he dedde whan he was aloon and idill, he answered thus: I am never the lesse aloon, though that I be aloon, ne the lesse idyll, though that I be idyll. This woorde hatthe doon myche goode to many a man and yet shalle doo, and it hatthe ben gretely praysed and autoriȝed with seintis and prophetis. Tullius, the whiche was oon of the wysest philoȝo[f. 57v]phres that ever was, remembred this woorde and praysed it and seide: A goode Godde, what this is an hye woorde, a woorthye, and a wyse of a goode man that whan he was idyll than was hee mooste besye, for than treted hee and ordeyned his greete besynesses and his grete quarellys; and whan he was aloon than was he never þe lesse aloon, for he was with the beste freende that he hadde, that was, with hymselfe to whom he spake prevylye and homelylye. Therefore thees ii thynges the whiche setteth the foole in sorouwe and in noyaunce setteth hym this in soolas and in ioye, the whiche is idilnes and [solitude]. Seint Ambros geyne taketh this woorde and prayseth it and seithe thus: It nedith not to Cypion too haue lerned al aloon to be aloon whan he is aloon and not idill whan that he is idill, for this woorde is true in a goode man that is cristened, wise, and iuste. For whan he is aloon than is he prevyly with Godde, and whan he is idill than treeteth he in grete besynes and in grete quarellys and kepeth his parlement betwene Godde and hym. And therfore seythe Seneque that ther is noothynge soo mooche worthe to man the whiche God desyreth as to speke litill to othir and myche to hymselfe. And Seint Bernard seithe that a goode man is never soo welle at ease as in his owne hous, that is, whan he is hoomly in his conscience with hymselfe, for than speketh hee with the mooste veraye freende that he hatth, that is, to hymselfe. But an eville man and a foole hatthe never wors beynge than in his owne hous. And thereof it cometh that ther is soo myche pepill the whiche con not be in reste ne aloon, for theye fynde noo solas in theymselfe. And therfore seke theye owteward. And for to flee idilnes theye doo idelnesse. Theye hereth, seyeth, and pleyeth at the deez and atte the tables and hereth romaunses fulle of fables. Theye speketh of tryffles and iaapes and maketh grete [f. 58] waste and grete largesse of the precious tyme, of the whiche theye shalle haue yette fulle grete nede, and theye lese the tresor of the precyous herte and fylleth it ayein with vanite. Theye oopyn the castelle, and their enemyes entreth into it. Theye calle theym idyll woordys. But theye be not alloonly idyll withoute more, for theye be harmefull and perlyous, as thoo that voydeth the herte of alle goodnes and filleth it with alle evylles as with siche as that theye moste yeve compte of afore God at the daye of doome, as that the gospell seythe, the whiche is not ellys to seye an idyll woorde is noon other thynge but a noyous woorde, a dyssehonest woorde, or an vnprofitable.

[Of Foly Feruentnesse or Ardentnesse to Do Well]

As that slouthe is synne, soo it is a foolysshe feruentnes and indiscrete. There be som that wille in noo wise condescend to theyre flesshe, but theye defule it be fastyng, be wacche, [be] penaunce that theye doo withoute discrecion. And that is right a grete syn. For as Seint Bernard seithe: Whoosoo distroyeth his bodye and feebleth it be vndiscrete desire or feruentnes to doo welle soo that goostely goodnesses be empeched, he taketh from his bodye myghte and strenghthe to doo weele, from his sperit good desire, from his neghborugh good example to worshipp Godde. And thus it is sacrilege, for he hatth filed and distroyed the temple of Criste Iesus, that is to seye, his bodye. And in alle thees thyngys he is culpable ayenst Godd. Seint Poule seythe that oure seruice sholde be resonable, that is to seye, [be] discrecion. Speke be discrecion. And God wille that a man serue hym be reson. He wille that a man distroye vices and not his bodye be to grete chargynge with penaunce but be reson and be temperance, soo that if any begynne any goodnes or seruice that he maye performe [f. 58v] it. Also a man is a resonable creature. And therfore he sholde werke and serve be reson. And he oughte moore to folwe wysedom and moore to doo be reson þan be strengthe, for the feende, ageyns whom wee haue euer batayle, feyghteth moore be subtilte and be malyce than be strenghth. And therfore we oughte the moore to defende vs ayeins hym be reson and be witte than be strengthe. For as wee rede in the Booke of Sapience: Wytte is better than strength and a wise man than a stronge. Wherefore it behoueth that the conuersacion of a wyse man fare as the clymbeyng oppon a ledder, where a man ought to clymbe be reson and discrecion. For if he falle into any sekenes there where that he falleth and descendeth alle downe be fooly feruentnes it is wors than it was atte the begynnynge. Aftir folye and indiscrete feruentnes often pryde and veinglorie folweth and commeth. Wherefore noon sholde distroye his bodye bot gouerne it be reson, and thoo fastes and penaunces that men doo be doon be discrecion and mekenes. For as Seint Austin seithe: Whoosoo gloryfyeth hym of a goode dede maketh of vertu synne. Theye doo alsoo ayeins the ordenaunce of hooly churche, for theye bere the crosse afore the lyghte [...] the whiche is wors. That is to seye that theye doo penaunce withoute discrecion and at the begynnyng take armes soo hevye that theye the whiche sholde kepe theyme and defende theym froo theyre enemyes be theyme theye be often taken as be vnpacience and be noyance. And it seemeth to som that theye maye not be hoole if theye be not mansleerres of theyre bodye be fastyng and be penaunce. And theye thynke that men sholde withdrawe the substance of the bodye froo the sonne of Godde, and yette theye were worthye to ete goolde and to drynke bawme. And notwithstandyng the delyte of metys men oughte greetely doubte. For men taketh mete often to delicious and with to grete feruentnes, and the consolacion that men hatth often in delicious metis taketh aweye ofte goostely consolacion. And alsoo Seint Bernarde seithe: The goostely consolacion is too delicious. Yette [f. 59] noon sholde seke in metys ne in oother thynges to bodyly delite. But men sholde and maye take siche as is nedeful to the sustenaunce of the bodye, soo that a man maye serve, prayse, and thanke his maker and that a man take it not with too grete feruentnes ne in to grete quantite. And whoosoo taketh it thus, it is noo synne, but it is rather meede. Yet ther be som men that be goode and mercyfull to oother and cruel to theymselfe. And whoosoo be evill to hymselfe to whom is hee goode? Seint Bernard seithe that a man sholde not alweye troste to fylle his bely and to doo alle his wille. A man sholde rather gouerne it and refreyne it be reson.

[Of the Synne of Couetice and of Branchettis Therof]

The v heede vice is covetice, the whiche regneth in the worlde that nowe is moore than any oother vice. Be the whiche it sheweth that the woorlde ageth and is in his laste aage. For the woorlde fareth as man. In a mannes yougthe reigneth more iolynes and lecherye than any oother vice; whan hee [f. 59v] is in myddel aage, reigneth in hym pride and ambicion; and whan he is oolde, scornes [and] covetice. And the worlde in his first aage was corromped with lecherye, for the whiche the floode come and drowned alle. After that reigned pryde and ambicion as longe as the iiii emperoures were in theyre dominacioune oon after anoother: first the Calden, aftir hym he of Grece that ouercome the Calden, aftir theym the Gregoys, and than the Romaynes. Nowe atte the laste is come Dame Auarice, the whiche is nowe lady, maistras and quene of the worlde. For as Salamon seithe: To haue goode, alle the worlde obeyeth. An Ierom[ye] seithe that froo the litel vnto the myche alle theye studie in auarice. This maistras hatthe a fulle grete scole and many scoleris bothe hye and lowe and of alle maner of pepille, anamly thoo that han avowed to lyve withowte propre goodes. Theye rynne to the scole of Dame Auarice, be the whiche it sheweth welle that the ende of the worlde approcheth, for it brenneth alle with auarice. And the holye man seithe that whan a man aageth oother vicis aageth. But the moore that the man aageth, thee moore auarice yongeth in hym. Alsoo auarice is a love to haue dissordonatly. And this disseordonat desire sheweth hym in ii maneres, in getyng fervently and withholdyng strey[n]ingly and too dispende it scarcely. Thees ben the ii branchis whiche groweth of this evil roote, of the whiche the firste is called coveitice. Coveitice is that meruelious beeste that Seint Iohn speketh of in the Pocalipse, the whiche hadde an heede lyche a lyon and a bodye of a liparde and feete of a bere and it hadde vii heedys and x hornes. And vppon hym was a woman of folye and of vntrowthe, the whiche was called Babiloine, the moder of malice and of vicis that be in erthe. And shee was cladde in a purpil clothe of golde and helde in hir hande a drynke of the whiche she yaf drynke to alle pepille. This woman is Dame Auarice, the whiche assotteth and maketh dronken alle the worlde and is the mooder of alle malice. And the drynke that shee helde in here hande is clere as goolde. This is the witte of the worlde, whereof euery man wolde drynke. The beeste on the whiche shee sat is coveitice, whiche hatthe the heede of a lyon. For the heedis of the worlde be covetouse, feerse, and cruel as lyonnes. [f. 60] And it hadde the bodye of a liparde, whiche is alle grene of the eville parte. Thoo be the mene marchaundes, þe vsurreris, the whiche be false and ful of deceite. The feete of a bere be the comune pepille, the whiche douteth not to doo synne and harme for to gete goode noo more than the beere doothe strokys and betynges soo that hee maye geete anythynge. The vii heedis be the vii dedely synnes, the whiche groweth alle of this evil roote. For this see wee oopinly that covetice setteth a man in pride, in envye, in ire, in slouthe, in glootounye, and in lecherye, as it sheweth in many woomen, the whiche for pouertee putteth theyre bodyes to lecherye. And therefoore seithe Seint Poule: That is the roote of alle evilles. The x hornes be the x maner of synnes of covetice, liche as x smal braunches.

[Of Symonie, the Whiche Is þe Firste Branchet]

The firste lityl braunche is symonye. This is whan a man wil bye goostly thyngys. Thoo be theye that bye and selle oordres and oother sacramentis and thoo that be theire yftes and be theyre promyses and theyre strengthe doon soo myche that theye or oother be chosen too dignitees of hooly chirche and han benefices or entren in religion. Hee deviseth not diuerse cases þat bee in simonye because that theye longen moore to clerkes than too layemen. And this booke is made proprely for laye pepill, the whiche in iii cases sholde specially kepe theym froo synne. Oon is whan theye wille helpe theyre freendis to clymbe intoo dignitees of hooly chirche. Anoother is whan theye yeve theym prebendis the whiche be of theyre yifte. The thirde is whan theye yelde their childer into abbeyes. In thees iii pointis somtyme theye yeve or receyve evil yiftis or evil prayerres or evil seruice, and thus theye synne be simonye.

[Of Sacrilege, the Whiche Is the Seconde]

[f. 60v] The seconde litill braunche of covetice is sacrilege. That is whan a man breketh or treteth vilaynously holy thyngys or persones [or] blessed places of hooly chirche. And covetice maketh this to be doon, liche as prestis for wynnynge synge too masses on oo daye. And thoo that receyve oure loordys bodye in dedely synne doo gretter sacrilege þan though theye serued it in myre. Theye be not quite of this synne that dispendeth the goodes of holy chirche in pride, in lecherye, and in oother eville vsages, no theye that take of thoo the whiche han noo power to yeve, ne thoo alsoo that withholdeth or withdraweth or payeth evil theyre rentys, offringgys or oother rentys of hooly chirche. And it is not oonly thefte withoute moore, but it is sacrilege, whiche is a gretter synne a grete deele. Syche synne doo theye that for covetice breeketh þe feestis that men sholde kepe. For seintys han theire libertee liche as the place and the persoones.

[Of Malignite, the Whiche Is the Thirde]

The thirde lytil braunche is malignitee, whan a man is soo vntrewe that he ne resoigne, *id est*, [...] to doo an horrible synne or harme to anoother for lytil wynnynge, liche as theye doon that for moneye maketh the feende to be called and maketh enchauntementis and loketh in swerdys and thoo that werrieth and brynneth townes and chirches and doothe hundreth poundes worthe of harme where theye haue noothynge of profite and thees carterris that steleth wyne oute of tunnes and that for a certeyne draughtis the whiche theye drynke and englotte theye hynder þe wyne of x *li* and [thoo] that purchace pletoures for too wynne with and thoo that accuseth the pore pepille to theyre loordys for lytylle wynnynge that [f. 61] theye take of coste. Syche maner of pepill bee bounde too restore al the harmes that theye haue doon to oother be wronge, be theye not veryly oute of theyre witte and moore vnhappy than oother synneres, the whiche bereth aweye the syn of the whiche oother hatthe the avayle.

[Of Raveyne, the Whiche Is the Fourthe]

The fourthe lityl braunche is raveyne. This is the grettest raveyne and cruelte of alle oother, that is of thoo that dispoyleth the dede, whan the sone robbeth the fader and the fader the sone or the husbond the wife or the wyfe hir husbonde. The moore freendly that theye haue been in theyre lyves, the gretter enemyes be theye atte the deethe. Of this synne be theye not quyte that be evil executoures, the whiche suffreth and delayeth testamentis and putteth theyme in foryetilnes and recketh not of the caytif soules, whiche brynneth in purgatory be theyre defautis. In siche synne be ryche men, the whiche taketh on the righte hande and on the lifte, as landys, vignes, and oother thynges, and [f]leethe the poore pepille, the whiche theye sholde keepe, but the shrede theyme be taxes, be corues, *id est*, be enhaunsynge theire rentis, be constreynynge theyme to make amendes, and be evil costomes and in moo than an c maneres that theye vmbethynke theym in for to take the poore pepil liche as men take litill fysshes. In this chapiter of covetice theye stodye nyghte and daye. And he is the beste clerke amonges theym that beste con [f]lee and make his lande moste worthe. To this synne longeth the synne of thoo that seeth the poore dye for hunger and han noo moore pytee than of an hounde and that taketh aweye þe hyres froo theym that deserve it. This synne is felawe to manslaughte. [f. 61v] And Seint Iame seithe that it is cryed harrowe oopin afoore Godde, liche as doothe the bloode of man that men sleeth. Syche be thoo that wille not paye that whiche the sholde, but theye con soo myche of iapes and of whyles that a man woote not where to haue theyme. Theye breeke covenantes and promyses, feithe, lawe, and oothe, and a man maye not haue right of theyme. Theye be wers than robberris, for that whiche robberrys bereth aweye costeth not to gete it but that the whiche theye paye evil costeth myche to gete it. And in the ende syche tyme is that a man leeseth booth coste and catell. And alle that be theye bounde too yeve ayeyne to thoo of whom theye haue hadde it.

[Of Thefte, the Whiche Is the V]

The fyfthe litell braunche is thefte. There be oo maner of thefes of whom men doothe iustice. And alsoo there be som that be covert theefes, the whiche stelith herytages, as theye be that remeueth boonde men and maketh theyme free and theye be boonde the whiche steeleth froo theyre loordes and froo theyre heyrys, and the wyfe the whiche knoweth welle that shee hatthe geten hir childe in aventure the whiche bereth therytage and disseheriteth the right heyris. Alsoo ther be oo maner of theefes the whiche thynketh not to stele grete thynges but theye stele polayle froo theyre neghboroughes, sheefes in hervest, peerys, applys, and oother thynges, for the whiche men curse. Syche theefes be theye that holdeth thynges and knoweth welle whoos theye bee and yeveth theym not ayeyne. Men calleth theym litil theefes, but theye be strenger theefes than the toother. For he is noo stronge theefe that steeleth greete thynges but hee that hatth ferventnes and covetice too steele. And certys it cometh of greete couetice and of righte an evil herte [f. 62] whan for a theeft of iii *d* a man yeveth to the feende bothe bodye and soule. Alsoo ther bee oo maner of homly theefes, the whiche steeleth not froo straungeres but froo theyre loordes. Too this synne religious pepil taketh theyme the whiche be appropred. But yet only their synne is moore than thefte, for theye be theefes and sacrileged and to blame for brekyng of theyre avowe. And alsoo there [be] a maner of sotil theefes, the whiche sotylly be wyles deceyveth symple pepill. In this konnynge, Dame Auarice hatthe many disciples. For in alle craftes and marchaundyses there be to many wyles and disceytes and theftes. Therfore Godde seithe in the gospelle that his hous, hooly chirche, is there where men make an hirne of thefes, for euery creature stodyeth to begyle his felawe. Alsoo ther be oo maner theefes be feleshipp, as thoo that councelleth too doo thefte and thoo that defendeth theyme in theyre malice and thoo that receyveth theym in theyre houses and thoo that serueth theym and gedreth theyme togeder and evil iustices the whiche suffreth theyme to reigne be theire shrewedenes. For the wil neyther haue the peyne ne coste to prison theyme ne to doo iustice.

[Of Vsure, the Whiche Is the VI]

The vi litil braunche is vsure, the whiche is thefte, but that oonly ther is a differens betwene the vsurer and the theef. For the theefe whan he steleth in oo towne he steeleth not in anoother; the vsurer somtyme steeleth in moo than an c townes. The theef steeleth not alweye; the vsurer doothe anamly sleepynge. The scripture seithe that, what that euer a man maye thynke of temperal avayle, if he that leneth atteyneth to any encrece and taketh it because of his leenynge be it in yifte, seruice, or in any oother bounte, al is vsure. Ther bee som vsureres as thoo that oppon catelle taketh the multiplyinge of theyme. And alsoo ther be som withhholdynge vsurerys as thoo that wil not yeve ayeine [f. 62v] that the whiche theye haue hadde of theyre auncestres that whan it be vsure. Theye be in grete peril, for theye wille neyther knowe ne beleue that theye be bounden to yeve ayeine that the whiche theye wan not. But theye seye comunly: Whoosoo brewe it, lete hym drynke it. And som seye alsoo: Lete the wed goo. Whooso drynke it, he most paye. Alsoo ther be som vsurerys whiche luste not to lene with theyre owne handys, but theye make it to be lent be her neghborughes, be their childer, or be theyre cosynes. Syche be grete men the whiche susteyneth Iues and Saraȝynes for yeftes and raunsomes that theye haue of theyme. Also ther be som vsurers, marchaundys that wil lene to a tyme, and though theye boughte it vil theye wil sylle myche the derer because of the longe leenynge. This is soo spredde throughoute the worlde that vnnethe ther is any marchaundyse but that there is som maner of vsure, not as myche but in marchaundyse of mostard ther is som. For whoosoo leneth he hatthe gladly moore wynnynge than he that borweth. There be alsoo som maner of vsurers be feleshipp the whiche taketh theyre moneye to marchandys on this condicion, that theye maye be felawes with theyme in wynnyng but not in leesyng, and thoo that lete theyre beestys to hyre with this, that if a beste dye a man shalle yeve the valewe therfore, and bee oother covenantes that theye vmbethynke theyme moore sootelly than any clerke can discrye. Alsoo ther be som vsurers of alle craftys thoo the whiche doo noo werke but if ther be som maner of vsure. Whan theye wyl delve theyre vygnes or eyre there landys, theye take heede whan that the pepyll be nedy. Than make theye marchandyse with theyme that if theye paye theyre moneye afore theye wille have ii penyworth of werke for oon. Alsoo ther be oother maneres of vsurers, the whiche sette pepill on werke withowte covenant makynge what theye shalle haue, and whan evyn cometh there where the man hatthe deserved to haue v or vi *d* hee hatth but iiii or lesse. And somtyme theye most take theyre evil stuffe, the whiche theye ouerselle [f. 63] theyme, in brede, in wyne, and in oother goodes, that if theye hadde theyre moneye drye theye sholde employe it better. Thus the poore pepille hatthe a pore iorneye and a pore wagys and an evyl. And knowe wel that this is ayeins Godde fulle strongely.

[Of Chalenge, the Whiche Is the VII]

The vii lityl braunche is chalange, that is to rynne oppon anoother wrongefully. To this synne longeth the [tricheries], disceytes, and the falsenes the whiche falleth in plee. In this connynge, Dame Auarice hatthe a grete scoole bothe of clerkys and of layemen, the whiche stodyeth in ryghtes and in lawes not oonly for to holde righte but for to pervert it. Of this synne fals pleyneres be not quite, the whiche trauayleth and chalangeth wrongefullye; theye seke false iuges and vnkonnynge or fere iuges and fals peticions, fals letteres, and fals wittenesses. Syche be suterys the whiche seyeth and denyeth that the whiche is right. Theye seke disceytes and delayes for to take from oother that the whiche is theyres. Syche be fals wittenesses [the whiche] disseheryte pepil and taketh froo theyme that the whiche is worthe m^{l} marke for the wynnyng of v *s*, the whiche theye haue for to forswere theyme and for to leese theyre soules. And alsoo ii fals wittenesses doothe more harme than alle a contre maye amende. False notaryes also doothe myche harme be covetice. For theye make fals letteres, and theye take for theyre knowelechyng moore than theye deserue. Fals aduocattys synne in many maneres. For wyttynglye theye receyve evyl causes and techeth to theyre clerkys malices and wyles whanne theye seke evyl delays and seythe lyes and aleggeth þe contrarye of righte and distorbeth the makyng of pees and taketh grete sallaryes and leeseth causys be necgligens and vnknowynge. Fals iuges syn also whan theye hynge moore on that oo partye than of the toother partye, outher for goode, for hate, for love, or for prayer, and theye receyve yeftys for quarell withoute reson and causeth grete spence to be maade and [f. 63^{v}] taketh bothe of that oo parte and of the toother. And alle thees maner of falsnesses and of chalengys, whan it cometh to iugement of the sowle, alle thees persoones of the aforeseyde be not oonly hoolden to yeve ayein that the whiche theye haue evyl getyn but with that alle the harme that oother hadde be theym moste be restored.

[Of Briberie, the Whiche Is the VIII]

The viii braunche is blandesshinge. And that is whan pepill be alyed togeder and sholde kepe feithe and trouthe euery too oother and theye labour and stodye howe theye maye begyle theyr felawes. In this scoole Dame Auaryce hatthe many scooleres. A man sholde kepe feythe and trouthe to Godde, for that aliance is everlastynge. For in Godde is neyther deceit ne blandeshyng but he is often blandeshed. For whoo is he that setteth hert, bodye, tyme, and witte withowte blandshyng and feintise to serue hym? We be alle of Caymes hous, of whom auarice began, the whiche offred to God litil shevys and wide. Oo goode Godde of hevyn the whiche clotheth and fedith vs al that we neede, what oure covetice doothe vs myche shame and shenshippe. Thowe yevest vs newe gownes, and we wille not ȝefe the ayein oure oolde. Thowe fillest vs oure gernerys, and thowe dyest for hunger afore oure yen. Thowe ȝefest vs fro ȝere to ȝere alle that ever the erthe berith, and the ix partees thereof sufficeth vs not but wee take froo the the x the whiche thowe haste holden to thyn vse in token that thowe arte lorde of alle. Nowe feir swete Criste Iesus, the whiche be thy dethe conqueridest the rentes that clerkis of hooly chirche hatthe for to serve and worshipp the with and to sustene with thye poore pepill, what thowe haste litil parte of that the whiche is thyne. Vnnethe men wil lete the o bene in thyn owne felde, for pride, glotounye, lecherye, and auarice bereth alle awaye. Thowe canste weele hire. On the same [f. 64] wise thowe shalt compt wele whan theye moste ȝefe acompt of that the whiche theye haue reseyvid. Betwene prelatis and theyre subgettis sholde be gret aliaunce and betw[e]ne princes and thoo that theye haue to gouerne. As to prelatis and erthely loordis, theye sholde truly kepe theyre subgettys and defende theym, gouerne theyme, counsel theym, and helpe theym. And the subgettis sholde obeye and serve theyme. Betwene the deciples alsoo sholde be gret aliaunce. And al theese sholde besyly and withowte synne teche theyre deciples. Alsoo ther bee myche pepil and felawes the whiche kepeth neyther feithe ne trouthe to felawes. Theefes shalle iuge sige pepil atte the daye of doome. For theefes whan theye haue stoolyn kepeth feithe and trouthe on too an nother. Trouthe of feleshipp is wretyn in the hert of man. And there be ii pointis in the lawe of kynde of the whiche the too pointe seithe thus: Take hiede that thowe doo not to an nother a thynge that thowe woldest not men didde to the. The toother point seithe this: In that which thowe wilte be reeson that anoother doo to thee, take heede to thye power to doo the same to hym. If I knewe al the blandeshynges that happeth in al feleshippes, I shoolde be wyser than nede were to me. And if I wolde set theym writyn in my booke, it sholde be fuller than it sholde be or than neded to me.

Off Disceite, LXXIe

The ix litil braunche is guyle and disceit. Ther be nowe oo maner of pepill that be gret deseyuerres, as these grete loordes the whiche taketh ȝiftes and seruices of thoo that hatth neede of theire helpe and euer taketh and euer promisseth and atte the laste they haue but federis and woordis, as the foxe seide to the larke. Alsoo ther bee some stronge deseyueres, as be theese ypocrites, the whiche be their contenaunces and theire lowlynes wynneth rentes and dignitees, and whan theye han getyn it the penaunce is doon. Alsoo ther be some stronge dissey[f. 64v]ueres, as be theese losengeris that seithe soo many white woordes or blak, the whiche hatthe their tonges araied to lye and to seye what that a man wil here, and maketh to beleve that the swan is blacke and the crowe white, as the foxe didde the ravyn whom he sawe hoolde a peece of chese in his beeke. Oo birde, seide hee, what thowe art feire and white. If thowe kowdest synge, thowe sholdest passe alle birdes. And than he reioyssed hym and openyd the beeke [to synge]. And the cheese felle fro hym, and the foxe cawght it anon. This is of Ysopeis fablis, but the example is noo fable, that siche foxes and siche flatererris berith aweye grete rentes and gret ȝiftes and theye be euer grete maisteris in grete courtes wher ther lacketh but oo thyng, as Seneque seith, that is to seye, on to seye trouthe.

Off Evil Craftys, LXXII

The x litil braunche of couetice longeth to al [evil] craftes that a man lerneth and maintenyth for to wyn with, as theese courteyoures the whiche sessith not to begyle pepil and theese championes that kylleth iche oother for money and theese fals moneye-makerys and diz makeris and chapelet makeris of floures. Wee haue now named and noumbred the branches that cometh of the roote of covetice. Wee shalle nowe speke of the seconde braunche, the whiche is proprely called covetice.

The Seconde Principal Braunche of Couetice, LXXIIIe

The covetous pepil be takyng, and the desirous pepil be holdyng. This vice is ful perlious, for the holdyng man is holden. Richesses holdeth hym as [f. 65] a snare a birde and a prison a theef. The riche man hatthe no richessis but as a theef hatthe, the whiche hatthe an halter aboute the necke and the feete in stockys, for he maye meve noo hande for to ȝif ne foote for to goo but there where his richessis commaundeth. And the more richesse he hatthe the strenger he is holdyn and charged with fere of thought of sorwe and synne. And he goothe ever from evil to wers, for the more þat he hatthe the more sotile he is and the more kepyng. This syn is foule and vile and shamful. For alle the worlde haloweth siche a man and pointeth hym with the finger, and al creatures rynneth oppon hym and shalle accuse hym at the daye of doome. For al thyng is maade to serve man and man to helpe iche oother, but the covetous man levith al feleshippe and lifeth be hymselfe as a cursed man. And he is putte to the moste [vile] thraldom and the hardest þat is, ayeins God, aȝeyns nature, and aȝeyns reson, for the richessis of whom he hatthe made his God is but donge and myre, and that the whiche he sholde fyle vnder his feete he hatthe soo reisid it ouer his hede that he derre not touche it ne ȝif it ne selle it ne lene it ne meve it ne dispende it but with grete fere kepith it as his lorde and worshippeth it as his god and proprely setteth in it that the whiche he sholde set to God, that is to seye, feithe, hoope, and luf ouer al thynge. Take heede nowe howe this synne blyndeth a man. He loofeth richesses moore than his soule, and neverthelesse he putteth ther where he woote wel that he shalle leese it and wil not put it there where he knoweth wel he sholde not leese it. And with that wherewith he myght bye hevyn and lif at ease and at worshipp he bieth helle and lyfeth with shame and disease. This is a fulle perlious vice, for siche a man is euer drowned in his richesses. And soo it shewith, for he doothe as a man that drowneth hymselfe. What that euer he hatthe, it is al kepte; nothynge maye ascape hym. This syn setteth a man in the theefes pitte and in the strengest preson that the feende hatthe. This synne is right foule and right grevouse to theym that hatthe richesses rightfully getyn, as oure loorde sheweth vs in the gospell of the laserur the whiche was saved and the riche man that was dampned not oonly for that the whiche he hadde taken and stoolyn but because that he wolde noothynge departe to poore pepil ne too the laser that laye at his gate. But this synne is x tymes grevouser to thoo that hatthe the goodes of God. Thoo be thee goodes of hooly chirche, of the whiche theye be not lordys but keperris withowte moore and dispensatoures of pore pepil to whom proprely theye longe, alle that euer hooly [f. 65v] chirche hatthe and al that euer covetouse pepill withholdeth and dispendeth in evil vsages. This is not oonlye covetice, but it is thefte, robborye, and sacrilege, as seintis seithe. Of thoo that withholdeth ȝerely that the whiche theye haue wonne vntruly, I seye not that theye maye ȝif anythynge of that the whiche is not theyres. For of theyme is a rewle set in the oolde lawe and in the newe it is confermed, soo that euery man maye lightly see it. For theye moste ȝelde it aȝein or be hanged. Oure loorde seithe in the gospelle that the feende the whiche is loorde of hym that is covetouse and that holdeth the scole of covetice is kalled Mammona. Noon maye wel serve God and hym this togeder. And it is no merveyle, for theye be contrarie bothe in theire willes, services, commandementis, and doctrinis. Godde techeth trouthe, sothefastnes, and iustice; and the toother techeth falsenes and blaundesshyng. God commaundeth and seithe: Of that the whiche thowe hast getyn truly ȝif and lene gladly and make thyn availe and tresor in hevyn. For that the whiche thowe haste vntruly getyn thowe haste no powre therof. Mammona commaundeth and seith: Holde wel that thowe haste, for as myche as thowe haste as myche art thowe worthe. If þou be poore, thowe shalt be holden wers than an hounde. Whoosoo is not stuffed and stored, he is shente. Thowe wotest not what hyngeth ouer thyn yee.

Many aduersiteis maye come to the: hungeres, sekenesses, diuers besynessis. Alle goothe to a goode ende. If thowe haue noght, what maiste thowe doo atte thy dethe? Wilt thowe that thy soones be rẹbawdes? Where maiste thowe doo a feirer almes than to helpe theyme? Be siche exortacion he enchaunteth hym soo myche that he taketh from his herte pitee, mercy, and charitee, the whiche is the louf of God and of his neghbourgh. And whan he hatthe rased from his herte the roote of pitee thanne maketh he hym a veraye scoller and techeth hym his commaundementis, his wiles, and his deceitis for to gete and geder togedir regratories and subtelteis for to restreyne and for to spare, and hee maketh hym too louf this goode soo myche that he suffreth hym not to ete his fylle ne he dreedeth ne beleveth noo man ne he doubteth neyther blame ne shame ne deethe ne daye of doome ne helle. His first commaundement is to kepe wel his. The ii^{e} that he lesse it not in his handis. The iii that he encrese it dayly. The iiii that he ʒif not ne doo noon almesse. The v that [f. 66] he lene not ne pleye the courteise ne that he set not at his feete that the whiche he kepeth in his handis. And this is the cruellest commaundement that Mammona commaundeth the covetouse man, for the caytyf holdeth this good in preson to his dampnacion. And he seeth his neghborughes greved be vsureris dayly, and he suffreth it whan with his he myghte delyuere theym saf and gete almes of Godde and worshippe of the worlde. But he hatthe no powre, for his maister defendeth it hym. The vi is that he ʒelde ayeyn nothynge vnto the deethe. But whan thowe haste, seithe hee, assigned to thye childer that ther is nothynge left the but a litil and that thowe seist dethe approche, thowe shalt sende for thy preste and confesse the. Soo shalt thowe doo thy power to ʒelde aʒeyn. And thowe shalt begyle God, for he maye noothynge aske the over thy power. And thus for oo peny thowe shalt be delyuered and quit. This techyng holdėth vsureris oueral thoo to whom the feende hatthe doon any grace, for he promysseth theym that theye shalle ende wel whan theye haue not whereof. Other hee bryngeth into wannehope and seithe to theym: Whan shalle alle this be ʒoldyn aʒeyin? Doo as thowe doest and let that be. The laste commaundement is that he take noothynge for to ease his bodye with. And he defendeth hym mete and drynke and maketh al his moneye to faste and to curse hym and maketh theyme theefes. And the lenger he lifeth, þe moore waxeth his fere, his anguisshe, and his sorwe, anamly whan he seeith deethe. There is to harde a disseuerance. As Salamon seithe: He [lesith] al thynge in right harde afflicciones, for he seeithe iii deethes before his yeyen: the deethe of helle, the deethe of bodye. And the iiie deethe tormenteth hym more than any of the toother ii. That is the deethe the whiche desceuereth hym and his goode. Thowe seeist nowe to what deethe goode bringeth a covetouse man and too what ende. The ende is evil; rightwis is [the] partye. The feende that berith aweye the soule is foule. Woormes hatthe the caroyne [...] and his kynne on the thirde parte for to cacche his goode. And ȝit is ther noon of theese iii feleshipes wolde ȝif their part for any of the toother ii.

[f. 66v] Off [Thyngys] That Causeth Covetise, LXXIIII

We wil speke nowe of thyngys that causeth this synne, for we haue spokyn of many maner of covetises. The first thyng is to feleshipp with covetouse pepil and desirous. For as qwik cooles kyndelith dede if theye be put togeder soo covetous and desirous pepil doothe theym that feleshipeth with theym. For as Ecclesiastes seithe: Whoosoo touchith lightly the [pitch is defiled], and whoosoo feleshipeth with proude pepil becometh proude. And therefore he bideth alsoo that a man shalle not holde feleshippe with riche pepil, that is to seye, with couetouse pepil. Wherefore Seneque seithe that the example of the couetouse and of the lecherous man causeth myche harme to be doon. The seconde thynge is too thinke oon richesses. Of the whiche the wyse man in his Prouerbis seithe: Reyse not thyn yen, that is to seye, thy desyre to thynge that thowe maiste not haue. The thirde thynge is to haue too gret louf too worldly ioye and worshipp. The fourthe thynge is disordenat louf to his childer. And certis it is no louf to geder togyder and to geete richesses too his childer shrewdely. It is rather haate, for it ledith bothe theym and their childer to helle. Wee shalle shewe yowe an example of an vsurer that hadde too sonnes. Of the whiche the tone wolde noothynge haue of his fader because he wiste welle that he hadde evil getyn it but maade hym an hermite. The toother abode with his fader. His fader died, and he hadde the remenant. And a litil after that the soone dyed. Whan þe hermite wiste that his fader and his brother was dede, hee was fulle soory, for he supposid certeynly that theye were dampned. Hee maade his prayeris too oure loorde that he woolde shewe hym in what state theye weere. He was ravisshed and lad to helle and sawe theyme commynge oute of a pitte enbrasid togeder, bytynge iche oother. And the fader seide to the soone: Cursed be thowe, for I was an vsurer for thee, and I am dampned. The soone seide ayein to his fader: Cursed be thowe, for hadde thowe not evil getyn it, I hadde not evil kepte it ne haue be dampned.

Off Remedies ayeins the Synne of Couetise, LXXVe

[f. 67] Nowe that wee haue spokyn of the vice of couetise and of thynge that causeth the synne of couetise, wee shal telle some remedies whereby men maye eschewe this vice. The firste remedie is to thynke euer or often of deethe. Wherfore Seint Ambrose and Seint Ierome seithe: Hee dispiseth and setteth lightly at nought alle temporel thynges, the whiche thynketh euer that he most dye. For hee woote welle that he shalle noothynge bere with hym whan that he shalle dye and that hee muste leve alle. Therfore deethe shewith vs proprely to dispise al richesses and delites and alle worldely ioyes. For there is noon if he wist veryly that he sholde dye within viii dayes that euer wolde doo diligens to haue siche thyngys if he hadde witte and reeson in hym. And ther is noon that hatthe the respite of viii dayes, noo not oo daye ne only on houre. Anoother remedye is to considre and to thynke oon the deethe of Criste Iesus. Hereof Seint Bernard seithe: It is grete abusion that a litil glas of erthe, the whiche euery man is, wil be riche, for whom God wolde be poore. That hee was pore it shewed whan hee toke oure poore nature and suffred in hym alle the pouertees that wee suffre bodyly in as myche as that he was man, safe only ignorance, synne, and sekenes. Anoother remedye is to considre and thynke oppon the riches of hevyn. Whereof Seint Gregory seithe: Whan men coueyteth and desireth goostely goodes, the whiche is grete ioye of hevyn, theye set noo prise be temporell goodes. Anoother remedye is that a man putte his hoope in God. And than God shalle purvoye for hym that the whiche shalle be needeful to hym alleoonly soo that he serve hym and kepe his commaundementis. For as oure loorde seithe in the gospell: A man maye not serve to loordes atte ones, that is to seye, God and worldely richesse. And therfore seithe he a litel after in þe same gospell: Be not to besye to thynke what ʒe shalle eete ne what ʒee shalle drynke ne howe yee shalle be clothid, for oure fadir of hevyn woote wel what is needefull to yowe, and he shalle ʒif it yowe soo that ʒe serve hym as yee sholde. The laste remedye is that a man be almesse and be oother goodnes and be prayeris or be oother dedes of mercy maye gete grace of Godde, [f. 67v] the whiche sufficeth to hym that hatthe it to delyuere hym from alle evillis and snaris of couetise and desires. Wherfore oure loorde seithe in the gospelle that it is fulle harde for a riche man too entre into hevyn. And his desiple seide: Whoo shalle be safe than? And oure loorde answered and seide: It maye not be that a riche, couetous man of hymselfe maye delyuere hym from his richesse ne withdrawe hym from his couetise. And therfore the synne of couetise and of negardshipp is gretely to doute, fro the whiche God of his grace preserve vs.

Off the Synne of Lecherye, LXXVIe

The scripture seithe that the feende sleepeth in the synne of lecherye because that in this synne a man ʒefeth to hym hoolly bothe bodye and sowle. For of alle the membris that a man hatthe [f. 68] he doothe sacrifice, offrynge, and seruice too the feende and for þe grete conquest that he hatth thereinne. For in oother synnes he taketh the pepil be oon and oon, but in this he taketh theym be too and too, ʒea sometyme be iiii and iiii, thoo that doo þe synne and the bawdes that causeth it and alle thoo that sustene it. I speke not of the moder that sellith hirre doughter ne of the husbonde that suffreth his wiff, for that is treson and mordre. Alsoo presteis and iusticeris that suffreth bordelles and evil ostries, theye be felawes and partoneris of alle the synnes that be doon there. Of the whiche wee reede in the oolde lawe that whan the childer of Ysrael conquered the lande beȝonde the see a fals prophete Balaan taught Kynge Balaac howe hee sholde disconfit theym. He maade to be sent into þe oste feire ȝonge women because that theye sholde synne with the men. And soo didde some of them. And therfore theye loste the louf of Godde, the whiche ledde theym afore or that theye synned. And than God commanded to theym that were maistres of the ooste that alle thoo that hadde synned with the women sholde be sleyn. And ther dyed xxiiii ml on a daye. After þat ȝit it sufficed hym not, but he commanded that alle the princes and the keperris sholde be hanged afore alle the worlde. The hooly man seithe there that if princes and prelattis vnderstode wel this woorde theye wolde not desire so manye prelasies as theye doo. This vice is principally devised in ii braunches of lecherye, oon of the hert, anoother of þe bodye.

Off Lecherye of the Herte

Many men and women in the worlde ther be that kepeth their bodye from that deede but the hertis be fulle of the dede. This lecherye hatthe iiii degreis. For the spir[i]t of fornicacion the whiche servith too enbrace in their hertis the fire of lecherye is called the foule feende amonge oother feendes that servith of oother vicys, liche as a maister werkeman amonge oother werkemen. He this whan he tempteth in this foule synne, first he bringeth into theire hertis þouȝthis and figures and maketh that caityf persone be it hee or shee to thynke theroon. After the ii is þat [f. 68v] the caytif dwelleth in his thoughtes and delites, allethough hee woolde not doo the dede for c *li*. This delit, this abidynge therin, and this thought maye be dedly synne, soo grete the delit maye bee and the thought. The thirde degree is the assentynge of the herte, of reson, and of the wyl. And siche assentynge is dedly syn, for after the assentyng commeth the desire and the greete ferventnes that theye haue too synne and coveyt in this and that and doo moo than xx or xxx synnes whan theye be amonge theese ladyes and ientil-women, the whiche be fulle perlious whan theye araye theym dishonestly and behaueth theyme iolylye for too make musardis too muse. And ȝit theye wene not too synne because theye haue noo wille too doo the synne of lecherye. Oo feende, what thowe art sottyle. If shee hadde stoolyn or takyn a sheepe from hir neghborough, shee wolde be fulle sorye, for shee sholde knowe wel that shee hadde synned dedly. And wheder is a man better or a shepe? Shee hatthe noo membre in hir bodye but that it is a snare of the feende, as Salamon seithe, the whiche oughte wel to knowe it, for he was takyn with siche wyles that for alle his greete witte he was deseyvid. But the herte seithe þat he is a grete [net], the whiche grypeth alle, fro whom lytyl fisshes maye not ascape. On the same wise, non herte maye from this fonned woman, for shee desireth greetely that euery creature sholde haue desire to hirre. This is the pecok that reyseth and shewith his tale and hatthe grete glorye whan men prayseth it. On the same wise, hatthe this fonned woman. Nowe, caityf, telle me: Whoo shalle ȝelde aȝeyn to God xx or xxx soules that thowe haste takyn from hym, the whiche he boughte aȝeyn with soo preciouse a goode as with the preciouse bloode of his side? Thowe shalt never be confessid, for thowe thynkest not therof ne thowe wootest not what thowe shalt seye atte the daye of doome whan God shal aske thee of theyme. Whan I remembre in myn herte the synnes that the worlde doothe and howe God leseth soules, me semyth that the proudest synne that is is the pride and the boste and the lewde araye and the disordenat behavyng of theese lewde ientilwomen and theese contirfetid guyses, the whiche me semeth theye stodieth on noon oother thynge but howe þat [f. 69] theye maye take from God the soules for whom hee dyed on the crosse. What shalle this caityf seye that in theire folyes hatthe wasted theyre liff, the whiche hatthe be nettys and snarys of the feende and cause of the ledynge of soo many soules to helle, of the whiche shee knoweth not the nombre? And nevertthelesse shee moste answere for the synne and restore the harmys.

Off Lecherye of the Bodye, LXXVII[e]

The lecherye of the bodye is devised in lecherye of yen, of eerys, of mouthe, of handis, of feete, and of easses of the bodye and of veleins lecherye. Seynt Peter seithe that theye be grete fooles the whiche hatthe their yen soo ful of lecherye and of aduoutery and of fornicacion that theye coveite and desire alle that euer theye see that is feire. And thus cometh louf into the herte be the wyndowes, that is too seye, be the yen. And therfore be theye soo besye to goo too festes and too karolles, too see theire harme and theire deethe, as Kynge Dauid didde, the whiche be a looke felle into iii dedly synnes: in aduoutery, in treeson, and in manslaught. And there where glotonye tastith the bodye doothe the moore, but the herte be the yen doothe moore than c synnes on the daye. And that the whiche theye haue seen on the daye, the feende puttith it theym in myende on the nyght, wakynge or sleepynge. And the synne that he hatthe hunted and takyn he bringeth it hoome as a foxe and deliteth hym therin. Lecherye entreth often into the herte be the wyndowe of þe erris to thoo that gladly hereth speke of louf whan theye here songes and karolles, pipes and taboures, the whiche be brondis of the feende alle kyndelyd with the fire of lecherye to spreede it in the hertis of lecherouse pepil. Lecherye of the feete wee see al daye. Theye lepe; theye trippe; theye daunce too mydnyght. It pleyseth theym soo [f. 69v] myche that theye shal never be weery. In lecherye of the mouthe syn theye that gladly synge songys and karolle and seye that theye louf paramours. Oo goode Godde, this is not to louf paramours, but it is dedly haate and trayson. Hiere wise Salamon what he seithe: Sone, seithe hee, looke thowe trost not thy dedly enemye whan he resoneth the swetely, for his woorde is outeward feire and swete but inwarde it hatthe vii traysones the whiche be in the herte. See and vnderstande nowe howe myche this sweete woorde is worthe. Whan men seye: Louf me paramours, I vnderstande þerbye veleny, for it is as myche to seye as though he seid: For the louf of me, I wil thowe lese thy chastite and thye worshippe and become an evil woman and a bordeler and lif with shame. This is o point. Alsoo I wil that for my louf thowe shalt forsake paradis and everlastyng ioye, soo that thowe shalt never haue parte therof noo moore than Iudas that betrayed Godde. After that alsoo that thowe forswere paradis too be banysshed oute of Goddes feleshipp and al seyntis and oute of alle goodnes of hooly chirche and too lese thye parte of alle the goodnes that men doo thoroughoute the worlde, soo that thowe shalt haue neyther parte ne helpe therof. Alsoo that thowe shalt leese alle the goodenes that euer thowe didest. Alsoo that thowe shalt yelde the to the feende bodye and soule and doo hym homage with alle thye membris and to be of his feleshipp. Alsoo that thowe for the louf of me to be as longe in helle as God shalle be in hevyn. Alsoo I wil that thowe reneye Godde and the blessed Virgin Marie and the Cristen feithe. Alle theese thyngys requireth hee be the swete woorde of louf, whan he boweth to the veleyny that I haue spoken of afore. And whan she granteth to hym and consentith to his wille, she grauntith hym al theese vii vicis. I am too sorye whan I hiere siche a lye and siche a blame seide, whan men calleth the foulest and the shamefulest dede that is be soo ferre, soo holye, and soo sweete a name as is to louf paramours, the whiche never noon didde but oonly Criste Iesus that loufed vs to the deethe, not as oon of vs loufeth anoother for availe that hee hadde of vs but purely for louf. Is not that than a grete synne too put soo hooly a name to serve [f. 70] too so foule a thynge and to soo foule a crafte wher ther be soo many synnes? For theye swere and forswere and lye for noght. Theye breke feithe and oothe and deceyve symple woomen and taketh froo theym their soule and the worship of the worlde and putteth theym to shame and too poore dayes. And therin syn theye dedly whan theye putte theym in synne of consentynge and than make therof gawdis and iapes and reyseth blame of theym. To lecherye of the bodye longeth al thynge by the whiche the flesshe is mevid and desireth siche dedes as proude pepil be of mete and drynke, softe beddes, delicious thyngis, and al maner of idil thyngis. For glotonye and slouthe servith proprely too lecherye. And whoosoo kepith hym not froo theese ii it is but folye to wene to kepe hym froo the thirde. After al theese evilles cometh lecherye of handis, touchyngis the whiche be somtyme soo foule and soo vileins that ther cometh gretter syn þerof than is aduoutery or fornicacion. For the flesshe of man and of a woman is of the nature of ii precious stones that men calle [t]e[rre]boles. And in the ton is the visage of a yonge man, and the toother hatthe the visage of a virgine. Whan euery of theym ar be theirselfe, theye be colde as oother stoones; and as sone as men putteth theyme togeeder, ther spryngeth oute fyre and flavmbe. Wherefore Seint Poule seithe, ther where he commandeth chastite too be kepte, hee techeth ii thyngys, of the whiche the ton seithe thus: If thowe wilt kepe thy bodye chastly, touche no woman but if shee be thyne. The toother seithe: If thowe wilte ouercome temptacion of lecherye, be fleyng thowe shalt [ouer]comme it and not be strengthe. Flee fornicacion, and flee thyngis of whiche wee haue spokyn. That is to seye, kepe the hert besyly from evil thoughtis, the yen froo beholdyng, þe errys fro heryng, the mouthe fro spekyng lecherye, the feete fro goyng to evil places, the handes froo evil touchyngys, the bodye fro idilnes and froo to myche leyser; and than put thye bodye and thy soule in the kepyng of God and of oure lady and goo often to the welle of hooly confession.

Off Braunches of Lecherye, LXXVIII

The synne of lecherye is devised in xv braunches opon the statis of persones þat doothe it, the whiche goothe clymyng from evil to wers. The first is of [f. 70v] man and woman that is not bounde in mariage ne to religion. The seconde is of a comvne woman the whiche is fouler. And for the fouller thynge that a man leseth his soule the more shame he doothe to God and ioye to the feende, and in soo myche the synne is the gretter because that somtyme siche women be of religion and maried and theye refuse noon, neyther broother ne coosyn ne fader ne sone ne noo kynne. The thirde is of a man wydower and of a woman wydowe. This synne is ful grete for the hye astate of wydowhode be the whiche men geeteth a coroune of lx preciouse stoones. The iiii is of a virgine whan men take from hirre the tresor of virginite and the coroune of c preciouse stoones and doothe hir siche harme that noon maye restore it to hirre. The v is of a woman maried. This synne is avoutery. And it is ful grevous for it encloseth in hym many grete synnes. That is to seye, lecherye and thefte, for the bodye is not hirres; it is hirre husbondes froo whom shee stellith it whan shee abaundoneth hirre to an nother. Alsoo ther is trespassyng of feithe and sacrilege whan a man levith the hooly sacrement of mariage. And also somtyme falleth therof disheretyng and fals mariag. The vi is as double to hym whan it is of a man maryed to a woman maryed. The vii is whan a man doothe to his owne wiff thynge disordeyned and defended ayeins nature of man and ayeins ordre of mariage. Of this synne seithe Seint Austin that he sholde doo lesse harme too be naturelly with his mooder than in siche maner too be with his wedded wiff. A man maye slee hym with his owne swerde; evyn soo a man maye lye with his owne wiff and synne dedly. Therfore the toother ȝere God smote with an evil deethe thee son of Iudas, the whiche was son to hooly I[ac]ob. And the feende strangeled vii husbondis of the hooly ientilwoman Sarra, the whiche after that hadde yonge Thobie. For al the sacramentis of hooly chirche men sholde trete hoolyly and haue theym in grete reuerence. The viii is of a man to his gossep or to his goddedoughter or of the godson to the childer of the godfader or the godmooder. For siche persones maye not medil togeder withowte the same synne in mariage. Thee ix is of a man with his kyn. And this synne heyueth or loweth after that the kyn is nere or ferre. The x is of a man with his wiffes kyn. This synne is gretter than the toother afoore. For whan a man hatthe parte of any woman oother in mariage or ellys he maye not after that haue noone of hirre cosynes. And if [h]ee take any the mariage is noon; he most [f. 71] leve hirre. And if hee take a wiff and after that he hatthe parte of his wyfes kyn, he leesith the right that he hadde too his wiff in so miche that he ought never moore too haue parte ne feleshipp in hirre, if shee require it not afoore. The xi is betwene clerkys ordred and women. This synne encressith and loweth after the persoones be that doothe it and after the dignitees that theye haue. The xii is of men of the worlde too religious women. And this syn hyueth and loweth after the persones be that doothe it and after the hyenes that theye be of and the digniteis that theye haue. The xiii is of prelattis, the whiche sholde be forme and example of hoolynes and clennesse afore al the worlde. And therefore this synne is to grete and to horrible. The xiiii is of men of religion with women of religion. This synne is felawe to the syn of a wedded man too a weddid woman. The xv is the vile foule synne that men sholde not name. And it commeth in many maneres that the feende techith it to pepil. Bot with Goddys leve this booke shalle teche it too noon. But I wil wele that thoo that be culpaple be soo aduertised and that theye maye knowe that this is the synne for the whiche God maade for to reyne fyre and bremston opon Soodom, Gomorre, Adama, Seboyon, and Segor. Theese v citeis sanke intoo the grounde. This synne is soo foule, the scripture seithe, that the feende, the whiche louffeth but filthe, purchasith it, and tisseth it, is ashamed whan men doothe it for the filthe that is soo greete. Oo goode Godde, howe stynkyng is it than tofoore God and his aungellis, and what hee oughte to haue grete sorwe the whiche hatthe doon siche thyngys.

Off Remedies aȝeins the Synne of Lecherye, LXXIX

Whoosoo wil kepe hym froo the synne of lecherye hee mooste kepe hym froo thee causes that draweth and ledith a man to this synne. And specially aȝeins this synne ther be iii remedyes. For the synne of lecherye is liche a fire, for whan the potte with woortis standeth aȝeins the fyre and that it boyle soo faste to it goo over, therfore is iii remedies: [f. 71v] to caste colde water in the pot or withdrawe the woode of the fyre or ellys to drawe the pot moore abacke froo the fyre. On the same wise men sholde doo ayeins this synne of lecherye. For whan men felith theym tempted with the syn of lecherye, oo consel ther is for to renne to colde water to caste opon hym or to caste hym in it, or he sholde take goode discipline and stronge abstinence or ellis to haue in mynde þe peynes that men deserve for that synne. As men fynde in *Vitis Patrum* of a goode man that was grevously tempted with a woman that he hadde herborghed in his house for Goddys sake. And whan he felt hym thus tempted, hee lighted a candell and brent al his fingeris. And be the woo that he felte in his fyngerys he was delyuered of the temptacion. And leuer he hadde to goo to paradis withowte fyngeris than into helle with alle his fyngeris. The secounde remedye aȝeins this synne is to withdrawe from his bodye too delicious metis and drinkys, specially siche as meve moste to lecherye, as stronge wynes and poigniant sauses be. The thirde remedie is a man too withdrawe hym froo the fyre of lecherye. As Seint Poule seithe and techeth vs ther where he seithe: Flee fornicacion and approche it not. For Seint Ambrose seithe: A man maye stryve with alle vicis and goo aȝeins theym and haue nere bataille with theyme, but froo this a man maye never soo welle defende hym as be fleynge. Three resones ther be whye a man sholde flee this synne. The firste is because that lechery is the fyre, and the man is herdis in the fyre. The seconde reson is because that this synne is to foule. For liche as it is not goode to werstyl with a man al fulle of myre, for a man sholde shende hymselfe than, on the same wise men sholde drawe abacke and flee this synne for þe filthe therof. The thirde reeson is because it is not goode to feight nere with his enemy, the whiche is siche that the nerer men aproche the more waxeth his strenghthe. And that is lecherye. And he that gothe aȝeins that enemy leesith the more his strengthe, that is the bodye of man, the whiche afore was stronge and in peesse. And in aprochyng this enemye he ioyneth to hym and maketh as a pees with hym because that he obeieth to hym and doothe his wille. But ther be iii thyngys the whiche deceyvith some pepil aȝeins this remedye. Firste the holynes and the bountee that men holde in some women, of the whiche Seint Ierome seithe: If thowe wilte seke a chaste louf to thyn herte, seke the woman that thowe shalt see of goode conuersacion, and ȝit goo not often there where shee is. The [f. 72] toother thynge is that a man troste not to myche in his chastite. Wherefore Seint Ierome seithe: Truste not to myche in thy chastite and suffre lityl or noght woomen to disporte theym in thyn house. For thowe art not hoolyer than Dauid ne wiser than Salamon ne strenger þan Samson, and notwithstandyng al iii were deceyved be woomen. The iii reson is whye sometyme men ar deceyved be woomen it is þe lynage. Therfore men sholde not troste to myche therin. As Seint Ierome seithe: Ne bee with woomen aloone what that euer shee bee ne sette the not nere hirre. And also a man sholde flee the placis where hee sholde see woomen, ne hee sholde not be seyn of woomen. And specially it is to flee placys where karolles be ledde for synnes that men doo there and maye doo. And bothe theye that lede it and thoo that beholdeth it doothe amysse, and that it is grete harme and grete synne to karolle. Seint Austin witnesseth it and seithe that it were better on the Sondaye to eree and too delve than too karolle. For sen that men defendeth bodyly labour on Sondaye and at festys, the whiche myght be too the worshipp of God or too his neghborugh or prophit to hymselfe, howe than was this labour too karolle graunted the whiche is to the disworshippe of God and of seintis and to the dampnacion of hym and of his neghborghes? Hardyly it was never granted. Alsoo thoo that karoleth doothe aȝeins the commandementis and aȝeyns the sacrementis of holy chirche in many maneres. Firste theye doo aȝeyns the sacrement of bapteme, for theye breke the covenantys that theyre godfaderes and godmoderes seide for theyme that theye forsooke the feende and alle his werkys and alle his prides. And the feendes pride is karolles. And thoo that doothe theyme be monkes and nones of the feendes. And thoo that beholdeth theym and that be aboute theye be as paryshones to þe feende and haue parte of alle the evilles that theye doo þat leedeth the karoles, and sometyme theye doo wers. [f. 72v] That karoles be the feendes possessiones it shewith because that men torne on the lefte side. Of the whiche the scripture seithe: The weyes that tornyth on the right hande Godde knowith thoo. Thoo that turneth on the lefte hande be contrarious and evil, and God hateth thoo. Aȝeyns the sacrement of ordre doo theye that lede karoles and doothe as the feendes ape, for theye doo siche service to the feende as clerkys and pristys doo to God. And often be theire songe and theire karoles the songe of hooly chirche is often dispised, for it happeth oftyn that thoo þat sholde be at the chirche and at evynsonge abideth stille in karoles. Aȝeyns the sacrement of mariage syn þey that make karoles, for ther be many causes to doo aȝeyns the trouthe of mariage and many steryngys be many songes that men seye and synge. Alsoo theye doo aȝeyns þe sacrement of confession. For men defendeth and sholde defende karoles to theym that confessith theyme, for alle thoo that karoleth synneth with alle theire membris in passyng qweyntly, in mevyng theire armys and in shakyng, and in spekyng dishonestly, in hyryng, in seynge, in qweynte and ioly arayes wherin theye synne dedly, and soo doo theye that seeyth the dedly synnes be the noble arayes and the mevyngys to syn of lechery and too dampnacion.

Of the Synne of Glotonie, IIII^{XX}

The laste vice is glotonie. This vice is ful plesant too the feende. For as the scripture seithe it sleepeth alweye in moiste places as a swyne doothe. It fleeth sure places, that is to sey, soobre [f. 73] hertys. Wherof wee reede in the gospel that oure loorde ȝeaf the feende leve to entre into swyne, and whan he was entred he drowned theyme in the see in tokyn that he hatthe leve to entre intoo glotounes, the whiche leedith swynes life, and to drowne theyme in the see of helle and to make theyme eete soo myche too they breste and drynke soo myche too theye drowne theymselfe. Whan a champion hatthe overthrowen his felawe and holdeth hym be the throote, he maye not welle ryse. On the same maner it fareth be hym that the feende holdeth in this vice. And therefore he rynneth gladly to the throote as the woolfe doothe to strangle a sheepe, liche as in paradis he did to Adam and to Eve and as he wende to a don to Criste Iesus whan he tempted hym in deserte. This vice displeseth God gretely, for it doothe hym ful grete shame whan he maketh a sacke fulle of donge his God, that is to seye, his belye, the whiche he trusteth, loufeth, and serveth moore than God. God commandeth hym to faste, and the beely seithe to hym: Thowe shalt not; certis thowe shalt rather eete longe and be leyser. God commandeth hym to rise eerly. His bely that lyeth be hym seithe to hym: Thowe shalt not; I am too fulle; I moste sleepe. The chirche doore is not ȝit opyn. It shalle abide me wel inowe. And whan he hatth slepte soo myche that he maye no more, he riseth and begynneth his matins and his prayeris, seyinge: Oo goode God, what shalle men ete todaye? Shalle we fynde ought that goode is? After his matines he begynneth laudes: Oo God, what we hadde goode mete ȝisterevyn; I sawe never erste siche meete. And howe trowest thowe compleynyth hee his synnys? Alas, seithe hee, I was tonyght nere dede. The wyne of ȝistirevyn was to stronge. Myn heede akith. I shal never bee at ease to I haue dronken. Here is an evil god; he bryngeth a man too shame, as it shewith be these rebawdes opon whom al the worlde cryeth and hateth. For first hee haunteth the tauernes. After he is a pleyer at the diz. Than sellith hee al that he hatth and becommeth a rebaude or an hullour or a theef, and soo men hange hym. Howe it bringeth hym too pouertee men seeth it dayly. It maketh hym too selle londes, heritages; it disheryteth his childer; it taketh aweye his goodez; it shendeth the bodye; it taketh froo hym his reeste, his sleepe, myght to faste, and wil to serve Godde; it maketh hym febil, hevye, and seeke, and bryngeth hym to pouertee [f. 73v] and to deethe. Seint Gregore deviseth this synne in v braunches for in v maneres men synne in glotonye: be eetyng or drinkyng or because that men eete oute of tyme or withowte mesure or to hastely or too delyciously. It is a greete synne and too foule a vice in a man of aage that he may not abide the right houre of eetynge. It coometh of greete likerousnes of the throte whan a man rynneth the whiche is stronge and hoole to mete afore the right houre withoute a resonable cause, as doomme beestes doo. Fulle grete synnes cometh of this costome, and this vsage becometh as nature froo the whiche men maye not withdrawe theym. Wherfore it happeth that siche men hatthe alweye hunger afore tyme and seithe that he hatthe too evil an heede. And he seithe soothe, for siche hatthe he made it. Hee seithe hee maye neyther faste ne doo penaunce. Hee breketh and draweth hym from hooly fastes, the whiche be commanded in holy chirche. Wherfore siche pepil knoweth wel that theye lif not liche Cristen pepil but as doome bestes, the whiche eteth nyght and daye and alweye whan talent taketh theyme or rather for theye abide not to talent taketh theyme. And therfore siche pepil eteth never goode morsell for theye haue not the right sause camelyn, the whiche maketh al metes sauory. That is to seye, talent is not medelid therwith, of the whiche men seye a goode woorde that plente sauoureth not. For a goode man hatthe moore delite whan he hatthe fasted and a poore labourer whan he hatthe laboured too eete his peese or his woo[r]tys than a likerous man hatthe to eete lampreys or fesantes and he that gothe on foote to drynke colde water than the gloton hatthe to drynke stronge wyne. If hee dampned hymselfe alon, it were the lesse charche, but he wil haue feleshipp too doo as hee doothe, the whiche he draweth froo weldede and leedeth theyme with hym to helle, for he maketh theyme too breeke fastes and too doo glotonyes fro the whiche theye wolde kepe theyme ne were evil feleshipes. For drynkeris and likerous pepil amonge oother synnes that theye doo theye doo on the whiche is kalled proprely the feendes crafte, for theye drawe froo goode dedes thoo that louf to doo welle. Theye seye theye maye not faste, but theye lye. For the litel louf that theye haue to God maketh theyme too doo and to seye soo. For if [f. 74] they loufed as myche the veraye ioye of hevyn as the vainglorye of the worlde liche as theye faste for temporell besynesse somtyme to it be nyght, as wel woolde theye faste oo daye for the louf of God if theye loufed hym as myche. This vice is right grevouse in a yonge man, but it is myche grevouser in an aged man. Wherfore Ysaie the prophete seithe: A childe of an c ȝere is cursed. He calleth hym or hir a childe the whiche wil alweye haue breede in the hande. Thowe shalt wit that liche as it is synne to eete too erly soo it is synne to eete to late if it be not doon for some nesessite. Wherfore siche pepil that loufeth to wacche so myche be nyght and wasteth the tyme in idilnes and goothe late too bedde, theye synne in many maneres, first in that theye waste the tyme and maketh it beestely in as myche as theye make of the nyght daye and of the daye nyght. Siche pepil God cursith bee his prophete Ysaie. And Dauid seithe it in the Sauter: Thowe sholdest on the daye doo wel and on the nyght thanke and worshipp God. And in the Booke of Iob God prayseth myche the wit of the cok the whiche goothe to his reste atte the sonnegoynge-adowne and at mydnyght refressheth hym and begynneth to synge, and whan it is daye he forȝeteth not too ryse betymes to seke his mete and to kepe his hennys. But theye doo neyther the ton ne the toother. For whosoo than leyeth hym downe he moste sleepe whan he sholde wake and whan hee sholde worshippe and prayse God. And thus leeseth he al his tyme, for he leesith bothe the nyght and the daye. Alsoo in siche wacchyngis men doo myche evil, pleye at the chesse and at the tablis, and speketh many iapes and folies. Thus the caytif wasteth his tyme and his wit and angreth God and grevith his bodye and ʒit more his soule. Theye be therfore blessed the whiche of childehoode be taught to lede a goode lyf in rewle and oneste and to reste betyme and to rise betyme as al religious pepil doo and as birdys doo the whiche techeth vs too ryse betymes and too prayse Godde.

Too Eeete Outeragyously afore Tyme, IIII^{XX}I

[f. 74^{v}] The seconde braunche is to eete outeragiously and to drinke oute of mesure. Thoo be veryly glotones the whiche al glotyth as doothe the putok or the cormeraunt. It is seide of a nyce man that is a sot that he woote never whan he hatthe etyn inoughe. Vnnethe is ther in the worlde amonge a ml iii that knoweth wel this mesure and þat kepeth it withoute doynge amysse. Therfore oure lyf is sorwful and oure condicions perlious. For the flesshe fareth as an evil womman the whiche wil alweye be lady and maistras too whom a man is bounde in siche maner þat he maye not leve hirre, be shee goode or evil. But whooso wil lerne this mesure he moste knowe and vnderstande þat ther be many maners of liferris in this worlde. Some lyfe after the flesshe, some after iolynesse, some oppon ypocrisye, some oppon covetise, some oppon phisike, some vppon theire curtesye, some after that theire synnes requireth, and some vppon the sperit and vppon the louf of God. Thoo that lyffeth after the flesshe, as Seint Poule witnessith and seithe, theye slee the soule, for of theyre bely theye make theire god. Theye holde neyther reeson ne mesure. And therfore theye shalle haue peyne withowte mesure. Thoo that lif opon theire iolynesse and wil holde felishippes maye nor can holde no mesure. Thoo that lyf as ypocrites, theye haue ii mesures, for the ii feendes the whiche tormenteth ypocrites is ful contrarious the ton to the toother. The ton seithe: Eete inowe þat thowe maye be feire and fat. The toother seithe: Thowe shalte not. Thowe shalt faste that thowe maye be pale and lene. Thus theye comand theym ii mesures, oon litil and scarse the whiche theye vse afoore the pepil, the toother goode and large the whiche theye vse whan noon seeth theyme. And whan theye haue geetyn the praye that theye haue longe chassed thanne caste theye aweye the scarsnesse and kepeth the largenesse. Thoo that be ledde be couetise hath siche mesure as theyre purs ȝifeth theym, for that is ladye and commaunderesse. Wherfore betwene the pors and the covetous gloton is a goode disputacion. The belye seithe: Y wil be fulle. The porse seithe: Y wil be fulle. þe belye seithe: I wille that thowe eete, drynke, and dispende. þe porse answerith: Thowe shalt not, for I wille that thowe kepe and spare. What shalle that caityf doo that is bonde to thoo ii evil lordes? He doothe ii mesures to make his pees. The mesure of his bely in anoother mannes howse is goode and large. The mesure of his porse in his owne house is [f. 75] woofull and scarse. Thoo that lif after theire phisike holdeth the mesure of Ypocras, the whiche is litil and streyte. Wherfore theye be often pale and lene, for theye doo neyther the wil of the flesshe ne the wil of the soule ne the wil of God but that the whiche Galyen commandeth. Thoo that lif opon theire oneste theye be thoo that holdeth the mesure of reeson and as to the worlde lifeth worshippfully and eeteth at due houre and tyme and curteisly and meryly takith aworthe siche as theye haue. Thoo that lifeth after that theyre synnes requireth holdeth siche mesure as is charched theym in penaunce. Thoo that lif oppon the sperit be thoo that is ledde be loufe and that the Holy Goste techith to holde ordre and reson and mesure and religion. Theye be loordes of their bodyes the whiche theye discipline and teche, soo that theye aske noon outrage but doothe alle that the sperit commandeth withoute grucchynge or geyneseyinge. Siche pepil men sholde louf and holde dere and holde and kepe and norisshe siche bodies. Theye maye oonly holde the rewle and the mesure that God ȝeaf too his aposteles whan he sende theyme to preche and seide to theym: Oueralle where yee goo eete and drynke siche as ȝee fynde. For a goode seruaunt deservith welle his mete. Therfore God commanded that men sholde not bynde the mosel of the oxe the whiche laboreth the cornes. Thowe maiste wel see nowe apon that the whiche wee haue seide that the feende hatthe many wyles to take theym be the throote that servith of this crafte. For fyrst he shewith wynes and metes the whiche be feire and behovely, as he didde the appil to Eve. And if that be not worthe to hym: Eete and drynke, sẹithe hee, as theye and thoo other doo. Thowe moste holde this feleshipp. Wilt thowe that menne mokke thee or that men holde thee for a papelart? Or ellys he seithe to hym: Thowe moste kepe the helthe of the bodye. He hatthe noothynge that hatthe not helthe. Thowe synnest grevously if thowe be a mansleer of thyselfe. Or he seithe to hym: Thow sholdest sustene thye bodye. Beholde the goodnes þat thowe haste doon. Thowe eetest not for thye de[li]t but for to serve God and to helpe thye neghborughe. Thowe owest thy strengthe to God, as Dauid seithe. And Seint Poule seithe that penaunce of bodye is [f. 75^{v}] lytil worthe, but dedis of pitee is myche worthe. Siche resones be soo attaigneyng that the wysest and the holyest be sometyme deceyved. This bataile is ful envenimouse whan a man maye not breke it atte oo strooke, as a man doothe the bataile of lecherye be sight of chastite, but he moste kepe the felde to the ende. And it happeth often that men wene to haue ouercomen this bataile whan after men falle fouler. And therfore the bataille is þe more perliouse. For the feende somtyme reculeth the better to assaile and restith hym the better to flee and makith a man faste soo myche that he castith hym in langoure and in siche sekenes that he moste seke grete delites, and than assaileth he hym hardily and ouercometh hym shamfully.

Too Eete Too Fervently, IIII^{XX}II

The iii braunche of this vice is to rynne too mete too fervently as a hounde to carayne, liche as Esau for a disshefull of soo foule potage as is the meete of lentilles, *id est*, [...] soolde his asse be siche a covenaunt that never after he myght recouere it. The sperit of man sholde be the asse and lorde of the house and the bodye his seruaunt. Bee glotony hee lesith his asse. For the bodye is lorde and the sperit seruaunt. And thus the firste man in erthely paradis loste his dignitee whan hee soolde hym and vs for an appil be siche covenant that never sithen man of his ligne recoueryd hoolly this dignitee but Criste Iesus and his sweete mooder. The scripture calleth siche veleins houndes whan theye rynne too the meete as houndes too the carayne. And the gretter that this ferventnes is the gretter is the synne. For as it is no synne to haue richesse but to louf it to myche, evyn soo it is noo synne too eete goode metes but to eete to fervently and to glout[on]ously. Alle meetes be goode to goode pepil and to the whiche vseth theyme clenly, that is to seye, be reeson and be mesure and with hoolynes and fere of God. For howe that ever it bee, a man sholde alweye haue fere too mystake hym in eetyng and drinkyng [f. 76] and woofull that a man is in thraldome too norisshe the bodye. A man sholde prayse God for his goodenes and of his ʒiftes and thanke hym that soo myche swetnes hatthe maade for to serve and too norisshe and too feede man with. And be the swetnes of the meete that maye not fylle man sholde thynke on the swetnes of God [and] on that mete that filleth the herte. Therfor in houses of religion men reede atte meete because that whan the bodye taketh his meete on the too part the soule to take his on the toother parte, that is, the hooly woorde of God be þe whiche man lifeth, as God seithe in the gospell whan the feende tempted hym with glotony.

Too Eete To Nobilly, IIII^{XX}III

The iiii braunche is the synne of thoo the whiche wil liffe to nobilly and pleye the ryche man, as the riche man didde of whom the gospelle speketh that euerye daye he lifed nobilly. But his delites were chanched intoo tourment for o drope of water alonly the whiche he asked c ʒere agone he hatthe it not ʒit, with the whiche he wolde a kelyd his tonge that brente in the fyre of helle. The scripture seithe in the Booke of Sapiens that in what that euer God doothe he kepith iii thyngys: weight, nombre, and mesure. Aʒeyns theese iii thyngys syned that meteʒeifer in as myche as he weyed neyther the pryse ne the taste of the throote and what goode he myghte a doone with that he dispended and wasted folily be his throote. Is it not grete synne and oultrage whan a man for to fille his belye wasteth and dispendeth wherewith he myght sustene hymselfe and fede x porc men? Herefore the scripture calleth the belye an vsurer because liche that as the vsurer putteth the pepil in pouertee soo doothe the belye the whiche cryeth alweye: Brynge. Nowe take heede here of the curtesye of God, of the sotilte of the feende, and of the foolye of the worlde. The thynge that be moste nessessarie and profitable to mannes bodye be thoo that God hatthe maade moste plente of, as is breede, peesyn, and wortys, and comune flesshe, the whiche is of litel coste, but plentee sauoureth not, and þat causeth the feende the whiche setteth before theym lucys and lampreis and wynes for to make theym to synne in many maneres: first in grete dispenses, after that in vsyng it too feruently and with to grete delit, alsoo in the veinglorye that theye haue [f. 76^{v}] therof. For this is not only for likerousnes of the throote but for pride that theye haue therin. Theye seeke metes of dere coste rather than though theye myght haue it for lityll. Therfore theye doo this withowte weight and withoute nombre of meses and withowte mesure of metes and of tymes the whiche theye vse in eville woordes and than in drinkes.

Off Likerousnes, $\mathrm{IIII}^{\mathrm{XX}}\mathrm{IIII}$

The v braunche is the cur[iosite] of glotones, the whiche thynke of noothynge but for to delite theire places. Theye be proprely likerous that stodye in siche a scole. For Seint Poule calleth it the prudens of the flesshe, the whiche is dethe too the soule. This clergye is soo mounted that euery man rynneth thertoo, greete and litill, soo that noon lifeth opon nature. And that is noo merveile for in the cradylle men ʒefeth yonge childer wyn too drynke the whiche be not wonte to assay it too theye be xv ʒeere olde. Howe sholde he faste [on] breede and water the whiche hatthe lerned in the cradille too drynke wyn? In theese iii thyngys lieth anamly the synne of siche pepil þat thynke soo besily: first in the besynes that theye haue too purchace, after that in the grete delit that theye haue to vse it, and than in the ioye that theye haue too remembre it. Whoo maye remembre the besynes and the desires that theye haue and the thoughtis and the sighyngis that theye make, alsoo what diligens and cur[iosite] þey doo that theyre metes maye be wel arayed euery in his right [s]auoure and howe theye maye make diuerse meses and gwyses for to delit withalle the palaice? Whan the mesys comyth oon after an nother, triffles [and] iapes cometh withalle. And than theye mysseye and dispise theire neghboroughes alweye in the werste wyse that theye can but never speke of theyre goode dedes. And thus the tyme goothe, and the caytif forȝetith hymselfe. Reson slepeth, and the stomak cryeth: Ladye þrote, ȝe slee me. I am soo fulle that I am a poynt to breste. And the lykerous mouthe answerith: If thowe sholdest breste, ȝit wil I not leve this goode morsell, ne this goode wyne shalle not ascape me. After þe likerousnes that cometh atte mete commeth the ioye that theye haue to remembre it. Than wolde theye that theye hadde a nekke like a crane because the morcelle sholde longe dwelle in thee throote and a bely like a cowe because that theye myght eete alle. Nowe haste thowe herde the synnes that cometh of glotonye and likerousnes. And because that siche synnes groweth in tauernes the whiche is welle of synne, therfore I wil [f. 77] speke of the synnes of the likerousnesse of the tauerne.

Off Synnes and Harmys That Men Doo in the Taverne, IIII^{XX}V

The taverne fareth as a welle of the whiche spryngeth alle synnes and harmes. For ther is the feendis scole where his litil disciples stodyeth in his chapelle, where men doothe his service, and ther where men doothe opyn miraclys siche as longeth too the feende. ȝee knowe welle that at the chirche God is wonte to shewe his vertues and too doo myraclys, to make the blynde to see, the crookyd too be redressid, madde pepil to haue witte, the doome too speeke, the deffe to hiere. But the feende doothe evyn the contrarie. Whan the gloton goothe too the taverne, hee goothe right and welle. Whan hee commeth aweye, he hatthe noo foote that maye bere hym aright, but hee maketh of o weye tweyn. And whan he goothe theder, hee herith and seeth and vnderstandeth and spekyth welle. Whan he commeth therfroo, he hatthe loste al that. For hee neyther hirith, seeth, ne vnderstandeth, ne maye not speke, for bothe his tonge and his reeson is bounde. He hatthe neyther witte ne mende, and alle is loste be glotonye. Siche be the miracles that men doo there. Feire sire, what lessones be redde there wher men lerne al harlotrye and glotonye and too mysseye, to lye, too swere and forswere, too boule, too amisse, too baret, too putte to shame and too pouertee oon anoother? There riseth noyses, chidyngis, medleis, manslaughter, werris, and hates. There lerne men to stele and too take from oother and too make hymselfe be hanged. Nowe telle me wheder synneth moore the maisteris or the disciplis, that is to seye, the drinkeris [or] the tavern[er]is or the loordes that sustene theyme. The drinkeris drinketh and swere etc. The tavernerys resseyvith theym in theire howses and maketh it a denne for theefys and a strengthe for the feende for to werre with God and his seintis. And the baily and the prouoste and the seriant and the loorde seeth it and herith it and consenteth thertoo and al thoo loordis that luf soo myche rentes and issues and the amendes of the tavernes that theye haue for the mysdedis that men doo there. Whether is better, he that holdeth þe foote or he that fleith it? Theye flee God alle qwycke and dismembre hym and his swete mooder and al the seintis of hevyn. And it is noo dowte but that alle thoo that susteyneth theym bee [f. 77v] partoneris too al the synnes that men doo there. Certis if men did or seide as myche shame too their flesshely fader as men doo too oure fader of hevyn, and too theire moderes as men doo too owre ladye, and too theire pagys as men doo to seintys of hevyn, theye sholde derly amende it. And alsoo loordes wolde sette oother counsell therin than theye doo heerein. In alle theese treis and smale branches that wee haue rehersed and in alle the branches that wee have nombred be many lefys but litil fruit. God ʒif vs grace too make siche fruit that alle wee maye be savyd. Hee graunte vs that for his bountee, hee that dwellith hye in the trinite the whiche lifeth and reigneth and shalle reigne in *seculorum secula*. Amen.

Off Remedies aȝeyns That Synne of Glotonye, IIII^XX^VI

We haue nowe spokyn of the vice of glotonye. Nowe wil wee speke of remedyes aȝeyns that vice. The firste remedye is to here and vnderstande the woorde of oure loorde. This remedye oure loorde techith vs in the gospelle there where he seide too the feende whan he tempted hym in the vice of the throote whan he had fasted xl dayes [and] hee seide too hym thus: Man lifeth not alonly be breede but be the woorde that cometh owte of the mouthe of Godde. That is too seye that no moore than a man maye lif bodyly withouten breede noo moore hee maye lif goostely withowte that hee hiere hooly scripture redde, whiche is the woorde of Godde the whiche causeth oftyn bodyly meete to bee forȝetin. The seconde remedye is too occupye hym in some goode dede. For as Salamon seithe: Desires sleith slowe pepill, the whiche wil noothyng doo but coueitith and desireth likerousnes. The eris desirith too hiere; þe yen coveitith vaniteis; the mouthe to engloute delicious metys. But some goode occupacion the whiche is to doo goode dedis restreyneth siche desires. The iii remedye is too thynke what the flesshe shalle be aftir the deethe, for it shalle be wormys meete. The [f. 78] iiii remedye is to take heede of the harmys that cometh and maye come of outeragious drinkyng and eetyng that men doo. First ther men lernyth and geteth deethe too the soule and after that oftyn deethe to the body, and thus men lesith bothe bodye and soule be glotonye. The v remedye is to thynke on the deethe of Criste Iesus that hee suffred hymselfe and that hee suffrith ȝit in his membris, that is too seye, in poore pepil of this worlde, the whiche suffreth myche hunger and colde and many oother diseassis that theye haue in theire bodyes. For the whiche men oughte too withdrawe theyme from outerages that theye doo in eetynge and drynkynge whan theye remembre theyme of the pouerte of Iesus Cristes poore pepil, the whiche vnnethe maye haue any breede. It is fulle grete merveyle of the riche pepil of this worlde that theyre consience remembrith theym not oftyn howe theye withdrawe from Goddes mouthe and putteth it in the feendes throote. That is to seye þat theye feede the feendes childer and theye lete Goddis childer dye for hunger. The chief and the laste remedie aȝeyns this vice is the grace of God. Therfore whoosoo is entechid with this vice hee sholde be in prayer and require the grace of Godde, the whiche restreyneth the feruentnesse of the throote. For as Seneque seithe: Whoosoo wil lif in delites withouten ende he sholde withdrawe hym from siche delites and froo siche bodyly covetises froo the which hee maye not withdrawe hym withowte special grace of oure lorde.

Off Synnes of the Tonge, IIII^{XX}VII

Whoosoo wil knowe the synnes of the tonge hee moste thynke and thynke aȝein the woorde what it is and whense hit cometh and what harme it doothe. For it maye happe that the [f. 78^{v}] woorde is synne and evil in hymselfe because that it is evil. And alsoo it happith that it is synne because that it cometh of right an evil herte. And it happeth alsoo that the worde is synne because þat it doothe grete harme, be it never soo feire polisshed. Thowe shalt nowe knowe þat an evil tonge is the tree that Godde cursed in the gospelle because he founde noothynge therevppon but levys. Be the levys is vnderstonden in hooly writ woordys. And as it is and harde thynge for to nombre the levys, soo it is and harde thynge for to nombre the synnes. But wee wille sette x chefe braunches the whiche groweth of this tree. And theese x braunches maye be called thus: idilnesse, avauntynge, flaterynge, backebytynge, lyynge, forswerynge, stryvynge, grucchynge, rebellynge, blamynge.

Off Idyll Woordys, IIII^{XX}VIII

Thoo that abaundoneth theym to speke idil woordys falleth into full grete harme, the whiche theye perseyve not. For theye leese the precious tyme of the whiche ȝit hereafter theye shalle haue fulle greete nede, and theye leese the goodnes that theye myghte and sholde doo, and theye leese the tresor of the herte and filleth it with vanite. Theye vnhylle the potte and letith flyes goo intoo it. Theye calle theyme idille woordis, but theye be not. Theye be rather ful costelewe, perlious, and harmeful, as þoo that voydeth the herte of alle witte and as thoo of þe whiche hee moste ȝif acommpt of euery woorde atte the daye of doome streitly afoore Godde, as hee seithe in the gospelle. It is not a litel thynge of the whiche men moste ȝif reeson and commpt in soo hye a courte as tofore God and alle the loordes of hevyn. In theese idyll woordys men synne in v maneres. For ther be somme woordys vaine, of the whiche some tonges be soo fulle that spekyth a[f. 79]fore and behynde the whiche fareth as a mylle that maye not be stylle. And also ther be some idille wordys, as in theyme that telleth gladly tydyngys the whiche setteth oftyn in disease the hertys of thoo that herith theyme and maketh the telleris of theyme to be holden fals and lierris. Alsoo ther be some faire woordes and tales wherein many oon hatthe vayneglorie, the whiche that can telle theym sotilly for to make the hererris to laughe. Alsoo ther be iapes and trifflis ful of harlotrye and of lyes that theye kalle idille woordes, but truly it is not soo. Theye be raþer fulle stynkyng and fulle grevouse. Alsoo ther be some as gawdys and scornynggys that theye seye of goode men and woomen and of theym that wolde doo welle because that theye myght drawe theyme too theyre acorde and too withdrawe theyme froo the goodnes that theye haue conceyved. Theese be non idille woordys. For thowe art as a mansleer if thowe with thy tonge withdrawest man or childe froo goode dede. And Godde kanneth the as myche thanke as the kynge woolde doo if thowe haddest kylled his soone or stoolyn his tresor.

Off Avauntynge, IIII^{XX}IX

After this cometh the synne of avauntyng, the whiche is fulle grete and fulle fowle and ful foliche and fulle veleins. It is ful greete for he that vaunteth hym is properly a theef to Godde and wolle take froo hym his glorie, as wee haue seide longe agon. It is a ful foliche synne for of the goodenes wherewith he myghte geete hevyn hee ȝeefeth it for a lityl wynde. And alsoo it is a fulle foule syn for the selve worlde holdeth hym for a foole and for veleins and for nice. This branche hatthe v leffis, that is to seye, v maner of vauntynggis. Oon is of thynge that is paste. This synne is in theym the whiche wille gladdely reherse theire dedes and theyre worthinessis in siche as theye weene theye haue wel doon or wel seide. The toother is of present temmps. [f. 79v] This is the synne of thoo whiche doothe noothynge gladly ne peynyth theym too doo welle ne to seye welle but oonly where men hirith or seeth theyme. Theye avaunt theyme euer, wheder it be in dooyng, daunsyng, or syngyng, and [s]elleth al that euer theye doo for nought. To this longeth the synne of theyme that vaunteth theyme of the goodnes that theye haue or that theye wene to haue as of theyre noblesse, of theyre richesse, and of theyre worthynesse. Theye fare as the cokkowe, the whiche kan not synge but of hymselfe. Thiii leef is in thoo the whiche be ouerhoopeyng and seithe: I shalle doo this and that; I shalle make hilles and velyes. The iiii leef is more subtile, that is of theyme the whiche derre not for shame prayse theymselfe, but what that euer any ooþer seieth or doeth alle theye blame and dispice as though it were not worthe too that the whiche they can doo and seye. The v leef is mooste subtile, as whan theye wolde preyse theymeselfe and derre not doo it oopynly, theye doo it contrariously and maketh theyme meeke and seieth that theye be soo evyl, soo synful, and soo vnkonnyng thre tymes moore than theye be because that men sholde prayse theyme and holde theyme meke. Alas, seith Seint Bernard, what this is an harde vauntyng. Theye make theyme feendes because that men sholde holde theyme angellis and maketh theym evil because that men sholde holde theyme goode. And ȝit men maye not angre theyme moore than for to seye: ȝe seye soothe. Too this longeth the synne of theyme that sekyth avocatis for too prayse theyme [and] for too crye theyre [obleys] be the whiche mouthe theye speke the moore hardily.

Off Flaterynge, IIII^{XX}X

Flatererris be norices too the feende, þe whiche ȝifeth his childer sowke and bringeth theyme too sleepe in theire synnes be theyre feyre syngyng. Theye anoynte the weye of helle with hoonye, as men doothe to the bere, because that synneres sholde goo thedir the moore hardily. This synne is devided in v partes as in v lefys. The firste synne in this braunche is in [f. 80] flatererris that whan theye see that hee or shee [that] wolde be praysed hatthe doon anythynge wel or seide welle anoon theye goo and telle it too theymeselfe because they sholde haue veinglorye therof, but theyre shrewdenesse wille theye never telle theyme. The ii syn is in theyme the whiche encressith the litel goodes þat theire childer doo or seye double foolde and putteth thertoo soo myche o theyres that ther be moo lesyngys þan soothes. And therfore in holy scripture theye be called fals witnessis. The iii synne is whan theye make a man or a wornman to vnderstande that ther is in theyme myche goodnes and grace, of the whiche ther is noon. And therfore the scripture calleth theyme enchantours whan theye enchant a man soo myche that theye beleve theyme moore than theymselfe and that he belevith better that the whiche he hierith than that þe whiche he seeth and knoweth. The iiii synne is whan theye synge alweye *placebo*. That is too seye, my [l]orde doothe welle; my lorde seithe wel and torneth al too weele what that ever a man doothe and seithe, be it goode be it evil. And therfore theye be called echo, that is the sowne the whiche resowneth in hye hilles and acordeth it to what that a man wille and seithe it, be it wel be it evil, be it goode be it fals. The v synne is of flatererris, the whiche defendeth and ascuseth and couerith the synnes of theyme that theye wil flatere. And therfore in scripture theye be called tailles, for theye couere the harlotrye of the synnes of riche men for some temporel availe. Wherfore theye be likenyd to the tayle of a shee foxe, *id est*, goupil, for theire deceit and theire trecherie.

Off Bakbytyng, IIII^{XX}XI

Losengiers and evilseiers be of o scole. Theye be the ii meremeidynes of the whiche wee fynde in thee Booke of Bestes that ther be a maner of beestes in the see that men calle meremaydynes the whiche hatthe bodye of a womman and tayle [f. 80v] of a fisshe and cleys liche an egle, and theye synge soo swetely that theye make marynerys for too sleepe and þan devoureth theyme. Theese be losengeris that with theyre feire syngynge maketh the pepil too sleepe in theyre synnes. There be oother maner of monstres of the see that hight meremaidynes the whiche rennyth as an hors, some-tyme fleith, the whiche hatthe soo stronge venym that noo triacle maye avayle, for dethe cometh or that a man felith the bytynge. Theese be evilseierris, of whom Salamon seithe that þey byte as a serpent in trayson. And that venym kylleth iii atte oo strooke: hym that mysseieth, hym that hiereth it, and hym of whom men misseiethe. Theese be thoo alsoo the whiche knaweth and missehandelith goode religious pepille, the whiche be dede as too the worlde. Theye be more cruell than helle, the whiche devoureth noon but shrewis, but theese devoure goode pepil. Wherefore theye passe the sowe that hatthe pigges, the whiche wil right gladly bite a man that is clothid in a white gowne. Theye doo alsoo as a flye that maketh his neste and resteth hym in the ordure of a man. Theye fare alsoo as a botte that forsaketh floures and loufeth donge. In this braunche be v levis. The firste is whan theye contreve lesynges and evilles for too hurte and too reyse blame of oother. The ii is whan theye telle forthe the evylle that theye hire of oother and adde thertoo moore. The iii is whan he quenchith and settith atte noght alle the goodnes that a man hatthe and maketh it to be holden evil. He this eteth the man al hoole. And these oþer eteth hym not, but theye bite hym in takynge oo peece froo hym. The fourthe is proprely detraccion, whan hee withdraweth and cutteth any peece of the pepill and of the goodnes that theye doo and of the goodnes that þey hire seye of oother. Ever theye contreve aȝens it and putteth forthe a mese. Sertis, seithe hee, it is true. Hee is a fulle goode man. I louf hym ful wel. But he hatth in hym siche a default and that forthynketh me. He this is the scorpion that flatereth with the face and envenymeth with the tayle. The v is whan hee perverteth and torneth to the wers partye al that he hirith and seeth that man maye torne to welle or evil. And therfore he is a fals and an vntrewe iuge.

Off Lyinge, IIII^{XX}XII

[f. 81] A lye falseth a man liche as a man falsed the kynges seel or the popes bulle. And because that siche a man maketh false moneye and berith false letteris, atte the daye of doome he shalle be iuged as a falseire. A lyer is amonge men as a fals penye amonge goode pens and as chaff amonge corne. A lyer resemblith his fader, the whiche is the feende, as Godde seithe in the gospelle. For he is a lyer and fader of lesynges, as he that fonde and forged the firste lesyng and alweye ȝit forgeth. The feende sheweth hym in many fourmes and chaungeth hym in many gyses for too deseyve the pepil, and soo doothe a lyer. This braunche hatthe iii smale braunches. For ther bee some þat be fervent lyerris and some þat be hevy lyerris and some þat be noyouse lyerris, and in al theese is synne. For as Seint Austin seithe: He þat lyeth although hee helpe anoother be his lye ȝit he doothe his owne harme. Therfore fervent lyes is synne. But hevy lyes is gretter synne, as lies of ministrellis and of losengeris and of iaperris, the whiche telleth lesyngys and iaapes and bourdes for to soolas withalle the pepill. And dowte not it is boothe synne to the seyer and too the herer. But noynge lies is dedly synne whan men seithe theym visily and wytyngly for to harme oother therwith. Too this branche longeth alle falsnesses, fikilneses, disceites, and wyles that men doo thorougheoute the worlde for to deceyve or harme any oother, oother in bodye or in sowle or in goode or in name, wheder that euer it bee.

Off Periurii, IIII^{XX}XIII

It is an evil thynge for to lye, but ȝit it is a wers thynge a man too forswere hym. It is to perlious a thynge to forswere. And therefore oure lorde defendeth it soo myche, not but that in some point a man maye swere withoute synne [f. 81^{v}] aȝeins the opinion of lolleris but because that ofte sweryng maketh often forsweryng and often to synne men sholde kepe theyme therfroo. For in v[ii] maneres men synne in oothis. First whan men swere feruently, be it in dispite or willyngly, soo that hym semeth that men deliteth therin.

Therfore Seint Iames defendith it, not only sweryng whan nede is but the likerousnes and the wil to swere. Alsoo whan men swere lightly for noght and withoute reeson it is defended in the ii commandement of the feithe that Godde wroote in the stone tablis with his blessed fynger. Alsoo whan men swere custumabilly atte euery woorde. For ther be somme soo evil taught that theye can noothynge seye withoute swerynge. Siche pepil God hatthe in too grete dispite, for alleweye and for nought in witnes of alle that theye seye þey calle hym. For to swere is not ellis but for to calle Godde to witnes. The cause oughte to be ful grete and resonable and true where men derre calle soo grete a lorde to witnesse as Godde is and that bothe hym, his moder, and his seyntes. Also whan men swere folyly. And that happeth in many maneres: whan men swere folyly for angre and for that wherof a man repenteth hym after, or if men swere a thynge þat men maye not kepe withowte synne (siche oothis men sholde restreyne and doo penaunce for the foly oothe), or whan men swere certeynly for a thynge whereof a man is [not] certeyne though that it be true, or whan men swere be the sonne that shynyth or be this fyre that brenneth here or be my heede or be my moders soule or my faderis or be other thyngys liche. Godde forbedith siche oothis in the gospelle. For to siche thyngys that I wolde conferme I sholde not drawe too witnesse but the souerayne trouthe, that is God the whiche knoweth alle, not only pore creatures the whiche be but vaine, for whan I swere bisily be theym I doo one of the worshipes too theyme that I sholde doo proprely to God. But whan men swere by the gospelle men swere be hym too whom the wordes longeth, for whom theye bee wrytyn. Or whan men swere be hooly relikes or be seintes of hevyn men swerith be Godde the whiche dwelleth in theyme. Alsoo whan men swere veleinsly be God and be his seintis. In this part Cristen pepil be wers than Sarazines, the whiche in noo maner wille suffre men to swere veleinsly be Mahomet as Cristen pepille doo be Criste Iesus. For theye wil brisse noon of his membris, but Cristen pepil brekith [f. 82] theyme smaller than men doo porke in the bocherye. þeye aske noothynge of oure ladye, but theye breke hy[rre] soo velenisly, bothe hy[rre] and oother seintys, that it is merveyle þat

Cristen pepil suffreth it. Alsoo whan men swere falsly or berith fals witnesse or whan men swere fals wittyngly in what wyse that it be [...] oother be crafte or soophyme. For as the right scripture seithe: Godde the whiche louffeth symplesse and trouthe vndirstandeth the woorde and reseyvith the oothe in siche wyse as hee vnderstandeth it the whiche vnderstandeth ne seketh but wel and that vnderstandeth it simply and withowte disceite. The debonartee of God is fulle greete whan siche men swerith that the whiche theye woote wel is not true or promyseth a thynge that theye maye not holde that thee feende strangeleth theyme not anoon. For whan he seithe: Soo God me kepe or soo God helpe me and lieth, hee putteth hym owte of the grace and the helpe of oure loorde. Thus than of veray right he sholde leese witte and mynde and boody and goode and soule and al that he holdeth of God. The laste branche of this vice is whan men trespasse the feithe and that the whiche a man hatthe p[ro]misshed in his beleve outher be feithe or be oothe. For feithe lyed and oothe trespassed theye be as alle oone.

Off Chydynge, IIII^{XX}XIIII

Seint Austin seithe: Ther is noothynge that the feende louffeth soo myche as chydynge. Doute not but that this crafte pleesith the feende myche, the whiche louffeth noothyng but werre, and it displesith Godde gretely, the whiche louffeth but peese and acorde. This branche is devised in vii smale branches, of the whiche the firste is too strive, the seconde to chide, the thirde to thwarte, the foureth too seye evil, the fyfthe too reproche or reprove, the vi^{te} too manace, the vii^{the} to reise discorde. Whan þe feende seeth louff and acorde amonge pepil, it displesith hym myche, for hee doothe gladly his power to make theyme at discorde and for the stryve. And the feende begynneth too enbrase the fyre of ire and of evil wylle. Wherfore after contec and strif commeth noyse and chydyng, liche as a man whan he [f. 82^{v}] kyndelith fyre, after the smooke cometh owte [þe] flaumbe. Stryfe and chidyng [i]s whan oon seithe too anoother: It is soo; it is not; it was; it was not. Chidyng is whan oon lyeth anoother and spekyth grete woordys too hym. After this commeth disdeyne, that is whan thee tone poynteth the toother and spekith right felly. For ther be some soo felle that theyre tonges be sharper than sharpe rasorres and swyfter than fleyng arwes. Syche men be liche the portespine whan hee is smytyn with a thorne, the whiche is al cladde with alles, for hee is too felle and too sone angrye. For whan he is angryd hee shooteth the pryckes of his body and smyteth bothe on the right syde and on the lifte. Also hee is liche a felle curre, the whiche abayeth and biteth al thoo that he maye. After that commeth cursyng, that is whan one curseth anoother. And this synne is soo greete that the scripture seithe that whoosoo curseth his neghborgh hee is cursed of God. And Seint Poule seithe that siche pepil maye not haue the kyngedom of hevyn. And he seith that theyre mouthes fareth as a potte that boyleth ouer the fyre and spredith the boylyng ouer here and there and skaldeth thoo that be abowte it. Than cometh reproches, that is whan men reprocheth a man of his synnes, the whiche ȝit is gretter synne, and whan men reprovith hym of his folyes and of his pouerte or of his pore kynne or of any oother default þat is in hym. Sometyme than commeth manaces, and than begynneth melleis and werres. But above alle the synnes that we haue rehersed here is werste the synne of theyme that with theyre tongys susteynyth and mainteynyth discordis, and mevith evil willes aȝeyns theyme that were frendes togeder, and that distorbith pees and concorde. Godde hateth siche pepil, as the scripture seithe.

Off Grucchynge, III[I]^{XX}XV

[f. 83] Oftyn wee see that thoo the whiche derre not answere begynnyth too grucche and grinde betwene þeyre teethe. Therfore after stryfe wee set the synne of grucchynge. That this syn is grete shewith vs the vengeance that Godde doothe and was wonte too doo or taake, as hooly writte remembrith. For be this synne the erthe opyned and swalowed Dathan and Abiron, and theye discendid al qwik intoo helle. For this synne alsoo God sent fire from hevyn, the whiche brente Chore and alle his felawes ii^{c} and l of the grettest that was in the oste of oure loorde in desert. Be this synne alsoo the Iewis loste the lande of behest that God had promissed too theyme, soo that iic vi thousand that Godde hadde castyn from the thraldom of the kynge of Egipt and the whiche he hadde norysshed xl ȝere with manna of hevyn entred not into the hooly lande but oonly ii the whiche highte Caleph and Iosue. But alle dyed with woo in deserte. This synne hatth ii branches, for ther is grucchyng aȝeins God and aȝeins man. This synne reigneth in many maneres, as in seruauntis aȝeins theire loordes and in ientilwomen aȝeins theire ladyes and in childer aȝeins the fader and the mooder and in poore pepille aȝeins riche, in communes aȝeins knyghtis, in laye pepil aȝeyns clerkys and prelatis, in cloisteris aȝeins theyre abbotes, priouris, and officeris. And this grucchyng groweth in siche persones oother of inobedience because men make too harde commandementis or of slowthe because that men be too slowe or of inpacience because that men folweth not al theyre willes or of envye or felnes because that men avaunseth oon moor þan anoother and in many oother evil maneres. Grucchyng aȝens God hatthe ȝit many moo causes, of the whiche cometh impacience. For whan a man hatthe loste grace and wisdome he wolde be maister of God. For what that euer God doothe if hee doo not as hym liste anoon he gruccheth aȝeins God and ageyne his seintis and seithe the apes pater noster, not only the apes but the fendes. For liche as the Hooly Gost [f. 83v] techith and makith his chosyn to synge in theire hertis the swete worde of hevyn, the whiche is *Deo gratias*, for what that ever hee doothe to theyme and for what that ever he sendeth too theyme, evyn soo the shrewe makith his disciples too synge on the songe of helle, the whiche is grucchyng, that shalle euer dwelle in helle. And of what that ever God doothe if it be not holly too theyre liste anoon theye grucche. Truly a man is ful lewde and owte of his witte the whiche wil that God ȝif hym acompte of what that ever hee doothe. If he sende pouerte, aduersite, sekenes, derthe, reyne, droughte, ȝif hee ȝefe to oon and take froo another, if al be not doone at his liste, anoon he taketh aȝeyns God and gruccheth aȝeyns God and kan hym noo thanke. What merveyle is it though God venge hym oon siche pepill the whiche woolde take his lordeshippe froo hym?

Off Rebellynge, IIII^{XX}XVI

It is an evil thynge to grucche, but it is werse to rebelle. Rebellynge is a vice that cometh of the herte that is rebellious and harde and contrarious and diuers, the whiche wil ever that his wille be doon and his sentence kepte. For he wille that oother obeye to hym, and he wil obeye to noon. This is the herte of the whiche Salamon seithe that it maye not fayle to haue an evil ende. And as hee is grucchynge aȝeins God and man soo is he in herte rebelle aȝeins God an man. This vice hatthe iiii branches. For siche hertis be rebelle and contrarious too beleve counsell an to doo the commandement of God and too suffre chastisement and too reseyve techynge. If any of theyre frendes wolde counselle theyme and telle theyme and shewe theyme theyre avayle, theye wil not hire it; but because that theye speke it theye wil rather doo the contrarie. On the same wise too the counsell of oure loorde theye be oftyn rebellis and contrarious. [f. 84] If men counseille theyme anythynge to soulehele, theye wille not doo it but rather iapeth therat. And alsoo theye be rebelle too the commandementis of oure loorde to the whiche theye be bounde. And the feende putteth before theyme soo many lettyngis outher of febilnesses or of ȝougethes or of oother maner of evil resones that at the laste theye doo right nought. Also whan men chastice theyme and reproveth theyme theye defende theyme as borris, soo that theye knowe neyther theymeselfe ne theyre folyes. And the moore that þeye excuse theyme, the moore theye encrese theyre synnes. Oon the same whise theye fare whan Godde chastiseth and beteth theyme. Maugre of hym theye be wonte to seye, maugre of hym that, maugre of thee toother. What wil God with me doo? What haue I mysdon too hym? Thus doothe the foole. For that the whiche sholde bee tryacle to hym it torneth hym too venym, and the medecyn that sholde heele hym ȝeefeth hym dethe. After this ther be some of soo dyuerse wit that theye withholde noo goode techyng but alweye defendeth theyre sentensis, whatsooever theye bee, soo that oftyn theye falle in erroure and in fals opiniones and in mysbelevys.

Off Blaspheme, IIII^{XX}XVII

Blaspheme is, as Seint Austin seithe, whan men beleveth or seieth thyngys of Godde the whiche is not nor that men sholde beleve ne trowe and whan men belevith not that the whiche men sholde beleve and trowe. Specially wee calle blaspheme whan men seieth amys of God or of his mooder or of his seintis or of the sacrementis of hooly chirche. This synne is doon in many maneres: outher whan men doothe it with avice, as lollerris and mysbeleverris doothe, or whan men seieth it be covetice for wynynge, as enchantures and sorseris doothe, or whan men seieth it for ire or despite, as pleyerris doothe the whiche swerith soo veleynly by the boody of Criste Iesus and soo veleynisly mysseieth of God and of his swete mooder that it is horrible [f. 84^{v}] too hire. Theye be liche woode houndes that biteth and knoweth not oure loorde. This synne is soo grete that sometyme God ponyssheth it al opynly as we haue seide afore whan that we spake of evil [Iewis]. Godde seithe in the gospelle of this synne that it is never forȝovyn in this worlde ne in the toother; that is to seye, vnnethe it happeth that it is forȝovyn. Wee haue nowe reherced x maner of synnes of the tonge, of the whiche the firste is idilnesse and the laste blaspheme. And perauenture this it is the whiche Salamon seithe. For the begynnynge of an evil tonge is folye and in the ende right thikke erroure.

Here endeth the vii dedly synnes and alle theyre branches. Whoosoo wolde stodye welle in this booke, he myght profit gretely and lerne to knowe al maner of synnes and too confesse hym wel. For noon maye confesse hym wel ne kepe hym froo synne if he knowe it not. Nowe than he that redith in this booke sholde diligently take heede if he be culpable of any of theese synnes aforeseide. And if he fele that he be culpaple in any, he sholde repente hym and diligently confesse hym and than kepe hym fro theyme vnto his power and from oother of the whiche he is not coulpable. God oughte gretely to be praysed and mekely to be thanked of theyme that hatthe been kepte therfroo.

Off Profit of the Tonge, IIII^{XX}XVIII

Nowe I wille shewe yowe a litil howe yee sholde speke diligently and kepe youre woordis. For the scripture seithe that thowe shalte be iustified or condempned be thye woordis. Truly it is a grete shame a man to be condempned be his woordis. Therfore I counsel yowe to kepe youre mouthes not oonly from veleynyes woordis but alsoo from idill woordis, lyche as Seint Ierom seithe. Idil woordis is that the whiche berith [f. 85] no prophit. And some pepil ther be that settith theese venial synnes at nought, and alsoo theye thynke not of that the whiche Godde seithe in the gospelle that of al the idil woordys that a man spekyth he shalle ȝif acommpt at the daye of doome. And the glose seithe a woorde the whiche is gretely to doute that oure loorde takyth hiede soo nere and soo streitly to oure woordis, oure thoughtis, and oure deedis that ther is noon soo subtil a thought ne soo litil but that at the daye of doome it shal be rehersed and iuged. Thynke than howe cruelly veleyns woordis shalle be iuged and dampned and woordis of grucchyngis and of bakbitynggys, standyng that oure loorde shal iuge soo streitly idil woordis. Kepe yowe from litil synnes, yf yee wil flee the grete. Mooreouer ther is anoþer thynge that sholde withdrawe vs myche from idil wordys, that is be a litil deuote prayer wee maye gete grace of oure loorde and the kyngedom of hevyn. Alsoo to seye goode woordis wee maye ȝif cause of helthe too many oon, and alsoo wee maye socoure and helpe the soules in purgatorie, the whiche hatthe grete neede therof, delyuere theyme, and alegge theyre peynes. Truly it cometh of grete corrupcion and of gret defaut that is in vs and wee be gretely too blame ayenst Godde whan wee soo gladly speeke of triffles and of harlotrye and idil woordys, standyng that we maye avayle soo myche with goode wordys bothe to vs and too other and make so myche fruit. In this it shewith welle that a man is myche to reprove and too blame the whiche employeth his mouthe in idill wordes and nedeth not. For he maye fynde and gedir in his mouthe viii maner of fruittys right worthye and right preciouse, be the whiche his sperit maye be worthy and fulfilled not oonly froo ȝeere to ȝeere ne froo moneth to moneth ne froo daye to daye but euer. Of this fruit is writen in Salamones Proverbis: Euery man, seieth he, shalle be fulfilled with the fruit of þe mouthe. The firste fruit is to prayse Godde, the seconde to thanke Godde. The preciousnes of this fruit sheweth and is in the treis of paradys, that is in angellis and hooly soules the whiche berith swete fruite, for theye doo never but prayseth and thanketh Godde, [f. 85v] as the prophete seithe. The thirde fruit is prayer. The dignite of this fruit a man maye knowe in this, that angellis berith it to hevyn and presentith it to oure loorde. Certis it is a ful preciouse iuelle whan soo ientil messangeres presenteth it to God. The iiii fruit is confession. The preciousnes of this fruit sheweth in þis, that oure lorde wil euer haue it afore his yeien. As a riche man whan men bryngeth too his borde dyuerse metes he kepeth and setteth before hym of the feirest, oon the same wise oure loorde wil ever haue before hym the fruit of confession because it is feire. The v fruit is temperance, the whiche is in this, that a man spekyth neyther to myche ne to lytel and that his woordes be resonable and true and that theye be to the praysyng and to the glorye of oure loorde. The sixte fruite is abstinence in eetyng and drynkynge. The prescyousnes of this fruit sheweth in þis, that abstinence is of soo grete vertue that it lengthet mannes lyfe, as Salamon seithe. The vii fruit is to teche his neghbourgh what he sholde doo and howe he sholde leff. This fruit made specially the tree of liff, whiche is the sone of the blessid Virgine Marie, as that he seithe in the gospelle. The viii fruit is whan a man seeith that men doothe velenye and wronge to God and too his neghbourgh and that he reproveth and argueth and spekyth aȝeins it. The preciousnes of this fruit sheweth in this, that men fynde but fewe that hatthe it. For men see but fewe of thoo that hath this fruit. ȝit let euery man take heede to haue this fruite ȝif he wil be wise.

Off the Gardyn with the Treys of Vertu, IIII^{XX}XIX

We haue soo longe goon spor[r]ynge forthe that be the grace of Godde wee bee commen to the drye tree. This tree is a tree the whiche in his ȝougthe was planted on a goode riuiere, as the prophete Eȝechie discryveth it right wel, and right wel nooriched and right comly, soo that in height and feirnes [f. 86] it semyd oon of the trees of paradis. This tree, as Salamon seithe, florissheth as an almander, that is too seye, feire and welle. But it hasteth it to fast, as Ysaie seieth. For ther come an hoote brennyng wynde that al toscorkelid it, as the forseide prophete Ȝechie seithe. For cause of the whiche anoother prophete that hight Iooel wepid and cryed and made grete sorowe in his booke. For as Seint Ierom seithe: Hee that sholde profit, encrese, and multiplie as a palme tree is nowe becomen as a genepre, the which berith feire flowres and noo fruit, ne it berith noothynge, ne noothynge is worthe but too the fyre. This tree sheweth vs the state and the lif of man, howe his liff is goode and hooly and waxeth and propheteth in grace and in vertues and in goode deedes and florissheth right wel and ȝeefeth goode sauour overalle. But there where hee is ȝit in his firste floure, as Iob seithe, commeth a brennyng wynde of right grete ferventnesse that it rasith fro hym his floures and brisseth his branches, soo that hee abideth drye and barhayne and is goode too caste downe and too cutte and to putte to the fyre.

Off the Tree of Liffe, C

This tree of lif to speke gostely began feire and welle too caste spryngys of vii vertues the whiche answerith too the vii chief vices. But the brennyng wynde of grete feruour and of selve-wit and of ondiscrecion corrompeth it and maketh it to become vice. For folysshe mekenes becommeth pusillanimite, *id est*, waiknes of herte, be vndiscrecion and selve-wit; fooly louffe becommeth cruelte; [...]; fooly largesse, prodigalite, *id est*, [...]; fooly worthynesse, cruelte; fooly chastenes, vntrouthe; fooly abstinence, pestilence. Nowe vnderstande welle that whan the feende seeth Goddis seruaunt as a ȝonge novice and seithe hym nyce and perceyvith that on the left side he maye not overthrowe hym in vices [f. 86v] ne in synnes of the whiche wee haue spokyn howe hee couereth hym than with a mantel of vertu and in spice and liknesse of goodnes asaileth hym more sotilly on the right side than on the lefte. Hee sheweth hym nowe howe he sholde haue grete mekenes that parfitly sholde overcome pride and al his doughteris. Than he maketh hym to disp[r]ise hymselfe and too lye of hymselfe and too dispyse hymselfe, soo that he wenyth too be not worthe, neyther in power ne in konnyng, in soo myche that he falleth in pusillanimite, that is, intoo a default of herte. Hee beholdeth than soo myche his defautes and the perilles that theye be in the whiche doothe grete goodnes that hee there not helpe hymselfe with noo grace that Godde hathe ȝovyn hym but rather hideth his lordes tresor, wherwith he sholde wyn and helpe bothe hymselfe and oother, as didde the shrewe that Godde reprovith in the gospelle and calleth hym vntrue seruaunt and evil and slowefull and not profitable and commaundeth hym too be ledde intoo the dirkenesse of helle. But veraye mekenes ne vertu is not getyn thus. For hee that wil geete a goode name moste nedis entre intoo the felde. Wherfore ther is noon soo hardy as is the veraye meeke. For as Seint Bernard seithe: In as myche as the iuste man hatthe lesse truste in hymselfe in litil quarellis, in as myche he hatthe the gretter feithe in grete emprises to God, as it shewid in the blissed Virgine Marie, the whiche of grete mekenes is praysed abowe alle oother that ever where after Godde.

Off Fooly Louff, CI

Moreover whan this ȝonge seruaunt withowte reeson and withowte mesure beholdith envie he begynneth to hate it soo egirly that he falleth intoo a foolysshe louff. For whan he sholde louff his neghbourgh as hymselfe, hee begynneth to louff hym more than hymselfe. For in right and wronge he seithe hee shalle louff his frende. And this foole willyngly putteth his soule in synne for to kepe this fonned frendeshipp. This louff is lewde and disordenat. [f. 87] For next Godde above al thynge thowe sholdest louff thy soule and after thy soule thye neghbourghe, as Seint Austyn seithe. Wherfore if thowe luff thy neghbourgh moore than Godde or than thye soule, thou arte not in charite. Therfore Godde seithe in the gospelle that noon maye be his deciple if he hate not fader and moder and kyn and frende, not the persones but the vicis. Alsoo ther be debonaire fooles the whiche hateth soo myche felnesse that for to kepe the louff of pepil theye leese oftyn þe louff and the pees of God, liche as whan theye see evillis and synnes the whiche theye myght and sholde fordoo, theye kepe theyme stille for too haue pees. This deboneirnes is to cruel, as Seint Austin seithe. Wherfore men be wonte to seye that a piteouse moder maketh a tigneuse, *id est*, a lewke, doughter. Is it not gret vntrouthe if thowe see and hire that men doo shame to thy fader of hevyn and thowe suffrest it debonairly and makyst a contenaunce as though it longyd nothyng to the? Of the whiche Iohn with the gylte mouthe seithe a goode woorde. A man that lightly forȝeteth and forȝefeth his owne wrongys it is a grete vertu and deboneirnesse, but for to be deboneire in shames and wronges doon to God it is right a grete vntrouthe and a shrewdenes. Therfor evyn as ther is noon soo hardy as is a veray meke man evyn soo ther is noo[n soo rigorous] in iustice as is the veraye debonayre, as it shewid be Moyses the whiche in witnesyng of hooly scripture was þe moste debonaire that was in the worlde in his tyme, but to venge synne men founde noon soo cruelle ne siche a iusticer as he was. Oo feire swete Criste Iesus, in the tyme that nowe rynneth this vertu is tourned right bestely. For ther is noon that setteth stoore to venge the shames that men doon to thee, but euery man wolde venge his owne wronge withoute reeson and withowte mesure.

Off Foly Worthines, CII

[f. 87v] The vice of idilnes and of slowthe answerith ȝit to the vice of foly woorthines, the whiche is a fulle perlious vice. Liche to hym þat is rengeid in a bataile and wil kepe noon ordre but wil take his owne wille withowte leve or counsell for to gete a name, evyn soo farith it be theym that doothe too grete penaunces withoute counsell and be desires or singulerteis or desgysynesses waccheth, fasteth, worshipeth, weepeth, werith the haire, and sleeth the body. Theye weene to be ouercommen if theye passe not oother, and theye maketh of theyre bodyes sacrifice the whiche theye sholde kepe to serve Godde. As Samuel the prophe[t] seithe: Whoo-soo makith sacrifice of his owne wit aȝeyns reson and obedience, he maketh offryng to the fende and not to God. And that is to vnderstande in clergie that he doothe ydolatrye.

Off Fooly Largesse

Avarice on the toother part answerith ȝit too the vice of prodigalite that is fooly largesse. The covetouse raveyneth al and kepeth that the whiche is his and that the whiche is not his. The large foole ȝefeth not but spendeth al that he maye gete with his handes, bothe that the whiche is not his and that the whiche is his. The large gothe the mene weye, the whiche taketh aweye noothynge. But that the whiche he hatthe sufficeth hym, and he ȝefeth his goode wysly and gladly and with goode herte and there where he sholde yif it and as myche as he maye and liche as he sholde.

Off Fooly Chastite, CIII

Aȝens lechery groweth fooly chastite, oother of the hert or of the bodye. Foly chastite of the body is in theim that be in mariage [f. 88] the whiche doothe not too theyre felawes as that theye sholde ne as that mariage requireth. And that is a roberie and an vntrouthe. For in there hertis theye require folyly chastite and clennes. For as soone as theye begynne to doo penaunce theye wene to be angellis the whiche draweth theym to deethe. Than whan foule thoughtis commeth too theyme the more that the feende seith that theye be angry the gladder he is and the more assaileth theyme bothe wakyng and sleepyng and putteth theyme intoo a sorowe and into an hevynesse and into a streit consience and a lewde. And of siche it fareth alsoo as of theyme that wenyth too make theire hous soo clene that ther sholde leve noo doste ne poudere therin, but the more theye clense it the moore ther cometh intoo it be the sonne-bemes. Thus it fareth be some nice hertis and novices that woolde haue the clennes of parfyt pepill or that theye be clenne. And whan theye fele a castyng aȝeyn of clerenesse as howe that God sheweth theyme theyre defaultis anoon theye wille confesse theyme for too remeve the house of the herte the whiche theye slee and that bothe theyme and oother. And the moore that tho hert to[r]n and retorne the more powderes and thoughtis theye see, þe whiche the feende maketh too come too theyme for to put theyme intoo an evil weye and too withdrawe theyme from the goodnes that theye myght and sholde doo.

Off Folye Abstinence, CIIII

On the toother parte, to the vice of glotony answerith the vice of [austerite], be the whiche a man is as a mansleer of hymselfe and vntrewe to Godde, whan he taketh from hym his goode seruaunt, that is too seye, his owne bodye. And this is oone of the strengest wiles that the feende hatthe, as Seint Bernard seithe. For whan he maye not overthrowe the knyght, he peynyth hym to kylle his horse. That [f. 88v] is to seye, whan he maye not overcommen the corage þat worthy and feruent pepille hatthe than he peyneth hym to take fro hym his bodye. Thus synnes and vices gothe oute of the weye, some on the right syde and some on the lifte, but vertu gothe evyn the kyngys hyeweye. Vertu is the tree that sholde growe on height because it attaigneth vnto hevyn. And therfore his branches he moste fulle besyly cutte and redresse bothe on the right side and on the lefte.

That This Lyff Is But Deethe, CV

Shee dyeth in vice that hatthe not lerned too dye. Lerne too dye and thowe shalt can lyffe, for noon can lif wel that hatthe not lerned to dye. And he is called a veray caytif that can not lif and derre not dye. If thowe wilt lif freely, lerne to dye meryly. If thowe aske me howe men lernyth it, I shalle telle it the anoone. [f. 89] Thowe shalt knowe that this liff is but deethe. For deethe is but a ful short passage. Euery creature knoweth that. Wherefore men seieth of a man whan he dyeth that he passith and whan he is dede that he is paste. Truly this lif alonly is but a passyng, yea, yea, and that a ful short passage. Euery creature knoweth that. Wherfore men seithe of a man whan he dyeth, for al the liff of a man thowe he lifed m^{l} ȝere yit that sholde not be as only a moment to regarde of the tooþer lyf, the whiche shalle euer laste withoutyn ende, oother in tourment or in euerlastynge ioye. This is welle witnessyd to vs be emperoures, kyngys, and princes that sumtyme hadde the worshipes and thee glorie of this worlde the whiche in helle howleth, cryeth, wepith, and seithe: Alas what avayleth nowe to vs oure power, worship, noblesse, richesse, ioye, and boste? Alle is paste sonner than a shadowe or a birde fleynge or an arowe oute of a bowe. Thus oure liff is paste. Nowe were we borne and anoon dedde; alle oure lyf was not a litil moment. We be nowe in euerlastynge tourment. Oure ioye is tourned to sorwe, oure karolles to wepyng. Chapelettis, roobes, disportis, festes, and al oure goodes failleth vs. Siche be the songes of helle, as the scripture witnessith to vs for to shewe vs that this liff is but deethe and a fulle shorte passage and that deethe is but a passage and to liffe is but for to passe. Than too liff is but for too dye. And that is as true as the pater noster. For as soone as thowe began to liffe, thowe began to dye. For al thyn age and thy tyme that is paste deethe hatthe conquerid it and kepeth it. Thowe seiest that thowe haste xl ȝere. Thowe seiest not true. Deþe hatthe theyme and wil never ȝif the theyme aȝeyn. Therfore the wit of the worlde is foolye. For these clere seerris theye see not. Nyght and daye theye doo oo thyng. And the more that theye doo, the lesse theye knowe it. Ever theye dye, and theye can not dye. For nyght and daye thow dyest, as I haue seide to the. In another maner ȝit I shalle teche the this konnyng, that þou maiste haue the knowyng wel to dye and too liff. Hire nowe and vnderstande. Deethe is but a disseueryng of the bodye and of the soule. This knoweth euery man. Wyse Caton nowe techith vs: Lerne, seiþe [f. 89v] he, to dye. Depart oftyn thi spirit froo thy bodye, as many of these grete philosophris didde the whiche hated soo myche this lyfe and dispreysed so myche the worlde and soo myche desired deethe that with theire owne wil theye kylled theymselfe. Yit it vailed not, for theye hadde noo grace ne the feithe of Criste Iesus. But hooly men the whiche of iii deethes hatthe passed tweyne, for theye be ever dede froo synne and froo the worlde. Nowe vnderstande the thirde deethe, the whiche is the disceueryng of the soule and of the bodye. Betwene theym and paradis is but a litil walle, the whiche theye passe thorough be desyre and thought. And though the bodye be on this side, the herte and the sperit is on the toother syde. There haue theye theire conuersacion, as Seint Powle seithe, theire solas, theire ioye, theire confort, and alle theire desire. And therfore hate theye so myche this liff, the which is but deethe, and desireth bodyly deethe. For that is a ientilwoman the whiche bryngeth ioye to alle hooly pepill and putteth theyme into blisse. To goode men deethe is ende of al eviles and havyn and entre of alle goodnes. Deethe is a ryver, the whiche departeth dethe and liff. Deethe is on this side; liff is on the toother syde. But wyse worldly pepil, the whiche seeith soo clerely on this syde the ryver, seeith noothyng on the toother side. And therfore the scripture calleth theyme foolys and blynde. This deethe calle theye lyff, and deethe the whiche is too goode men begynnyng of liff theye calle it an ende. And therfore hate theye soo myche deethe, for theye knowe not what it is ne on the toother syde the ryver theye haue not conuersid. For he that goothe not oute knowith but litil. Wherfore if thowe wilt knowe what is goode and what is evil, isse oute of thyeselfe, isse oute of the worlde, lerne too dye, disseuere thye soule be thought, sende thyn hert intoo the toother worlde, that is to seye, intoo hevyn, intoo helle, and into purgatorie. And ther shalle thowe see what is goode and what is evil. In helle shalt thowe see moore sorwe than men can devise, in purgatorie moore tourment [f. 90] than men maye endure, in paradis more ioye than men maye devise or desire. Helle shalle teche þe howe men vengeth dedly synne. Purgatorie shalle teche the howe men vengeith and clensith venial synne. In paradis thowe shalt opynly see howe that vertu is a goode dede and hyly rewardid. Thus in theese iii thyngys is alle that behovith too knowe howe too liff and too dye wel.

Howe Man Sholde Flee Synne, CVI

Nowe take hiede ȝit a litil and noye the not with theese iii thyngys, that is to seye, with helle, purgatorie, and paradis, because that thowe maye lerne to hate synne. Ones on the daye forȝete thy bodye and goo into helle in thy lifyng that thowe goo not theder in thye dyynge. Hooly men and wise didde soo fulle oftyn. For there shalt thowe see al that euer the herte hateth and fleeth: faute of al goodes, plente of al evilles, brennynge fire, stynkynge bremstone, horrible feendes, hunger and thriste the whiche maye not be staunched, diuers tourmentis, wepyngys, and sorwes more than herte maye thynke or tonge devise. And theye shalle ever endure withowtyn ende. And therfore siche peyne is called everlastyng dethe. For there men dye alweye in lyffyng, and theye lyfe alweye in dyynge. Nowe than whan thowe seest alonly that on dedly synne moste be bought so dere, thowe sholdist rather suffre to be sleyn al qwyk than to concent alonly to one dedly synne. After this than goo intoo purgatorie. And ther shalt thowe see þe peyne of soules the whiche hadde repentaunce here but theye were not fully purged. Therfore theye doo there the remenaunt of theire penaunce vnto the tyme that theye be as clere and clene as theye were the tyme and the houre that theye come oute of the funte of bapteme. But that penaunce is ful horrible and fulle harde. For alle þe [f. 90v] martirdomes that seintis suffred ne al the sorwes that womman hatthe in trauaylyng of childe is but a batthe in colde water vnto þe regarde of þat fourneys wherein soules brenneth to that theye be purged holly as golde is fyned in fyre vnto the tyme that men fynde noo moore too fyne þerfroo. For that fyre is of siche nature that whatever it fyndeth in the soule of [filthe] of dede, of worde, or of thought that longeth to synne, oother litel oother myche, alle it brenneth and purgeth. And al venial synnes, the whiche we calle smale synnes, be ponysshed and venged there, the whiche wee dide besyly and often, as thoughtis fooly, idill wordes, iapes, triffles, and al oother vanitees vnto that in the sowle ther bee noothynge too purge and that it be worthy too entre into hevyn where nothynge entreth but if it be right veryly cleere. They dowte this fyre, the whiche too theire power kepeth theyme fro venial synnes and þat kepeth theire hertis, theyre bodyes, and theyre mouthes holyly and kepeth theym holly from alle synnes and liffeth as theye sholde dayly dye and come to Goddes iugement and because that noon maye only liff withowten synne. For Salamon seithe: VII tymes on the daye the rightwys man falleth in synne. Therfore be holly confession and be wepyngis and be prayeris theye doo theyre peyne too wesshe theyme and to rise and too amende and to iuge theymselfe soo that theye abyde surely the laste iugement. For whoosoo iugeth hymself verily here he shalle noo fere haue of dampnacion at the daye of iugement. Thus men lerneth to knowe evil and too flee it and to hate al synne lytyl and myche and to conceve the hooly fere of Godde, the whiche is the begynnyng of hooly lyff and of al goodnes.

Howe Men Lerneth to Doo Welle and too Liff Welle, CVII

[f. 91] It is not inoughe to leve evil if men doo not goode dedes and seke vertuz, withowte the whiche no man maye lif aright. Therfore if thowe wilt lerne to liff wel oppon vertu, lerne thus too dye as I haue taught the. That is to seye, desseure the sperit fro thye bodye be thought and be desire; goo oute of this dedely worlde; goo intoo the lande of liff where that noon dyeth ne ageth, that is to seye, into paradis. There men lerne goodnes, wisdom, and curtesye, for ther maye no veleny entre. There is the gloriouse feleshipp of [God] and of his sweete moder and of angellis and of seintis. Ther above haboundeth al goodnes, beaute, richesse, worshipp, glorie, vertu, louffe, wit, and euerlastyng ioye. There is neyther ypocrisye ne deceit ne losengerie ne discorde ne envye ne hunger ne thrist ne heete ne colde ne sorwe ne evil ne fere of enemyes but euer festes, mariages, and songes and ioye withowten ende. This ioye is ther soo gret that whoosoo hadde tasted o drope of the leste ioye þat is there hee sholde be so dronkyn with the louff of God that alle the ioye of this worlde sholde be to hym but tourment and stynke; riches, donge; worship but filthe. And the grete desire that a man sholde haue to come thedir sholde cause hym c foilde more feruently to hate synne and too louff vertu than alle the fere of helle sholde doo, off the whiche I haue spokyn and touched afore, for louff is myche strenger than is drede. Thus than the liff is feire and honest whan a man fleeth evil and doothe welle not only for fere of dampnacion but for the desyre of hevyn and for the louff of Godde and for the gret clennes that is in vertu and goode liffe. For he that is ledde be loufe rynneth faster and lesse grevith hym than it doothe hym that servith God for fere. The hare and the grehounde rynneth, the toon for fere the toother for desyre. The toon fleeth; the toother chasseth. Hooly men rynneth as the grehounde dooth, havyng ever theyre yen to hevyn, where that theye see theyre praye that theye chase. And for that forȝete theye alle oother goodes, liche as the gentil hounde doothe whan he seeth his praye a[f. 91v]fore his yen. This is the liff of fine lufferes and of ientil sette hertis the whiche louffeth so myche vertu and honeste and soo myche hateth synne that though theye wiste certeinly that noo man sholde wite it ne that God sholde not venge it ȝit sholde theye not lyste to doo synne. But alle theire thought and alle theyre peyne is too kepe and too araye clenly theyre hertis that theye maye be worthye to haue the blisse and the ioye of paradis, into the whiche noon herte entrith that is veleyns, foolysshe, ne proude, for the feleshipp than sholde be myche the wers.

Howe Men Commeth too a Goode Liffe, CVIII

I haue nowe shewed the howe men lerneth too dye wel and too liff wel. But thowe shalt wite that the begynnyng for too come too goode liff and too geete vertu is for a man to knowe not alonly what is good and what is evil but that a man sholde knowe and deme certeinly what is evil and what is goode and too devise the [verraye] goodes from the shewyng of the evyl and the grete goodes from the lytil. For that thynge the whiche a man knoweth not is neyther hated ne desired. And therfor thowe shalt knowe that liche as the scripture seithe ther be some that be called litil ȝiftes of God, the whiche men calle litil goodes, and somme gretter and some gretest. And it is ful soothe that alonly there be verraye goodes of the whiche al the worlde is nerehand deceyvid, for theye ȝif the grete goodes for the lytil or ellys the grettest goodes for the mene goodes. For this worlde fareth as a fayre where that many fonnyd marchaundis bee, the whiche bieth glasses for sapheris, laton for golde, bledderis for lanternys. But he is a verreye goode marchaunde that of euerythyng knoweth the propre vertu and the value. The Hooly Gooste techith vs this. And anoother maister lerneth and techeth vs too knowe grete thyngis from litil, preciouses from vile, and swetnes from bitternesse.

Off Litil Goodes, CIX

[f. 92] The calleth the litil goodes temporell goodes, goodes of fortune [the whiche] with alle hirre whele dayly taketh and ȝifeth and tournyth vppe soo doun. These be noyouse stoones the whiche [musardis] bieth for rubies and for sapheris and for emerawdis. Theese be as iuellis to childer the whiche God ȝif vs for too solace vs and too drawe withalle oure louffe to hym because he knoweth wel that we be feeble and tendre and that wee maye not holde the sharpe weyes of angwisshe and of martirdome as didde the goode knyghtis of Godde, the whiche tooke the kyngedom of hevyn be strengthe and conquerid it be theyre worthinesse. Therfore theese be not grete goodes ne verraye goode. For if theye be veray goodes than was the son of [Godde] Crist Iesus a foole that chase poverte and sharpenes and refused ioye, worshippe, and richesse. Alsoo if theye be veray goodes than is not al veraye goodes in hevyn, ne Godde is not parfitly blessid, the whiche of sich goodes vseth noon. And mooreouer than Godde is vntrue and vnkynde that taketh siche goodes from his frendes and ȝif theym more largely to his enemyes. Alsoo if theye be veraye goodes than al theese seintes and theese wyse clerkys and theese grete philozophres were foolys, the whiche fledde theese goodes and dispised it as dounge. Alsoo ȝit if theye be veraye goodes than lieth Godde and hooly chirche and hooly scripture, the whiche calleth theyme lesyngys, shadowe, and vanitee, nettis and liaines of the feende. And that is as true as the pater noster. For theye be the fendes wylys be the whiche he deceyvith man in moo than m^{l} maneris and takyth and byndeth and holdith. But the wyse marchandes tho be the worthye men that the Hooly Goste techith and enlumineth be veray knowyng, the whiche knoweth theymeselfe oueralle and woote what euerythyng is worthe. þeye see and vnderstande right wel that al the worlde is not o goode morselle for to feede with the herte of man and that ther is þerin myche evil and litil goode. And because þat theye beholde the perillis and the evilles that is therin and knoweth that it is true that men be wonte to seye, þat whoosoo ȝefeth not that he louffeth reseyvith not þat the whiche he desireth, theye make to God a game of þe paume whan that theye ȝif the worlde for hevyn and noght for alle richesse, as myre for golde, and levith al delites and worshipes for to enryche God and becommeth pore too wynne Godde and for to gete hevyn therwith. This [f. 92v] is the feirest and the clenest and the moste honest lyffe that is in this worlde. Oother ther be that seeth þat in many maneris men maye doo theyre availe with temporelle goodes, whoosoo myght haue theyme and not louff theyme. For God commaundeth not to leve al. þey maye haue it and litil preyse it. Theye maye vse it and a litil louff it, as hooly Abraham, Iob, and Dauid didde and many oother the whiche eschewed þe perillis of hit and didde theyre availe with the goodes that Godde hadde ȝovyn and lente vnto theyme. For þeye can bye hevyn therwith. Theye were wonte too bye aȝen theire synnes with it and too helpe theyre neghborghes and the more to prayse, too louff, to þanke, to worshipp, to drede, and too doubt Godde for it, for the grete perilles that theye be in. And the more theye meke theymselfe whan theye see theire febilnesse and theyre grete pouerte and theyre defaultes, whan that theye derre not goo the streit weye, standyng that theye wil suffre soo lytil for God, the whiche ȝaf and le[f]te and suffred soo myche for theym. Theye knowe this wel, but it is ful harde too doo. For it is a lyghter thynge for to leve at onys al the goodes of the worlde for Godde than to haue theym and not too louff theyme.

Off Goodes of Nature off Meene Goodes, CX

The meene goodes be goodes of nature and techynge: of nature, as beaute of bodye, worthinesse, strengthe, debonairte, clere witte, myende, and al siche goodes as man geteth be techyng or be stodye or bee goode costomes, as goode condicions be and some maner of vertues. But ȝit theese be not veraye goodes. For theye make not hym that hatthe theyme parfitly goode. For many kyngys, emperoures, and philozophris and gret clerkys, the whiche hadde myche of siche goodes, be dampned in helle. Alsoo oure lorde ȝefeth siche goodes to his enemyes as well as too his frendes and too Saraȝins and to fals Cristen pepil [f. 93] as too goode. Alsoo theye be noo veraye goodes the whiche faileth and that men maye lese wheder theye wil or noon. And though that a theef maye not steele it ne take it aweye, neverthelesse yit at the laste dethe takyth theyme aweye. Moreover veraye goodes helpeth euer and noyeth never. But truly siche goodes and siche foreyn graces oftyntymes doothe harme and noyeth theym that hatthe theym if theye vse theyme not wel whan theye avaunteth theyme and enprideth theyme and dispiseth oother therfore. For hee the whiche God hatthe ȝofyn siche graces and siche goodes as I haue above rehersed, that is to seye, for to serve God and to helpe his neghborghe therwith, if he vse theyme not truly, he shall be in the grefouser torment and the streitlyer. He moste ȝif answer and acommpt at the daye of doome what hee hatthe doone and what he hatthe wonne with the goodes that God hatthe lente hym for to multiplye it.

Off Verray Goodes, CXI

I have nowe shortely shewed to the whiche be litil goodes and mene goodes. Nowe wil I shewe the whiche be veraye goodes and rightwys goodes, the whiche maketh hym goode that hatthe theyme and withoute the whiche was never noo goodnes. Men calleth theese goodes the grace of Godde and vertu and charitee: grace because it ȝiffeth liff and helthe too the soule. For withoute these goodes the soule is deede. For as the bodye is dede withoute the soule soo the soule is but dede withoute the grace of Godde. It is called vertu because it arayeth the soule with goode condiciones. It is called charitee because it ioyneth the soule to Godde and maketh it as al oone. For charite is not ellys but a dere vnite. This is the ende; this is the perfeccion; this is the blessidnes to the whiche wee sholde take heede. Theese olde philizophris were gretely deceyvid that soo besyly disputed and sought whiche was the verraye goodnes in this liff and that myght ȝit never fynde it, for somme [f. 93v] set it in the delit of the bodye and some in richesse and somme in clene liff. But the grete philosophre Seint Poule the whiche was ravisshed vnto the thirde hevyn techith vs be many resones that the souerayne goodnes in this liff is the quene of vertues, Dame Charitee, for withoute this, seithe hee, noo goode is noughte woorthe. And whoosoo hatthe this hatthe al oother. And whan ooþer shalle faile, this shalle never faile. For above al the grete goodnes that is, this is ladye. Wherfore this is the grettest goodnes that is vnder hevyn. And because that thowe wilte the more louff and seke this goode abowe al oother goodes the whiche is called vertue and right goode I wil ȝit shewe þe the value therof. Men be wonte for to devise iii maner of goodes: worshipful goodes, profitable goodes, and delitable goodes. Ther be no moo goodes ne vauntagis but theese iii thyngys. And this seest thou opynly in worldly goodes that noon desireth noo thynge but if hee suppose that it be worshipful, profitable, or delitable. A proude man sekyth worshipful thyngys, a covetouse man profitable thyngys, a delicious man delitable thyngys. And what that ever theye seke vainly is vertu verily. For vertu is a thynge worshipful, delitabil, and profitable.

That Vertu Is Ful Worshipfull, CXII

That vertu is right worshipful thowe maiste knowe in this wise. Ther is in the worlde vi thyngys gretly belouyd and desyred because that theye be worshipfull, that is to seye, beaute, wit, power, worthynes, freedom, and nooblesse. These be vi wellys of vanite of the whiche riseth gret plente of veinglorie. Beaute is a thynge gretely beloffed, for it is a thynge that is myche worshiped. And neverthelesse the beaute that the yen of the herte seeth and louffeth is short and voide and a thynge [f. 94] that is false, for ther is neyther hee nor shee that is feire. But oure yen be febil the whiche seeth but the skyn withoute. For a feire bodye is but as a faire sacke ful of dunge and as a dungehylle in a ȝerde. Alsoo this beaute is short and voide, for it fliteth and faileth anoon, as a floure of the felde dooth. Alsoo soone as the soule departith, the bodye lesith al his beaute. Wherfore al the beaute that the bodye hatth the soule ȝefeth it hym, and thorough the soule hatthe he beaute. And therfore he is a foole that ioyeth hym of beaute of bodye. But beaute of the soule is veray beaute the whiche waxeth ever and shalle never faile. That is the veraye beaute wherbye God is pleised that seeth the herte. This beaute ȝeldeth and ȝifeth to the soule grace and mede and the louff of Godde, for it reformeth it and callith it aȝeyn and ȝifeth it his right preynte, that is to seye, the likenesse of his creature, the whiche is feire withoute comparison. And whoosoo resemblith hym moste is feyrest. Wherfore the feyrest thynge that is vnder Godde is a soule, the whiche hatthe parfitly his right forme and his right prynte and his right clerenesse. The colour of a floure, the clerenesse of the sonne, the figure of man, plesans of preciouse stoonys, or what feirnesse that ever the bodyly yee seeth, it is but harlotrye and filthe too regarde of the soule. For what that ever any man maye thynke of beaute vnder Godde, it maye not compare thertoo.

Off the Wit of the Soule, CXIII

Clergie and wit is a thynge that is myche worshiped. But if thowe wilte be verily wyse and lerne hye clergie, doo soo that thowe maiste haue veraye goodenes, that is too seye, grace and vertu. For that is veray wisdom the whiche enlumineth the hert of man as the sonne doothe the worlde and as the sonne causeth the clerenesse of the moone. For the scripture seithe that the wit of the worlde is but folye, [f. 94v] childehoode, and woodenesse. It is folye in theym that louffeth the woorlde and his beaute the whiche can not knowe the daye froo the nyght ne the nyght froo the daye ne iuge betwene gret and litel ne betwene preciousnes and filthe. Theye weene of the mone it weere the sonne. For theye wene of the worshipp of the worlde that it were verraye blisse, of a litil appil that it weere a montaigne. For theye weene of the worlde that it were a grete thynge, the whiche too regarde of hevyn is but as a litil appil. Theye weene of glas that it were a saphere and that theyre myght and strengthe weere fulle grete, þe whiche is febiler and freller than any glas. Alsoo the wit of the worlde it is childehoode in theym that be soo wyse to delite theyre bodyes, the whiche liffeth as childer that wil not doo but theire owne wille. In siche persoones reeson is deede. And therfore liff þeye as beestes, for theire wittis ar soo corumped and soo bestely that theye fare as a seke man or a woman with childe, the whiche fyndeth more sauour in a soure appil than in brede of wheete and as a childe doothe in colys than in goode meete. Siche pepil wil not beleve þat ther is more ioye and delit to se[r]ve and to louff Godde than to doo the wille of theyre caroyne, for þeye can not iuge betwene the swete and the soure. Alsoo this witte is woodnesse in theyme that be soo subtile to fynde malice and too deceyve and too hyndere oother outher be plee or be force or be deceyte that theye neyther thynke ne stodye but for to vaunce theymselfe and too hynder oother. This witte, as Seint Iame seithe, is the witte of the fende, the whiche peyneth hym euer to deceyve and too hynder oother. But the veray witte þat the Hooly Goost ȝifeth and techith the Godes frendes is to knowe withowte myssetakyng what eueryethynge is worthe. He sheweth that the worlde in value is vile and that the blisse of the worlde is vaine and that richesse is filthe and delites bitter. Alsoo hee maketh theyme to fele that the louff of God is a thynge veray, preciouse, and sweete, for it filleth, norissheth, [f. 95] and susteyneth the herte. Precious[e], for a man maye eesyly by God and al that he hatthe. [Sweete], for this is the hande that maketh alle thynge sweete: laboures, sorwes, teris, wepyngis, chames, and martirdommes and al maner of peynys. And what that any man maye thynke, this maketh it sauoury and swete as suger. And this is the witte and the wisdom of the whiche groweth veray blisse in conscience.

Off Verraye Woorthinesse, CXIIII

Alsoo vertu and charitee ȝifeth veraye worthinesse. Ther is noo right veraye worthines but in Goddis knyghtis that the Hooly Gooste debbith with vertu and charitee. Ther bee iii partes in worthynes: hardynes, strengthe, and stedfastnes.

Ther is noon right worthye that hatthe not theese iii thyngys, that is to seye, to be hardye and worthy too vndirtake gret thyngys, stronge and myghty in pursuynge it, stedefast and stabill too performe it. But ȝit withoute witte and his purviance noon of al theese iii thyngys vayleth. For as the Booke of Knyghthoode seithe: In ooþer quarellis whan men missetakith theyme men fyndeth amendement whatsooeuer it be, but errour in bataile may not be amendid, for it is anoon soore boughte. Foly emprise is þer where that lieth litel availe and myche coste and peril and peyne. Syche be the emprises of thoo that men calle woorthy and hardye as too the worlde, the whiche putteth body and soule in synne and in peril and in peyne for to gete withalle a litil loos, the whiche is fulle vaine and litil while lesteth. But vertu maketh a man of grete herte and of wise emprise whan it maketh a man the whiche is but erthe soo hardy that he derre vndertake to conquere so grete a thynge as is the kyngedom of hevyn and al the fendis of helle the whiche ar fulle stronge too ouercome. This emprise is goode and wise. And therin is litel perill or peyne [f. 95v] but ioye, worshipp, and blisse withowte mesure. And whosoo hatthe not vertu hatthe noo grete herte but farith as he that is ferde of nought. Siche bee thoo that doubteth soo greetely the evillis and the aduersiteis of the worlde and that be aferde to lese that the whiche theye maye not longe haue. He hatthe noo greete hert the whiche ȝifeth it for nought, as theye doo that settith theyre hertis to louff worldly thyngys, as goodes of fortune, the whiche in trouthe be noght too regarde of the veraye goodes of blisse. Wherfore siche pepill farith as a childe þat louffeth better a mirrour than a reaume and a litil appille than al his heritage. But vertu ȝefeth right a grete herte, for vertu maketh hevyn too be getyn, the worlde to be dispised, gret deedis of penaunce to be borne, and al the evillis of the worlde gladly to be suffrid and endured for Goddys sake, and to withstande al þe asautis of the feende. Wise Seneque seithe that werris, myshappes, sorwes, ne what that ever fortune maye doo ne manace theye haue no more power aȝeins vertu than oo drope of water hatthe aȝeins al the see. Vertu makyth a man hardye as a lyon, stronge as an olyfaunt, stabille and enduryng as the sonne, the whiche is not werye and ʒit euer it rynneth. Wherfor ther is noo worthynesse but in vertu.

Off Verraye Lordeshipp, CXV

Alsoo ther is no veraye lordshipp but in vertu. He is a grete lorde too whom alle the worlde obeieth and servith. Grace and vertu ʒiefeth siche lordeshipp too man. For Godde setteth man goostly in his right state where he was firste. Too siche lordeshipp and too siche worshippe man was maade. For he was lorde of al the creatures of the worlde that was vnder hevyn to whom al thynge obeied and nothyng myght noye hym. And this is þe veraye state of man and his right [f. 96] lordshippe. But hee loste this lordeshipp be synne, the whiche he maye not recouere but be vertu. For vertu reysith a man hye and setteth the worlde vnder his fete and makyth hym to be conuersant in hevyn. Vertu makyth man moore veray lorde of the worlde than þe kynge is of his reaume. For of worldly goodes he hatthe as myche as his hert desyreth. He hatthe þere his vsage and his sustenaunce and as myche as he wille haue, moore sufficiantly than hatthe the kynge. What that euer goode pepill hatthe or evil pepill, al is his. For of al thynge he makyth his availe and prayseth and thanketh God of al thynge and the more louffeth hym, dredeth hym, and servith hym in that that he seeth, beleveth, and knowith þat alle creatures is made for to serve hym. [...] withoute the whiche noon ys a lorde verily. For he is emperoure of hym-selfe, þat is to seye, of his bodye and of his herte, the whiche hee iustifieth and with the whiche he doothe his wil. For his hert and his wil is soo ioyned to God þat what that ever God doothe al is goode to hym and pleeseth hym gretely. And therfore his hert is ever in pees, and hee gouernyth it after the wil of Godde. And what that euer God doeth to his bodye it pleysith hym gretely. This is the lordeshipp that vertu ʒiefeth to hym that hatthe it, of the whiche Seneque speketh, the whiche seithe: Grete worshipp and a grete empire I shalle ʒif the, that is to seye, to be emperoure of thyselfe. O lorde Godde, what ther be many kyngys and barones in the worlde that hatthe reaumes, castellis, and citeis the whiche be not lordes of þeyre hertis. For theye torment theymselfe oftyn be ire or be evil wille or be covetise or be desyris the whiche theye maye not fulfille.

Off Verraye Freedome, CXVI

Alssoo noon hatthe freedom if he haue not grace and vertu. Wherfore if thow wilt wit what the verraye freedome of man is, thowe shalte [f. 96v] wite and vnderstande that man hatthe iii maner of freedomes: oon of nature, the toother of grace, the thirde of blisse. The fyrste is free wille, be the whiche he maye frely chese wheder he wylle doo goode or eville. This freedom hatthe hee of Godde soo freely that noon maye doo hym wronge ne al the feendis of helle maye not enforce the wyl of man to doo synne withoute his agreyng, for if a man didde evil aȝens his wyl, it were no synne. For Seint Austin seithe: Ther is noo synne in þat the whiche a man maye not eschewe. And this freedom hatthe euery man. But it is soo bounden in childer and in follis and in madde pepill the whiche hatthe noon vsage of reeson that theye can not cheese the goode from the evil. This freedom in partie is takyn fro man whan hee synneth dedly. For he sellith hymselfe for the delite of synne and ȝeldeth hym to the feende and becommeth seruaunt to synne, soo that he maye not as he wolde put froo hym that the whiche he hatthe than deservid if the grace of God helpe hym not. The seconde freedom is that the whiche goode men hatthe in this worlde, as thowe that God hatthe freid be grace and be vertu from the feendes servage and froo synne soo that theye be noo seruauntis thertoo, ne worshipeth not sylfer ne goodes of fortune, the whiche deethe maye take aweye. But theire hertis be soo reisid to Godde that theye sette not a strawe be the worlde. And theye doubte neyther kyng ne erle ne myshappe ne pouertee ne deethe, for theye be than halfe deede and hatthe deseueryd þeyr hertis fro the worlde the whiche theye haate. And theye desyre bodyly deethe, as the goode laborer doothe his paiement and the bayly his hervest and thoo that bee in tourrment of the see goode havyn and presoneris theire delyuerance and pilgrimes theire contree. These be parfitly free as that any man maye be in this worlde, for theye dowte ne drede [f. 97] nothynge but Godde. And theye be in grete hertis reste, for theye haue sette it in God. And theye be in paradis be desire. And siche freedom commyth be grace and be vertu. But ʒit al this freedom is but servage to regarde of the thirde freedom, the whiche theye haue that [b]e holly departed froo the body and be with Godde in his blisse. Theye be veraly [free], for theye be parted from alle tourmentis and from al fere of deethe and of synne and frome worldly perillis and from the wrecchidnesse of al peyne of the herte and of the bodye withoute retournynge. From the whiche thyngys noon is free in this worlde be he never soo parfit.

Off Verraye Noblesse, CXVII

Whoosoo maye haue the seconde freedom of grace and of vertu of the whiche I haue spokyn, he shal come to grete noblesse. Verraye noblesse commeth of a ientil herte. Noo hert is ientil if it louff not God. Wherfore ther is no noblesse but in servyng and louffyng Godde ne evil wille but in the contrarie, that is to seye, to greve Godde and to doo synne. Ther is noon verye ientillesse of the bodye. For wee bee al childer of oo moder, that is to seye, of erthe and of myre, of the whiche al wee toke flesshe and bloode. Of this side ther is noon veray ientil ne free. But oure fader the kynge of hevyn, the whiche formyd the bodye of slyme and of erthe, he made the soule to his ymage and too his liknesse. And evyn as the flesshely fader [f. 97v] is fulle gladde whan his son resemblith hym evyn soo farith it be oure fader of hevyn, the whiche be his scriptures and be his messages sessith not to somounde vs and to praye vs to doo oure deuoire and to sette oure peyne to resemble hym. And therfore he sent vnto vs his blessed son Criste Iesus into erthe for to bringe to vs the veraye example be the whiche wee shalle be reformed too his ymage and to his beaute, as theye be that dwellith in the hye citee of hevyn. Thoo be the angellis and the seintis of paradis, where iche of theym the hier and the nobiler that theye be the moore nobilly theye bere the liknesse of that feyre ymage. And therfore holy men of this worlde settith þeyre hertis and dothe theyre peyne to louffe and to knowe Godde and in dede hooly to clense theyme. For the clenner the herte is in as myche the moore opynly seeth it that faire face of Godde, and the verilier that it resemblith hym the moore fervently it louffith hym. This is the veraye noblesse that God doothe. And therfore Seint Iohn the apostle seithe right wel that than wee shalle bee Goddis childer, and wee shalle resemble hym proprely whan we shalle see hym opynly. That shalle be in his blisse, whan wee shal be in paradis. For here noo man seeth the beaute of God opynly but as it were in a mirrour, as Seint Poule seithe, but than we shalle see hym clerely face to face. The veray noblesse of man, as I haue seide vnto the, is be grace and be vertu, and it is fulfilled in blisse. This noblesse the Hooly Goste settith in hertis that hee pourgith in clennesse and enluminith in [v]erite and fulfilleth in charite. These be the grettest goodnesses that God doothe to aungellis, as Seint Denis seith, be the whiche theye resemble to theyre maker. And thus be grace and be vertu the Hooly Gooste werkith in the hertis of worthy men, be the whiche theye be refor[f. 98]myd to the ymage and to the liknesse of God as myche as man maye be in this liff. For hee reysith theyme soo in Godde and enbrasith theyme soo in his luff that theire vnderstandynge, theire entent, theyre wille, and alle theire mynde, that is to seye, theire remembrance is conuertid to God. This luff and this desyre the whiche cometh therof ioyneth and settith the herte soo too Godde that it maye wilne noon oother thynge but that the whiche God wille. For ther is but oo wil betwene hym and God. And than hatth he the ymage and the liknesse of Godde as myche as men maye haue in erthe. And this is the grettest noblesse and the hyest gentillesse to the whiche a man maye clymbe and atteyne. Oo goode God, what theye be ferre froo that hyenesse, thoo that maketh theyme soo queynte with soo pore noblesse that theye haue of theyre mooder the erthe the whiche berith and norissheth as weele swyn as it doothe kyngis. And ȝit theye avaunt theyme of theyr gentillesse because theye weene to bee of a gentil lyne as of that syde. This kynrede can theye compte too welle, but too the toother syde theye take noo hiede whense the veraye nooblesse and the gentil kynrede cometh too theyme. Theye sholde take heede too the veray example of Criste Iesus, the whiche louffed and worshiped his mooder moore than ever dide any oother man. And ever whan men seide vnto hym: Syre, ȝowre mooder and ȝoure cosynes askith after yowe, hee answerid: Whoo is my mooder, and whoo be my cosines? Whoosooever doothe the wille of my fader of hevyn, he is my broother, my moder, and my sister. For þis ys þe noobil side and the gentil kynrede from the whiche commeth and groweth too the herte veraye blisse, liche as doothe of the toother noblesse veinglorie, pride, and vanite.

That Vertu Is Right Profitable, CXVIII

[f. 98^{v}] I haue nowe wel and sufficiantly shewid vnto the that ther is noo goode right worshipfull but vertu and charitee, that is too louff Godde. And that ther is noon oother goode profitable Seint Poule witnessith vnto vs: If I hadde, seithe he, in me soo myche wit as that I cowde al clergie and al langagis and spake as wel as any man or angell maye speke and that I knewe the counsellis and the secretis of God and delyuered my bodye too martirdom and ȝaf al that I haue too poore pepille and if I be meracle made hillys leepe from oo place too an nother, if I hadde not the vertu of charytee, alle the remenaunt vailed not. Nowe take hiede howe Seint Poule, whom wee sholde beleve, hatthe rehersid heere to vs the grettest goodnes that man maye doo and that moste maye profite and availe, that is to seye, penaunce of bodye too suffre martirdom, too helpe thee poore, to conuerte synneres, and konnyng of al langagis. And he seithe that al these goodnessis vaileth not withowte charitee. If siche goodenessis vailith not, howe than sholde oother lesse goodenes availe? This same maist thowe see be reeson. It is a grete while agoon men seide þat a man is as myche worthe as his lande is worþe. And that is as true as pater noster. Whoosoo vnderstandith wel howe and whye a man is ought or nought oother somwhat, or moore or lesse, doute not but that it is vnderstandyn be charite and be þe louff of Godde. For whoosoo hatthe mooste therof mooste is worthe, and whoosoo hatthe leste leste is worthe, and whoosoo hatthe noght noght is worthe. And though a man haue never soo myche of temporelle goodes, as golde and sylfer, or richessis or goostely goodes or naturel goodes, as crafte, engin, wit, clergie, strengthe, and worthinesse, or any oother goodes, whye sholde I seye that theye [f. 99] profit hym whan that he is the more cruelly dampned because that he vsith theyme not aright, that is to seye, the goodes that Godde hatthe lente hym to wyn withalle? Alsoo if hee doo bodyly werkys, as doothe laborers and seruauntis, or if he doo goostly werkys, as to faste, too praye, too be porely clothid, too were the haire, if it be withowte charite, to seye verely, it vaylith hym not. For he shalle never haue the more mede ne be the nerer God for al that. Hee shalle rather haue dampnacion. And he shalle be dampned if he dye withoute charitee. But he that hatthe parfit vertu and charitee of what that ever God sendith too hym in this worlde, he maketh his avayle therwith and getith hym grace and blisse. Chartee is the goode marchande, the whiche wyneth overalle and leesith never. He byeth alle goode geffare and makyth alle his. And neverthelesse hee hatthe alweye his peny aȝein, that is to seye, the louff of his herte, the whiche is Goddes peny, with þe whiche men bieth al the goodes of the worlde and notwithstandyng it abydeth euer stylle in the coofer. Louff hatthe in euery place his cheffare. Charitee wynneth in euery quarell. Hee hatthe the victorie in alle batellys. Hee makyth that as myche vaileth the fastyng of oo daye in some man as in anoother al a lentyn and that as myche avayleth the ȝefyng of oo peny in some man as þe ȝefyng of a c *li* in some oother and to seye o pater noster as though anoother seide a sauter. And this is for noon oother cause but because that a man is worthe as myche as his dedes be worthe. For the moore veray louff that he hatthe the moore louff wynneth he dayly. Alsoo it is the peyse in Seint Michellis balaunce. For whan it comyth that euery man shalle take his wagis, noon oother thynge maye weye there but louff and charitee. And therfore seye I that ther is non goodnes profitable to seye verely and rightfully [f. 99v] but feire louff and charitee.

Off Delitable Goodes and That Vertu Is Delitable, CXIX

Liche as Godde maade man of body and of soule, evyn soo he ȝaf hym ii maner of delitable goodnessis for to drawe his hert withalle vnto hym in whom is alle verraye delites. Goodnessis outeward commyth by the v wittis of the bodye, as be seyng, heryng, smellyng, tastyng, and felyng. The v wittis fareth as a conduit, wherethorough the delitable goodnessis of the worlde rynneth intoo the herte for too ease it and delite it in the veraye delites the whiche be in the louff of God. For al the worldly delites that the v wittis hatthe is butte as oo droope of dewe too regarde of the welle of the grete see whens that al goodnes strecchith. A droope of dewe whan a man seeith it oo ferre is liche a precious stone. And whan a man wenyth to take it, it falleth too thee erthe and commyth too nought. Thus fareth it be the v wittes. Whan men thynkith, fygureth, and desyrith theyme, they seme fulle preciouse. And whan a man holdeth theyme, anoon theye be loste and commyth to noght, as dremys and thoughtis of delitis paste, and as the dreme of a nyght thowe seest that al is noght. Thus soone theye passe, and thus soone theye come to noght. Theye maye in no wisse fullefille the. Nowe than if ther be thus myche swetnesse in oo drope, what is than the swetnesse of alle the welle? And therfore the hooly wyse men in this worlde in al that ever theye see or sauour in delitable goodnessis of this worlde theye prayse God and the moore coveitith the louff of hym. And the swetter that theye see the droopes, the moore theye desire to comme to the welle. And because that theye knowe that the moore that men louffe the droope the moore forȝetith men the welle and that the more þat men desyre worldly swetnesse, the lesse men desire the swetnesse of Godde and of hevyn, ther[f. 100]fore as litil as [theye] maye theye take or vse flesshely delites, the whiche commyth be the v wittes. Oo goode Godde, what theye be foollis and bestis, the whiche knoweth well that the bodye of man is the foulest and the poorest creature that is and that the sperit, that is to seye, the soule of man is the noblest thynge and the hyest creature that maye be, and notwithstandyng theye maye not beleve but that the goodnes the whiche commeth of þe bodye is as swete and as delitable as is that the whiche commeth of the sperit, the whiche be veray and cleene and euerlastyng goodnesses and maye the hert saoule and fulfille. Sich goodnessis God ȝifeth to man in this worlde whan he ȝifeth hym pees of hert and victorie of his enemyes and blisse of conscience, as whan he fulfilleth his herte with louff and goostely ioye and makith it dronkyn with a mervelouse swetnesse, soo that he maye not continue hym to fele hymselfe. To siche ioye ne too siche delite maye noo comparyson be founde in worldly ioyes ne delites of this worlde, the whiche be but droopes to regarde of the welle. Wherof oure lorde spekith in the gospelle: Whoosoo shalle drynke, seithe he, of the welle that I shalle ȝif hym, it shalle become a welle the whiche shalle make hym lepe intoo euerlastyng liff. That is the welle of ioye and of charite, the whiche maye fille and saoule the herte and noon oother thynge that is. Dauid hatthe tasted of this welle, the whiche seid in the Sauter: A goode Godde, what the multitude of thy swetnesse is ful grete, the whiche thowe kepest too thy seruauntis and ȝifest to thy frendes. And truly whoosoo had wel tasted and sauoured that swetnesse that God ȝiefeth too his frendes, he sholde despise the ioyes and delites of this worlde, and he sholde cheese and withholde gostely ioye, and hee sholde doo as hee þat bulteth mele, the whiche deseuereth the floure of the bran, and as he that maketh oyle, the whiche taketh the pure grese and levith the groos mater. For ioye of the herte, the whiche commeth of the louff of Godde, is veraye parfit ioye, as the Prouerbis seithe, the whiche seithe that noon hatthe parfit ioye if it come not of louff. And siche ioye in scripture is called oyle, as oure lorde seithe be the prophete: I shalle, seithe hee, ȝif the oyle of ioye for penaunce of weepyng. With this oyl[e] be theye anoynted that God hatthe maade kyngys and lordis of the worlde and of theymeselfe. And than is hee a parfit Cristen man whan he is anoynted with this [f. 100v] hooly creme. For of creme is seide Criste, and of Criste is seide Cristen. And whoosoo is anoynted with siche oynement, that is to seye, with gostely ioye and with the louff of God, he liffeth in Godde and Godde in hym, as þe postel Synt Iohn seithe. And this is the lif of a Cristen man, that is to seye, to speke verily the liff of man. And this lif is blessid the whiche Cristen men sholde beleve and desire for to gete withal euerlastyng liff. For he is not in lif but in langoure the whiche liffeth euer in charches, thoughtes, and angwisshe. That is not the liff of a man but of a childe that nowe weepeth and nowe laugheth, nowe at ease, nowe at vnease, nowe angrye, nowe pesid, nowe in ioye and in festis, and thus soone in hevynesse. Therfore whoosoo wil lede a goode liff hee sholde soo seke that he myght haue the veraye goodnesse. And than sholde he haue a liff bothe worshipful, delitable, and profitable. And than sholde he liff as a man, that is to seye, surely, wisly, meryly, withoute angre, withoute errour, withoute sorowe. And siche liff a man hatth outher be grace or be vertu and ellis not.

[Of the Tree of Vertues, CXX]

[f. 101] I haue nowe generally shewed the thee dignitee, the valu, and the bountee of vertue and of charite and whye men sholde gete theyme. For to haue theyme commyth greete availe, bothe ioye, worshipp, and euerlastyng liff. But because that men knoweth not soo welle a thynge in general as theye doo in especialle, therfore myn entent is here to speeke of vertu the moore specially soo that euery creature that wil stodie in this booke maye ordeyne and lede his liff in vertu and goode dedis. Or ellis it vaileth hym litel to knowe goodnesse, if he doo it not. For as Seint Iame seithe: Whoosoo knoweth goodnesse and doothe it not, he synneth and dooþe amisse. He is a foole that knoweth þe right weye and wetyngly goothe oute therof. Hooly scripture likenyth the liff of a goode man and of a goode womman to a feire gardyn fulle of grenesse and of feire treys with goode fruit. Wherefoore Godde seithe in the Booke of Louff: My sistir, my louff, thowe art a gardyn closid with ii closeris, that is to seye, with the grace of Godde and with aungell. This gardyn is planted with the goode gardiner, that is to seye, with God, whan he weeteth the herte and maketh it softe and tretable as waxe chawfed and goode lande arayed and woorthye too be planted with goode ympes. These ympes bee the vertues that the Hooly Gooste dewith with grace. The sone of God, whiche is the veraye sonne be the vertu of his clerenesse, makith theyme too profit and waxe on hight. Three thyngys ther be that be necessarie too alle thyngys that groweth on erthe, that is to seye, covenable erthe, norisshyng moistnesse, and mesurable heete. Goostely, withoute these iii thyngys the treis of vertu maye not waxe, profit, ne fructifie.

These thyngis makith the grace of the Hooly Gooste to comen intoo the hert and maketh it alle too refresshe, too floorisshe, and to fructifie and maketh there as right a delitable paradis ful of goode and preciouse treis. But liche as Godde planted erthely paradis ful of goode treis and with fruit and in the myddes he planted a tree that men calle the tree of liff because that his fruit hadde vertu to kepe the liff of theyme that sholde eete therof from dethe, from sekenesse, from agyng, and fro febilnesse, soo gostely doothe the goode gardiner, that is to seye, God the fader in the herte of man. For there hee hatthe planted treis [f. 101v] of vertu and in the myddes the tree of liff, that is to seye, Criste Iesus, the whiche seithe thus in the gospell: Whoosoo eteth my flesshe, seithe hee, and drynketh my bloode, he hatthe everlastyng lyff. This tree be his vertu refresshith and [e]nbelesshith al this paradis. And be the vertu of this tree al the toother treis groweth, profiteth, florissheth, and fructifieth. Alle that ever is in this tree it is goode. This tree is goode to preyse and to louff for many thyngys: for the roote, for the tymber, for the floure, for the smelle, for the leeff, for the fruit, and for his feire shadowe. The roote of this tree is the right grete louff and the outeragiouse charite of Godde the fader. For he louffed vs soo myche that he ȝaf and delyuered his dere sone Crist Iesus to deethe, too martir, and to tourment for to bye aȝein withalle his evil seruauntis. The prophete spekith of this roote and seithe that a virgine sholde sprynge of the roote of Iesse. This worde of Iesse is as myche too seye as a braser of louff. The tymber is his preciouse flesshe. The herte of this tree was his hooly soule in whom was the preciouse moistenesse of the wisdom of Godde. The berke was his feire conuersacion owtewarde. The gomme and the dropyngys of this tree were iiii preciouse thingis of right grete vertu the whiche degouted of his precious membris, that was, water, teris, swete, and bloode. The levis were the hooly wordis, the whiche heelyd alle sekenessis. The floures were the hooly thoughtis, the whiche were al feire and onest and berynge fruit. The fruit were the xii apostelis, the whiche fedde and norisshed alle the worlde with theyre techynge and theire examplis and theire goode werkys and beneficis. And the branches of this tree in oo maner be al the chosyn that ever were, be, and shalle be. For as he seithe to his postlis: I am, seith he, the veraye vine, and ȝe be the branches. In anoother maner the branches were likenyd to the feire vertues and the glorious examples that he shewed vnto vs in dede and taught to vs be vertu of the mouthe. Tho were parfit vertues and ful of veraye blissednesse, the whiche he shewed to his prevy frendes, that was, to his xii apostlis, the whiche hee ledde homly to the hye hylle. And, [f. 102] as the gospell seithe, there he sette hym downe and his disciples aboute hym. And than he openyd his mouthe and his tresor the whiche he hadde hidde in his herte and seide vnto theym thus: Blessid be the pore in sperit, for the reaume of hevyn is theires. Blessid be the debonaire pepil, for theye be loordes of the erthe. Blessed be thoo that weepe, for theye shalle haue the comfort of God. Blessed be thoo that hatthe hunger and the thriste of rightwisnesse, for theye shalle be saouled. Blessed be thoo that shalle be mercifull, for theye shalle fynde mercy. Blessid be thoo that be clene in herte, for theye shalle see God opynly. Blessid be the pesibble, for theye shalle be called Goddes childer. These be the vii branches of the tree of liff of the sone of Godde, Criste Iesus. In the shadowe of this tree a goode herte sholde shadowe hym and beholde the feire branches, the whiche berith the fruit of euerlastyng liff. In these vii woordes is enclosed al the hyenesse and þe perfeccion of grace and of vertu and of veraye blessidnesse as myche as men maye haue in this worlde and atteyne to in the toother. These be the vii rewlis of this liff, the whiche the veraye Salamon techith to his childer. And this is the veraye philosophie that the maister techith to his deciples. In theese vii branches, as hooly men seieth, is enclosed al the some of the newe lawe, the whiche is the lawe of louff and of swetnesse. It maye wel be seide newe, for it maye not age. It is newe and degysee from oother lawes. For lawe is seide because it byndeth. But oother byndeth and this vnbyndeth; oother charchith and this discharcheth; oother manasseth and this p[rom]ysseth; in oother is plee, in this is pees; oother hatthe feere, this hatthe louff, in oother is cursyng, in this is blessyng. Wherfore it is blessed and fulle of blessidnesse. And therfor Salamon seithe that he is blessid that kepeth it. For hee that hatthe it he hatth wonne the tree of liff. Theese vii wordes that God maade be called blessyngis, for theye make men blessed in this worlde, as man maye be in this liff, and moore blessed in the toother. Thowe haste nowe herde what the tree of liff is that is in the myddes of paradis the whiche God planted in þe hooly soule. In the shadowe of this tree, the treis of vertu groweth and profiteth and berith fruit, that Godde the fader, the whiche is the grete gardiner, planted [f. 102v] in this gardin and moisteth theym with the welle of his grace, the whiche maketh theyme too refressh, to wax, and too profite and kepeth theyme in qwiknesse and in liff. This welle devidith hym in vii ryueres; thoo be vii ȝiftes of the Holy Gooste, the whiche moisteth this gardyn. Take heede nowe of the curtesye of oure right goode maister Criste Iesus, the whiche cometh to the worlde to seke and to saue that the whiche was loste, because that he knoweth wel oure pouertee and oure febilnesse, that wee maye falle of oureselfe, but wee maye not rise ne releve of oureselfe ne comme oute of synne ne gete vertu ne come to a blessid liff ȝif it come not be his ȝifte and grace. Therfore he sessith not to somon vs to require hym and to praye hym. And he p[romiss]ith vs that if wee require hym of anythynge that is goode to vs that wee shalle haue it. And ȝit hee doothe more curtes[y]e than soo. For he is oure aduocat and formeth vs oure peticion the whiche wee cowde not forme if he ne were. The peticion that he formed with his blessid mouthe is faire and goode and short and atteignyng. That was the pater noster, wherein is vii peticiones be the whiche we beseke oure goode fader of hevyn that he wille ȝif vs the vii ȝiftes of the Hooly Gooste, the whiche maye deliuere vs from þe vii dedly synnes and drawe theyme oute of oure hertis and in theire place plante and norisshe the vii vertues þe whiche maye leede vs to the vii blessingys of perfeccion and of hooly liff, be the whiche wee maye haue the vii promisses that he promised to his chosyn in the vii wordis aforeseide. For the whiche oure entent is with þe helpe of the Hooly Gooste to speke firste of the vii peticiones of the pater noster, after that of the vii ȝiftes of the Hooly Gooste, and than of the vii vertues the whiche be aȝeins the vii dedly synnys, wherof wee haue spokyn afoore. Theese vii peticiones be evyn as vii right feire maydenys, the whiche sessith not too carye the qwycke wateres of these riueres for to moiste therewith the treis the whiche berith the fruit of euerlastyng liff.

Howe Men Expoundeth and Vnderstandeth the Pater Noster, CXXI

[f. 103] Whan a man settith a childe firste to lettre, atte the begynnyng men lerneth hym his pater noster. Whoosoo wil konne this clergie he moste become meke as a childe. For to siche scoleris oure goode maister Criste Iesus lerneth this clergie, the whiche is þe moste profitable clergie that is and the feirest whoosoo vnderstandeth it wel and kepith it. For siche ther be þat weneth to knowe it and too vnderstande it wel the whiche knewe never but the barke withoute, that is to seye, the lettere the whiche is goode, but that vayleth litil to regarde of the mary, the whiche is ful sweete inward. It is ful short in worde and ful longe in sentence, light to seye and soutil too vnderstande. This prayer passith alle other in iii thyngys: in dignitee, in shortenesse, and in profite. The dignite is because that Godde the son made it too Godde the fader in worde. Godde the Hooly Gooste is that the whiche men asketh there. Also he woolde that it sholde be shorte because that noon sholde ascuse hym of the lernyng and because that noon sholde be anoyed for to seye it gladly and often and for to shewe that Godde the fadir hirith vs gladly whan wee praye to hym with goode herte, for hee reckith not of longe riott ne of rymes ne polisshed woordes. For as Seint Gregor seithe: Verily too praye is not to seye feire wordes polissed with the mouthe but too caste compleyntes and deepe sygheyngis of herte. The value and the profit of this prayer is soo greet that it encloseth in shorte woordes al that euer man maye desire with herte and require be mouthe, that is too seye, that men maye be delyuered from alle evillis and fulfilled with al goodnes, as that the pater noster seithe.

Howe Men Vnderstande the Pater Noster

Oure fader that art in hevyn. Take heede howe oure goode advocat and oure goode maister Criste Iesus, the whiche is the wisdome of God the fader and that knoweth alle the lawes and the vsages of his courte, howe hee techith the to plete [f. 103v] wel and wisly and to speke shortly and sootilly. Truly þis firste woorde that thowe seiest, if it be wel pursued and vnderstanden, it shalle ȝif the al thy cause. For Seint Bernard seithe that the prayer the which begynneth with the swete name of the fader ȝifeth vs hoope to gete al oure prayeres. This swete name, the whiche maketh al the remenaunt swete, sheweth the what that thowe sholdest doo and ledeth the to þat the whiche thowe sholdest beleve. Two thyngis ther be that savith man. On is whan that he beleveth wel and rightfully, and anoother is whan that hee doothe that the whiche he sholde doo. Whan thowe callest hym fader, thowe knowelechist that he is lorde of the howseholde of hevyn and of erthe and cheveteine and welle and begynnyng of al creatures and fro whom that al goodnesse cometh. And thus knowest thowe his myght. After that, standyng þat he is fadir, he is ordenour, gouernour, and purveyour for his meny, anamly for his childer and for his goode men that he hatthe made and sette to his liknesse. And thus knowlechist thowe his wisdom. Also sen that he is fader [be] nature and be right, he louffeth al that the whiche he hatthe maade, as the Booke of Wisdom seithe, and he is softe and debonaire. And alsoo he louffeth and norissheth his childer and doothe for theyre availe better than theye can devise and as a goode fader beteth theyme and chastissith theyme whan theye doo amisse and gladly reseyvith theym whan theye come to hym aȝein. And thus knowest thowe his bounte and his deboneirnesse. I haue nowe shewed the of this woorde that thowe seiest fader his myght, his wisdom, and his bounte. On the toþer parte it remembreth the of thyeselfe, as thye noblesse, thye beaute, and soo myche richesse. Gretter noblesse maye not be than to be son to soo gret an emperoure as God is. Gretter beaute maye not bee than rightfully to be like to hym, the whiche beaute is so greete that it passeth the beaute boþe of man and of angelle. Therfore this woorde [f. 104] fader remembreth the that thowe art his son. Wherfore thowe sholdest peyne the to resemble hym as a goode childe sholde resemble to his fader, that is to seye, to be vigorouse and stronge and myghty to doo welle and to be wyse and wel-avised, large, curteise, softe, and debonair, clene and withowte veleny, liche as he is, and that thowe hate synne and harlotrye and al evil, as he doothe, soo þat in no wise thowe doo no folie. And than euery tyme that thowe seiest thye pater noster this woorde remembrith the that thowe art his right son and that thowe sholdest resemble to hym be nature, be commandement, and be right and that thowe sholdest owe to hym bothe louff, reuerence, worshipp, drede, seruice, and obeissance. Thynke than whan thowe seyist thye pater noster too be a goode sone and a true to hym, if thowe wilte that he be a goode and a deboneir fader too the. Men seith to a newe knyght whan he entreth intoo a tournement: Thynke whoos son thowe arte. Thus than thowe seest wel howe this firste woorde is swete and howe it amonestith the to be valiaunt, worthy, and wyse and techith thee what thowe sholdest be.

I aske the nowe whye and wherfore þou seiest oure fader and not my fader and whom thowe feleshipest with thee whan thowe seiest ʒif vs and not ʒif me. I shalle telle the if thowe wilt. Noon sholde seye my fader but oonly hee that is his sone be nature withoute begynnyng and withowte endyng, the veraye son of God. But wee be not his sonnes be nature save in as myche as wee be made to his liknesse, and soo be Sarazines. But wee bee his sones be adopcion, that is to seye, be avowery. This is a woorde of lawe. For after the emperoures lawe whan a man hatthe no childe he maye chese the son of a pore man and make hym his son and his eyre be adopcion, that [is] be avowery, soo that hee shalle be avowed for his son and shalle bere his heritage. Godde the fader didde [f. 104v] this grace to vs withoute owre deserte, as Seint Poule seithe, whan he made vs the whiche were poore and naked and childer of ire and of helle come too bapteme. Wherfore whan wee seye oure fader and that we seye ʒif vs, we feleshipp to vs al oure brether of adopcion þe whiche be sones of hooly chirche be the lawe þat theye reseyve in bapteme. This woorde than sheweth to vs [the] largesse and the curtesie of Godde oure fader, the whiche ʒiffeth gladlier gret thyngis than litil and too many þan to oon alone. Therfore Seint Austin seithe that a prayer the more it is seide in comune the more it is worthe, liche as a candell is better employed the whiche servith an halle fulle of pepille than þat the whiche servith but to oo man alone. This woorde monestith vs to ȝif hym thankyngys with alle oure hertis for this grace þat he hatthe doon to vs, be the whiche wee be his sones and his heyres, and that we ought right fervently to louff oure eldest brother Criste Iesus, þe whiche hatthe feleshiped vs with hym in this grace. This woorde amonestith vs to kepe the Hooly Gooste diligently in oure hertis, the whiche is oure wittenesse of this adopcion, and as a plegge, as Seint Poule seithe, be the whiche wee bee alle brether, greete and smal, pore and riche, hye and lowe, boothe of oo fader and of oo moder, that is to seye, of God and of hooly chirche and that noon sholde dispice oother but iche helpe oother, as doothe the membris of oo bodye, as Seint Iames seithe. And alsoo it is grete availe to vs. For if thowe putte thye prayeris in comune thowe haste parte of al the comunaltee of holy chirche, and for oo pater noster that thowe seiẹst thowe shalte haue moo than an hundreth thousand. Alsoo this woorde ouris techith vs anamly to hate iii thyngys: pride, hate, and covetice. Pride putte a man oute of feleshippe, for hee wyl be alone above al ooþer so[o] that he wolde haue no felawe. And þat is contrarie to this woorde oures. Hate also putteth a man oute of feleshippe, and that is whan oon werreieth another or somtyme al other. And this is contrarye to the same woorde. Covetise putteth a man oute of feleshippe, for he wil neyther haue his deedis ne hymselfe conuersyng with oother. Thus he is contrary also to the same worde. And therfore siche pepil hatthe neyther parte ne helpe of [f. 105] the hooly pater noster. Alsoo this woorde ouris sheweth vs that God is ouris if we wil, bothe the fader and the sone and the Hooly Goste, that is to seye, if wee k[e]pe his commandementis. And thus seithe hee in the gospelle.

Howe Men Vnderstandeth *Qui Es in Celis*

Whan I seye: *qui es in celis*, I seye ii thyngis. Liche as I seye: The kynge is atte London, I seye that he is a kynge and that he is atte London, on the same wise, whan I seye: the whiche arte in hevyn, I seye that he is and that he is in hevyn. Wee fynde writyn in the seconde booke of the feithe that Godde apperid too Moyses vppon an hylle and seide to hym: Goo thy weye intoo Egipte and seye too Kynge Pharaon on my behalfe that he delyuere to the my pepil, the childer of Israel, from the seruage that he kepeth theym in. Sire, seide Moyses, if men aske me youre name, what shalle I seye? I am þat I am, seide Godde. Thus shalt þou seye to the childer of Israel: He that is sendeth me to yowe. Goode hooly clerkys seith nowe that amonge alle the hye names of oure lorde this is the firste and the moste propre and that mooste verily techith vs what Godde is. For al oother namys theye speke outher of his bonte or of his wisdom or that he is siche and siche, as he is right goode, he is right wise, he is right myghty, and many oother woordys that men seieth of hym, the whiche telleth not proprely the trouthe of the beyng of Godde. But wee be rude and bostous to speke of siche thyngys. But wee speke rather of God thus as men be wonte to seye of a man whoos name theye knowe not, liche as men seye: He is a kynge; he is an erle; he is soo grete, so feire, so large, and many siche thyngys, be the whiche howe soo it bee men maye knowe the man, allethough þat men telle not yit verely his name. Alsoo, whan wee speke of Godde, wee fynde many names [f. 105^{v}] that sheweth to vs some maner thynge of Godde. But ther is noon soo propre as this woorde þat is ne þat soo proprely ne soo briefly ne soo atta[ign]yngly and soo soutilly shewith theyme to vs not oonly in so myche as oure vnderstandyng shewith it to vs and maye strecche. For Godde is he that is aloon, as Seint Poule seithe. And to seye verely, he is aloon, for he is aloon euerlastyngly and withouten ende. That maye noo man seye of noon ooþer thynge. Alsoo he is veraly aloon, for he is veraye and trouthe. Al thynge that is made and al creatures, as Salamon seithe, is voide and nought to regarde of hym and to nought sholde come whens that theye come, if he sustenyd theyme not be his myght. Alsoo he is aloone in stabilnes and stedfastnesse, for he is euer in oo plite withowte chaunchyng, withoute mevyng, withoute trouble in any maner. Al oother thyngis be meve-able, as Seint Iame seithe, in theyre nature in some maner save only he. Therfore he is proprely called þat is. For he is veraly withoute any dowte, withowte vanite, stabilly withoute mevyng, euerlastyngly withoute begynnyng and withoute endyng. He was aloone and shalle be alone withoute begynnyng and withoute endyng. For hee hatthe noo passyng. Thowe sholdest nowe vnderstande here that ther is noothynge moore certeyne than that þat God is, but ther is noothynge soo harde to knowe as howghe and what thynge that God is. Therfore I counsell thee that thowe muse not to myche in serchynge this mater, for thowe maist goo too myche oute of the weye. Holde the content for too seye to hym: feire fader that art in hevyn. And ȝit forsoothe he is oueralle present, in the see, in erthe, and in helle, liche as that he is in hevyn. But men seye that hee is in hevyn because that hee is there mooste seyne, knowen, and worshiped. Alsoo he is in hevyn [gostely], that is to seye, in hooly hertis, the whiche be hye, clere, and clene as hevyn is. For in siche hertis hee is seeyn, knowen, dredde, worshiped, and louffed. Thowe haste nowe these iiii wordes: *pater noster qui es in celis*. The firste somonneth the to worshipp Godde; the seconde too louff Godde; the thirde to doubte Godde, for though that he be oure fader ȝit he is rightwisse and not meveable; thee fourthe for to vigoure the, for sen that he is soo hie [f. 106] and thowe soo lowe if thowe be not worthye and vigorouse thow shalt never come there where he abiteth. The firste also shewith vs the lengthe of his terme, the seconde the largesse of his charite, the thirde the depnesse of his [v]erite, the fourth the heighthe of his mageste. Whoosoo hadde weele atteyned too theese iiii thyngys withouten doubte hee sholde be blessed.

Howe Men Vnderstande *Sanctificetur Nomen Tuum*

Thowe haste herde nowe þe prolouge of the pater noster, the whiche is liche the entre of a towne. Oo goode Godde, whoosoo cowde welle this songe he sholde fynde fulle swete notes therinne. In this songe be vii notis. Thoo be the vii peticiones the whiche p[urcha]seth the vii ȝiftes of the Holy Gooste that raseth and draweth oute of the herte the vii heede vicis and planteth therin for theyme the vii vertues be the whiche men cometh to vii blessyngys. Of these vii peticiones, iii the firste maketh man hooly as he maye be in this liff. The toother iiii makith theyme parfitly iuste. And alle the holynesse of man the whiche is maade to þe liknes of Godde after iii thyngys that is in a soule—mynde, vnderstandynge, and wyl—it is in iii thyngis. That is to seye, that the soule be parfitly purged in wille, parfitly enlumined in vnderstandyng, parfitly confermed in mynde in Godde and with Godde. And the moore habundantly that the sowle reseyvith these iii ȝiftes of Godde the more proprely it approchith to his right naturel beaute as too the liknesse of the fader and of þe sone and of the Hooly Gooste. That is as whan God the fader confermyth hym his mynde, Godde the sone enlumyneth hym his vnderstandyng, Godde the Hooly Gooste purgeth hym hys wylle. These iii thyngys require wee in the iii woordis of the firste peticion of the [f. 106v] pater noster. For whan wee seye: *Sanctificetur nomen tuum*, wee shewe curteisely to oure goode fader oure principal desyre, the whiche wee sholde ever haue, that is to seye, that his hooly name be halowed and confermed in vs. Than whan we seye: *Sanctificetur nomen tuum*, wee seye: Sire, this is oure souerein desire. Wee require above al thynge that thye blessed name, thye goode renoune, thye knowleche, and thye feithe maye be confermyd in vs. In this peticion wee require the firste and the principal ȝifte of the Holy Gooste, the whiche is the ȝifte of sapience, that fermyth and confermyth the hert in God and ioyneth it soo to hym that it maye not be depar[t]ed ne desseueryd. Wisdom is seide of knowyng savouryly. For whan a man reseyvith this ȝifte he tasteth savourisly the swetnesse of Godde and feelith it as the swetnesse of goode wyne is felt better be taste than be sight. But ȝit because that thowe shalt the better vnderstande what is to seye: Thye name be halwed in vs, thowe shalte wite that this woorde hooly is as myche for to seye as clene, as [withowte] erthe, as dedicat to the service of Godde, as dyed in bloode, and as confermed. In these v maneres the Hooly Gooste haloweth the herte of man be the ȝifte of sapience. Firste it clenseth and porgith it, liche as fire clensith, porgith, and fynyth golde. After that it putteth it from the erthe, that is to seye, from erthely louffe and from alle flesshely affeccion and makyth alle too fade that it was wonte afore for too louff, liche as water is fade to hym that is wonte too goode wyne. Alsoo he [d]edifieth it al holly to the service of Godde. For hee putteth it from al besynessis and chargis and settith it hooly to thynke on Godde and too louffe hym and too serve hym, liche as a chirche is [d]edified too the seruice of Godde. Alsoo hee dieth it in bloode. For hee setteth it in soo fervent a louff and in soo sweete a devocion of Criste Iesus that whan it thynketh of hym and off his passion hee is died and wette with þe precious bloode that Criste Iesus shedde for hym, liche as a soppe of hoote brede is whan me putteth it in wyne. This is a newe bapteme. For too dyee and too baptise it is al oone. Alsoo hee confermeth it soo in Godde that noothynge maye desioine it ne disseuere it. I wil nowe than seye this woorde: Thy name be halowed in vs. That is to seye: ȝif vs the sperit of sapience be the which [f. 107] we maye be fyned as golde and clensed from al harlotries, wherethurgh wee maye be soo dronken of thye louff þat al oother swetnesse maye be bitter to vs, wherebye wee maye soo be ȝovyn to the and to thye service that wee maye never take heede of oother and that not oonly withouten moore wee maye be wesshyn but dyed in greyne and baptised and renewed with the bloode of Criste Iesus be devocion of louff, that the name of oure fader be soo confermed in vs that he maye be oure fader and wee his childer and his heyres, and that wee maye be soo confermed that noothynge that maye comme maye disioine this stedfastnesse ne this grace. The grace of Godde is fulle grete whan the wil is soo rooted in hym that it maye not qwake for noo temptacion. But ȝit it is a gretter thynge whan men is soo confermed in his louffe and dronken of his swetnesse that theye fynde neyþer soolas ne conforte but in hym. For than the herte is parfitly confermed whan the mynde is soo stedefaste too hym that it maye thynke of noothynge but of hym. And this require wee of hym whan wee seye: *Sanctificetur nomen tuum*. Sire, thye name be halowed in vs.

Howe Men Vnderstande *Adueniat Regnum Tuum*

This is the seconde peticion of the pater noster, where wee praye that the kyngedom of Godde maye come to vs and that it maye be in vs. Oure lorde in the gospell seithe to his disciples: The kyngedom of Godde is nowe within yowe. Vnderstande wel nowe howe that maye be. Whan Godde ȝefeth a grace that men calle the sperit of vnderstandyng vnto the hert, liche as the son putteth aweye the derkenes of the nyght and wasteth the mystes and the clowdes in the mornyng, [f. 107v] on the same wise this sperit wasteth al the derkeneses of the herte and sheweth hym his defaultes and his synnes and doste and powder oute of nombre, liche as the bemes of the sonne sheweth the doste that is lowe in a house flore. Alsoo on the toother part he sheweth not only withoute moore that the whiche is within hym but that þe whiche is in helle vnder hym and that the whiche is above hym in paradis and that the whiche is abowte hym, as al feire creatures that holly prayseth Godde and berith hym withnesse howe he is myghty, wyse, feire, deboneir, and softe. And the moore he seeith theese creatures, the more he desyreth to see hymselfe. But he seeith that hee is not clene ne worthy to see hymselfe. Than chawfeth the goode true herte and angreth with hymselfe. Than he taketh his pikkes and maketh hym redy and begynneth to delve and to myne and too entre intoo his hert. And ther hee fyndeth soo many synnes, vices, and defaultes and poudere of tribulaciones, of charges, of thoughtes, and of evil willes that he is angry and soo hevye that he taketh a pensifnesse in hymselfe, soo that he begynneth verily to clense his herte and too caste oute al his harlotries, the whiche in hymselfe taketh the sighte of Godde from hym. And that doon he p[ar]elleth hymselfe with veraye confession. And whan he hatthe longe myned and caste oute alle his harlotryes than fyndeth hee pees, soolas, and reste in so myche that hym semyth al the worlde ys but as an egge to regarde of that clerenes and of that pees that he fyndeth in his herte. And this aske wee whan that wee seye: *Adueniat regnum tuum*. That is to seye, plesith it vnto the feire swete fader that the Hooly Gooste wil enlumine, clense, and purge soo myche oure hertis that theye maye be woorthy too see God and that hym liste to come and too dwelle with vs as kynge and lorde and gouernoure and commandeoure, soo that al the herte maye be his and he kynge therof and that wee may euer see hym in this everlastyng liff and haue the kyngedom of God in vs. And therfore seithe oure lorde [f. 108] in the gospelle that the kyngedom of God [i]s liche a tresor hidde in a felde, that is to seye, in the herte of a goode man, the whiche is gretter than alle the worlde.

Howe *Fiat Voluntas Tua* Is Vndirstanden

This is the iii peticion of the pater noster, where we require that the wil of Godde be doon in vs liche as it is doon in hevyn, that is to seye, as it is in seintis and angellis that be in hevyn, the whiche be soo enlumined and confermed in Godde that theye maye willne noon other thynge but as Godde wille. This prayer maye wee not haue but ȝif wee haue the ȝifte of counsell, the whiche is the thirde ȝifte of the Hooly Gooste, the whiche techith vs his goode wille and conuertith oure caytif wille and confe[r]mith it to his goode wille soo that in vs be no propre witte ne selfe-wille but alonly his and that it maye holly be ladye of al the hert to doo in vs what that shee wylle, liche as shee doothe and ys doone in hooly angellis of hevyn the whiche doothe ever hire wille withoute mistakynge or geyneseyyng. Thowe haste now herde iii the firste peticiones of the pater noster, the whiche be hyest and moste worthy. In the firste we aske the ȝifte of wisdom, in the seconde the ȝifte of vndirstandyng, in the thirde the ȝifte of counsell, as I have seide and shewed too the afoore. ȝit wee require not these iii thyngis too haue theyme parfitly in this dedly lyff. But wee shewe to oure fader oure desires the whiche be or sholde be to the entent that these iii prayers maye be fulfilled in vs in euerlastyng liff. And in the toother iiii that folwith after here wee speke anoother langache, for wee seye opynly to oure fader: ȝif vs, forȝif vs, kepe vs, and delyuere vs. For ȝif we [f. 108^{v}] hafe not theese iiii prayeris of hym, wee be dede and evil stedde in this worlde, for theye be ful nessessarie to vs in this dedly liff.

Howe *Panem Nostrum Cotidianum* Is Vndirstanden

Owre goode maister techith vs ful mekely for to speke whan he lerneth vs to seye: Feire fader, ou[r]e dayly brede ȝif vs todaye. What maye the sone aske lesse of his fader than brede alonly to passe þe daye withal? He asketh noon outrage, neyther wyne, flesshe, ne fysshe. He requireth but brede withoute any moore and not for a ȝere ne for a wooke but withowte any moore to passe the daye withalle. Me semeth nowe that this is but a lytel thynge that wee aske, but truly wee require a ful grete thynge. For whan a man requireth of an abbot the brede of his abbeye, he requireth brotherhoode and feleshipp and part and right in alle the goodes of the howse. Thus is it here. For whoosoo hatthe the graunte of this brede hee hatth brotherheed and feleshipp and part and right in alle the goodes that be in hevyn. This is the brede of that blessed covent, the brede of hevyn, the brede of angell, the delectable brede, for it ȝefith goode liff and kepith the soule from deethe. This brede is veraye mete, for it stancheth alle the hunger of the worlde and filleth a man soo that he hatthe inough. And soo doothe noon oother mete but this. This is the brede and the mete that thowe takest in the sacrament of the auter, the whiche, as the scripture techith, thowe sholdest ete hastely and glotonously as a likorouse man doothe goode mete, the whiche sometyme swaloweth doune the goode morsell withowte chewyng. That is to seye that thowe sholdest take this [f. 109] mete with grete ferventnesse of herte, and with grete desire thowe sholdest swalowe it doune withoute chewyng, that is to seye, too beleve holly that it is the veraye boodye of Criste Iesus and the soule and the godheede al togeder withowte any serchyng in thyeselfe howe that maye be. For Godde maye doo more than man maye vnderstande. Also men sholde eete this mete as the oxe doothe the gras the whiche he swolweth. That is to seye that a man sholde remembre swetly and softely in parties al the bounteis of oure loorde and al that Criste Iesus suffred in erthe for vs. And than the hert holdeth the right sauour of this mete and conseyvith of God a right feruent louff and a right grete desire to doo and to suffre inoughe and al that he maye for hym. And al this maketh the vertu of this brede. For this is the brede that conforteth and strengtheith the herte to be right stronge and too suffre and to doo grete thyngys for the louff of Godde. But this maye not be withowte the iiii ȝift of the Hoolye Gooste, that is the ȝifte of strengthe, the whiche armeth Goddes knyghtes and maketh theyme to rynne too martirdom and maketh theyme for to laughe aȝeyns theyre tormentis. Thowe maiste wel see nowe howe curteisly wee aske the ȝifte of strengthe whan wee aske this brede. For as bodyly brede susteyneth and conforteth the boodye soo the ȝifte of strengthe maketh the herte stronge to suffre and to doo grete thyngys for God. We calle this brede oures, for it was maade of oure paste. Nowe blessed be that goode womman that put of hirre floure thertoo, the whiche was the blessed Virgine Marie. It is oures, for it was sothyn and fryed for vs, soothyn in the wombe of the Virgine Marie, fryed in the same panne [of] the cros, as that he seithe in the Sauter, truly fryed in his owne bloode. And that didde he for the gret feruent louf that he hadde to vs. This is the biscuit wherewith he stuffeth his shippe, that is too seye, hooly chirche for to passe withalle the grete see of this perlious worlde. For hee lefte it vs too take be his leve and at his laste testement as the grettest tresor that hee myght leve to vs and ȝaf it as the feirest ivel that he myght ȝif vs for that [f. 109v] wee sholde kepe it for his louff. It is also verily oures, for ther is noon maye take it from vs aȝeyns oure wille. Wee calle it oure dayly brede, that is to seye, for euery daye, for that is þe distribucion that Godde ȝefeth euery daye to his chanones that syngeth his matines and doothe his service, that is to seye, to alle goode Cristen pepill, the whiche euery daye deuoutly and swetly for veray louff hatthe mende and remembrans of his passion. The substance of the pr[o]vendre we shal take at oure hervest in hevyn whan we shalle see hym opynly in his beaute as he is. And therfor it is seide dayly for it is nessessary to vs dayly. And euery daye men sholde take [it] ovther in the sacrement of the auter as prestes doo or ellys goostely be right feithe. This brede is right precious and right noble and right wel arayed. This is kyngly mete in the whiche is al maner of sauoures and deliciousnessis, as the Booke of Wisdom seithe. This is no mete for boyes ne to ȝefe to lewde pepill ne too carles ne too harlotes but too noble and ientil and curteis hertis, that is to seye, the whiche is gentil be grace, noble be goode liff, wesshyn and clene be veraye confession. Seint Matthu in the gospell spekith of the vertu of this brede and calleth it brede abovesubstanciall. That is to seye that it passeth alle above substances and surmounteth ferre al creatures in vertu and in dignite [and] in al maner of valu. He maye not better descrye it ne more sufficiantly than too calle it abovesubstancial. Men seye þat mete is substancial whan it hatthe substance inoghe and norisshynge. And the moore that it is norisshyng men seye that it is the moore substancialle. And because that this brede hatthe moore vertu and goodnes and norisshyng than man maye thynke or seye, men seye not alonly withowten moore that it is substancial, but men seye rather that it is abovesubstanciall, ouer vnderstandyng and supposyng. Wee require and praye oure fader that he wil ȝif vs this brede in this daye, that is to seye, in this dedly liff, soo that we maye make a goode iorney and the merilier abide oure hire, the whiche is the hyre that he ȝifeth to his werkemen at evyn, that is, at ende of theire liff.

[f. 110] Howe *Et Dimitte Nobis* Is Vnderstanden

In this peticion wee require oure goode fader of hevyn that he wil forȝif vs oure mysdedis as wee forȝif theyme that mysdoothe or hatthe mysdoon to vs. Wherfore wee seye thus: Feire fader, quite vs of oure dettis liche as we quite vs to oure dettures. Oure dettis is oure synnes that wee haue acroched or borwed vppon oure soules, the whiche is vppon the beste wedde of oure howse. Wherfore a synner for oo dedly synne that is to soone paste as to the delite and as too the deede is obliged to soo grete an vsure that he hatthe noo power to flee the peyne of helle, the whiche is withowten ende. Alsoo he oweth to Godde whom he hatthe grevid soo gret amendis that hee hatthe noo power to paye it. For in al his lyfe though he lifed c wynter or more he myghte not doo the penaunce for oo dedly synne if God woolde vse right iustice. And therfore hym behoveth to rynne aȝeyn to the courte of mercy and to aske forȝifnesse. For be the right of the courte of iustice the synner sholde be iuged and condempned to everlastynge deethe. And therfore oure good maister Criste Iesus techeth vs to aske pardon and aquitance whan wee praye too oure goode fader, the whiche is softe and meeke, large and curteise for to ȝif, to forȝif vs oure mysdedis as wee forȝif theym þat hatthe mysdone to vs. For ȝif wee forȝif not theym that hatthe mysdone to vs Godde shal not forȝif vs oure mysdedis, as he seithe hymselfe in the gospelle. Wherfore hee that seithe his pater noster and kepeth rancoure or felonye or hate in his hert he prayeth myche more aȝeyns hymselfe than with hymselfe. For whan he seithe as I forȝif, he prayeth Godde not to forȝif hym. And therfore as ofte as thowe seist thy pater noster afore God, the whiche seeth thyn herte, thowe sholdest forȝif thyne evil wille and caste al ire and rancoure oute of thyn herte, and ellys thi pater noster is more aȝeins the than with the. If thowe thynke [f. 110v] it harde and grevouse to caste al ire oute of thyn herte and too forȝif al evil wille to theym that hateth the or that hatthe doon evil to the or that wolde þe evil or that holly mysseth, thynke that God forȝaf his deethe to theyme that crucified hym for to ȝif the example to forȝif theyme that hatthe mysdone too the and too doo theyme the moore goode if theye haue nede too thee and alsoo the moore to praye for theyme that God wolde forȝif theyme. For as Godde seith in þe gospelle: It is noo gret thynge ne grete desert as too Godde to doo wel to theyme that doothe welle to vs and to louff theyme that louffeth vs, for soo doothe payenymes, Sarazines, and oother synneres. But wee that be Goddes childer be feithe and be grace and that be cristened and named of Criste Iesus and be heires with hym of the heritage of paradis on of vs sholde forȝif an nother. And wee sholde louff oure enemys, that is to seye, theyre persones and praye for theyme and doo theyme goode if we maye [and] if theye haue nede, for soo seith he and comm[a]ndeth in the gospelle. Therfore wee sholde alonly hate theire synnes and louff theire persones, the whiche be made to the ymage of Godde. Liche as oo membre of a bodye louffeth an nother, for if be aventure on hurt an nother as for that the toother membris vengeth theyme not, on the same wyse al wee bee oo bodye in Criste Iesus, as the postle seithe. And therfore euery of vs sholde louff oother and not on to hate and to greve wrongefully another. For whoosoo doothe so he is a mansleer and condempneth hymselfe, as the scripture seithe. Siche seithe theire pater noster that theye were better to be stille for theye meve theire iuge aȝeins theyme. In this prayer that wee make to Godde wee require of hym a ʒift of the Hooly Gooste the whiche is called the ʒifte of connyng that maketh a man sadde and konnyng. This sperit sheweth hym what he is and in what perille hee is in and whens he cometh and whider he [f. 111] gothe and what he doothe and howe myche he hatthe getyn and what hee howeth and whan he sholde make aseethe. And if he haue not whereof to paye than this sperit maketh hym to wepe and to sighe and too crye Godde mercy and to seye: Sire, forʒif me my dettis, for I am gretely endetted to yowe in my synnes for the harmes that I haue don and for the goodes that I haue lefte to doo and forʒetyn that the whiche I myght and sholde a doon and for the goodnesse that thou haste don to me and thye grete bounteis that I haue dayly reseyved þe whiche I haue evil vsed and with the whiche I haue served the ful evil. Sire, because that I haue not whereof to make payement, forʒif me that the whiche I owe to the. Whan this sperit hatthe enlumined hym soo that he knoweth his defautis than makith it hym to caste al haate and rancoure owte of his herte and to forʒif al his evil wil if he haue any. And if he haue noone, he is in very wille and purpose in his herte too forʒif ʒif any hatthe mysdoon to hym or wolde mysdoo to hym. And than maye he wel seye: Feire fader, forʒif vs oure defaultis and oure mysdedys liche as wee forʒif theyme that hatthe mysdone to vs.

Howe Men Vnderstande *Et Ne Nos Inducas in Temptacionem*

A scalte man dredeth hoote water. Soo he the whiche is sometyme fallen in synne whan the synnys be forʒovyn hym he is the meker and the dredefuler and the gretter fere hatthe of temptacion. Therfore pray I here for hym the whiche Godde hatthe forʒovyn his mysdedes that he kepe hym froo fallyng aʒein, and I seye thus: *Et ne nos inducas in temptacionem*. That is to seye, [f. 111v] right feire swete fader, lede vs not into temptacion. The feende is the tempter. For that is the crafte wherof he serveth in Goddes howse for to esprove newe knyghtis. And ʒit if temptacion were not goode and profitable to goode pepill Godde the whiche doothe al for oure profit wolde never suffre it for to come to vs. But Seint

Bernard seithe: Whan that the tempter smyteth vs on the backe, he forgeth vs oure crounes of blisse. The feende proprely tempteth a man for the entent that he myght drawe hym froo the louff of Godde. Therfore Seint Poule prayeth his disciples to be founded as toures and rooted as grete myghty trees soo þat no temptacion maye move theym ne shake theyme. Therfore in his peticion we aske in owre bataile the louff of Godde and the ȝifte of pite. This is a grace the whiche moisteth the herte and maketh it softe and pitouse and maketh it holly to be refresshed [and] to bere fruit and goode dedes inoughe outeward, and inward it stedfasteth his rootes in the erthe of liffyng pepille and maketh theym to bide faste, as goode cyment doothe wherwith men maketh walles ȝaraȝineis, the whiche no man maye distroye neyther with pike ne mattok ne engyne. Whan we seye than: *Et ne nos inducas in temptacionem*, that is to seye: Feire swete fader, make vs for to be stedfast and stabill in oure hertis be the grace of the ȝift of pitee that theye meve not for noo temptacion that maye come to theyme. We praye not that we shalle not be tempted, for that were a fowle prayer and a disonest and a shamefull, liche as the son of a worthy man that were newe made knyght wolde praye and seye: Feire fader, I praye yowe to kepe me and forbere me that I goo never too noo feightyng ne tournement. This were grete shame. Wherfore we wil wel be tempted, for that is gret profit to vs in many maneres. For wee be the meker and the ferefoler and the wiser in many wises and the worthier and the more proved. For as Salamon seithe: Whoosoo that hatthe not ben tempted he maye noothynge knowe verily but as a man knoweth the bataile of Troye be heryngseye whan he maye not knowe hymselfe ne his sekenes ne his enemyes ne theire sotilte ne howe God is true to helpe his frendes atte nede ne from howe many synnes and perilles he hatth often kept hym. For alle these causes he sholde never con louff God verily [f. 112] ne thanke hym of his goodnesse if he were not tempted. But wee pray hym to k[e]pe oure hertis that theye entre not into temptacion. That is to seye that theye consent not therto. For as of oureselfe wee be so pore and soo feble that we maye not withstande on houre of þe daye the assautis of the feende withoute helpe of oure lorde. And whan we fail hym wee entre into theyme. And whan he helpeth vs we withstande theyme and feighteth and overcometh theyme.

Howe a Man Shalle Vnderstand *Sed Libera Nos a Malo*

Seint Austin seithe that alle these oother vicis maketh vs owther to doo evil or leteth vs to doo wel. But alle the goodnes that men hatthe don and alle the ȝiftes that men hatthe geten pride desireth to distroie and too take aweye. And therfore whan Godde hatthe ȝovyn a man that the whiche he hatthe required in these vi peticiones aforeseide than at erst it is verily nede to delyuere hym from the shrewe and from his whiles. And therfore this peticion cometh forthe as the rerewarde: *Sed libera nos a malo*. Amen. That is to seye: Feire swete fader, deliuere vs of the shrewe, that is too seye, of þe feende and his wyles that wee lese not be pride the goodnesse that thowe haste ȝovyn vs. In this peticion wee praye hym to ȝif vs the ȝifte of hooly fere be the whiche wee maye be delyuered of the shrewe and of alle oother evilles, that is to seye, of alle synnes and perilles in this worlde and in the toother. Amen. Soo be it as wee haue seide, thus seithe this woorde *amen*. Thowe haste nowe herde the nootes that men be wonte to seye vppon this songe that Godde made, that is to seye, the pater noster. Take nowe goode heede that thowe conne synge theyme welle in thyn hert, for grete goode shalle come to the if thowe soo doo.

Here Endeth the Pater Noster

[f. 112v] And Here Begynneth the VII ȝiftes of the Hooly Gooste, CXXII

After the vii peticiones that be conteyned in the pater noster, wee oughte too speke with grete reuerence of soo hye a mater as is the right hooly ȝiftes of the Hooly Gooste liche as that he techith vs hymselfe. And wee shalle firste telle whiche be the vii ȝiftes, after that whye theye be called ȝiftes and whye ȝiftes of the Hooly Gooste, alsoo whye theye be [f. 113] vii and neyther moo ne lesse, and than of the goodenesse that theye doo to vs. It is a costome and a cortesye that an hye man and a riche and a worthye and a noble whan that he cometh to his wiff, the whiche he louffeth with alle his herte, to brynge hir of his iuellis. We reede that Ysaie the prophete sawe in writyng the blessed mariages that were made in the wombe of the blessed Virgine Marie whan the son of God tooke and wedded oure sister, oure flesshe, oure humanite, oure nature. And alsoo hee reherseth to vs the iuellys and the feire ȝiftes tha he broughte with hym for too ȝif to his wiff and to his kynne. And the prophete ful curteisly seithe thus that of the roote of Iesse shalle sprynge a virgine the whiche shalle bere the floure of Nazareth. That is to seye, of the right grete charite and of the right grete brasyng of the louff of Godd ther shalle come a virgine to vs the whiche shalle bere the floure of Nazareth, that is to seye, the floure of floures, Criste Iesus. For Nazareth is as myche to seye as flour, and Iesse is as myche to seye as an enbraser. And opon that flour he shalle reste the hooly gooste of wisdom and of vnderstandyng, the gooste of counselle and of strengthe, the goste of konnyng and of pyte, and the goste of the fere of Godde. These be the graces of the whiche he was al fulle from the oure that he was conceyved in the bely of his blessed moder. Liche as the grete see is ful of sprynge wateres and of al oother wateres bothe swete and salte wherwith it moisteth al the worlde, evyn soo doþe he, as Seint Iohn seithe, for he is soo fulle of grace, of vertu, and of trouthe that of his plente al we reseyve and take theese vii speritis and these vii ȝiftes in holy bapteme. But liche as bodyly graces the whiche Godde ȝifeth to a childe as in witt, in bounte, in strengthe, and in oother that he ȝeffeth as hym liste and sheweth it theym litil and litil too euery person as the childe waxeth and commeth forthe, evyn soo farith it be these vii goostely graces. After that euery persone profiteth in goodnes and arayeth his hert and ȝifeth hym to serve Godde, soo God ȝiffeth hym aȝeinward the more and the more of his grace. And these goodnesses sheweth vs this in werkyng iche after oother, liche as it pleisith the Hooly Goste the whiche departeth theyme as hym liste, as Seint Poule seithe. Wherfore these graces begynneth as vertues begynne lowe and cometh heyer, that is to seye, froo fere vnto wisdom. For fere is the be[f. 113v]gynnyng of wisdom, as Dauid seithe. But in Criste Iesus where dayly alle these graces and alle these vertuz right pleinly withoute any mesure. And therfore the prophete setteth theyme descendyng euery after the ordre of his dignite, liche as the vii peticiones afore bee sette after the ordre of theire dignitee, the heyest firste and the lower after.

Whye These Graces Be Called Ʒiftes, CXXIII

These graces be called ʒiftes for iii causes: first for their dignite and for their valu. If men in a kyngis courte ʒif to a pore man a cote or a dissheful of pese, that is nothyng worthy to be called a kyngis ʒifte. Therfore Seint Iame calleth al oother ʒiftes God ʒifeth bothe bodily and gostely not only ʒiftes but smale ʒiftes, the whiche be meveable and passyng. But these graces be called parfit ʒiftes. For he ʒifeth theym too no creature but there where hee ʒifeth hymselfe. The seconde reson is because that oother graces and oother goodnesses he leneth vs for to vse in this liffe, but these be veraye ʒiftes withowte mystakyng and withowte lesyng, for whan oother shalle faile theye shalle helpe vs. Wherfore theye be soo verily oures that we maye not lese theyme aʒeins oure wil as we maye doo oþer. The iii reeson and the principall is because theye be ʒovyn purely for louff. For whan a ʒifer taketh heede to his owne availe it is noo verey ʒifte but rather a marchaundise, or whan he loketh to reseyve for his ʒifte bounte or service it is as dette ʒolden aʒein. But whan the ʒifte cometh proprely and purely from the welle of louff withoute availe, withoute fere, and withoute any dette, than is it called a ʒifte. Wherfore the prophete seithe that a ʒifte withowte reseyvyng a ʒifte aʒein is a ʒovyn ʒifte, that is to seye, withowte reseyvyng any rewarde savyng alonly to gete withalle louff. On the same wise Godde ʒiefeth these ʒiftes purely for louff that hee hatthe too vs and for to gete withalle oure hertis and oure louff. And for this cause proprely be theye called ʒiftes.

[f. 114] Whye Theye Be Called Ʒiftes of the Hooly Gooste, CXXIIII

Bvt whye be theye called ʒiftes of the Hooly Gooste rather than ʒiftes of the fader or of the son, standyng that alle theire werkys and ʒiftes be in comune? For these ii causes:

On is that liche as dedes of myght be appropred to the fader and dedes of wisdom too the son evyn soo the dedes of bounte be too the Hooly Goste. For as Seint Denis seithe: Bounte is to sprede hymselfe. For if a man ȝif that the whiche costeth hym noght, it is noo grete bounte. But because that the Holy Gooste spredith hymselfe in oure hertis be these ȝiftes liche as be vii branches, as Seint Poule seithe, therfore be theye called proprely ȝiftes of the Hooly Goste. For he is the welle, and theye be the ryveris. The toþer reeson is because that the Holy Gooste is proprely the louff that is betwene the fader and the son and because that the louff is the propre and the principal and the first ȝifte that a man maye ȝiff, whoosoo wil ȝiffe rightfully. In this ȝifte men ȝiffeth al oother, and withoute this noon oother ȝifte is rightfully called a ȝifte. Therfore the Hooly Goste is proprely the ȝifte and the ȝifer, for he ȝifeth hymselfe and is ȝifen in euery of these vii ȝiftes that he ȝifeth vs for to conferme oure louff to his soo that it maye be confermed stedfastly and fynally and veryly and clenly.

Whye Theye Be VII Ȝiftes and No Moo, CXXV

The man is saved be ii thyngys, be fleyng evil and be doyng welle. The ȝifte of fere maketh vs to hate and too flee evil. The toother vi maketh vs too doo welle. The ȝifte of fere is [the usher with the] grete ma[sse], that is to seye, [with] the grete manace of the sentence of Godde and of the peine of helle the whiche he hatthe alweye vp [f. 114v] and redy. This is the wacche of the castelle the whiche slepeth never. This is the wedehooke of the gardyn the whiche raseth oute al evil herbis. This is also the tresorer the whiche kepeth the herte and al the goodes that is therin. The toother vi ȝiftes maketh vs to doo welle. Thowe shalt nowe witte that liche as the clerenes of the son which thowe seest with thyn eyen ȝifeth clerenesse to al the worlde and vertue and vigoure to alle thyngis that groweth in erthe and that liffeth in the worlde, on the same wise the Hooly Gooste enlumineth al thoo that be in hevyn and in erthe, bothe man and angell, the whiche be in grace. And liche as that þer is in hevyn iii statis of angellis, as Seint Denis seithe, of the whiche some be hyest, oother lower, and the thirde lowest. The hyest be as tho that be kyngys [counselle] in hevyn. Theye be alweye in God and nerre hym than oother be and seeth bothe hym and his secretes. The lower be as shrewys that kepeth and gouerneth the reaume and commeth and goeth and aprocheth to theym of the counselle, and that the whiche theye here they commande and maketh it to be doon of oother. The lowest bee as seruauntis and officeris the whiche hatthe craftes and offices and doothe theyre messages liche as men biddeth theyme. On the same wise and liche the same example ther be in Goddes childer iii astatis in erthe the whiche the Hooly Gooste gouerneth and ledeth, as Seint Poule seithe. On is in theyme that be in worlde and liffeth after the commaundementis of Godde and opon that the whiche theye beleve and here theire prelatis seye. The seconde be in the mydyll astate, the whiche gouerneth welle bothe theyme and oother and liffeth after the counsell of the gospell and not only after the commaundementis, but they have soo myche more. The thirde is in theyme that be parfit and setteth theyre hertis holly from the worlde, the whiche seeth Godde as mych as men maye see hym in this liff and hatthe theyre conuersacion in hevyn and the bodye in erthe and [f. 115] the herte with Godde. The Hooly Gooste techith these iii maner of pepill and gouerneth and ledeth theyme be vii ȝiftes and departeth his graces to euery of theyme as hym liste, as the postell seithe. The iii firste of these vii ȝiftes longeth to theyme that be of þe firste astate. That is to seye, the ȝifte of fere maketh theyme too flee and to hate synne and to louff Godde, the ȝifte of conyng techith theyme, and the ȝifte of pyte maketh theyme to doo worshipp. The oother ii that be heyer longeth to the hyer astate. That is to seye, the ȝifte of counselle gouerneth theyme, and the ȝifte of strengthe fulfilleth theire werkys. The ii laste longeth too thoo of the hyest astate. That is to seye, the ȝifte of vnderstandyng enlumineth theyme, and the ȝifte of wisdom maketh theym parfit and confermeth and ioyneth theyme with Godde. Ther is a reeson whye theye be vii. For the Hooly Gooste be theese vii ȝiftes raseth owte of þe hert the vii vicis and planteth and norissheth theraȝeins vii vertues contrarie too theyme the whiche maketh a man parfitly blessed. These be the goodnesses that the Hooly Gooste doothe too tho hertis [to] the whiche he dessendeth bee theese vii ȝiftes. But or wee descende to the vertues the whiche be contrarie to the vii vicis, that is to seye, the vii dedly sinnes, I wil telle the vii oother vertues, of the whiche iii be called devine and the toother iiii be called cardinales.

Off III Devine Vertues, CXXVI

The iii firste Seint Poule calleth hoope, feithe, and charitee. And theye be called devine because that theye sette the herte too Godde. Seint Austin seithe that feithe setteth vs vnder Godde and maketh vs to knowe hym for oure lorde, of whom [f. 115v] we holde al that ever wee haue of goodnes. He seith that hoope reiseth vs to God and maketh vs stronge and hardye too take on hande for hym that þe whiche passeth the strengthe of man. Charitee, seythe hee, ioyneth vs to Godde. Charite is not ellys but vnite, for it maketh God and the herte al oone, as Seint Poule seithe. Feithe [b]eholdeth in Godde souereyn trouthe; hoope, souerein hyenesse and souereyn mageste; charite, souerein bounte. These iii vertues be devised in iii degreis of louff. For iii thyngis causeth men to louff man: outher because that men hatthe herde goode of hym, or because that men supposeth too haue grete goode of hym, or ellis because that men reseyveth grete goode of hym. These iii maneres of louff bee in these iii vertues. Louff of feithe spekith and werketh. Louff of hoope felith the smell and seketh. Louff of charitee takith and tasteth and seeth and kepeth.

Off IIII Cardinall Vertues, CXXVII

Avncient philisophres spake myche of the iiii cardinall vertues, but the Hooly Gooste ȝifeth theyme and techeth theyme an hundrethfolde better. As Salamon seithe in the Booke of Wisdom, these vertues be called thus: The first is prudens, the seconde temperance, the thirde strengthe, the fourthe rightwisnes. These iiii vertues be called cardinales because theye be principal amonge þe vertus of the whiche the philosophres spake. For be these iiii vertues man is gouerned in this worlde liche as the pope gouerneth hooly chirche be his cardinalles. Prudens kepeth a man that hee be not deceyved be noo wyle of the enemy, temperance [f. 116] that he be not corromped be no shrewe, strenghth that he be not ouercommen be ire ne be hevines ne be fere. These iii kepeth a man in goode astate as anenst hymselfe. And iustice settith hym in ordre and in right weye anenst oother, for it ȝeldeth to euery person that the whiche is hisse. These be iiii toures in iiii corneres of the howse of a goode man, the whiche maketh the howse sure and stronge. Prudence be purveyance stuffeth hym aȝeins the perilles of the este, temperance aȝeyns evil he[e]tis toward myddaye, strengthe toward septentrion aȝeyns evil coldes, and iustice toward the weste aȝeyns evil reynes.

Off the Vertu of Prudens, CXXVIII

These iiii vertues hatthe diuerse offices. And theye dyuerse gretly in theire werkys, as an olde philosophre the whiche highte Platon seithe in his booke that hee made and devised it fulle sotilly and seithe that prudence hatthe iii offices. For be this vertu what that euer a man doothe, seith, and th[i]nketh al it gouerneth and ledeth and rewlith with the lyne of reson [...] and in al his werkis he purveieth hym that theye goo after the ordenaunce and the wille of God, the which seeth and iugeth al thynge. Me semeth he were a grete lorde that hadde this vertu aloone and that gouerned hym be these iii thyngys.

Off the Vertu of Temperance, CXXIX

The vertu of temperance hatthe iii officis. For what hert that hatthe this vertu he coveiteth ne desireth noothynge [f. 116v] that is to be repented, he passith in nothynge the lawe of mesure, and he refuseth alle covetises of the worlde. For whoosoo hatthe this vertu he kepith hym that he be not corrumped be iii thyngis the whiche shendeth the worlde, as Seint Iohn seithe, that is to seye, from flesshely synne, from pride of hert, and from worldly covetice.

Off the Vertu of Strengthe, CXXX

The vertu of strengthe hatth also iii offices. For the hert that hatth this vertu hee reyseth theyme hye above the perilles of the worlde; he doubteth noothynge but veleny; aduersite and prosperite he suffreth and berith withowte bowynge oother on the right syde or on the lefte. He sholde be a ful goode knyght that were wel proved in these iii thyngys. These iii vertues armeth, arayeth, and setteth a man as too iii parties of the herte, the whiche men calle louff, reson, and vigoure. Prudence kepeth reeson that it be not deceyved. Temperance kepeth louff that it be not corrumped. Strengthe kepeth vigorousnesse that it be not overcommen.

Off the Vertue of Iustice, CXXXI

Iustice maketh a man to liffe ordenatly amonge oother. For as Plato seithe: This is the vertu the whiche maketh a man to doo that the whiche he sholde doo too other, for it ʒifeth reuerence to thoo that be above hym, frendeshipp to thoo that be evynly to hym, and grace to thoo that be vnder hym. He [f. 117] seithe that be these vertues a man is worthy to be a gouernour, first of hymselfe and after that of ooþer. In these iiii vertues olde philosophres stodyed gretly, the whiche for to gete vertu and wisdom dispised and forsooke the worlde. And therfore were they called philisophres. For philosophie is as myche to seye as louff of wisdom. Oo good Godde, what we oughte to be ashamed and abasshed seeyng that theye wrote the whiche were paienymes and withowte lawe and that knewe nothynge of þe grace of Godde ne of the Hooly Goste as tho that were before the tyme of grace and notwithstandyng theye mounted vnto the hylle of perfeccion of liff with strengthe be theyre owne vertu and liste not only take heede of the worlde. And wee that haue veraye feithe and knoweth the commaundementis of God and haue the grace of the Holy Goste if wee wille the whiche maye profit moore in a daye than theye in a hole ʒere that wee t[o]ille vs and liff as hogges here benethe in the myre of this worlde. And therfore seithe Sint Poule that payenymes the whiche be withoute lawe and feithe atte the daye of doome shalle iuge vs þat hatthe the lawe and doothe litel therafter. But beecause that theye hadde not the right feithe ne the Holy Gooste theye myght not haue no verraye vertu of liff, though that theye were feire. For as myche difference as is betwene a quycke cole and a dede as myche is ther betwene vertu that hatthe charite and vertu that hatth noo charitee. For vertu that hatthe charitee is the vertu and the valu and the beaute of þe soule and of [other] vertues. Therfore Seint Austin whan he spekith of these vertues he deviseth theyme too iiii maner of louffes and for iiii thynges that veray louff doothe. Hee seithe that the vertu of prudence is the louff of the hert, the whiche wisly refuseth al that maye noye it and chesith al that [f. 117v] maye helpe it to haue that the whiche it desireth, þat is to seye, Godde. The vertu of temperance is the louff of the herte be the whiche a man ȝifeth hym holly and withowte corrupcion to that the whiche men luffeth, that is, to Godde. Strengthe is the louff of the herte be the whiche it suffreth vigerously al thynge that maye come for hym that [men] louffeth the whiche is Godde. Iustice is the louff of the herte be the which hee desyreth withowte moore to that the whiche he louffeth, that is, Godde. And therfore setteth he vnder foote al oother thyngys. Wherfore iustice setteth man in his right state, that is to seye, above alle thynge and vnder Godde. Withoute these iii[i] thyngys noon maye come to the hylle of perfeccion. For whosoo wille clyme soo hye atte the firste he moste looke too haue prudence, the whiche maketh hym to dispice the worlde, and strengthe withalle that it maye ȝefe hym a grete herte too vndertake grete thyngys. On the toother parte, he moste have temperance to conceyve that he be not soo gretely charched and alsoo iustice the whiche maye sette hym and lede hym in the right weye and shewe hym the kyngdom of God, as Godde didde to Iacob, as the Booke of Wisdom seith. Whoosoo myght haue thus these iiii vertues he sholde be blessed and right parfit in this worlde and after that in the toother. For hee sholde be in gostely ioye and in pees of herte. And alsoo he sholde habounde in Godde the whiche he sholde haue in hym in whom he sholde delite hym.

Off the Goodenesses That Vertue Doothe to Vs, CXXXII

Nowe that wee come aȝein to oure mater, lete vs praye with alle oure hertis too that Hooly Gooste the whiche techith hertis that he maye be oure aduocat too teche vs howe be these vii ȝiftes draweth he aweye [f. 118] the vii vicis and in stede of theym planteth and norissheth vii vertuez. The ȝifte of fere is the firste of the ȝiftes that casteth synne oute of the herte, as wee haue seide afore. But proprely it arasseth the roote of pride and planteth in his place the vertu of mekenes. Take heede nowe and vnderstande wel howe a synner that slepeth in dedly synne is like a dronken rybawde the whiche hatthe loste in the tauerne al that he hatthe and is soo naked and soo poore that he hatthe right noght ne thynketh not ne pleyneth hym not but weneth he were a grete lorde. But whan hee hatthe slepte and commeth to hymselfe than feelith hee his evil and knoweth his folie and pleyneth his harme. This is the firste ȝifte that the Hooly Gooste ȝiefeth to a synner whan he viseteth hym. For hee ȝiefeth hym his witte and his mynde and bringeth it aȝeyn to hym soo that he knoweth what goodes he hatth loste and into what pouertee he is fallen be his synne, liche as the [noble] mannes sone was the whiche had dispended and wasted his heritage in rybaudye in soo myche that he was feyne to lede swyne to theyre mete, as oure lorde setteth in an example in the gospell. Also as Salamon seithe. The synner is liche hym that is in yeynes and in stookes and in many wardes, as Seint Peter was in Herodes prison. And ȝit this caytif thynketh neyther of the provoste that holdeth hym ne of the gybet that abydeth hym but slepeth and dremeth that hee goo too festes and mariages. ȝit the [grace] of the Hooly Gooste fareth as the angell that woke Seint Peter and delyuered hym from Herodes handes. Nowe wake thowe synner and delyuere the from the handes of the feende. Alsoo as Salamon seithe: The synner fareth liche hym that slepeth in the myddes of the see, and the shippe perissheth. And he woote not therof ne hatthe noo feere, but whan the Hooly Gooste waketh hym than feelith hee, seeth hee, and knoweth his perille and begynneth to be aferde of hymselfe. Alsoo a synner farith as he that hatthe deethe vnder his clothis and wenyth to be hoole and [f. 118v] stronge. For he hatthe evil corrumped humeris in his bodye of the whiche he shalle dye within a moneth and wenyth too liffe xl wynter, as Seint Clement seithe in his verses of dethe. And he seithe thus: Putte from ȝowe, seithe he, triffles and iapes. For siche couereth me with his clothis that weneth to be stronge and hoole and too liffe noo lesse than xl wynter, þe whiche or viii dayes endeth his tyme. But the Holy Gooste fareth as a goode leche the whiche sheweth hym his sekenes and chaungeth his humeres and ȝiffeth hym soo bitter a drynke that he helith hym and ȝiffeth hym liff aȝeyn. Thus oure lorde troubleth that herte the whiche he wil hele, as Dauid seithe in the Sauter, and spredeth hym and bryngeth hym aȝeyn to knowe hymselfe, as hee didde oure firste fader Adam after his synne whan that he hidde hym amonge the treis of paradis. For the whiche he seide to hym: Adam, where art thowe? He asked be his angell other demandis of Habrahames wiff, the whiche hight Agar. Agar, seide hee, whens comest thowe? Where art thowe? Whider gooste thowe? What doest thowe? The Hooly Gooste asketh these iiii demaundis of a synner whan he waketh hym and reyseth hym and openeth the yen of his herte and ȝiffeth hym his witte and his mynde ayen. Where art thowe, caytif? seithe hee. Beholde in what sorwe and perill thowe art in this worlde, for thowe farest as hee that slepeth in the shippe the whiche perissheth and taketh noon heede ne felith not his perille. Whens comest thowe? Beholde, caytif, thy liffe that is paste, for thowe comest fro the feendes tauerne where thowe haste wasted thy liff and loste thy tyme and alle the goodes that Godde hadde ȝovyn the. What doest thowe? That is to seye, caytif, take heede howe febil thowe art bothe in body and soule. Thowe wenyst to be hoole and stronge. But peraventure thowe haste siche humores in thy body that shalle brynge the to thy dethe, and in thy soule thowe haste evil condiciones the whiche shall [f. 119] brynge the to the dethe of helle if the grace of God rescowe the not. Than where goest thowe? That is to seye, beholde, caytiff, howe thowe goest to dethe where thowe shalt falle into the handes of Herode, that is to seye, intoo the handes of the feende and vnto his meny. Thowe goest to the iugement where thowe shalt fynde the iustice soo cruell, soo streite, and so myghty. Thowe goest too helle where thowe shalte fynde brennyng fyre, stynkyng bremston, and a thousand tormentis the whiche shalle never sesse to tourment the. Thus the Hooly Gooste maketh the synner to opyn his oyen and to beholde above and vnder, before and behynde. These be iiii thondirclappes the whiche ferith the synner and maketh hym to tremble and to be aferde. In the iiii beholdyngys be iiii branches of the roote of mekenes, the whiche the ȝifte of fere planteth in the synneres hert whan that he visiteth hym.

Howe Holy Fere Groweth and Commeth intoo Man, CXXXIII

These iiii thoughtes aforeseide rasith oute of the gardin of the hert iiii rootes of pride. That is to seye owther that þe prowde man wenyth that pride is of value or that it is konnyng or richesse or ellys myght. These be the iiii hornes and the iiii corneres the whiche shent the [contre] that God shewed to Zakarie the prophete. [...] bee the iiii fevers the whiche come after for to overthrowe these iiii hornes. For whan a man thynketh whens he cometh and vnderstandeth and knoweth the filthe and the freelnes of his birthe howe that he was conseyvyd in synne of foule mater and herborwed in soo poore a loggyng and in soo grete pouerte borne and dede in soule or that he was seen of the worlde, in what peynes hee was norisshed, in what labour hee hatthe liffed, howe he hatthe loste his tyme, hee seeth the grete heepe of his synnes and of the goodnesses that he hatthe lefte to doo. Than the grace of Godde maketh hym to fele with his hert that he is not worthe. After that he thynketh where he is and seeth this worlde that it is but an exile and a desert fulle of lyones and of lepardes, a forest fulle of thefes and of snaris, a see [f. 119v] ful of tempeste and of perille, a forneys enbrased with fire of synne and of angwysshe, a filde of bataile where he moste liff in werre and feight with feendes the whiche be fulle wise, sotil, and stronge. Than the grace of Godde maketh hym too feele and too perceyve his ignorance and that he kan right noght. Alsoo whan he thynketh and vnderstandeth his synnes and his defaultes, howe fulle he is of synne and howe voide of al goodnes, than the Holy Gooste maketh hym to feele his pouerte and that he hatthe noght. Also whan he seeth before hym what part he goeth, he seeth deeth the which he maye not withsterte; he seeth the streite iustice of Godde be whoos hande he moste passe and seeth the [peines] of helle fro whom non may ascape that hatthe deservid it. Than God maketh hym to fele that the power of man is nought and that he maye nothyng doo. Soo whan he seeth, feleth, and vnderstandeth that hee is nought and that he hatthe nought, than begynneth he to be pore. These iiii thoughtes be iiii branches of the roote of mekenesse. This tree is be the welle of the fere of Godd with the whiche it is alweye moisted bothe in wynter and in somer, that is to seye, in aduersite and in prosperite. Thowe shalt nowe knowe that euery of these vertues ȝiffeth entent to speke of his degreis where it waxeth and profiteth and clymeth intoo the herte and in his workes and in his goode condiciones be the whiche it sheweth hymselfe outeward. For vertu waxeth hye as doothe a palme tree or a cedre tree or a cipres tree and thanne spredeth and casteth his branches overalle.

Off the Degrees of Mekenes, CXXXIIII

Off the vertu of mekenes Seynt Anseaume speketh and seithe that it hatthe vii degrees wherebye it waxeth hye or that it comen to perfeccion. The firste degree of mekenes is to knowe his default and his pouerte. For Seynt Bernard seith that whan a man knoweth hymselfe verily mekenes maketh hym to dispise hymselfe and to holde hymselfe a wrecche. This knowleche groweth of the iiii rotes aforeseide. Ʒit ther bee somme that knoweth welle ther defaultes and theire [f. 120] synnes, but theye fele theyme not. Therfore the ii^{e} degree is to fele and too pleyne his sekenes, his defaultes, and his pouertee. And whoosoo felith his woo and his pouertee rynneth gladly to a leche. For whoosoo felith his evil humores in his bodye hee is gladde whan he maye porge theym and caste theym oute. Therfore the iii degree of mekenesse is gladly to be clensed and porged and to be confessed of his synnes and his shrewdenesse. Alsoo ther be somme that knoweth and feleth wel theire defaultes and ys sory therfore and confesseth theyme welle, but theye wolde in no wyse that oother knewe it as theye doo. Therfore the iiii degree of this vertu is to wil to be knowen and to be holden for vile and for dispitable. But ȝit ther be some that knoweth, felith, and telleth welle theire defaultis and seieth welle: I am a shrewe and a synnere and siche and siche. But if anoother seide to theyme: Certis it is true that ȝe seye, theye wolde be fulle soory and angre theymeselfe to the deethe. And therfore the v degree of this tree is gladly to hire the trouthe of hymselfe and that a man sholde telle hym his defaultes. And this is that Seint Bernard seithe where he seeth that a very meke man wolde be holden for vile and not praysed for his mekenes. Therfore the vi degree is whan a man suffreth pasciently to bee vilensly entreted and as a persone dispitable, as Kynge Dauid didde, the whiche esyly suffred and herkenyd a seruaunt of his called Semoye, the whiche keste stonys atte hym and scorned hym as in disdeyne and seide to hym al the despite that he cowde. Ther is ȝit a degree the whiche is þe somme of perfeccion of this vertu, that is to seye, too wil and too desyre verily with herte withowte feyntise too be holden for vile and to be reviled and veleynsly treted. This is veraye pouerte of sperit and mekenesse of herte. The riche kynge of hevyn luffed gretly this povertee whan he come to seke it froo soo fere as froo hevyn to erthe. And he louffed it gretly with hert whan hee boughte it soo dere that alle that ever he hadde, anamly the gowne of his backe, he ȝeaff for to be veryly veraye poore. Hee louffed gretely mekenes. For he in whom was never synne and in whom whas never default put hym amonges theefes, that is too seye, amonge the childer [f. 120v] of Adam and clothed hym with the robe of synne and of shrewdenes for to be velensly treted. And he seide to his aposteles the eevyn of the cene: With grete desyre haue I desired this pase, tha[t] is to seye, this dethe, this shame, and this passyng. This tree maye waxe noon hyer. And whoosoo were encressed to this degree of mekenes withowten doubt hee sholde be blessed anamly in this worlde. For hee that seyeth thus maye not lye the whiche is the souereyne trouthe and that seid it with his blessed mouthe: Blessed be the poore in sperit. And howesooeuer it be he shewed it whan he seide: Lerne of me and of noon oother to be meke of herte as I am, and ȝe shalle fynde reste in ȝour soules. This rest and this blessednes howe it is and what it hight noon knoweth but hee that lerneth it. Therfore if thowe wilt knowe what thynge it is, peyne the hertely to conquere soo myche that thowe maye clymbe to the vii degree of mekenes, and than maiste thowe gedir fruit and ete of the tree of liff as Godde seithe in the Pocalipse.

Off the Tree of M[e]kenes, CXXXV

Off the tree of mekenes groweth vii braunches. For this vertu sheweth in vii maneres: first to worshipp Godde, to preyse oother, too louff pouertee, to serve gladly, too disp[r]ise hymselfe, too flee losengerie, and holly too truste in the ʒifte of Godde. The veraye meke worshiped Godde in iii maneres. For mekely he belevith hym in alle that ever he seithe and prayseth hym truly and prayeth to hym devoutly. First he worshiped Godde in as myche as that he belevith hym in alle that ever he seithe liche as a litel childe doothe his maister. And for this cause oure feithe hatthe mede. Soo whooso belevith God well hee doothe hym grete worshipp liche as he doothe grete worshipp to a man the whiche belevith hym be his symple woorde. And it is the begynnyng of weledede the whiche is nessessarie too alle thoo that wil be savid, as Seint Poule [f. 121] seithe. That is to seye that a man beleve Godde opon his symple worde that al that euer he seithe be [trouthe] withowte sekyng any oother reeson or any oother preve. For this cause these proude lollerris and heretikes be dampned for to myche serchynge, for theye wil not beleve God withoute goode plegge, that is to seye, if theye see not veray reeson in alle that he seieth but holdeth theyme to the qwyk reeson. Alsoo theye seye as the vsurer that holdeth hym too the plegge. For theye wil in noo wise beleve the symple worde. And of this cometh al maner of heresyes and mysbelevis. For the proude blynde the whiche wil compare theire wittes to the wisdom of God list to beleve nothynge that Godde seithe to theym ʒif he ʒif theyme not goode plegge, that is to seye, outhir qwike reeson or opyn miracle. But wee that kepe the veraye feithe belevith an hundrethfolde better that he seithe the whiche maye not lye than wee doo miracle, reeson, or þe same that wee see. Godde, the whiche shalle iuge euery persoone after his werkys, seithe that vs moste ȝif acommpt of euery idille worde att the daye of doome. The meke, the whiche seeth, herith, and belevith this, dredith and doothe his devoire to kepe his herte and his bounte and alle his werkys. Alsoo the veraye meke prayseth Godde truly for al the goodnesses that hee doothe dayly to hym and the whiche hee abideth, for the meke fareth yit as the poore man the whiche hatthe grete ioye of a litil almes and thanketh hertely his goodedoerris. Than whan the meke seeth that he is not worthe the brede that he eteth, he knowelecheth truly, belevith, seeth, and vnderstandeth that al is of the pure ȝifte of grace and not of dette what that ever Godde sendeth and ȝifeth to hym. And therfore he taketh noothyng to hym of his loordes goodes the whiche passith be his hande. Therfor Seint Bernard seithe that he is a true seruaunt. Also than he worshipeth God and prayeth deuoutly to hym, that is to seye, with verray teris the whiche cometh of the grace of Godde and of right felyng of herte. For hym semeth that he is liche a childe that is afore his maister al naked and that can not his lesson or that he is liche a poore man that is endetted and that is fallen into þe vsureris handes and hatthe not wherof to paye ne noo[f. 121v]thynge to qwyte hym with or that he is liche a proved theef the whiche is taken with moȯ than an hundreth mysdedes and hatthe the gebet aboute his necke or that he is liche a maymed man that lyeth at the chirche ȝeate the whiche hatthe noo shame to shewe his maymes too alle thoo that passe forby because that euery persone sholde haue pitee. If thowe wilt than lerne too praye and too worshipp Godde, these iiii shalle teche the: the childe, the dettour, the maymed man, and the theeff.

Howe and Wherein Men Sholde Worshipp Godde, CXXXVI

It is of a meke man the veray costome too prayse and too name and too put forthe oother and too prayse and too worshippe theym with mouthe and too doo theyme worshipp in dede. Hee farith as a litil flye þat maketh honye, the whiche fleeth stynkynges and folweth feldis floured and the dewed flowres of the whiche hee maketh honye to stoore withalle his house. Soo doothe a meke herte the whiche taketh noo heede of stynkyngis ne of otheris defaultes. But alle the goodnesses that oother hatthe taken heede of hee louffeth it and prayseth it and conceyvith the swetnesse of deuocion wherewith is hert is refe[i]t and his conciense fulfilled. ȝea truly, only of stoones and caliones hee can souke boothe oyle and hony, lyche as the Sauter techeth. For he seeth noon soo evill ne soo synfull ne soo dyuers but that he can drawe mater too prayse Godde therfore in his herte. In iii maneres he prayseth oother. For hee belevith better another mannes wit than his owne. He wil that oother mennes willes be sonner fulfilled than his. Hee trusteth better in oother mennes myght than in his. The whiche a prowde man doothe the contrarie, as wee haue shewed afoore. Alsoo he aloweth and prayseth oother be woordys, hee trusteth and prayseth the goodnesses that theye haue and doo, and hee ascuseth theire evilles and loweth and lesseth mene thyngys. Hee tenteth alweye too goodnes and torneth to the goode weye and too the goode partie. And this is aȝeyns iii evil condiciones of mysseyerres, the whiche reyseth evilles and loweth goodnesses and perverteth the mene thynges [f. 122] and torneth theyme bestely. Be dede he worshipeth and prayseth euery persone as hee oughte and maye doo withowte myssedede. And soo doothe not a prowde man, but evyn the contrarye, as wee haue shewed afore in the tretys of pride.

Howe Mekenes Maketh Oother too Bee Worshiped, CXXXVII

It is the costome of the veraye meke to haue al his goodnes behynde his backe and al his evil before his yen and the goodnes of oother before his yen and theire evilles at his backe. And hereof folweth þat the moore hee prayseth oother the more he disprayseth hymselfe. He farith as a covetous riche man the whiche hatthe ever his yee too the goodnes that ooþer men hatth and doothe, and alweye hym semyth that he hatthe noon therof. For as ther is an hooly pryde, soo ther is an hooly covetice and an hooly envie. Hee fareth as a kynges sone that is heire of a reaume, the whiche weepeth and cryeth and knoweth noothyng of his hyenesse ne of his richesse. He farith as a sympel shepe in whom al is goode and profitable, boothe wolle, flesshe, skynne, mylke, fruit, and donge, and neverthelesse it knoweth it not ne thynketh not theron. On the same wise holy Abraham, the grete patriarke, seide þat he was but asshes and powdre. And holy Iope that was soo grete in the worlde and soo hooly in Godde seide hymselfe: What am I but asshes and slyme, myre and rotenesse, venym and wynde and febill shadowe and a leffe that the wynde berith aweye and drye stobill þe whiche hatthe nought ne nought is worthe but to þe fyre? And as the veraye meke prayseth oother with herte, mouthe, and dede, as wee haue seide, on the same wyse hee disprayseth hymselfe in these iii maneres. It semeth too hym, as Seint Ierome seide of hymself, that wheder he ete, drynke, wake, or slepe that alweye the orible horne sownyth in his ere: Come to þe daye of doome; come thens to iugement. And because [f. 122^{v}] he wil not be iuged there hee cessith not too iuge hym here and too dampne and too argue his dedis and his woordes and tryeth and nombreth and weyeth and ȝeynweyeth and reprevith his thoughtis, for hee fyndeth myche more chaff than corne. And because he sholde not be iuged in the courte of iustice he wyl neyther leve litil ne myche but that it shalle be examined and iuged in the courte of mercy, that is to seye, in hooly confession. And whoosoo compteth truly in this courte he is quyte forever. But in the court of iustice the whiche shalle be at the daye of doome, whoosoo owe anythynge there he moste paye it, and ȝit hee maye never be quytte. And therfore he shalle be dampned. For hee moste paye or ellys be hanged or ellis abide the deethe of helle. Alas what shalle he paye that hatth noght but his necke charched with dedly synne? Whoosoo vnderstoode and felt these thynges he sholde be stylle and withdrawe hym froo mokkes and lyes that he contrevith aȝeyns veray meke pepill that dredith Godde, the whiche, because theye wolde kepe theyme clenly, confessith theyme often and gladly. But it vaileth litil to doo a goode iugement if the iustice after be not truly doon. And therfore evyn as the verray meke doþe veray iugement of hymselfe with contricion of herte and confession of mouthe, on the same wise he doothe veraye iustice in deede. For he iugeth hymselfe as a theeff and withowte feintise or ypocrysye putteth hym veryly to the gybet of penance.

Howe Mekenes Maketh Man too Disprayse Hymselfe, CXXXVIII

Whoosoo hateth pride louffeth pouerte, the whiche setteth the herte lowe. And therfore al that be veraye meke louffeth pouerte in sperit for iii thyngis, [f. 123] that is to seye, for perilles that be in richesses, for þe goodnes that is in goode pouerte, and because that God as longe as he was in the worlde louffed pouertee and ȝit doothe, as hooly scripture witnessith in diuers places, of the whiche he seithe in the Sauter that he herith þe desyres of the pore pepil and theire prayeris and purveyeth theire mete and arayeth it swetely and with a goode sauour. And he is theire refuge and shalle save theyme. Iob seithe that God is fader to pore pepill and hatth ȝovyn theym power to iuge oother. And oure lorde seithe atte the begynnyng of his sermon: Blessed be the pore pepil. And the riche be vnhappy whiche hatthe theire paradise here. For the veray paradis he hatthe ȝovyn to the pore, soo that theye maye ȝif it and sille it. But the worlde wil not beleve that Godde seithe that pouertee is blessed, for it is of the secrete counsellis of God the fader. Therfore Criste Iesus seithe in the gospell: Feire fader, I ȝelde to þe graces and thankes that thy secret hidde thingis to wyse pepill is shewed to the meke, the whiche seeth theym welle and belevith theyme welle and louffeth an hundrethfolde better theyre pouerte than the riche man doth his richesse. In iii maneres a man sheweth that he louffeth pouertee, whan hee louffeth and folweth gladly the feleshipp of pore pepill and theire liffe and theire coustume. He louffeth theire feleshipp as Criste Iesus didde as longe as he was in the worlde. For naturelly lames louff togedir and fleeth the feleshipp of grete cheepe. On the same wise meke pepil louffeth toogider and feleshipeth theyme gladly. The liff of a poore man is poore. For he seketh neyther metes precious ne outragious ne boste ne pride ne gaye gownez ne noo grete araye nouther in menye ne in festes ne in feleshippes. He is gladde if he haue alonly his sustenaunce withoute moore. Hee suffreth hunger and colde, thirste and hete, and scornes and many bitternesses. And alle these thyngys evil pore pepil suffreth aȝeyns theire wylle. The veraye meke suffreth and desireth gladly al for Godde. Also it is the costome of a pore man if he haue nought ne nought maye gete, he is not ashamed for to aske. Alsoo the veraye meke asketh alweye prayerys and orisones of goode pepil and of Goddes frendes there where he weneth that mooste goodnes is. And [f. 123v] he trusteth hym more to theire helpe than he doothe in his owne goodnes.

Howe Mekenes Maketh Pouerte to Be Louffed, CXXXIX

Pride louffeth hye places and mekenes lowe. This is a diamant of noble nature, the whiche liste not sitte in golde put in poore metall as iryn. Soo farith it be an hille of whete that is thresshed. The corne is vnder and the chaff above. But oure lorde shalle fanne his corne at the daye of doome, as he seithe in the gospell, and caste the chaff in the fyre and the corne in his garner. The purer that golde is, the hevyer it is; and the hevyer that it is, the sonner it goeth too the bottom. The meker a man is, the lower place he louffeth, as didde Criste Iesus [a]n his swete moder the whiche ȝeaf vs example to serve and to obeye and not oonly to the grettest but to the leste. And the moore dispitable that the service is, the gladlier the meke putteth hym thertoo. For to teche this, oure lorde Crist Iesus wolde weisshe the feete of his apostlis. Mekenes than is proprely moder to obedience and norissheth it and techeth it and kepith it that it be not corromped noþer be veinglorie ne be hevynes ne be selve-witte ne be his propre wille ne in non oother maner. It dresseth it, cheressheth it, and worshipeth it with alle worshipes.

Howe Mekenes Causeth to Serve and too Obeye, CXL

Obedience hatthe iiii garmentis, that is to seye, to obeye redyly, iustly, generally, and vigorously. And first þe meke obeyeth redyly, for tofore his owne yee hee is poore and naked and hatth not wherof to occupie hym for hymselfe. And therfor he is alweye arayed and redy as marineris be in a shippe. [f. 124] For as soone as theye hire a [whistle] o[f] þe gouuern[our] þey ryn and lepe as theye were woode. The meke obeyeth gladly. For he is liche hym that is hye sette the whiche is soo gladde whan hee hatthe reseyvyd the commaundement of his maister that he reseyvith with grete ioye bothe perillis, peyne, and dethe for the louff that he hatthe to obedyence. Therfor seide Dauid in the Sauter that he louffed better the commandementis that he ȝeaf hym than outher golde or precious stoonis. The meke obeieth simpilly, as the sheepe doothe the whiche the pasture ledith where hym liste and seith never: Why goo I sonner hider than theder? For hooly sympilnes is oon of the beste doughteres that mekenes hatthe. Mekenes is right true to God, as a goode lady is to hirre lorde the whiche wil pleese noo creature folyly but oonly hirre lorde. And therfore noon obeieth soo clenly with soo pure entent as doothe the veraye meke the whiche hateth not but to plese the worlde. Alsoo the meke is right iuste and swyfte as longe as the wil of God or of his prelat is in hym and that the vertu of obedience ledith hym. But whan his poore wil berith hym or ledith hym he is dulle and slowe to doo welle, liche as the sterre dooth that is called Saturne the whiche rynneth as myche in a daye with the firmament liche as the firmament ledith hym as it doothe in xxx ȝere in his proper terme and sercle and in his owne cours. Alsoo the meke obeyeth oueral generally ther where he supposith that it plesith God and in al thyngys, as an asse doothe the whiche berith too the mylle as gladly barly as whete and lede as golde and the pore manes corne as wel as the ryche. Alsoo the meke is ful stronge, for he chaungeth his strengthe intoo Goddes strengthe, as Ysaie seithe. And therfore ther is noothynge but that he maye bere, for Godde berith bothe hym and his dede. Alsoo he obeieth vigorously and perseuerantly, for he is not wery no more þan the sonne the whiche Godde condith and ledith. And the lenger he liffeth the moore waxeth his strengthe, as it doothe of the litil pissemere. Thus maist thowe see howe mekenes lerneth the too serve and too obeye Godde profitabilly.

[f. 124v] Howe Mekenes Maketh the Prayse of the Worlde to Be Fled, CXLI

The grete maister of mekenes, Criste Iesus, whan he hadde preched and fedde the pepil and helid the seeke, hee fledde vppe intoo the montaigne above the pepil for to be in orisones too teche vs too flee praysyngys and glosyngys. And therfore a true meke herte liche as he peyneth hym too doo welle whan hee obeyeth evyn soo he peyneth hym too flee losse and too [h]ide hym for the wynde of veinglorye and kepeth hym prevy for the rage and the tempest of evil tonges in the shadowe of the rooche. This rooche is Criste Iesus hymselfe, the whiche is the refuge of the garson of meke pepill. Theder fleeth the hecchehogges, as the Saulter seithe, the whiche be meke hertis charched with penaunce and with thornes and sharpenesses. þis is alsoo the douffe house whyder that the doufes of oure lorde fleeth and restith theym, that is to seye, meke symple hertis for the birdys of raveyn the whiche be fendes. Whan a meke herte hatthe doon soo myche that he is entred intoo the hoolys of this rooche as a doufe into his douff house, that is, whan hee remembreth welle the liff of Criste Iesus and his blessed passion, þan hatthe hee forȝetyn alle his sorwes and prayseth litil al that euer the worlde is worthe or that it maye doo. The herte that hatthe asaied this desirith nothyng soo myche as to be forȝetyn and loste as to the worlde. The worlde is to theym a chartre, only[nesse] paradise. For as wise Cypion seithe of hymselfe that hee was never the lesse alon thowe hee were alone ne besyer than whan he was idyll, for than was hee with his ii beste frendes, that is, hymselfe and Godde. Ther treteed hee of his grete besyinesses and of his grete causes for the whiche hym semyd al ooþer besynesses but iapes. Ther dyv[is]eth he with Godde and Godde with hym with hooly thoughtis and feruent desyres. There feleth he grete swetnesse of confortis that Godde ȝefeth too thoo that dredith hym, as the Saulter seithe. And than al langaches and al wordes greveth hym and noyeth hym if theye be not of God or to Godde or for Godde, lyche as the soule hatthe to louffe soulnesse [f. 125] and scilence. And than waxeth in his herte a shame the whiche is one of the feirest doughteres of mekenes, evyn as a ientilwoman that louffeth of louff ys ashamed whan shee is perceyved and shee [hyrith] alsoo whan men speketh therof. [Alsoo] whan shee hyrith that men spekyth of hym and of goodnesses that God hatthe sent hym. And ȝit notwithstandyng shee doothe as a maydyn fervently takyn with louff. For what that ever the world can speke shee seketh euer hirre hirnes and hir secret places as shee the whiche wolde not ellis but be ravisshed, as Seint Poule was.

Howe Mekenes Maketh Worldly Thyngys Not to Be Praysed, CXLII

With this costome and homlynesse that þis hooly soule begynneth to haue, it entreth into the selfe and is ravisshed into hevyn, ȝit beholdeth erthe froo ferre, as Ysaie seith, and seeth it soo litil to regarde of the largesse of hevyn and soo foule to regarde of that grete beaute and soo voide too regarde of that grete plente that than it disprayseth and dispiteth al maner of richesses, worshipes, beauteis, and noblesses that is in the worlde. Al semyth to hym but as the pleye of childer in the streete where theye travayle gretly and wyn nothyng. Hym semyth that al is but wynde, dremes, and lesyngis, as Salamon seithe. And than begynneth he to dye, as Seint Poule seithe, soo that shee is soo pore of sperit that shee hatth noothyng, for Godde hatth ravisshed and takyn aweye hirres and filled hirre aȝeyn with his, liche as he didde his apostelis at Pentecoste. Than the Holy Gooste ȝiffeth hyrre soo grete an herte that worldly prosperite ne aduersitee shee setteth not by a notte. She hatth soo grete a suretee of conscience that shee abideth hardely the dethe and soo gret a troste in God that ther is nothyng but that shee derre abyde and vndertake for Goddes louffe. For shee hatthe the feithe of the whiche Godde speketh in the gospell, the whiche is liche [f. 125v] mostard seede, by the whiche shee maye commande rochis and hilles to obeye to hirre and theye shalle obeye. Mustarde sede is litil, but it is fulle stronge and sharpe, for in the fourthe degree it is hoote, as phisissienes seye. Be the heete wee vnderstande louff. The firste degree of louff, as Seint Bernard seithe, is whan a man can not louff but hymselfe and his owne availe. The seconde is whan hee begynneth too louff God, and that is for his owne avayle. The thirde is whan he knoweth Godde and louffeth hym proprely for his bountee. The fourthe is whan he is soo taken with that hooly louff that he louffeth noon oother thyng but Godde too the whiche veraye mekenes leedeth a man. Thowe maiste nowe opynly knowe howe the poore pepill in sperit be blessed in this worlde. For theye haue voided and meked theyme soo myche that theyre spirites is alle neyntysshed. And the Hooly Goste hatthe filled the house aȝeyne and is lorde of the herte and enhaunseth soo myche hym þat enhaunseth meke pepill that he maketh hym a kyng of hevyn be hooly hoope and be suretee of conscience. And therfore oure lorde seithe that the kyngedom of hevyn is theyris not oonly with-oute moore be promyse but be certoine seisine, as he that nowe begynneth to reseyve the fruites and the rentes. Howe theye shalle be blessed in the toother worlde. And ȝit noo man maye knowe this parfitely vnto that he be there, for the herte of man maye not thynke it ne tonge devise it.

Off the Ȝifte of Pitee and of þe Vertu That Men Calle Mansuetude or Benignesse, CXLIII

The firste ȝifte of the Hooly Gooste maketh an herte meke and ferefull. And therfore it is called the ȝifte of fere. The seconde maketh an herte softe, deboneire, and petouse. And therfore is it called the ȝifte of pytee. This is a vereye moist-nesse and a triacle aȝeyns alle felonyes, anamly aȝeyns the synne of envye, and helith it parfitly. Wherfore the herte that reseyvith this ȝifte conseyvith a swete and a softe and a right temperat moisture. This is a goode louffe of the whiche groweth a feire tree and an hye and right welle-beryng fruit. This [f. 126] is a feire vertu the whiche men calle in Latyn mansuetude and benignite. This is swetnesse of herte the whiche maketh man humaine, *id est*, mankyndely, softe, charitable, deboneire, louffyng, and amiable, for it maketh man to louffe his neyghborghe as parfitly as hymselfe. This tree hatth vii degrees be the whiche it waxeth on height. These vii degrees Seint Poule sheweth to vs where hee meveth vs and prayeth þat wee sholde doo oure devoire too be al in Godde. That is to seye that wee sholde haue on herte, oon sperit, and oon louff in Godde. The firste cause why wee sholde be al one, hye and lowe, poore and riche, is because wee haue oo fader in hevyn the whiche made vs alle comunally to his ymage and to his liknesse. Therfore than sen al we haue oo creature the whiche made vs of oo mater and too oo forme and too on ende, that is to seye, that al we sholde be in hym, as he seithe in the gospell, it is grete cause that wee sholde louffe vs togedir. For euery beste louffeth his liknesse, as Salamon seithe. The seconde cause is because wee bee al cristened in oo bapteme bothe poore and riche. That is too seye that al wee be wesshyn with oo wesshyng, the whiche was with the precious bloode of Criste Iesus, and bought aȝeyne with on only moneye, and as myche coste oon as an nother. Euery of vs than ought gretely to louff and to worshipp oother the whiche Godde hatthe louffeth and praysed soo myche and made of soo greete dignitee. The iii cause is because al wee hoolde oo feithe and haue al oo lawe the whiche is al fulfilled. Seint Poule seithe: Louffe thy neyghborgh as thyselfe. Ther is noon quytte of this dette for ought he can doo. This dette euery persoone oweth too oother, and the moore hee ȝefeth the moore hee oweth. The iiii cause is because that wee haue al oo lorde the whiche is Godde of whom wee holde bothe bodye and soule and al that wee haue. Hee hatthe made al comunly and [wil] rewarde al largely thoo that hatthe kepte his commaundementis and that hatthe [f. 126v] louffed togedir truly. The v cause is because we bee al felawes in oure lordis oste and his knyghtis and his soudeoures the whiche abide al oon wagis, that is too seye, the blisse of hevyn where the louffe and the feleshipp shalle be parfit and confermed, the whiche shalle be wel begunne in this worlde. The vi cause is because þat alle wee liffe with oo gostely sperit as wee liffe with a bodily. Be this sperit al wee be Goddes childer be adopcion, that is to seye, be avowerie and childer of holy chirche, brether germeines of oo fader and of oo moder be a gostely brotherhoode, the whiche is as myche better than flesshely as gostely is better than flesshely. The vii cause is because that al wee be membris of oo boody of the whiche Criste Iesus is the heede and wee bee the membris, the whiche liffeth with oo mete, that is too seye, with the holy flesshe and with the precious blode of Criste Iesus, the whiche louffeth vs soo myche and hatthe vs in soo grete cherte that he ȝifeth vs his bloode to drynke and his flesshe to eete. Seint Poule remembreth vs this louff that he sheweth to vs because that qwyker reeson ne feirer example of veray frendeshipp maye he not shewe to vs. If thowe wilt thynke wel on these vii resones aforeseide, thowe shalt fynde vii causes of frendeshipp the whiche cometh of the ȝifte of pytee.

Off Branches of Frendeshipp, CXLIIII

Off this stokke groweth vii branches. For this vertu sheweth hym in vii maneres liche as men knowe the louff that is betwene the membris of on bodye be vii maneres. First oo membre forberith anoother and kepeth it too his power þat it doo it no harme, anguysshe, ne hurte. In this vnderstande wee the innocency that on of vs sholde kepe to anoother. For this commandement is writen in the herte of euery persoone that þou shalt doo too noon oother that thowe woldest not [f. 127] haue don to the no more than thowe woldest thye right hande smote thye lefte. Alsoo what anguissh that oo membre doo too anoother it suffreth softely and vengeth it not. The membris fele noo mevyngys ne withholdyng oon aȝeyns anoother. In this vnderstand wee parfit deboneirnesse, the whiche hatth iii degrees. The first is that a man sholde not venge hym; the seconde, that a man sholde not kepe angir longe; the thirde, that a man sholde fele noo mevyng of ire noo of hate too his neyghborghe for nothynge that hee doothe. Alsoo the membris obeye al to theyre souereyne, for to theyr power theye doo al þat the hert commandeth theym and that the yen techith theyme. In this vnderstand wee the vertu of obedience of the whiche wee haue spokyn afore the whiche sholde be araied in louff and charite, as Seint Petir seithe. Alsoo oo membre louffeth anoþer and servith it withowte daunger or geynseyyng. In this vnderstande wee the vertu that men calle charitee. Than whan a man louffeth and socoureth gladly ooþer with the power that Godde hatthe ȝovyn hym or consellith and techith theyme with wit that he hatthe or chastisseth and redresseth foles be the auctorite that he hatthe or if he ȝife and depart largely with the goodes that he hatthe for Goddes sake, men seye than that he is fulle charitable. And thus commandeth Seint Peter that of siche thyngys as Godde hatthe ȝovyn vs that wee sholde ministre theyme too oure neyghborghs. Wherfore Tullus the philosophre seithe: Wee sholde fele that al that euer is and groweth in the worlde al is made to serve man, and men be engendred one for too helpe anoother. Lete vs than, seithe hee, doo that for þe whiche wee were made and borne, and lete vs seke the comune profit. For Seint Poule seithe that alle wee be membris of oo bodye. Alsoo al the membres felith and rehersith to theyme that the whiche man doothe to euery membre be it goode or evil, ioye or anguysshe. Whan a man smyteth the foote, the mouthe seithe: ȝe hurte me. In this we vnderstande þe vertu [f. 127v] of veray pite that wee sholde haue comunly, the wyche hatthe ii offices, as Seint Poule seithe, to be glad of the goodes that oother hatthe and too be sory of the evilles that oother hatthe and doothe, suffreth and felith. Alsoo if a membre be seke or wonded al the toother helpeth it that it maye be hoole. In this vnderstande wee the vertu of iustice and of correccion withoute þe whiche the body of hooly chirche myght not endure. For the roten membre sholde shende oother. Whoosoo wil than knowe howe he myght chastie his brother, repreve or ponysshe his neyghborghe or his soget, take heede of hymselfe. Whan a membre is seeke or wonded, the herte felith hevynes and hatth grete compassion. And for the grete louff that he hatthe to it, he putteth his hande þertoo ful softely. And also as Seneque seithe: Liche as men doo with the bodye, men sholde on the same wise entrete softely with the herte. For correccion sholde come with veray louff and with grete compassion, and with grete fere a man sholde put his hande therto. Also the membris worshipeth and forberith on anoother. For as Seint Poule seithe: Euery of vs sholde doo reuerens too oother and forbere oother. Anamly thoo that hatthe moste nede for to be forborne as siche as be febilest and porest men sholde moste forbere theyme. Wherfore as bones bereth tender flesshe and postis an house soo worthy men and wyse sholde euer forbere fooles and febill pepill. This is evyn aȝeyns mysseyerris that soo gladly klatereth forthe the evill and the defautis that theye see in oother. Alsoo oo membre defendeth an nother atte nede and putteth hym forthe for hym. For atte nede men seeth what a frende is. Whan oo foote halteth, the toothe[r] helpeth hym, and as soone as men smyteth the heede the hande putteth hym forthe too defende it. In this vnderstande wee pure and parfit frendeshipp. For the whiche Godde seithe in the gospell that gretter frendeshipp maye not be than too put his liffe for his frendes. This frendeshipp veray Criste Iesus shewed to vs, the whiche put his liff and his body to dethe for vs. And that didde hee for too ʒif vs example, as Seint Petir and Seint Iohn seith, that God set his soule for vs. On the same wise wee sholde sette oure soules for oure brethir, that is to seye, for oure [f. 128] neyghborghes, if wee be veraye membres of the bodye of the whiche he is heede. Whoosoo hadde this vertu, I wolde seye pleinly that he were blessed. This is the vertu that oure goode maister Criste Iesus techith vs whan he seith: Blessed be the deboneire, for theye shalle be in possession of the erthe. Vnderstande nowe wele this blessidnes that deboneire pepill hatthe in this worlde, for thoo that be parfitly deboneire be euer in possession of þe erthe. This is to vnderstande in iii maneres. That is to seye, of [...] lifferris. For liche as the erthe is an habitacion for men and bestis, Godde hymselfe is the heritage for lifferres, that is to seye, for seintis and goode men. And because that God the whiche is the erthe of lifferres hatthe deboneire pepill in his hande and in his possession. [...] as the Sauter seithe. The deboneire, seithe he, shall haue the erthe in possession and in heritage. And Seint Austin seith that noon shalle haue God in possession but if he be firste in [hymselfe]. Alsoo deboneire pepill hatthe here the erthe of theire hertis in possession, for theye be veraye lordis of theire hertis. But ire and felnesse maistreth shrewes. And deboneire pepill maistreth evill condiciones. And Salamon seithe that he is better that maistrieth his herte than hee that taketh castell and citees with force. Alsoo deboneire pepil be lordes of the erthe, that is to seye, of erthely goodes, for if theye lese theyme theye wille never the more be troubled ne angred. But thoo that wille be angrye whan theye leese theyme theye be noo lordis but seruauntis. And therfore it is right that thoo that hatthe goodes temperell and spirituell and theymselfe in possession that theye haue atte laste the erthe of lifferris, that is to seye, Godde hymselfe in possession. But nowe take heede and vnderstande that Godde ȝifeth to poore pepill hevyn and the erthe too deboneire pepill. Where than shall covetouse and felle pepil be but in helle and in torment?

Off the Ȝifte of Kunnyng and of the Vertu of Equite, CXLV

[f. 128v] The firste ȝifte of the Holy Gooste maketh man meke and ferefull. The seconde maketh hym softe and petouse. The thirde maketh hym connyng and clere-seeyng. And therfore men calleth it the ȝifte of konnyng, for it maketh man very konnyng and wise in alle thynges. For this ȝifte whan it dissendith intoo the herte araseth and casteth oute the synne of ire and of felnesse, the which troubleth the herte and maketh a man al woode soo that hee seeth neyther to conduite hymselfe ne noon oother. But this ȝifte enlumineth the herte on euery parte soo that it maye not be deceyved of noobodye. Wherefore Seint Iohn seithe in the Pocalipse that hooly men the whiche were fulle of these iii ȝiftes were al fulle of yen bothe before and behynde. And an angell shewed a stone to Ȝacharie the prophete wherein was vii yen, the whiche be vii beholdynges that goode men hatthe. For theye see within theyre hertis and aboute theyme, that is to seye, vnder and above, afore and behynde, on the right syde and on the lefte. This ȝifte is liche the maister of werkys, that is to seye, of the vertues of the soule, for hee maketh alle with poynte and with ligne and with rewle and with leede and with the lityl ligne. Firste he taketh his pointe and prycketh it and doothe as the wise man seithe: What that euer thowe shalt begynne take heede to the ende, to what conclusion thowe shalt comme. After that he streccheth his lyne, for hee goothe forthe be right deuocion and not only as the serpent nor as the snake. Than maketh hee al with rewle the whiche maketh the walle egal and pleyne, for he louffeth the comune liff of goode pepill withowte fyndyng of novelryes. Alsoo hee provith ofte his werke with a litil lyne and lede, for hee taketh heede that his toure hyngeth neyther on the right syde ne of the lefte, on the right side be prosperite ne on the lefte be aduersitee. Thus than this is the prioure of the cloister of the soule the whiche kepeth the ordre and maketh it to be kepte overalle, firste in the herte and after in oother offices. In this herte is ii sides: the vnderstandyng and the wil, the reson and the affeccion. Whan these ii sides acordeth, [f. 129] theye make feire seruice, feire songe, and a ful swete melodye. That is to seye, whan [t]he wil will as the vnderstandyng techith of goodnes, and affeccion felith alle þat reson vnderstandeth. Vnderstande nowe wel of these ii sides the whiche be in the soule howe theye sholde accorde. In the too syde be iiii sisteres, and in the toþer be oother iiii. For reson hatthe iiii offices, that is to seye, to serche, too iuge, too remembre, and too shewe that the whiche it vnderstandeth be worde. This ȝifte techith reeson that the whiche it sholde seke and lerne and in what ordre, in what maner, and too what ende. And this is ful grete nede, for the mystakyng in siche thynges is ful perliouse. It maketh reson to vnderstande and too lerne that the whiche is necessarie and profitable and honeste, and it withdraweth the contrarie. Aa goode Godde, what man leseth and despendeth his tyme gretly in lernyng thyngis the whiche is not worthe but too synne and too vanite. But the Hooly Gooste be þis ȝifte techith lightly and maketh a man too lerne ordenatly that the whiche is mooste necessarie too the soule and that the whiche ledeth mooste too the louff of Godde and to doo al too a right entent and too a right ende, that is to seye, too the worshipp of Godde and for profit of his soule and for to helpe his neyȝghborghe. Alsoo it maketh reeson to serche wel the trouthe of thyngys and anamly howe it sholde beleve. Too beleve wel is whan man beleveth symplye al that euer Godde seide and commaunded withoute to myche sekyng and enserchyng the counsell of Godde and the depenes of his iugementis and the hyenesse of his mageste and the reeson of his sacrementis. Also to beleve wel is whan men beleveth not to sone ne too late ne too euerythynge ne too noothynge, for boothe the ton and the toother is vice, as Seneque seithe.

Howe Man Sholde Behaue Hym, CXLVI

After goode serche cometh goode iugement. Too iuge welle longeth that a man shal not afferme noothynge too he haue wele sought it and that he haue serteinte therof. And a man sholde not entremete hym to iuge that þe whiche longeth not to hym, as thyngys hidde or defuse [f. 129^{v}] and entenciones of hertis. And thyngys that men maye tourne on the right syde and on the lefte men sholde euer vnderstande thoo too the [goode] partye. Wherfore this sperit be this ȝifte maketh reeson too iuge welle and too knowe rightfully and too distinge betwene goode thyngys and evylle, betwene gret evillez and lesse, betwene litil goodnesses and gretter. For it maketh euerythynge to be praysed after his right value.

Howe Man Sholde Behaue Hym too the Woorlde, CXLVII

After that it maketh reeson too be remembred. For it maketh a man to remembre al that is nedefull to hym, as Godde seithe in the gospelle. He moste remembre thyngys that be paste. It maketh hym to dresse and too vnderstande thyngys that be present. It maketh hym to thynke afore and too purveye for thyngys that be to come. Theese be iii partes of the vertu of prudence vppon the philosophre seyinge.

Howe Be the Vertu of Equite Men Sholde Take Heede to Fooles, CXLVIII

Than it maketh reeson to speke be mesure and gladly to be stylle and to speke wisily, soo that the worde maye comme to the ly[m]e or that it come to the tonge and that it be peysed as goode moneye and proved as Salamon seithe. That is to seye that it bee of goode mater as of goode metal, of goode forme, that is, that it be seide in goode maner and that it haue his right weyght and his right nombre, soo that it haue neyther too litil ne too myche and that it be wel employed. For goode moneye ne goode woordis sholde not be ȝovyn for noght. Wherfore Godde seithe to vs in the gospelle that we shalle not caste oure precious stoones afore hogges. This ȝifte ordeyneth and acordeth the toother partye of the herte, that is to seye, the wil where ther is iiii [f. 130] parties alsoo: louff, fere, ioye, and woo. That is to seye, man sholde louff that the whiche he sholde and as he sholde. And a man sholde neyther haue woo ne fere but of that þe whiche he sholde and as he sholde and as myche as he sholde. And a man sholde neyther haue ioye ne delyte but in that hee sholde and as he sholde and as myche as he sholde. Whan these iiii parties be tempred than men seye that a man is temperat, lyche as men seye of a roote and of an herbe that it is temperat whan it is neyther too colde ne too hoote, ne too drye ne to moiste. And liche as in the bodye of man al maladyes cometh be distemperaunce of these iiii qualitees or of these iiii humores, on the same wise intoo the herte of man commeth alle evilles and al synnes be the distemperaunce of these iiii humoures. Whan these ii sydis of the herte be wel sette and acorded, that is to seye, the reeson and the wille, than is man sette in hymselfe. These be ii branches of the roote of a fulle feire tree the whiche is of a ful feire vertu that men calle equite. Equite is called verily that the whiche men doothe in iustyce, right, and trouthe, in iugement not to softe ne too rude, withowte bowyng too any partye, either too one or too oother. And that is whan a man goothe forthe qw[i]ck[l]y and right as a lyne. For equite is noon oother thyng but vnite, that is too seye, equalite. Whoosoo hatthe this vertu he is a goode iuge and a wyse, for hee doothe nothynge but that it is wel soughte and examined liche as a goode iuge sholde doo.

Off Braunches of Equite, CXLIX

The firste degree than of this vertu is that a man be a goode iuge of his owne herte. For hee sholde entre into hymselfe and beholde his conscience and examine wel his thoughtes and his willes, wheder theye be goode or eville, and ordeyn al to the beholdyng of reeson, soo that wille and reson be holly at oon acorde. For as Seint Bernard seithe: Vertu is noon oother thynge but the assentyng of reeson and of wille, [f. 130v] that is to seye, as whan [t]he wil withoute geynseyng wil doo and seye and put it in dede that the whiche reson seithe, sheweth, and techith.

The Seconde Degree of Equite

The seconde degree of the vertu of equite is a man to be a right iuge and holde [þ]e ligne right betwene hym and þat the whiche is vnder hym, that is to seye, his bodye that hee hatthe in kepyng, the whiche he sholde soo norisshe that it myght serve hym and soo discipline and chastie it that it wil obeye. For reeson sholde be as a true arbetrore betwene the spirit and the flesshe, the whiche be euer contrarie and the whiche sholde safe the right bothe of the ton and of the toother in siche wise that the sperit sholde be a goode loorde and the bodye a goode seruaunt. It is ful grete nede nowe in this partie too holde oueral equite and right mesure in etyng and drynkyng, in clothyng and in arayyng, and in al thyngys that the body asketh, for it enclineth often to to myche rather than to to litil. Also he moste condite and gouerne wel the v wittys of the bodye be reeson and equite, soo that iche of theyme serve of his office withowte syn and withowte myssetakyng, as the yen in beholdyng, the erris in heryng, the nese in smellyng, the mouthe in tastyng and spekyng, the handes and alle the body in touchyng. Whan these v wittys be wel kepte, than is the castell ferme and wel assured. For these be the ʒeatis of the soule; these be the wyndowes wherebye dethe entreth ofte into the soule.

The Thirde Degree

The thirde degree of this vertu is whan a man is a goode iuge betwene hym and that the whiche is afore hym. Thoo bee temperell thyngys the whiche dis[f. 131]troyeth often the bodye and the soule whan man setteth hym to myche theropon, as vsureris and covetous pepill doo and al thoo that louffeth the worlde to myche, the whiche hatthe theire hertis soo laced in the fendes nettes, as Iob seithe, that is to seye, in plees and quarell and forein besinesses of the worlde that theye maye not entre intoo theire hertis ne ordeyne theire liffes. Wherfor it folweth that it is true that wise Seneque seithe þat be this al we synne and goo owte of the weye. For to these parties of liff euery person is diligent and thynketh thervppon. But too sette his liff sadly and holly noon is diligent ne thynketh thervppon. Men ought not than too sette theyre hertis to myche vppon foreine thyngys. For whosoo setteth hym to myche the[r]vppon he falleth in charches and covetices of the worlde, the whiche is roote of al vicys, as wee haue shewed longe afore.

The Fourthe Degree

The fourthe degree of this vertu is a man too see clere on his right syde. That is to seye that hee take heede to the goodnesses the whiche be on his right syde and that he take his example ever of wyse men and goode men. But ȝit on this syde thowe moste holde equite and discrecion, for al the pepill maye not goo o weye ne al the goode pepil and wise hatthe not oo grace, liche as al the membris of oo body hatthe not on office. Many an hert is vnknowynge hereof, as the Booke of the Collacion of Hooly Faderis seithe, the whiche tretith of the perfeccion of vertues. For whan theye see a parfit man that avayleth in oo thynge, anoon theye bowe thertoo and wolde be liche hym. And whan theye see anoother that in other wises doothe myche goode, anoon theye wolde doo after hym and renneth after hym and soo to the thirde and too the fourthe. And thus theye reste vppon noon. Siche pepil farith as a ȝonge grehonde, the whiche is ȝit al vnkonnyng and renneth after euery game and [f. 131v] euery beste that cometh afore hym and doothe but maketh hym weery and lesith his tyme. Of this Ysope setteth a fabille of the hounde and of the asse. The whiche asse sawe euery tyme that his loorde come home the hounde comyng aȝeins hym and made hym grete ioye. The asse thought: Thus sholde I doo, and than my lorde woolde louff me, for he ought too make me gretter ioye that servith hym dayly than to the hounde the whiche servith hym of noght. Within a lytel tyme after, the asse sawe his loorde comme, and he ranne aȝeins hym and leide his feete in his nekke and began too make gret noyse and ioye. The seruauntis the whiche sawe that ranne with levoures and stavys and beete the asse to he hadde evyn inowe. And thus of the whiche he wende to haue hadde worshipp and avayle hee hadde shame and harme. Be siche fablis somtyme goode men were wonte to teche theyre menye. Be this example he shewed to theym that theye sholde not strecche too siche graces the whiche theye maye not atteyn too. And the same Salamon taught his sonne: Sone, seithe hee, lifte never thyn yen to richesses, that is to seye, too graces that thowe maye not atteyn too. And therfore it is grete nede to haue discrecion too see of whom a man sholde take example.

The Fifthe Degree of Equite

The v degree is a man too see clere on his lefte syde. For he sholde take heede of fooles and shrewes the whiche be as on the lefte side for theye be on the werse syde. Hee sholde take heede too theyme firste for to haue pite and compassion of theym. Alsoo because that he sholde not folwe theire perdicion ne theire folye liche as wise Salamon didde, the whiche seide: I passed, seide he, be þe vigne and the felde of the slowe fole, and I sawe that al was ful of nettelis and thornes. Therin lerne I wit and forsighte. For men be wonte to seye: He is softly chastyed that be oothir is chastyed. Alsoo because that men louff moore Godde be whom men be quytte of theire synnes and of theire perrilles. But a man oughte gretly in this syde to kepe equitee and discrecion. For whan I see the foole and the slowe persone I sholde haue pitee and compassion and not iape theyme ne scorne theyme. I sholde ever hate the synne and louffe the persone. And I oughte gretly too take heede in myn herte too wilne too [f. 132] dampne noon ne compare me too noon be hee never soo evill, for siche is evil toodaye that toomorowe maye be goode and siche is goode todaye that tomorowe maye be eville. Alsoo I oughte as myche as I myghte withowte mysdede in myselfe too weepe and too condescende after theyme in dede and in worde for to wynne theyme too Godde and too withdrawe theyme froo synne. For as Seneque and Seint Gregorie seithe: Wee maye not reyse theyme that be fallen if we wil not bowe vs too theyme.

The VI^{te} Degree of Equitee

The vi^{te} degree is the vi ye, that is to seye, too see clere behynde theyme. For the enemye seeth vs and wee maye not see hym. Oure enemyes be the fendes, the which be stronge and wise, subtil and diligent for to deseyve vs. For theye cesse neyther nyght ne daye but ever be in aweyte for to deceyve vs be theire craftes and be theire enginis, the whiche theye vse in mo than ml maneres, as Seint Gregorye seithe. The feende seeth the state of man ful sotilly, bothe his manere and his complexion and to what vice ho is mooste enclined outher be nature or be costome. And on that side he assaileth hym strongely: the colrique man with ire and with discorde, the sanguyn man with iolines and lecherie, the flematique with glotonye and slouthe, the malencolye with envie and hevynes. And therfore euery persone ought to defende his castel moste on that parte that it is febilest and feighte moste aȝeyns that vice that hee seeth hym moste asayled in. And vnderstande welle that he spareth noon, for hee is hardy and sharpe and entreth as he that assailed the son of God, Criste Iesus his loorde. Knowest thowe, seithe oure lorde to Iob, in howe many gyses he disgyseth hym? As whoo seye, noon knoweth it but I. For as Seint Denys seithe: Alle angellis bothe goode and eville and alle the sperites of men is as a goostely mirrour. For evyn as a mirrour anoon reseyvith alle formes and prentes that cometh before it soo doothe the sperit of man be it slepyng or wakyng. Nowe than take a mirrour and sette it before an nother mirrour. Anoon the formes that were in the ton thowe shalt see in the toother. On the same wyse men seye that the feende sheweth too a soule siche formes and siche [f. 132^{v}] figures as hym liste whan Godde suffreth hym and the soule reseyvith theyme. Siche is maugre his as to the thought or to the ymaginacion, as whoo seye, maugre of me I moste see and reseyve in the pirle of the yee the forme of the thynge that commeth before it. It is a right grete grace of the Hooly Gooste too vnderstande welle al the langachis [of the feende] and to knowe al his dedes. For as Seint Bernard seithe: It is to harde and too subtile a thynge to konne distinge betwen the thoughtis that the herte fantesieth and thoo that the enemye setteth therin. Whan he commeth as a felawe or a frende [or] as a marchaunde and he sheweth howe the synnes be plesant and delitable, a man maye knowe it lightly. But whan he cometh liche an angell and sheweth goodnes for to torne it too eville, than the temptacion is strengest. And therfore Seint Iohn seithe that a man shalle not beleve al speritis or that a man haue provid theyme. But doo as thoo that hatthe a goode confessoure, an hooly man and a wise and welle provid in siche causes, too whom theye shewe often and besyly al theire thoughtes that cometh to theire hertis bothe goode and eville. For as Salamon seith: Blessed be thoo that alweye douteth theym. And in an nother place he seithe: Doo be counsell that the whiche thowe shalt doo, and after the counselle thowe shalt not repente the.

The VII Degree of Equite

The vii degree of equite is an ye þat hee moste haue, whoosoo wille haue this vertu. It is hee that beholdeth hye the whiche hatthe euer God before hym. Of hym this spekith oure lorde in the gospelle: If þyn yee be symple and clene, thye bodye is al clere and shynyng; and if thye yee be foule and diuers, thye bodye is dymme and derke. That is too seye, if the entent of thyn herte be simple and clene and goothe right forthe as a ligne thoroughe al these vii degrees that wee haue spokyn of, al the hepe of al his werkys and vertues shalle be feire and clere and plesant to God. And if the entent be [f. 133] wronge or forked or if it foilde aȝein as doothe a sercle, al the consciense and the hepe of vertues is derke. For withowte a right entent almes becometh synne and vertu vice. The entent is meke and goode whan a man doothe goode dedes verily for God. It is clovyn a twoo whan men desireth of the to parte to God and of the toother parte too the worlde. It is wronge whan it is doon for to plese the worlde or of veinglorie. And it torneth ageyne as a sercle whan a man doothe his owne avayle in alle that euer hee doothe. Thowe haste nowe herde the vii degrees wherebye this tree waxeth on height.

Howe Man Sholde Behaue Hym and Defende Hym froo the Feende, CL

The braunches of this tree be the vii principal vertues the whiche answereth too vii capital vicis, as humilite aȝeyns pride, frendeshipp aȝeyns envye, deboneirnes aȝeyns fellenesse, worthinesse aȝeyns slouthe, largesse aȝeyns covetice, chastite aȝeyns lecherie, sobirnesse aȝeyns glotonye. These vii vertues kepeth and conditeth the sperit of konnynge, the whiche ledith theyme be the weye of equite, as Salamon seithe. Be the whiche weye discrecion and reeson, the whiche is the chariotter of vertues and gouernoure of the soule, as Seint Bernard seithe, ledith and conditeth theyme soo that theye goo not oute of the weye neyther on the lefte side ne on the right. And thus theye profit, wax, and berith plente of fruit in somer. Than because that the vertu of equite shewith hym be discrecion in alle the werkys of oother and withowte this alle oother vertues leseth the name of vertu and becommeth vice, I maye wel seye that bee oo weye these forseide [vertues] be the vii braunches of equitee and al the fruit of goode werkys the whiche groweth of theym longeth too this tree. Vnderstande nowe wel the grete maister of vertues the whiche spekith to vs of this vertu. For hee seeth not in his rewle: Blessed be thoo that overalle holdeth equite and that hatthe discrecion and mesure in al thyngis withoute mystakyng. For soo [f. 133v] sholde wee not wynne gretely, for ther is noon but that somtyme missetaketh theyme in many maneres. And therfore oure goode maister Crist Iesus conforteth vs ful sweetly whan hee seith not: Blessed be thoo that synneth not ne that doothe not amysse but doothe al equite and be ligne. But he seith fulle curteisly to confort synneres: Blessed be thoo that weepeth, for theye shalle be conforted. That is to seye, tho be blessed thath seeth and vnderstandeth and knoweth wel theire defaultis and al these vii pointis of equite the whiche wee haue rehersed here and that weepeth and is soory for theyme because that theye fynde soo often inequite and fyndeth it where theye sholde fynde equite. For the worlde is therfore called the vale of terres, for noon that is in the worlde maye lyff withoute terris that hatthe reseyved the ȝifte of konnyng of the whiche wee haue spokyn afore. But rather, as Salamon seithe, hee that seeth the sorwes of the worlde moste haue the more sorwes, terres, and wepyngis in herte. Thus this worlde begynneth to noye. And the more that this liff noyeth, the more men desire the toother. And thereof groweth oother teres for the desire of the toother liff. Thowe shalt now vnderstande that ther be vi maner of terres the whiche hooly men in this worlde hatthe be the ȝifte of konnyng. The firste commeth because men see that theye haue often and many tymes grevid Godde be thought, be woorde, and be deede. The ii[e] commeth because that men taketh heede of the horrible tourmentis of euerlastyng helle, of the whiche euery persone sholde haue grete feere. The iii cometh for the evilles that men see the goode pepill suffre. The iiii commeth for the synnes that evil pepil doo. The v is for this liff that noyeth and for the tooþer that is delaied. The vi commeth of devocion and of grete plente of ioye and of the presence of Criste Iesus and of the felyng of the Hooly Gooste. And thoo that thus weepeth bee verily blessed, for theye shalle be conforted, as the scripture seithe, liche as the norice conforteth the childe that weepeth. For shee wypeth his yen and kisseth it [f. 134] and with strengthe maketh it too laughe. Thus as I haue seide oure loorde shalle doo to theyme that weepeth in this worlde. For he shalle wype theire yen soo that theye shal never weepe ne theye shalle neyther fele evil ne woo but they shalle euer bee with Godde in ioye and in laughynge and in euerlastyng pees.

Off the Ȝifte of Strengthe and of Worthynesse, CLI

We haue nowe spokyn of ȝiftes and vertues the whiche gouerneth thoo that l[i]ffeth in the worlde in the lowest parte of þe iii astatis of whom we haue spokyn. Whe shalle nowe with the helpe of the Holy Gooste speke of ȝiftes and vertues that more proprely longeth to thoo that dispiceth the worlde and tenteth to the hye hille of perfeccion. Of theym Iob seithe propirly that the liff of man in erthe it fareth as knyghthoode. Take heede nowe of a ʒonge burgeis and a newe knyght. Thes ii hatthe ful diuerse thoughtes and diuerse desyres. The burgeis desireth to be a marchant and to wyn and to geder togyder. And the ende of his entent is to be riche and to be worshiped in þe toune. The newe knyght goothe al anoother weye. For he desireth to [doo] curtesye, and to ʒif largely and too vndertake knyghthoode and too goo to armys, to suffre hardenys and too shewe worthynesse, to gete a name and to come to hye astate. These ii astates wee see opynly in ii maner of pepill, of the whiche the ton be thoo that wil kepe theyme wele fro synne, doo penaunce, ʒif almes, holde the commandementis of Godde and of holy chirche, and it sufficed theyme withal if that theye myght safe theymeselfe at the laste. Theye be in goode astate and maye wel safe theymeselfe. The toother be thoo that is noyed with the worlde for the perilles, peynes, and synnes that is therin, of the whiche it is al [f. 134v] ful soo that noon maye haue pees of herte ne hole consciens. Oo the tother part theye see that ther is noo tresor maye compare to the louff of Godde, noo swetnesse soo grete as pees of herte, noo worldly ioye maye compare to the ioye of a clene consciens. It semeth to theyme and soothe it is that whoosoo myght haue these iii thyngys he were a grete lorde and gretter than an emperoure. But þis is soo grete a thyng that þer is but fewe of thoo that derre take on hande to doo this emprice. But whan Godde ʒifeth a man this grace and this ʒifte that men calleth the sperit of strengthe, he ʒefeth hym a new herte, a nobil herte and an hardy, noble for to dispice al that the worlde maye ʒiffe or promyse, hardy for to suffre al the evilles that the worlde may manace. Of this hardinesse speketh oure lorde whan he seieth: Blessed be thoo that hatthe hunger and thirste of iustice. Salamon seithe that he is iuste that dispiseth his harme for his frende, that is to seye, for Godde the whiche is the veray frende. And Seint Bernard seithe that he is not iuste that seeth not and feleth and vnderstandeth in his herte that he is endeted to Godde to louffe hym above al thynge. He that veryly desyreth with alle his herte to ʒelde þis dette to Godde he is oon of theym off whom oure lorde spekith of in the gospelle whan he seithe: They be blessed that hatthe hunger and thirste of iustice. For iustice maye not be doon ne this dette maye not be fully ȝolden in this worlde, but it is desired in this worlde and payed in the toother. Therfore oure good maister Criste Iesus seith not: Blessed be thoo that shalle doo this iustice and that shalle ȝelde this dette. But he seith more curteisly as he that knoweth oure pouertee: Blessed be thoo that hatthe hunger and thirste to ȝelde this dette. For hee requireth not his dette, but it sufficeth to hym if wee haue goode wil and desyre to ȝelde it. Howe sholde I seye that he were iuste that ȝeldeth not that the whiche he sholde ne hatthe neyther wil ne desyre to ȝelde it? Whan this desire is verily in the herte, it moste nede shewe it in dede. As Salamon seithe: None maye hide fire in his lappe but if his gowne brenne. This may [f. 135] not be shewed withowte vertu and worthynesse. For be wittenessez ne pletyngis men provith not that a man is a good knyght but be suffryng and enduryng and in doyng many dedis of armys. And this is the iiii vertu that the Holy Goste ȝifeth too man for to arase withal holly the iiii vice, that is to seye, the synne of slokynes or of slouthe. This vertu is of soo gret dignite that amonge al oother vertues this aloonly berith the name of vertu. For vertu and worthynesse is al one. This vertu God ȝifeth too his seruauntes whan hym liste to make theyme knyghtis as he didde his aposteles atte pentecoste, of whom wee reede that theye were siche cowardis that theye dorste not come oute of theire houses too theye were armed with this vertu. But sitthyn theye went makyng grete ioye whan men didde theyme any duresse or shame.

Off Degrees of Strengthe and of Worthinesse, CLII

[...] philosophres and philosophie setteth the vii point thertoo. The firste point of worthinesse theye calle it magnanimite; the seconde, troste; the thirde, suerte; the fourthe, pascience; the fifthe, constance; the sixte, magnificence. The vii^{te} that oure maister ioyneth thertoo is called hunger and thirste of iustice. Men maye not soo propirly name these vertues in Romaunce as the vnderstandyng of these wordis seith it in Latin.

Off Magnanimite, CLIII

Magnanimite is hyenesse, gretnesse, and noblesse of corage be the whiche man is hardye and of grete emprise. This vertu hatthe ii partis, on to dispise grete thyngis, anoother to chese and to vnder[f. 135v]take gretter thynges. Of the firste parte, Seint Austyn seithe: Worthinesse is al that euer corage dispiceth, the whiche is not in his power, that is to seye, al that hee maye lese aȝeyns his wille. A[nd] Seneque seithe that in worldly thyngys is noothynge soo grete as an herte that dispiseth grete thyngys. The philosophre of þe seconde part seithe that magnanimite is a resonable emprise of thyngys hye and ferefull. Whoosoo hatthe this vertu he beholdeth the worlde fro fere, as Ysaie the prophete seithe, and thus the worlde semeth to hym as litil as a sterre doothe to vs. Wherfore al the worlde and al the [charches] of the worlde semeth to hym as noght. And therfore he setteth be theyme no more than be the webbe of an eraigne. For the whiche Salamon seide whan in his thought he hadde torned vp soo downne al the worlde and al þe statis of foolles and disputed of wise pepill, hee seid thus his sentence: Vanite of vanites and al that euer I see is vanite. That is too seye, the worlde is vanite, and also it is al ful of vanite, and man hymselfe for whom the worlde is made hee is alsoo holly vanite, for in hym is al maner of vanite, as the Saulter seithe: Vanite be mor[t]alite, for his liff fleeth as a shadowe; vanite be bisinesse, for his besynesses fareth as dremes; vanite be iniquite, for synne maketh hym more noughty than anythynge that is in the worlde. Nowe than the firste parte of this vertu is that [it] maketh the worlde to be dispised liche as men doo here after philosophres, paienes, and hooly Cristen men. The thother partee is that it maketh the weye of perfeccion and the weye that is soo harde, soo sharpe, and soo fereful to chese. That is the weye the whiche ledeth to the hille of God. This is the weye of perfeccion. This is the weye of the counsellis of oure loorde the whiche he shewed to his aposteles on the hille of the whiche this trete spekith. This weye chase theye to whom it sufficed not alonly to kepe withouten moore the x commaundementis of Godde to the whiche theye be bounden, but theye wille fulfille the counsell to the whiche theye be not bounde be dette as thoo doo that leve al that theye haue for Godde and abaundoneth theyme to dye for the louff of Godde [f. 136] the wiche dyed for theyme or to goo over the see as pepill doo that forsaketh and dispiseth for Godde al that ther is, boothe goode and frendes, and maketh theymeselfe bonde too oother the whiche were free, and maketh theyme pore that were riche or myght be riche, and putteth theyme to suffre grete sharpenesses the whiche hadde grete delites in the worlde as many that be in religion or in sharpenesse of penaunce in herte and in bodye. For it vaileth litil to be in sharpenes of penaunce ne in religion if the herte be not there. For the habite maketh not the monke ne the armes a knyght but the goode herte and the worthynesse of armes.

Off Troste of Worthinesse, CLIIII

The seconde degree of worthynesse is troste. For whoosoo hatthe vndertake a goode liff hym behoveth to haue his purpose stedefaste and to haue goode troste in Godde that he shalle performe to hym that the whiche hee hatthe begonne. This vertu that men calleth troste is right necessarie ageyns the assautis of the worlde, of the flesshe, and of the fende, whiche assaileth a man strongelyest at the begynnyng. The flesshe seithe to hym: I maye not endure this liff and leve myn olde custumes. The worlde rynneth after too drawe hym aȝein, liche as men rynneth after a theeff whan hee scapeth owte of prison. The fende seith to hym: Caytiff, what wilt thowe doo? Wilt thow kylle thyselfe? Thowe maiste save the wel ynoughe oother weyes. These be the firste assautis that the newe knyghtis of oure lorde suffreth, the whiche desireth to conquere the kyngdom of hevyn. But whan he setteth hym to Godde be goode and stedefast troste hym therre not recche. For hee is right a true frende the whiche knoweth and maye and wille kepe theire goodenesses. And whoosoo that God will helpe, none maye noye hym.

[f. 136v] Off Suerte of Worthines, CLV

The thirde degree of worthynesse is surenesse. As the philosophre seithe: Suertee is a vertu be the whiche a man douteth noon evill that is afore his yee. And this is the thirde goodnesse that þe ȝifte of strengthe doothe. For the Hooly Goste whan hee armeth Goddes knyghtis with his vertu first hee ȝifeth hym a noble hert for to vndertake gret thyngis. After that he ȝiffeth hym anoother grete ferventnesse and a grete desire to pursue it and a grete troste to acheeve it. And than he maketh hym sure as a lion soo that he hatthe neyther fere of perill ne of peyne ne of dethe ne of tourment but rather desireth theyme liche as newe knyghtis doothe tournementis. And soo didde martires as it shewith in theire lives, of whom we rede of Seint Agathe that with as grete ioye she wente to turmentis as that shee hadde goon to festes and to mariages.

Off Pascience, CLVI

The fourthe degree is pascience. Liche as the Hooly Gooste maketh his knyght sure for too abide tornementis and wayes the whiche to hym be for to come, on the same wyse he maketh hym stronge and pascient whan theye comme. And this is the fourthe degree that theye calle pascience. Be this vertu a man ouercometh al his enemyes: the worlde, the flesshe, and the feende and al that theye maye doo or seye. For this is a shelde of golde to hym that suffreth for the louff of Godde the whiche couereth hym oueralle, as the Saulter seithe, soo that noo strooke maye hurte ne trouble the herte. Noon hatthe this vertu but thoo that hatthe ben tempted. For as Seint Poule seithe: Tribulacion bryngeth pascience as that the fire maketthe twelle harde. Noon hatthe victorie withoute pascience. For whoosoo lesith pascience he is ouercommen. [f. 137] Withoute pascience noon maye comme too perfeccion. And therof wee see example in al maner of craftes that men doo with hande. A peesse suffreth myche fire and many strookes or that it be sette on the kyngys borde and a chalis also or that it be blessed and sette on the aulter. A tounne suffreth many a grete strooke or þat wyn be put therin and scarlet gretely defouled with the fullers feete or that the kynge were it. Thowe maiste fynde as many of these examples as ther bee craftes in London. Be this vertu a man is stronge as iryn, the whiche soupleth al oother preciouse metalles; as golde, the whiche the more that it is in the fire the purer, the clerer, and the more traictable it is;

as the salemandre is, *id est,* [...] þat liffeth in the fire; liche as the fisshe þat baigneth and norisshith hym in wateres.

Off Constance, CLVII

The fifthe degree of this vertu is called constance. This is a vertu that maketh the herte ferme and stable in Godde, as a toure that is founded on a rooche and as a tree that is rooted in goode erthe the whiche mevith hym not for no wynde that maye blowe nor for noon aventure that maye come goode ne eville. Noon cometh too a victorie withoute this vertu. For whan Goddes knyght hath doon any woorthinesse than the feende assailleth hym be veinglorie. Wherfor Dauid seithe in the Saulter þat the feende ouerthroweth the goode stronge pepill on the [right] side be aduersite and the right stronge on the lefte side be veinglorie. Seneque prayseth gretly þis vertu the whiche seithe that ther is noo vertu but that the whiche goothe forthe proudly betwene the to fortune and the toother, that is too seye, betwene the goode and the evill and with grete dispite bothe of þe ton and of þe toþer.

Magnificence of Worthinesse, CLVIII

The vi degree of worthinesse is called magnificence. Theye discrie this vertu thus: Magnificience is of a hye besinesse blessedly achevyd. Oure grete philosophre Criste Iesus calleth this vertu perseuerance [f. 137v] be the whiche Goddes goode knyghtis endureth and abideth vnto the ende and goothe in the hyeweye of perfeccion, the whiche he hatthe vndertakyn. Seint Poule seith of this vertu that alle oother rynneth but this wynneth the spere. They feighte al, but this hatthe the coroune and the victorie. Al theye werke, but this berith aweye the hire at evyn. For as oure loorde seithe: Whoosoo perseueryth vnto the ende hee shalle be saffe and noon oother. Ferther these philosophris cowde not shewe ne trete of the vertu of worthynesse. But the disciples of oure maister Criste Iesus goothe ferther forthe. For whan theye hadde gedered al togyder than thought theyme theye were newe to begynne. The vertu and the worthynesse of philosophres was for to ouercomme vices and for to acquere vertues. But the worthinesse of holy men is for to ouercome these vices and to gete these vertues and principally therwithal for to holde iustice and trouthe toward Criste Iesus. He is not iuste that ȝeldeth not that the whiche he sholde vnto his power. And truly it is a thynge ful iuste and resonable that I ȝif my liff and my deethe for hym that ȝaf his liff and his deethe for me. And as myche as hee is more worthe than I in as myche am I redeveable to hym be right iustice, as Seint Anseuume seithe. A man maye desire this vertu, but ther is noon that here maye sufficiantly ȝelde it ne plainly paye it, liche as wee haue seide afore.

The VII Degree Is Hunger and Thirste of Iustice, CLIX

And herfore the vii degree of this vertu is that the whiche oure maister ioyneth thertoo to whom the philosophres myght not atteigne whan he seide: Blessed be thoo þat hatthe hunger and thirste of iustice. Thoo be verily blessed that be mounted to the vi degrees of worthynesse and that hatthe hunger and thirste and grete desire to mounte vnto theire power to the vii degree.

[f. 138] Off the Tree of Worthinesse, CLX

In this tree wee fynde vii branches as ther be in oother. For in vii maneres a man knoweth the vertu and the worthinesse of oure lordis good knyght. For be vii maner of batailles theye come to vii victories. Be vii maner of victories theye come to vii maneres of corounes, the whiche be vii hirres of the whiche Seint Iohn speketh in the Pocalipse. For as that Seint Bernard seithe: Hee is too fonned and a grete foole that withowte victorie wenyth to haue [...] victorie. Wherfore Seint Poule seithe that no man shalle haue a coroune [...]. That is to seye, vppon the lawe of the felde to prove them but if he [sholde doo] as theye the whiche auncientl y at Roome was wonte to doo. That [i]s to seye, it be[f. 138^{v}]hovyd that hee that set hym in the felde for to conquere a name ouercome al thoo that the maister of the felde made for to come thedir. The maister of oure felde the whiche provith the newe knyghtis, as it is writen in the Booke of Kyngis, that maister is right trewe, as Seint Poule seithe, and knoweth wel the power of euery persone. For the whiche he suffreth that noon enemy tempteth vs ouer oure power ne noon aduersite too assaile vs but that wee maye ouercome if we wylle with the helpe of Godde, the whiche in oure bataille encresseth strengthe to vs, as Seint Poule and Seint Iohn seithe, as wee haue devised and seide: vii victories and vii corounes that we shalle haue, that is to seye, vii maner of hirres the whiche Godde promisseth too tho that shalle overcome.

The Firste Bataille of Penaunce, CLXI

The firste bateille that a Cristen man hatthe is aȝeyns dedly synne. Ther is noon that is ouercomen in this bataille the whiche wil not consente to synne. He ouercometh the bataille the whiche is light to ouercome to vigorous hertis and noyouse and slowe and sloggy too thoo that be lache in Goddis seruyce, the whiche be not fulle coilde be fere ne fulle hoote for the louff of Godde, as Seint Iohn seithe. He that falleth in this bataille and is ouercomen hatthe myche moore to doo to reise hymselfe and too feighte with hymselfe than hee that is standyng. For hee hatthe noo power to reise hymselfe ne too defende hym if Godde strecche not his hande to hym be grace. For liche as a fisshe be his owne wille entreth intoo a maske and maye not gete owte too men caste hym owte, on the same wise a man falleth in synne be his owne wille, but he maye not gete oute withoute the wille of oure lorde and withoute his helpe, the whiche ȝifeth hym the armoure of penaunce whan it plesith hym be the whiche hee maye ouercomme his enemy. This is the armoure þat the postle Seint Poule commandeth for [f. 139] to take in this bataille. For a man vnarmed is noght in bataille. Thowe shalte nowe knowe that a man too be wel armed for too ouercome synne hym behovith to haue iii thyngys the whiche is in veraye penaunce. The firste is repentance of herte, the seconde confession of mouthe, and the thirde is sufficiant satisfaccion in the worlde. Be dede of these iii thynges is the haubergion of penaunce determined. If oon of these iii thyngys faile, the armure is al false, and he that werith it is ouercomme.

Off Repentance, CLXII

Repentaunce asketh grete sorwe and grete weymentacion of herte because that man hatthe grevid Godde. And the more that man hatthe grevid hym soo the moore sholde be his sorwe. Dauid repented hym thus the whiche seide in the Sauter: I labored and travailled in my weymentaciones. Therfore euery nyght I shalle wesshe my bedde and my couche with my terris. He that hatthe grevid Godde be dedly synne hee sholde weyle with depnesse of herte soo that is herte sholde melte al in terris, and with grete sorwe and sighȝyng he sholde crye Godde mercy as his theef, as his mordorer, as his traytoure the whiche hatthe deservid the gebet of helle. The synner is a theef to Godde. For his loordes goodes the whiche be but lente hym for to wynne with, as goddes of fortune, of grace, and of kynde, hee hatthe dispent theym folyly and in evill vse and set al at hazarde. Alsoo hee is a morderer of the kyngys doughter, that is to seye, of his soule, the whiche he hatthe kylled be dedly synne. Alsoo he is traytour to Godd. For the castel of his herte and of his bodye, the whiche Godde hatthe takyn hym to kepe, hee hatthe ȝoldyn it too hys dedly enemy, that is to seye, to the feende. Hee ought to haue gret sorwe that is in siche plite. Hee sholde often wesshe wele his bedde with his terris, the whiche is his conscience. Siche teres chasseth the enemy of helle froo the herte liche as hoote water chasseth an hounde froo the kechyn. Also after repentaunce sholde come confession. For that is the [f. 139v] goode chamberer the whiche clensith the house and casteth oute harlotries with the besom of the tonge, of the whiche Dauid spekith. Vnderstande nowe welle howe a man sholde confesse hym.

Off Confession, CLXIII

Iff confession sholde availe too helthe of soule, it moste haue vi condiciones. The firste is that it be don wisly. This konnyng is in ii thyngys, the firste that a man take heede to whom a man sholde confesse hym. Seint Austin seithe that liche as a man wolde doo for too eschewe bodyly dethe he sholde doo for to eschewe the deethe of the soule. A seke man for too eschewe deethe and for too haue helthe seketh gladly the beste and the wisest leeche that he maye fynde. On the same wise Seint Austin seithe that whoosoo wil confesse hym wysely and fynde grace too Goddewarde he sholde seke siche a confessour as koude bynde and vnbynde, that is to seye, siche as can wel knowe the synne and counsel the synner and that hatthe power too asoile and too ȝif penaunce. After that he that wil confesse hym wisely, hee sholde diligently thynke on his synnes toofore that he come to confession, and he sholde serche al his herte and his concience howe he hatthe grevid Godde and his blessed moder and his seyntis and with grete fere remembre al his liffe, as the goode kynge Ezechie didde that seide thus: I remembred al my ȝeres with grete bitternesse of herte. A synner sholde entre intoo his house, that is to seye, intoo his herte, not only passyng forby as a ioglour that abideth not gladly in his owne house, for he hatthe noo wers house than his owne. But he sholde abide there and beholde al his defaultis, of the whiche he sholde ȝif acommpte too Godde and reeson to his provoste, that is to seye, too his confessoure. And hee sholde thynke of hymselfe as he that hatthe to commpte of his receitis and dispenses before his lorde. Wherfore hee sholde diligently beholde the beynge of his concience that he faille not of his compte. For ȝif he faile of his commpte Godde wille not faile of hisse.

[f. 140] To Conffesse Hym

A man whan he hatthe thought diligently on his synnes and remembred howe and howe often and in howe many maneres he hatthe grevid Godde and howe grevously he hatthe synned and howe longe he hatthe dwelled in synne, thanne a man sholde confesse hym hastely and anoon. And this is the seconde condicion that sholde be in confession. For the kynge roose at mydnyght for to confesse hym, as he seithe in the Saulter, soo hee aboode neyther a moneth ne halfe a ȝere. And the wise man seithe in anoother place of the scripture: Tarye not to conuerte the to God, ne seke not lengtheyngis ne fleyngys ne delayes froo daye too [daye]. For the abidyng is fulle perliouse for many causes. First for the condicion of synne, for synne is a brennynge fire whiche maye not be staunched but be confession. Hee were a grete foole that sawe his howse brenne and ranne not faste to the water. Also syn is a ful gret sekenesse, and confession is the medicine. And forsoothe hee praysith lytil his sowle that seeth it seeke to the deethe and desireth it not to be hoole. Alsoo deethe the whiche is soo nere and spieth the synner oueralle sholde meve hym too confesse hym. For he knoweth neyther the tyme ne the oure ne the daye whan dethe shalle come, the which vndertaketh the synner ther where that he taketh noon heede. Therfore whoosoo knewe whan hee sholde dye he woolde make hym redye in al the haste he myght, as I suppose. Alsoo ȝif the synner sawe the peril that hee is inne in the prison of synne in the throote of the lyon of helle and of the dragon the whiche wolde devoure hym, he wolde crye confession too Godde in al the haste that he myght. Alsoo if he sawe the grete goodes that he hatthe loste be his syn, as euerlastynge goodes, goostely goodes, his tyme, and hymselfe, the whiche he myght fynde be confession, hee were a fulle greet foole if hee hasted hym not too torne aȝene after the mercy of Godde, the whiche abideth hym at his doore, as the Pocalipse seithe. For the lenger that Godde forberith the synner, the moore cruelly he smyteth hym whan hee seeth hym slowe [f. 140v] and necligent. Liche as an archere, the depper that he draweth his bowe, the soorer he smyteth. And forsoothe he hatth his bowe bente and drawen, as the Sauter seithe, for too slee synneres, if theye kepe theyme not. Alsoo whoosoo taryeth to longe fro confession he for[ȝ]eteth often his synnes, soo that vnnethe it happeth that he is well confessed, for he forȝeteth ful many synnes of the whiche he shalle never vmbethynke hym. And thus he shalle never repente hym ne shalle not be confessed. For thus it is too hym ful grete perille.

Howe Confession Sholde Be Clere

Also whan he is afore his confessour, he sholde confesse

hym faste and openly. That is to seye, hoo sholde telle his synnes clerely, anamly soo that the confessour maye see the charge and the hert and the entent of hym that confesseth hym. For the seke man sholde discouere his sekenesse to his phizisien, or elles the phizisien may not werke ne the surgeun vppon the disese but if he see the wounde. And therfore Boece, the wise man, seithe: If thowe wilte, seithe hee, that the phizisien shalle hele thee, thowe moste shewe hym thy woundes. Wherfore these trowantis oughte too teche the too confesse the, the whiche sheweth theire pouertee and theire sekenesse and sheweth the fowlest owteward for to haue almesse. Thus sholde a synner discouere his synne for to haue mercy. And this is the thirde condicion that sholde be in confession.

Off Hoolle Confession

Alsoo a synner sholde confesse hym holly. And this is the iiii condicion that sholde be in confession. For hee sholde telle al the synnes grete and litille and the circumstances of the synnes. Wherfore hee sholde firste take heede of the vii dedly synnes of the whiche wee haue spokyn afore and holly con[f. 141]fesse hym of euery of theyme after that hee felith hym coupeable withoute hydyng, fauoryng, or defendyng hym of anythynge and withoute accusyng any oother. Dauid confessed hym thus the whiche seide in the Sauter: I shalle confesse me, and I shalle telle my synnes aȝeins me and not of oother, as ypocrites doo the whiche setteth the feyrest outeward and that sheweth theire goodnesses and hideth theire evilles and accuseth oother of that the whiche theye be moore coupeable. For theye see right well a mote in theire negȝborghes ye, but theye see not a myllestone in theire owne. Siche is the pharaseye of the gospelle, the whiche remembred his goodnes and dispised the seculer man that mekely bette his blame and cryed [mercy] afore Godde in the temple and seide thus: Sir, haue mercy on this synner. A synner sholde iuge hymselfe afore Godde and not ease his synne but greve hymselfe and thynke on it withowte lyinge. Alsoo confession sholde be hoole togeder and not devided too dyuers confessoures. For a man sholde seye al to oo priste and not o part to on, anoother parte to anoother.

Godde setteth nought be siche shrifte. Alsoo hee sholde not only telle the synnes but mooreouer al the circumstanses the whiche encreseth the synnes. For a synne is gretter in oo persone than in anoother, as in a man of religion than in a seculer, in a prelet than in a lower degree, in a grete loorde than in a simple man. Alsoo it is gretter syn in oo place than in anoother, as in the chirche or in hooly placis, and in oo tyme than in an nother, as in lenten or at festful dayes. Alsoo whan a man synneth wityngly he synneth moore than whan it is be ignoraunce. Alsoo a man sholde telle the condicion of the synne. For it is gretter synne in a maried woman or in a mayden or in a womman of religion or in a persone set to bee a preste or a dekyn. Or after that the ordre is the lesse or the gretter is the synne. [Alsoo] if the synne be ageyne nature or vppon nature. Alsoo howe ofte a man is fallen in synne and howe longe he hatthe dwelte therin. Alsoo a man sholde telle if he haue stryvyn litil ageyns the temptacion, for somme ther be that abideth not the temptacion, or if a man cause the syn or if a man be fallen into the temptacion be his owne purchasyng. Alsoo the cause and the entent that mevid hym too seye or to doo syn and al oother causes and circumstaunses that maye encresse the synnez. Alsoo men sholde reherse to rynne be þe membris wherwith theye haue synned. A man sholde [f. 141v] first goo too the herte and telle his thoughtis what theye bee wheder flesshely or gostely as aȝeins the feithe or of veineglorie or of envie or of rancure or of oother maneres of the whiche ther be to many. The flesshely thoughtis longeth too the delit of the flesshe. A man sholde take goode heede of al his thoughtis if ther be any consentyng or longe abydynge in the delite the whiche sometyme is as myche as the consentyng [and] of al siche thoughtis man sholde confesse hym. Alsoo a man sholde take heede if hee haue synned with the membris of the bodye. For man maye synne with theyme in many maneres, first with the heede, wherevppon men maketh often to grete besynesse and too grete coste, as those ladyes doo that arayeth soo besyly theire heedes with precious arayes for pure vanite, for to be the more pleesaunt, and for to drawe men to synne, with the whiche theye synne ful grevously, anamly thoo that make soo greet hornes with theire heere or with any oother thyngys that theye be like to folisshe women. Ther is vanite inoughe aboute these heedes in waysshyng, in kemyng, in lokyng in mirroures, wherwith Godde is fulle often grevid. Men be not quyte of this vanite that putteth soo grete besynesse to looke in mirroures, too keme, and to araye wel theire heedes. Of siche vanitees men sholde confesse theyme. After this men sholde rynne to the v wittys of the bodye, wherewith men synne ful often, as be the yen in foly lokyng or be the erris in foly heryng, as to be glad to hire mysseyerris, lyerris, losengeris, and oother folyes or with the mouthe in foly spekynge or in to myche drynkyng and etyng or with the nesse [in] delitynge hym in goode smellis or in folily and disonestly touchynge hymselfe or any ooþer. A man sholde alsoo confesse hym of owterages that he hatthe doon in roobes, in hoosyn and shoon, and in al oother defautes of the whiche a man remembreth hym. Thus the confession is veraye whan a man telleth alle his defautis litil and myche. And this is the iiii condicion that sholde be in confession.

Meke Confession

[f. 142] The v condicion is that a man sholde confesse hym mekely. For a synner spekith to Godde that seeth his herte. Wherfore the confessoure is but the ere of God. For that the whiche hee herith he knoweth it nat os man but as Godde. And therfore a synner sholde meke hym as myche as hee myght afore Godde. And hee sholde telle his synnes with grete fere and opyn al his herte tofore hym, as the scripture seithe. Liche as a man spilleth a pot ful of water, whan the water is spilt, ther abideth neyther colour as is in mylke ne sauoure as is in hony ne smelle as is in wyne, evyn soo a man sholde withholde noothynge of the synne after that a man hatth tolde it in confession, neyther the coolour ne the sauour, that is to seye, the maner that a man hatth hadde in spekyng or in beholdyng or in suyng evil feleshipp or in any oother thynge that is colour of synne. Alsoo a man sholde leve þe savoure of synne. He hatthe sauoure of synne that thynketh of the synnys that he hatthe doon and that the thought is as plesans to hym. But he sholde thynke of hys synnes with grete fere and with grete sorwe and confounde hymselfe. He oughte afore Godde to haue grete shame in hymselfe and purpose never to retorne to synne thoughe a man sholde dismembre hym. Also a man sholde flee and leve the smelle. Ther be some that levith wel theire synnes but gladly theye hire speke therof, the whiche theye sholde rather haue grete abhominacion.

The VI Condicion That Sholde Be in Confession

The vi condicion that sholde be in confession is that a man sholde confesse hym often for many causes. Firste for to gete the moore grace and clennesse, as a towelle the whiche is white be often waysshynge. Alsoo for venial synnes wherein a man falleth often. And whoosoo often foulleth hym, often sholde weisshe hym, lyche as a shippe moste often be pvmped for the water that alweye entreth intoo it. Also for to put the feende fere froo hym. A birde gladly [f. 142v] draweth hym fere froo the place where men taketh his egges froo hym. Alsoo for to lerne to confesse hym wel, for vsage maketh maister as it sheweth in other craftes. Alsoo because that a man forgetheth often his synnes, hee sholde ofte confesse hym. Alsoo because a man knoweth not wheder he hatthe ben wel confessed and wel repentant or not, this a man sholde ofte recouere that the whiche he hatthe lefte vnsufficiantly doon. Alsoo for too meke hym and for to gete the more mede. For þe whiche men asked an abbot whye he confessed hym soo often, and he answered and seide: Because I haue ever fere that I be not wel confessed. Also it remembreth me often of somme thyngys that I haue not seide. And because that froo confession I rise ever for to meke me.

The Lettynggys of Confession, CLXIIII

Thowe haste nowe herde howe a man sholde confesse hym. Thowe shalt nowe knowe that v thyngys specially letteth veray confession. The firste is shame that a man derre not telle his synne for shame. That maketh the feende the whiche putteth shame before hym for to close withalle his mouthe, liche as a theeff doothe that casteth a litill frosshe in an houndes throote, for that litil frosshe is of siche nature that it maketh an hounde mvet whan it is casten in his mowthe. But a synner sholde thynke that the shame that hee hatthe too telle his synne is a grete parte of thee amendes. Alsoo a synner sholde gladly haue a lytel fere for too eschewe the grete shame atte the daye of doome, the whiche the synner abideth whan al the worlde shal see his synne. The seconde thynge is evil fere too doo grete penaunce the whiche the feende putteth in the synneres ere, seyyng thus: Thowe maiste not doo sharpe penaunce, ne thowe maiste not leve thye costomes. Siche pepil be liche an eschewe hors the [whiche] is aferde of the shadowe that hee seeth. And forsothe al the penaunce that a man maye doo in this worlde is but as a shadowe too regarde of the penaunce of helle or of purgatorie. The iii thynge is evil louff. For the feende hatthe soo enlaced the synner that hee [f. 143] louffeth soo myche his synne that he wil not leve it. Soo he thynketh that hee sholde confesse hym for nought, hee that slepeth in his synne as an hogge doothe in mire. The iiii thyng is hoope of longe liff for the whiche the feende seithe to hym: Thowe art a ȝonge man. Thowe shalt liffe longe. Pleye þe and doo thy wille. Thowe maiste confesse the al betyme. But he taketh noo heede too deethe that awayteth hym, the whiche shalle take hym sonner than he weeneth. For Godde the whiche promisseth pardon too thoo that shalle repente theyme promisseth theyme not to toomorwe, as Seint Gregore seithe. Wherfore sometyme it happeth that the feende pleyeth hym with a synner as the katte doothe with a mouse. Whan he hatthe takyn it and longe pleyed therwith, than hee eteth it. The v thynge is whannehoope wherein the feende putteth a synner. But he sholde thynke that Godde forȝiffeth soone thoo that repenteth theyme and þat hee is gladder to ȝiff vs pardon than wee be to aske it.

Off Satisfaccion, CLXV

After confession cometh satisfaccion. That is the amendes oppon the arbiterment and the counsell of the confessoure the whiche sholde iuge the mendement after the missedede, outher in fastyng or in almesse or in prayer or in oother thynges after that the synne requireth. For as a seke man sholde gladly obeye to a phisissian for too have helthe, on the same wise it is goode to doo the commaundement of his goostely fader for profit of his soule. Thowe haste nowe herde the thyngys the whiche holly maketh the haberion of penaunce wherewith God armeth the newe knyght for the toother bataille that hee hatthe ageyne synne. And whoosoo overcommeth this bataille hee setteth noo stoore of the secounde dethe, as Seint Iohn seithe. The firste is the deethe of synne the whiche a man ouercometh [f. 143v] be penaunce, be the whiche a man escheweth the secounde deethe of helle the whiche maye not dye. This is the firste branche of the tree of worthinesse too hym that wille ouercome this bataille.

Off the II Bataille, CLXVI

After this bataille cometh anoother. For whan a man repenteth hym of his synne than commeth a newe striff too his owne herte as too thynke what penaunce he shalle doo or what liff he shalle leede. Ther be many of thoo that in this batalle be recreauntis. For as Godde seithe in the gospelle: Nowe theye beleve; nowe theye myssebeleve. Nowe theye wil; nowe theye wil not. Nowe theye purpose, nowe not. And therfore theye be liche a fane that standeth on a chirche the whiche torneth with euery wynde. But whan hee setteth hym too Godde and affermeth his herte and his goode purpose, than is this bataille wonne. And than Godde maketh hym ferme and stabill as a pelir in his temple, that is to seye, in hooly chirche, as Seint Iohn seithe. This is the secounde victorie and the wagis that he kepeth for hym.

The Thirde Bataile, CLXVII

After this bataile cometh the thirde bataile that a man hatthe with his owne flesshe, þe whiche pleyneth and gruccheth gretely whan it begynneth to fele hardnesse and sharpenesse of penaunce, and it striveth gretly for to come ageyne too his olde costomes. The flesshe is the evil woman of whom Salamon spekith. Whosoo doothe mooste hirre wylle werste hatthe therof, and the moore contrarie it is to hym. And whoosoo suffreth his flesshe too ouercome hym he entreth intoo a ful foule and a ful grevouse [f. 144] thraldom, the whiche was signified be Sampson the fort as that because he lete a woman ouercomen hym, he loste the here of his heede where his grete strengthe was and the yen of his forhede and [the] strengthe of his bodye and felle intoo the handes of his enemyes, the whiche made hym dye a shameful deethe. Al this doothe the feende goostly to hym that suffreth his flesshe ouercome hym. Whoosoo ouercometh this bataile, Godde promisseth hym the white gowne of chastite and of innocencie, as the Pocalipse seithe.

The IIII Bataile, CLXVIII

After this bataile commeth the worlde and Dame Fortune with alle hirre wheele, the whiche assaileth man on the right side and on the lefte, the whiche be ii ful stronge batailles and where myche pepill be ouercomen. And ʒit ther be moo ouercomen on the right side than on the lefte, as the Sauter seithe. For the bataile is myche strenger that commeth of worshipes and of richesses and of delites that the feende offreth and putteth forthe than that is that commeth of aduersite, as of pouerte or of sekenesse that Godde sendeth. And he that ouercommeth the firste bataile fleith and dispiseth with his herte worldly prosperitees. Godde promysseth hym worshipp and hyenesse in hevyn. For he shalle make hym sitte with hym in his trone, as the Pocalipse seithe.

The V Bataile, CLXIX

Too hym that shalle ouercome the toother bataille the whiche is on þe lefte side in the aduersitees of this worlde Godde promisseth too hym hidde manna, that is too seye, the grete swetnesse and the grete delite of paradis that noon maye take fro hym. For be manna the whiche was soo swete that euery sauour was founde therein siche as theye wolde is vnderstanden the grete swetnesse and the grete delite [f. 144v] that Godde promisseth to his frendes and hideth and kepeth to thoo that ouercometh the aduersitees of this worlde.

The VI Bataille, CLXX

The vi bataille is ful stronge, that is to seye, aȝeyns the shrewys that be in this worlde the whiche be membris of Antecriste, that be theyre strengthe werreyeth goode men as tirauntis didde in olde tyme and heretikes in olde tyme goode Cristen men and as in the ende of the worlde the membris of Antecriste shalle werre goode Cristen pepill that vnethe any shalle derre clayme hym cristined for the myght of Antecriste and of his membris. This is the beste that Seint Iohn sawe werrey saintes, of the whiche wee haue spokyn longe agoon. The membris of this beste sheweth theym euer in evill princes and in eville prelattis, the whiche be theire covetise revith, fleeth, and eteth theyre soiettis and doothe theyme diseasses and grete myschevis inowe. And he that shall ouercomme this bataille Godde promisseth hym that he shalle haue power ouer his enemys, as Seint Iohn seithe in the Pocalipse.

The VII Bataille, CLXXI

After al these batailles cometh the laste, the whiche is the strengest. For the feende whan he seeth that a man is mounted vppon the hylle of perfeccion and that he hatthe ouercomen al the forseide batailles than he assayleth hym be veinglorie and be presumpcion. For hym semeth that he is a ful goode man and wel with Godde because that he hatthe don and suffred soo myche for hym. Be the whiche some-tyme he falleth froo as hye to as lowe as Lucifer didde. And therfore it is grete neede for a man to be wel-avised too de-fende hym froo veinglorie the whiche maketh the rerewarde, for the venym lyeth in the tayle, and nere the havyn [f. 145] often the shippe perissheth the whiche goothe surely on þe hye see. Wherefore it behovith hym too dresse his saille, that is to seye, his entent to the havyn of savacion, the whiche is to Criste Iesus, be the wynde of fervent louff and of grete desire. This is the ende of iustice of the whiche wee haue spokyn afore the whiche commeth of the ȝifte of strengthe and of the vertu of worthinesse, as a goode and a worthy knyght that hatthe a goode herte and an hardye and that hatthe ben in myche worshippe and hatthe grete liste and desire too shewe his strengthe in tornementis and batailles to gete hym a name. And forsoothe whoosoo hatthe grete louffe too Godde and grete liste and desire of his owne savacion, he ouercommeth lightly this laste bataille. He neyther willneth ne desyreth in this liffe but that the whiche is to the worshipp and to the glorie of Godde and to savacion of his soule. Whoosoo wynneth this bataille hee hatthe getyn the goode wagis of the whiche Seint Iohn spekith where oure loorde seith in the Pocalipse: To hym that shalle overcome this, I shal ȝiff hym mete of the tree of liff the whiche is in the middes of paradis. That is Criste Iesus the whiche ȝiffeth everlastyng liff by the whiche alle seintis liffeth in euerlastyng ioye. And there theye be fulfilled and fedde. And this is the blessyng that oure goode maister Criste Iesus promisseth to his knyghtis whan he seithe: Blessed be thoo that hatthe hunger and thriste of iustice, that is too seye, too louff and too serve Godde, for theye shalle be fedde with the fruite of the tree of liff. This is the ende and perfeccion of þis vertu to the whiche the ȝifte of strengthe ledeth a man.

Off the Ȝifte of Counselle

As the Hooly Gooste ȝiffeth strengthe and vigour to take on hande grete thyngys, on the same wise he ȝiffeth counsell be the whiche man cometh to goode conclusion of that the whiche he hatthe take on hande. This the whiche is called the ȝifte of counsell is a grete grace that the Hooly Gooste ȝiffeth be the whiche a man hatthe grete avisement and grete deliberacion [f. 145v] in that the whiche he vndertaketh and that hee be not to hasty in his emprises. For as the philosophre seithe: Grete thyngys be not doon be bodily strengthe ne be armes but be goode counsell. For of an evil counselle a man repenteth hym after. And therfore Salamon seithe: Doo noothynge withoute goode counsell, and after that dede thowe shalt not repente the. This grace is shewed in man in iii maneres, firste in sekyng good counsell. Thobie counselled soo his sonne: Feire sone, seide hee, aske euer counselle of wise men. And Salamon seithe: Where ther is noo goode goouernance, the pepill perissheth and is discoun[f]it and mate. But he is save that hatthe goode gouernaunce and goode counsell. Wyse Thulles seithe that litel vaileth armes owtewarde if ther be no goode counsell inwarde. But kepe the, seiþe the scripture, from evil counselloures. And counsell not with fooles, for theye louff not but that the whiche plesith theyme and not that the whiche plesith Godde. Alsoo the scripture techeth that a man sholde beleve goode counselle of auncient pepill and not in ȝouthe, the whiche is not provid in besinesses necessarie. For in auncient pepill that hatthe seen and proved necessarie thyngys is the witte and also the counsell. Wherfore because that Roboam, Salamon is sone, lefte the counsell of auncient pepill for the counsell of ȝouthe he loste the grettest partie of his reaume.

To Examine His Counselle

Alsoo whoosoo hatthe this ȝifte hee examineth the counsell that men ȝiffeth hym and thynketh with grete deliberacion, that is too seye, with grete avisement wheder a man counsell hym well and truly or noon. For he sholde not beleve the counsell of oo man ne of ii though theye be homly with hym and his frendes. Wherefore Seneque seithe that a wise man examineth his counsellis and belevith theyme not lightly. For he that beleveth lightly fyndeth often siche as decevith hym.

[f. 146] To Beleve His Counsell

Alsoo whoosoo hatthe this ȝifte hee obeieth too goode counsell whan he fyndeth it. For hee seketh counsell for noght that hatthe noo liste too doo therafter. Therfore Salamon seithe that a foole thynketh that hee is in the right weye, but a wise man hireth goode counsell the whiche fooles dispiseth. The mooste profitable counsell that he maye haue is the counselle that oure goode maister Criste Iesus, the whiche is the wisdom of Godde the fader of whom cometh alle goode counsellez, brought vs from hevyn, hee that is tonge of the counsell þat hee ȝiffeth vs in the gospell whan hee seyeth too vs: If thowe wilte be parfit, goo and selle al that thowe haste and ȝiff too the poore and come after me, and thowe shalte haue grete tresor in hevyn. Take heede and thynke whoo ȝiffeth this counsell. For it is, as I haue seide, the wisdome of Godde the fader, the tonge of counselle, the whiche is verraye Godde and verraye man that come into erthe for to counsell the and for too teche the the weye and the right patthe too goo intoo paradis. And that is the patthe of pouertee whider that the Holi Goost leedith tho that he inlumineth be the ȝifte of counsell. Forsoothe oother menys ther be be the whiche men maye welle be saued and be an noother weye as be the weye of the commandementis of oure lorde. Or a man maye saue hym be mariage or be widowhoode or with richesses of this worlde whan a man vseth theyme rightfully. But the Holy Gooste be the ȝifte of counselle ledeth and conditeth moore rightly and moore surely be the paththe of veraye pouertee be the whiche a man dispiceth and putteth vnder foote the woorlde and al covetise for the louff of Godde. This ȝifte raceth oute of the herte the synne of covetise and planteth ther aȝeynwarde a fulle feire tree the whiche is þe vertu of mercy, that is to seye, too haue woo and compassion of ootheres evill.

Off Mercy

[f. 146v] This tree hatthe [v]ii degrees as oother hatthe whereby it groweth and profiteth. Thees be vii thynges the whiche mevith a man gretly too mercy and too haue compassion of ootheris evill. The firste thynge that draweth a man to mercy is nature. For as the Booke that Speketh of Nature of Bestes seyth: No birde eteth anoother birde that is of his nature. Alsoo the same booke seith that oo mere norissheth the foole of anoother whan shee is dede. Alsoo men hatthe provid often that wolves norissheth ientilly theire childer and defendeth theyme from oother bestes. Man than oughte wel to haue pite and compassion of otheres evil likly to hym in nature. For wee be alle of oo nature and al made too oo forme and too oon example, as wee haue seide longe afore.

The ii^{e} thynge that sholde drawe man to mercy and too compassion of ootheres evill is grace, because wee be al membres of oo bodye, that is to seye, of hooly chirche. And bee that grace oo membre naturelly hatthe compassion of an nother. Alsoo wee bee al bought with oo prese, that is to seye, with the precious bloode that Criste Iesus shedde opon the crosse for to bye vs aȝeyn from euerlastyng deethe. Than whan the sone of Godde was soo mercyfull and soo pitous to vs wee oughte wel too haue pite on of an nother and euery of vs too socoure and too helpe oother. Alsoo wee bee breether of oo fader and of oo mooder be feithe and be grace, for wee be the childer of Godde and of holly chirche. And oo broother oughte to helpe an noother. For atte neede men seeth what a frende is. The iii thynge that sholde meve a man to mercy is the commaundement of hooly scripture the whiche commaundeth and techith the dedis of mercy above alle oother dedis. Wherfore wise Salamon seithe: Looke, seithe hee, that thyne heede be not withoute oyle. Be the oyle that norissheth fire in the lampe is vnderstanden mercy, the whiche sholde ever be in thyn heede. And liche as oyle in the lampe surmounteth al oother licoures, evyn soo mercy sourmounteth oother vertues. And liche as oyle kepeth fire in the lampe and whan the oyle failleth the fire gothe oute, evyn soo mercy kepeth in the herte the louff of Godde. And whan mercy faileth, the louff of Godde faileth, as Seint Iohn seithe. Whoo shalle, seithe hee, see the nedy haue nede [f. 147] and defaute, necessite and disesse, and shette froo hym the doore of his herte, that is to seye, whoosoo hatthe not pite and wil not helpe hym if he maye, howe, seithe he, is the louff of Godde in hym? As whoo seye, it maye not be, for in his herte the oyle of mercy is failled. Alsoo goode Thobie taught his sone and seide thus: Feire sone, be merciful as longe as thowe maiste. If thowe haue goodes inoughe, ȝif largely. If thowe haue litil, of that litil ȝif gladly. And oure lorde seithe in the gospell: Goo and selle al that thowe haste and ȝif to the poore. This is the vertu that hooly scripture prayseth mooste generally. For it is the vertu that plesith Godde, as the scripture seithe. Wherfore Godde seith be þe prophete: I wil, seith he, mercy and not sacrifice. And Seint Austin seithe: Ther is noothynge that maketh man soo amiable to

Godde as pite. Miche pepill doothe sacrifice in fastyng, in pilgrimage, and in sharpenesse of bodye, but to doo almesse theye be dulle, scarse, and streite. Alsoo myche pepill to whom Godde hatthe ʒovyn largely of temporell goodes doo sacrifice not only to God but to the worlde, in as myche as theye dispende folily theire goodes in vanitees [and] in forfetis for [pride] of the worlde, but to ʒif for God theye be harde as an a[d]amant stone. Alsoo liche as mercy pleisith God soo it displesith the feende, for it is the armure be the whiche it is sonneste ouercomyn, as a glose opon the Sauter seithe. For it maye not suffre the odure of that oynement noo moore than þe botirflie maye doo the smelle of the vine that florisshet. Iudas might not suffre this smelle whan Marie Magdaleyne anoynted the heede of Criste Iesus with the preciouse oynement, for hym thought it was thynge loste. Hee hadde lever hadde the moneye in his purse for covetice. Of siche pepill a feende is loorde and maister that is called cloosepurse, the whiche an hermite sawe that he hadde the office too close purses of oother because theye sholde not be opyned for too ʒiff almesse. The iiii thynge that sholde meve man to doo mercy is the largesse of Criste Iesus, the whiche ʒiffeth largely to al pepil after that theye be, as Seint Iame seithe, and maketh his sonne shyne bothe vppon goode and opon evil, as he seithe in [f. 147v] the gospell. Than sithyn that he is soo large to vs that he ʒifeth vs al that euer wee haue of goodenes, euery of vs sholde be large and curteis to oother and iche helpe oother. For he commaundeth it in the gospell whan he seithe: Be ʒe mercifull liche as ʒoure fader of hevyn is mercyfull. The sone sholde resemble his fader, and ellis he sholde goo oute of the ligne. And therfore the wise man seithe in the scripture: Be ʒee petiful and mercyfull too faderlesse childer, as thoughe ye were fader to theyme. The v thynge that sholde meve man to mercy is the worshipp of Godde. For as Salamon seithe: He worshipeth Godde that doothe wel to the poore. For what that a man doothe too the poore he doothe it too Godde, as that hymselfe witnesseth in his gospelle: That, seithe he, the whiche ʒe haue doon to one of the leste ʒe haue doon it to me. Pore pepil be oure lordes meny. Whoosoo worshipeth theyme with the dedis of mercy, he worshipeth

God. For whooso worshipeth the seruauntes, he worshipeth the loorde; and whoosoo doothe shame to the seruauntes, he doothe shame to the lorde. Hereof haue wee a feire example of that goode loorde Seint Martin, to whom Godde aperid the nyght after that he hadde ȝovyn his mantell to a poore man. And hee was lapped in the mantell and seide to his angell: Martin hatthe clothid me with this mantell. The vi thynge that sholde meve man to mercy is fere of iugement. For as Seint Iame seithe: Iugement withoute mercy shalle be doon too thoo that doothe not mercy. And he seithe in the gospelle that whan the daye of doome shalle comme the sentence shalle be ȝovyn aȝens thoo that hatthe not doon the dedes of mercy. And God shalle make a deffe ere to strette pepill, as it shewith in the gospell in an example that he setteth of a riche man that voided a laȝar that was atte his ȝeate. Because that hee denyed hym his almes, Godde denyed hym a drope of water whan hee was in the fyre of helle. Evyn soo shalle hee doo atte the daye of doome to strette an covetouse pepill that hatthe not þe condit of mercy, [f. 148] the whiche counditeth soules to paradis and maketh theym a weye too come before God, as the scripture seithe, liche as a man maketh a weye to hym that bringeth a feire present whan that he opyneth hym the gate. Truly he shalle be verily acursed to whome pite turneth the backe that daye whan Godde shall ȝif fereful sentence. And alsoo it shalle be ferme and stabill and confermed be righ[t]vissnesse, for it shalle never after be called aȝein. And he shalle doo this iustice as a kynge and than caste his grete cours as a grete bisshopp and a souerayne pope. For he is bothe kynge and bisshoppe, as the scripture seithe, for hee toke humaine nature of the lynage of kynges [and of bisshoppes]. This course shalle be caste as of a bisshopp for thoo that shalle be on the lefte side. Noon shalle be outetaken ther. These shalle be the shrewes the whiche he shalle curse for theire vntrowthe. And he shalle seye vnto theyme thus: Go, ȝe cursed, intoo the grete stynkynge fire of euerlastyng helle in derke shadowes, the whiche is ordeyned for false orible feendes and for thoo that hatthe doon outragis. Alas this sentence, thoughe it be shorte, it shalle be fulle noyouse and grevouse whan he shalle caste theyme oute of his feleshipp. Soo harde a departyng ought gretely to be douted. The vii thynge that sholde gretely meve a man too mercy is the fruit that groweth of that tree the whiche sheweth in many maneres. First because that mercy geeteth forȝifnesse of synnes, for the whiche mercy hatthe letteres of pardon and of indulgence. For Godde seithe in the gospelle: Blessed be the mercyfull, for theye shalle haue mercy. Alsoo the same lettere seithe that ȝif on of vs forȝiff anoother God shalle forȝiff vs and elles not. Mercy is a goode marchant that wynneth oueral and lesith noo tyme. For as Seint Poule seithe: Mercy is goode to al thynge. Mercy it is that wynneth temporelle goodes and goostely goodes and euerlastynge goodes. Of temporell goodes, seithe Salamon: Worshipp Godde with thy substaunce. ȝiff to the poore of thi goodes, and Godde shalle fille aȝeyn thy gernerys and thy celleris with wyne. But vnderstande welle þis woorde that he seithe of thy goodes and of noon others, as thoo doo that wil doo almesse of that the whiche [f. 148^{v}] theye haue be raveyne or be vsure or be an eville cause and maketh often large thonges of oother mennes ledder. But ȝif of thyn owne that thowe haste truly, for thowe art bounde to ȝiff ageyne the toother. And ȝit he seith that thowe shalt ȝiff to the poore and the nedy and not too the riche. And Godde shalle ȝelde it too thee aȝeyn, as he seithe in the gospelle. Mercy is a seede that fructifieth better in lene erthe than in fatte. Wee haue in scripture many feire ensamples howe that mercy multiplyeth temporell goodes, of the whiche here nowe I wille shewe some. Men seye of Seint Germain d'Auxerre that whan he come froo Roome atte þe comynge oute [of] Mylan in Lombardie he asked his dekyn if he hadde any silfer. And he answerd and seide that he hadde but iii *d* for Germane had ȝovyn it al to pore pepill. ȝit he seide God had ynoughe too feede theyme with that daye. The dekyn with grete woo and grete grucchynge ȝaf ii^{e} and kepte the thirde. Whan theye wente on þeire weye, a seruaunt of a riche knyght brought theym from his loorde [c]c *li*. Than he called his deken and seide to hym that he hadde taken a peny aweye froo the poore pepill, for ȝif he hadde ȝovyn thee iii pens þis goode loorde had sent vs [cc]c *li*. Also Seint Gregore telleth that Boniface whan he was a childe was soo pitouce that oftentymes he ȝaf his cote too poore pepill notwithstandynge that his moder bette hym often therfore. It felle on a daye ȝit that the childe sawe myche poore pepille that hadde disease. Hee aspied whan his moder was not nere, he ranne too the gerneres, and that the whiche his mooder hadde geder togeder the ȝere afoore hee ȝaf it to the poore pepille. And whan his mooder come and knewe the dede, shee was al oute of hirre mynde. The childe prayed too oure loorde for helpe, and anoon the gerneres were pleyne fulle. Alsoo, as men seye, ther was a poore man that herde his preeste seye in a sermon that Godde seide in the gospelle howe Godde sholde ȝelde an hunderethfoolde for that the whiche a man ȝiffeth [f. 149] for hym. The poore man hadde a cowe. And be his wyfes counsell he ȝaf it to his curat, weenyng to have c therfore. Whan he hadde a grete whyle abiden and that the promisse taried, he wende that his curat had disceyvid hym. Wherfore he thought to slee hym. He roose in a mornynge for too slee his preste. And whan he was in the wey thederwarde, he founde a grete quantite of goolde. And that tyme he thought that Godde hadde sente hym that and kepte hym his promise, soo he torned aȝeyn in pees. Also men telleth of an nother. Because that hee hadde herde the woorde of the gospelle that Godde ȝaf c folde for on, he ȝaf his cowe to a riche preeste. The preste toke it gladly and sent it to the pasture with oother that hee hadde. Whan evyn come, the poore mannes cowe come to his olde house and broughte with hirre al the prestes kyen to the nombre of an c. And whan the goode man sawe that, he thought that it was the promise of the gospelle that Godde hadde ȝovyn theym to hym. And afore the bisshopp theye were iuged to hym aȝens the preste. These examples sheweth wel that mercy is a goode marchande whan it multiplieth temporell goodes. [...] and euerlastyng goodes. Wherfore Seint Poule seithe that it is goode to al thynge, for it ȝiffeth liff of grace [in] present and at the laste euerlastynge ioye. And therfore Dauid seithe in the Saulter that God louffeth mercy and trouthe. For it shalle ȝif grace in this worlde and ioye in the toother. Alsoo for to conclude al it kepeth a man from alle evilles and from alle perilles and from goostely dethe, that is to seye, from syn and from bodyly deethe. For myche pepille hatthe ben reysed aȝeyn for the dedis of mercy that theye haue doon, of the whiche ther be many examples in seintis liffes. And alsoo it delyuereth the froo the deethe of helle. For almesse delyuereth the and kepeth the from al synne and from deethe and defendeth the soule that it goo not intoo the derkenesse of helle. Thow haste nowe herde the degrees of the tree of mercye wherby it groweth and profiteth. Nowe behouyth to see of the braunches of this tree wherebye it shewith hym and spredith hym.

[f. 149v] Off VII Braunches of the Gostely Dedys of Mercy, CLXXII

This tree hatthe moo braunches than þe toother aforeseide. For it spredith ferther than the toother doothe. Therfore it hatthe branches on the right side and on the lefte. On the right side be goostely dedys; on the lefte be bodily dedis the whiche longeth too the bodye. The firste of the vii braunches of the right syde of this tree is too ȝiff goode counsell for the louff of Godde purely too thoo that hatthe nede and not for covetice to wynne temporelle goodes, as evill men of lawe doo, the whiche taketh with bothe the handes and for siluer ȝiffeth often ful evill counsell or for ȝiftes or for fere or for fauoure of [riche] men. But thoo that hatthe Godde afore theire yen the whiche counsellith synneres to comme oute of synne and thoo þat bee oute of synne to kepe theyme therfroo, theye doo the firste dede of mercy of the right syde. The iie braunche is too teche wel thoo that a man hath too teche, as prelates theire sogettis the whiche theye sholde fede with goode techyng and with goode examples, alsoo masteres theire disciples in konnyng and in goode condiciones, alsoo as faderes and moderes theire childer too that entent that theye maye kepe theyme froo syn and that theye maye vse theyme to doo weele and to kepe theym froo lyyng and sweryng, from evil games, and from evil feleshipp. Anamly the childer of riche men sholde be beste taught in goode dedis. For a childe wil euer holde his firste forme as a shoo doothe. And therfore men sholde enforme theyme too doo welle. For as the prouerbe seithe: He that lerneth a koltte for too endente aye whilest he dureth he wille to it tente. The iii braunche is to correcte and too repreve fooles and shrewes of theire folyes. And that longeth specially too prelattis and to princes, the whiche sholde chastie theire soiettys whan þeye knowe that theye be evill. For whan theye suffre synnes there where theye maye amende it, theye [f. 150] be parteners thertoo. Neyther prelat ne no worthy man sholde suffre aboute hym noo shrewdenes too his knowynge. For ȝiff he haue evil meny aboute hym and hee knowe it or suppose it and hee sette not remedy therfore, it is a signe that hee is noo goode man. For men be wonte too seye: siche loorde, siche menye. And after the loorde, the meny disposeth theym. Ȝit it happeth often that the loorde is wrongely defamed thourgh his evil meny. And, therfore, louff ne fere ne familiarite of person sholde not lette a loorde for to putte aweye syn from aboute hym, for hee sholde dowte and louff moore Godde than man. Men sholde louff the persones and hate the synnes. And alsoo prelates and princes and oother loordes sholde knowe þat of this parte ignorance shalle not ascuse theyme, for theye be bounde to knowe howe theire pepill demenyth theyme in theire offices and in theire howses. And [theye] sholde serche it be goode trewe pepill the whiche dowteth and dredeth Godde. Wherfore theye shalle not be quytte atte the daye of doome for to seye: I knewe not therof. The iiii braunche is to comfort poore pepil and thoo that be in tribulacion or in aduersite with goode woordis that theye dispeyre not and that the herte faille theyme not. Seint Poule commandeth thus, the whiche seithe: Conforte thoo that be febill of herte. And Salamon seithe that he that is in disease of herte shalle reioysse hym with goode wordis. For as he seithe hymselfe: Liche as the herte deliteth hym in goode smelles, soo the soule feelith gret swetnesse in goode counsellis and in goode woordis of a veraye frende. And that is hee that louffeth in aduersite as hee doothe in prosperite. For atte nede a man seeth what a frende is. An thowe shalt wite that iiii thyngys ther be the whiche conforteth a man gretely that is in aduersitee. The firste thyng is to thynke on the peynes of helle, the whiche be soo sharpe that al that ever a man maye suffre in this worlde is but as a softe oygnement too regarde of that peyne. For the whiche Seint Austin seithe to oure lorde: Sire, here brule me and al tohewe me rather than ȝe sholde dampne me euerlastyngly. It is goode too suffre the ȝerde of [f. 150^{v}] chasticement for to escape withalle the spere that sleeth euerlastyngl[y], that is to seye, the deethe of helle the whiche maye not dye. God sheweth grete signe of louff too thoo the whiche hee sendeth temporelle aduersite. For oure loorde seithe in the scripture: I chastie thoo that I louff. An ox that men will slee is made fat, but hym that men wil kepe is put to gresse and too drawe in the plowghe. The kynge sheweth hym grete signe of louff too whom he drinketh and sendeth his cuppe. The cuppe of oure lorde to whom he drinketh is the tribulaciones of this worlde. This is the firste sause with the whiche theye sholde ete this mete that thynketh of the peynes of helle. This is vinegre sause the whiche taketh aweye the sauour of goode wyne. The ii^{e} cause that conforteth in tribulacion is to thynke of the ioye of hevyn. For Seint Gregore seithe: Whan a man hoopeth too haue a goode hire, it alleggeth myche his trauaylle. The iii thynge is to thynke of the passion of Criste Iesus, the whiche he suffred for vs. Ther is noothynge that easeth soo myche temporelle peynes and tribulaciones as that doothe. And that is wel figured to vs in scripture there were the childer of Israel come to a water, þe whiche was soo bitter that theye myght not drinke therof. Godde shewed Moyses a stycke and bade hym put it in the water. And whan he hadde put it therin, it was alle swete. The bitter wateres be the tribulacions of the worlde. The sticke that made it swete is the cros wherevppon the son of God hange for vs. For whoosoo thynketh welle on that sorwe that he suffred on the cros ther is neyþer peyne, ire, ne tribulacion ne temporell aduersite but þat it is softe and easy too suffre. The iiii thyng is to thynke what good tribulacions and aduersitees doothe to vs if wee suffre theyme paciently, for tribulacion provith Goddes knyght. A knyght knoweth not his strengthe vnto þat he hatthe ben empressed. Therfore Seint Poule seithe that pacience provith a man. And the angel seide [f. 151] to Thobie: Because that thowe sholdest be pleysyng to Godde, it behovith þat temptacion sholde prove the. Alsoo temptaciones porgeth a soule. Seint Gregore seithe that tribulaciones be as medicines the whiche helith sekenesses of synne. As the scripture seithe: A grevous sekenes maketh a man often soobre, where synne maketh a man ofte dronken. Wherfore Seint Gregore seithe: Lete not that be an harde thynge too the, the whiche thowe suffrest in thy body owteward whan thowe art heled inward of the sekenes of synne. Also be tribulacion man wynneth a coroune of blisse. These iiii thoughtis aforeseide conforteth gretely thoo that be in aduersitee. The v branche of gostly mercy is too forȝif his evil wille. As Seint Gregore seithe: Whoosoo ȝifeth his pens or his almes too poore pepil and forȝiffeth not his evil wille, his almes is not worthe, for Godde accepteth not the ȝifte of the hande as longe as fellenes is in the herte. Wherefore Godde weyeth the ȝifte after þe wille. And therfor oure lorde seithe in the gospell: If on of yowe, [s]e[i]the he, forȝif not anoother, Godde ȝoure fader shalle not forȝiff yowe. For the which hee that wille not forȝiff seithe aȝeins hymself euery tyme that he seithe his pater noster. For he prayeth that oure lorde shalle forȝiff hym liche as hee forȝiffeth his evil wille. The vi branche of mercy is too haue pite and compassion of synneres and of thoo that be in tribulacion or in pouerte or in aduersite. For o membre sholde sustene the sekenes of another. Wherfore Seint Poul seide: Whoo is seke and that I am not seke with hym? And Seint Gregore seithe: The parfiter that a man is, the more he felith in hymselfe the diseses of oother. The vii branche is to praye for synneres, anamly for his enemyes. For oure loorde commaundeth soo in the gospelle: Prayeth, seithe hee, for thoo that doothe yowe harme, and soo shalle ȝee be the sonnes of youre fader that is in hevyn. As whoo seye: ȝe be not elles Goddes childer. And if ȝee be not Goddes childer, ȝe shalle no parte haue in his heritage. Thus it is grete almes and grete availe [f. 151v] to praye for synneres and for his enemyes. These be the vii braunches o the right side of this tree.

Off Branches of the Dedes of Mercy That Longeth to the Body, CLXXIII

As this tree hatthe vii branches on the right side soo it hatthe vii on the lefte. Thoo be vii dedis of mercy, the whiche kepeth the bodye liche as the toother kepeth the soule. The firste branche is to fede the poore and thoo that be diseassed. This commandeth vs hooly scripture in many placys. Firste where Thobie seide to his son: Ete thi brede with the nedye that dyeth for hunger. And Salamon seithe: If thy frende have hunger, ȝif hym mete; and ȝif he haue thirst, ȝif hym drynke. Alsoo oure lorde seithe in the gospelle: Whan thowe shalt make a grete dyner, calle thertoo the poore and the febil, the halte and the lame and the blynde, and thowe shalte be blessed. For theye maye not ȝelde it the, but Godde shalle ȝelde it the in the resurreccion. That is gretely ageyns riche men that doo grete outrages in goode metes for pompe of the worlde and haue no pite of the poore. But theye ought to haue grete fere that it happe not of theyme as it didde of the riche gloton of whom Godde speketh of in the gospelle, the whiche ete dayly deliciously and plenteuously and lete the poore lazar die for hunger at his gate. But at the deethe of the ton and of the toother ther was a grete chaunge. For the lazar was borne to hevyn with angellis and the gredy gloton with his beree was not put in Cristen beriell for he was cursed be the auctorite of Godde. But he was in stynkyng helle when he hadde nede of o drope of water too kele with his tonge. A goode Godde, though alle the water of the see [r]an opon his tonge, it sholde not ȝit be keelid in this euerlastyng fire the whiche maye not be qwenched. What sholde than a drope of water doo thertoo? Therfoore it is goode to feede the poore, wherethorugh man escha[f. 152]peth the peynes of helle and wynneth the blisse of hevyn, as oure lorde seithe. For the whiche oure lorde shalle seye atte the daye of doome: Come ȝe blessed of my fader intoo the kyngdom of hevyn. For whan I hadde hunger, ȝe ȝafe me mete; and whan I hadde thirste, ȝe ȝaf me drynke; for that the whiche ȝe didde too the poore, ȝe didde it to me. The ii^{e} branche is to clothe aȝen the poore that is naked. That is to seye that man sholde ȝif theyme al maner of cloothyng. Thobie taught his son soo: Feire sone, covere the naked with thy gowne. And Ysaie the prophete seithe: Whan thowe seest the poore naked, covere hym. The cloothyng that men ȝiffeth too the poore is a memorial too the poore, for hee prayeth for hym that doothe hym good. The iii braunche is to lene too poore pepil at theire nede and too forȝiff theyme theire dette whan theye maye not paye it. For it is not alonly almesse for to ȝiff, but it is grete almesse for to lene withoute vsure and withoute evil entente purely for the louff of Godde and also for to forȝiff his dette whan the poore man maye not paye it. This is that the whiche Godde commaundeth in the olde lawe ther where he seithe: If on of thy brether falle in pouertee, thyn herte shalle not be the harder to hym ne thowe shalt not withdrawe thyn hande froo hym, but thowe shalt opyn it too the poore and lene hym that the whiche he hatthe nede of. And oure loorde seithe in the gospelle: Lene, seithe hee, to hym that hatthe nede withouten hoope of temporell wynnyng, and Godde shalle ȝelde it to yowe. This is opynly aȝeins vsureris, the whiche wil euer haue moore than theye lene oother in pens or in seruice or in oother thyngys. But Godde commaundeth to lene too the poore purely for Godde, and Godde shalle ȝelde aȝein the vsure. Or if the poore to whom thou haste lente maye not paye the that he oweth the, thowe sholdest forȝif hym, for oure loorde seithe soo in the gospelle: If on of vs forȝif not anoother, Godde shalle not forȝif vs. The iiii branche is to visite the seke. That is a dede that plesith Godde gretely, more than fastyng or trauayle temporelle or bodily. Of the whiche men fynde in *Vitis Patr[u]m* that an hermite asked a fader wheder hadde more [f. 152v] mede he that fasted thrise in the woke and trauailled and labored with his handis or in oother wyse or he that visited or served seeke pepille. The goode man answerid that he that fasted and trauailed, though he hange hymselfe be the nesethrilles, hee myghte not compare to hym that seruyth seeke pepill. And therfore, seithe Iob, visite thy likenes, that is to seye, the seke the whiche is like to the in nature, for he is man as thou art. And soo thowe shall not syn, for God shalle kepe the fro syn for doyng of that dede. And Seint Iame seithe that it is a hooly religion and a clene afore Godde to visitee faderles childer and wydoues in tribulacion. Of the whiche men telleth of a grete synner that wente over the see and put hym in an hospitall too serve seeke pepill. Opon a tyme it fel that he hadde gret abhominacion of a seke persone whoos feete he waysshed anoon aȝeins his herte. Hee dranke fulle his throote of that water. And whan he hadde dronken it, he felt it right swete and right softe and right welle-smellyng aboue al the goode oignementis that ever he felt. And that was a signe that for that dede his synnes were forȝovyn hym. Alsoo for that dede a man geteth grete perfeccion of hooly liff. Wherefore the wise man seithe in the scripture: Noye the not too serve seeke pepill and poore, for therby shalt thowe be confermed in the louff of Godd. Alsoo a man geth wagis therbye, as the gospelle seithe, and seintes witnesseth it be scriptures. Oure lorde ȝiffeth vs ensample therof in the gospelle, the whiche touched meselles and heled theyme. The seruaunt ought not to haue disdeyne ne shame to visite seke pepill ne too serve theyme whan the loorde of hevyn and of erthe come into the worlde for to serve theyme. For the whiche he tooke forme of a seruaunt, as Seint Poule seithe, for to serve vs that were seke be synne. The v branche is to herbergh trauaylyng men be the contre and poore pepill that hatthe noon houses. This is oon of the dedes of mercy that plesith Godde moste, as it sheweth in examples of scriptures, first of Abraham that reseyvid angellis in likenes of pilgrimes. And theye promissed hym that his wiff Sarre the whiche was olde sholde conseyve a sone. Alsoo Loth [f. 153] because that he reseyvid poore pepille and kepte hospitalite reseyvid angellis, the whiche delyuered hym froo the perille of Sodome. And therfore seithe Seint Poule: Leve not hospitalite be the whiche myche goode pepil hatthe pleysid Godde soo that theye kepte angellis in stede of poore men. It is no merveyle though siche pepil reseyvid angellis, for theye reseyvid oure loorde, as he seithe in the gospelle: Whoosoo reseyvith ȝowe reseyvith me, seithe hee. For that a man doþe too the poore, he doothe too hym, as he seithe hymself. Of the whiche Seint Gregore seithe of a goode man, the whiche was fulle pitouse and fulle gladly reseyvid poore pepil as he was acostomed to doo, and whan he wende to a ȝovyn on water that was diseassed the whiche was with hym there as he tourned hym he that was there in liknes of a pore man vanysshed, of the whiche he merveyled gretly. And in the nyght oure loorde apperid to hym and seide to hym that oother dayes he hadde reseyvid his membris but that daye he hadde reseyvid hym in his owne persone. Alsoo hospitalite is myche better than abstinence or oother labour. Wherof men fynde in *Vitis Patrum* that in Egipte was an hooly fader the whiche reseyved al trauaillyng men that hadde nede and ʒaf theyme gladly of siche as he hadde. It befelle that a man of grete abstinence was herberghed in his house, the whiche wolde faste and wolde not ete atte the prayer of the goode man that hadde reseyvid hym. Than he seide to hym: Goo wee vnder ʒone tree withoute, and lete vs praye too oure loorde that the tree maye bowe to hym that plesith hym mooste. Whan theye hadde made theire prayeris, the tree bowed to hym that reseyvid the poore man and not to hym that didde the grete abstinence. Ther be many oother feyre examples of hospitalite, but it were to longe to telle theyme. The vi branche is to visite and to confort þoo that be in preson and to delyuere theyme if a man maye. Too this counsellith vs Seynt Poule the apostell, the whiche seithe: Vmbethynke ʒowe of thoo þat be in prison liche as that ʒe were bounde with theym ʒoureselfe. That is to seye, visite and conforte theyme [f. 153^{v}] liche as ʒe wolde men visited and conforted yowe if ʒe were bounden in preson. Thobie didde thus, the whiche wente too al thoo that were in preson and in bondes and visited and conforted theyme. And Salamon seithe in his Proverbis: Delyuere, seythe hee, thoo that men lede too the deethe. Wherfore Daniel the prophete deliuered Susanna froo deethe, and oure loorde delyvered the womman that was taken in avoutre, the whiche after the lawe sholde haue ben stoned. This is not only seide because that men sholde not doo iustice of evildooerris, but in this he maketh a tooken what iuges sholde be and howe theye sholde iuge the pepill. Therfore in this example he techeth iiii thyngys that euery iuge sholde haue and kepe in iugement. The firste thynge is grete deliberacion and grete advisement of grete counsell. Wherfore Iob seide: I shalle serche right diligently þe mater that I knowe not. And this is vnderstanden in that oure loorde whan the Iues hadde accused the womman hee wrote in the erthe with his blessed fyngger. Be the whiche we vnderstande discrecion and deliberacion. For hee ʒaf not anoon his sentence. The ii^{e} thynge is right entente that a man flit not for prayer ne for ʒifte. And that is vnderstanden in that whan he hadde writen hee stoode vpright. The iii thynge is goode liff and goode conscience. Elles theye sholde haue grete fere of this sentence of the gospelle the whiche seithe: Siche iugement as ʒe shal doo of oother, men shalle doo of ȝowe. And Seint Poule seithe too an evil iuge thus: In that, seithe hee, that thowe iugest oother, thowe dampnest thyselfe, for thowe dooeste the same for the whiche thowe condempnest and iugest theyme. Wherefore oure loorde seide whan hee stode vppe: Hee of ȝowe, seide hee, that is withoute synne caste too hirre the firste stone. And whan theye herde that sentence, theye wente alle aweye feire and softely, one after anoother, for theye were gretter synneres than shee that theye woolde a dampned. The iiii thynge is pytee and compassion þat the iuge sholde haue of hym that hee sholde deme. For he sholde meve hymselfe moore be mekenes and mercy than harde hymselfe be hardnes in iustice. For iustice withoute mercy is crueltee, and mercy [f. 154] withowte iustice is lachesse. And therfore the ton of these ii vertues is goode. But neverthelesse the scripture setthe that mercy surmounteth iustice. And Seint Iohn with the mouthe of golde seithe that at the daye of doome it shalle be better to ȝif cause too mercye than of to harde iustice. And Seint Iame seithe þat iugement withoute mercy shalle be doon to hym that doothe noo mercy. And therfore oure lorde whan hee stoode vppe bowed hym aȝein to the erthe and delyuered the woman. For that the iuge sholde be compassion meve hym toward hym that he sholde iuge. For if he iuge evil, he shalle be iuged at þe daye of doome. And therfore he sholde iuge with grete fere and as aȝeyns his wille. Nowe than it is grete almesse to visite presoneres and to by theyme aȝein and to delyuere theyme. And therfore oure lorde wolde discende into helle for to delyuere the soules of seintis that were there. The vii braunche is to bery dede pepil. Thobie is gretly praysed in scripture for that dede the whiche beried poore pepill and lefte his mete. Of the whiche men rede in the Booke of Kynde Bestes þat dolphines, whan theye see a dolfin dede, theye gader theyme togeder and berith hym too the boþom of the see and berieth hym there. If nature and pite meve Ives and Zarazins and myssebeleverris to doo this, gretly ought pite in forme of Cristen feithe meve to doo this the whiche knoweth that þeyre bodyes shalle be reysed and gerdouned with the soules. And therfore whoosoo louffeth the soule of his neȝghbourgh, he louffeth the bodye, and he oughte to bery al the mankynde that he myght. Thowe haste nowe herde the vii branches of the tree of mercy, the whiche be the vii dedis of bodily mercy.

Off Almes and Whereof a Man Sholde Doo It, CLXXIIII

Bvt because ther be miche pepil that lesith ther almes and mich oother goodnesses that theye doo [f. 154v] and for that theye doo not as theye sholde doo, therfore wil I shortly shewe howe men sholde doo almesse so that it maye be profitable and plesyng too Godde. Wherfore whoosoo wil doo almesse, he moste take hede of iii thingis. First whereof hee doothe almesse, for hee sholde doo it of his owne of þat he hatthe getyn wel and truly and not of anoother mannes good. For Godde setteth not be an evil ȝifte. Almesse that is doon of stollyn thynge or of briberie or of ravyne plesith not God. Wherfor the scripture seithe: Thowe shalt not doo to Godde sacrifice of an oxe ne of a shepe wher ther is in it any spotte, for Godde hatth grete abhominacion of siche sacrifice. And the wise man seithe in scripture: Whoosoo doothe sacrifice to Godde of a poore mannes catelle, hee doothe as hee that kylleth the son tofore the yen of his fader. And Seint Austyn seithe that siche be ȝiftes as that men taketh merily and oother þat be taken wepyngly be noone. And therfore euery man sholde take heede wherof hee doothe almesse.

Howe and to Wham a Man Sholde Doo It

Alsoo he sholde take heede to whom he doothe it. Wherfore the scripture seithe: Take heede to whom thowe shalt doo welle. Doo welle too a goode man. For thowe sholdest doo wel too goode men and ȝiff not too shrewes because of theire shrewdenes, as thoo doo that ȝiffeth to rebawdes and to ministrelles. For men sholde ȝiff theyme right nought for siche causes, for it is grete synne, as seintis seithe. But whoosoo ȝiffeth ought too theyme not only for cause of theire shrewdenesse but for pite and compassion of theire pouerte and of theire wiffes and theire childre if they haue any or for theire faderes and theire moderes or for any oother goode cause as for to drawe theyme froo synne, it is wel doon. Therfore almesse sholde be ȝovyn too the poore and moore too thoo that be veray pore in herte and wille the whiche hatthe lefte for God þat [f. 155] theye hadde or myght haue than to thoo that be not poore in wille but poore of necessite. Nevertheless, men sholde ȝiff theym gladly, anamly to the poore that is shamefaste and too faderlesse childer and too wydowes and too oother that be diseassed whan a man seeth that þeye haue nede and that a man maye doo it. Soo if men be bounde too strangeres above al oother than a man is bounde too fader and too moder whan a man seeth theire nede, for nature techeth it and God commaundeth it. Men redith of a cygoigne, *id est*, a gresse birde, that it norissheth his fader and his mooder whan theye bee olde and maye not purveye for theymselfe. Wherfore nature techith that a man sholde doo wel to fader and too moder. And whoosoo doothe not is vnnatural and aȝeyns nature and synneth aȝeins Godde that commaundeth to worshipp fader and moder. And therfore it is goode right that hee missehappe that missedoothe too fader or too moder, as it hatthe falle ofte.

The Maner of Doynge of Almesse

Alsoo men sholde take heede howe a man sholde doo almesse and the maner therof. The scripture seithe that iiii condiciones ther be in doynge of almesse. The firste is for to ȝiff it gladly and hertely. For Godde taketh more heede of þe herte than of the hande. Therfore Godde taketh noo heede in his sacrifice howe greete thyngis men ȝiffeth but with what herte, as it sheweth in the gospell of the poore woman that hadde but ii peitevines, thee whiche shee offred in the temple. For the whiche oure loorde seide that shee hadde leide moore than alle the toother that hadde leide grete thyngis. For sometyme an halfe peny that a poore man ȝiffeth for the louff of Godde plesith more Godde than though a riche man ȝaf an hundreth marke of moneye with chidynge or with hevinesse of herte and withowte deuocion. And therfore seithe the wise man in scripture: Make, [f. 155v] seithe he, feire chere and glad in al thy ȝiftes. And Seint Poule seithe that Godde louffeth the ȝiffer that ȝiffeth curteysly and gladly. Ther be some pepil soo vilens too poore men that anoon theye reprove theyme vilensly and calleth theym trowauntis and seithe to theyme soo many reproches and fellenesses or that theye wil ȝif theyme oughte that the moneye is dere bought. Siche almesse plesith not Godde. And therfore the wise man seithe in the scripture: Bowe, seythe hee, thyn ere too the poore man withowte hevinesse, and answere hym deboneirly. The ii^{e} thynge that behovith hym in almesse is too doo it soone and hastely. Wherfore Salamon seithe that thowe shalt not seie: Frende, goo and come aȝein tomorwe and I shall ȝif the. Whan thowe maist, ȝif it hym sonner. And in anoother place he seithe: Differre not thye ȝifte fro the nedy. That is to seye, make hym not abide whan thowe maiste ȝif it hym. This is aȝeins myche riche pepil that maketh poore men to crye soo moche that hatth to doo with theym and delayeth theym soo myche. And soo often theye moste praye and require or that theye wil ought doo that theye selle theyme to dere the bounte that theye doo to theyme. For Seneque seithe: Noothynge is derrer bought than that the whiche cometh be prayer. And this is the prouerbe þat men seithe: Too dere hee bieth that asketh. Alsoo euery man sholde hastely doo wel as longe as he liffeth and is hoole for his soule sake. Wherefore the wise man seithe in scripture: Feire soone, seithe hee, doo welle if thowe haue wherewith. Offre to God worthy offryngis as longe as thowe liffest, for deethe taryeth not. And in another place hee seithe: Feire sone, doo welle too thy frende afore the deethe, that is too seye, to thye sperit to whom thowe sholdest doo wel afore the deethe. Thye true frende is Criste Iesus too whom thowe sholdest doo welle afore thy deethe in doynge almesse for the louff of hym to his poore pepil. For that thowe doest too poore men thowe doest too God, as he seithe in the gospelle. Wherfore the almes that a man ȝiffeth in liff and in helthe is better than that the whiche is doon after the deethe, liche as a lanterne that is borne afoore a man conditeth hym [f. 156] better and moore surely than that the whiche a man berith behynde his backe. And therfore Seint Poule counsellith vs to doo welle as longe as wee haue the tyme that Godde hatthe lente vs. The iii^{e} condicion that sholde be in almesse is that a man sholde ȝif largely after þat he hatthe. Wherfore the wise man seithe: ȝiff too Godde after that he hatthe ȝovyn the. And Thobie seithe: Be pitous and mercyfull after thye power. If thowe have myche goode, ȝif largely. ȝif thowe haue litil, ȝif gladly, merily, and curteisly. Therfore euery man sholde ȝiff after his astate and after that Godde hatthe ȝovyn hym. Men fynde of a kynge of whom a poore man asked a peny, and he answerid hym that soo litil a ȝifte longeth not to a kynge. And also men rede of Alixandre that he ȝaf a cite too a seruaunt of his. And whan he wolde a refused it because hym semyd it was a grete thynge too take siche a ȝifte, Alixandre answerid hym: I take noo heede what ȝifte longeth to the too take but to me to ȝif. The iiii condicion is that the almes be doon mekely and in deuocion, soo that a man seke no veineglorie and that a man dispise not the poore man too [whom] he ȝiffeth it. Ne for noon almesse that a man doþe in dedly synne lete hym not presume to be savid. Ther be some pepil that ȝif theye doo almesse will þat euery man wite it. But the wise man seithe that a man sholde hide the almesse in the bosom of thee poore man. For as Seint Gregore seithe: It sufficeth too the goode man that hee see it, of whom he abideth his hyre. And therfore seithe oure lorde in the gospelle: Whan thowe shalt, seithe hee, doo almesse, lete not thi lefte hande knowe what thye right hande doothe, soo that thyn almesse be in secretenesse, and thy fader of hevyn that seeth it in secretnesse shalle ȝelde it the. That is to seye, whan thowe shalt doo almesse, take heede that veinglorie the whiche is vnderstanden be thy lefte hande be not medelid therwith, but doo it in right entent the whiche is vnderstanden be the right hande. I seye not that men sholde not doo almes and good dedes sumtyme afore the pepil for too ȝiff goode example wherethorugh Godde sholde be praysed. For oure loorde seithe thus in th[e] gospell that wee shall doo oure goode dedis tofoore theyme because that Godde maye be praysed and glorified and not for þe [f. 156v] prayse of the pepill. A goode seruaunt oughte haue noo shame to serue his lorde afore the pepill for to worshipp hym. Wherefore oure loorde seithe in the gospelle: Whoosoo shalle haue shame of me afore men, I shalle haue shame of hym afore angellis. This is evyn for thoo that levith to doo wel opynly because that theye sholde not be holden ypocrites. And therfore seithe Seint Gregore that men sholde doo soo his werkys opynly that inwarde the entent maye be right. Alsoo whoosoo wille doo almes hee sholde doo it soo that hym oughte not to dispise the pore man too whom he ȝiffeth it. Therfore the prophete seithe: Dispise not thy flesshe, that is to seye, the poore man the whiche is like too thee and of siche nature of flesshe and of bloode and of myre as thow art. Ther be somme that dispiseth poore men and liste not to speke to theyme, and if theye doo theye speke bostosly and proudely too theyme. Iob didde not soo the whiche seide that hee dispised never begger that wente by the countre though hee were naked but rather ȝaf hym clothis and mete. An hooly man thoughe he were a kynge and a grete loorde ȝit sholde he haue no shame of pore men, as some grete lordes doo in this worlde the whiche welle doo almesse too pore pepill and neverthelesse theye haue theyme in dispite. And if theye were verily meke theye had lever haue the feleshipp of goode men that be pore for Godde, the whiche might wel edifie theyme be examples and be wordis, than many riche men that theye haue abowte theyme where ther is but flaterie and covetise and vanite and doothe theyme myche harme and letteth theyme too doo myche goode. Alsoo ther is miche pepil that doothe almesse, but ȝit theye leve not theire synnes. Siche almesse shalle not save theyme. And if theye died in siche plite, theyre almesse sholde not kepe theyme froo dampnacion. Therfore siche pepill fare as thoo that bieldeth theire house on the too side and breketh it on the tother side. And therfore the scripture seithe: If thowe wilt plese Godde, haue firste pite and mercy of thy soule. For whoo[f. 157]so is evil and vntrue to hymselfe, to whom sholde he be goode and true? seithe the scripture. As whoo seye: He maye not be goode and true to an nother that is evil and vntrue to hymselfe. I haue nowe shewed the inoughe of the degrees of the tree of mercy and of the braunches and of the fruit that cometh therof in þis worlde and in the toother. Dauid in the Sauter speketh right wel to vs of the fruit of this tree where he seithe: Hee is blessed that tenteth too the poore and too þe nedy, that is too seye, that abideth not too the poore man aske hym but rather ȝiffeth it hym withoute askynge. Hee doothe wel that ȝiffeth a poore man that asketh, but hee doothe better that ȝiffeth withoute askynge. And of hym seithe the Sauter: Hee is blessed that tenteth to poore men. And whi he is blessed, he seithe after in the same verse: For Godde shalle delyuere hym on the evil daye from his enemyes. That shalle be atte the daye of doome, the whiche shalle be harde and evill too shrewes that shalle be dampned for the dedis of mercy that theye haue not donne. Wherfore the iuge shall seye that daye: Goo, ȝe shrewis, intoo euerlastynge fire with the feendes. For I hadde hunger and thriste, and ȝee ȝaf me neyther mete ne drinke. I was seeke: ȝe visited me not. And thus he reproved them in the dedis of mercy, the whiche theye haue not doon. And therfore þey shalle be delyuered too theire enemyes, the whiche be the fendes of helle, froo whom thoo that be pitouse and tenteth too poore pepill shalle be delyuered that daye and they shalle be putte in possession of the kyngdom of hevyn, as oure lorde seithe in the gospelle. For he shalle seye too thoo that hatthe doon the dedis of mercy: Come, ȝe blessed childer of my fadir, reseyve ȝe the kyngdom that I haue arayed for ȝowe froo the begynny[n]g of the worlde. For that the whiche ȝe haue doon too pore pepille, ȝe haue doon it too me. Godde shal doo theyme grete worshipp the whiche shalle thonke theym for the dedis of mercy and shalle ȝiff theym euerlastyng liff. And therfore seithe he in the gospelle: Blessed be the mercyfull, for theye shalle haue mercy. Because they haue lengthed the liffes of poore pepille be theire almesse, it is good right and reson that Godde ȝiff theyme longe liff, that is too seye, everlastyng liff the whiche is withoute ende. Because theye hadde pitee of the membris of Criste Iesus in [f. 157v] erthe and visited, conforted, and susteyned theyme in theyre aduersitees, it is goode reeson that at the laste ende hee doo theyme mercy. And soo shalle hee doo whan he shall ȝiff theyme euerlastynge blisse [where] mercy shalle condit theyme and herberghe theyme.

Off the Ȝifte of Vnderstandyng and of the Vertu of Chastite, CLXXVI

Holy scripture techith vs ii maner of liffes be the whiche men cometh too euerlastynge ioye. The firste is called actiue because it haboundeth in goode werkys and maketh a man tente too the profyt of hym and of his neghborughe. The seconde is called contemplatiue because that it is in reste of goode werkys outewarde and tenteth but to louff and to knowe Godde. For the whiche it is idil outeward and tenteth but too Godde liche as in a sleepe, but it is waked inward to thynke on Godde and to louff hym and too desire but to see hym and forȝeteth al oother thyngys for hym, soo that he is al ravisshed and set in Godde and desireth too be departed fro the deedly body for too be holly with Criste Iesus, as Seint Poule seithe. The firste bataile is in the felde of dedes, where the knyghtis of Godde provith theym and maketh theyme [lowed]. The seconde resteth hym with Godde in the chambre of clene conscience. The firste tenteth too feede Godde with goode dedes. The seconde tenteth too be fedde and saouled with Godde be veraye goostly confort. Wherfore the firste is signified be Martha, the whiche was besy too feede oure lorde, as he seithe in the gospell. The seconde is signified be Mari, the whiche sat atte feete of Crist Iesus and herkenyd his wordis. The firste is [weye] and entre to the seconde. For none maye come to contemplatiue liff but if hee be firste wel proved in actiue liff, as Seint Gregore seithe. The ȝiftes and the vertues that wee haue spokyn of longeth too the firste liff that is called actiue. The ii^{e} laste liff, of the whiche wee shalle speke with the helpe of Godde and of the Hooly Gooste, longeth [f. 158] to the contemplatiue live the whiche is the secounde liff, that is too seye, the ȝifte of vnderstandynge and the ȝifte of wisdom. This liff is in ii thyngis, as we haue touchid afoore, that is to seye, too haue Godde in right knoweleche and in parfit loue. The ȝifte of vndirstandyng ledith too perfeccion of right knowlech. Firste we wille nowe speke [of] the ȝifte of vnderstandynge, as that the Hooly Gooste shalle teche vs. This ȝifte of vnderstandynge opon the seyinge of mastres and of seintis is not ellis but a light and a clerenesse of grace that the Hooly Gooste sendeth intoo the herte. Be the whiche the vnderstandynge of man is qwik and reysed too knowe his creature and goostely thynges and al thynges that longeth too souleheele, too the whiche naturell reeson ne vnderstandynge maye not come, for bodyly it maye not be seen ne knowen. This ȝifte is proprely called light, for it purgith the vnderstandynge of man from the derkenesse of ignorance and from spotys of synne. For as bodily light putteth aweye derkenesse and maketh bodyly thyngys clerely too be seen, soo this goostely light purgeth the vnderstandynge of man that it maye clerely and certeynly knowe his creature, as men maye knowe in this liff, and oother goostely creatures, as angellis and soules bee, and oother thyngis longynge to helthe of the soule, as the articles of the feithe be of the whiche alonly as of theire parte wee haue spokyn and treted longe agon. This know-leche is but in a conscience wel purged and clensed. For as a seeke yee and a webbed and blered maye not wel beholde bodily thyngis if it be not wel porged of al dymnes of webbis and of al sekenesses, on the same wise the vnderstandynge of man as of hymselfe maye not wel beholde ne knowe goostely thyngys if it be not wel purged of al spottys of erroure and of harlotrye be veray feithe the whiche purgeth the herte, as the scripture seithe. But the ȝifte of the Hooly Gooste of the whiche wee speke parfiteth this purgacion and this clennesse in the herte to that ende that the hooly soule the whiche is purged and enlumined with this light of vnder-standynge maye comen too knowe Godde and that the whiche is necessarie and profitable too sauacion of it. [f. 158v] And this is the blessednesse that oure lorde speketh of in the gospell whan he seithe: Blessed be clene hertis, for theye shalle see veraye Godde [in] presente be feith enlumin-ed with the ȝifte of vnderstandynge. And after the deethe theye shalle see hym opinly, as Seint Poule seithe. This ȝifte putteth aweye al harlotrye and clensith it parfitly of al spottis, specially from the spotte of the syn of lecherie. For whoosoo is spotted with siche a spotte hee is verely blynde and hatthe loste the yen of the herte, that is too seye, reeson and vnder-standynge soo that he maye notte knowe his creature ne thynge that torneth to helþe of his soule. But he is liche a beste that hatthe neyther wit ne reeson in hym. Wherfore Dauid seiþe in the Sauter that a man to whom Godde hatth don siche worshipp that hee hatthe made hym to his ymage and liknes wherbye he maye knowe Godde and louff hym, the whiche he hatthe doon to noo beste but too man. Ȝit he forgeteth his creature and the curtesye that he hatthe doon to hym and he is comen like a lewde beste the whiche hatthe neyther reson ne vnderstandyng. The syn of the worlde that mooste maketh a man to resemble a foule beeste and a slutty is the syn of lecherye, of the whiche wee haue spokyn longe afoore in tretyng of vicis. The ȝifte of vnderstandynge, the whiche is contrarie too that harlotrie, raseth from the herte the synne of lecherye and planteth therin clennes and oneste. Of the whiche groweth a feire tree, that is to seye, the vertu of chastite be the whiche men commeth too that blessyng that Godde promisseth too thoo that kepeth clennesse of herte whan he seith: Blessed be clene hertis, for theye shalle see Godde, because theye haue the yen of the herte wel purged and enlumined with the ȝifte of vnderstandynge. This tree encresseth and waxeth as the toother aforeseide doothe be vii degrees, the whiche bee vii thyngys that vaileth gretly to kepe chastite.

Off Chastite, CLXXVII

[f. 159] The firste degree of chastite is clennesse of conscience. That is the roote of this tree, for withoute clene conscience ther is no chastite that plesith Godde. This honeste and this clennesse requireth that a man shalle kepe his herte from evil thoughtes, that he consente not to theyme, and from evil desires of his herte. For whoosoo consenteth to theyme, he is not chaste though he kepe hym froo the dede, for thourgh the consentynge withoute moore he maye be dampned. Three thyngys vailleth gretly to kepe chastite. The firste is gladly to here the worde of Godde and sermons. Wherfore oure loorde seithe in the gospelle to his desciples: Al ȝe, seithe he, be [clene] by the worde that I haue seid to ȝowe. For the worde of Godde is liche a mirroure wherein men seeth the spottis of theyre hertis. The secounde thynge is veraye confession the whiche is the veray lauoure where men sholde wesshe often with grete sorwe of herte and with gret repentaunce soo that a ryver of terris might rynne fro hym be the condite of his yen, and soo shalle hee be savid from al synnes. And therfore seithe Seint Bernarde: Louff confession if thowe wilt haue beaute, for confession is not withoute beaute. The iii thynge is remembrance of the passion of Criste Iesus. For noo temptacion ne noon evil thought maye not abide in the herte that thynketh and remembreth often of the deethe of Criste Iesus. For that is the armure that the fende dowthet moste, as be the whiche he was overcomme and looste his power. This is right wel signified to vs in the scripture of the serpent of brasse that Moyses be the commaundement of oure lorde reised soo hye o the perche that al the worlde sawe it, and al thoo that behelde it were hellyd thorough the peintures of the serpent. The serpent of brasse hungen on the perche betokeneth the bodye of Crist Iesus that hange on the cros that was the serpent withowte venym of the whiche was made thee triacle of oure helthe. Whoosooeuer felith hym smy[f. 159[v]]tyn and envenymed with the peyntures of the venymous serpent of helle, that is too seye, the feende, take heede be veraye feithe too the serpent of brasse. That is to seye that hee vmbethynke hym of the passion of Criste Iesus and anoon he shall be helyd and delyuered from temptaciones of the feende. The ii[e] degree wherby this groweth and profiteth is too keepe the mouthe from wordes that be evil and veleyns, the whiche torneth to ribaudy and to dishoneste, for be thoo belewes and be that wynde the fire of lecherye is often kyndelid. Wherefore the scripture seithe that the worde of a lewde womman is brennynge as fire. And Seint Poule seithe that evil woordes corrompeth goode condiciones. And therfore whoosoo wil kepe chastite, hee moste kepe hym from siche woordes. And whoosoo gladly herith theym and seeth theym it sheweth that he is not chaste, for oute of a vessell maye not come but siche as is þerin. If the woordes be foule and veleins, it is an open signe that harlotry and veleny is in the hert, for after the haboundaunce of the herte the mouthe speketh, as oure loorde seithe in the gospell. The iii[e] degree is to kepe welle alle the v wittes of the bodye: thee yen from foly lokynge, the erris from herynge lewde wordis, the handes from lewde touchyngis, the noose from to myche delytynge in swete smellis, the taste from to miche delytynge hym in goode metes. These be the v ȝatis of the citee of the herte wherbye the feende entreth oftentymes. Theese be also v wyndowes whereby deethe entreth often into the herte, as the prophete seithe. Many a goode man hatthe ben takyn and deceyvid the whiche were stronge and myghty because theye kepte not wele these gatys. If thowe wilte haue examples, thynke that noon was stronger than Sampson ne holyer than Dauid ne wisser than Salamon, and neverthelesse theye were alle overthrowen be women. Forsoothe if theye hadde kepte wel these gatys, the enemye hadde not takyn soo greete a forteresse. For Seint Ierom seithe: The toure of the herte maye not be takyn if the gatis bee not opyned to the feendes oste. The iiii degree for too putte aweye the fire of lecherye is too take aweye the fyre and the kynde[f. 160]lynge that norissheth that fyre, that is too seye, delytes and eases of the bodye the whiche enbraceth and kyndelith the fyre of lecherye and corrompeth chastite. Wherefore Seint Bernard seithe that chastite perissheth in delites. And therfore whoosoo wil kepe hym from brennynge hee sholde putte aweye the kyndelynges be abstinence and be sharpenesse of bodye. Wherfore the scripture seithe that childer that were norisshed with grete mete and wolde not vse delicious metes were saued in the fornesse of Babiloine. By the whiche is vnderstanden the syn of lecherye the whiche is quenched be abstinence and be sharpenesse of bodye. But fat metes and stronge wynes kyndelith it and norissheth it, evyn as fatnesse and gresse kyndelith fyre. The v degree is too flee evil feleshipp and causes of synne. Myche pepil synneth thorough evil feleshipp the whiche sholde not ellys falle. Liche as levain corrompeth paste and draweth it too sauour, soo evil feleshipp corrompeth the goode name of a persone. A rotyn appil if it be longe amonges hoole roteth the toother. A quicke coole setteth sone other dede colys o fyre whan it is put to theyme. Therfore the Sauter seithe: Thow shalt be hooly with hooly pepil and a sherewe with sherewes. As whoo seye: If thowe wilt kepe the clene and chaste, folwe the feleshipp of goode pepil. For if thowe louff the feleshipp of evil pepil, thowe shalt be siche as theye be. For whoosoo louffeth the feleshipp of fooles, hee moste be a foole, as the wyse man seithe in the scripture. Alsoo he moste flee the causes of synne, as to speke previly with a womman in suspecious places prevely and alon togeder. For whan a man hatthe tyme and place, it ȝefeth cause too synne. Of the whiche wee rede in the Booke of Kyngis that Aman the whiche was Dauidis son, whan he hadde his sister alone, hee corromped hirre. Therfore seithe Seint Poule: Flee fornicacion, that is to seye, causes that maye lede the to the synne of lecherye. For a man maye noo better ouercome the synne of lecherye ne kepe chastitee than for too fle suspecious feleshippes and the causes of the synne. Wherfore the angell seide to Lothe that hee sholde goo oute of the citee of Sodom and from al the marches. For it sufficeth not too leve evil feleshippes [f. 160v] ne the synne but if he leve not the marchis of synne, that is to seye, the causes. Men seith þe potte goothe soo longe too the water that at the laste it cometh brokyn hoome, and soo longe fleeth the botirflye aboute the fyre to that he brenneth hym. On the same wise, men maye soo longe seke the causes of synne that theye maye falle therin. Soo whoosoo wil kepe hym fro brennynge, he moste drawe hym from siche fire. The vi degree is too be ocupied in goode honest ocupaciones. For the feende the whiche shalle never sleepe whan hee fyndith a man idil and slowe too doo wel hee setteth hym in his occupacions and overthroweth hym lightly in synne. Wherfore the scripture seithe that idilnesse [and] necgligens and slowe too doo wel is mastres of myche evil. And therefore seithe Seint Poule: ȝiff, seith hee, no place to the feende. That is to seye, be not idil that the feende fynde a place too tempte ȝowe in. For Seint Ierom seithe: Doo, seithe he, euer some goode occupacion that the feende maye euer fynde the ocupied, for he that is idil maye not longe kepe hym oute of synne. Wherfore the prophete seith that the cause of the synne of Sodom was pride and plente of brede and idilnes. That is to seye that they dranke and ete and didde nought by the whiche theye fel in that foule synne that is not for to name. Soo fareth myche pepil that lesith theire tyme and emploieth it in vanitees and in outeragis of mete and of drinke and in lewde games and in iolynes of songes and karolles and in oother disportes and lewde desires. In siche vanitees theye waste theyre tyme. And therfore theye falle ful lightly in many foule and vilens synnes and often intoo the pitte of helle. For as Iob seithe: Theye lede theire liff in ioye and in disporte and in delites and in games that in o pointe alone falleth intoo the pit of helle. That is at the point of deethe, too the whiche theye take noo heede. The vii degree is deuote prayer, the whiche is myche worthe and ouercometh al synnes, anamly the synne of lecherye. For the whiche Seint Ambros seithe that prayer is a goode shilde aȝeins al the dartis of the feende. And Isidore seithe that it is a remedye aȝeins al temptaciones of synne whoosoo torneth to prayer as soone as the feende saileth [f. 161] the herte. For prayer vsed or vsynge of prayer quencheth al the assauttis of synne. Prayer is fulle myghty anenst Godde whan it is approprid with iiii thyngys, liche as with iiii pilleris. The firste is right feithe. Wherfore oure lorde seithe in the gospelle: In what that ever ȝe aske in youre prayeris, haue goode feithe and stedefast beleve in Godde, and ȝe shall haue what that ever ȝe aske. And Seint Iame seith: A man sholde aske of Godde with stedfast feithe withowte doubtyng. For whoosoo goothe doutynge, he fareth as the flode of the see the whiche the wynde ledith too and froo. And therfore hee that goothe doutyng getith nothynge of Godde. The ii[e] cause that sholde be in prayer is hoope to haue that the whiche a man asketh. Therfore the Sauter seithe: Haue goode hope in Godde, and hee shalle ȝiff the that thow askest hym. Therfore seithe hee in another place: Loorde, haue mercy of me, for myn herte tristeth in the. Grete hoope than causeth vs too require of hym the whiche in promisyng deceyvith not, whan he seith in the gospelle: Whoosoo asketh, he hatthe; and whoosoo seketh, he fyndeth. Loo, what bounte Godde doothe to hym. This is to vnderstande that whoosoo asketh wissely and seekyth diligently and calleth perseuerantly maye not faile. As whan theese iii thyngys be in prayer – with, diligens, and perseuerance – Godde hirith it anoon. Fele that thowe aske wisly. For myche pepil asketh that be not herde because theye forme evil their peticion. Wherfore Seint Iame seithe to thoo that knoweth not what theye aske: ȝe aske, seithe hee, often of Godde, but ȝe gete nought because ȝe can not aske. Some ther be that asketh hyer than longeth to theyme. Therfore whoosoo wille wisly praye to Godde, kepe hym froo presumpcion that he wene noo grete thynge of hymselfe, as þe phareseye didde, the whiche vaunted in his prayer and dispiced oother. But men sholde mekely praye too Godde and iuge hymselfe afore Godde, the whiche seeth the herte and knoweth the sekenesses and the defautis and knoweth what nede wee haue better than wee doo oureselfe. Take heede of these poore beggerres howe theye shewe theyre sekenesses and theyre defaultis for too meve the pepil withal to theymwarde in pitee. Soo sholde a man doo a[f. 161v]fore Godde mekely [to] shewe his defautis and his synnes to remembre theyme al there for to gete grace and pardon of Godde. And some ther be that can not aske but vile thyngys and smale, as temporelle goodes be. Godde the whiche wil ȝefe the a gretter thynge wil not plese the with a litil, as men doo a childe, but he will that thowe aske hym grete thyngys that maye be profitable to helthe of thy soule, as his grace and his blisse. For whoosoo asketh of Godde richesse or worshipp or deethe of his enemyes, hee sendeth to Godde foule prayerris. And therfore he hirith theym not. Wherefore Seint Austin seithe: Holde, seithe hee, for grete thyngis þe goodes the whiche hee ȝiffeth as wel to shrewes as to goode men. As whoo seye: Men sholde not sette be these transetorie goodes the whiche Godde ȝefeth as wel too shrewes and ȝit more as too goode men. And therfore goode men lerneth too dispise that the which shrewes hatthe desire too. As Seint Ambros seithe: Whan thowe prayest to Godde, aske grete thyngis, as siche be as that lasteth euer withouten ende and not transetorie thyngis, for siche prayer goothe not to Godde. And therfore oure goode master techith vs to aske wisly and sheweth vs oure demande whan hee seith thus: If ȝe aske anythynge of my fadir in my name, he shall ȝif it yowe. He asketh in the name of Criste Iesus that asketh that the whiche longeth to helthe of his soule. For Iesus is as myche to seye as helthe. And he techeth vs in the gospell what thynge we sholde aske whan hee seithe: Seke firste the kyngedome of Godde and his iustice, and ȝe shalle haue alle temporell thyngis too avauntage. For as men be wonte to seye: Too the gretest loorde men sholde alweye rynne. We haue nede of ii thyngis, that is to seye, of goostely goodes and of temporell goodes. But wee haue moore nede of the goostely goodes. And therfore firste and principally we sholde seke thoo, and Godde shalle ȝif theyme to vs. And the temporelle goodes wee shalle haue to avauntage. Wee sholde not make temporell goodes principall as covetouse pepille doo, the whiche seketh noon oother liff but that the whiche shalle ascape theyme and lightly faile theyme wheder theye wille or noon. But the kyngedome of hevyn the whiche is euerlastyng ioye [f. 162] wee sholde seeke firste be merites and be goode deedis, be the whiche a man maye come too that kyngedom that shalle never faile. And whoosoo doothe thus, Godde ȝiffeth hym too avauntage the temporell goodes, for hee ȝiffeth too theyme sufficiantly to theyre vse. For thoo that dredith and louffeth Godde failleth noothynge, as the scripture seithe. But as too the covetouse pepill of the worlde, the more they haue, the more theye nede. And whoosoo hatthe moste pepill behovith mooste mete. And whoosoo hatthe mooste hors hym behovith the moo pagis and stablis. And Ierom seithe that the negard failleth boothe that hee hatthe and that he hatthe not. Nowe thynke than whan thowe wilt praye too Godde too aske wisly, diligently, ententively, and perseuerantly, and he shalle ȝif the al that shalle be nedefull too thy profit and to helthe of thy soule. The iii thynge that sholde be in prayer is deuocion of hert, that is too seye, too reyse his herte to God withowte thynkynge anyewhere ellis. Therfore oure lorde seithe: Whan þou shalt praye, goo intoo thi couche (that is to seye, intoo thyn herte) and cloose the doore opon the (that is too seye, put oute al flesshely thoughtis and foule and velenis) and soo preye too thye fader secretely. And Seint Ciprien seithe: Whoosoo wil praye to Godde sholde putte, depart, from his herte al seculier and flesshely thoghtis, soo that the herte thynke of nought ellys but on his prayer. Howe wenest thowe, seithe hee, that Godde herith the whan thowe hirest not thyselfe? And Ysidore seithe that than wee praye verely whan we thynke of noght elles. And Seynt Austin seithe: What aveyleth, seithe he, to meve and to bete þe lippes whan the herte is doomme? Siche difference as is betwene chaff and corne, betwene bren and floure, betwene the skynne and the beste, siche difference is betwene the sowne of prayer and deuocion of herte. Godde is noo gote to be fedde with levys. Godde cursed the tree where he fonde but levys. Evyn soo, prayer the whiche is al in levys of woordis withoute deuocion of herte plesith not Godde but rather displesith hym. Hee torneth his erre therfroo soo [f. 162v] that he here it not. For hee vnderstandeth noo siche langache. And whoosoo prayeth to Godde withoute deuocion of herte, hee speketh giberisshe too Godde, as hee that speketh halfe Ynglisshe and halfe Frenshe. With the mouthe he speketh to Godde, but the herte speketh another langache, for he thinketh ellyswhere. Wherfore hym semeth that siche pepill that prayeth soo iapith hym, liche as he that wyl iape a deffe man meveth his lippes alonly and maketh contenaunce of speche and speketh not. Too siche pepill, Godde maketh a deffe erre. But a prayer that cometh parfitly of the herte Godde hireth that. For as hee seithe in the gospell: Godde is a sperit, and therfor whosoo wille be with Godde he moste praye to hym in sperit and in trouthe. Dauid in the Sauter techith vs to praye devoutly to Godde. Sir, seithe hee, my prayer be set before ȝowe as incens. Encens whan it is on the fire smelleth swete. Soo doothe prayer whan it cometh of the fervent herte of louff. If it come not froo the herte, it fareth as a messingere that cometh not gladly afore a kynge but if he haue letteris or goode knowleche. Prayer withoute deuocion is as a messanger withoute letters. Whoosoo sendeth siche a messanger too courte, hee doothe evil his erande. For comunly as men seye: Whoosoo sendeth a foole, folye hatthe. Whoosoo wille than praye verily to Godde, hee sholde praye to hym with depenes of herte, as Dauid didde in the Sauter: Sir, here my voys, for I crye too yow with depenes of herte. In the feruentnes of louff is the crye of the herte, Seint Austin seithe. Siche vois and siche crye plesith hym and not the noyse of florisshed woordis. Wherefore Seint Gregore seithe that too praye verily it is not alonly in many feted and polisshed woordis, but it is in weymentaciones and co[mpun]ciones of sorwe and of repentaunce of herte. Siche cryes chasseth aweye theefes, that is to seye, feendes the whiche wayteth to robbe vs. And therfore wee sholde often crye and weepe to Godde that he kepe vs froo siche theefes. Dauid cried to God therfore and seide: Sir, saue me froo perilles of wateres the whiche be here entred vnto myn herte. And the disciplis of oure loorde whan theye sawe the tempest and þe [f. 163] see vppon theym theye cryed and seide to hym: Sir, save vs, for wee perisshe and be in grete perille. For these iii thyngys that I haue seide here men sholde crye to Godde too save vs from these iii perilles:

from theefes of helle, from fire of covetise and of lecherie, and from floodes of evill thoughtis and of temptaciones.

Off Prayer, What It Sholde Be, CLXXVIII

Thowe shalt nowe knowe that in al tymes and in alle placis men maye praye to Godde. But in especiall men sholde praye too hym in the cherche on Sondayes and atte festes ordeyned too praye, too serve, too prayse, and to worshipp God and the moore devoutly to doo gostely dedis. What shalle he doo with theym that doothe grete synnes on Sondayes and at festes and wasteth theyre tyme in vanitees and in folies and doo wers atte festes than on oother dayes? Verily theye shalle be moore punisshed and dampned than Iues that breketh theyre sabat. Thus the principalle festes that be set in hooly chirche is set for to praye and to worshipp and to thonke Godde of the grete bountees that hee hatth doon to vs, as hooly chirche remembreth atte siche festes as at cristmes at the natiuite whan hee was borne of the Virgine Marie, atte ester whan he roos froo dethe too liff, atte the ascencion whan he stey intoo hevyn, atte pentecoste whan hee sent the Hooly Gooste too his apostlis. Alsoo the festes of seyntis be stablisshed for to worshipp Godde and the seintis for the miraclis that he didde for too conferme oure feithe. And therfore we shold kepe the festes of seintis and to praye theyme that theye socour vs anenste oure loorde that worshippeth theyme soo myche in hevyn and in erthe. Therfore he synneth fulle grevously that kepeth not the halydayes. For he doothe ayeinste the commandement of Godde. Whoosoo wil than kepe the halydaye as he sholde, hee sholde kepe hym froo thyngis that displesith Godde and his seintis and employe the tyme in prayer and praysyng and thankyng Godde of his goodnes and here sermones and tente too oother goode dedis. Also whan men be in the chirche theye sholde beehaue theyme honestly and doo worshipp and reuerens to Godde and to seintis. For the place is hooly and stabled for too praye to Godde and not for to iangle ne for to triffle ne for too laughe. Wherfore oure lorde seithe: Myn hous is an hous of prayer. And therfore men sholde seye ther [f. 163v] noon oother thynge but that for the whiche it is ordeyned. As Seint Austin seithe, he that sholde come afore a kynge in his chambir for to aske any grace he oughte too be wel warre to seye anythynge that sholde displese the kynge. Myche more oughte he too take heede that goothe to the chirche, the whiche is the chambir of Goddes hous, to doo or to seye anythynge afore Godde or afore his angellis that sholde displese theyme. Godde wil not that men make of his hous neythir booþe ne market. For the whiche the gospelle seithe that hee droff oute of the temple þo þat sould and bought þerin. For hee wil not þat men make ther noo seculer plee ne noise, but he wil þat men tente þer to praye devoutly to Godde and to prayse hym and to thanke hym of alle his goodnesses. There men sholde put oute al evil thoughtis and thynke on his maker and of the bounte that Godde hatthe doon too hym and doothe dayly and remembre his synnes and his mysdedis and his defaultis and meke hym afore Godde and require hym of pardon and of grace to kepe hym froo synne and preserve hym in goode dedis vnto his ende. These loordes and these ladyes sholde forȝete there theire glorie and theire power and theyr dignite and their hynesse and thynke that theye be afore a iuge that shall set theym to compte of the goodes that he hatthe doon to theyme, of the dignitees þat he hatth set theym, in howe theye haue vsid theym, and shalle ȝiff theyme wagis after that theye haue deserved. Wherfore theye sholde gretely meke theyme to Godde and not ioye theyme of theyre hyenesse ne of theire feyr araye ne of theire feire roobis [be þ]example of Kynge Dauid whan he prayed to Godde and dispised hymselfe in soo miche that he seide afore Godde: I am, quod he, a litil worme and noo man. In this he knowleched his litilnes and his filthe. For as a worme is a thynge litil and dispiteful and groweth alle naked of the erthe, soo a man hymselfe is a thynge vile and poore. For whan he entreth intoo þe[x]ile of this worlde he bryngeth noothynge ne noght berith aweye. Naked he entreth, and naked he shalle goo oute. Wherfore Seint Bernard seithe: What is man but a foule sede and a sacke fulle of donge? Also these grete ladyes that cometh soo arayed to the chirche with golde and silfer and with precious stoones afore Godde theye sholde take ensample of Queen Hester þat didde of hirre precious stoones, roobes, and hirre precious arayes whan shee come to praye to oure loorde and meked hirre and knowleched hirre pouerte afore Godde: Sire, thowe knowest that I haue al tokyn of pride. But ʒit [f. 164] the ioye of araies and of iuellis that me moste put opon myn heede I haue theym in grete abhominacion. Truly soo hatthe Godde grete abhominacion of thoo that ioyeth theym in siche thyngis and that arayeth theyme to shewe theyme too fooles. God hatthe not to doo with siche araye in his chirche but of a meke herte and of a clene consciens. Seint Poule techeth ful wel howe goode women sholde araye theyme whan theye come to praye too Godde. Hee seithe: Theye moste haue an honeste clothyng withoute outrage. That is to vnderstande after that the person requireth. For that the whiche is outerage in oo persone is noon in another. Ther longeth moore too a queen þan doothe to a symple ladye or too a burgeisesse. Alsoo hee techeth that theye sholde be of symple beholdynge, that is to seye, meke and shamefast and not the forhede set vppe ne popped, as lewde wommen be that goothe þe necke strecched oute as an herte on a lande and lookyng o trauerse as an hors of pris. Alsoo he wil not þat theye be too besy to araye ther heedes with golde and silfer ne with precious stoones. And ʒit he wille that at the chirche theire heedes be couered soo that be theyme noon be evil sette and that theye ʒif noo cause too thoo that seeth theyme too thynke eville. But theye shold be arayed as goode women that sheweth the bountee of theyre hertis be goode dedis. And therfore seith Seint Ambrose: Whoosoo wille be herde in prayer it behovyth to put froo aboute hym al signes of pride. And he sholde bowe hym to Godde be veraye mekenes for to meve God too mercy. For as he seithe: Proude clothynge geteth nought anenst Godde, but it ʒifeth cause to deme evil of hym or of hyrre that werith it. I haue nowe shewed the iii thyngis that sholde be in prayer: feithe, hoope, and deuocion. But ʒit too the entent þat prayer maye be parfitly acceptable and agreable to God and pleysynge and worthy too be herde, it moste haue iiii thyng, that is to seye, ii wynges too brynge it tofore Godde. The ii wyngys is fastynge and almesse. Withoute these ii wyngys, prayer maye not flee too Godde. As Seint Amb[r]ose seithe: Goode lyvynge maketh prayer flee too

Godde, but syn letteth it and draweth it abacke. Wherfore thowe shalt wite that in ii maneres prayer is letted, as Isodore seythe, owther because that a man cessith not of evil deede or because that a man wil not forȝif his evil will. For evyn liche as an oignement is noght too heele a wounde ne noon oother medecyn as longe as the iren is within it, on the same wise prayer [f. 164v] vayleth not ne profiteth to hym tha seith it as longe as he hatthe shrewdenes in his herte. And therfor seithe the prophete: Lifte, seithe hee, ȝoure hertis and ȝoure handis too Godde. He lifteth his herte and his handis to Godde that susteyneth his prayeris be goode dedis the whiche be don with goode conscience. For Godde herith not a prayer that cometh of a conscience fulle of harlotrye and of synne. Hereof haue we example in the gospelle, the whiche seithe þat the ȝeate was closed to the fole virginis that hadde theire lampes voide and seide vnto theyme: *Nescio vos*; I woote not what ȝe be. For Godde knoweth not but thoo that serveth hym truly, the whiche hatthe theire lampes ful of oyle as the wise virginis hadde, that is too seye, that hatthe theire hertis ful of pitee and sheweth it in goode dedis. Siche pepil herith he, and too siche pepill openyth hee the ȝeate and gladly resceyvith theire prayeris. I seye than þat prayer the whiche is rested opon these iiii peleris is fulle myghty anenste Godde, as I haue seide afore, for it geteth of hym lightly that the whiche is nedefull be it too the bodye or too the soule, as the scripture seithe. Wherfore Seynt Iame seithe that the prayer of a goode man vailleth myche, for it vailleth too hele al sekenesse boothe of bodye and of soule. Therfore hymselfe seithe that prayer that cometh of feith helith the seke man. And ȝif he be in synne theye shalle be forȝevyn hym. The scripture seithe that Moyses ouercome Amalech and alle his oste not only be bataile but be hooly prayeris. For as an hooly man seithe: An hooly man praynge too Godde vaileth moore and moore maye doo þan many ml synneres maye doo in feyghtyng. The prayer of a goode man persith hevyn. Howe than sholde theye not ouercome enemyes in erthe? A goode persone getheth more of hevyn in praynge in on houre þan a thousand knyghtis geteth of erthe be armes in alle theyre lyffetyme. And therfore it is goode to gete þe prayeris of goode pepille, specially of coventis of religion the whiche be assemblid for to serue Godde and too praye for theire goodedoerris. For as the scripture seithe: ȝif þe prayer of a goode man vailleth myche to Godde, myche moore vailleth þe prayer of many goode men. For as an hooly man seithe: It maye not be but that the prayeris of many goode men moste be herde. For the prayerris of a [f. 165] covent is sonner herde of the abbotte than the prayer of a monke aloone. On the same wyse, Godde hirith sonner the prayerris of thoo that be assemblid for too serve hym than of oother. Wherfore he seithe in the gospelle: ȝif ii of ȝowe accorde togyder too require of me anythynge resonable, what that ever yee require my fader shalle graunte it ȝowe. I haue nowe tolde thee of vii degrees wherebye the tree of chastite waxeth, groweth, and profiteth. Nowe behoveth to telle of the branches the whiche be vii statis of pepill þat bee in this worlde.

Off Chastite in Maydenhode, CLXXIX

The firste astate is of thoo þat be hoole of bodye and haue kepte theire maydenhoode but notwithstandyng theye be not bonde thertoo but that maye be maryed. In that state, men sholde kepe theym clene of herte and of bodye. Wherfore the childer of rich men sholde haue goode keperris and honeste, the whiche sholde be nere theyme and to be diligent too teche theyme and too kepe theyme from evil feleshypp and froo synne. For evil feleshipes shendeth often childer and techeth theym evil games, as wordes of shrewdenes and of rebaudie, lewde tochyngis and dishonest be the whiche theye falle in the synne of legerie, the whiche is aȝens nature, of the whiche wee haue spokyn in thee tretice of vicis. And therfore it nedeth not nowe too remembre it, for the mater is not feire. And therfore men sholde teche childir welle and chastie theyme and holde theyme nere to theyme as longe as theye be ȝonge and vse theyme to holde and too kepe goode techyngys. For as Salamon seith: What that a childe lereth in his ȝougthe, hee wille k[e]pe it in his age. And it is not a litil thyng too vse theme welle or evil in theire ȝough, but it is alle. For as men seyth: Whoosoo lerneth a kolte to amble hee wil kepe it whilest that he endureth. Siche forme as the shoo taketh at the begynnynge, it kepeth alleweye. Than in siche state chastite hatthe nede of goode kepynge. For ellis it maye soone be loste.

Off Chastite Corromped, CIIII^{XX}

The seconde state is in thoo that be corromped of bodye and hatthe loste theire chastite and theire maydenhode withoute þat theye were euer maried or bounde with thee [f. 165^{v}] liein that myghte let theyme, and neuerthelesse theye be confessed and repentaunt of theyre synne. In this state men sholde kepe chastite and haue stedefast purpose and wil never to fal in synne of his bodye but kepe hym too his power withoute this that he maye marye hym and he wille. And he that in this state wil kepe his chastite he moste defolle his flesshe and chastie it be sharpe fastynggys and be penaunce. And this is the secounde braunche of this tree.

Off Chastite in Mariage, CIIII^{XX}I

The iii state is in tho that be bounde in mariage. And that state men sholde kepe chastly saunec þe dede of mariage. For the ton scholde truly kepe theym to the toþer withoute doynge wronge on too an nother. And the lawe of mariage requireth this that the ton sholde haue feithe and trouthe too the toother of his bodye, for after that theye be flesshely ioyned togeder theye be oo bodye, as the scripture seithe. And therfore the ton sholde louff the toother as hymselfe, for as theye be oo bodye theye sholde be oo herte be trewe louff, and theye sholde never devide theyme neyther in herte ne in bodye as longe as theye liffed. Wherfore theye sholde kepe þeyre bodyes clenly and chastely save in the dede of mariage. And therfore Seint Poule seithe that women sholde louff and worshipp theire husbondes. And theye sholde be chaste and kepe theyme from al oother save from theire husbondis. And theye sholde be sobre in drinkynge and etynge, the whiche is a grete kyndelynge of the fire of lecherye. On the same wise, men sholde kepe theyre bodyes chastly that theye bandoune theyme too noon oother women but too theyre owne. Mariage is a state of grete auctorite, for Godde stablisshed it in erthely paradis in the state of innocency afore that man hadde ever synned. And therfore men sholde kepe it holyly because that Godde stablid it. Also it is a state of grete dignite, for Godde wolde be borne of a womman maried, that was, of the Virgine Marie. For the whiche the virgine made of mariage a ma[n]tell vnder the whiche the son of Godde wolde be conseyved and born. Vnder this mantelle was hidde the secretis and the raunson of oure helthe. Therfore men sholde worshipp it and kepe it clenly. Alsoo men sholde [f. 166] kepe it hollyly because of the holynes therof, for it is oon of the sacramentis of holy chirche betwene Godde and the soule. Wherfore the state of mariage is soo holy and soo honest that the dede the whiche was dedely syn oute of mariage is withoute synne in mariage and not oonly withoute synne but it maye be doone to gete withal the mede of euerlastynge liff. And thowe shalt knowe þat in iii^{e} cases men maye doo the dede of mariage withowten synne [...] in entent too haue issue too serve Godde [and] too that entent mariage was firste ordeyned. The ii^{e} cas is whan the ton ȝeldeth his dette too the toother. And rightwisnes sholde meve the to this the whiche ȝeldeth to euery persone his right if theye aske it or require it outher be mouthe or be signe, as wommen doo that be shamefast too aske siche thyngis. Whoosoo refuseth it to the toother þat requireth it synneth, for hee robbeth hym and doothe hym wronge of his owne thynge, for the ton hatthe right too the bodye of the toother. But he that ȝeldeth that the whiche he sholde doothe wel and rightfully whan hee doothe it in siche wise and deservith grete mede anenste Godde. For rightwisnes meveth theyme to doo it and not lecherye. The iii cas is whan a man requireth his wyff of that dede for to kepe hirre of siche synne, anamly whan hee seeith that shee is soo shamefast þat shee wylle never require hym of siche thynge and dredith that she myght lightly fal in synne if he required it not of hirre. Whoosoo in siche entent ȝeldeth and requireth siche dette he synneth nothynge. But he maye deserve therein grete mede of Godde, for pitee meveth hym too doo it. In these iii cas is no syn in the dede of mariage. But in oother wyses men maye synne outher venially or dedly and specially in iii cas. The firste cas is whan men requireth not in siche dede but his delite and his lecherie. And in siche cas men maye synne venially or dedly. Venially whan [t]hee delit passeth not the boundes ne the termes of mariage, that is to seye, whan the delit is soo grete soget to reeson soo that hee that is in siche state wolde not doo siche a thynge but with his wiff. But if the delit and the lecherye be soo grete in his wiff þat reeson is þer soo blynded that he wolde doo as myche þowe shee were not his wiff, in that cas he synneth dedly, for siche lecherie passeth the boundes of mariage. For þe whiche God angreth hym ofte with siche pepill and ȝifeth [f. 166^{v}] grete power too the feende to noye theyme. Alsoo men maye synne ther in oother wise, that is too seye, whan the ton draweth the toother aȝeins nature and oother weyes than nature of man or lawe of mariage granteth. Siche pepill synneth moore grevously than these oother aforeseide. But thoo that in theire mariage kepeth the fire of oure loorde and kepeth theire mariage clenly as it is ordeyned, siche pepil plesith Godde. The ii^{e} cas wherein men maye synne in mariage is whan a man goeth too his wiff in siche tyme as he sholde not, that is too seye, whan shee is in the sekenes that is wonte comunly to come too woomen. Thoo þat spareth not theire whiffes whan they knowe þat theye be in that plite synneth grevously. And therfore God defendeth that a man sholde feleshipp with his wiff whan shee is in that plite. For the whiche the wiff sholde telle it too hir husbonde whan shee is in that plite that he myghte forbere [hym to be with] hirre atte that tyme, for he ought too forbere hym. Alsoo theye sholde bothe spare the dede of mariage in hooly tymes, as in grete solempne festes, the better to entent to praye and to serve Godde. Alsoo in tymes of fastynge comanded be hooly chirche men sholde forbere that dede not for that it is synne to doo siche dedis in siche tymes. In siche entent men maye doo it, but somtyme men sholde forbere it though that men myght wel doo it [and] that hee maye doo it withoute synne, ȝit he sholde forbere it the better too gete of Godde that the whiche a man asketh, as Seint Austin seithe. Alsoo in the tyme that a woman lithe in gesyne or nere here delyuerance than namly men sholde kepe theyme froo that dede of mariage for honeste and for the perille that maye bee therin. Men fynde in the Booke of Nature of Bestes that the olephaunt abideth not with his femmale as longe as shee is with hir birdeyn. Be reeson a man sholde be more temperat than a beeste. And therfore hee sholde suffre the more. Neverthelesse, I seye not that he synneth if hee doo the dede of mariage in siche tymes for a goode cause or for a goode entent of þe whiche Godde is iuge. The iii cas wherein men maye synne grevously is whan it is in hooly place. For in hooly placis as in chirches the whiche bee appropred to serve God men sholde not doo there the dede of mariage for the reuerens of the place and for that siche thynge maye be syn in oo place and in oo tyme [f. 167] the whiche is noon in anoother.

Off Chasti[t]e of Wydowhoode, CIIII^{XX}II

The iiii astate is of thoo that hatth ben in mariage but deethe hatthe desseuered the tone froo the toother. And he that abideth oo-lyve sholde kepe hym chastly as longe as hee is in the state of wydowhoode, the whiche is a state that Seint Poule prayseth gretely. For he seithe too widowhoode that it is right that theye holde theym in that state if it plese theyme not to be maried. But it is better to theyme too be maried than to be brent. Thoo brenneth theym that consenteth to syn. For he setteth ofte his herte in the synne of lecherie be wille or be desire. And better it were too marie hym than in siche fire too brenne hym. And this is too vnderstande be thoo that be in state of simple wydowhoode, not be thoo that be bounde in that state be vowe soo that theye maye not vnbynde theyme after the vowe ne marye theyme withowte synne. But neverthelesse the vowe is symple, that is too seye, whan it is made prevyly. Allethough that theye synne dedly that after that vowe marieth theyme, notwithstandynge hee sholde abide stylle in mariage if ther bee noo empechement. 3it hee sholde doo his penaunce for the vowe brokyn. But whan the vowe is solempned be the hande of the prelat or be [pro]fession of religion or be hooly ordre þat men hatthe resceyved, as subdekyn, dekyn, or preeste, than the mariage is noon. Thoo that cometh toogeder in siche mariage moste be departed, for theye maye not be saved in siche state. The state of þe tortille sholde meve too kepe the state of wydowhoode. As the Booke of the Nature of Bestis seithe: After that þe tortille hatthe loste his make, hee wil never feleshipp hym with noon oother, but he wil alweye be solitarie and flee the feleshipp of oother. Ther be iii thyngis þat longeth too thoo that be in the state of wydowhoode. The firste is too hide hymselfe prevyly in his howse and sue not suspicious feleshipp. Of this haue wee example be Iudith, the whiche was a widowe and a fulle feyre womman, of whom men reede in scripture that shee kepte hir clos in hirre chambir with hirre maydenis. For the whiche Seint Poule repreveth yonge women þat be idil and to besy and to goo and too come and iangleresses [f. 167^{v}] and to miche spekeres. For theye sholde be clos in theire houses and tente to doo goode dedis, as Seint Poule techith. The ii^{e} thynge is to tente to praye to Godde and gladly too be at the chirche in deuocion and in teris, as men reede in the gospelle of Seint Luke of that godde wydowe þat hight Anne that shee departed not froo the temple and served Godde daye and nyght in fastyng and in teris. The iii thynge is sharpenes of liffe. For as Seint Poule seithe: The woman that is a wydowe the whiche norissheth here liff in delites, shee is dede be synne. For as Seint Bernard seithe: Chastite peris-sheth in delites liche as hee perissheth that is in the water the whiche is soo longe vnder that hee lesith his brethe. Noon maye haue his heede in the water, that is to seye, his herte in the wateres of delites of this worlde but that he lesith his breethe, that is to seye, the grace of the Holy Gooste be the whiche the soule liffeth in Godde. Too this state alsoo longeth meke cloothynge and not prowde ne besye [be þ]example [of] Iudith, the whiche lefte hirre feyre roobes and hirre riche arayes whan hirre loorde was dede and tooke state of simple wydowhoode, the whiche is more signe of weepynge and of woo than of ioye and of vainglorie, be-cause that shee luffeth chastite and wolde kepe it al hirre liffe. Shee werid the haire and fasted dayly, save at festes. And ȝit shee was yonge, riche, feire, and wisse. But bounte of herte and louff of chastite made hirre too doo that. For whoosoo wil kepe chastite sholde liffe thus in siche state. And this is the iiii branche of the state of chastite.

Off Vi[r]ginite, CIIII^{XX}III

The v state is virginite. In this state be thoo that kepeth and hatthe kepte and purposeth euer too kepe theire bodyes al theire liffes withoute corrupcion holly for the louff of Godde.

This state is gretely to prayse for his virginite, for his beaute, and for his bounte. For siche state maketh hym that kepeth it wel like too angell of hevyn, as hooly men seithe. But virginis hatthe thus myche moore than angellis, for aungell liff withoute flesshe, but virginis hatthe victorie of theire flesshe. And it is grete merveyle that theye maye kepe soo feble a castelle as the bodye is aȝeins soo [f. 168] stronge an aduersarie as the fende is, the whiche seketh al the wyles that he maye for to take this castell for to robbe the tresor of virginite. That is to seye, the tresor of the whiche oure loorde speketh in the gospell, the which seithe þat the kyngdom of hevyn is like too the tresor that is hidde in the filde. The tresor that is hidde in the felde is virginite hidde in the bodye, the whiche is like a felde that a man sholde ere be penaunce and sowe it with labour of gode dedis. This tresor is like to the kyngedom of hevyn. For the liffe of virginis is like to the liffe of aungellis, virginis of the whiche oure loorde seithe in the gospell that in the resurreccion theye shalle not haue as theye haue here but theye shalle be as aungellis of hevyn. Alsoo this state is gretely to prayse for his beaute. For the feirest state that is in erthe that is virginite clenly kepte. Of the whiche Salamon seithe merveylyng in hymselfe in the Booke of Sapience: O, seithe hee, what it is a faire thynge a chaste lignie with clerenes. For than chastite and virginite is feire whan it is clere be goode dedis and be a good honeste live. Liche as the clerenes of the sonne maketh a feire daye, soo the clerenesse of grace and of goode liff maketh virginite feire and plesaunt to Godde. Wherfore Seint Ierome seithe that the vertu of virginite is ful faire and ful clere afoore Godde and afore aungell whan it is withoute spotte and withoute filthe. For whoosoo is hole of bodye and corromped of herte, he is like a whited sepulcre the whiche is feire and white owteward and inward fulle of bones and of rotenesse. Virginite is as a white gowne wherein a spotte is fouller and more shewyng than in another gowne. This gowne ought too be kepte welle from iii spottis: fro myre, froo bloode, and froo fire. These iii spottis defouleth gretely this white coote. The spotte of myre is the covetice of the worlde, the whiche sholde not be in an herte that wolde pleise Godde in this state of virginite. For noon maye pleise Godde and his enemye. As Seint Gregore seithe, he sheweth welle that he is not Goddes frende the whiche wille pleise the worlde that is his enemye. For Seint Iohn seithe: Whoosoo wille be frende too the worlde he shalle be enemye too Godde. And Seint Poule seithe: If I wille pleise worldly pepille, I shalle not be Goddis seruaunt. A tookyn that men wil plese the worlde and that the herte is not holly to Godde is to grete araye and too besy araye aboute his bodye, for noon sholde never seke beaute ne curiosite of roobes ne of arayes if hee supposed not to be seen of pepille. But [f. 168v] whoosoo moste seketh outewarde that beaute moste lesith inwarde þat be the whiche men pleiseth Godde. Seint Bernard seithe too þoo that seketh preciouse gounes and feire arayes for to be plesaunt to the worlde and for to shewe theymeselfe: ȝe be, seithe hee, the doughterz of Babiloine, that is to seye, of confusion, for theire glorie shalle torne theyme to confusion and too euerlastynge shame if theye be not wel ware. Theye cloothe theyme, seithe hee, with preciouse roobes and with porple. And vnder þoo roobes þe caroyne is often poore and naked. And outewarde theye shyne with golde and with silfer and with preciouse stoones. But theye be vile and foule afoore Godde be evil condicions. Seint Bernard seithe this of thoo þat arayeth theyme þus for an evil entent and that doothe moore than theire astate asketh. But the glorie of the doughter of the kynge of blisse is inward in clene consciens and in feire vertues where there is no covetice but too plese Godde. And soo the spotte of myre shendeth it not. Alsoo in this state men sholde kepe theyme froo the spotte of bloode, that is to seye, from thoughtes and from flesshely desires. Wherfore Seint Ierom seithe that siche virginite is offrande and sacrifice too Godde, the whiche is not spoted in the herte with evil thought ne in the bodye with evil lecherie. For as he seithe hymselfe: Virginite of bodye is not worthe the whiche is corromped in the herte, liche as fruit is not goode thoughe it be feire withoute whan it is rooten and mouled within. Alsoo in this state men sholde kepe theyme from the spot that cometh of þe fire. The fire that oftentymes bruleth and brenneth þe white cote of virginite and of chastite is gladly to here speke and to herkyn wordis that maye meve to synne. For as Seint Poule seithe and oother tymes wee haue seid it afore: Evil woordis corromped goode maneres. And therfore Seneque seithe: Kepe the, seithe he, from evil woordes the whiche be not honeste, for whoosoo habandoneth hym to theyme he becometh vnshamefaste and bolde. That is to seye that hee lesith shame and falleth the lightlyer in synne. And therfor whoosoo wille kepe clenly the white cote of virginite, he moste kepe hym fro spekyng and from heryng siche wordis wherewith that men maye outher bryn theym or brule theym. [Prive] catte bruleth hirre skyn oftener than doothe wilde. Virginite amonge oother vertues is likenyd too a flour de liz, the whiche is a feire floure and a white. Therfore oure loorde seithe in the scripture be the mouthe of Salamon: [f. 169] My louff is liche þe floure de lis amonge thornes. The specialle louff of oure loorde is a soule that kepeth virginite. For that is a vertu be þe whiche the soule geteth mooste specially the louff and þe familiarite of oure loorde. For the whiche Seint Iohn þe vangeliste, the whiche was a virgine, amonge ooþer was moste familiar with oure loorde. And oure [loorde] shewed hym gretest signe of louff and grettest familiarite, as he seithe in the gospelle. And he was called amonge the toþer disciples hee þat Criste Iesus louffed moste. Not but þat he louffed the tooþer wel but he louffed hym moste specially for his virginite. This flour de liz kepeth his beaute amonge the thornes of temptaciones of þe flesshe. For þe flesshe is but as a dongehille the whiche berith ne bringeth forthe as of hymselfe but netlis and thornes, the whiche be evil mevyngis þat often priketh þe sperit. But the flour of virginite setteth not be the þornes, for it is rooted wel in the louff of Criste Iesus, the whiche defendeth it from the thornes of temptacion. This flour sholde haue vi levis and iii gylte greynes withinne. The firste leef is holnes of bodye, that is to seye, the bodye to be hole withowte corrupcion of lecherie. For if a virgine were holly corrumped aȝeins hirre wille shee sholde not þerfore lesse the wagis of virginite. Wherfore Seint Luce seide to þe tyraunte: If þou corrompe me aȝeins my wille, it shalle be to me double chastite, as too þe corone of blisse. The ii^{e} leef is clennes of herte. For as Seint Ierom seithe: It is not worthe to haue virginite of body to hym that hatthe wil to marie hym. He seithe this too thoo that hath vowed chastite. For whoosoo voweth too kepe virginite or chastite, he sholde kepe his herte and his bodye clenlye and chastlye. The iiie leeff is mekenes. For virginite prowde plesith not Godde. And þerfor seithe Seint Bernard: It is a fulle feire thynge too haue mekenes with virginite. And the soule in whom is mekenes plesith Godde ful gretly. For mekenes ȝefeth a lawde to virginite, and virginite embelissheth mekenes. I der wel seye, seith Seynt Bernard, that withoute mekenes virginite hadde never plesed Godde. The iiiie flour de liz of virginite is the fere of God. For thoo that be purely virginis ar wonte to be ferefulle and shamefaste. And it is noo merveyle, for theye bere a fulle precious tresor in a fulle febill vessell. Wherfore the quene, the Virgine Marie, was alweye hidde and hadde ful grete fere whan the angell perid too hirre. But the fere of Godde is the tresorer the whiche kepeth the tresor of virginite that the feende maye not stele it. For it kepeth the ȝeatis of the castelle of the herte where þe tresor of [f. 169v] virginite is cloosid. The ȝeatis of þe castelle of þe herte where the tresor of virginite is be þe wittes of the bodye. These ȝeates kepeth the fere of oure loorde that theye be not openyd to the feende [b]e veine besynesse to hire or to see or too speke or to goo into suspeciouse feleshippes. Specially too see and too hire vanitees of þe worlde it is often weye to [the] synne of lecherie. Wherfore men rede that Iacobes doughter wente musyng besyly too see the women of the countre that shee was of, the whiche was ravisshed and corromped be the princes son of þe londe. And therfore whoosoo wil kepe virginite moste withdrawe his wittes gretly and kepe hym fro vaine besynes. And men doothe this be the holy fere of oure loorde, the whiche is ever aferde to greve Godde. This is the witte of þe v virginis. Of the whiche oure loorde seithe in the gospelle that the kyngedom of hevyn is like to x virginis, of the whiche v be wyse and the tother v foles. Here he calleth the kyngdom of hevyn hooly chirche, the whiche is here beneþe where ther be goode and evil, fooles and wise, the whiche be membris of hooly chirche be the feithe þat theye resceyvid in bapteme. The v wise betokeneth þoo that kepeth welle and governeth the v wittis of þe bodye wherof wee haue spoken longe afore. The v fooles betokeneth thoo that kepeth theyme folyly. The v leeff is sharpenesse of liff. For whoosoo wil kepe virginite hee moste mate his flesshe gretely and put it vnder foote be fastynge, be wakynge, and be prayer. Sharpenes of liff is liche an hecche for to kepe the gardyn of the herte that evil bestes entre not into it. Thoo be þe enemys þat desyreth but for to stele the tresor of virginite. And therfore siche tresor sholde be wel closed and wel hidde that it be not loste. For whoosoo lesith it maye never recover it no more than a lampe whan it is broken maye be made holle. The vi leeff is perseuerance, that is to seye, to kepe that the whiche a man hatthe promissed to Godde. For the whiche Seint Austin in the Booke of Virginite seithe where he spekith of virginis: Folewe, seithe he, þe lamme, þat is to seie, Criste Iesus in kepynge stedfastly þat the whiche ȝe haue vowed to Godde. Doo fervently as miche as ye maye that the goodnes of virginite perisshe not in yow. For ye maye doo nothynge be the whiche it maye be recouered aȝein if ȝe lese it, as wee haue seide in the example of the lampe. And Seint Bernard seithe also: Stodie ȝe in perseuerance. These vi leefes aforeseide embelesshith gretly þe flour de liz of virginite. But too þis flour longeth iii gilt greynes to be withinne, the whiche betokeneth iii maneres of louff in Godde. For virginite withouten the louff of Godde is as a lampe with[f. 170]oute oyle. [...] where shette oute froo the mariage. And þe wyse virginis the whiche filled theire lampes with this oyle entred with þeire husbondes to the mariage. The iii^{e} maneres too louff Godde the whiche be signified be the iii greynes be thoo þat Seint Austyn techith whan he seithe thus: Thowe shalt louff Godde with al thyn vnderstandynge withowten erroure, with al thy wille withowte geyneseynge, with alle thy mynde withoute forȝetynge. In siche wyse the ymage of Godde is parfyt to man vppon iii dignitees that be in the soule, that is to seye, myende, vnderstandyng, and will. Whan þese iii thynges be set wel to Godde in these iii wyses that Seint Austin seithe than be the greynes of þe flour de liz wel gilte with the golde of charite, the whiche ȝefeth beaute, bountee, and valve to al vertu. For withoute þis golde noo vertu afore Godde is neyther feire ne preciouse. Seint Bernard seithe oother weys of the maner too louff Godde and seithe þus: O thowe Cristen man, seithe hee, lerne howe þou sholdest louff Criste Iesus. Lerne to louff swetely, wisly, and strongely, wisely that thowe be not deseyved be nysete and swetely þat þou be not mevid be pro[s]perite, strongely that thowe be not ouercomme be aduersitee. Thus the flour de liz is feire whan it is siche as wee haue seide. The iii^{e} reeson why the state of virginite is gretely too prayse is for his bounte, for þe profit þat cometh therof. For virginite is a tresor of soo grete valwe that it maye not be praysed. Wherfore þe scripture seithe that noothynge is worthe to be counterpeysed too a chaste herte. This is to vnderstande be the chastite of virginite. For above al oother statis virginitee berith the grettest fruit. Thoo þat be in mariage and kepeth it as theye þat sholde doo þey haue xxx fruitis. Thoo þat bee in wydowhoode theye haue lx fruitis. But thoo þat kepe virginite theye haue an hundreth. For oure loorde seithe thus in the gospelle that þe sede the whiche felle in goode erthe fructified on the to parte in xxx and on the tooþer parte in lx and on the thirde parte in an hundreth. These iii noumbres, xxx, lx, c, longeth to þe statis aforeseide. The noumbre of xxx the whiche is of x and of iii, for threis x maketh xxx, longeth too the state of mariage, wherein men sholde kepe the x commaundementis of the lawe in the feithe of the trinite. The noumbre of lx the whiche is gretter of x and of vi, for vi tymes x maketh lx, longeth to þe state of wydowhoode. For in that state men sholde kepe the x commaundementis. And therwith men sholde doo þe dedis of mercy of the whiche wee haue spokyn afore. But [f. 170^{v}] the noumbre of a hundreth the whiche is the grettest of the iii is the moste parfit. For it representeth a figure bon gire, *id est*, rounde, the whiche is the feirest amonge ooþer figures and moste parfite. For as in a rounde figure the ende torneth aȝein to his begynny[n]g soo fareth this. For x tymes x maketh an c, the whiche betokeneth the corone that the wyse virginis be coroned with. And ȝit for al that in the state of mariage or in the state of wydowhoode men maye wel wynne the corone of blisse and haue more mede anenste Godde than many virginis hatthe. For ther be many of thoo that hatthe ben in mariage and in wydowhoode the whiche in paradis be nerer to Godde than many virginis. ȝit virginis hatthe a speciall coroune above opon the coroune of blisse the whiche is commune to al seintis because that seintes hatthe specialle victorie of theire flesshe. Ther shal theye be soo wel-beseyen and soo nobilly arayed with a special clothynge, soo gentil, soo feire, and soo comly that no tonge maye devise it. And therfore I wil no moore seye but that the scripture seithe that spekith of feire cloothyngis, the whiche theye haue moore specially than thoo of the toother statis hatthe aforeseide. And ȝit þe scripture seithe that theye shalle synge newe songes and soo melodiouse þat noon shalle synge siche the whiche be not of theire astate. This newe songe that theye shalle synge signifieth a newe ioye and a special wagis þat theye shalle haue because þat theye haue kepte wel the state of virginitee. This is the v degree of chastite and the v braunche of þis tree.

Off Chastite þat Sholde Be in Clerkis, CIIII^{XX}IIII

The vi state wherein men sholde kepe chastite is in clerkys ordred, as in subdekenes, dekenes, prestes, and prelates. Al þoo be bounde to kepe chastite for many causes. Firste for the ordre þat theye haue resceyvyd, the whiche requireth al holynes, for the sacrement is soo hye and soo hooly that tho þat resceyvith it be soo bounde too keepe chastite that theye maye not marie theyme. Alsoo for the office þat theye haue, for theye be appropred to serve Godde in his temple and in his house and too handel and to ȝif with theire handis halowed thyngis, as vessellis sacred, the chalis, the corparax, and that the whiche is a gretter thynge withoute comparison, the bodye [f. 171] of Criste Iesus that prestes sacreth and resceyvith and ȝiffeth too oother. Theye oughte nowe þan too be fulle hoolye and fulle clene because of the loorde whom theye serve the whiche is hooly and hateth vnclennes. Therfore he seithe in the scripture: Be ȝe hooly, for I am hooly. And siche loorde siche maynye, and because of the place where theye serve, that is, the chirche the whiche is hooly and [d]edified or dedicat too serve Godde. Men fynde þat amonge payenymes the prestes þat serveth in the temple kepeth chastite and be devided from oother because theye sholde not leese theire chastite. Miche moore withoute comparison oughte Cristen prestes to be clene and chaste that serveth in the temple of oure loorde, the whiche is halowed and appropred too serve Godde. ȝit theye sholde be alsoo clenner and withoute synne because þat theye serve atte Goddes boorde of his cuppe, of his breede, of his wyne, and of his mete. Goddes boorde is þe auter. His cuppe is the chalys. His br[ee]de and his wyne is his propre bodye and his owne bloode. Theye ought gretly þan to be clene and hooly thoo þat doo siche service to God. Wherfore Seint Poule seithe þat the bisshopp and þe ministres of whom wee speke the whiche bee ministres of hooly chirche ought too be chaste. This chastite was signified in þe olde lawe wherfore Godde commaunded too þoo þat sholde ete of þe lambe the whiche betokenyd the bodye of Criste Iesus that þeye sholde girde wel þeyre [reynes] with. þe girdel þat þe ministres of hooly chirche sholde girde þeym with theire [reynes] is chastite, the whiche restreyneth þe lecherie of þe flesshe. Therfore Godde commaunded Aron þe whiche was preste and bisshopp þat he and al his childer sholde be clothed in longe cotis and girde þervppon with white lynen girdell. Aron and his childer þat served in þe temple betokened þe ministres of holy chirche þe whiche sholde be clothed in longe cotys of chastite þat betokeneth þe white lynen girdell. For liche as a lynen towaile or þat it be white moste ofte be betyn and wasshen, evyn soo þe flesshe moste be betyn and waisshyn be discipline and be sharpenesse and often to waisse his hert from evil delites and fooly desires be veraye confession or þat men maye haue þe white cote of chastite. But this cote sholde haue a white girdell above. þat is to seye þat chastite sholde be kepte streytly and wel restreyned be abstinence as fere as reeson will the whiche is þe bocle of þis girdle. [f. 171v] Men maye it seye ooþer weyes þat þe lynen coote betokeneth chastite of herte. The girdel above betokeneth þe bodye the whiche sholde restreyne þe desires of þe flesshe for to kepe þe chastite of the soule. And anamly it is betokenyd to vs in þe aube and in þe girdell þat þe ministres of holy chirch werith whan þeye sholde serve at þe auter. For theye sholde be chaste in herte within and withowte in bodye. It is a ful foule spotte of synne anamly of þe synne of lecherye in the ministres of holy chirche, as þe scripture seithe, for liche as the yen conditeth þe boodye and sheweth hym þe weye where hee sholde goo soo prestes and oother ministeres of holy chirche sholde shewe þe weye of helthe to ooþer pepil. And liche as a spotte is fouler in the yee than in anoþer membir of þe bodye, soo the spotte of lecherye is fouler and more perlious in clerkis, prestis, and prelatis than in oother laye pepil. Also theye of holy chirche sholde be mirroures of þe worlde in whom laye pepil loketh and taketh example of þeyme. And whan þe mirroure is foule, men seeth wel þe foule spotte that is þerin. But he þat loketh in sich a mirrour seeth not his owne spotte no moore þan he seeth in a mirrour þat is foule and derke. But whan þat mirrour is feire and clere and right clene þan maye hee wel see and knewe his owne spotte. On þe same wise, whan þe prelat is of a goode name ther men sholde take example of good liffyng. Alsoo þeye sholde be ful holy and clene because theye clense ooþer and maketh þeym hooly. For as Seint Gregor seith: The hande þat is foule and mirri may not do aweye the filþe of anoother ne clense ooþer. And scriptures seithe that he þat is foule maye not make another clene. This is too vnderstande as be his merite. For þe sacrement þat is made or ministred be þe hande of an evil preste is never þe wers in the selfe ne þe lesse vertuos ne þe lesse myghty to make holy þo þat resceyvith it than þat the whiche is made be the hande of a goode ministre. For the shrewdenes of þe ministre enpeirith not þe sacrement ne þe bounte þerof ne it amendith it not. But neverþelesse þe shrewdenes of þe ministre maye enpeyre oother be evil example and edifie þe bounte be example of goode liffyng. Therfor þan because þat þeye clense and maketh oother holy or because theye ministre the sacrementis [f. 172] of hooly chirche, theye sholde be holyer and clenner þan oother. For if theye be wers theye shall be moore ponysshed þan oother. This is þe vi branche and the vi state wherein that men sholde kepe chastite.

Off Chastite þat Be in Religious, CIIII^{XX}V

The vii state wherein men sholde kepe chastite is þe state of religion. For thoo þat be in that state hatthe vowed and promissed to Godde þat theye shalle liff chastly, to þe whiche theye be holden and bounden be siche vowe that theye maye never mary theyme after þat theye be professid. And if theye mary theyme, it is noo mariage. And þerfore theye sholde put grete peyne and diligens too kepe theyme chastly and for theire state þe whiche is a state of holy perfeccion. For þe hollyer þat þe state is, the fouler and the gretter is þe synne, liche as a spotte is fouler and moore shewyng in a white gowne than in anoother. And fro þe hyer þat a man falleth, the sorer is þe hurte. And for to ouercome theire aduersarie, that is, the feende þe whiche peyneth hym moste to tempte and to ouerthrowe pepil of religion and ioieth hym moste whan he maye ouercome on of theyme þan he dooþe of another astate. For liche as aungell of hevyn hatthe grete ioye of a synner whan he repenteth hym and doothe penaunce, evyn soo ioyeth feendes whan theye maye ouercome and ouerthrowe a goode man. And of þe gretter astate and þe more parfit þat he is, the more ioye haue theye whan þeye maye deceyve hym, liche as a fissher hatthe gretter ioye to take grete fisshes þan litell. Men rede in *Vitis Patrum* þat an holy man tolde howe he become a monke and seide þat he was a payenymes son þe whiche was a preste to ydoilles. And whan he was a childe on a tyme hee entred intoo a temple prevyly with his fader. Ther sawe he a grete feende the whiche was set in a [prive] place and al his mayny aboute hym. Ther come one of his princes and worshiped hym. Than hee þat sat in the trone asked hym wens he come, and he answerid þat he come froo a lande where he had purchased and meved grete werres soo þat myche pepil was dede and myche bloode shedde. The maister [f. 172v] asked hym howe longe he hadde ben þeraboute. Hee answerid þat he hadde ben aboute it xxx dayes. The maister seide to hym: Haste þou done no more in soo longe a tyme? Thow shalt be betyn. þan he commaunded hym to be betyn and to be ferde evil withal. After hym þat come another that worshiped hym as þe firste didde. The maister asked hym whens hee come, and he answerid þat he come froo þe see where he hadde made many tempestes and brokyn shippes and drowned pepil. The maister asked hym: In howe longe tyme? He answered: In xx dayes. And anoon hee made hym be bette as the tooþer was because he hadde don soo lytill in soo longe a tyme. Than come þe thirde that seide þat he come from a citee where he hadde ben atte a mariage. Þer hadde [h]e caused and meved strives and debates soo þat miche pepill was dede, and amonge al ooþer he hadde sleyn the husbonde. The maister asked hym howe longe he hadde been þeraboute. Hee answerid: X dayes. þan he commanded þat he sholde be wel beten. Atte the laste come anoother afore þe prince and worshipped hym. And [he] asked hym whens he come. He seide þat he come froo an hermytage where hee hadde ben xl yere for to tempte a monke with fornicacion, þat is to seye, with þe synne of lecherie. And he had don soo myche þat the same nyght he hadde ouercomen hym and ouerthrowen hym in þat synne. Than the maister leped vppe and halsed hym abowte þe necke and kissed hym and sette his coroune on his heede and made hym sitte by hym and seide to hym that he hadde don a grete thynge. Than the goode man whan he hadde seen and herde this thought it was a grete thynge to be a monke, and for þat cause hee become a monke. Men maye see nowe in þese examples that feendes hatthe grette ioye whan þey maye in syn overthrowe a monke of religion. For after þat a monke be entred into religion he is as he þat is entred intoo a felde for to feight with þe feende. Wherfore whan oure loorde wolde be tempted of þe feende, he wente intoo a deserte, for the desert of religion is a felde of temptacion. Religion is called deserte, for liche as deserte is a place sharpe and drye and fere from alle pepill soo þe state of religion sholde be sharpe and drye be sharpenes of liff the whiche is a stronge hecche aȝeins evil bestis and a stronge armure aȝeins the fende. This is the remedye a[f. 173]ȝeins the sinne of lecherie. For whoosoo wille stanche the fire of lecherye he moste withdrawe the kyndelynge, the whiche be the delites of the flesshe. þat is to seye þat a man of religion sholde kitte it aweye be fastynge, wakynge, be terres, and be discipline. Ellis þis fire maye not be staunched. Whoosoo wil take a castel or a citee, as myche as he myght he sholde withdrawe fro theym mete and drynke and water for too enfamine theyme. For whan the castelle is famined, it maye not be kepte aȝeins his aduersarie. Evyn soo thee castelle of þe bely, the whiche is þe forteresse of the flesshe, maye not defende it aȝeins þe sperit of þe soule whan it is famined be fastyng and be sharpe abstinence. The state of religion sholde be sette soo fere froo þe worlde that he the whiche is in siche state sholde fele noothynge þerof. Wherfore he sholde be dede as to þe worlde and liff in Godde, as Seint Poule seithe. For liche as hee that is dede bodyly hatthe loste al the bodily wittes – seynge, spekyng, tastyng, hyrynge, and smellyng – thus þe religious as too the worlde sholde be dede, soo þat theye sholde fele noothynge þat longeth too syn, soo þat hee maye veryly seye this worde that Seint Poule seith of hymselfe: The worlde, seithe hee, is crucified to me and I too þe worlde. He [wolde] sey as þat þe worlde helde hym for vile and abhominable liche as men holdeth hym þat is crucified for his evil dede. Thus sholde he hate þe worlde that is in state of perfeccion, þat is to seye, the covetice and the shrewdenes of þe worlde þat he fele not þerof be dede ne be desire, soo that the conuersacion maye be in hevyn, as Seint Poule seiþe of hym and of ooþer þe whiche be in þe state of perfeccion. Oure conuersacion, seithe hee, is in hevyn. For though þe bodye be in erthe, the herte is in hevyn. A goode religious sholde in erthe haue nothynge propre, but he sholde make his tresor in hevyn. As þe gospell seiþe: If þou wilte, seithe hee, be parfite, goo and selle al that thowe haste and ȝiff it too poore pepill. The tresor of a religious man is veraye pouertee, the whiche cometh of goode wille, as an holy man seithe in *Vitis Patrum*: Pouertee, seithe hee, is þe moneye wherwith men bieth the reaume of paradis. Therfore oure loorde seithe: Blessed be the poore in sperit, for the kyngdom of hevyn is þeires. Forsoothe, whoosoo is pore of sperit, that is to seye, of wille hee desireth in this worlde neyther delites ne richesses ne worshippes but forȝeteth al for Godde. Thus sholde a goode religiouse [f. 173v] man doo, the whiche wil assende in the hylle of perfeccion. Wherfore þe angell seide to Loth whan hee was goon oute of Sodome: Reste the not, seiþe hee, nere þe place þat þou art comen oute of, but saue þe on þe hille. For he þat is comen oute of þe conuersacion of the worlde sholde not holde hym nere þe worlde be wil ne be desire but besye hym as myche as hee myght to þat he be in the hille of perfeccion. There sholde hee take heede to his helthe withowte lokyng behynde hym.

Lothes wyff behelde the citee þat brent behynde hirre, þe whiche shee was comyn oute of. And therfore was shee chaunched intoo an ymage of a salt stone. Loothes wiff betokeneth þoo þat after that theye be gon oute of þe worlde and be entred into religion be wille and be desire the whiche hatthe þe bodye in þe cloister and the hert in the worlde. Theye be liche þe ymage of salte the whiche hatthe but the liknes of þe man, and also it is harde and colde as a stone. Soo be siche pepill colde in the louff of Godde and harde withoute moisture of pytee and of devocion. Wherfore theye haue but þe habite of religion. The ymage was of salt, the whiche in scripture betokeneth wit and discrecion. For liche as salt ȝeffeth sauour, soo a man sholde haue witt and discrecion in his dedis and in his wordes. This ymage of salt sholde than ȝiff vnderstandynge and example to þoo of religion that hatthe lefte the worlde that theye torne not aȝein too that the whiche theye haue lefte. And therfore seithe oure loorde in the gospell to his disciples þat folwed hym: Vmbethynke ȝowe, seide he, of Lothes wyff. That is to seye, take noo heede of the liff of the worlde the whiche ȝe haue lefte for me, þat ȝe lese not þe liff of grace and of ioye as Lothes wiff loste the liff of the bodye because þat she tooke heede to þat the whiche shee hadde lefte. Wherfore oure loorde seithe in the gospell that he þat putteth his hande to þe plowe and looketh behynde hym is not worthe to have þe kyngedom of hevyn nor of Godde. For liche as hee þat kepeth the plough looketh euer before hym for to erre wel, soo sholde hee doo that putteth his hande to the ploughe of penaunce or of religion, the whiche sholde alweye haue the yen of the herte, that is to seye, the vnderstandyng too that the whiche is afore and not to that the whiche is behynde, that is too seye, too euerlastynge goodes, the whiche in the herte sholde be tofore, and not to temporell goodes that sholde be behynde, that is þe worlde [f. 174] and al his couetice, the whiche is not to prayse. And he sholde alweye goo befor hym. And hee sholde ever haue his entent, the whiche is the right yee, that is to seye, his desire in hevyn. But myche pepill of religion setteth the plough afore the oxen, the whiche is theire hurte. For ther bee many that desireth temporelle thyngys moore than spirituell. Þey sette before that the whiche theye sholde put behynde, temporell goodes before, euerlastynge goodes behynde. Siche religious pepill be in grete perille of theire dampnacion, for theye haue but þe habit of religion. Be the example of Seint Poule, a goode religious man sholde forȝete the worlde and sette it behynde hym and haue alweye the euerlastynge goodes afore his yen and goo ever forthe froo vertu to vertu too þat he come to þe Mon[tio]ye, that is too seye, to þe hille of euerlastyng ioye, where he shalle see Godde clerely and louff hym parfitly. This is þe blissednes to the whiche the ȝifte of vnderstandyng bringeth thoo þat kepeth clennes of herte and of body, as wee haue shewed and seide afore. This blessednes begynneth here. For theye be clensed from derkenes of erroure as to þe vnderstandyng and fro spotes of syn as too þe wille. And therfore see theye Godde be feith enlumined with the clerenes of Godde, the whiche cometh of the ȝifte of vnderstandyng wherebye man knoweth his creature and þat the whiche longeth to helthe of his sowle withoute doutynge and withoute fallyng and withoute brekyng the feithe of Criste Iesus, wherein theye be soo stedefastly grounded that theye wille not parte þerfroo for dethe ne for tourment. And þerfore tho þat be clene of hert be blessed in this liff, as wee haue seide. Wherefore oure loorde seide to Seint Thomas: Because, seide hee, that thow haste seen me thowe haste leved me, but blessed be tho þat hath not seen me bodily and b[e]levith me certeinly. And this blessednes shalle be parfit in euerlastynge liff with tho þat be clene of herte, the whiche seeth it here be feithe neverthelesse but derkely, but ther theye shalle see it face to face, opinly, as Seint Poule seithe. This is þe blessednes of aungellis that they shalle see and of seintes the whiche shalle see Godde in the face, wherein that aungellis and seintes beholdeth theyme and merveileth theyme, and theye maye never be fulle of the behaldyng of hym, for þer is al beaute, al bounte, alle swetnes, welle of euerlastynge liff, and al that ever herte maye wilne and desire of goodnes. But I seye [f. 174v] litill. For as the scripture seithe: Dedly ye maye not beholde, ne ere here, ne herte of man thynke that the whiche Godde ordeyneth for his frendes. Wherfore Seint Anseaume seithe: Soule, seithe hee, lifte vp thyn vnderstandyng þer above and thynke as myche as þou maiste howe myche and howe grete and howe delictable is þe goodnes þat kepeth þe ioye and þe delit of al goodenesses. Not only siche delit and siche ioye as men fynde in this worlde, but as miche gretter as the creature is gretter than the creatures, soo myche is the ton gretter than the toother. O, seithe he, man, feture of man, what goost thowe follying for to seeke dyuers goodes to thye sowle and to thye bodye? Louff o goode the whiche is al goodes and þat sufficith to þe. This is the goode þat God graunteth to his frendes, that is, hymselfe the whiche is souereyne goode of the whiche al oother risseth as riueres doothe of a welle. This blessed vision is the blessednes that thoo abide that kepeth here clenly bothe herte and bodye.

Off the ȝifte of Wysdome, CIIII^{XX}VI

The laste and the souereigne ȝifte and the hyest is the ȝifte of wysdome, the whiche is a grace þat the Holy Goost ȝiffeth too a contemplatif hert. Be the whiche he is soo ouertakyn with the louff of Godde that he desireth ne requireth noon other thynge but to see hym and too haue hym and to delit in hym and to dwelle with hym. This is þe somme of perfeccion and the ende of contemplacion. The ȝifte of vnderstandynge of þe whiche we haue spokyn afore maketh Godde to be knowen and gostly thyngys, as be sight and be simple beholdyng. But the ȝifte of wisdome maketh it to be felt and knowen be taste. Wherfor wisdom is not ellis but a sauoury knowleche, the whiche with sauoure and with grete swetnes of hert tasteth it. For he þat sauoureth and tasteth wyne knoweth it al oother weyes [t]han hee þat seeth it in a feire verre. Many philozophris knewe Godde be the scriptures, liche as thorough a mirrour wherein theye looked be feithe and be vnderstandynge, his worthinesse, his bounte, his witt, his beaute. Therfore theye knewe it wel be sight and symple beholdynge of vnderstandynge and naturel reson, but theye felt never noght be taste of swett [f. 175] louff ne be deuocion. On the same wise ther be many Cristen men, bothe clerkys and layemen, þat knoweth it wel be feithe and be scripture, but because that theire taste is vnordinat be syn theye maye not fele it no more than a seke man fyndeth sauour in goode mete. And the ȝifte of wisdom the whiche setteth the ȝifte of the Holy Gooste parfitly in the herte purgeth it and clensith it of al harlotry of synne and reyseth soo the sperit of man that he ioyneth hym with God be a grete louff soo þat he is al oon with Godde. And he vmbethynketh hym but of that the whiche he louffeth, that is God alonly. This is þe laste degree of the ledder of perfeccion that Iacob sawe slepyng, the whiche atteigned to hevyn, wherby aungelles monted and descended. The degrees of this leder be þe degrees of the Hooly Gooste of the whiche wee haue spokyn. Be these vii degrees mounteth angellis. Theye be thoo that ledeth angellis liff in erthe be clennesse of conscience the whiche hatthe theire hertis in hevyn be desiryng it whan theye goo profityng fro vertu to vertu too þat theye see Godde opinly and parfitly. But whan theye be monted to þe laste degree, theym behovith somtyme too descende be mekenes, for the parfiter þat a man is the more he is obeying and þe lesse prayseth hymselfe. Therfore men be wonte to seye: The moore he is woorthe, the lowlyer he is. Wherfore a goode parfit man sholde be as a tree that the moore it is charged with fruit the more it boweth to the herthe. Also men maye vnderstande this be the descendynge of angellis. For goode men the whiche in erthe ledith aungellis liff be theire holynes whan theye be mounted to þe souerein degree of contemplacion theder as the ȝifte of wisdom ledith, he the whiche sholde be ioyned to Godde soo þat hee forȝetith al that is vnder God for þe grete swetnesse þat the herte felith the whiche is thus ravisshed in Godde þat it passeth alle oother delite. A reeson ther is whye he moste descende from soo hye a degree of contemplacion whider that the ȝifte of wisdom ledith hym. The answer is for the corrupcion of the flesshe is soo grete þat the sperit in this dedly liff maye not longe abide in soo hye astate of contemplacion ne sustine þat grete swetnesse the whiche passeth al the delites that men maye fele in this worlde, as theye knowe that hatthe proved it. Therfore the conterpeise of the flesshe is soo hevy [f. 175v] that it dredith the evil sperit wedir it wil or noon. And therfore this grete swetnesse that a contemplatiff herte felith be the ȝifte of wisdom in this dedly liff is but a litil taste whereby men sauoreth and felith howe

Godde is softe and easy, liche as a man tasteth the sauour of wyne or that he drynke his fille. But whan he shalle come too that grete tauerne where þat the grete haboundant tauerner is soo habaundoned, þat is to seye, in euerlastyng liff where the Godde of louff, of pees, of ioye, and of soolas is soo haboundant too euery creature that al theye shalle be filled, as the Saulter seithe, soo that hertely desyres shalle be fulfilled. For Godde shalle make a floode of pees to descende opon his frendes, as the prophete seithe, of the whiche they shal be dronken. Of this dronkenes, Dauid in the Saulter spekith and seithe thus of the blisse of paradis: Sire, al shalle be dronken of the greete plente that is in ȝoure house. And ȝe shalle ȝiff theyme drinke of the floode of yourre swetnesse and of youre delite. For with yowe is the welle [of liffe] that maye not dye. Of the whiche welle above al the seintis that is in paradis riseth a floode of ioye, of delit, and of pees soo greet þat al tho þat shall drynke therof shalle be dronken. This is the pees and the blessednes the whiche is in the worlde that is for to come. For too haue þat and to wynne it, men sholde liff sobirly, as Seynt Austin seithe. For þer is noon that drinketh of þis ryuer of pees ne that is dronken of þat plente of ioye but if he kepe sobirnes. For that is the vertu that the ȝifte of wisdom planteth in the herte aȝeins the outerage of glotonye. For wisdom techith sobirnes, as Salamon seithe.

Howe Sobirnes Setteth Mesure in Vnderstandynge, CIIII^{XX}VII

Sobirnes is a fulle precious tree, as the scripture seithe, for it kepeth the helthe of the soule and of the bodye. And of glotonye and of outeragiousnes of mete and drinke cometh myche harme and sekenesses and often deþe. For be to myche drinke and be too myche mete dieth ofte myche pepill. And oftentymes sodeyn dethe taketh theyme liche as men taketh fisshe with beite, that is to seye, with the mete in the moothe. Firste sobirnes taketh heede too reeson and too þe vnderstandyng [f. 176] of his freedom the whiche dronkenes taketh fro hym. For hee þat is dronken is soo ouertaken with wyne þat he lesith boþe reeson and vnderstandynge and

[b]eeth as he that is drouned in wyne. The seconde goode þat sobirnes doothe is þat it delyuereth a man from to foule a thraldome, that is to seye, froo the thraldom of the wombe. For gloutones and outeragious pepill of metes maketh of theire wombe theire Godde, as Seint Poule seithe. Truly he fouleth hymselfe gretely that serveth soo foule a loorde as is his wombe, of þe whiche maye nothynge come oute but harlotrie and filþe. Sobirnes kepeth a man in his lordeshippe. For the sperit sholde be lorde of the bodye and the bodye sholde serve the sperit. And this ordre kepeth wel sobirnes. The þirde goode that sobirnes doothe is þat it kepeth þe ȝeate of þe porche of chastite aȝeins the feendes oste, that is to seye, the mouthe, the whiche is maister ȝeate of the castell of the herte, the whiche þe feende assailleth as myche as he maye. But sobirnes denyeth hym the ȝeate, that is to seye, the mouthe. And whan the ȝeate of the mouthe is opyn, the oste of syn entreth lightly. And he that kepeth not his tonge feighteth for noght aȝeins oother synnes. Whoosoo hatthe this vertu hatthe the lordeshippe of his bodye, liche as þe maister hatthe þe maistri of his hors be the bridill. Sobirnes hatthe the firste bataille in the oste of vertues and kepeth and defendeth oother vertues. Wherfore the feende tempted oure lorde firste toward the mouþe whan he seide to hym þat hee sholde make brede of þe stones. Hee assayled alsoo þe firste man toward the mouthe and ouercome hym, for he openyd to hym thee ȝeate of his castell whan he consented to þe temptacion. In this nature techeth vs that men sholde ete litill and drinke litil, for nature is sustened with litil and be to myche mete it is corromped. The scripture techeth vs sobirnes in many manerz and be many examples, as theye maye see that maye vnderstande scriptures and that kepeth the liff of holy pepill. Alsoo al creatures techith sobirnes, for in alle creatures Godde hatthe set right mesure, as Salamon seithe in hooly scripture. Sobirnes is too kepe right and mesure the whiche holdeth euer the mene betwene myche and lytil. But in these temporell goodes that the whiche is too litill too on is to myche too an nother; that the whiche is outerage in a poore man of[tesythe] sholde be fulle litille too a riche man. But sobirnes setteth mesure oueralle. Seint Austin seithe that þe vertue [f. 176v] of temperance and

of sobirnes is a louff þat beholdeth Godde entierly and withdraweth vs froo this louff here benethe, that is to seye, froo þe louff of this worlde, the whiche trobeleth miche the herte and setteth it in vnease and taketh from it the right knowleche of Godde and of hymselfe, liche as þat men seeth not clerely in trouble water. But the louff of Godde the whiche is clensid from alle erthely louff and from al flesshely louff setteth þe herte in pees. For it setteth the hert in his propre plas and easeth it, that is to seye, in Godde. There it restith and is in pees and hatthe no ioye ne reste but there. Wherfore oure loorde seithe in the gospelle: ȝe shalle be empressed in this worlde, but in me ȝe shalle fynde pees. And Seint Austin seide: Sire, myn herte maye not be in pees vnto þat it reste in yowe. Siche louff risseth not of the erþe ne of þe mareis of this worlde, but it discendeth froo that hye rooche [vppon] the whiche is set and founded the grete citee of hooly chirche and of paradis. This is Criste Iesus, [vppon] the whiche is sette and founded stedfastly be right feithe stronge castellis, the whiche be hertis of goode men. Froo that hye rooche descendeth that welle of louff intoo an herte þat is porged froo worldly louff. That welle is soo clere and soo stille that the herte knoweth hymselfe and seeth þerin hymselfe and his creature, liche as men maye see a thyng in a feire welle that is right clere and stille. On þat wel resteth the herte after the trauaille of goode dedes, as wee reede of oure loorde Criste Iesus, that whan he hadde goon so myche that he was wery he rested hym and sette hym on the welle. The welle [vppon] the whiche a goode herte sholde reste hym is the louff of Godde. That welle is soo swete and soo amerous that he that drinketh þerof forȝeteth al oother swetnes and al oother sauour. That welle feleth not the [myre ne the erthe] ne þe mares of this worlde. And therfore it is swete and sauoury to drinke, for the lesse þat þe welle feleth of the erthe the better and the softer it is to drinke. This is the welle of wit and of sauour. For whoosoo drinketh therof hee knoweth and feleth and sauoreth the grete swetnes þat is in Godde. And this is the chef wit of this worlde and of man for to knowe wel his creature and to louff hym with al his herte. For withoute þat philozophy al oother witte is but folie. Siche witte putteth the Hooly Gost into the herte whan he ȝiffeth it the ȝifte of wisdom, [f. 177] the whiche fedeth þe herte with gostely ioye and ȝifeth it drinke and maketh it dronken of holy louff. This gostly witt that cometh of the parfit louff of Godde maketh the herte sobre and temperat and mesured in alle thynge soo that the herte that is in siche state is in pees as þat men maye be in this dedly lyff. For in this worlde none maye liff withoute tourment or withoute some bataille of temptacion, the whiche God sendeth for to prove with his knyghtis because that they sholde covnne vse vertues and theire armes, for theye maye not ellys be goode knyghtis. And therfore men were wonte to make tournementis in tyme of pees. But whan a goode knyght hatthe wonne the tournement, he retourneth to his inne where þat he resteth hym there wele at ease. Soo doothe a goode herte whan it hatthe wel foughten and ouercomme the tormentis of temptacion. He commeth aȝein to hymselfe and resteth hym with Godde, the whiche stedfasteth hym after his trauaile soo that hee forȝeteth al the trauailles that he hatthe hadde and thynketh but on Godde, where he fyndeth al that he desireth. This is the fruit that the tree of sobirnes berith, the whiche cometh of the ȝifte of wisdom, as I haue afore bothe seide and shewed. Sobirnes is not ellis but for too kepe right mesure in al thynges. But specially men sholde kepe mesure in vii thyngis, the whiche be as vii degrees be the whiche the tree of sobirnes groweth and encressith.

The Firste Degree of Sobirnes

The firste degree of sobirnes is a man to sette mesure in his vnderstandyng, specially in pointis and articlis of the feithe of the whiche wee haue spokyn afoore. He passeth mesure þat wil seke naturel reeson in that the whiche is above reeson and above þe vnderstandyng of man, as lolleris doothe and mysbelevyng pepil, the whiche wil mesure the feithe after theire vnderstandynge and theire reeson. Theye sholde mesure theire vnderstandynge and theire reeson after the feithe, as goode Cristen men doo. Therfore Seint Poule seithe that men sholde not bee wyser than reeson bringeth to theyme but be wise be sobirnes after the mesure of the feithe that Godde hatth ȝovyn vs. And Salamon seithe to his sone: Feire sone, seithe hee, sette mesure too thy witte. That is to seye þat [f. 177v] thowe be not soo selfe-willed ne soo sette in thi presumpcion that thowe [f]lette not to beleve goode counsell and but as that thowe maye leve thyn owne witte for to beleve and obeye too a better than thyne. And specially in þe articlis of the feithe a man sholde leve his owne witt and remeve his vnderstandynge and put it intoo thraldom of the feithe, as Seint Poule seithe. Spute not ne seke naturell reeson where none is, as besy and malencolious pepil doo the whiche be liche to thoo þat seketh þe molle in mollehilles or too hym þat seketh þe skyn in the egge or to hym þat seketh þe cloude in the resshe.

The Seconde Degree of Sobirnesse

The seconde degree of sobirnes is a man to put mesure in apetite and in goode wille of desire that a man lete not the bridelle rynne to myche too flesshely desires and to þe covetice of this worlde. Folwe not, seithe he, þe desires of thyn herte ne thye covetises. Torne thy wille that thowe fulfille it not and set the vppon goode reeson. For if thowe doo þe desires of thyn herte, thowe shalt glade thyn enemyes, that is to seye, feendes, as hee gladeth his enemy aȝeyns whom he sholde feighte whan he feleth hym overcomyn to hym. He ȝoldeth hym too the feende as ouercomen, þe whiche consenteth too his eville desires. Therfore seithe Seint Peter þe postle: I coniure ȝowe, seith hee, as strangeris and pilgrimes that ȝe kepe ȝowe from flesshely desires, the whiche is the feendes armie aȝeyns the soule. He þat is a pilgrime in a straunge contre wher many theefes and robberes bee, the whiche spieth pilgrimes and wayteth the weyes, hee kepeth hym gretly that hee falle not in the theefes handes and thynketh myche howe hee maye goo surely. Alle the goode men in this worlde be pilgrimes and strangeris. Theye be strangeris, for theye be oute of theire countre, that is to seye, oute of paradis, the whiche is the contre and the right heritage of goode men. And theye be pilgrimes, for theye thynke not but for to doo theire iorneye vnto þat they maye come too theire heritage, that is to seye, to the citee of paradis, the whiche goode pilgrimes seketh, as Seint Powle seithe, þat hatthe noon heritage ne wil noon haue in this worlde. Siche pilgrimes as wil goo surely putteth theyme in goode feleshipp. That ledith theym right and conditeth surely is feithe and louff. Feithe sheweth þe [f. 178] weye to þe pilgrime, but louff ledith hym soo that the weye costeth hym litil or nought. Whoosoo hatthe þat feleshipp setteth not be the theefes that wayteth the weyes whiche be the feendes þat taketh and robbeth al thoo þat goothe in theire feleshipp. Theye bee thoo þat here wil doo theyre desires the whiche putteth theyme into the handes and the snaris of the feende. But feithe and louff of Godde withholdeth the herte and retorneth it from evil thoughtis and from fals desires soo þat theye consent not too theyme liche as men withholdeth a birde be gesses that he maye not flee atte his wille. And ȝiff it be not withholden be gesses of feithe and of louff it fleeth perlyously soo þat it lesseth þe selfe and often falleth intoo þe snares of þe fouler of helle, the whiche be feendes þat hunteth not but for to take siche birdes. Therfore goode men and wyse withholdeth theire willes, theire thoughtes, and theire desires be temperance and be sobirnes. Wherfore Seneque seithe: If thowe wilte be soobre and temperat, kit aweye and withdrawe thye desires and set a bridill too thye covetises. For liche as an hors is holden be the bridelle that hee goo not atte his wille, soo a man sholde holde aȝeyn his hert be the bridill of soobirnes that he baundon it not to the wille of the covetise of þe worlde.

The Thirde Degree of Sobirnesse

The thirde degree of sobirnes is to sette and to kepe mesure in woordes. Wherfore Salamon seithe that a wyse man and a well-taughte tempereth and mesureth his woordes. And Seint Ierom seithe that in fewe woordes is proved the liff of man. That is too seye, opon the woordes men maye knowe the wytte and the foolye of man liche as men knoweth an hogge be the crie of the tonge if he be clene. And therfore seithe the wyse man in scripture that the woordes of a wyse man be peysed in the balance of discrecion and of reeson soo that ther be not to repreve. Ther be some pepill that maye not be stille and taketh noo heede what theye seye bee it trewe be it false, the whiche fareth as a mille that alweye torneth after the cours of the water þat is withoute a scluse, for theye haue as many woordes as ther cometh water to the mille. But a wyse man setteth a scluse of discrecion for too holde in þe outeragious and the lewde woordes þat theye passe not be the [f. 178v] mille of the tonge. And therfore seithe the wyse man in scripture: Lete not the water goo, that is too seye, withholde thye woordes with the scluse of discrecion. For as Salamon seithe: Whoosoo leteth the water goo at his liste it causeth ofte plee and striff and myche harme, the whiche cometh of an eville tonge, as I han shewed longe agone in the tretice of vices where I spake afore of þe syn of þe tonge. Therfore the wise man seithe fulle wel in scripture: Set, seithe hee, thye wordes in balance and a goode bridelle in thye mouthe and take heede þat thowe falle not be þy tonge afore thyn enemyes þat spieth the. For whoosoo weyeth not his woordes in the balaunce of discrecion and withholdeth not his tonge from evil woordes, hee falleth lightly in the handes of his enemies the whiche be feendes þat waiteth vs and spieth vs oueralle. Whan enemyes þat werreyeth a castell fyndeth the ȝeate opyn, theye entre lightly. And therfore seithe Dauid in the Sauter: I haue, seithe hee, set garde on my mouthe aȝeins myn enemyes, the whiche bee feendes that be euer aȝeins me. The garde of the mouthe is reeson and discrecion the whiche examineth the wordis whan theye goo oute of the mouthe. That is the balance of the whiche the wyse man speketh, as I haue seide afoore, where the woorde sholde be peysed or it be seide. And thowe shalt wite that trouthe holdeth his balaunce right, for trouthe accordeth the entent of the herte [...]. And this balaunce sholde not hynge neyþer on the right side ne of the lefte. Neyther for louff ne for prayer of persone ne for temporell availe ne for hate of oþer men sholde not lette to seie trouthe there where men sholde and whan nede is, but lyes and falsnes men sholde not seye for none.

The Fourthe Degree

The fourthe degree of sobirnes is that as men sholde kepe mesure in spekynge soo men sholde kepe it in hyrynge and herkenynge. For men maye as welle synne in evill hyrynge as in evil spekynge. Wherfore hee þat herith gladly mysseyerris is partoner of the synne and felawe to hym þat seithe it. For noon wolde gladly seye evil of oother anamly toofore a grete man ȝif hee supposed not too pleese hym that herith it. Wherfore an hoolye man seithe that ther sholde be none mysseyer if þer were none mysseherer. These grete men sholde gretely take heede what theye hire and whom theye beleve, [f. 179] for theye fynde fewe þat seeth theym trouthe but flatererris and lierris in theyre courtes be greet chepe. The grettest derthe that theye haue aboute theyme is of trouþe and of soothenes. And therfore be theye often deceyved, for gladly theye here and lightly beleve that the whiche plesith theyme. Seneque seithe that grete loordes failleth not but sotheseyerris, for lierris haue theye grete chepe. Men sholde ever haue theyre erris opyn gladly too hire goode woordes that vaileth too soulehele and cloos to lewde and to evil wordes the whiche maye noye and maye not helpe. Wherfore þe wise man seithe: Stoppe ȝoure erris with thornes and hirre neyther mysseyerris ne evil woordes ne evil tonges. An evil tonge is the tonge of the serpent of helle the whiche e[n]venemed hym that hirith it. Aȝeins that tonge men sholde stoppe their erris with thornes, that is too seye, with the fere of God or with the thornes wherewhith Godde was corouned be remembrance of þe passi[on] of Crist Iesus. For whoosoo hadde fere of Godde and remembrance of the passion of oure loorde, hee wolde not gladly hirre mysseierris ne flatererris ne lewde woordes ne dishonest. Also men maye vnderstande this woorde, stoppe thyn erris with thornes, þus: The thornes þat pricketh betokeneth harde wordes and sharpe of þe whiche men sholde repreve mysseyerris and make theyme be stille, and men sholde make countenance not to be gladde to hire it. Whoosoo coude stoppe his erris þus hee sholde not gladly hire ne remembre thynge þat sholde displese Godde, and alsoo he sholde be welle-tempered in hyrynge and herkenynge.

The Fifthe Degree

The fifthe degree is to kepe mesure in cloothynge and in precious roobis, wherin men passeth often mesure and dooþe myche outerage. And because þat the outerage is grete synne and ȝefeth often cause too other for to synne, men sholde kepe mesure in siche thyngis. For if too precious and to beesy arayes were noo synne oure loorde hadde not spokyn soo actaignyauntly þerof in the gospelle aȝeyns the evil riche man the whiche clothed them with [f. 179v] right precious pourple. And truly he is a grete childe of witte þat prydeth hym for his gowne. Siche garmentis and siche vsage of roobes is a signe the whiche was not founde but be the synne of oure firste fadir for to couvir his confusion and oures. Whan a man seeth a beere arayed it is a tokyn þat ther is a dede bodye therin. Soo it falleth often that vnder feire cloothis þe soule is dede be synne anamly in hym or hirre that ioyeth theym and prideth theym therin. If the pecok be proude of his taile and the cocke of his combe it is no merveyle, for nature ȝiffeth hym and he doothe after nature. But man and womman the whiche hatthe reeson and witte and woote wel that nature ȝaf hym not siche cloothyng hee sholde not be proude of þe araynge of his bodye ne of the queintises of his heede. Therfore the wyse man seithe in scripture: Ioye the never in feire cloothis. And Seint Poule seiþe that women sholde araye theym with sobirnes, that is to seye, be mesure withouten outerage after þat the state of the persone requireth. Truly it is not withoute outerage þat oo persone shalle haue soo many arayes and roobes for his bodye and of dyuers maneres with the whiche myche pepill myght be susteyned with the surfet. Ȝit if theye were atte the laste ȝovyn for Godde it were somwhat, but theye be ȝovyn to ribaudes, the whiche is grete synne. Therfore men sholde kepe mesure in siche thyngis after that the state of the persone requireth, as I haue seide afoore.

The VI Degree of Temperance and of Sobirnes

The vi degree of temperance and of sobirnes is that euery man kepe mesure and goode maner in his countenance and in his behavynge. Wherfore Seneque seithe: If thowe be soobre and temperat, take heede that the mevyngis of thyn herte and of thy bodye be not foule nee vngoodly. For of þe foule ordenaunce of the herte cometh foule ordounance [of] þe bodye. Ther be somme soo enfantesied and of soo nyce maneres þat theye make theyme be holden for fooles. It longeth gretly too a man of valu and of grete astate too be wel sette and mesured in al his dedes and in al his seynggys and of feire countenaunce afore al pepil soo þat noon maye take evil example in hym and that hee be not holden neyther for a foole ne for a childe. Wherfore Seint Poule seide of hymselfe: Whan I was, seide hee, a childe, I didde as a childe; but sithen þat I come to age of man, I lefte alle my childehoode. For whoosoo holdeth a man of age a childe, hee holdeth hym for a foole. And therfore seithe Seint Poule: Be not a childe of witte, but in malice be litil. It is nowe a feire thynge and an honeste and a profitable and a worshipful to man and to womman [f. 180] anamly too grete pepill to kepe resonable mesure in behavynge and in countenaunce and that men be wel sette afoore Godde and afoore the pepill. This is the vi degree of this tree.

The VII Degree of Equity

The vii degree of temperance is to sette mesure in drinkynge and etynge. For the outerage of drinke and of mete doothe myche harme to the bodye and too the soule, as I haue seide longe afoore. Therfore oure loorde seithe in the gospell: Take ȝe heede that ȝoure hertis be not grevyd ne charched with glotonye ne with dronkenes, that is to seye, that ȝee doo noone outerage of drinke. Sobirnes kepeth mesure in drinkynge and in etynge that men doo none outerage. Of outerages þat men doo in drinke and in mete therof haue I spoken inoughe in the tretie of vices whan I spake of the syn of glotonye, to whom this vertu of the whiche I speke here is in especial contrarie. And therfore I wille noo more speke therof. Nowe haste thowe herde the degrees whereby this tree groweth and profiteth. And if thowe wilt knowe the branches of this tree, beholde al the toother vertues. For as I haue seide and shewed afore, this vertu is mesured amonge al the toother vertues for the whiche I wil set noon oother branches but the vertues aforeseide. This tree berith ful feire fruit and ful sauoury, that is to seye, pees of herte, as I haue seide afoore and touched. For hee that hatthe this vertu he hatthe dese[vr]ed his herte froo the louff of the worlde and ioyned it soo too God be charitee, the whiche is Goddys dere louff, that hee forȝethet al oother thynge that is not set to Godde. And in siche wise the herte resteth it in Godde where he hatthe al his conforte, his ioye, and his delit, the whiche passeth al oother delite. Siche conforte, siche delite setteth þe Hooly Gooste in a herte þat is parfit in the vertu of sobirnes the whiche cometh of the ȝifte of wisdom, as I haue seide afoore. Sertis whoosoo myght haue and feele siche pees of herte as that he myght reste it in Godde the whiche is the ende and the fulfillynge and the somme of his desires he were right happy in this worlde and in the toþer, for he sholde haue wonne the blessednesse that God promisseþ in the gospell too thoo þat withowte brekynge shalle kepe þis pees, whan he seithe: Blessed be the pesible, for theye shalle be called Goddis childer. Thoo be pesible, Seint Austin seithe, þe whiche setteth al the mevyngys of the herte vnder the lordship of right reson and of the sperit. Thoo be called right Goddes childer, for theye bere the likenes of theire fader the which [f. 180v] is the Godde of louff and of pees, as Seint Poule seithe. Wherfore pees and the louff of Godde is the thynge that maketh it to be moste like to Godde and the contrarie too þe feende the whiche is enemy to Godde. Alsoo theye be called Goddes childer, for theye folue theire fader nereere þan oother. For pees and louff foloweth nereerre þan any ooþer vertu. Alsoo theye doo the dedes of theire fader. For Godde come never intoo erthe but for to make pees betwene Godde and man, betwene man and angell, and betwene man and hymselfe. Therfor whan he was borne angellis sange: *Et in terra pax hominibus* because of the pees that Godde hadde brought in erthe. And therfore than because þat the pesible sekyth but pees and purchasseth it of Godde as myche as theye maye and of þeyre negheborughes and of theymeselfe, theye be called Goddis childer. Theye be blessed in this worlde specially be grace. þis blessednes shalle be parfite whan theye shalle be in pesible possession in the heritage of theire fadir, that is to seye, of the kyngdom of hevyn where theye shalle be in sure pees and where alle delites shalle be complised. For there maye neyther be evil ne woo ne aduersitee but haboundance of al goodnes and plentee of blisse and ioye withouten ende. That shalle be a worshipful pees, a delitable pees, and an euerlastynge pees and a pees that surmounth and passeth alle wittes. It passeth alle oother woordes. For herte maye not thynke ne tonge devise what thynge Godde ordeyneth for his freendes. And therfore I wille no more seye but he[re] shalle ende my mater to the glorie of oure lorde where al the worshippe is, the whiche lede vs intoo his feleshipp there where euerlastyng liff is. Amen seye euery man.

A frere off the ordre of prechoures made and compiled this booke opon the gospell and opon holy scripture and auctoriteis of seintes atte þe requeste of Kynge Phelip of Fraunce in the ȝere of oure lorde m^{l}ii^{c}iiii^{xx} and ix. *Deo gracias.*

Textual Notes

All French and Latin readings are taken from MS P.

9 dedly synnes generall] generall synnes, *Fr.* pechies mortelz generalment, *see notes.* **15** Of *follows* the, woodenes *begins new line.* **48** hatthe to] hatthe of to, of *expuncted. Chapter 36 is lacking in both table and text.* **86** whiche *supplied, see notes.* **127** right worshipfull] right and worshipfull, *Fr.* bien honourable. **149** fere *supplied, Fr.* paour. **161** mekenes *supplied, Fr.* humilite. **164** vii] vi. **171** clerely] cherely. **208** bataile *supplied, Fr.* bataille. **212** gostely] flesshely *supplied from the text, Fr.* espiritueles, *see notes.* **214–8** *items reversed to coincide with text, see notes.* **243** whiche *supplied, Fr.* qui. **255–6** *supplied from table of contents.* **272** metemus] metuemus. **284–5** honor] homo; premium] primum; presistens] prestens, *see notes.* **315** viam] via. **316** to *supplied, Fr.* cestadire. **327** hadde labored] hadde labrd labored, labrd *expuncted.* **396** the snare] brethe, *Fr.* lain, *see notes.* **408** mariolos] mariobe. **409–10** interficiam eam] interficiam meam; de medio populi mei *supplied.* **414–5** et execratis] extracis, et *supplied.* **415–6** mendacibus] mandacibus. **416** erit *supplied.* **435** and *supplied, Fr.* et. **438** ceteris] teris. **459** be] b. **498** iuged] in god, *Fr.* adiugie. **542** quod] qui. **594** whiche is but] is *inserted by caret.* **602** they] ther, *Fr.* ils. **604** we *supplied, Fr.* nous. **612–3** In genesi legitur fiat lux *supplied.* **616** percussum] precussum. **636** Apocalipsim] Apocalipsi. **637** que] qui. **645** debemus] de bonis. **646** Dominica] Dominica festinare, festinare *expuncted.* **647** procedamus] damus. **650** citharisantes] extharisantes. **651** ridentes] ridantes. **651–2** et alia multa dicit que homines in festo faciunt *supplied;* vero] non. **657** commendans] commendas. **667** smotte] shette, *Fr.* ferue. **671** was *supplied, Fr.* nen demoura oncques nul. **710**

is] they, *Fr.* est. **723** the] th *with bar through ascender.* **748** folysshe] foysshe. **751** estamme] destamme, *see notes.* **764** iii] iiii. **818–9** sanguinis] sanguis. **840** the whiche] be the whiche. **896** many ... sonez] many or be ther sonez men, *transposition, Fr.* moult dommes et de filz; they] ther. **908** gretnes] grettest, *Fr.* grandeur. **939–40** wonte to seye] wonte to to seye. **941** made man] ego made man. **957–8** abusage and of] abusage of, *Fr.* abusage et de. **966** inuito] merito. **975** baraturs] baratus. **985–6** moneye my] moneye my my *catchword.* **997** vii] iiii. **1030** noye othir] noye non othir, *Fr.* nuire a autri. **1035** for no] or for no. **1036** thynge] thyge. **1038** be. But] be for but, for *expuncted.* **1042** that a man] that whan a man, *Fr.* car un homme. **1073** losengery] losengerys. **1092** and coveitith] and coveithi coveitith, coveithi *expuncted.* **1114** and than] and h than, h *expuncted.* **1137** omnium] omni. **1146** vii] ii, *see notes;* foure] fourthe. **1164** persone] sone persone, sone *expuncted.* **1223** general] generally, *Fr.* general. **1272** draweth *supplied, Fr.* trait. **1304** if *supplied, Fr.* se. **1306** gevist *added in margin, in contemporary hand.* **1334–5** surte of] of *supplied, Fr.* de. **1362** ioye *supplied, Fr.* joie. **1376–7** *uncentered title written directly under* brerys. **1391** men disordenatly] men disorte disordenatly, disorte *expuncted.* **1409** angellis and] and *supplied, Fr.* et. **1438** brere] dewe, *see notes.* **1443** gardner] gardne. **1467** *supplied from table of contents.* **1509** if *supplied, Fr.* se. **1536–7** the whiche *supplied.* **1578** made me *supplied, Fr.* me fist. **1603** that *supplied, Fr.* que. **1621** more *supplied, Fr.* plus. **1651** that is] that that is *catchword.* **1703** be] doo, *Fr.* seroies. **1731** of Bountez] of bount bountz. **1735** thee] that, *Fr.* pour toy. **1761** or *supplied, Fr.* ou. **1763** the coventis] th coventis, *expanded stroke crossing* h. **1773** promyseth] prayseth, *Fr.* promet. **1777** for to gouerne] for for to gouerne *catchword.* **1787** made *supplied, Fr.* fait. **1907** Of Renoyng, the Whiche is the Thirde] Of Wodenesse, *supplied from table of contents, see notes.* **1918** he trespasseth] he trsp trespasseth, trsp *expuncted.* **1931** liche] siche. **1965** Despite] Renoying, *supplied from table of contents, see notes;* is *inserted by caret.* **1977** Dauid didde] Dauid seide didde, seide *expuncted.* **2042** Gods wourd *later hand, original erased or washed out.* **2045** prais hym *later hand.* **2046** as *later hand.* **2049** lawe *later hand.* **2049–50** sermons preched *later hand following an erasure;* evill *later hand.* **2076** kepe his horse] kepe hi his horse. **2078** that geteth] that geth geteth, geth *expuncted.* **2081** with feendes] with feed feendes, feed *expuncted.* **2104** toure] woodnes, *see notes.* **2106** tresor] trsor tresor, trsor *expuncted.* **2111** whan þat] whan tha, tha *expuncted;* þat *inserted by caret.* **2150** answere] answre. **2174** suffrith] susfrith. **2190** lefte] leste. **2197** whiche *supplied, Fr.* qui. **2212** manye] maye. **2215** wher] when, *Fr.* ou. **2217** whiche *supplied, Fr.* qui. **2231** departet] deparet. **2283** theye putte] theye put that theye putte. **2296** belies] blies. **2328** disfiguryngys] difiguryngys. **2414** and *supplied, Fr.* et; in siche karolles putteth theym] putteth theym in siche karolles, *transposition.* **2429** coroune] coronice, *Fr.* couronne. **2434** Lady Fortune] Lady of Fortune, *Fr.* Dame Fortune. **2475** the relief] th relief, *no cross bar.* **2478** wolde emploie] wolde emplie emploie, emplie *expuncted.* **2487–8** and sperid with] and *and* with *supplied, Fr.* et decouppee a. **2493** where he] where we he, we *expuncted.* **2548** be *supplied, Fr.* par. **2571** noble] notable, *Fr.* noble. **2603** in the] in in the *catchword.* **2626** þt bachelor *in margin (next to* hym*) in later hand.* **2662** anamly] a *expuncted and* & *inserted just before in margin in later hand.* **2664** his] his and his. **2667** wolde God] wolde a God, a *expuncted.* **2669** be] to, *Fr.* par. **2682** was] as *expuncted,* er *written above in later hand.* **2695** abaundoned *expuncted apparently in later hand,* acompanyed *written in margin in later hand.* **2696** feste] d *appended to* feste *and* þeym *written above line in later hand.* **2697** and thowe] and *crossed out apparently by later hand.* **2698** with] with *cancelled,* vnto *written above line in later hand, see notes;* in drawyng *expuncted, apparently in later hand;* aȝeyns] after *inserted by caret in later hand.* **2699** O] o *expuncted,* a *inserted by caret in later hand.* **2701** abaundoned *caret and insertion* and geven *in margin in later hand.* **2702** in] in *expuncted;* to *inserted by caret above* in. **2715** gostely] especially, *Fr.* espirituelement, *see notes.* **2742** she] he *expuncted,* she *inserted by caret.* **2764** as] a *expuncted,* as *inserted by caret.* **2798** Capt 27 *before* The thirde braunche *in later hand.* **2824** Whoosoo] whoosoo hame of, hame of *expuncted.* **2828** hounte] bounte, *Fr.* honte; hounte] bounte, *Fr.* honte. **2856–7** turneth] ascapeth turneth. **2858** theye wolde] theye wode wolde, wode *expuncted.* **2861** the better] þe the better *catchword.* **2870** nowe is] nowe is nowe. **2878** feleshippeth] felshippeth. **2880** *supplied from table of contents,* capt 29 *inserted in later hand.* **2898** he knewe] he kewe welle knewe, kewe welle *expuncted.* **2910** begynnyng] begynnyg. **2926** to] to to; seythe *supplied, Fr.* dit. **2927** anamly to] to anamly to. **2985** men haue] men hou haue, hou *expuncted.* **2986** witnes] vertues, *Fr.* tesmoignage. whiche *supplied, Fr.* qui. **3000** a more *supplied, Fr.* une plus. **3029** *supplied from table of contents,* Capt 30 *in margin in later hand.* **3054** they] ther. **3090** litil *supplied, Fr.* peu. **3102** *supplied from table of contents,* Capt 32 *in margin in later hand.* **3159–60** it blyndeth] it is blyndeth. **3174** soule] toon, *Fr.* ame, *see notes.* **3178** and coveyteth] and coveyth coveyteth, coveth *expuncted.* **3181** evyll] goodnes, *Fr.* le mal. **3188** enchaunted] enhuaunsed, *Fr.* enchante. **3233** a *inserted by caret.* **3268** fareth] saweth, *Fr.* sont. **3274** righte grete] grete righte grete, *first* grete *expuncted.* **3277** of] of of *catchword.* **3279** tree] man, *Fr.* arbre. **3285** *supplied from table of contents.* **3297** nater] mater, *Fr.* nature. **3332** he goostely] he hooly goostely, hooly *expuncted.* **3333** wyl not] wyl noon, *Fr.* ne veult. **3336–7** *supplied from table of contents,* Capt 34 *in margin in later hand.* **3343** Another ire] Capt 35 *in margin in later hand.* **3358** Somtyme men seye] Capt 36 *in margin in later hand.* **3363** Somtyme men seye] Capt 37 *in margin in later hand.* **3367** Somtyme men seye] Capt 38 *in margin in later hand.* **3371–2** Somtyme men seye] Capt 39 *in margin in later hand.* **3376–7** Somtyme men seye] Capt 40 *in margin in later hand.* **3378** werre *supplied, Fr.* guerre. **3381** thorne] glorye, *Fr.* espine. **3382–3** *supplied from table of contents,* Capt 41 *in margin in later hand.* **3393** meveable] meveable be the, be the *expuncted.* **3396** sootenes] sostenes, *Fr.* suavite. **3404** Ieromye] Ierom, *Fr.* Iheremie. **3410** boterel. Also] *mark for* id est *followed by space of approximately eight letters between* boterel *and* Also. **3430** *supplied from table of contents,* Capt 42 *in margin in later hand.* **3443** *supplied from table of contents,* Capt 43 *in margin in later hand.* **3451–22** *supplied from table of contents,* Capt 44 *in margin in later hand.* **3459–60** *supplied from table of contents.* **3473–4** heede, seythe] feythe, *Fr.* par mon chief dit le diable. **3497** hym *supplied, Fr.* lui. **3522** *supplied from table of contents.* **3526** men] men men. **3546** *supplied from table of contents.* **3551** neyther] neyther ev, ev *expuncted.* **3554** deemeth] dremeth, *Fr.* iuge. **3578** *supplied from table of contents.* **3581** ii] iii, *Fr.* deux. **3582** Goostely a] a goostely, *metathesis.* **3584** wyt] wyl, *Fr.* cognoist. **3585** as] al, *Fr.* comme. **3590** seeth] sleeth, *Fr.* voient. **3593** the bodye] they bodye. **3605** irreguler. Be] irreguler (*mark for* id est *followed by space of approximately eighteen letters*) Be. **3608** not *supplied, Fr.* nest il mie homicide. **3612** irrogularite] irrogalite, *Fr.* irregularite. **3622** afore Godde that] aftyr that Godde, *Fr.* devant dieu qui. **3642** *supplied from table of contents.* **3668** *supplied from table of contents.* **3677–8** comforte and] comforte & and. **3686** longaigne] longage, *Fr.* longaigne. **3691** *supplied from table of contents.* **3704** Patrum] patrem. **3723** nedye] remedye, *Fr.* souffretteux. **3728** remedye that] remedye is that. **3739** *supplied from table of contents.* **3742** ennoy] ennoyeth, *Fr.* ennuy. **3745** thys] thye. **3779** *supplied from table of contents.* **3781** weykly] weylly, *Fr.* tiedement. **3790** fayleth *supplied, Fr.* Quand elle fault force fault. **3801** *supplied from table of contents.*

3803 *supplied from table of contents.* **3811** thynke *supplied, Fr.* penser. **3813–4** precyous thynge] precyous tyme thynge, tyme *expuncted.* **3816** wagiz] watz, *Fr.* loier. **3837** *supplied from table of contents.* **3854** *supplied from table of contents.* **3878** goode feelde] goode feed feelde, feed *expuncted.* **3884** sterveth] setteth, *Fr.* se defenist. **3885** dede] drede, *Fr.* oevre. **3891** charches] hertis, *Fr.* cures. **3892** his yee] his eye yee, eye *expuncted.* **3896** not *supplied, Fr.* na pas. **3901** *supplied from table of contents.* **3902** vi] vii. **3911** dedely] deely. **3922–3** *supplied from table of contents.* **3956** seyeth] yeveth, *Fr.* dit. **3974** morne] more, *Fr.* demain; *space of two or three letters follows.* **3986** knowe *supplied, Fr.* saches. **3992** perdicion] pardoon, *Fr.* pardon, *see notes.* **3993** of good] of god good, god *expuncted.* **3995** *supplied from table of contents.* **4024** gremercy] gremcy gremercy *catchword.* **4034** *supplied from table of contents.* **4040** nis] is, *Fr.* ne soit. **4065** *supplied from table of contents.* **4074** *Latin supplied from P to fill space of approximately 25 characters.* **4077** be iuste] be of iuste, be *inserted by caret,* of *expuncted.* **4085** forsoothe sloggy] forsoothe sloggy that is to seye, that is to seye *expuncted* **4098** is *supplied, Fr.* est. **4102** costum] eetyng, *see notes.* **4105** commeth of] commeth not of. **4107** if *supplied, Fr.* se. **4108** of tendernes] oft of tendernes. **4119** *supplied from table of contents.* **4128** slowe] showe. **4131** vigorous] rigorous, *Fr.* viguereux. **4133** God] seye, *Fr.* dieu. **4138** whan] whant. **4143** *supplied from table of contents.* **4150** bowynge is nere] bowynge that he is nere, *Fr.* qui est aussi enclin est pres de trebucher. **4166–7** *supplied from table of contents.* **4174** it *supplied, Fr.* la. **4187** slowly] be essensynge, *Fr.* peresceusement, *see notes.* **4194** erres] ernest, *Fr.* erres. **4200** he] and, *Fr.* il. **4211** ne *supplied, Fr.* ne; more *supplied, Fr.* plus. **4226** *supplied from table of contents.* **4257** acciduell in] *mark for* id est *followed by space of approximately nine letters between* acciduell *and* in, *see notes.* **4262** techynges maye] techynges that maye. **4273** ye] theef, *Fr.* oeil; is] us, *Fr.* est. **4300** solitude] besynes, *Fr.* solitude, *see notes.* **4335** *supplied from table of contents.* **4339** be] of, *Fr.* par. **4349** be] to, *Fr.* par. **4385** bawme *space of approximately 39 letters follows, see notes.* **4402–3** *supplied from table of contents.* **4410** and *supplied, Fr.* et. **4420** Ieromye] Ierom, *Fr.* Iheremie. **4421** fulle grete] fulle a grete. **4431** streyningly] streyingly, *Fr.* restraignament. **4463** *supplied from table of contents.* **4480** *supplied from table of contents.* **4483** or blessed] in blessed, *Fr.* ou. **4484** prestis for] prestis doo for. **4492** rentys, offringgys] rentys as offringgys, *see notes.* **4498** *supplied from table of contents.* **4500** resoigne to] *mark for* id est *between* resoigne *and* to *without interven-*

ing space. **4509** thoo *supplied, Fr.* ceulx. **4517** *supplied from table of contents.* **4251** sone] sonn sone, sonn *expuncted.* **4530** fleethe] sleethe, *Fr.* escorchent. **4537** flee] slee, *Fr.* escorchier. **4540** þe hyres] þe th hyres, þe *inserted by caret,* th *expuncted.* **4554** *supplied from table of contents.* **4576** Too] too synne, synne *expuncted.* **4579** be *supplied, Fr.* sont. **4593** *supplied from table of contents.* **4618** vil] evil, *Fr.* vil. **4647** *supplied from table of contents.* **4649** tricheries] touchementis, *Fr.* tricheries. **4660** the whiche *supplied, Fr.* qui. **4662** of v] of o v. **4683** *supplied from table of contents.* **4710** shalt compt] shalt con compt. **4712** betwene] betwne. **4751** to synge] *supplied, Fr.* pour chanter. **4759** evil *supplied, Fr.* mauvais. **4783** creatures] cratures creatures, cratures *expuncted.* **4787** vile] *supplied, Fr.* vil. **4794** and proprely] and pro proprely, pro *expuncted.* **4866** theym saf] theym faste saf, faste *expuncted.* **4887** lesith] shewith, *Fr.* perd. **4893** rightwis] rightwisnes; the *supplied, Fr.* la departie est iuste. **4898** Thyngys] Synnes, *Fr.* choses. **4906** pitch is defiled] peis lieth downe, *Fr.* la pois se conchie, *see notes.* **5005** men] women, *Fr.* garcons. **5020** spirit] spirt. **5048** net] kynge, *Fr.* rais, *see notes.* **5065** ientilwomen and] ientilwomen haue and. **5101** karolle] karolles, *Fr.* dansent. **5129** whan she] whan he she, he *expuncted.* **5156** terreboles] feboles, *see notes.* **5165** ouercomme] comme, *Fr.* vaincre. **5208** Iacob] Iob, *Fr.* Iacob. **5220** hee] yee, *Fr.* il. **5288** The thirde] *space of approximately three letters between* The *and* thirde. **5388** his] this, *Fr.* ses. **5396** first hee] first at hee. **5424** pepil eteth] pepil eth eteth, eth *expuncted.* **5431** woortys] wootys. **5560** delit] debt, *Fr.* delicter. **5579–80** lentilles soolde] *mark for* id est *together with space of approximately eleven letters between* lentilles *and* soolde. **5593** gloutonously] gloutously. **5603** and *supplied, Fr.* et. **5615** kelyd his] kelyd haue his, haue *expuncted.* **5633** þat *inserted by caret.* **5645** curiosite] curtesye, *Fr.* curiosite. **5653** olde] oldere, *Fr.* devant quinze ans; on *supplied, Fr.* en. **5661** curiosite] curteseye, *Fr.* curiosite. **5663** sauoure] fauoure, *Fr.* savour. **5665** and *supplied, Fr.* et. **5701–1** drinkeris or the taverneris] drinkeris in the tavernis, *Fr.* les buveurs ou les taverniers. **5743** and *supplied, Fr.* et. **5824** and lierris] and of lierris, of *expuncted.* **5856** selleth] felleth, *Fr.* vendent. **5857** To this] to this to this. **5879** and *supplied, Fr.* et;. obleys] wafris, *see notes.* **5889** that *supplied, Fr.* que. **5903** he seeth] he hierit seeth, hierit *expuncted.* **5904** lorde] borde. **5915** goupil] goul goupil, goul *cancelled and expuncted.* **5965** falseire] fals heire, *Fr.* faulsaire. **5994** vii] v. **6016** not] *supplied, Fr.* nest mie. **6032** pepille doo] pepille brekyth theym smaller doo, brekyth theym smaller *expuncted.* **6035–6** hyrre] hym, *Fr.*

la; hyrre] hym, *Fr.* elle. **6053** promisshed] p *plus five minims* sshed, *Fr.* a promis. **6069–70** commeth noyse] commeth cometh noyse, cometh *expuncted.* **6071** þe] ys, *Fr.* la. **6072** is] as, *Fr.* est. **6075** the toother] the thoo toother, thoo *expuncted.* **6102** IIII] III. **6203** veleynisly] veleyinsly, *metathesis.* **6204** Dame Anne is acquainted *in later hand two lines below end of text.* **6208** Iewis] gameys, *see notes.* **6210** toother] too toother, too *expuncted.* **6301** sporrynge] spornynge, *Fr.* esponnant. **6334** prodigalite] *mark for* id est *together with space of approximately fifteen letters follows.* **6345** disprise] dispise, *Fr.* desprisier. **6397** noon so rigorous] noo kynge, *Fr.* nul si roy, *see notes.* **6418** prophet] prophe. **6456** torn] ton, *see notes.* **6463** austerite] dronkelewnesse, *Fr.* austerite. **6488–9** Every ... dyeth *barely cancelled and expuncted.* **6534** theire solas] theire ioye solas. **6589–90** trauaylyng of] trauaylyng of of, of *expuncted.* **6594** filthe] gouernance, *Fr.* roul, *see notes.* **6629** God *supplied, Fr.* dieu. **6637** be so] be sholde be so, sholde be *expuncted.* **6653** praye] praye whan. **6672** verraye] greete, *Fr.* vray. **6691** the whiche *supplied.* **6693** musardis *supplied, Fr.* les musars. **6702** Godde *supplied, Fr.* dieu. **6716** theye be] theye be theye be, *second* theye be *cancelled and expuncted.* **6750** lefte] leste, *Fr.* laissa. **6800** in richesse] in *inserted by caret.* **6816** worshipful, profitable] worshipful thyngys profitable, thyngys *expuncted.* **6820** profitable] profitable That vertue is ful worshipfull. **6883** serve] seve. **6898** Preciouse] preciously, *Fr.* Precieuse. **6899** Sweete *supplied, Fr.* Douce. **6942** maketh hevyn] maketh maketh hevyn. **7002** þat *inserted by caret.* **7031** be holly] he holly. **7032** free] parfit, *Fr.* frans. **7045** verye ientillesse] verye ientil of ientillesse. **7078** verite] merite, *Fr.* verite. **7210** theye] I, *Fr.* ils. **7248** oyle] foyle; oyle] oylo. **7264** hee] hee he, he *expuncted.* **7271** *text supplied from table of contents, rubricated numeral from margin.* **7291** he weeteth] he weth weeteth, weth *expuncted.* **7315** enbelesshith] cnbelesshith. **7376** promysseth] punysseth, *Fr.* promet. **7384** the tree] the liff tree, liff *expuncted.* **7398** gete] getu gete, getu *expuncted.* **7401** promissith] punisshith, *Fr.* promet; require hym] require vs hym, vs *expuncted.* **7403** curtesye] curtesle. **7477** be *supplied, Fr.* par. **7524** is *supplied, Fr.* cest. **7532** the] oure, *Fr.* la. **7557** soo] som. **7568** kepe] kpe. **7578** pepil] pepil of. **7599** attaignyngly] attayngly, *Fr.* ataignanment. **7612** nature] nature or. **7628** in hevyn gostely, that is to seye, in hooly hertis] in hevyn, that is to seye, in gostely men in hooly hertis, *see notes.* **7640** verite] merite, *Fr.* verite. **7649** purchaseth] perseth, *Fr.* impetrent. **7658** purged] purged and; enlumined] enlumined and. **7679** departed] deped *with bar across descender of* p. **7686** withowte] hooly in, *Fr.* comme sans terre. **7694** dedifieth] edified, *Fr.* dedie. **7697** dedified] edified, *Fr.* dedie. **7701** þe *inserted by caret.* **7757** taketh] taketh taketh. **7758** parelleth] pelleth, *see notes.* **7773** is] as. **7785** confermith] confemith. **7807** oure] oue. **7847** 3ift *abbreviation for* is *not expanded.* **7859–60** panne of] panne and vn, *Fr.* paele de. **7875** provendre] prvendre. **7878** it *supplied, Fr.* le. **7890** and *supplied, Fr.* et. **7892–3** substancial] substancialis. **7900** 3if vs this brede in this daye] 3if vs today this brede in this daye. **7954** and *supplied, Fr.* et; commandeth] commendeth, *Fr.* commande. **7958** if be aventure] if he be aventure. **8001** esprove] desprove, *Fr.* esprouver. **8008** prayeth] seith prayeth. **8014** and *supplied, Fr.* et. **8040** kepe] kpe. **8060** of the feende and his wyles] of the feende & his wyles, of the feende & his wyles, *latter cancelled.* **8071** Pater Noster] Pater Noster CXXII. **8138** leneth] lerneth, *Fr.* preste. **8184** the usher with the] for hym to troste the in; masse] manace; with] in, *see notes.* **8200** counselle *supplied, Fr.* conseil. **8240** to the whiche] the whiche, *Fr.* ou. **8255** beholdeth] he holdeth. **8286** heetis] hertis, *Fr.* chaleurs. **8295** thinketh] thnketh. **8343** toille] trille, *see notes.* **8354** other *supplied, Fr.* autres. **8365** men *supplied, Fr.* on. **8370** iiii] iii. **8406** noble mannes sone] notable mannes sone, *Fr.* fils au prodomme. **8415** grace] werre, *Fr.* grace. **8432** as a] as as a. **8472** branches of] branches of of. **8481** contre] pes, *Fr.* pays. **8492–3** his hert] his his hert; worthe] worthe where, where *expuncted.* **8508** peines] frogges, *Fr.* paines, *see notes.* **8539** porged] sporged. **8571** childer] chider childer, chider *expuncted;* childer of] childer of of *catchword.* **8575** that] thas. **8590** Mekenes] mkenes. **8593** disprise] dispise, *Fr.* disprisier. **8594** *first* in] in to. **8597** to *inserted by caret.* **8607** trouthe] medeful, *Fr.* verite. **8662** of otheris] of oheris otheris, oheris *expuncted.* **8665** refeit] refert, *Fr.* refait. **8706** febill shadowe] shadowe and febill, *Fr.* umbre fieble. **8778** these] these these. **8786** Maketh *inserted by caret.* **8797** an] in, *Fr.* et. **8814–5** whistle of þe gouuernour] strok on þe gouernayle, *see notes.* **8859** hide] bide, *Fr.* repondre. **8876** onlynesse] only of, *Fr.* solitude, *see notes.* **8882** dyviseth] dyveth, *Fr.* devise. **8891** hyrith] sessith, *see notes.* **8892** Alsoo *supplied, Fr.* aussi. **8937** and is] and b is, b *expuncted.* **8990** wil *supplied, Fr. future* guerdonnera. **9020** anguysshe] anguysshe an, an *expuncted.* **9055** al the] al the the. **9088** toother] toothe. **9114** hymselfe *supplied to fill space of approximately ten letters, Fr.* en la sienne. **9170** the] he, *Fr.* la volente. **9171** of] & of, *Fr.* de. **9195** enserchyng *suspension on* g *not expanded* (*translates Fr. infinitive* encerchier). **9209** goode *supplied, Fr.* en la bonne partie. **9227** lyme] lyne, *Fr.* lime. **9237** iiii] iiii iiii *catchword.* **9259** qwickly] qwcky.

9272 the wil] he wil. **9277** þe] be, *Fr.* la. **9314** thervppon] the vppon. **9324** oo grace] oo mesure of grace, *see notes*. **9330** doo after] doo myche goode after, myche good *expuncted*. **9418** of the feende *supplied, Fr.* au diable. **9422** or] and, *Fr.* ou; and he] and for he. **9465** konnynge] konnynge conditeth these vii vertues, *see notes*. **9476** vertues *supplied, Fr.* vertus. **9526** liffeth] louffeth, *Fr.* vivent. **9529** more proprely] more longeth proprely, longeth *expuncted*. **9537** doo] be, *Fr.* faire. **9544** if that] that if, *transpostion*. **9551–2** noo worldly] noo worl worldly, worl *expuncted*; the ioye] the louff of godde ioye, louff of godde *expuncted*. **9615** And] as, *Fr.* et. **9622** charches] hertis, *Fr.* cures. **9627** vanites] vanitates. **9632** mortalite] moralite, *Fr.* mortalite. **9636** it *supplied, Fr.* elle. **9688** hym anoother] hym *inserted by caret*. **9724** salemandre is þat] salemandre is (*misplaced mark for* id est *followed by space of approximately eight letters*) þat. **9736** right side] lefte side, *Fr.* destre. **9747** be the whiche Goddes] be the whiche Goddes be the whiche Goddes *catchphrase*. **9786** hirres] hireres, *Fr.* loiers. **9792** sholde doo *supplied, Fr.* souloit estre. **9793** is] as. **9833** haubergion] haubegion haubergion, haubegion *expuncted*. **9909** daye *supplied, Fr.* jour. **9939** for3eteth] foreteth, *Fr.* oublie. **9967** hydyng] hyndryng, *Fr.* celer. **9978** mercy *supplied, Fr.* merci. **9998** Alsoo] as, *Fr.* apres. **10,007** reherse to] reherse þe to, þe *expuncted*; to *inserted by caret*. **10,015** and *supplied, Fr.* et. **10,036** in *supplied, Fr.* en. **10,111** whiche *supplied, Fr.* qui. **10,124** promisseth] propmisseth. **10,130** thoo] too thoo, too *expuncted*. **10,174** whoosoo suffreth] whoosoo doothe mooste suffreth, doothe mooste *expuncted*. **10,179** the strengthe] his strengthe, *Fr.* la force. **10,187** man] man be the. **10,285–6** noo goode] noo goode goode, *first* good *expuncted*; discounfit] dicounsit, *Fr.* desconfit. **10,319** brought vs from hevyn] the whiche he brought vs from hevyn. **10,344** vii] ii. **10,352** theire] theire þeir, þeir *expuncted*. **10,402** and *supplied, Fr.* et. **10,403** pride] poure, *Fr.* boban. **10,404** adamant] alamant. **10,412** lever] lever on. **10,455** þe *inserted by caret*. **10,462** rightvissnesse] righavissnesse, *Fr.* justice. **10,467** and of bisshoppes *supplied, Fr.* et des evesques. **10,505** of *supplied, Fr.* de. **10,512** cc] x^c^, *Fr.* deux cens, *see notes*. **10,514** ccc] x^c^, *Fr.* trois cens, *see notes*. **10,550** in present] he present, *Fr.* en present. **10,577** riche *supplied, Fr.* riches. **10,614** theye *supplied, Fr.* ilz. **10,637** euerlastyngly] euerlastyng liff, *Fr.* pardurablement. **10,670** pleysyng to] pleysyng to to. **10,684–5** the 3ifte of] the the 3ifte of. **10,687** seithe] felthe. **10,733** ran] kan, *Fr.* couroit. **10,773** Patrum] patrem. **10,782** art] ara *plus vertical stroke of* t art, ara *plus vertical stroke of* t *expuncted*. **10,794**

dede a] dede ma a, ma *expuncted*. **10,820** a man doþe] a man the which doþe. **10,871** theye] theye the, the *expuncted*. **10,909** of] of of. **10,969** Maner of] Maner doy of, doy *cancelled*. **10,970** Alsoo *preceded by two cancelled lines*, seith that iiii condiciones ther be in doynge of almesse cat. **11,041** whom *supplied, Fr.* qui. **11,059** the] th. **11,066** seithe] seithe seithe. **11,082** welle doo] wil welle doo, *Fr.* bien font. **11,090** theye leve] theye lve not leve, lve not *expuncted*. **11,126** begynnyng] begynnyg. **11,140** where *supplied, see notes*. **11,158** lowed] solitarie, *see notes*. **11,165** weye] liff, *Fr.* voie. **11,177** of] *supplied, Fr.* du don. **11,194** alonly as of theire] alonly of as theire, *transposition*. **11,211** in *supplied, Fr.* en present. **11,226** hym and] hym that is and whan. **11,254** clene] mastris, *Fr.* netaies. **11,302** herte] herte and. **11,364** and] is, *Fr.* et. **11,429** mekely to shewe] mekely shewe, *Fr.* humblement demonstrer. **11,527** sholde praye] sholde than praye, than *expuncted*. **11,529** feruentnes of louff] feruentnes of the herte of louff, *Fr.* ferveur damour. **11,534** compunciones] corrupciones, *Fr.* compunction. **11,586** heede that] heede he that. **11,610** be þexample] example, *Fr.* a lexemple. **11,616** þexile] þe ile, *Fr.* lexil. **11,620** that cometh soo arayed] that cometh soo arayed that cometh soo arayed. **11,659** thyng] thyngys, *Fr.* chose. **11,662** Ambrose] Ambose. **11,683** he] the, *Fr.* il. **11,698** sholde theye] sholde þan theye, þan *expuncted*. **11,707** that] that that. **11,737** kepe] kpe. **11,738** thyng] thyngis. **11,748** liein] *possibly* liem, *Fr.* lien. **11,781** mantell] matell. **11,794** and *supplied, Fr.* et. **11,805** not lecherye] not lege lecherye, lege *cancelled*. **11,818** thee] hee, *Fr.* le. **11,842** hym to be with *supplied, Fr.* se sueffre destre avec. **11,849** and *supplied, Fr.* et. **11,868** Chastite] Chastie. **11,889** profession] confession, *see notes*. **11,905–6** iangleresses and] iangleresses and and *catchword*. **11,922** and] and state and. **11,923** be þexample of] example be, *Fr.* a lexemple de. **11,933** Virginite] *a letter between* i *and* g *erased and not replaced*. **11,960** thynge a] thynge of a. **12,026** Prive *supplied, Fr.* prive. **12,034** Iohn þe] Iohn the þe, the *cancelled*. **12,035** loorde *supplied, Fr.* seigneur. **12,078** be] he. **12,080** to the synne] to see synne, *Fr.* au pechie. **12,140** prosperite] propriete, *Fr.* prosperite. **12,168** begynnyng] begynnyg. **12,170–1** al that] al this that, this *expuncted*. **12,200** handel and] handel fulle and, fulle *expuncted*. **12,207** he] he he. **12,210** dedified] edified, *Fr.* dedie. **12,220** breede] brde, *Fr.* pain. **12,228** reynes] handis, *Fr.* rains, *see notes*. **12,310** liche] for liche. **12,316** prive *supplied, Fr.* repost. **12,335** he] be. **12,340** he *supplied, Fr.* il. **12,377** *erasure of one letter space before* and. **12,380** be dede *between* be *and* dede *scribe expunged two or three letters that are smudged.* **12,384** wolde sey] whoo sey, *Fr.* vouloit dire. **12,407** þe place, þe *inserted by caret.* **12,410** desire] desiren. **12,415** a *inserted by caret.* **12,416** gon oute] gon outhe oute, outhe *expuncted.* **12,444–7** whiche in] whiche is not to prayse in; that is þe worlde] the which is þe that is þe worlde, the which is þe *expuncted, Fr.* cest le monde; the whiche is not to prayse *supplied from previous line, Fr.* que ne prise rien. **12,460** Montioye] moneye, *Fr.* montioie. **12,478** belevith] blevith; parfit] parfitly, *Fr.* parfaicte. **12,485** maye] maye maye. **12,520** than] whan. **12,521** the] theire, *Fr.* les. **12,522** as thorough] as thoug thorough, thoug *expuncted.* **12,584** welle of liffe] of liffe *supplied, Fr.* fontaine de vie. **12,609** beeth] fleeth, *Fr.* est. **12,646** oftesythe] of þe self, *Fr.* moult de fois. **12,664** vppon] vnder, *Fr.* sur. **12,665** vppon] vnder, *Fr.* sur. **12,676** vppon] vnder, *Fr.* sur. **12,680** myre ne the erthe] bloode, *Fr.* fanc ne la terre, *see notes.* **12,711** right mesure] right and mesure, *Fr.* droite mesure. **12,718** of the whiche] of the whiche of the whiche. **12,730** flette] lette, *Fr.* flexisses. **12,794** that a wyse] that in a wyse. **12,802** Ther be some pepill that] that ther be some pepill, *Fr.* Aucunes gent sont qui. **12,863** envenemed] evenemed, *Fr.* envenime. **12,866** passion] passis, *Fr.* passion. **12,867** the] the þe. **12,918** of *supplied, Fr.* du. **12,957** desevred] deserved, *metathesis, Fr.* dessevre. **13,002** here] he, *Fr.* icy.

Explanatory Notes

All readings from the French are taken from MS P unless otherwise indicated.

1–4 *Title.* The title follows V. All the other MSS (with the exception of R, which lacks both title and table of contents, and S, which is mutilated) associate the *Miroir* with the *Somme le Roi*: *Icy commencent les chapitres du livre qui est appelle le mirouer du monde que aucuns appellent vices et vertus les autres lappellent le somme le roy* (f. i[a]). Following the table of contents V adds *Icy fine la table des rebriches de ce livre appelle le mirouer du monde et dautres des vices et vertus* (f. 4[a]). On the confusion of titles in MSS of the *Miroir* and *Somme* see Brayer, 'Contenu,' 60–4, and Kosmer, 'Style and Iconography,' pt. 2, 12–14. On mirror-imagery in titles see Bradley, 'Backgrounds,' and Grabes, *Mutable Glass*, 276, who, however, appears to confuse the *Miroir du Monde* with the *Image du Monde*; and, more generally, Torti, *Glass of Form*, 1–35.

5–254 *Table.* The French tables divide into three groups: P, Q, and ACDNUV. (R lacks a table and S's table, if it existed, has been lost to mutilation.) B, although it has no direct source in the extant MSS, follows the tradition of ACDNUV and is particularly close to V with which it shares, as noted below, two unique errors (ll. 212, 213–18). The chapter headings of the text, however, appear to derive from the P-tradition, which provides individual rubrics for each of the commandments, articles of the faith, petitions of the Pater Noster, branches of equity, and points of confession.

9 The French adverb *generalment* is rendered by the adjective *generall*. Translate: 'taken collectively, in general.'

12 *the whiche*: on this combination – the usual form in the *Mirroure* – which was particularly frequent in fifteenth-century prose see Mustanoja, *Middle English Syntax*, 198–9, and Fischer, 'Syntax,' 303.
17 *too*: 'second.' On the use of cardinals for ordinals, which occurs frequently in the *Mirroure*, see Mustanoja, *Middle English Syntax*, 306.
31 *losengiers*: 'deceitful flatterers.' The form is taken straight from OF *losengier(s)*. Cf. l. 105. The chapter number (XXIII), lacking here, appears in the text. Its omission accounts for the misnumbering of chapters through XXXV (l. 47). Correct numeration resumes at chapter XXXVII (l. 48).
37 *fore*: 'fear' (*paour*). The scribe occasionally writes *o* for *e*, for example, *bordolere, certoine, disordonat, irrogularite, monoy, mordorere, oyen, partoner(is), purvoye, renoyinge, robborye, rovers, whoder*. There is no other occurrence of *fore*. The overwhelmingly dominant form *fere* occurs seventy-six times, *fire* occurs once.
47–8 Chapter XXXVI is lacking in both the table and the text. There is a similar omission in V.
49 *branchettis*: 'small branches' (*branchets*), one of the kinds of sin. Not recorded by MED. *Branchelet* is found in Lydgate's 'Ballade in Commendacion of Our Lady' (l. 44). *branchettis* is repeated in ll. 58 and 76, and *branchet* is used in l. 77. Both forms are taken directly from the French. Cf. AND, s.v. *branchet* n.
59 *lewkenes*: 'tepidity.' Not recorded by MED as a noun referring to a branch of the sin of sloth.
75 *feruentnesse or ardentnesse*: 'ardor, zeal.' MED does not record *feruentnesse* as a noun in this sense; nor does it record *ardentnesse*, the earliest citation of which in OED is 1632.
84 *briberie* translates the French *boi(s)die* 'fraud, deception, betrayal.' MED glosses *briberie* only in the sense of 'robbery' or 'something stolen.' This usage occurs in l. 10,927.
86 *whiche*: *qui* (so all tables except P which has only *des mauvais mestiers*).
88–9 A chapter heading, *Off Remedies ayeins the Synne of Covetise, LXXVe*, appearing in the text, has been omitted here. The French table correctly reads *Des remedes contre le pechie davarice*. The following chapter, *Off the Synne of Lecherye*, is numbered 76 in the text, but the chapter that follows it, *Off Lecherye of the Herte*, is unnumbered. *Off Lecherye of the Bodye* is numbered 77, coinciding with the table.
92 V's *Des branches de luxure* is repeated in the following line (93), omitting the chapter on the remedies.

95–7 *Outeragiously* 'excessively, immoderately' and *nobilly* 'sumptuously' are first cited by MED with reference to food c. 1475. The earliest citation to *feruently* with the implication of gluttony is c. 1450 (*Alphabet of Tales*).
105 *losenge*: 'deceitful flattery.' The form is taken from the French. In MED it appears only as *losengerie*.
118–9 An unnumbered chapter heading, *Of Foly Largesse*, appearing in the text has been omitted here. The French table has *de prodigalite*.
125 *mene goodes*, that is, goods of nature. MED lacks the term.
138 *yftes* should perhaps be emended to the dominant form *yiftes*.
142 *devine* is not recorded by MED with reference to the theological virtues. For its use in this sense see *Myrour* 87/9 and *Speculum Vitae*, ll. 1777, 1780. Cf. l. 8245.
166 *mansuetude or benignes or frendeship* meaning 'love of one's fellow man, fellow-feeling, beneficence' closely renders the French *mansuetude ou benignite ou amistie*. MED does not identify this synonomy for the Gift Virtue corresponding to pity. *benignes* (which reappears as *benignesse* in l. 8948 and *benignite* in l. 8959) is unknown to it. OED cites *benigness* c. 1731 meaning 'quality of being benign.' There is a single reference in MED to *beningnesse* 'good will, benignity' c. 1450.
175–7 *Howe man sholde behave hym ... goode and wise examples*: ACNQV *Comment len se doit avoir envers les choses du monde et comment len doit prendre des bons et saiges examples*; P *Comment on se doit avoir au monde*; DU *Comment len se doit avoir envers les choses du monde et comment on doit prendre garde et example des bons et des saiges*, RS om.
197 *vii condiciones*: so CDNUV, A *vi*, PQRS om. Six conditions (cf. l. 9868) are discussed in the text.
208–9 Four chapter headings omitted here (P *Du don de conseil*, *De examiner son conseil*, *De croire son conseil*, and *De misericorde*) appear in the text as four unnumbered heads: *Off the 3ifte of Counselle* (l. 10,268), *To Examine His Counselle* (l. 10,300), *To Beleve His Counsell* (l. 10,310), and *Off Mercy* (l. 10,343).
209 *dedis*: perhaps an eyeskip. The French reads *Des degres de misericorde*.
212 *gostely*: all MSS read *espiritueles* except V, which has *corporelles*, evidently the reading of B's exemplar.
213–18 The emended order that coincides with the text is found in all MSS except V.

221–2 *clene*: 'cleanness, moral purity' (*nettete*). MED, s.v. *clene* n. The only previous instance of its use as a noun in this sense is *Trinity Homilies* (c. 1225).
228 V adds *de leurs meres*. If the phrase appeared in Scrope's exemplar (assuming he is the translator of the *Mirroure*), its omission here may reflect his long-held resentment against his mother's acquiescence in the sale of his wardship to Sir William Gascoigne. See above, 'Introduction,' 22.
257 Matthew 19.17.
258–9 Hassell B93 (*qui le bien voit et le mal prend fait folie en bon escient*); Morawski 1853. Cf. Whiting F431 (He is a fool that leaves the better and chooses the worse). *lerneth* miscontrues *prent*, which was read as, or confused with, *aprent*.
260–2 Ecclesiasticus 15.18.
269 Whiting D278 (Do well and have well); Hassell B92; Morawski 1843.
271–2 Galatians 6.9.
273 *Fynde* meaning 'acquire' loses the force of the biblical metaphor.
273–8 *vnderstandyng*: 'intention' (*entencion*). MED, s.v. *understonding* n. 9. *vnderstandyng* is properly the subject of the sentence, the translator having been led astray by the faulty reading of *pour ce que* for *pour ce* in all MSS except D: *pour ce que lentencion de chascun prince qui donne ses commandemens et met ses loys et ses ordenances et ses establissemens a garder en sa terre doit estre de atraire et de admener le peuple a faire oevres vertueuses*. For the comparison between earthly and heavenly government see *Dives* 1.5.
284–5 Cicero, *Pro Milone*, 97, based on Aristotle, *Nicomachean Ethics*, 4.3.10–11: *sed tamen ex omnibus praemiis virtutis, si esset habenda ratio praemiorum, amplissimum esse praemium gloriam*. Cf. Tilley H571 (Honor is the reward of virtue); Walther 37279 (*Honor coronat virtutem*). The proverbial text is garbled in the *Mirroure* (*Quia homo est primum virtutis prestens in bono*) and in the majority of the French MSS: AP *Quia honor est premium virtutis presistens in bono*, CN *Quia honor est premium virtutis persistens in bono*, RUV *Quia homo est primum virtutis persistens in bono*, Q *Quia honor est premium virtutis prestestens in bono*, D *Quia honor et primum virtus persistens in bono*, S om.
285–9 Isaias 33.22. The sentence lacks a verb, *cest* having been misconstrued as *that is to seye*. The French reads *Chere gent, nostre prince, nostre sire, nostre roy, qui nous donna ses commandemens,*

ses lois, ses establissemens cest (D *est*) *nostre seigneur Ihesu Crist si comme dit ysaye le prophete* and so on. *Dere pepil* (*Chere gent*): an indication, here and subsequently (for example, ll, 316, 330, 341 *sir*(e), 318, 325 thowe, 342 *me*, 345, 366, 368 *I*), that the exposition of the commandments originated with an oral instruction. For its indebtedness to Bonaventure's *Collationes* see below ll. 378–88, 944–56, 967–87.

293–4 Jeremias 7.3, 26.13. The attribution to Isaias is erroneous.

298–305 Matthew 19. 16–17.

310–14 I John 5.3. *Canonique*: 'epistle' or 'canonical epistle.' The form and meaning are unknown to MED and OED, both citing *canonic* in a different sense from Caxton onwards. AND cites *canonical* as an adjective (*epistre canonical*) but not as a noun. MED (*canonial* adj.) cites a single instance of *canonial epistle* from the *Ancrene Riwle*.

315 Psalm 118.32.

325–7 *And if ... right large*. B follows the French MSS, all of which lack a main verb except U, which reads *Cest pour quil est tres courtois et tres large*.

330–1 *Sir, it is not liche*, that is, like the preceding example.

344–5 *Bot I seye: He vndidde the snare*: *I seye* should perhaps be deleted as needlessly repetitive and the text emended to read *Bot he undidde the snare*, in accordance with the French: *Je di que non fait mais il declaire les las ou nous pourrions cheoir*. *a*: 'have.' The loss of *h* from forms of 'have' (ll. 380, 1508, 1676, etc.) and the pronoun 'his' (ll. 1055, 8665, 9844) occurs occasionally throughout the text. Cf. also *arlotries* (l. 2768), *orrour* (l. 815). For the instability of initial *h* in Middle English see Milroy, 'Sociolinguistic History,' and 'Middle English Dialectology,' 197–201, and LALME IV.320 for its dialectal distribution.

346–7 *a man sholde not doo ... men didde to hym*: Matthew 7.12, Luke 6.31. Whiting D274 (Do as you would be done to); Hassell F4; Morawski 724.

352–3 Exodus 20.3, Deuteronomy 5.7.

353 *ii goddes*, but French *divers dieux*. *Deus* was evidently read for *divers*. The error is repeated in ll. 388–9.

370–6 On the conflicting medieval theological views of the nature of the eucharist see Rubin, *Corpus Christi*, 14–35.

378–88 Tubach 1602, 3129; Gregg D12. The story is taken verbatim from Bonaventure, *Collationes De Decem Praeceptis*, 3.14. *Of whom men remembre* clumsily renders *Dont on recorde*. *torned*, that is, returned (*retourna*). *on the to knee*, that is, on one knee, presumably

because the priest is no longer bearing the host. *It is writen ... Crist Iesus*: Philippians 2.10, Romans 14.11, Isaias 45.23.
388–9 *Thowe shalt not love ii goddes* misconstrues *tu nauras pas divers dieux. Namras* was read for *nauras* and *deus* for *divers*. Cf. l. 353.
389–92 Isaias 41.22. There is a similar condemnation of sorcery in the *Treatise on the Commandments* (Royster, 'Treatise,' 13).
395 *fendesse* is not recorded by MED.
396–7 *for the whiche she toke the snare of the fende* translates the French *dont elle se prist a lain. lair* 'brethe' was evidently read for *lain*.
397 Genesis 3.5.
405–6 *trauailleth* renders the French *vont conseillier*, the translator interpreting *vont* to mean 'resort (to),' but neglecting to translate *conseillier*.
407–10 Leviticus 20.6. *de medio populi mei* is supplied from P. The phrase is translated in l. 413.
413 *in* translates Latin *de*, French *du*; see also in l. 10,293.
414–17 Apocalypse 21.8.
421 *envenimoures*: 'poisoners' (*envenimeurs*). Not recorded by MED. The only citation in OED dates from 1598.
425 Ezechiel 18.4, 20 (here misattributed to Paul). After *morietur* the French adds *La seconde mort est la separacion du corps et de lame*.
427 The source of this quotation is the responsory of the burial service, beginning *Libera me, Domine, de morte eterna* based on Romans 7.6. *Holy Writ* is erroneous. All MSS read *sainte eglise* except Q, which has *le scripture*, but without *sainte* and the Latin quotation.
437–8 Augustine, *Enarrationes in Psalmos*, 77.20 (PL 36, col. 996).
439 *maketh his god of his bely*: Philippians 3.19.
445–6 Exodus 20.7, Deuteronomy 5.11.
448 *iii maner of pepil*: the transgressors of this commandment are described in ll. 448–65, 466–503, 540–8. Cf. *Dives* 2.1: *In þre maner Godis name is takyn in veyn, þat is be myslyuynge & be mysspeche and be mysherynge*. In a similar vein, Owst, *Literature*, 418–19, cites Bromyard to the effect that Jews, unlike Christians, flee blasphemy.
453–4 *houndes ... maistris*: McCulloch, *Medieval Latin*, 110–11.
459–61 Whiting H571 (A mad hound cares for neither friend nor foe (bites his own master)).
465 Matthew 15.4.
472–6 Tubach 2789 (Jew at dice-playing). Its direct source is probably

Jacques de Vitry (Crane 218, 91). The story is also found in *Doctrinal of Sapience*, chap. 50 (Gallagher, 158), and in British Library, Harley MS 463, f. 17^b.

482–99 Tubach 1272 (Shooting at father's corpse). See Stechow for a comprehensive account of the sources of this tale and its widespread appearance in literature and art. *iuged*: 'legally decided' (*adiugie*). B's reading, *in God*, is clearly a scribal error, *u* having been read as *n* and *e* as *o*.

500–1 *Salamon and of ii women*: 3 Kings 3.16–27. The story is recounted at length in the *Miroir*.

505–9 Matthew 5.34–6.

518 *vesyly*: 'intentionally' (*apenseement*). MED does not cite the aphetic form in this sense, but it cites *aviseli* (2c) meaning 'intentionally' or 'deliberately' from *The Pilgrimage of the Lyfe of the Manhode*, l. 2336. Cf. l. 5982.

519–20 *notwithstandyng for noght or for some evil cause: touteffois pour nient ou pour aucune mauvaise raison*, that is, every time for noght or for some worthless reason. Cf. *Ayen* 6/27–8: *alneway uor naȝt oþer uor some skele kuede* and *VV* 2/4–5: *for nouȝt or for þing þt is worþ. touteffois* was mistakenly rendered by its alternative meaning 'yet, nevertheless.'

527–35 After *sware* the French adds *ou le livre sur quoy il jure*. The same observation, recalling Proverbs 6.1–2, is made by *Fasciculus Morum*, Book 3, chap. 4, ll. 17–23 (Wenzel, 164, 166): *Et hic adverte quod scienter menciens cum periurio primo obligat se diabolo, et quando cum manu librum tangit vel rem sacram, tunc per illam manum retinet eum diabolus donec ad penitenciam redeat; et in tantum quod cum cibum capit, de manu diaboli capit; similiter si se signet aut huiusmodi faciat, totum de manu diaboli est. Unde Proverbiorum 6: 'Defixisti apud extraneum manum tuam, illaqueatus es verbis oris tui, et similiter captus propriis sermonibus.'*

535–40 A variant of Tubach 3704. Cf. *Speculum Laicorum* (Welter, 91, no. 470a) where the perjurer's hand burns away; in a late version it shrivels (Herbert, *Catalogue of Romances*, 410, no. 9). Caesarius of Heisterbach, *Dialogus Miraculorum*, 7.44, tells the grim tale of a man who was struck dead for a false oath.

542 Apocalypse 3.1.

550–1 Exodus 20.8, Deuteronomy 5.12.

552–60 Exodus 20.9–11, Deuteronomy 5.13–15. The passage is based on Augustine, *De Genesi ad Litteram*, 4.11 (PL 34, cols 303–4).

Ecclesiastical prohibitions against *opera servilia* on Sunday are discussed by Huber, *Geist und Buchstabe*, 49–222, and Rordorf, *Sunday*, 154–73. On the names for the Sabbath and their significance see Rordorf, *Sunday*, 274–93.

563–4 Ezechiel 3.27. The shortened form *Eze* appears only in DV.

565–72 For the general concern over the neglect or abuse of the Sabbath and the specific complaint against tavern haunting see *Dives* 3.6, the *Treatise on the Commandments* (Royster, 'Treatise,' 21–2), the pulpit denunciations cited by Owst, *Literature*, 434–41, and Parker, *English Sabbath*, 11–15. The subject recurs in ll. 5685–719.

568 The superfluous conjunction *which* destroys the syntax of the sentence and is not supported by the French: *Cest contre moult de pecheurs qui au iour de diemence et des festes de dieu et de la benoite vierge marie et des sains et des saintes de paradis ne sont pas en pais mais suivent les caroles et les tavernes et les bordeaulx et degastent le temps que dieu leur a donne pour dieu servir et pour emploier en bonnes oeuvres*, and so on.

573–6 Cf. Matthew 18.28.

582–8 Cf. *Dives* 3.5: *Also God byddith þat men schuldyn beþinkyn hem to halwyn wel þe halyday for in þe halyday, namely on þe Sonday, men schuldyn drawyn here wittis togedere from þe world & beþinkyn hem ȝif þei haddyn ouȝt trespasyd þat woke be recleshed or be couetyse or be lecherie or ony oþir wise & askyn God forȝifnesse.*

589–90 Psalm 94.2.

590–3 *Truly oure festes ... for to come*: Colossians 2.16–17. Cf. *Dives* 3.22.

603 *inowe*: an error (repeated in l. 877) for *nowe* 'then, at that time.' Cf. MED *nou* adv.

604–7 Luke 16.24.

607–10 On the origin and rationale of the Sunday observance see Baukham 'Sabbath and Sunday,' 232–40, and Bacchiocchi, *Sabbath*, 270–302, 308.

610–58 The familiar attribution to Augustine of the historical events that Sunday commemorated appears to derive from *Sermones de Diversis* (appendix), 280.2 (PL 39, col. 2274), and *Epistolae*, 2.55 (PL 33, cols 204–23). Similar material is found in Ambrose, *Enarrationes in Psalmos*, 43 (PL 14, cols 1090–1); Isidore, *Etymologiae*, 6.18 (PL 83, cols 760–1); and, among later writers, in Pseudo-Alcuin, *De Divinis Officiis*, 27 (PL 101, cols 1226–7), Jonas Aurelianensis Episcopus, *De Institutione Regia*, 16 (PL 106, col. 304), Theodulf, *Capitular*, 24 (PL

105, col. 198), and, in greater detail than the preceeding works, the sixth-century Irish 'Epistle Concerning Sunday' (O'Keefe, 'Cain Downaig,' 198–201). The passage in the *Mirroure* bears a particularly close resemblance to one in the late fourteenth-century *Manuale Sacerdotum Parochalium, De Die Dominica Observanda* (British Library Harley MS 4172, ff. 48[a]–49[a]): *Augustinus ponit multa signa hoc ad quod dies dominica est veneranda in qua visa fuit prima lux sicut in genesi legitur. In hac enim die multa et magna mirabilia pro nostra salute fecit dominus. In die dominica requievit archa post diluvium. In die dominica pluit dominus manna de celo filiis Israel in deserto. In die dominica percussum est mare rubrum per manum moysi et transierunt ebrei c milia armatorum et cecinerunt canticum domino. Et iterum percussit mare Moyses et reversum est mare in locum suum. Mersus est Pharao cum curribus et equitibus suis et non est relictus ex eis unus. In die dominica percussit moyses petram in deserto et fluxerunt quattuor flumina. In die dominica natus est Christus ex virgine Maria. In die dominica baptizatus est Christus et spiritus sanctus venit super eum in specie columbae. In die dominica fecit dominus vinum ex aqua in cana galilee. In die dominica saciavit dominus v milia hominum de v panibus etc. In die dominica surrexit dominus. In die dominica venit dominus ad apostolos ianuis clausis. In die dominica confederavit pacem inter celum et terram et inter angelos et homines inter deum et hominem inter corpus et animam sicut apostolus dicit: Ipse est pax nostra qui fecit utrumque unum. In die dominica misit spiritum sanctum in apostolos. In die dominica in pathmos insula apocalipsim revelavit Johanni evaungelistae. In die dominica raptus fuit Paulus in tertium celum et audivit archana dei que non licet homini loqui sicut ipsemet dicit. In die dominica dominus noster Ihesus Christus venturus est in magestate sua cum angelis suis quando reddet unicuique iuxta opera sua. Ante dominicam passionis non appellabatur dominica ex prima Sabbati. Septem dies habet ebdomada sex ad operandum dominis, unam dedit nobis ad operandum ad remocionem malorum. Adveniente sancta die dominica festinare debemus in sancta die, id est, recedentes ab opere ad ecclesias procedamus. Non enim ab opere tantum est recedendum sed a malis et a peccatis. In die dominica quosdam videbis coreas ducentes alios citharizantes quosdam in armis plaudentes alios ridentes et proximis detrahentes et alia multa quae homines in festis faciunt et hec sunt gravia peccata et gravibus penitenciis digna. Si vero ad ecclesiam veniunt vident ibi dominum Ihesum Cristum et sanctus*

spiritus presencialiter ibidem assistit et angeli descendunt et alia multa dicit comendans qui ecclesiam humiliter et devote frequentant vituperantes facientes vanitates in tali sanctissimo. For the early history of this tradition in the West see Cobb, 'Christian Year,' 404–5, and Thomas, *Sonntag*, 39–47. A comparable tradition in the Jewish Midrash is discussed by Dugmore, *Influence*, 26–7. According to Parker, *English Sabbath*, 18, the tradition continued in Reformation and post-Reformation Sabbatarianism. *In genesi legitur fiat lux* is supplied from the French; it is, in fact, translated in ll. 661–2. *in armis plaudantes*: so all MSS (CNRUV *plaudentes*) except D *alios manus plaudentes*. There is a brief notice of the *Manuale* in Boyle, 'Study of the Works,' 70, and Pantin, *English Church*, 278–9.
661 Genesis 1.3.
664–5 Genesis 9.12–17. *departed hym* 'spread out' (MED *departen* v., 1a(f)) misconstrues *recedit*, a variant of *recidit* 'happened, appeared.' The arc was generally interpreted in biblical exegesis as a sign of divine promise.
665–6 Exodus 16.14.
666–71 Exodus 14.21–8, Psalms 95.1, 149.1. *smotte* translates *ferue* which was read as *ferme* (hence B's *shette*).
671–3 A conflation of Exodus 17.6 and Genesis 2.10.
673–4 Matthew 1.25.
674–5 Matthew 3.15–16.
675–7 John 4.46. *strete*: ACNPQU *rue*, RV *ville*, DS om. Although MED provides a meaning of *strete* (2d) as 'town, village,' it seems likely that this is an instance of the translator's characteristically close adherence to his French source.
677–8 John 6.9–12.
678–80 Matthew 21.1–10.
680–1 Matthew 28.1–8.
681–2 John 20.19. *the ȝatis shette*, that is, when the gates were shut.
682–5 A paraphrase and conflation of 2 Corinthians 5.18–20, 1 Corinthians 6.16–17, and 1 Timothy 1.1.
685–7 Acts 2.1–4.
687–8 Apocalypse 1.1.
688–91 2 Corinthians 12.4.
691–3 Matthew 24.30–1, 25.31–46.
704 *some that drawe aweye othir* attempts to render the spurious Latin reading *extharisantes* in l. 650. The French MSS properly read *citharisantes*, which is translated *[les uns] qui sonnent et harpent.*

718 *some necessite* translates *aucune necessite* found uniquely in D; other MSS read *grant necessite.*
719–23 The division of the commandments into two groups – the first three ordering man's relationship to God, the last seven ordering man's relationship to neighbours – derives from Augustine, *Sermo*, 9.5 (PL 38, col. 79).
723–4 Exodus 20.12, Deuteronomy 5.16.
732–5 John 19.25–7.
735–40 Tubach 4644. Although all but one of the French MSS read *grue* ('crane') – the sole exception is D (*signoigne*) – the story is actually told of the stork (*cyconia*) and goes back to Aristotle, *Historia Animalium*, 615b; Aelian 3.23; and Pliny, *Historia Naturalis*, 10.32. It is also found in Ambrose, *Hexaemeron*, 5.16 (PL 14, col. 229); Bartholomaeus Anglicus, *De Proprietatibus*, 12.8; Jacques de Vitry 260 (Crane, 109); *Novus Physiologus*, ll. 817–28; Grosseteste, *De Decem Mandatis*, 4.16; and *Dives* 4.3. See also McCulloch, *Medieval Latin*, 174; Friedmann, *Bestiary*, 296–7; Rowland, *Animals*, 161. A similar story is told of the hoopoe in *Physiologus*, 10 (ed. Carmody, 21–2). See also McCulloch, *Medieval Latin*, 126–7; Friedmann, *Bestiary*, 224–6; Dawson, 'Lore of the Hoopoe,' 126–42. Little or no distinction was made between the two birds. Cf. Hassig, Bestiaries, 93–103.
743–4 1 Timothy 5.3–5. Here the statement is more generally applied to the relationship between children and parents.
747–63 Tubach 2001 (Father in stable). The story is taken directly from Peraldus 2.6.3.37, but versions of it appear in a large number of medieval story collections, among them, *Alphabetum Narrationum, Liber Exemplorum, Manuel des Péchés, Speculum Laicorum*, and *Handlyng Synne*, as well as among the exempla of Jacques de Vitry and Odo of Chriton. There is a shorter version of the story in *Dives* 4.4. *olde clothis the wiche was called estamme ou flossoye, stamyne or boltel* renders a passage that varies in the French: A *unq viel habit qui est appelle estamne*, C *une vielle vesture qui estoit appellee estanine ou flochee*, D *ung drap qui estoit appele estamne ou floschee*, N *une vieille vesteure qui estoit appellee estamne ou floschaye*, P *une vieille flochee ou estanine* [possibly *estamne*], Q *une vielle vesteure qui estoit appellee estamine ou flossaie*, R *une vieille couverture de flossoie*, U *une vielle vesture qui estoit appellee estamme ou flocsee*, V *une vieille couverture ou flossaie*, S om. *estame* 'combed wool' is clearly an error for *estamine* which, like *flossoye*, refers to a garment or covering of coarse light woolen or cotton cloth that was also used as

a horse blanket. Q uniquely preserves the correct form, CP nearly so. RV omit the word altogether. *Estamme* is rendered as *slavaine* in l. 758. *Destamme* of the English manuscript (l. 751) has been emended to *estamme*, the translator having mistaken the preposition *d(e)* as the first letter of the French word. There is a similar error in l. 8001 (*esprove/desprove*). Cf. Godefroy, s.v. *estame* n., *estamin(e)* n., *flassaie* n., *flassart* n.; Zangger, s.v. *étamine* n.; Cotgrave, s.v. *estamine* n.; Tobler-Lommatsch, s.v. *estamine* n., *flassaie* n.; AND s.v. *estamine* n.; Douet-D'Arcq, s.v. *estamine* n. (374), *flocées* n. (376); OED, s.v. *stamin* n.; and MED, s.v. *bultel* n., *stamen* n., *sclavin(e)* n., the latter two not provided with the precise senses of *estamine* and *flossaie* employed in the text.

763–4 Ecclesiasticus 3.14. Ecclesiastes and Ecclesiasticus are frequently confused in the *Mirroure* and its source.

765–70 Hebrews 13.17. *be*: all MSS read *sont*, perhaps in error for *font*.

776 Luke 11.2.

779–80 Hebrews 4.13.

782 Exodus 20.13, Deuteronomy 5.17.

786–7 Cf. ll. 346–7 and *n*.

792–4 1 John 3.1.

800–3 1 Peter 1.18–19.

804 *principal chambir of Goddes hous* loosely renders *principal manoir et maison de dieu*. On coordinates resolved as genitives see Ellis, 'Choices of the Translator,' 42*n*47. For other instances see ll. 1505, 4083, 4778, 8862.

818–19 Genesis 4.10. The others – they are generally considered to number four rather than three – are the crimes against nature of Sodom and Gomorrha (Genesis 18.20), the oppression of the laboring poor (James 5), and the oppression of widows and orphans (Psalm 93.1–6).

822–3 1 John 3.15.

824 *thought afore*: 'premeditated' (*apensee*).

825 A sentence has been lost after *commandement*: *Et celui qui porte ire encontre autri longuement tenue et enracinee de long temps en son cuer cest rancure et hayne qui est pechie mortel et encontre cest commandement.*

829 The repetition of *to noye any* after *indignacion* is redundant and receives no support from the MSS: *Mais indignacion qui passe legierement*, and so on. It is probably an eyeskip and should perhaps be deleted.

830–1 *withoute consentyng of aforethought* translates *sans consente-*

ment delibere et apense. MED cites a single instance of the phrase *malice afore thought* 1472–3 (*afore-* pref., 2). The only form of the noun is *forethought* cited uniquely from Idley (c. 1450).
834 Exodus 20.19, Deuteronomy 5.18.
840 *lytil*: ACDNPQ *mains*, RUV *plusers*, S om.
845–6 The five kinds of carnal sin discussed here are simple fornication (ll. 847–906), adultery (ll. 906–13), violation (ll. 913–22), incest (ll. 922–7), and unnatural vice (ll. 927–60). Raptus, normally included in medieval treatises on sexual abuse, is omitted in the *Miroir*.
850 *lightnes of the flesshe*: 'wantonness, promiscuity' (*legierete de la char*). Not recorded by MED. OED cites *lightness* in this sense from 1516 and the phrase *lightness of bodie* under 1541.
878 *multiplie for fruite be man* is an incorrect rendering of *pour lignie multiplier par home*. *pour* appears to have been construed as a preposition.
880 *the ofte beyng*, that is, frequent intercourse (*le souvent hanter*). For this expression see Adams, *Latin Sexual Vocabulary*, 177. MED does not record the phrase. For excessive coitus considered as a cause of infertility see Cadden, *Sex Difference*, 243.
898–9 Ecclesiasticus 23.19.
899–900 Ecclesiasticus 16.3.
900–1 1 Corinthians 7.7, 25–35.
905–6 *hous propre, hors propre, wyf propre*: postpositional adjectives are frequently employed in the *Mirroure*. Cf. *chirche general* (l. 1223), *lordshipp gret* (l. 1543), *leche fried* (l. 1717), *man reneyed* (l. 1916), *besinesses necessarie* (l. 10,294), *virginite prowde* (l. 12,060), *vessellis sacred* (l. 12,201). Occasionally, they bear plural French-type endings (*preciouses* (l. 6688), *germeines* (l. 9000), *ȝaraȝineis* (l. 8018)). For the latter see Mustanoja, *Middle English Syntax*, 277, and Fischer, 'Syntax,' 214.
912 *stablisseth*: 'settles an inheritance on' (*establist ses heritiers*). The earliest citation in MED to this sense is c. 1475.
914 *corrompyng*: 'violation of chastity' (*corrumpement*). Not recorded by MED as a verbal noun in this sense.
915–19 Genesis 34.2, 25–9. *Sichion*, that is, Sichem. Perhaps a scribal error.
920 *violens*: 'force, rape.' Not recorded by MED as a verb in this sense.
921 After *sacrilege* the French adds: *Ou se cest violence ou force comme se une pucelle estoit ravie par force de la maison de son pere. Cest Raab.* The reference is to Joshua 2.

925–7 1 Corinthians 5.5.

928–33 From the time of Philo and Josephus in the first century A.D. the sin of Sodom and its neighboring cities was identified with homosexual practice, so provoking the wrath of God by virtue of its enormity and shame that he destroyed them. The homosexual interpretation of the Sodom story became strongly entrenched in medieval Christian thought. In Genesis 19.24–6 the destruction of Sodom and Gomorrah and the turning of Lot's wife into a pillar of salt are recounted. The other cities – Admah, Zeboim, and Zoar – are identified in Genesis 14.2. In the French they are named *Adaya*, *Seboyon*, and *Segor*. The source of the phrase *syn aȝens nature* is Romans 1.24–7. *the worst* echoes Genesis 13.13: *sodomitae pessimi erant*. Brundage, *Law, Sex*, 13–14, finds in Plato's *Laws* the origin of the belief that homosexual acts are unnatural. Peter Damian, *Liber Gomorrhianus*, 1 (PL 145, col. 161), regarded sodomy as the gravest violation of nature, and, since he is expicitly cited in l. 945, he may be deemed the source of the like opinion expressed in ll. 927–8. Peter Lombard and Albertus Magnus shared Damian's view (Bailey, *Homosexuality*, 19–20; Boswell, *Christianity*, 316; Bullough, 'Sin against Nature,' 64–5). On post-exilic Jewish and patristic and medieval attitudes towards the sin of Sodom see Bailey, *Homosexuality*, 9–28, 64–120; Goodich, *Unmentionable Vice*, 25–63; Bullough 'Sin against Nature,' 59–64; Payer, *Bridling of Desire*, 40–4, 135–9; and Brundage, *Law, Sex*, 57, 121–2, 174, 212–14, 313–14, 398–401, 472–4.

937–8 Augustine, *Confessiones*, 3.8 (PL 32, col. 689).

944–56 Peter Damian, *Liber Gomorrhianus*, 21 (PL 145, col. 182). Its direct source, however, is Bonaventure, *Collationes De Decem Praeceptis*, 6.15. The Latin tale is about masturbation – see the reference to the *touchyngis with handes* in l. 958 – but is here employed as a further caution against homosexuality.

946 *and*: the French reads *en penitence tres aspre*. *en* seems to have been misread as *et*.

957 *abusage*: 'sexual misconduct' (*abusage*). Not recorded by MED. *incontinence* denotes 'impurity.'

962 Exodus 20.15, Deuteronomy 5.19.

965–6 Raimundus de Pennaforte, *Summa de Paenitentia*, 2.6.1, col. 528.

967–70 Peter Lombard, *Sententiae*, 3.37 (PL 192, col. 832), commenting on Exodus 12.35–6, by way of Bonaventure, *Collationes De Decem Praeceptis*, 6.17.

971–9 Bonaventure, *Collationes De Decem Praeceptis*, 6.17.
972–9 *In this commandement also is forbedyn opyn raveyn ... to hym that wolde paye* partly misconstrues the French: *En cest commandement est deneee rappine aperte comme quant on tolt a autri sa chose a force apertement sicomme font ces larrons couvers, et fraude et barat sicomme ceulx qui vendent leurs choses par condicion ausquelz on adioint couvenant pour decevoir sicomme est marchandise a terme ou len donne la chose a celui qui la croit pour cent solz que on don[ne]roit a celui qui paieroit pour cinquante solz. larrons* refers to the *men* who are guilty of *opyn raveyn* (l. 973), whereas *fraude* and *barat* refer to the deceptive practice described in ll. 974–9 and condemned as usurious (McLaughlin, 'Teaching of Canonists,' 119–20). *takith* (l. 974) means 'take by force, seize' (*tolt ... a force*).
979–81 *In siche wise ... the tyme*: profiting from a loan was deemed usurious partly on the ground that, as enunciated by William of Auxerre and Innocent IV, it violated a universal law against the sale of time which is common to all. Cf. *Tabula Exemplorum* 304 (Welter, 82), quoting William of Auxerre (*Summa Aurea*, 3.48.3, 391): *Usura: item faciunt contra legem universalem, quia vendunt tempus quod est commune omnium creaturarum* and Bonaventure, *Collationes De Decem Praeceptis*, 6.18: *Usura, in qua id quod venditur, est commune, scilicet tempus*. The same point is made in ll. 991–2. Relevant texts are assembled and discussed by Noonan, *Scholastic Analysis of Usury*, 43–4; McLaughlin, 'Teaching of Canonists,' 111; Ibanès, *Doctrine de l'Église*, 19–20; and Delumeau, *Sin and Fear*, 222.
981–3 Bonaventure, *Collationes De Decem Praeceptis*, 6.18. *of weyght and of mesure*: Leviticus 19.35–6, Deuteronomy 25.13–15. The object of a loan applied only to things that could be counted, weighed, or measured, according to the pronouncements of medieval canonists. See McLaughlin, 'Teaching of Canonists,' 100, citing, among others, Huguccio, *Summa*, f. 217[b]: *Mutuum enim consistit in his rebus quae pondere, numero vel mensura constant veluti vino, oleo, frumento, pecunia numerata, aere, argento, auro*, and so on, *the which thyng fewe marchandes eschewe* misconstrues the French *la quelle chose pou eschiuent les marchans*, that is, little do merchants eschew such (fraudulent) transactions. *besinesses* (*besongnes*) is not recorded by MED in the sense of 'transactions.' The earliest citation in OED is 1727.
983–7 *Also in the hous and in the clothyng ... thowe wynyst but not of me*: the distinction is between a contract of rent or hire and a loan of

money or other commodity such as wheat or wine. In the former there is a transfer of use for which it is proper to receive payment. In the latter there is a transfer of ownership, and the demand for payment is therefore illicit. What was 'mine' has become 'yours'; for the use of money or other commodity is inseparable from its consumption; indeed, use is consumption. After *eschewe* (l. 983) there is a long omission that introduces the argument. The entire French passage taken from Bonaventure, *Collationes De Decem Praeceptis*, 6.19, reads: *Mais pourquoy nest ce usure se je prens louage de mon cheval ou de ma maison ou de ma vesteure sicomme je la prens de ma monnaie? Je respons que du cheval et de la maison et de la vesteure est trait lusage et peuent* (D *puet*) *empirier et amenuisier de lusage mais* (D *de*) *la monnaie nest pas aussi. Car elle na fors lusage de mutacion et nest fors muee en autre qui autant vault comme celle feroit se elle estoit vendue en icelui temps. Item en la maison et en la vesteure etc.* (ACD *qui*) *est fait aprest* (ADNQ *ou*, C *et*) *en ouvrage en la quele chose la value nest pas tenue mais en la peccune ou la monnaie ma chose est faicte. Et pource en ta chose par ton sens tu gaignes non pas de la mienne* (NP *mienne*, CQRV *moye*, ADU *monnoye*, S om). The translator whose exemplar must have read *moye* 'mine' failed to recognize it as a possessive. On the distinction between a lease and a loan see McLaughlin, 'Teaching of Canonists,' 100–2, and Noonan, *Scholastic Analysis of Usury*, 39–51.

991–2 *But the vsurer ... reste of the nyght*: *Tabula Exemplorum* 304 (Welter, 82): *Item usurarii vendunt lucem et requiem, lucem diei et requiem noctis.*

994–5 Jeremias 16.13.

995–6 Cf. *Tabula Exemplorum* 15 (Welter, 5): *Item nota quod in vanum dicitur requiem pro usurario, quia neque nocte neque aliquo festo dedit requiem quin semper usura curreret.*

997–8 Ezechiel 7.13.

1002–20 Tubach 5027. An extremely popular tale, it appears in a large number of story books, as Herbert notes (*Catalogue of Romances*, 53, no. 84). Its source in the *Miroir* may be Jacques de Vitry 207 (Crane, 86–87). *templis* (l. 1012) departs from the French *cheveulx*. On the matter of restitution see ll. 4604–9*n*.

1026–7 Exodus 20.16, Deuteronomy 5.20.

1033–4 Augustine, *Contra Mendacium*, 1.12 (PL 40, col. 537). Cf. Raimundus de Pennaforte, *Summa de Paenitentia*, 1.10, col. 380, and *Decretum*, C.22.2.5 (Friedberg 1, col. 868).

1035–9 Augustine, *Enarrationes in Psalmos,* 5.7 (PL 36, cols 85–6). Cf. Raimundus, as above, and *Decretum,* C.22.2.14 (Friedberg 1, col. 871).
1049–51 *And for this cause ... venym in the mouthe*: Peraldus 2.9.2.5. Cf. Augustine, *In Iohannis Evangelium Tractatus CXXIV,* 42.11–13 (PL 35, cols 1703–5) and Isidore, *Sententiae,* 2.30.5 (PL 83, col. 632).
1051–4 John 8.44. Whiting D186 (The devil is a liar and the father of lies).
1054–7 Tubach 3102, 4053. Its direct source is *Tabula Exemplorum* 168 (Welter, 46).
1057–8 Isidore, *Sententiae,* 2.30.1 (PL 83, col. 632); Jerome, *Epistolae,* 6 (PL 22, col. 337); Werner M23.
1059 *trueseyrres:*'speakers of the truth' (*les vrais disans*). Cf. MED s.v., *seier* n. (a) 'a seyer of trouth' (c. 1450).
1059–61 Isidore, *Sententiae,* 2.55.2 (PL 83, col. 727).
1061–5 The story is taken from *Tabula Exemplorum* 165 (Welter, 46). An earlier version is in Petrus Alfonsi, *Disciplina Clericalis,* 11.
1077–8 Exodus 20.17, Deuteronomy 5.21.
1090–1 Matthew 5.28.
1093 *with the yee of his herte* misconstrues the French *avec elle de son cuer,* confusing *elle* 'her' with *oeil* 'eye.'
1100–1 Exodus 20.17, Deuteronomy 5.21.
1107 *the sertein consentyng and the full thought* mistakes the French *le consentement apense et certain. full thought* may be a scribal error for *forethought. apensee* was translated as *thought afore* in l. 824.
1110–23 The source of this story has not been identified. MED does not record *almesse* (*ala(u)mosne*) in the sense of 'almsgiving' or 'charitable event.' *brothirhode* (*frayerie*) refers to a parish confraternity devoted to charitable activity.
1137 James 2.10.
1138 *Feithe,* but French *loy,* which was evidently read as *foy.* The same error occurs in ll. 1281, 6000, 7575.
1145–7 The meaning is that the first article pertains to the Father, the next seven to the Son, and the last four to the Holy Ghost. The numerical error derives from the French texts, all of them corrupt except D: *dont le premier appartient au pere, les autres deus ensuians au filz, le quart au saint esperit.* D properly reads *les sept au filz.* The correct reading is also found in *Ayen* 11/32 and *VV* 6/26–7.
1149–51 For the tradition, originating with Rufinus's *Commentarius in symbolum apostolorum* (PL 21, col. 337) and the Pseudo-Augustinian

Sermo de symbolo (PL 39, col. 2189), that each of the apostles composed an article of the creed, see Kelly, *Early Christian Creeds*, 1–6; Bühler, 'Apostles,' Gordon 'Articles,'; Kosmer, 'Style and Iconography,' vol. 1, pp. 35–41; *Othea* 36/3–5 and *n*; *VV* 6/30–2; and *Ayen* 12/2–3 and *n*. Like *Ayen* and *VV*, the *Mirroure* follows the apostolic order of the eighth-century *Sacramentarium Gallicanum*. D assigns the second article to St Andrew and the fourth to St John the Evangelist.
1158 *beyng* (*essence*) is not recorded by MED as a synonym of *godhed*.
1195 Resumptive pronouns occur occasionally throughout the text. Cf. ll. 2782, 5440, 9844.
1223 *chirche general*, that is, 'the universal church' (MED, s.v. *general* adj, 4b). All the French MSS read *general* except D, which has *generallement*, an error that was probably in B's exemplar.
1229 *holy unccion* 'extreme unction': apparently the first appearance of the phrase, which is cited by MED only from *The Assembly of the Gods* (c. 1444).
1251–7 Apocalypse 13.1–2. On the adoption of the beast rising from the sea as a structural image in treatises on the vices, see Newhauser, *Vices and Virtues*, 163–5.
1263 *A leparde hatthe diuers coloure*: Bartholomaeus Anglicus, *De Proprietatibus*, 18.67. Cf. Collins, *Symbolism*, 89; McCulloch, *Medieval Latin*, 150–1.
1265–9 On the strength of the bear's feet see Aristotle, *Historia animalium*, 594b; Pliny, *Historia Naturalis*, 8.54; Isidore, *Etymologiae*, 12.2.22 (PL 82, col. 437); Hrabanus Maurus, *De Universo*, 8.1 (PL 111, col. 223); *Novus Physiologus*, l. 268. See also White, *Bestiary*, 45; McCulloch, *Medieval Latin*, 94; and Friedmann, *Bestiary*, 194–7.
1270–1 On the fierceness of the lion see McCulloch, *Medieval Latin*, 137–40; *Gesta Romanorum* 104; White, *Bestiary*, 8; Friedmann, *Bestiary*, 229–53. *for his grete cruelnes*: Whiting L308 (As cruel as (a) lion(s)); Hassell L65.
1271–85 The sources of the symbolization of the seven heads and ten horns of the beast to represent the deadly sins and the violation of the commandments have their origin in Richard of St Victor, *In Apocalypsim Joannis*, 4.1 (PL 196, col. 799). See Bloomfield, *Seven Deadly Sins*, 85; Kosmer, 'Style and Iconography,' vol. 2, 42–3.
1281 *feithe*, but French *loi*. See l. 1138*n*.
1288 Whiting G96 (He that gives not which he loves has not what he desires).
1309–10 Morawski 1805 (*Qui a le vilain a la proie*).

1313 Matthew 7.17. Cf. Hassell A161 (*De bon arbre précieux fruit*).
1313–14 *Evyn soo ... evil liffe*: possibly a paraphrase of Matthew 12.35.
1315 Augustine, *De Civitate Dei*, 15.22 (PL 41, col. 467).
1319–23 Genesis 2.9, 17; 3.1–24. A subordinate clause has been partially lost after *the tree of dethe*: *pour ce que son fruit donne mort qui ne peut mourir*.
1324 *trees*, that is, the trees whose fruit they were permitted to eat, as D makes clear: *des arbres qui leur estoient ordonnes a menger*.
1326–30 Unlike the *Somme*, the *Miroir* abandons the image of the beast of the sea for the image of the trees of good and evil. The schematization of vices and virtues in the form of trees as a means of elucidating their complex hierarchical relationship was frequently employed as a pictorial and literary device in pastoralia. See O'Reilly, *Iconography*, 323–74, and Newhauser, *Vices and Virtues*, 160–1. The image of the two trees may have originated with Conrad of Hirsau's *De Fructibus Carnis et Spiritus* (PL 176, cols 997–1006).
1333–4 Romans 7.18–25.
1352–3 3 Kings 3–9. *an*: 'and' (ll. 2758, 3446, etc.); *tha*: 'that' (ll. 2524, 2795, etc.) On the loss of stops in Middle English see Milroy, 'Middle English Dialectology,' 197, and LALME IV.313.
1355–7 Romans 14.17.
1366–7 *Whoso knowith ... to bataile*: cf. Hassell C268 (*La connaissance de son ennemi est la moitié de la victoire*).
1373–5 Proverbs 24.30–1. *a wel set man*, but French *cuer bien afaitie*, maintaining the image of the heart begun in l. 1331.
1380 *evil gresse groweth faste*: Whiting W170 (Evil weed is soon grown).
1387 *chief vicis*, that is, the cardinal (or capital) sins often confused with, or used interchangeably for, the deadly (or mortal) sins (l. 1377). Cf. Bloomfield, *Seven Deadly Sins*, 43.
1407 *it is the begynnyng of alle synnes*: Ecclesiasticus 10.15.
1408–10 Isaias 14.12–15. *for his grete beaute and wit*: William of Auxerre, *Summa Aurea*, 3.2, 50–1.
1418–20 Deuteronomy 6.5.
1421–2 *lecherous bodye* translates *le lecheur de corps*, presumably a debauchee. The phrase is not recorded in MED.
1425 *os* 'as' is a form characteristic of Norfolk and neighboring areas. See LALME IV.313. It appears again in l. 10048.
1435–45 Thorns and briars are used to signify the corruption and baseness of sin throughout the *Mirroure*. Cf. ll. 2212, 2217, 3381, 3878–

9, 9364. They apply to illicit desires in ll. 12,041–7. On the biblical and medieval backgrounds of these metaphors see Eberly and Chamberlain, '"Under the Schaddow,"' 15–21.
1438 *brere*: V *rosay*, ACNP *rouchay*, Q *rousay*, R *rousier*, U *rouse*, D *rouce*. *roray* ('dewe') was evidently read for *rosay*. *rouces* is translated correctly as *breris* in l. 1440.
1443 *goode gardner*: John 20.15.
1446 *springlyngis*: 'shoots' (*getons*). Not recorded by MED.
1469 A likely allusion to the legend of the devil's daughters (the number varies from four to nine) who are married to various classes of men. It is recounted in the *Tabula Exemplorum* 58 (Welter, 19); Jacques de Vitry 244 (Crane, 101–2, and *n*, 235–6); and other exempla and sermons. There is a versified French version, *Mariage des neuf filles du Diable*, spuriously attributed to Robert Grosseteste. Pride is called the eldest of the devil's daughters in *Handlyng Synne* (l. 2993), adapted from the *Manuel des Péchés* (c. 1260–70), and in a collection of fifteenth-century homilies cited by Owst, *Literature*, 96. Cf. Tubach 1452; Bossuat 3479; Hauréau, 'Les Filles,' 225–8; Bourgain, *Chaire Française*, 220–2; Bloomfield, *Seven Deadly Sins*, 129, 136, 141–2, 172, 397 *n*109; and Newhauser, *Vices and Virtues*, 194 *n*26.
1473–4 *Pride is the quene ... of vicis*: Hugh of Strasbourg, *Compendium Theologicae Veritatis*, 3.15; William of Auxerre, *Summa Aurea*, 12.4, p. 393.
1498–1501 *We see al daye ... lefte pride* mistranslates the French: *Ce veons nous tous les iours que une personne qui tout son pouair son avoir et son corps met a acquerir boban. Je suis lomme du monde, dira il, ou il a mains dorgueil. son avoir* was apparently read as *savoir* and translated as a finite verb.
1504–5 *al triacle torneth to venym*. Whiting H433, s.v. 1532, quoting More's *Confutation* 422 (Turnyng all honye into poyson). *chastisment of techyng*: *doctrine et chastiement*, the copulative translated as a preposition. Cf. ll. 804, 4083, 4778, 8862.
1507–10 The passage is based on Bernard, *De Gradibus Humilitatis et Superbiae*, 17.45 (*Opera* 3, 51): *Multis modis fiunt excusationes in peccatis: Aut enim dicit qui se excusat: Non feci aut feci sed bene feci aut si male: non multum male aut si multum male non mala intentione. but that I ... never wers* paraphrases the French: *A cestui mal fussent ores tous nos maulx atournes*.
1520 *synnes*, but all French MSS read *parties* except V *branches*. *pechies* may have been read for *parties*.

1523 *plante*: 'shoot' (*geton*). MED, s.v. *plaunt(e)* n., 1c.
1534–66 An abbreviated version of the popular sermon of the redemption, *Rex et Famulus*, inspired by Bernard's *In Annuntiatione Dominica*, Sermo 1 (*Opera* 5, 13–29). The text appears in Immaculate, 'Four Daughters,' 952–4. On its complex history see Sajavaara, *Chateau d'Amour*, 54–90.
1536–7 *the whiche was bothe pore and bonde* is an independent sentence in the French: *Un garcon ot en son hostel et serf.*
1541 *bailie*: In one of the many versions of the fable, *Les Quatre Sereurs* (Långfors, *Incipits*, 181–3, 221–48), the king appoints the thrall seneschal of his country.
1545 *a grete theef* does not appear in the French: *et avecques celui moult grant quantite de fourbetures. roveres*, that is, 'reavers' (*fourbetures*). *hym that*: For other instances of this collocation see above, 'Introduction,' 21 and *n*116.
1555–6 *and for his iustice and grete trouthe and taken heede of hym* misconstrues the French *et pour sa grant iustice loiaute garder.*
1557 *ientilles*: not recorded by MED in the sense of 'favors' (*courtesies*).
1561 *plees* mistakes French *explois* 'revenues.'
1566 *mystirman*, but French *menestreel* 'servant.'
1575 *in blode of baptesme* mistakes *en saint batesme, saint* having been read as *sanc de.*
1578 *grace* in French reads *graces*, referring to the gifts of the Holy Ghost.
1581 *v besantis*: Matthew 25.15–21.
1633 On the image of the exemplary mirror see Bradley, 'Speculum Images,' 10.
1638 *dungehille vnder a snowe*: cf. Whiting S441 (Snow makes a dunghill white).
1643 *dayly*, but French *tousiours.*
1649 *thurgh þe caytyvous pride of this worlde* misconstrues *pour acquerir le chetif boban du monde, pour acquerir* having been read as *pour ce que.*
1652–3 *streccheth forthe*: a past participle rendering French *estendues.* Cf. *contrevith thyngis* (ll. 1945–6).
1656 The phrase *be smale parties* is not recorded in MED.
1663–4 Whiting T533 (One good turn asks another); Hassell B142; Morawski 1146.
1664–5 *to hym ... doon to hym* is an awkward rendering of *Qui moult*

fait pour moy moult lui doy rendre. Cf. Whiting D274 (Do as you would be done to).

1671 MED does not record *advises* (*avis*) in the sense of 'goods, material benefits.' Godefroy, s.v. *avis* n., *'portion de bien qui un pere assigne à ses puinés.'*

1676 *boole* translates *beuf*, the reading unique to D. The other MSS read *boterel* 'toad.'

1691 Here, and throughout the text, *Yngelond* is regularly substituted for *France*.

1698 *tormentis*: 'tournaments' (*tournois*). MED, *tournament* n, provides two examples of this uncommon variant derived from Medieval Latin *tormentum*. Du Cange cites a single Anglo-Latin source.

1702–3 *repent the* misconstrues *respond toy*, 'hide yourself.'

1703 B's reading of *doo* for *be* (*seroies*) may be due to eyeskip (l. 1704) or more likely to confusion of the letters *s* and *f*, as also in ll. 769, 5663, 5856, 6750, 10687, and 12646.

1706 The unusual spelling *thee* for *the* occurs twenty-six times in the *Mirroure*, for example, ll. 4428, 4815, 5207. Not in MED. OED cites a single instance from *Cursor Mundi*.

1714 *forȝeth*: a contracted form of *forȝeteth* 'forgets.'

1717 *leche fried* mistakes French *leschefrite* 'dripping pan.' Godefroy, s.v. *lechefreit* n. The word was also used for a variety of dishes consisting of sliced meat and other ingredients (cf. MED *leche*^{2} n., b, and OED *leach*^{1} n., 2).

1727 *thanke*, but French *loer* 'praise.'

1728–30 Psalm 9.1–2.

1746 *Torkys* and *Sarrazins* are synonymous, meaning little more than disbelievers or pagans. Cf. Daniel, *Heroes and Saracens*, 8–9, and Jones, 'Conventional Saracen,' 202, 204.

1758–9 *vii houres of the daye* refers to the seven daily services of the divine office, that is, matins and lauds (treated together), prime, terce, sext, none, compline, and vespers.

1760–4 *Truly he is a velein ... or othir weyes whoso can: Et certes moult est le cuer mauvais et villain qui celle bonte oublie ou qui le puet faire et ne veult dire ces sept heures du iour ou par nombres de paternostres sicomme font ces convers de cisteaulx ou en autre maniere qui le scet. le cuer* is rendered as *he. the coventis of Celestinis* replaces *ces convers de cisteaulx*. The Celestines (also known as the Hermits of St Damian and as the Hermits of Morrone) were a continental branch of the Benedictines centered in Paris and noted for their asceticism and piety. Henry V endeavored without success to found a house in England. Cf. Heath, *Church and Realm*, 273; Knowles, *Religious Orders*, vol. 1, 175, 181–2, 276; Wylie, 214, 230–1, and *History of England*, vol. 2, 352–64; Catto, 'Religious Change,' 87, 110–11; *Gesta Henrici Quinti*, 186–7. *Convers* were professed laybrothers (later laysisters) in auxiliary service to a religious house. They were particularly numerous and influential in the Cistercian order, which employed them in a variety of tasks and often gave them administrative control of the temporal affairs of the community. The institution of Cistercian lay brotherhood declined after the thirteenth century. See Donnelly, *Decline*, especially 15–37; Lescher, 'Laybrothers,' 65–6, 70–1; and Lekai, *Cister-cians*, 337. There is a further reference to *convers* and *converses* in l. 5334.

1774 *wagis*: a plural used as a singular. MED, s.v. *wage* n., 2a.

1793–4 *Some be pore and beggaris, and some be pore and laborerris: les uns sont poures et mendians, les autres sont poures laboureurs.* The *and* between *pore* and *laborerris* should probably be deleted.

1797–8 For *thy rentis* and *thy lordshipis* the French reads *terres rentes et seignouries*. Possibly a scribal omission.

1798 *Seynt Martinis Feste*, that is, Martinmas, 11 November, when fairs were regularly held.

1807–8 *It is goon ... that I have named to thee*: *Or a mil ans que nul de tous ceulx que je tay nommes nestoit.*

1821 Tilley H492 (The hog never looks up to him that threshes down the acorns). *glene*: 'acorn' (*glan*). Not recorded by MED or OED in this precise sense. Cf. AND, s.v. *glan* n.

1832 *whoso wel luffeth seldom forȝeteth*: Whiting L565 (He that loves leally forgets late); Hassell A63; Morawski 1835. *seldom* mistranslates *envis* 'reluctantly, hardly' (so all MSS except D *tart* 'late'). Godefroy, s.v. *envis* adv. The translator was unfamiliar with the word. Cf. ll. 4136, 6478, 9226.

1835–7 *Oo God, howe shal I doo ... the veray kynge of iustice* is taken from Thibaut d'Amiens, *Prière*, 5.49–54: *E, Deu, que ferai?/ Comment finerai/ Al jor de juise?/ Coment conterai/ Al juge verai/ Al roi de justise?* (Bec, *La Lyrique Française*, 81–2).

1847–9 On the exorcistic rite of baptism see Cramer, *Baptism and Change*, 14 n17: *Renuntio tibi, Satana, et omni servitio tuo et omnibus operibus tuis.*

1873–4 Cf. Whiting F380 (Folly to begin and more folly to continue).

1875 The proper and precise title of this chapter appears in the table.

Of Vntrouthe adopts the heading of NPQR *De Desloyaulte*. Other MSS correctly read *De Forsennerie*.

1879–80 *liche the pismere ... in somer for the wynter*: Proverbs 6.6–8; *Physiologus*, 11 (Carmody, 22–4); Isidore, *Etymologiae*, 12.3.9 (PL 82, col. 441); and Bartholomaeus Anglicus, *De Proprietatibus*, 18.53. Cf. also Tubach 266 and McCulloch, *Medieval Latin*, 82–4.

1898–9 Luke 16.2. *bataille*: so all MSS except DP, which preserve the correct reading *baillie* 'stewardship'.

1902 *Now haste thowe mused and thy tyme vsed* is quoted from Thibaut d'Amiens's *Prière*, I.7–8: *Assez ai musé/ Et mon tens usé* (Bec, *Lyrique Française*, 80).

1903 *hired* misinterprets French *aloue* meaning 'consumed, squandered' (unrecorded by MED) rather than 'rented.' *tyme wasted*: *temps gaste* (so all MSS except V *sens gaste*).

1907 The misleading heading of the text, *Of Wodenesse*, reproduces the error of NPR *De Forsennerie*. The table has the correct title.

1912 1 John 3.8 (here misattributed to Paul).

1917 Although the terms *lollerie* and *loller(r)is* in English documents are properly taken to refer in a pejorative manner to the heresy associated with John Wycliffe and his followers, in the *Mirroure* they invariably translate the French *bougrerrie* and *bougre(s)* and are employed as no more than general words of opprobrium for heresy and heretics. Cf. ll. 1948, 1950, 6199, 8608, 12,720. The single instance (l. 5992) in which *lolleris* clearly refers to English heretics represents a departure from the French text. On the origin and use of the terms *loller*, *lollerie*, and *lollard* in English and on the continent see Lerner, *Heresy*, 40–1; Kurze 'Festländischen Lollarden'; Workman, *John Wyclif*, vol. 1, 327; Deanesly, *Lollard Bible*, 70 *n*1, 273–4; Aston, *Lollards and Reformers*, 1 *n*1, 8, 9; and Hudson, *Lollards*, 45, and *Premature Reformation*, 2–4.

1926–7 *Cambriche* and *Chartirhous* replace French *Paris* and *Cisteaulx*. The Carthusians were highly esteemed in England for their austere piety. See Knowles, *Religious Orders*, vol. 2, 129–38, and vol. 3, 222–40. Tanner, *The Church*, 124–5, notes that they were particularly popular in Norwich, despite the fact that no house was ever founded there. Cf. above, 'Introduction,' 24–5.

1942–3 *therfore his othe standeth to noon availe*, not in the French, is an infrequent instance of the translator's expansion of his source.

1945–6 *contrevith thyngis*: 'fabrications' (*choses controuvees*). Not recorded by MED. Cf. *strecceth* as a past participle in l. 1652.

1954–61 Augustine, *De Gratia et Libero Arbitrio,* 1.20 (PL 44, col. 907); *In Joannis Evangelium Tractatus,* 7.7 (PL 35, cols 1440–1).
1965 NPR read *De Renoierie,* the source of B's error. Other MSS properly read *De Despit.* The table, too, has the correct heading.
1968–71 *Thowe shalte ... as to thy creature*: so all MSS except D, which provides a fuller and more coherent text: *Or doiz tu scavoir que tu doiz premierement porter honneur a ton createur et puis aux sains angelz et archangelz et puis aux glorieux sains et sainctes and puis apres aux gens. A dieu premierement comme a ton createur.* Cf. *Ayen* 20/18–21 and *VV* 16/1–3.
1977–9 Psalm 122.1–2.
1979–86 The translator mistakes the French, owing perhaps to an eyeskip that resulted in an improper division of the two sentences. The French reads: *Et cest un des plus grans sens qui soit et qui plus retrait de pechie quant lomme pense quil est devant les yeulx de nostre seigneur qui tout voit et tout met en escript plus diligemment que nul ialoux ne seroit de sa femme mesmes les pensees du cuer. Dont ceulx qui ont le cuer net ilz ont tele honte se dieu voit en leur cuer une pensee villaine comme tu auroies se tout le monde veoit tes villains membres.* The phrase *veleins membris,* that is, genitalia, is not recorded by MED.
1992 *baronage,* here and in l. 1999, translates *compaignie,* that is, the angels or hierarchy of heaven. MED, s.v. *barnage* n., 1b.
1995–6 Whiting M73 (Every man for himself); Morawski 45 (*A la cort le roi chascuns i est por soi*). Cf. Chaucer's *Knight's Tale* ll. 1181–2.
2001 *besynes* translates the French *besogne* 'need.' MED records the meaning under *besoignes* n., a, but not under *besinesse.*
2003 *Parceval, Rouland, Olyver*: heroes of the *Conte del Graal* and the *Song of Roland.* Cf. *Dives* 1.51: *ȝyf þey ben þer a lytil while, hem þynketh wol longe. þey han leuer gon to þe taverne þan to holy chirche, leuer to heryn a tale or a song of Robyn Hood or of some rybaudye þan to heryn messe or matynys or onyþing of Goddis seruise or ony word of God.*
2004–5 *childe that maketh lesynges* attempts to make sense of a garbled text, *enfant menteur,* found in the French MSS. The original must have read *enfaumenteor* 'sorcerer.'
2005–6 *For these pepil be in gret perille* does not appear in the French.
2006–10 *Thynke nowe ... oryson to hym* abridges the French: *Or pense pour dieu nest ce pas grant despit de dieu quant tu ne veulz aler au moustier pour celui veoir qui tous les jours vient des cieulx pour te*

veoir ne tu ne veulx parler a lui quant il parle a toy ne tu ne veulx parler a lui en confession ne en oroison?

2011 *thow sellist ... the asse,* that is, hold in contempt, treat as a fool. OED, s.v. *ass* n., 1c, cites the proverbial expression from Topsell (1607). It is not recorded in MED. Hassell B66 (*Tenir pour bête*) may be a variant.

2018–19 Isaias 1.2. After *thus* the French adds *en la personne de dieu.*

2019–21 The English renders the French awkwardly: *Lomme het moult dieu qui de lui ne veult oir parler en bien et peu lui chaut se on dit honte de dieu devant lui. hym of* is a rare instance of metathesis.

2029–30 Deuteronomy 16.16.

2044–6 Saracens were generally represented as singing and dancing around their idols. Cf. Jones, 'Conventional Saracen,' 212. *howte* has a dismissive implication.

2048–50 The English alters the French: *Apres tu dois oir au diemenche les commandemens et les festes anoncier et oir nommer les excommenies ad ce que tu les puisses escheuer.*

2053–9 On the exclusion of excommunicates from religious services and their attempts to insinuate themselves into their congregations see Vodola, *Excommunication,* 54–8, and Logan, *Excommunication,* 13–14. *He farith ... in spite of the.* The French reads *Cest aussi comme se celui qui est bani de France sembatoit en la sale a paris devant le roy pour lui faire honte. pleye hym* mistranslates *sembatoit* meaning 'insinuate himself' or 'steal into.' The translator may have confused *embatre* with *embelir. as who seye ... in spite of the* paraphrases *pour lui faire honte.* Here, and throughout the text, *London* is regularly substituted for *Paris.*

2063–4 *hirre matines .... and hire service* refers to the Little Office of the Blessed Virgin Mary (cf. Wieck, *Time Sanctified,* 60–72, 159–71). Saturday was dedicated to Mary because of her belief in Christ's promise to rise again. Cf. MED, s.v. *ladi(e)* n., 4d.

2066 *hym,* that is, the guardian angel.

2066–9 Bernard, *Sermones In Psalmum Qui Habitat,* 12.6 (*Opera* 4, 460).

2072–3 1 Peter 2.17 (here misattributed to James).

2078–9 *hotte* 'basket' misconstrues French *hoe* 'pickax.' *or with his barowe* does not appear in the French.

2086–7 *faster than a trot*: cf. Hélinand of Froidmont, *Les Vers de la Mort,* 15.7: *Certes je queur plus que le pas. ioye,* but French *compte.*

2104 *toure*: *forteresse*. So all MSS except V, which reads *forsennerie*, the reading of B's exemplar.
2108–9 Luke 11.21. *the stronge soule* misrenders *le fort arme*, 'the strong man of arms.' *arme* was confused with its homonym meaning 'soul.'
2114 *whereto he shal becomme*, that is, what will become of him (*quil deviendra*). Cf. l. 3730.
2119 *on the rowe*, but French *en renc*, that is, 'in an assembly.' *banc* may have been read for *renc*.
2125–7 Cf. Whiting H343 (The hen lays and cackles and the chough comes and reaves her of her eggs).
2127–31 A garbled and inaccurate rendition of the French. The sense is that braggarts make use of flatterers to proclaim their achievements and serve as their advocates: *Ca pechie est moult lait a celui qui par sa propre bouche se vante mais il double quant il loue les losengiers et aucuns pour crier et dire leurs fais et en font leurs advocats qui pour eulx mentent et perdent iceulx leurs ames aussi.*
2134–5 *homly with the feende* misconstrues *prevos au diable* 'the devil's magistrates.' *Prevos* was evidently read as *prives*.
2138–9 Matthew 2.16–18.
2148 *steyne* mistranslates *estaindre* ('destroy, quench'), confusing it with *teindre*. The error is repeated in l. 3272.
2156 *confesse* mistakes French *conseille*, possibly a scribal confusion of *f* for *s* and *ss* for *ll*.
2164–8 Bernard, *De Gradibus Humilitatis et Superbiae*, 17.45 (*Opera* 3, 51). *with his beeque and with his cleys*: cf. Whiting T417 (tooth and nail). *beeque*: a variant French spelling of *bec*. Not in MED.
2184 For the lives of Andrew and Lawrence see *Legenda Aurea*, chaps 2, 117. Andrew is not mentioned in the *Miroir*.
2202 *þat overthroweth and that be overthrowen* renders the French *qui trebuchent et sont descendus.*
2208–10 *Thus it fareth ... with grete sorwe* is an inexact rendering of the French: *Ainsi est des richesces de cest monde ou il monte a grant loisir et en grant paour et descend a grant doleur.*
2215 *stately*, but French *reales* referring to royal foundations. Not glossed by MED in this sense.
2231–2 *what that ever*: For the metathesis of the generalizing pronoun see OED *what*, IV.C.4(c), citing only two later instances from the Stonor Papers (1464) and Caxton's *Game of Chess* (1481).

2253 *for he oweth his feithe to God and to kepe holy chirche*: *Car il doit la foy de dieu et sainte eglise garder*. For the construction in which 'to' occurs before the infinitive when its object preceeds it, see Mustanoja, 'Features of Syntax,' 74–5.

2258–9 The reference (here misattributed to John the Baptist) is to 2 Timothy 2.3. *his*: 'is.' Cf. *herthe* (l. 12,552), *hothe* (l. 511), *howest* (l. 1672), and *howeth* (l. 7972). For the appearance of excrescent *h* in Middle-English see Lass, 'Phonology and Morphology,' 61–3, 157n, 2.4.1.2, and Milroy, 'Middle English Dialectology,' 199.

2263 *peny*: Matthew 20.9.

2264 *And ȝit therfore it shal not leve ...*, that is, the true bliss of heaven does not preclude worldly praise and glory.

2275–6 On the policy and practice of employing excommunication as a punishment for the failure to pay debts, including debts to usurers, see Vodola, *Excommunications*, 30, 129–30, 149, 176–7, 182. The obligation to discharge debts made on pledge to usurers is discussed by McLaughlin, 'Teaching of Canonists,' pt 1, 108, and pt 2, 15–17.

2296 *theye make god of their belies*: Philippians 3.19.

2299–2300 For the construction *vs moste doo* see the 'Introduction,' above, 21–2. An analogous construction to express obligation or necessity ('us is to donne') is discussed by Fischer, 'Syntax,' 336, and Visser, *Historical Syntax*, vol. 1, 351–3, who cites a late Middle-English instance in *Knyghthode and Bataile* (c. 1475).

2309 A sentence has been omitted after *pleser*: *Ainsi y mettent corps et ame et chatel tant que leur hostel en devient gaste et leurs maismes en ont grant defaulte.*

2311–12 McCulloch, *Medieval Latin*, 189. Cf. Whiting W466 (To spare no more than the wolf does the sheep); Hassell L84.

2318–19 On the peacock's pride in its tail see Pliny, *Historia Naturalis*, 10.22; *Tabula Exemplorum* 92 (Welter, 29); Bartholomaeus Anglicus, *De Proprietatibus*, 12.32. Cf. Whiting P71 (as crank [proud] as a peacock), P73, quoting Caxton's *Ovyde* 131: *more orguyllous than a pecock whan he is presed for his fair taylle*; Tilley P157. See also White, *Bestiary*, 149; McCulloch, *Medieval Latin*, 153–4; Friedmann, *Bestiary*, 284–5.

2228 *disfiguryngys* does not appear in MED as a verbal noun.

2330 Matthew 25.12.

2354 Whiting R53 (as sharp as a razor); Hassell R5; Tilley R36. Cf. Psalm 51.4.

2355 A clause has been lost or omitted after *trees*: *ou entre ceulx qui fovent en la vigne.*

2359–60 Matthew 12.36.
2369 *curtesies*: 'salutations' (*salus*). Not recorded by MED in this precise sense.
2372 *flaile*: 'leper's clapper' (*flavel*). Not recorded by MED with this meaning.
2374 *shewed*: 'viewed with favor.' MED, s.v. *sheuen* v., 1a.
2384–8 There is a considerable lacuna in B at this point. The French reads *Et quant le diable a tousiours este seigneur et maistre de celle lengue comment cuides tu quil sen dessaisisse et cesse* (D *rende*) *au iour de la mort quant ilz auront plus grant besoing* (D *mestier*) *deulx confesser et sans vraie confession nul ne puet venir a vraie fin? Pense en quil peril ceulx sont qui ne sont mie seigneurs de leur lengue. Car ilz lont pieca donnee au diable qui en fait son chalemel et ce deust estre le chalemel du saint esperit. hors* and *nyȝghtyngale* are mistranslations of *chalemel* 'pipe' or 'shawm.'
2388 *lif*, but French *viennent* which may have been read as *vivent*.
2391–4 Bernard, *Sermones super Cantica Canticorum*, 11.1 (*Opera* 1, 54–5).
2395 After *songes* the English omits a transitional sentence: *Il est trois manieres de chansons.*
2396 *hymselfe*, that is, God (P *soy*, NV *dieu*, ACDQRSU *luy*).
2408–11 Augustine, *Contra Julianum Pelagianum*, 4.14 (PL 44, col. 770).
2414–16 *and tho that hireth ... the feendes seruice*: *et ceulx et celles qui les escoutent et qui en teles chansons et en teles caroles se mettent ilz font proprement le service au diable.*
2421 The adverb *lachely* is unrecorded by MED.
2424 *seruice*: 'serve, worship.' Not recorded by MED as a verb in this sense. *hoope*: 'think, believe' (*cuident*).
2451–4 Luke 14.12–13.
2460 Cf. Whiting A149 (to mowe like an ape).
2461–99 For condemnations of pride in clothing see Owst, *Literature*, 390–411 and index under costume. Cf. also ll. 11,982–12,000.
2462 *wherein* should perhaps be deleted. The French reads: *Apres en celles beles robbes ilz ont leur tres grant gloire.*
2462–7 Gregory, *Homiliarum in Evangelia*, 2.40.1655 (PL 76, col. 1305). The biblical references are to Luke 16.9 and Matthew 11.8. *of that*: 'because.'
2480 *fyne marchandis* loses the sardonic force of *fin frepier* ('excellent second-hand clothes dealers').
2486 *botonettis* does not appear in MED.

2494–9 Isaias 3.18–23. After *thorw it* the French adds *mesmes les aguilles dont elles atachent leurs gimples, les espingles et les mirouers noublie il mie.*
2501–5 Apocalypse 18.7. *his lif* translates *sa vie* where *his* (*sa*) refers to the soul.
2512–13 *For theye make ... it is not he,* that is, 'For they make him believe that he is not the person he is.'
2514–15 Whiting C574 (To say the crow is white), S931 (A black swan), quoting Trevisa's translation of Bartholomaeus Anglicus, *De Proprietatibus*, 12.12 based on Isidore, *Etymologiae*, 12.7.18 (PL 82, col. 461): *For noo man fyndyth a blacke swanne*; Tilley S1027. Cf. ll. 4746–7: *the swan is blacke and the crowe white.*
2516 Whiting H111 (As dreadful [timid] as a hare); Hassell L48; Tilley H147.
2518–21 *They make of evil wel ... the sotted foole dothe or seithe*: Isaias 5.20–1. *al dremes torneth theym to goode* echoes Chaucer, *House of Fame*, l. 58. Cf. Tilley D588 (Dreams go by contraries).
2524–31 A version of Babrius 18 ('Sun and North Wind in Contest'). Cf. also Aesop, *Complete Fables* 73, and Avianus 4. *bise,* a keen north wind, appears elsewhere only in Havelok. MED and OED, s.v. *bise* n.
2531 A portion of the text has been lost here, perhaps owing to an eyeskip: *Bise qui tant est un vent dur et aspre est verite qui tant est aspre et dure et haye nommeement a ces grans cours quant celle vente. harre*: 'chill, biting' from Middle Dutch *hare* meaning 'sharp wind, bitter cold.' See Bense, s.v. *haar* n., noting that its usage is confined to the North and Northeast; Wright, s.v. *haar* n.; SND, s.v. *haar* n., 1. Not recorded by MED. OED, s.v. *haar* n., cites it as from 1671 with the meaning 'wet mist or fog.'
2535–6 *But praysyng the whiche is the hye wynde of noone: Mais losenge est le chaud vent de midi.* The introduction of *the whiche* destroys the syntax of the sentence and is unsupported by the French MSS.
2538–40 4 Kings 20.12–18
2543–4 The reference is to Lamentations 1, 2 generally rather than to a particular chapter or verse.
2569 Whiting S181 (To follow one like his shadow); Tilley S263.
2586 *Laurens Garin*: PS *loheren garin*, CN *loherain garin*, V *lorrain garin*, Q *loherain guerin*, D *lorrain guerin*, U om. The reference is to an early chanson de geste entitled *Mort de Garin Le Loherenc*, an

account of a war between the Lotharingians and the Bordelais. *Laurens* mistakes French *lorrain*.

2589–636 The story of the Unfaithful Spouse is taken from Ezechiel 16, as is indicated in ll. 2667–72. For the original foundling motif the *Miroir* has substituted the introductory account of the prince's rescue of the maiden from robbers reminiscent of *Gesta Romanorum* 117. *bacheler* (*vavaseur*): a household knight frequently employed in the administration of royal estates. See Bean, *Lord to Patron*, 22–32, and Coss, 'Literature,' 112–21.

2652–4 Proverbs 6.16–17, 16.5.

2655–6 James 4.4.

2656–7 1 John 2.15.

2658 Matthew 6.24.

2660–1 A paraphrase of Luke 23.34.

2678–717 Ezechiel 16.3, 7–20, 32–52. The corrector's substitution of *vnto* for *with* (l. 2698) receives support from DNRV (*a toy*) as against ACPQSU (*avec, ovec, avecques*), the reading in the translator's exemplar, and accords with the reference to Ezechiel 16.33–4. *praysyng* (l. 2698) confuses *loier* 'payment, recompense' with *louer* 'praise.' *in drawyng aȝeyns the costome of lyght women*, that is, contrary to the usual behavior of prostitutes. *Sodome and Gomorre*: Genesis 18.20. *flesshely nature* (l. 2714) mistakes the French *contre nature charnelment*, destroying the contrast between *charnelment* and *esperituelment* (*gostely*) which was misread as *especialment*. *flesshely* and *nature* should perhaps be transposed.

2751–2 Cf. *Summa Virtutum* 2.367–8: *Vel ypocrisis dicitur ab 'ypos,' quod est sub, et 'crisis,' aurum, quasi sub-auratus.*

2754–5 Matthew 23.28.

2755 John 14.17.

2758 Job 20.5.

2759–62 *That the worlde is an ypocritt ... contirfet thyngis* mistakes the French: *Cest vray que le monde est ypocrite et sourore car nous veons au monde cest en ceulx qui aiment le monde richesces dehors et pourete dedans et moult de si fautes choses*. The contrast is between appearance and reality. MED, s.v. *poverte* n., 3b 'sinfulness of heart or soul.'

2766 *the trouthe of holynes*, but French *la verite ne la saintete*. *de* was read for *ne*.

2769–71 Matthew 23.27–8. *ful of harlotrie* delicately abridges the French *plains dordure et de pueur et de pourreture*.

2771–2 Matthew 7.15.
2774–5 *Liche as the wolfe ... a lambe hathe*: Albert the Great, *De Animalibus*, 22.114. Cf. also Luke 10.3.
2777 *veray lambe Criste Iesus*: John 1.29.
2780 *tho that seme ypocrites* departs from the French *qui font lez pechies coiement* (V *secretement*), that is, who sin secretly, losing the force of the fine distinction drawn in the following sentence.
2788 *apys to the feende*: cf. *Summa Virtutum* 2.393: *symia diaboli.*
2795 After *see it* the French adds: *Et pource leur couste il moult car il advient tousiours que tous ypocrites sont avaricieux* and after *monoy*: *Et de ce dont ilz peussent le ciel acheter ilz achetent enfer.*
2797 2 John 8.
2801–2 Matthew 12.33.
2805–7 Cf. Hassell A162 (*De mauvais arbre mauvais fruit*), A163 (*De mauvais arbre ne vient nul bon fruit*); Morawski 520.
2808–10 Cf. Matthew 13.20–2, Mark 4.16–19.
2816 After the second *syde* the French adds: *Et ceulx qui se craignent sont trop desloiaulx.*
2824–6 Luke 12.9.
2827–9 *theye vndirstande of worshipp that it were hounte and of hounte that it were worshipp*: so all MSS (*quilz entendent honneur que ce soit honte et de honte que ce soit honneur*) except S, which has *bonte* for the first *honte*, and R, which has *bontes/bonte* for *honte/honte.*
2845 *meke*, that is, 'modest.' MED, s.v. *meke* adj., 4c. The earliest recorded use with reference to clothing is 1500.
2851 *iobbardis*: 'sanctimonious hypocrites' (*beguins*). Not recorded by MED in this sense. Cf. *Ayen* 26/23 and *VV* 22/5.
2869–70 *enforced ayein* (*renforche*), that is, subjected to added force or constraint. The precise application to the sentence of excommunication is not recorded by MED.
2872–4 Jeremias 15.10.
2875–9 *Noon therre shewe me frendeshipp ... that sheweth contenaunce of love: Nul nose a moy monstrer amistie ne marchaunder ne prester a usure. Adoncques est la sentence moult aggravee quant lomme est si excommenie que tous sont excommenies qui avecques lui sont en compaignie et qui sont de sa maisine et qui lui monstrent semblant damour.* On the public ostracism of excommunicates see Vodola, *Excommunication*, especially 48–54, and Logan, *Excommunication*, 14–15.

2888–9 Augustine, *In Epistolam Joannis ad Parthos*, 8.9 (PL 35, col. 2040). Q attributes the statement to John Chrysostom.
2891–4 Gregory, *Moralia*, 8.48 (PL 75, col. 851).
2896 *withlettyng*: 'obstruction, obstacle,' a nonce word not recorded by MED or OED, translates the French *avecques empeschement*.
2897–900 Ambrose, *De Moribus Brachmanorum* (PL 17, col. 1139). Cf. *Fasciculus Morum*, 4.4.136–43. The comment to Alexander is made in direct and familiar discourse in the French: *Dieu est appareillie de toy donner sapience mais tu nas lieu ou tu la puisses recevoir.*
2903–4 Wisdom 1.4.
2906 Ecclesiasticus 10.15 (here misattributed to Ecclesiastes).
2909–15 Bernard, *In Natali Sancti Andreae*, Sermo 2.7 (*Opera* 5, 439). *the corner of the cros*: V *le bout du bras de la croix*, ACNPRSU *le cornuel de la croix*, Q *humilite*. According to Bernard, the four corners of the cross stand for *continentia, patientia, prudentia*, and *humilitas*. After *herte* (l. 2912) D adds *contra orgueil.*
2919–20 Job 41.25.
2920–2 Gregory, *Moralia*, 34.23 (PL 76, col. 750). The attribution to Augustine is erroneous.
2926–8 Ecclesiasticus 13.24 (here misattributed to Ecclesiastes).
2933–5 Psalm 9.9–10.
2935–6 Psalm 118.78.
2937–8 Psalm 73.4, 23.
2945–7 Psalm 73.23.
2953–4 Job 31.27.
2960 John 15.5.
2961–2 Isaias 26.12.
2964–6 Unidentified.
2967–70 Apocalypse 18.7.
2970–2 Luke 1.52.
2976–7 Isaias 42.8.
2982 Deuteronomy 32.35
2984–7 Romans 2.15, 9.1. B's reading of *vertues* for *witnes* (*tesmoignage*) is clearly a scribal error.
2988–9 1 Corinthians 4.4–5.
2989–92 *And also I derre not iustyfye me ... that I knowe not meselfe: Je ne mose en ce point iustifier car dieu qui tout voit et tout scet ce qui est fait et a faire voit en moy tel chose et congnoist que je ne congnois mie.* The subordinate clause lacks a verb, owing to the loss of the repetition of *seeith* and *knoweth* required by the French.

3005 *likned,* but French *divisee.*
3014 *shineth clere be nyght and not on the daye* refers to the *ignis fatuus* or the phosphorescence of decaying matter.
3022 Whiting W675 (To be worm's food (meat)). The aphorism is repeated in ll. 3069 and 5757.
3023 *religious*: so all MSS except V *orgueilleux.*
3024–5 Pseudo-Jerome, *Regula Monachorum,* 19 (PL 30, col. 368).
3026 A phrase has been lost after *troubled: a lexemple de la benoite vierge.* The biblical reference is to Luke 1.26–38.
3037–8 Matthew 6.1–4 (here misattributed to John).
3042 *discende*: 'proceed (to consideration of)' (*descendre*). MED, s.v. *descenden* v., 7a. Cf. l. 8241.
3046–7 Boethius, *De Consolatione Philosophiae,* 3, pr. 6.
3049 *kynge of glorye*: Psalm 23.10.
3050–1 Psalm 113(2).1.
3054–7 Gregory, *Moralia,* 24.8 (PL 76, cols 297–8); *Homiliae in Evangelia,* 1.7 (PL 76, col. 1103).
3059–61 Ecclesiasticus 13.1 (here misattributed to Ecclesiastes).
3062–4 Psalm 17.26–7.
3065–71 Pseudo-Bernard, *Meditationes Piissimae De Cognitione Humanae Conditionis,* 3.8 (PL 184, col. 490). The passage incorporates the quotation attributed to Jerome. A similar passage taken from Origen, *Homiliae in Ezechielem,* 9 (PG 13, col. 734) is quoted by *Othea* 27/17–23. Cf. also *Summa Virtutum* 2.140. The references to *mire* (l. 3068) and *ashes* (l. 3069) recall Genesis 18.27 and Job 30.19. *wormes mete*: Whiting W675 (To be worm's food [meat]). *harlottrye* (l. 3071): 'filth, excrement' (*ordure*). MED records this sense from 1467.
3071–2 Micheas 6.14. The attribution to '*Mathias*' is possibly a scribal error. The French MSS read *Micheas.*
3078–80 Augustine, *De Agone Christiano,* 11 (PL 40, col. 297); *Sermones de Scripturis,* 123.1 (PL 38, col. 684).
3085–6 Psalm 30.24.
3086–8 Isaias 2.12–21.
3096–8 Augustine, *In Iohannis Evangelium Tractatus,* 1.15 (PL 35, cols 1386–7).
3103 Whiting E136 (Envy may not die); Hassell E56; Tilley E172.
3104–6 Isaias 14.12–15.
3109–10 Wisdom 2.24 (here misattributed to Paul).
3112–13 Romans 6.9.

3132–3 *he hateth but the weele of other*: cf. Augustine, *Enarrationes in Psalmos*, 104.17 (PL 37, col. 1399).
3136–9 Matthew 12.31–2
3151 *flytte*: 'change (his) behavior' (P *flexir*, NRUV *flechir*, ACDQ *fleschir*, S om).
3159 *it blyndeth*: *it* is the object of *blyndeth*.
3161 *donne mouse* mistakes the French *chauve souris* 'bat.' The confusion of *chauve* 'bald' with *chanue* 'white-haired' also occurs in *Dicts* 80/7, as noted, above, in the 'Introduction,' 20. Cf. Whiting S892 (The sun's light is never the worse though the bat flees from its bright beams); Tilley O92 (As blind as an owl [bat]); ODEP, 66; Rowland, *Animals*, 7. Fischer, 'Animal References,' 88, miscatalogues it as a mouse. Cf. MED, s.v. *chanué* adj.; AND, s.v. *chanu* adj., *cauf* adj., and *cauf sorice* n.
3162–3 Pseudo-Dionysius, *De Divinis Nominibus*, 4.19 (PG 3, col. 783).
3174 B's *toon* results from a misreading of *lune* for *lame*. The French reads *Or regarde comment en lame a trois vertus*.
3192 *streccheth it into evylle wittys* misconstrues *entent en mauvais sens*. *entendre* was evidently confused with *estendre*. The error is repeated in l. 7601.
3196 *The deedys*, that is, of others.
3197 *thikke* mistakes the French *pesme* 'evil, dire' (ACNPQSU *pesme*, DV *mauvais*, R *corrumpu*), which was clearly confused with *espés* (*spes*) meaning 'thick, dense, populous.' Cf. Godefroy, Tobler-Lommatsch, AND, s.v. *espés* adj. The error is repeated in ll. 3222, 6215.
3208–9 Cf. Whiting G459 (As swift as a greyhound); Hassell L39.
3218–20 Matthew 20.15.
3226 *whan*: perhaps *wha[n]*. A light stroke through the ascender of *h* extends to the *n*.
3247–8 Matthew 12.34. Whiting A22 (Of the abundance of the heart the mouth speaks); Hassell B151.
3250 Psalm 10.7. *bonte* (*bounte*) has been misread for *bouche*. The error is repeated in l. 8626.
3251–2 *with his boost*, that is, with his deceptive or fraudulent speech, translating French *par boidie*. *boost* is not glossed by MED in this sense.
3254–7 Apocalypse 16.13.

3263 *moyen* is not recorded by MED as an adjective in this form, which is taken over directly from the French. OED cites it as from 1481 (Caxton).
3264–6 Mark 4.26–8.
3272 *steyne* mistranslates *estaindre,* the same error that occurs in l. 2148.
3274–9 Matthew 2.16. Nearly all of the three examples of malice have been lost here. The French reads *Lune fu du roy herode qui tua les innocens car par lenvie quil ot de Ihesu Crist pour lui estaindre qui estoit aussi comme en herbe et en bon commencement de bien faire. Il fist tant de murdres et si crueulx. Lautre envie fu du diable contre eve qui estoit en fleur et en estat de bien profiter. La tierce fut lenvie des juifs contre Ihesu Crist qui estoit en estat de perfection qui faisoit tant de biens qui estoit aussi comme larbre par creu et fruit meur.*
3291–3 Gregory, *Moralia,* 5.46 (PL 75, col. 730).
3294–5 Ecclesiasticus 13.19. Whiting B129 (Every beast loves its like); Hassell P34.
3306–8 Psalm 118.63.
3310–14 1 Corinthians 12.12–20.
3320–2 2 Corinthians 11.29.
3345 A portion of the French text has been lost in this sentence: *Et dois savoir que cestui vice a cinq degres en diverses manieres de personnes et cinq degres en diverses manieres de ire.*
3354 *fellenes*: 'ire, wrath' (*felonie*). Not in MED in this sense, although it cites *felli(che)* adv. with the meaning 'fiercely, angrily.'
3360–1 Isaias 57.20. *blustrynge*: 'tempestuous' (*bruyant*). Cf. MED, s.v. *blusteren* v., 1 'blow violently,' but not with reference to the sea.
3363–4 *Somtyme men seye this fareth a man* follows the text of CDNQS: *A la fois on dit auxi est il de lomme.* APRUV, however, appear to preserve a better reading: *A la fois aussi on dit de lomme. this*: 'thus' as in l. 10,084. On the dialectal distribution of this usage see LALME IV.315.
3381 *espoire* (hence B's *glorye*) was read for *espine* 'thorn-bush.'
3404 Lamentations 1.10. ACNPQRSUV *Iheremie,* D *Ieroisme.*
3404–9 A paraphrase of Galatians 5.17–23.
3410 Whiting T343 (To boll like a toad); Hassell C339. *boterel*: 'toad' (*boterel*: so all MSS but D *crapault*). The translator was unfamiliar with this obscure Picard word whose only other appearance in Middle English is *Ayen* 187/29. A similar error occurs in l. 10,408.
3412–13 *strengthe, for ... moste doute* appears to follow the eccentric

reading unique to MS R: *force quant il na vertu ne pouair sur son courage quil ne puet vaincre* (so PU, ADQV *dompter*, CNS *danter*, R *douter*).

3453 *branche*, but French *guerre*. Probably an eyeskip.

3461–2 See ll. 6057–6100.

3476–7 *Truly thowe shalt tomorowe ... whate thowe arte* departs from the French: *Certes tu parleras le matin a sa maisine sique il le pourra bien oir. Voisin(e)* may have been read for *maisine*.

3505–6 *to I haue cleered myn herte* translates *iusques ad ce que jen voie mon cuer esclarcy. cleered*: 'calmed' (*esclarcy*). MED *cleren* v., 3c.

3516–18 Cf. Midrash Rabbah, *Esther* 7.13, 97–8. The devil is called an avenger in Psalm 43.16–17 and Apocalypse 12.10.

3518–19 *But he this ... that dothe thus* misconstrues the French: *Mais il ne se prent a filz ne a pere sicomme fait celui. se prent* 'considers, takes account of' was evidently misread as *reprent*.

3523–4 Hassell L73 (*De legier pleure à qui la lippe pend*); Morawski 512; Tilley L330.

3530–2 Leviticus 19.18.

3539–42 Ecclesiasticus 25.1–2. *neghborughshipp*: 'neighborliness' (*voisinage*). MED, s.v. *neigheborshipe* n.

3543–4 *betwene nere-dwelleres and neghebourghes*: *entre prochains et voisins. nere-dwelleres* does not appear in MED.

3553–5 The French reads *L'orgueilleux lui tolt sa gloire, l'envieux qui iuge le cuer son iugement, le ireux sa vengance aussi comme sa haulte iustice. iustice* and *doome* should perhaps be transposed.

3569–73 Matthew 2.16. *he dedde slee* (l. 3570): a unique use of 'do' in its auxiliary function.

3576 *thugh* should perhaps be emended to *thurgh* (cf. ll. 1649, 3675). The loss of medial *r* occurs occasionally in the text and may have been weak in the scribal dialect. Cf. the textual notes to ll. 5431, 6456, 6883, 7785, 9314.

3577 *kynge*, that is, Herod (Acts 12.21–3).

3587–9 Ecclesiasticus 34.25–7.

3589–90 *Decretum*, I.86.21 (Friedberg, vol. 1, 302) by way of Bonaventure, *Collationes De Decem Praeceptis*, 6.11.

3593–625 The source of this passage is Bonaventure, *Collationes De Decem Praeceptis*, 5.7–10.

3594 *treted* 'drawn' (*traitie*) is not recorded by MED. Cf. Godefroy, s.v. *traitier* v.

3611–13 *In that caas ... longeth to hym*: *En ce point il ny a coupe ne irregularite se il fist bien son devoir et ce que a lui appartenoit.*
3658 Whiting N43 (In the neck).
3666–7 Wisdom 6.5–6.
3669–90 The source of this passage is Gregory, *Moralia*, 31.45 (PL 76, cols. 621–2). The concatenation of the vices is discussed by Wenzel, *Seven Deadly Sins*, 4.
3695–9 Augustine, *De Peccatorum Meritis Et Remissione*, 2.11 (PL 44, col. 161). Peraldus 2.9.4.1 attributes the statement to Gregory.
3702–3 Proverbs 15.1, 25.15.
3703–7 *Vitae Patrum*, 5.569 (PL 73, col. 867).
3715 *ryghtwys*, but French *sage* 'wise, experienced'. MED does not define *ryghtwys* in this sense. Possibly an eyeskip (*rightwis*).
3717–19 Job 2.10.
3720 There is a lacuna after *vs*: *Dieu les nous donne; Dieu les nous tolt a sa volente. Benoit soit dieu de quanquil nous fait.*
3723 Proverbs 19.22.
3726–8 Augustine, *Enarrationes in Psalmos*, 25.2.3 (PL 36, col. 189).
3730 *weretoo we shalle torne*, that is, what will become of us. Cf. l. 2114.
3731–4 Ecclesiasticus 28.6–8.
3744 Whiting H408 (To sleep like hogs); Hassell P245.
3750 *herbes*, but French *arbres* which was evidently read as *erbes*.
3751 *doome beestis*: cf. Job 12.7.
3752–3 Proverbs 6.6.
3759–60 Isaias 14.12–15.
3767 After *examples* the French adds: *ou pour paour denfer ou pour amour de dieu.*
3177 Gradon (*Ayen* 34/16*n*) suggests that *pointis* may refer to the dots on dice.
3791–5 Apocalypse 3.16.
3795–7 *Apothegmata Patrum*, Poemen 111 (PG 65, col. 350). Cf. ODEP, 72 (To a boiling pot flies come not).
3802–4 *The seconde lytyl branche is tendirnes the which is a full grete synne* introduces the discussion of idleness in the English manuscript, masking the loss of a full page of text. It is likely that *tendernes* ended on the recto of one page and *the whiche* began on the recto of the next, the verso having been lost in between. Waldron, 'Manuscripts,' 291–2, notes a similar occurrence in a copy of John Trevisa's translation of Higden's *Polychronicon* (British Library, London, Additional MS 24194,

f. 214 recto and verso). He concludes that the omission occurred 'because of the scribe's inadvertence not because of a gap in the exemplar or interruption in his supply of copy: namely that it occurs between the recto and verso sides of one folio ... Everything points to an accidental omission on the part of the scribe of A.' A third instance of such inadvertent scribal omission occurs in the *Towneley Plays* manuscript (Henry E. Huntington, San Marino, MS 1). According to Stevens, 'In copying his exemplar onto folio 5 verso, the scribe unaccountably skipped a page. He apparently discovered his mistake as he proceded onto folio 6 recto, where he then inserts the missing page out of sequence. Thereupon he inserted a red lower case "a" in the upper left-hand margin of folio 6 recto and a "b" in the same location of folio 5 verso, and in the upper left-hand corner of folio 5 verso, he inserted the following words in red: *[M]d that this syde of the leyfe [sḥ]uld folow the other next syde [ac]cordyng to the tokyns here maide [an]d then after al stondys in ordre.* The tokens, of course are the "a" and "b" he has marked on the two pages' ('Towneley Plays,' 167). The lost chapter on *Tendirnesse* reads in the French *Le second ramcel est tendresce. Car quant [le] diable entre ou cuer comme le ribauld ou four couste lui convient pour lui reposer. Celle couste est la tendresce de lomme et de la femme. La gist et chante et se deduit et enchante celle chetive ame et lui dit: Tu as este souef nourri. Tu es de trop fieble complexion. Tu ne pourroies ce souffrir. Veillier, traveiller, jeuner. Matin lever et ces autres duretes que ceulx sueffrent qui ce ont apris. Tu seroies tantost mort. Il na rien qui na sante. Bon chastel garde qui son corps garde. Ce dit le diable au chetif ou a la chetive qui se pert. Il te convient avoir robbe nette chaude en yver et froide en este. Garde toy de ces froides viandes et sur toutes choses de boire froit vin et mauvais. Car il atrait les mauvaises humeurs et le bon vin nourrist le corps et fait le bon sang. Par foy ceci droites merveilles le diable est devenu phisicien. Ainsi engraisse il les pourceaulx contre la feste quil fera quant ilz mourront. Hee dieu comme cy a mauvais phisicien. Les autres garissent les malades et cestui fait les haities malades et langueureux et les gete en tele paralisie quilz ne se pevent aidier de membre quilz aient et les fait fort malades et tout adcertes languir et mourir a honteuse mort ancois quil en soit temps et ancois heure et tele mort est moult honteuse quant on se tue a ses deux mains et fait on tant que le corps est si pesant et si plain et le cuer si failli et si vain quil ne puet le corps servir et le corps ne veult le cuer de porter. Car il est si seigneur et si maistre et tant demande de repos et de delices*

quil en pert le talent de mengier et tout delit et tout repos et en la fin le corps et lame.
3804 The discussion of idleness begins *Le tiers ramcel est oysviete qui est moult grant pechie ...*
3805–7 Genesis 3.19.
3807–9 Matthew 8.30–2. After *hogges* the French adds: *et y maine vii compaignons et y est mester et tient lescole.*
3809–10 Whiting D182 (The devil finds work for the idle).
3827–8 Cf. Whiting L405 (He that lives [loves God] best prays best). *prayeth* and *doothe* should perhaps be transposed.
3833–4 1 Corinthians 11.28–9.
3840–3 Luke 22.46, 1 Peter 4.7. *he hym*, that is, he himself (*lui mesmes*).
3848–50 Psalm 5.3.
3851–3 A sentence introducing the fourth kind of *hevynesse* has been lost or omitted after *swetely*: *Apres ce que si envis et si peresceusement se lievent matin pour dieu servir. swete*: 'sweat, perspiration' (*sueur*), following the French, which perhaps should have read *sommeil ou sueur* as in the *Somme* tradition. Cf. *Ayen* 31/29–30: *zwot oþer ane slep*; *VV* 27/15–16: *slep or a swot*. The full sentence reads: *Ilz aiment mieulx perdre trois messes que une sueur quant elle vient au matin*, that is, they would rather lose three masses than toil in the morning. Peraldus 2.5.2.3 warns against sleeping in the morning: *Tempus etiam in quo dormiendum non est, tempus matutinum est. Illud enim tempus non est somno occupandum.*
3865–7 4 Kings 5.11.
3867–70 Hebrews 1.11–12. Cf. also 2 Corinthians 5.2–4, Colossians 3.9–10.
3870–3 Isaias 10.13–14.
3880–5 Psalm 77.20–42.
3886–7 *bowe his eerys*, that is, 'give ear, listen' (*encliner ses oreilles*). Cf. MED, s.v. *bouen* v., 5b. The meaning is that the sinner refuses to seek after wisdom and rejects the instructions of a father as given in Proverbs 4.20.
3890 *the*, that is, them (*se*). Possibly a Lincolnshire dialect form. Cf. LALME IV.14.
3890–3 *caste* translates *degout* meaning 'drain water'. Not recorded by MED in this sense. B's reading, *hertis*, confuses *cures* with *cuers*. The identical error occurs in l. 9622. The French reads *Et de celui qui voit le*

degout de la maison cest a dire les cures du monde qui lui crevent les yeulx.
3903–6 Wisdom 17.14–20. *good* translates *bien* or *biens* (D alone reads *Dieu*), which here is probably intended to mean 'goods, property' rather than the biblical sense of 'soul'. *he* (l. 3906) refers to *good* (l. 3905). *Ayen* 32/7 has *god* for *good*; *VV* 27/27 *erthe.*
3912 *ouer his heede with a swerde drawen*: Whiting S979 (To have a sword over one's head).
3912–14 Whiting S419 (To be afraid of a snail).
3915 *hissyng of gees*: Whiting G381 (Not to dare go for the goose that blows (hisses)).
3920 *stronge as an vnycorne*: Pliny, *Historia Naturalis*, 8.31; *Physiologus*, 16 (Carmody, 31–2); Isidore, *Etymologiae*, 12.2.12–13 (PL 82, cols 435–6); Bartholomaeus Anglicus, *De Proprietatibus*, 18.80; White, *Bestiary*, 20–1. See also McCulloch, *Medieval Latin*, 179; Rowland, *Animals*, 152–7; Friedmann, *Bestiary*, 302; Henkel, *Studien*, 168–71. Whiting U4 (As fierce as a unicorn); Hassell L40.
3924 *begynnyng*, but French *amendement*. Possibly an eyeskip (cf. *begynnynge*, l. 3921).
3929 *understandyng*, but French *amendement*, which was probably read as *entendement.*
3929–30 Hassell D119 (*Qui tost donne deux fois donne*). Cf. Whiting G76 (He that gives a gift by time his thank is the more).
3930–1 The adverb *withdraweyngly* is not recorded by MED.
3932–3 Whiting P48 (As sooth as the paternoster); Hassell P76; Di Stefano, *Dictionnaire*, 653.
3950–1 Ecclesiasticus 30.16.
3959 *dawe* renders French *beguin* meaning 'hypocrite' or 'fool,' here probably the former. MED (*daue* n., b) does not record the first sense and only hesitantly records the second, citing a single instance from the *Towneley Plays*. *beguins* had been rendered by *iobbardis* in l. 2851.
3960–1 Augustine, *De Disciplina Christiana*, 12 (PL 40, col. 676). Whiting L237 (A good life a good death); Hassell V91; Tilley L39.
3961–4 1 Corinthians 15.36–8. Cf. Proverbs 24.30–1.
3970–1 *an oolde roile to amble*: Whiting H513 (A horse that ever trotted is hard to make amble); Tilley F408. *an oolde dogge to wepe*, although reminiscent of Whiting D313 (It is hard to make an old dog stoop) and Tilley D500 (An old dog will learn no tricks), misconstrues the French *vieil chesne a plaier* meaning 'an old oak to bend.' Cf.

Whiting O11 (While an oak is a young spire it may be wound into a withe). For a similar mistranslation of *ploier* ('to bend') see l. 9378.
3992 *perdicion*: B's reading, *pardoon*, adopts the corrupt reading of the French MSS (*pardon*) which apparently resulted from the earlier loss of a suspension mark.
3997 *delayinglye* is not recorded by MED as an adverb.
4000 First *he* refers to God, as the French makes clear: *Dieu est trop debonaire*.
4010 *besye, diligent*: the collocation of English and French favored by the translator ('Introduction,' 21). The French reads simply *qui est si diligent de garder son cuer. desire* renders *affaitier* 'to devote himself to, to give himself up to.' Not recorded by MED in this precise sense. Cf. l. 8366*n*.
4026–8 Proverbs 24.16.
4028–33 Matthew 18.18, 21–2.
4040–6 Peter Lombard, *Sententiae*, 3.27.5–6 (PL 192, col. 815), based on Matthew 22.37. The attribution to Augustine is erroneous.
4048 *verse*, that is, a verse from the Psalms (*miserele*).
4056 Whiting C77 (To make castles in Spain); Hassell C100.
4059–64 *thoo that ... confesse theym soo often* awkwardly translates the French: *ceulx qui bien aiment dieu et qui bien congnoissent leurs defaultes et treuvent plus a confesser en un jour que les autres en un an qui goute ny voient et qui a paine font rien ou il nait un pechie et se merveillent de ce que les autres se confessent si souvent.*
4074 Matthew 6.10.
4083 The three kinds of snares are *synne, vsage*, and *feblenes*, the last coordination expressed as a genitive dependence. The French reads *pechie, acoustumance et fieblesce*. Cf. ll. 804, 1505, 4778, and 8862.
4087–8 *kynnes in his handys ... morfewe in the necke*: mistakes the French *guerillons es mains et les buyes es pies et la meule au col liee*. The translator seems to have taken *guerillons* and *buyes* 'clamps, shackles' and *meule* 'millstone' to mean, respectively, 'chilblains' (*kynnes, moules*) or 'scurvy eruption' (*morfewe*). Part of his difficulty stems from his confusion of *m(e)ule* 'millstone' with *m(o)ule* 'chilblain.' The alternative translations provided for the phrase *buyes es pies* – the first correct, the second incorrect – must surely reflect his general uncertainty with the French. MED, s.v. *dogge* n., 4 'clamp,' *morphea* n., 'morphea,' and *mule* (2) n., 'chilblain.' For *kynnes*, a northernism that does not appear in MED, see Halliwell, *Dictionary*,

vol. 2, 494, and OED *kin* 'chilblain.' OED provides a single instance of *gin* (5b), a southern form, meaning 'fetter,' as from 1663.

4094–6 Possibly Bernard, *Sermones de Diversis*, 12.3 (*Opera* 6[1], 129), echoing Genesis 3.17–19. *sauour of his bodye* mistakes French *sueur* (sweat) *de son corps*.

4098–103 Bernard, *Sententiae*, Series Secunda, 47, 119 (*Opera* 6[2], 35, 47). The story is told of the eagle and the raven in the bestiary (McCulloch, *Medieval Latin*, 123, 161). B's reading, *eetyng*, confuses *amorson* with *morson*.

4113–14 Bernard, *Sermones Super Cantica Canticorum*, 33.10 (*Opera* 1, 240–1). *dismesureth* does not appear as a verb in MED. There is a single reference in OED dating from 1598.

4125–8 Aristotle, *Historia animalium*, 579b; Aelian 4.34; Pliny, *Historia Naturalis*, 18.7; Bartholomaeus Anglicus, *De Proprietatibus*, 18.65. Cf. McCulloch, *Medieval Latin*, 138.

4128–9 Proverbs 6.6.

4133 The translator read *dit* for *dieu*.

4133–40 *Syche mevyng cresceth euer ... noo power too hurte hym* clumsily translates the French: *Car tel mouvement croist tousiours qui est selon nature si comme il appert en la pierre qui descent de hault. Et plus vient de hault et plus tost vient de grant radeur. Mais quant elle monte en hault pource que envis le fait tant plus monte et plus lachement se muet. Aussi comme la pierre dune perriere quant elle a tant monte comme elle puet plus se elle frapoit un homme qui fust en hault elle nauroit pouair de lui blechier. hym* (l. 4134) is a reference to *la pierre*, as are *he* and *it* in ll. 4135–6. *vice*, translating *envis*, 'reluctantly,' is spurious. Cf. ll. 1832, 6478, 9226.

4142 *vigorousnesse*: 'moral strength.' The only citation to this word in MED is *Promptuarium Parvulorum* (c. 1440). Cf. l. 8321.

4144 *defauteth* is not recorded by MED in the sense of 'fails to fulfill an obligation.'

4145–7 Whiting E90 (Who serves not to the end loses his reward), S163 (Who serves and does not full-serve loses his shipe [wages, hire]); Hassell S82; Morawski 2138. *deserueth*: 'serves to the end,' 'completes the task' (*parsert*). Not recorded by MED in this sense. *the knotte* must mean 'field of battle,' 'midst of battle,' or 'midst of the game' as the context and the variant French readings make clear: APU *lemprise ou la partie*, NRS *lemmain*, QV *lenvy*, C *le moins*, D *au meilleu du jeu*. MED, s.v. *knotte* n., 2c, citing only *Knyghthode and*

Bataile (l. 2916), glosses (perhaps incorrectly) as 'result of a battle, outcome.'
4148–9 2 Timothy 2.5. *sheweth*: 'shuns, avoids' (*moustre*). The earliest citation in MED to this sense is 1500.
4149–50 *And whoosoo boweth beste he maye be nere to falle* misconstrues the French: *Et mur qui sencline puet estre pres de cheoir. mieux* may have been read for *mur.*
4152 *if hee abide to praye* misconstrues *sil demeure apuier*, that is, 'to prop (himself) up.' *apuier* was read as *a prier.*
4154–8 Daniel 2.32–3. Details of the biblical narrative are garbled.
4176–8 Ecclesiasticus 22.1–2. *myyry* (*emboees*) is not recorded by MED in the sense of 'made of clay.' *bowellys* misconstrues *bouse de vache* 'dung.'
4179 *shamefulle*: 'rebuking.' MED records the sense under the adverb *shamefulli* and the noun *shame*, 6a, but not under the adjective.
4185–7 Ecclesiasticus 33.5. *slowly*: *parescheusement*, which was read as *par esconsement*, resulting in the translation 'be effenynge.' B's reading, *essenynge*, is a scribal error. *brayinge*: 'creaking' (*brait*). Not in MED with this precise meaning.
4190 After *theye* a portion of the sentence has been lost: *de ceulx qui sont entour lui que ilz lui sont sans pitie, de ceulx qui de soubz lui sont que ilz ne le scevent servir ...*
4201 *bodyly strooke* renders French *le cop de la mort. Othea* 25/11 (MS L) also has *bodely* in the sense of 'deadly.' Not glossed by MED in this sense. Possibly *mort* was misread as *cors.*
4216 *vntrowth* 'evil, wickedness' renders French *dissolus.*
4220–1 Whiting H571 (A mad hound cares for neither friend nor foe [bites his own master]).
4229–32 Jerome, *Epistolae*, 125.11 (PL 22, col. 1078).
4235–45 Tubach 275. The source is *Vitae Patrum*, 3.516 (PL 73, col. 780).
4250–1 2 Thessalonians 3.10.
4251–2 Ecclesiasticus 35.12. After *doo* the English has lost, or possibly omitted, the completion of the statement: *Car en enfer ne seront nulle fors oevre ne raison ne sapience ne science qui te puissent excuser ne deffendre. Car le serf qui scet la volente de son maistre et ne la fait sera batu en moult de tourmens.*
4254–5 Augustine, *Enarrationes in Psalmos*, 36.16 (PL 36, col. 372).
4255–9 *Vitae Patrum*, 3.516 (PL 73, cols 780–1). Judging from the lacuna, the translator was unfamiliar with the meaning of *acciduel*

'slothful' (*assiduel*). MED lacks the form. After *dowte* the abbot's statement continues in the French: *Car se tu les avoies bien diligenment regardes se ta chambre estoit toute plaine de vers iusques au col tu seroies en ta sele ou en ta chambre sans accide et san peresce.*

4263 *shewe theym lyghte,* that is, enlighten them (French *les enluminent*).

4265–7 Cf. Whiting T187 (Three things cause a man to flee from his own house); Tilley H781.

4273–4 Jeremias 3.51. *theef* (B) is undoubtedly an eyeskip (*theefes* l. 4272).

4279–81 John 15.5.

4281–6 Cicero, *De Officiis*, 3.1.1. On the source and widespread use of this statement in medieval literature see the series of notes by Allen, Brewer, Cook, Cooper, Lowes, MacCracken, and Tatlock.

4288–9 *prophetis*, but French *philosophes*. The substitution of *prophete* for *philosophe* occurs also in l. 8149. *praysed and autorized* expands French *loe*. Cf. MED, s.v. *auctorisen* v., 3 on the use of *autorized* in the sense of 'given validity, endowed with authority.'

4289–4300 Cicero, *De Officiis*, 3.1.1. *solitude*: so all MSS except DU, which have *solicitude*, the erroneous reading of B's exemplar.

4300–4 Ambrose, *De Officiis Ministrorum*, 3.1 (PL 16, cols 145–7).

4308–10 Seneca, *Epistolae*, 105.6.

4310–16 Paraphrases of this statement appear in Bernard, *In Festivitate Omnium Sanctorum*, Sermo 2.6 (*Opera* 5, 347), *Epistolae*, 311.1 (*Opera* 8, 240), and, perhaps even more closely, in Pseudo-Bernard, *Domus haec*, Proemium (PL 184, col. 507).

4316 Possibly a lacuna. After *hous* the French adds: *en guise de menestrel. Quant il treuve un mauvais hostel et un mauvais homme et un fol et son anemi mortel il parle a lui.*

4330–1 Matthew 12.36.

4340–5 A paraphrase of Bernard, *Sermones super Cantica Canticorum*, 33.10 (*Opera* 1, 240–1). *vndiscrete desire or feruentnes* (ll. 4341–2) expands the French *indiscrecion*.

4348–9 Romans 12.1.

4361–2 Ecclesiastes 9.16 (here misattributed to Wisdom).

4372–3 Augustine, *Sermones de Diversis*, 143.2 (PL 38, col. 785). The statement appears in Peraldus 2.5.3.2 without attribution to Augustine.

4375 A phrase has been lost between *afore the lyghte* and *the whiche is wors*: *ou sans lumiere.*

4385 The end of one sentence and the whole of the next have been lost – or possibly omitted – after *bawme*: *si comme dit saint bernard. Donne moy, dit il, un de tes disciples si comme fu thymotee et je le paistray dor et la buvreray de basme.* Bernard, *Sermones super Cantica Canticorum*, 30.12 (*Opera* 1, 218).
4389–90 This statement cannot be found among Bernard's works. It derives from Peraldus 2.5.1.4, and it also appears, but without attribution, in *Summa Virtutum*, 8.163–4.
4398–9 Cf. Whiting G353 (How shall one do good to another who can do no good to himself).
4399–400 Bernard, *Sermones de Diversis*, 19.1 (*Opera* 6[1], 161), *Sermones super Cantica Canticorum*, 82.6 (*Opera* 2, 296).
4407–11 For the traditional division of life into three (four or seven) ages and the moral flaws attributed to each of them, see Burrow, *Ages of Man*, 5–11, 36–54, 69–71, and an appendix of *loci classici* (192–202), including Aristotle, *Rhetoric*, 2.12–14; Horace, *Ars Poetica*, ll. 156–78; and Ptolemy, *Tetrabiblos*, 4.10.
4413–17 *After that ... the Romaynes*: an awkwardly slavish and partly inaccurate rendering of the French: *Apres regna orgeuil et ambicion tant comme les quatre emperieres furent en leur seignourie lun apres lautre premier les caldeens apres celui de grece que les caldeens vainquirent apres les greioys et apres les rommains.* The translator's difficulty appears to have arisen from a misreading of *emperieres* as *empereres*. *Calden*, that is, Babylonians, with whom the Chaldeans were often confused. *he of Grece* (*celui de grece*) refers to the kingdom of Alexander. *dominacioúnes* should read *dominiones*: possibly a scribal error. The concept of the four World Empires derives from the interpretations of Nabuchodonoser's dream in Daniel 2. See the studies of this tradition by Rowley, *Darius the Mede*, 61–160, and Swain, 'Four Monarchies,' 12–21.
4419 Ecclesiastes 10.19.
4420–1 Jeremias 6.13.
4427–8 Ecclesiasticus 11.16.
4429 *a love to haue dissordonatly* mistakes the French *amour davoir desordenee*.
4431 *ii maneres*: so all MSS except D *trois manieres*. *Ayen* 34/28 and *VV* 30/13 correctly read *þri (þre) maneres*. *streyningly*: 'tightly' (*restraignament*). Recorded by MED as from 1500 with the meaning '? under compulsion.'
4434–7 Apocalypse 13.1–2, 17.1–6.

4450 *grene*: AQSV *vert*, CDN *vair(e)*, PRU *vairole*. Although Guillaume le Clerc, ll. 2029–36, lists green as one of the variegated colors of the panther, it is probable that *vair(e)* or *vairole* 'furry' preserves the correct reading. The source of the statement has not been identified. *eville parte* (*male part*) is not recorded by MED.
4454–5 *anythynge*: P *avoir*, ACDNQRSUV *miel*. Was *rien* read for *miel*?
4460–1 1 Timothy 6.10.
4487 *serued* mistranslates *getoient* ('threw').
4491–3 *ne thoo also that withholdeth ... or oother rentys of hooly chirche*: *ne ceulx aussi qui retiennent ou forcoeillent ou paient mauvaisement leurs rentes* (D *dismes*) *leur offrendes et les autres rentes de sainte eglise*. The first *rentys* refers specifically to tithes, the second generally to other dues. MED records neither sense. For the second *rentys*, *Ayen* 41/20 and *VV* 37/17 read *ryȝtes* (*riȝtes*).
4500 *resoigne*: 'fears' (*resoigne*). Not recorded by MED. OED provides a single citation dating from 1500.
4503 *loketh in swerdys*: a form of divination or sortilegium, the sword being employed as an instrument of mirror-magic. See Owst, *Literature*, 277, and Duffy, *Stripping of Altars*, 71–5, on contemporary interest in, and ecclesiastical condemnations of, the practice.
4507 *a certeyne draughtis* paraphrases the French *deux septiers*. On the French origin and late Middle-English examples of this construction see Rissanen, 'Use of *One*,' 346–7.
4508 *englotte*: 'gulp down' (*engloutissent*) does not appear in MED. OED (*englut* v.) records it from 1491 (Caxton). Cf. ll. 5483, 5754. Neither MED nor OED cites *hynder* (*honnissent*) in the sense of 'spoil' (wine).
4511 *of coste*: 'apart, indirectly' (*de coste*). Not recorded by MED.
4525–6 The precise meaning of the phrase *putteth in foryetilnes* 'neglect' or 'disregard' is not recorded by MED. It is cited by OED (*forgetfulness* n., 4) as from 1576. The French reads: *qui les testamens detiennent, delaient, et mettent en nonchaloir*.
4527–35 *In siche synne ... as men take litill fysshes* renders the French: *En telz pechies sont les riches hommes qui tolent a destre et a senestre terres vignes et autres choses et escorchent la poure gent que ilz deussent garder et leur font paier tailles coruees et faulses amendes et mauvaises constumes en plus de cent manieres quil pourpensent pour la poure gent prendre aussi comme on prent les petit poissons*. *shrede*, echoing *fleeth* in the previous line, is not recorded by MED in the sense of 'fleece, strip of wealth.' *be enhaunsynge theire rentis* is

the translator's gloss on *corues*, a little-known word in Middle English, which actually refers to the exaction of unpaid labor (MED, s.v. *corve* n.). *rentis* stands for *rente servises*, services due to a lord, or money in lieu of services (MED, s.v. *rente* n., 4c). *be constreynynge theyme to made amendes* mistakes *faulses amendes* 'illegal fines.' *forcies* may have been read for *faulses*. *costomes*, that is, customary dues or 'aids,' were another form of taxation. On corve and customs see Duby, *Rural Economy*, 187, 204, 224, 269.

4542–3 James 5.4.

4563 *theefes*, but French *petis larrons* which is properly translated in ll. 4568–9.

4577 *appropred*, that is, in possession of the endowment or income of a parish church, translates French *proprietaires*. The implication is that such 'religious pepil' violate their vows of poverty.

4583–5 Matthew 21.13.

4598 *townes*: the French adds *a la fois*.

4599–603 Deuteronomy 23.19–20. The text, however, is closer to the general statements of the *Decretum*: *Quod autem praeter summam emolumenta sectari sit usuras ... Si feneraveris hominem, id est, si tu mutuum dederis pecuniam tuam, a quo plus quam dederis expectes, non pecuniam solam, sed aliquid plus quam dedisti, sive illud triticum sit, sive vinum, sive oleum, sive quodlibet aliud, si plus quam dedistis expectes accipere, fenerator eris, et in hoc inprobandus, non laudandus ... Qui plus quam dederit expetit, usuras accipit* (C.14.3.1); *Quicquid supra datum exigitur usura est* (C.14.3.2); *Esca usura est, et vestis usura est et quodcumque sorti accidit usura est; et quodcumque velis ei nomen inponas, usura est* (C.14.3.3) (Friedberg, vol. 1, col. 735). C.14.13.2 explicitly forbids the acceptance of gifts, however small. See McLaughlin, 'Teaching of Canonists,' 82 *n*6, 95, 98; Noonan, *Scholastic Analysis of Usury*, 104–5.

4603–4 *that oppon catelle taketh the multiplyinge of theyme*, that is, take their profit over and above the principal of the loan. Any addition to the principal constituted usury: *Quicquid sorti accidit usura est* (*Decretum*, C.14.3.3; Friedberg, col. 735). *multiplyinge* translates French *montes* 'interest' or 'increase.'

4604–9 On the restitution of usury, including that acquired through inheritance, see Raimundus de Pennaforte, *Summa de Paenitentia*, 2.7.11, col. 549. The issue is discussed by Noonan, *Scholastic Analysis of Usury*, 16–17, 19, 192 *n*88, and especially 75; De Roover, *Money*, 151–3, 157 *n*13; Tawney, *Religion*, 46, 49; and Ibanès, *Doctrine*, 98–9.

4610 Whiting B529 (As one brews let him drink); Hassell B172.
4611 *Lete the wed goo* mistakes the French *Va la chancon* 'Away with the cupbearer.' The translator confused *eschancon* 'cupbearer' with *escheance* 'inheritance, right of succession.' *Wed*, however, does not quite capture the meaning of *escheance*. Cf. Godefroy 9.510b *eschançon* n., 3.379c *escheance*.
4611–12 Whiting P455 (Who will drink, unbuckle his purse).
4612–14 *Alsoo ther be som vsurerys ... or be theyre cosynes* refers to illicit agreements to conceal the practice of usury and avoid its penalties. A chapter entitled *De His Quae Circa Parochianos Sunt Inquirenda* in Raimundus de Pennaforte's *Libellus Pastoralis*, 621–3, denounces the use of friends for this purpose.
4615–17 For the hostility against Jews as usurers – prohibitions against usury were deemed applicable to all – see Pirenne, *History of Europe*, 131–3; Noonan, *Scholastic Analysis of Usury*, 34–5; McLaughlin, 'Teaching of Canonists,' 138; and Ibanès, *Doctrine*, 16–17. *Saraȝynes* is obviously an error, but whether it is due to the deficiency of the translator or scribe is impossible to determine. The French properly reads *caoursins*, which is used in the general sense of 'moneylenders' rather than in its original and more restrictive sense of petty merchants from Cahors who engaged in the practice. On this term, as well as the status and protection conferred on usurers by medieval princes and magnates (*grete men*), see Pirenne, *History of Europe*, 132–4, 213–15; De Roover, *Money*, 99, 103–4; and Grunwald, 'Lombards,' 394–5.
4617–19 *Also ther be som usurers ... because of the longe leenynge* freely paraphrases the French: *Et si sont uns usuriers, marchans que on appelle termoieurs, et ceste pestilence est en eulx dacheter vil et de vendre plus cher pour le terme*. The English clarifies the meaning of the French and moderates its harshness. Buying cheap in order to sell later at a much higher price on the pretext of deferred payment was severely denounced as *turpe lucrum*. See McLaughlin, 'Teaching of Canonists,' 95, 117–19, and Baldwin, *Just Price*, 47–8. The earliest citation in OED to *vil* meaning 'cheap in price' (s.v. *vile* adj., 5c) is 1490 (Caxton). MED does not record this meaning.
4624–7 Medieval canonists regarded as illicit the formation of 'leonine' partnerships where the risks of loss were all on one side. See McLaughlin, 'Teaching of Canonists,' 104–5, and Noonan, *Scholastic Analysis of Usury*, 134–5.
4627–31 *to hyre* (*a mitoiere*) refers to the métayage system, whereby the landowner provides the farmer with stock and seed in return for a

fixed rent (*bail à ferme*) or a proportion – generally half – of the crop (*bail à part de fruits*) or the natural increase of the livestock (*bail à chaftel*). The latter, particularly where the farmer accepted full responsibility for losses, was regarded as usurious. See Sicard, especially 1398, and Robert of Flamborough, *Liber Poenitentialis*, 4.220 (Firth, 194 and *n*47). For the métayage system generally see Ganshof and Verhulst, 'Medieval Agrarian Society,' 324–6, and Duby, *Rural Economy*, 275–6.
4634–7 *Whan that the pepyll be nedy ... ii penyworth of werke for oon*: for short-term seasonal loans or advanced payments to impoverished peasants at high interest, repayable in money, kind, or labour service, see Duby, *Rural Economy*, 253–4, 349.
4639–40 *the man* abridges the French *le poure homme et la poure fame*.
4642 *ouerselle*: 'overcharge' (*survendent*). Not recorded by MED. The earliest usage cited in OED is 1580.
4643 *drye*: 'paid in cash' (*sec*). Not recorded by MED in this sense. OED, s.v. *dry* adj., 19, cites it as from 1574.
4664 *alle a contre*: for this construction see Fischer, 'Syntax,' 211.
4665–7 The French tartly observes that false notaries take twice (*deux fois*) what they deserve for their services.
4684 *blandesshinge*: 'deceit, betrayal, deception' (*boydie, boidie*). For this sense MED (*blaundishing* ger., b) offers, with a query, a single citation from Rolle's *Psalter*.
4692–4 Genesis 4.3–5. *wide*: 'worthless' (*vuide*), a variant spelling of 'void,' which is recorded by OED, s.v. *void* adj., 2c with a 1502 citation. MED does not record the variant under the adjective, but it cites 'wide' as a variant form of the verb 'voiden.'
4696 *shenshippe* 'disgrace', but French *boidie* 'deception.'
4709 *Thowe canste weele hire* misconstrues the French *Tu sces bien escouter*, confusing *escouter* meaning 'to hear' with a variant spelling of *escoter* meaning 'to pay scot,' here metaphorically, to pay a penalty for sin. MED, s.v. *scotten* v., 1c. Cf. Hassell E73 (*payer l'escot*); Whiting S97; Tilley S159.
4725–6 Whiting D274 (Do as you would be done to), listing both versions of the proverb.
4738–9 The reference is to the story of the fox who pretends to be dead (Tubach 2176) going back to *Physiologus*, 15 (Carmody, 29–30). Cf. Hassig, *Bestiaries*, 62–3.
4741 *lowlynesse*, here implying feigned humility, freely renders French *conchiemens* 'deception.' Not recorded by MED in this ironic sense.

4744 Whiting W627 (White words); Hassell P61.
4746–7 Cf. Whiting S931 (A black swan), C574 (To say the crow is white). Cf. ll. 2514–5 and *n*.
4747–52 Tubach 2177 (Fox, Raven, and Cheese) deriving from *Romulus*, 1.19 (Thiele, 58–61). See Hassig, *Bestiaries*, 65.
4755–7 Seneca, *De Beneficiis*, 6.30.3.
4761 *courteyoures*, translating *corratiers* meaning 'brokers,' does not appear in MED. Possibly, however, the translator may have confused *corratiers* with *correters* 'courtiers.'
4778–9 *fere of thought ... and synne* omits the French coordinates: *de paour et de pensee et de doleur et de pechie*. Cf. ll. 804, 1505, 4083, 8862.
4782 *pointeth*: 'points out' (*mostre*). Not recorded by MED in this sense. OED, s.v. *point* v., 10, cites the meaning as from 1489 (Caxton).
4809–13 Luke 16.19–31. *laserur*: 'leper' (*ladre*). Not recorded by MED in this form.
4823–5 Leviticus 6.1–5, Numbers 5.6–7, Luke 19.8–9.
4825–6 Whiting Y17 (Yield or hang); Hassell R24; Morawski 1571. Cf. l. 8727.
4826–9 Matthew 6.24, Luke 16.13.
4834–5 Matthew 19.21, Luke 10.21.
4838–9 Whiting M143 (A man is worth as much as his land is worth); Hassell H54.
4840 Whiting H576 (To be worse than a hound); Hassell C166.
4852–3 *for to restreyne and to spare* translates the French *pour estraindre et pour espargnier*. *regratories* refers to the practice of purchasing and selling commodities (usually victuals) at higher prices illegally achieved through forestalling the market. Cf. MED, *regratory* n., and Holdsworth, *English Law*, 375.
4859 After *almesse* the French adds *ne courtoisie*.
4887–8 Ecclesiastes 5.13. The erroneous reading *shewith* in B resulted from the confusion of pr. 3 sg. indic. *pert* 'loses' (*perdre*) with *pert* 'shows' (*paroir*).
4893 *the partye*: CNQRSUV *la partie*, AP *la departie*. Translate: 'it is a fair division of the inheritance.'
4895 There is a considerable lacuna here. The French reads *Les vers ont la charongne, les parens lavoir. Les diables se combatent pour celle ame tourmenter qui mieulx mieulx et les vers dautre part pour la charongne devorer et les parens pour son avoir happer*.
4905–6 Ecclesiasticus 13.1. Whiting P236 (He that touches pitch shall

be defiled); Tilley P358. The French reads: *Qui touche la pois de legier se conchie. couchie* was apparently read for *conchie* and *pais* for *pois.*
4909–11 Seneca, *Epistolae,* 7.7.
4912–14 Proverbs 23.5.
4919–35 Tubach 5027.
4942–5 Ambrose, *Enarrationes in Psalmos,* 36.76–7 (PL 14, cols 1005–6), Jerome, *Epistolae,* 53.10 (PL 22, col. 549). Cf. *Fasciculus Morum,* 4.11.24–6.
4947 *proprely,* but French *apertement* ('clearly').
4954–6 Bernard, *In Resurrectione,* Sermo 3.1 (*Opera* 5, 104).
4960–3 Gregory, *Moralia,* 8.26 (PL 75, col. 829).
4967–8 Luke 16.13, Matthew 6.24.
4969–73 Luke 12.22–30.
4978–83 Luke 18.24–7, Matthew 19.23–6.
4987–8 A paraphrase of Romans 13.11–14, John 8.44, Ephesians 2.1–3.
4998 *iusticeris*: not recorded by MED in the sense of 'judges.' See, however, OED, s.v. *justicer* n., 2, as from 1481.
5000–12 A conflation of Numbers 22–4 and 25.1–9. *louf,* but French *aide,* which was probably read as *aime. to theym that were maistres of the ooste* departs from the French: *a Moyse qui estoit maistre de lost.*
5012–14 *The hooly man,* but French *le sage* with the single exception of D, which attributes the statement to St John the Evangelist. The biblical reference, loosely paraphrased in the text, is to Apocalypse 6.15–16.
5031 *and,* but French *en* which would appear to be correct.
5044–8 Ecclesiastes 7.27; 3 Kings 11.
5048–9 Cf. Hélinand of Froidmont, *Les Vers de la Mort* 31.1: *Mors est la roiz qui a tot atrape. net*: DP *rais,* C *rays,* AV *roys,* RSU *roy,* Q *ray,* N om. *Roy* 'net' was confused with *roi* 'king.'
5050 *non herte maye from this fonned woman,* that is, 'none may escape the entrapment of this seductress.'
5052–3 Cf. ll. 2318–9.
5063–5 *proudest,* but French *le plus perilleux. the pride and the boste ... theese contirfetid guyses* translates the French *lorgeuil et le boban, le fol atournement et desordene aournement de ces dames foles et de ces damoiselles sotes et de ces desguises cointeaux. disordenat behavyng* 'dissolute conduct' mistakes *desordene aournement* 'excessive adornment,' and *contirfetid guyses* 'deceitful practices' mistakes *desguises cointeaux* 'elegant fashions.'
5077–80 2 Peter 2.14.

5082–6 2 Kings 11.
5091 *foxe*, but French *loupe*.
5103–7 Proverbs 26.24–5.
5114–15 Matthew 10.4, 26.14–16, 47–50.
5132 *ferre* 'fair' may be dialectal and so is allowed to stand, although it is more probably a scribal error for *faire/feire*.
5147 *proude pepil* mistakes the French *oultrages* 'excesses,' which may have been read as *outrageor(s)* adj., 'presumptuous, overweening.'
5152 *lecherye of handis, touchyngis* should perhaps be emended to *and evil touchyngis* in accordance with the French *la luxure des mains et des mauvais atouchemens*. Possibly a scribal omission.
5156 *terreboles* (DQ): fire stones whose properties are described in *Physiologus* 3 (Carmody, 13–14). See also McCulloch, *Medieval Latin*, 119; White, *Bestiary*, 226–7; Collins, *Symbolism of Animals*, 209–10; and Hassig, *Bestiaries*, 116–28. Continence is compared to a *terribolus* in *Fasciculus Morum*, 7.17.105–10. *feboles* (B) reproduces the spurious reading found in all French MSS except DQ. *terreboles* is unrecorded by MED.
5160–4 1 Corinthians 7.1.
5164–6 For the source of this quotation, see ll. 5277–82*n*. The attribution to Paul is erroneous.
5166 1 Corinthians 6.18.
5200 *disordeyned*: 'forbidden' (*desordenee*). Not recorded by MED in this precise sense.
5201–4 *Decretum*, C.3.7.11 (Friedberg 1, col. 1143), paraphrasing Augustine, *De Bono Coniugali*, 8.8 (PL 40, col. 379).
5204–6 Whiting M154 (A man may sin with his own wife and hurt himself with his knife).
5207 *son of Iudas*, that is, Onan (Genesis 38.8–10).
5208–9 Tobias 3.8.
5211–25 For impediments to marriage and bans on sexual contact between spiritual kinsmen see Lynch, *Godparents*, 258–81. *heyueth* (l. 5216) and *hyueth* (l. 5229) mean 'is more heinous,' a sense unrecorded by MED.
5236 *synne that men sholde not name*: an allusion to the sin of Sodom, narrowly interpreted as homosexuality, which Peter Cantor, *Verbum Abbreviatum* 138 (PL 205, col. 335), termed 'ineffabile.' The *Mirroure* expresses its disapproval more strongly, employing a phrase that also occurs in a letter of Honorius III to the Archbishop of Lund (4 February

1227) printed in the *Bullarium Danicum*, 1, no. 208, 178, and translated by Boswell, *Christianity*, 380.

5239–42 Cf. ll. 928–33.

5243–6 Romans 1.27.

5255–9 The same illustration occurs in *Fasciculus Morum*, 7.4.14–20. Cf. Whiting B506 (Take away the brands to quench the fire), P327 (When the pot boils the best remedy is to withdraw the fire).

5265–72 Tubach 4741. Its source is *Vitae Patrum*, 5.37 (PL 73, cols 883–4).

5277–8 1 Corinthians 6.18.

5279–82 This statement together with its attribution to Ambrose is taken from Peraldus 2.4.4.1. It is also found in *Fasciculus Morum*, 7.4.33–4. Its source is actually Caesarius of Arles, *Sermones*, 41.1 (CC 103, 180).

5299–301 Pseudo-Jerome, *Epistola ad Oceanum*, 3–4 (PL 30, col. 289).

5303–13 Jerome, *Epistolae*, 52.5 (PL 22, cols 531–2). Cf. Whiting S52 (As strong as Samson), S460 (As wise as Solomon), D26 (As holy as David); Hassell S34, S24. For Samson, Solomon, and David as exempla of lechery see Bloomfield, 'Piers Plowman,' 234. Cf. ll. 10,176, 11,306–7.

5317–19 Augustine, *Enarrationes in Psalmos*, 91.2 (PL 37, col. 1172). Cf. *Dives* 3.17.

5330–1 *theye forsooke the feende ... and alle his prides* is taken from the baptismal rite: *Abrenuncias Sathanae ... et omnibus operibus ejus ... et omnibus pompis ejus* (Maskell, *Monumenta*, 23). *pride/prides* render French *pompe(s)* 'the show(s) or spectacle(s) of the devil.' This meaning is given by MED not under *pride*, but under *pompe* n., 1e. Baptismal formulas of exorcism are discussed by Cramer, *Baptism*, especially 14.

5334 *paryshones to þe feende* paraphrases the French *convers et converses au diable*, that is, laymen and women who devote themselves to the service of the devil. Cf. ll. 1760–4.

5338–9 Proverbs 4.27.

5353–4 *in mevyng theire armys and in shakyng* inaccurately renders *en bras demener et dehocher*, confusing *dehocher* 'to bend' with *hocher* 'to shake.'

5356–8 *and soo doo theye ... and to dampnacion*: a garbled version of the French: *et font ceulx and celles pecher mortelment qui les regardent par ce quilz ont si nobles atournement et les esmeuvent a pechie de luxure et a dampnement.*

5361–2 2 Peter 2.22. Whiting S539 (To slumber like a sow in a slough). Cf. Pliny, *Historia Naturalis*, 8.77; Isidore, *Etymologiae*, 12.1.25 (PL 82, col. 428); Bartholomaeus Anglicus, *De Proprietatibus*, 18.85.
5363–6 Matthew 8.30–2.
5373–4 Cf. Whiting W466 (To spare no more than the wolf does the sheep); Hassell L84.
5374–5 Genesis 3.1.
5375–6 Matthew 4.1.
5377–8 Philippians 3.19.
5384 *The chirche dore ... opyn* departs from the French: *Le moustier nest mie lieure.* For a literal translation of the French see *Ayen* 51/2–3 and *VV* 47/23–4.
5405–8 Gregory, *Moralia*, 30.18 (PL 76, cols 556–7).
5425–6 *sause camelyn* – a blend of currants, nuts, bread, and spices – renders the French *saulse de citeaulx*. See *Curye on Inglische*, 4.149 and 213. MED, s.v. *camelyn* n.
5427 *talent*, but French *famine*. Possibly an eyeskip (l. 5424). Cf. Whiting H642 (Hunger is the best sauce).
5428 *plente sauoureth not*: Whiting P270 (Plenty is no dainty).
5428–31 Cf. Whiting M473 (Meat savors better to the hungry than the full).
5450–1 Isaias 65.20.
5459–60 Isaias 5.20.
5460–2 Psalm 91.2–4.
5462–66 Job 38.36 on the cock's intelligence. For the other details of cock lore see Ambrose, *Hexameron*, 5.24 (PL 14, cols 240–1); Bartholomaeus Anglicus, *De Proprietatibus*, 12.17; and Gregory, *Moralia*, 30.3 (PL 76, col. 529). Rowland, *Animals*, 24; McCulloch, *Medieval Latin*, 104; Friedmann, *Bestiary*, 203.
5483 Rowland, *Animals*, 30–1, 93. *glotyth*: 'swallow' (*engloutissent*). OED defines *englut* v. in this sense as from 1491. MED defines *glotien* as 'feed to repletion.'
5484 *sot* is not recorded by MED in the sense of 'one who eats to excess.'
5488 A transitional passage has been lost or omitted after *perlious*: *Car nous avons a gouverner nostre anemi mortel. Cest nostre corps que nous portons lequel nous devons vaincre et se nous lui laissons rien de nostre droit nous nous tuons.*
5495 *curtesye*: 'virtue, moral purity' (*courtoisie*). Not recorded by MED in this sense. Cf. *Ayen* 54/7 *onestete*, *VV* 50/7 *honestly*.

5497–9 Romans 8.13, Phillipians 3.19.
5514 *commaunderesse* is not recorded by MED.
5541–4 Luke 10.8. *sende*: 'sent' (*envoia*).
5544–5 Cf. Whiting S157 (A full good servant must have good wages); Hassell S80.
5545–7 Deuteronomy 25.4; 1 Corinthians 9.9; 1 Timothy 5.18. *laboreth* does not appear in MED in the sense of 'treads.'
5551 Genesis 3.1–6.
5561 Psalms 45.1, 58.10.
5562–3 1 Corinthians 13.3, Ephesians 2.9–10, Titus 3.5.
5570–2 Whiting R29 (A ram draws back to push his enemy the harder); Hassell R15; Morawski 875. *flee* mistranslates *ferir*, which was evidently read as *fuir*.
5578–81 Genesis 25.29–34. The account of Esau's sale of his birthright in *Genesis and Exodus* (c. 1250) contains, according to MED, the only other reference in Middle English to lentils as food. The translator was unfamiliar with the word.
5584–5 Genesis 3.
5588–9 Isaias 56.9–11. MED does not record *veleins* in the sense of 'gluttons.'
5605 *to take*: the only instance of the use of an infinitive for a finite verb in the text. *reprengner* may have been read for *reprengne*.
5605–8 Luke 4.1–4.
5611–16 Luke 16.24.
5616–18 Wisdom 11.21.
5624–7 Job 20.18–20.
5632–3 Whiting P270 (Plenty is no dainty).
5643 *drinkes*, that is, bouts of drinking with the implication of drunkenness, translating French *buveries* (*beveries*). PR emend to *renoierie* 'forswearing.' MED, s.v. *drink(e)* n., 3.
5645–6 *curiosite*: 'fastidiousness' (*curiosite*), misread here and in l. 5661 as *curtoisie* (B *curtesye*). *places*: 'palates' or 'throats' (*palais*) should perhaps be emended to *palaces*. MED, s.v. *palas* n., *curiousite* n., 4a.
5647–8 Romans 8.6.
5649 *mounted*: 'esteemed' (*montee*). OED, s.v. *mount* v., 13a and c, as from the sixteenth century. Not recorded by MED in this precise sense.
5651–3 Cf. Thomas Eliot's *Castell of Helthe* 2.19: *Galene also prohibiteth chylderne to drynke any wyne, forasmoche as they be of a hote and*

moyst temperature, and so is wyne: and therfore it heateth and moysteth to moche their bodyes, and fulleth their heedes with vapoures. More ouer he wolde, that yonge men shulde drinke lyttel wine, for it shall make them prone to fury and to lecherye: and that parte of the soull, whiche is callyd rationall, it shall make troublous and dulle. The passage summarizes Galen's treatise, *The Soul's Dependence on the Body*, 809 (*Selected Works*, 170), which, in turn, is based on Plato's *Laws*, 2.666[a].

5653 B's reading, *oldere*, possibly derives from a faulty scribal extension of a tag on final *e*.

5656 *besily*: 'intently' (*curieusement*). Cf. MED, s.v. *bisily* adv., 2.

5664 *gwyses*: 'dishes' (*desguisez*). Cf. MED, s.v. *gise* n., 4 'some kind of dish' (1475).

5685–5729 For contemporary fulminations against tavern-haunting see Owst, *Literature*, 427–30, 434–42.

5686 Whiting T48 (The tavern is the devil's schoolhouse).

5705 MED does not record *boule* as a verb. It records *amisse* as a verb, but not in the sense of 'to do wrong.'

5720 *fleith* and *flee* translate *escorche* and *escorchent* ('flay[s]').

5740–5 Matthew 4.1–4.

5751–2 Proverbs 21.25–6.

5753 B should perhaps be emended to read *þe yen coveitith [to see] vaniteis* in accordance with the French *les yeulx couvoitent a veoir vanites*.

5757 Whiting W675 (To be worm's food [meat]).

5779–83 Seneca, *Epistolae*, 7.8.

5783–5801 Peraldus added the sins of the tongue as an independent category to the other seven sins. On the origin and development of the concept of *verbositas* or *vitium linguae* among the moralists of the twelfth and thirteenth centuries see the study of Casagrande and Vecchio, *Peccati*, especially 103–35, Newhauser, *Vices and Virtues*, 195–6, and Craun, *Lies, Slander*, 10–72.

5792–4 Matthew 21.19.

5812–14 Matthew 12.36.

5819–20 Whiting C276 (Like the clapper of a mill that will not be still).

5832–3 *drawe theyme too theyre acorde*: Hassell C307 (*Traire a sa cordele*). *conceyved*: S *concepu*, AP *receu*, CDQRUV *conceu*, N om. Gradon (*Ayen* 58/28) glosses *conceyved* as 'devised.' MED, s.v. *conceiven* v., 6d.

5850 *worthinessis*: 'acts of chivalry' (*proesces*).
5856 *daunsyng*, but French *disant*, which may have been misread as *dansant*.
5861 Whiting C601 (The cuckoo sings only of himself).
5863 *I shalle make* misconstrues the French *feroy* 'I shall bear away,' as Gradon notes (*Ayen* 59/23–4*n*).
5873–6 Bernard, *Sermones in Psalmum Qui Habitat*, 11.4 (*Opera* 4, 451).
5879 *obleys*, that is, 'offerings' (*oublees*). The translator seems to have been aware of only the secondary sense of *oblee* as 'host' or 'wafer'; hence B's reading, *wafris*, which mistakes the meaning of the passage. MED, s.v. *oble* n.
5884–5 Tubach 520. Cf. McCulloch, *Medieval Latin*, 94; White, *Bestiary*, 47.
5896 Proverbs 6.19.
5899–5900 Isaias 47.10–12.
5904 Whiting P248 (To sing placebo); Hassell P188.
5908–10 *and acordeth it to what that a man wille and seithe it, be it wel be it evil, be it goode be it fals* mistakes the French *et sacorde a quanque on veult dire soit bien soit mal soit voir soit faulx. voir* 'true' was evidently read as *bon* 'good.' The superfluous *it* after *seithe* is probably an eyeskip by anticipation and should perhaps be deleted.
5912 Isaias 9.15.
5914–16 Cf. Albert the Great, *De Animalibus*, 22.146, on the fox using its tail to deceive its pursuers.
5918–24 *mermeidynes*, that is, sirens. Tubach 4495. The reference is to *Physiologus*, 12 (Carmody, 25–6). See also Bartholomaeus Anglicus, *De Proprietatibus*, 18.97; White, *Bestiary*, 134–5; McCulloch, *Medieval Latin*, 166–9; Henkel, *Physiology*, 173–5; and Rowland, *Animals*, 154–6. On the origin and development of the legend see Rachewiltz, *De Serenibus*, especially 64–112, and Hassig, *Bestiaries*, 104–15.
5926–30 The reference is to the serpent sirena described by Isidore, *Etymologiae*, 12.4.29 (PL 82, col. 446) and Bartholomaeus Anglicus, *De Proprietatibus*, 18.97. See McCulloch, *Medieval Latin*, 169–70; Rachewiltz, *De Serenibus*, 67–9; Hassig, *Bestiaries*, 237 *n*30.
5930–1 Ecclesiastes 10.11.
5934 *knaweth and missehandelith* misconstrues *demordent et demenguent* 'consume and devour.'
5838–9 Thomas Cantimpratensis, 4.4.9–10, based on Pliny, *Historia*

Naturalis, 10.83; Albert the Great, *De Animalibus*, 22.22; Vincent of Beauvais, *Speculum Doctrinale*, 16.100.

5939–41 *flye* misconstrues the French *huppe* 'hoopoe,' an uncommon word whose only appearance in Middle English is *VV* 59/24. MED, s.v. *houpere* n. On the tradition that the hoopoe nests in human ordure, see Isidore, *Etymologiae*, 12.7.66 (PL 82, col. 468); Bartholomaeus Anglicus, *De Proprietatibus*, 12.38; McCulloch, *Medieval Latin*, 126–7; White, *Bestiary*, 150; Rowland, *Animals*, 81–3; Henkel, *Physiologus*, 200–1; Hassig, *Bestiaries*, 93, 101–3; and Kunstmann 'Bird That Fouls.' Cf. Tubach 3475 (hoopoe invites a nightingale to his nest, but the latter finds it too dirty to stay in).

5941–2 Tubach 554. *botte*: 'dung beetle' (*escarbos*). Not recorded by MED with this meaning. Cf. Thompson A2433.5.4 (Why beetles live in manure); Tilley B221: The beetle flies over many a sweet flower and lights in a cowhard.

5946–7 *settith atte noght* (*nacomptent a riens*), that is, demeans his virtues and ruins his reputation. MED, s.v. *setten* v., 25a.

5948–9 *these oþer*, that is, detractors.

5956–7 Whiting S96 (The scorpion flatters with its head when it will sting with its tail). See White, *Bestiary*, 192; Friedmann, *Bestiary*, 289–91. Cf. Chaucer, *Book of the Duchess*, ll. 636–41.

5966–7 John 8.44. Whiting D186 (The devil is a liar and the father of lies).

5972–86 The three kinds of lies are helpful, pleasing, and harmful. Lines 5973–4 are taken from Peraldus, 2.9.2.5, but go back to the *Decretum*, C.22.2.13 (Friedberg 1, col. 871): *Fit etiam magistraliter ex verbis eiusdem Augustini alia distinctio brevior et tamen plenior; quia mendaciorum, aliud officiosum sive pietatis, aliud iocositatis*. B is garbled, owing to corruptions in the French text: *Car ilz sont unes menchonges ardans et si sont unes menchonges plaisans et unes menchonges nuisans et en toutes a pechie*. UV read *pesantes* for *plaisans*. *ardans*, in error for *aidans*, is translated as *fervent* and *pesantes*, in error for *plaisans*, as *hevy*. The passage is rendered correctly in *Ayen* 62/34–63/1 and *VV* 60/32–4 and is ultimately based on Augustine, *De Mendacio*, 14, 21 (PL 40, cols 505–6, 515–18). Cf. also Peter Lombard, *Sententiae*, 3.38.1 (PL 192, col. 833). *wheder that euer it bee* (l. 5986): *que le quelle soit*.

5987 The table of contents reads *Of Forsweryng*.

5990 Matthew 5.37.

5992 *aȝeins the opinion of lolleris* replaces the French *sicome dient les docteurs*, as noted, above, in the 'Introduction,' 18. On the Lollard opposition to oaths see Hudson, *Lollards*, 371–4. For other uses of the terms *lollerie* and *loller(r)is* see the note to l. 1917.
5992–3 Smith, 'Three Obscure Proverbs,' 442–3, cites numerous occurrences of the proverb originating in the Latin *Qui facile jurat facile perjurat*. Hassell J51 (*Qui volentiers jure, volentiers se parjure*). Cf. Whiting S938 (He that swears craftily manswears); Tilley S1030 (He that will swear will lie).
5997 James 5.12.
5998–6001 Exodus 24.12. *feithe*, but French *loy*. Cf. ll. 1138, 1281, 7575.
6006–7 *For to swere ... witnes*: cf. *Dives* 2.8: *And ouyr þat, ȝif þey sweryn fals þey clepyn God to witnesse of a þing þat is fals and seyn þat God wose name is trewþe beryth hem witnesse of a þing þat is fals.*
6015–20 A paraphrase of Matthew 5.34–6.
6023 *bisily* translates *apensement* ('with forethought'). Not recorded by MED with this meaning.
6025–6 *too whom the wordes ... theye bee wrytyn* misconstrues the French: *a qui lez parollez sont qui y sont escriptes*, that is, 'to whom the words written therein pertain.'
6030 Cf. Hassell J47 (*Pire que Juifs ou Sarrazin*).
6032–4 Cf. the *Treatise on the Ten Commandments* (Royster, 'Treatise,' 16): *Also, he þat sweres custumnabully. & haath in custom to swere & dismembur. & drawes lymme from lyme of oure lorde ihesu criste þat is he þat sweres by his herte & be his iȝen. and als be his armus. sydes. & wondes. & so of other dismembringe of him.* For similar sentiments see Owst, *Literature*, 414–25, and Hughes, *Swearing*, 59–62. Woodforde discusses wall and window paintings depicting the dismemberment of the deity. Cf. ll. 5720–2.
6034–7 *þeye aske noothynge of oure ladye ... Cristen pepil suffreth it*: *Ceulx ne demandent rien a nostre dame cestassavoir les sarrasins mais les Cretiens la despiecent si villainement et elle et les autres sains que cest merveille que cretiente le sueffre. þeye* (6034) refers to *Sarazines, theye* (6035) to Christians.
6039 A phrase has been lost or omitted after *that it be*: *ou apertement ou couvertement*.
6040–4 *Decretum*, C.22.5.13 (Friedberg 1, col. 886), incorporating a quotation from 1 Paralipomenon 29.17. Gradon (*Ayen* 65/3–8) explicates the lines as follows: 'The meaning is that, though a man swear

with the intention to deceive ... God ... will understand the oath in the sense in which a simple and honest hearer accepts it.' *scripture* is not employed elsewhere to refer to the *Decretum*. Cf. MED, *scripture* n.
6057–8 This statement is taken from Peraldus 2.9.2.10, paraphrasing Augustine, *Confessiones*, 3.3 (PL 32, col. 685).
6071 Cf. Whiting F194 (No fire without some smoke); Hassell F69.
6073 *lyeth*: 'give the lie to' (*desment*) or, as Gradon suggests, 'contradicts' (*Ayen* 2, 275, s.v. *lyexneþ*).
6075 *poynteth*: 'attacks' (*poignent*). MED *pointen* v., 1b 'stab verbally.' *Ayen* 66/9 has *peyneþ* and *VV* 64/1 *putte*.
6077–8 Whiting R53 (As sharp as a razor), A186 (As swift as an arrow); Hassell R5.
6078–82 Aristotle, *Historia animalium*, 623a; Pliny, *Historia Naturalis*, 8.53; Albert the Great, *De Animalibus*, 22.105. Cf. McCulloch, *Medieval Latin*, 124–5. *thorne* mistranslates *espie* 'lance,' which was evidently read as *espine*.
6082–3 Whiting H571 (A mad hound cares for neither friend nor foe).
6085–6 Psalm 100.5.
6087–8 1 Corinthians 6.9–10, Galatians 5.19–21.
6088–90 Job 41.10–12 (here misattributed to Paul).
6096–101 Proverbs 6.14, 16, 19.
6105–18 Numbers 11.21, 16.1–35, 26.9–10, 51, 65.
6120 *reigneth*: 'holds sway,' confusing *regne* from *regner* with the homonymic form from *reigner* 'argue.' *Ayen* 67/24 makes a similar error (*regneþ*), as Gradon notes. Cf. Godefroy, s.v. *raigner* v., and AND, s.v. *reigner*. The meaning is unknown to MED and OED.
6121 *ientilwomen* is presumably a euphemistic rendering of *chamberieres*.
6123–4 *in communes aȝeins knyghtis* departs from the French *en villains contre chevaliers*, converting a commonplace observation of the traditional resentment of the peasantry against the nobility into what is possibly a reference to the widespread dissatisfaction with the government of Henry VI, which erupted into the rebellion of the commons of Kent under Jack Cade in May–July 1450 and smaller uprisings intermittently throughout the early 1450s. For an account of these events and the tensions and divisions underlying the political upheavals of the reign of Henry VI, which may be adumbrated in this passage, see Harvey, *Jack Cade's Rebellion*, 37–191; Storey, *House of Lancaster*, 34–5, 43–52, 53–60; Jacob, *Fifteenth Century*, 483–501; Griffiths, *King Henry VI*, 301–94, 443–550, 610–65. The translation of

'*villains*' as 'communes' – the common people, with the clear implication of rabble – also occurs in *Othea* 32/11.
6136 *apes pater noster*: Hassell P74 (*Le paternôtre du singe*); Tilley A274; Di Stefano, *Dictionnaire*, 653. *fendes*: Whiting D214 (To murmur the devil's paternoster); Tilley D315.
6142 *too synge on the songe* preserves the phrasing of ACDNQRSUV *chanter du* (U *de*) *chant*. Only P reads *chanter le chant*.
6159–60 Proverbs 17.20, Wisdom 12.26–7.
6177 Whiting B394 (To defend oneself like the boar). Cf. Bartholomaeus Anglicus, *De Proprietatibus*, 18.7.
6184 *doothe* misconstrues *fait* meaning 'says.'
6192–5 Augustine, *De Moribus Ecclesiae*, 2.11 (PL 32, col. 1354); *Contra Mendacium*, 19 (PL 40, col. 546).
6197–204 Cf. *Dives* 2.2 for a detailed discussion of blasphemers and their motivations.
6205–6 Whiting H571 (A mad hound cares for neither friend nor foe).
6208 *Iewis*: P *jeulx*, V *juys*, NQ *gieux*, S *giex*, RU *juifs*, ACD *ieux*. B's reading, *gameys*, shows confusion between *jeux* and *jeulx* or *gieu* and *g(i)eu*.
6208–10 Matthew 12.31–2, Mark 3.28–30. Blasphemy against the Holy Spirit is denied forgiveness because it is regarded as a despair of pardon. Acts of repentance are possible but are rarely (*vnnethe*) pursued. On the consequences of the sin of blasphemy in this life – cf. Ecclesiasticus 23.14 – and at the Judgment see *Glossa Ordinaria* 6.7.a, commenting on Romans 2.5. There is an extensive discussion of the matter in *Dives* 2.4, 8.
6213–15 Ecclesiastes 10.13. *thikke*: cf. l. 3196*n*.
6230–1 Matthew 12.37.
6233–5 Jerome, *Commentarium in Evangelium Matthaei*, 2.12 (PL 26, col. 84).
6238–40 Matthew 12.36.
6240–4 *Glossa Ordinaria* 3.58.b, commenting on Job 31.
6267–8 Proverbs 12.14.
6270–3 Psalm 148.2.
6288–9 Ecclesiasticus 37.34.
6291–3 Genesis 2.9, Apocalypse 22.2–3.
6296–7 *that men fynde but fewe that hatthe it* misconstrues *que on en treuve pou*.
6300 The image of the Garden of Virtues, although suggested by earlier religious writers, chiefly Augustine and Hugh of St Victor, comment-

ing on occasional biblical passages that describe embryonic gardens, is first fully developed in the *Miroir*. See Kosmer, 'Style and Iconography,' 52–67, and 'Gardens of Virtue,' 302–3.

6302–6 Ezechiel 17.24, 31.3–9. Cf. Jeremias 17.8.

6306–7 Ecclesiastes 12.5.

6308–9 Isaias 17.11.

6309–10 Ezechiel 19.12.

6311–12 Joel 1.12–19. D has Amos for *Iooel*, the reference being perhaps to Amos 4.9.

6313–16 *Seint Ierom*: V *Ierome*, all other MSS *Iheremie*. *Seint* may be the translator's addition. The statement, which appears to be a fusion of Psalm 91.13 and Job 30.4, cannot be found in Jerome, although the general sense of it is contained in his commentary on Ezechiel 19.10–14 (*Commentaria in Ezechielem*, 6.19 [PL 25, cols 185–6]).

6320–5 Job 7.7, 14.1–10.

6330 *selve-wit*: 'self-wisdom, pride' (*propre sens*) which MED, citing the translation of the same passage in the *Myrour* (226/38, 227/2), glosses (perhaps inaccurately) as 'one's own knowledge and intelligence.'

6333 After *cruelte* the phrase *fole debonairete nicete* has been lost. The subject is discussed under *Fooly Louff* (ll. 6381–6406).

6345 *lye* is erroneous, the translator having read *amentir* 'lie' for *anientir* 'diminish (himself),' that is, decry his own conduct through an excess of humility. MED and OED gloss *anientishen* in this sense, but not *anienten*.

6353–7 Matthew 25.24–30.

6360–5 Bernard, *Sermo Dominica Infra Octavam Assumptionis*, 13 (*Opera* 5, 273).

6366 This chapter is entitled *Of Foly Frendeshipp* in the table of contents.

6374–6 Augustine, *De Moribus Ecclesiae*, 1.26 (PL 32, cols 1331–2).

6378–81 Luke 14.26. Whiting V30 (To hate the vice and not the persons); Tilley P238, F710.

6386 Augustine, *De Moribus Ecclesiae*, 2.16 (PL 32, col. 1367). Cf. Bernard, *Apologia ad Guillelmum Abbatem*, 8.16 (*Opera* 3, 95): *Talis misericordia crudelitate plena est.*

6386–8 Hassell M128 (*Mère piteuse fait sa fille tyneuse*); Cotgrave, s.v. *teigneux* (A tender housewife maketh a tainted household); Huguet, s.v. *Tigneux* (*Femme trop piteuse fait souvent fille tigneuse*); Tilley M1201; and ODEP, 628. *lewke* 'slothful' mistakes the meaning of *teigneuse* 'scabby,' which may have been confused with, or misread as, *segnicieuse*. Wartburg, s.v. *segnitia*, quoting the *Chroniques de Jean Molinet*, vol. 3, 253.

6392–6 Pseudo-Chrysostom, *Opus Imperfectum In Matthaeum*, Homilia 5 (PG 56, col. 668).

6396–402 Exodus 32–3. B's reading, *soo ther is noo kynge in iustice*, misconstrues *nul si roy* (D *royde*) *en justice* where *roy* (*royde*) is an adjective meaning 'harsh.'

6413–14 *þe desires or singulerteis or desgysynesses* renders the French *par hies* (D *privees*) *ou singulieres ou desguisees*. *desires* mistakes *par hies* 'by strenuous and abundant efforts.' MED does not record *desgysynesses* in the sense of 'eccentric or extraordinary behavior.' For contemporary counsels against excessive ascetic practices and intemperate private austerity see Constable, especially 'Moderation and Restraint,' 323–7, and *Othea* 66/5–8 and *n.*

6418–20 1 Kings 15.22–3.

6422 This title does not appear in the table of contents.

6451–5 *And whan theye fele ... bothe theyme and oother* mistakes the French, owing in part to a corrupt text: *Et quant ilz sentent une raiette de clarte que dieu leur monstre leurs defaultes tantost sen veulent confesser et lostel du cuer ramouner* (D *remouvoir*) *que ilz tuent eulz et autri*. The translator's exemplar must have read *remouvoir* as in D, a corruption of *ramouner* meaning 'to cleanse' or 'to sweep'; MED does not record *remeve* in this sense. The second *que* is used with the signification of a consecutive 'so that' rather than a relative conjunction. *castyng*: 'ray.' Cf. MED, s.v. *casten* v., 8a 'to shed light.'

6455–6 *And the moore that tho hert torn and retorne*: V *et comme plus versent telz cuers et renversent*, ACNQRSU *et comme plus versent ce cuer et renversent*, P *et comme plus cerchent ce cuer et recherchent*, D *et comme plus versent et renversent celui cueur*. B appears to follow an exemplar akin to V with *telz cuers* construed as the subject of *versent et renversent*.

6463 B's *dronkelewnesse* is erroneous and is supported by none of the French MSS, which read either *austerite* (ACDNPQRSU) or *austerite et fole abstinence* (V). It is possible that the exemplar read *asprece* (*aspresce*), which was either misread as, or confused with, *ivrece* (*iveresce*).

6466–7 Unidentified.

6478 *Shee* is retained, although it is clearly a scribal error. Cf. *VV* 68/21: *þe man ne die gladly*. *in vice* is an awkward attempt to construe *envis*

'reluctantly,' 'unwillingly.' Cf. ll. 1832, 4136, 9226. Whiting D240 (Learn to die and then you shall know how to live); Hassell M231.
6481–2 *If thowe wilt lif freely, lerne to dye meryly*: Seneca, *Epistolae*, 61.2.
6497–8 Whiting S185 (To pass like a shadow), F579 (To fly like fowls), A192 (To spring like an arrow from a bow).
6501–2 *Oure ioye ... to wepyng*: James 4.9.
6502–6 A paraphrase of Ecclesiastes 2.
6507 Whiting P48 (As sooth as the paternoster); Hassell P76.
6513 *clere seerris* is not recorded by MED. Cf. *Othea* 42/13: *clere seers*.
6520–1 Walther 5863.
6533–5 Philippians 3.20.
6544 Matthew 23.17.
6592 Whiting G298 (Gold is afonded in the fire); Hassell O64.
6594 *filthe*: CP *roul*, NRSU *rouil*, A *ruil*, V *roil*, D *roille*, Q *roye*. B's reading, *gouernance*, confuses *ruil* or *roul* with *riul*.
6607–9 Proverbs 24.16.
6620–65 O'Connor regards this chapter as a forerunner of the *ars moriendi* treatises, although, as she acutely observes, it is more concerned with the art of living than dying (*Art of Dying Well*, 18).
6656–7 *ientil sette hertis*: *cuers gentilz et afaicties*. The omission of the conjunction may be scribal.
6672–3 *the verraye goodes from the shewyng of the evyl* translates *le vray bien de laparent*. *greete*, B's reading for *verraye*, was evidently an eyeskip (*grete goodes*) by anticipation. *of the evyl* was evidently added to clarify the meaning of *shewyng*; it has no MSS support.
6675–8 1 Corinthians 12.1–11, Romans 12.3–8. *some gretter and some gretest* translates *uns moiens et uns grans*. Cf. Augustine, *Retractationes*, 1.9.6 (PL 32, col. 598).
6680 A phrase has been lost or omitted after *lytil*: *ou les moiens pour les petis*.
6681–2 Whiting W662 (This world is but a fair).
6692–3 *noyouse stoones*, but French *pierres luisantes* 'gleaming stones'. *nuisantes* was read as *luisantes*.
6712–15 1 Timothy 6.9, Ecclesiastes 7.1, Psalm 143.4, 8. *liaines*: 'snares' (*liens*). Not recorded by MED (s.v. *lien* n.) in this sense. AND, s.v. *lien* n., and Tobler-Lommatsch, s.v. *liien*.
6715–16 Whiting P48 (As sooth as the paternoster); Hassell P76.
6726–8 Whiting G96 (He that gives not what he loves has not what he desires).

6728 *game of þe paume* confuses *paumee* meaning 'bargain' with *paumee* referring to the type of game in which the hands strike the ball. MED, s.v. *paume* n., 5 citing Shirley (c. 1456).
6754 *Off Goodes of Nature* does not appear in the table of contents.
6801-5 1 Corinthians 13.1–8.
6820 After *profitable* the scribe wrote *That vertue is ful worshipfull* before realizing that it was the heading of the following chapter.
6829–30 *short and voide*, that is, short-lived and empty or devoid of value (*courte et vaine*).
6832–3 The French is more expansive, observing that if man possessed the eye of a lynx he would plainly see that physical beauty is *but as a faire sack ful of dunge*, and so on. *Ayen* 81/5–8 and *VV* 79/25–8 translate the passage in full.
6834–5 Whiting F318 (To fail like the flower). Cf. Hassell F97.
6843 *mede*, but French *verite*, which was evidently read as *merite*. There is a similar confusion in l. 8607.
6844 *callith it aȝeyn* mistranslates *rapareille* 'returns to its original state,' which may have been read as *rapeille*.
6859–61 A portion of the text has been lost after *and* (l. 6860). The French reads: *Car cest la vraie sapience qui enlumine le cuer de lomme aussi comme fait le soleil le monde. Ce sens passe le sens du monde aussi comme le soleil la clarte de la lune. causeth* alters the sense of *passe*. The statement derives from Isidore, *De Natura Rerum*, 18.3, 24 (PL 83, cols 991, 997).
6861–3 1 Corinthians 1.20, 3.19.
6866–7 *betwene preciousnes and filthe* misconstrues *entre le precieux et le vil*.
6889–90 James 3.15.
6892 *Godes frendes*: 'pious persons' (*amis de Dieu*). Cf. MED, s.v. *frend* n., 2b. The phrase goes back to Wisdom 7.27 and James 2.23.
6896–6905 Cf. Bernard, *Sermones super Cantica Canticorum*, 20.2–3 (*Opera* 1, 115–17).
6897–8 *for it filleth, norissheth, and susteyneth the herte* completes the meaning of *veray*.
6898–9 *Preciouse, for a man maye eesyly by God and al that he hatthe* renders the French literally: *Preciouse car on puet dieu et quanquil a acheter*, a strange mercantile metaphor to express the bestowal and beneficence of divine love.
6900 *hande*, but French *manne*, 'manna,' correctly translated in *Ayen* 83/7 and *VV* 81/25.

6903 Whiting S870 (As sweet as sugar).
6915–19 Vegetius, *Epitome Rei Militaris*, 1.13.
6946–9 Seneca, *De Constantia Sapientis*, 5.3–5.
6950 Whiting L314 (As hardy as a lion), Hassell L70; Whiting E65 (As strong as an elephant), Hassell E22.
6964 *setteth the worlde vnder his fete*, that is, 'makes him despise the world' (Gradon, *Ayen* 85/3–4*n*).
6974–5 *withoute the whiche noon ys a lorde verily* concludes a sentence that has lost its main clause. The French reads: *Apres il en a un autre empire moult grant et moult bel sans lequel nul nest a droit seigneur*.
6983–6 Seneca, *Epistolae*, 113.30.
7001 *agreyng*, that is, consent. MED gives this meaning not to the gerund, but to the verb (*agreen*, 2a).
7002–3 Augustine, *De Perfectione Iustitiae Hominis*, 2 (PL 44, col. 293).
7015 *sylfer*, but French *ne a or ne a argent*, the omission possibly the result of an eyeskip.
7017 Whiting S813 (Not set a straw). *strawe*, but French *bouton* (Hassell B166).
7041 Hassell G33 (*Qui le coeur a loial et fin, il est gentil [noble]*); Morawski 1418; Tilley C586.
7068–71 1 John 3.1–2.
7072–4 1 Corinthians 13.12.
7078–80 Pseudo-Dionysius, *De Caelesti Hierarchia*, 7.2 (PG 3, cols 219–26).
7105–10 Matthew 12.47–50.
7118–25 1 Corinthians 13.1–3.
7134–5 Whiting M143 (A man is worth as much as his land is worth).
7135 Whiting P48 (As sooth as the paternoster); Hassell P76.
7158–9 *geffare*: 'ware, merchandise' (*denrees*). Cf. *Ayen* 90/36 and *VV* 89/10*n*. The metaphor continues into the next sentence.
7164 *cheffare*: 'sales-price' (*ventes*), that is, 'his peny' (7160). Not recorded by MED in this precise sense. Cf. *Ayen* 91/3 *ȝales*, *VV* 89/15 *chaffare*.
7173 *Seint Michellis balaunce*: the scales of justice held by St Michael in scenes of the last judgment. See Kretzenbacher, *Seelenwaage*, 82–91; Réau, *Iconographie*, 2.49–50.
7190 *strecchith*, but French *descendent*.
7194 *fygureth* is not recorded by MED in the sense of 'imagine.'

7195–7 *And whan a man ... that al is noght* misconstrues the French: *Et quant on les tient tantost sont perdus et deviennent nient et songes. Pense du delit dantan et du songe de ennuit* (D *David*) *et tu verras que tout est nient.*
7224–5 *soo that he maye not continue hym to fele hymselfe* does not render the French *si quil ne se puet contenir ne lui mesmes sentir, contenir* having been read as *continuer*. Gradon (*Ayen* 92/32–3*n*) correctly interprets this passage to mean 'so that he cannot contain himself nor be aware of himself.'
7228–31 John 4.13–14.
7233–6 Psalm 30.20.
7243–6 Psalm 15.11. The attribution to Proverbs is erroneous. Cf. Whiting J63 (None has perfect joy if it come not of love).
7246–8 Isaias 61.3.
7253–6 1 John 4.16.
7260–4 Cf. Whiting N179 (Now this, now that). *at vnease*: the phrase is not recorded by MED.
7281–3 James 4.17.
7287–8 Canticle of Canticles 4.12–14.
7289–93 John 20.15. *weeteth*: 'softens' (French *amolie*). Not recorded by MED in this sense. Whiting W100 (As tretable as wax).
7306 *tree of liff*: Genesis 2.9.
7313–14 John 6.54.
7325–7 Isaias 11.1.
7328 *braser*: 'fire' (*brasier*). Not recorded by MED.
7333 *degouted of*: 'ran from' (*degouterent*). Not recorded by MED with this precise meaning.
7342 John 15.5.
7345–61 Matthew 5.3–10.
7367–8 Proverbs 9.1. *veraye*: '?wise.' Not recorded by MED in this sense. The French reads, perhaps erroneously, 'le vrai Salomen.'
7370 *branches*, but French *parolles*.
7379–80 Proverbs 29.18.
7397 *releve*: 'rise from sin' (*relever*). MED, s.v. *releven* v., 4a.
7421 *carye*: 'draw water' (*puisatier*). Not recorded by MED in this sense.
7428 Whiting C195 (As meek as a child).
7447–9 Gregory, *Moralia*, 33.23 (PL 76, col. 701).
7455 Matthew 6.9.

7456 *advocat*: 1 John 2.1.
7461–4 Bernard, *Sermones super Cantica Canticorum*, 15.2 (*Opera* 1, 83).
7474 *gouernour*: Wisdom 14.3.
7477–9 Wisdom 11.25.
7482 *chastisseth*: Proverbs 3.11–12.
7492–5 *Therfore this woorde ... to his fader*: Romans 8.15, 17.
7521 *that is be avowery* is the translator's addition.
7525–8 Romans 3.24, 8.15.
7535–8 Ambrose, *Commentaria in Epistolam ad Romanos*, 15.30 (PL 17, col. 177). The attribution to Augustine is erroneous.
7538–51 Romans 8.15–17, 12.4–5, 1 Corinthians 6.15, 12.12–20, Ephesians 1.14, 4.25. The attribution to James is misplaced. It properly belongs to ll. 7551–5 which paraphrase James 5.13–16.
7555–64 Only DU provide the source of these lines, the remaining MSS lacking the sentence explaining why hate militates against fellowship. The three sentences beginning '*And þat is contrarie*,' '*And this is contrarye*,' and '*Thus he is contrary*' have been added by the translator for emphasis and clarity. *conuersyng* misconstrues the French for 'sharing' (PQSU *communier*, V *communiquer*, ACD *communer*, RN om.) Cf. *Ayen* (102/34) *communy*, *VV* (101/4) *in comune*.
7565–9 John 14.5–21,15.10.
7571 Matthew 6.9.
7575–82 Exodus 3.1–14. *feithe*, but French *loi*. Cf. ll. 1138, 1281, 6000.
7599 MED does not record the adverb *attaignyngly*. It cites the unique form *atteinauntli* from *VV* 102/20 in the sense of 'effectively, successfully.'
7601 *strecche* mistakes French *entendre* 'comprehend,' which may have been read as *estendre*. Cf. l. 3192.
7601–2 Job 14.4 (here misattributed to Paul, possibly owing to a misreading of *Pol* for *Iob*; all MSS read *Iob*).
7605 Ecclesiastes 1.2.
7609–13 The bibilical reference to James 1.17 is misplaced and should appear at the end of the previous sentence as the French makes clear: *Car il est tousiours en un mesmes point sans soy* (D *loy*) *troubler sans soy* (D *loy*) *muer sans soy* (D *loy*) *changier en nulle maniere sicomme dit saint Jaques. Toutes autres choses sont muables en aucune maniere de leur nature.* Gradon (*Ayen* 104/10) notes that the passage refers to the divine attributes impassibility, immutability, and immovability.

The introduction of *or* into the text at l. 7612, as recorded in the textual notes, stems uniquely from the defective reading of V: *en aucune maniere ou en leur nature.*

7614–15 *vanite*: so all MSS except V, which reads *variete. mevyng* renders *muance* 'alteration, change.'

7628–9 *Alsoo he is ... as hevyn is*: *Apres il est es cieulx espiritueulx cest es sains cuers qui sont haulx et clers et nes sicomme est le ciel.* The adjective *espirituelx*, modifying *cieulx*, was mistaken for a noun.

7631–2 Matthew 6.9.

7643–4 Matthew 6.9.

7644 *the entre of a towne* misconstrues *lentree de la ville*, where *ville* is an alternate spelling of *viele*. Cf. *Ayen* 105/11 *an inguoinge of þe viþeele* and *VV* 103/33 *an entre of a fiþele.* The phrase means little more than 'the introduction of a song.' D emends eccentrically to *lentree de la vielle loy.*

7653–7 Augustine discusses the Trinity in terms of memory, intelligence, and will in *De Trinitate*, 4.6 (PL 42, col. 1042).

7680–1 *savouryly* is not recorded by MED in the sense of 'with spiritual understanding.' See, however, *savourli*, where the meaning is cited as from 1500. *savourisly* is not recorded by MED. OED notes its use by Caxton in a different sense.

7694 *dedifieth* 'dedicates' is first recorded by MED in this sense c. 1475.

7698–703 Apocalypse 1.5, 7.14.

7713 *greyne*: 'The most prestigious dye of the Middle Ages was kermes, obtained from an insect of the Mediterranean and the Near East, Kermes vermilio Planch. These small round insects were known as "vermilion" ("little worm") to the Italians (hence "vermilion") and as "grain" to the English' (Walton, 'Textiles,' 334).

7724 *stedefaste*: 'devoted to' (*aherse*). MED, s.v. *stedfast* adj., 2b.

7728 Matthew 6.10.

7732 Luke 17.21.

7758–9 *And that doon ... veraye confession*: P *Et ce fait il par la pele de vraie confession*, C *Et ce fait il prent la pele de confession vraye*, V *Et ce fait il lappareille de vraye confession*, NS *Et ce fait il o la pele de vraie confession*, AQ *Et ce fait il avecque la pele* (DQ *la palle, lappelle*) *de vraie confession*, RU om. *pelleth*, the reading of the text, may have resulted from a scribe's failure to notice a mark of suspension.

7761–2 Cf. Whiting A259 (Not worth an ay); Hassell O17.

7772–3 Matthew 13.44.

7776 Matthew 6.10.
7804 Matthew 6.11.
7819–22 John 6.32–5, 50–8.
7826–7 Exodus 12.11.
7836–7 Isaias 11.7.
7858–61 Gradon (*Ayen* 111/33–5*n*) comments: 'The reference is to Leviticus 6:21 ... and only indirectly to the Psalter. Gregory *Hom in Eziechelem*, 1 (PL XXXVI, col. 932) links Ezechiel 4:3 ... with Leviticus and with Psalm 68 (69):10, *zelus domus tuae comedit me* because the metaphor of the pan signified zeal.' Presumably *bloode* resulted from a misreading of *sanc* for *sain* ('grease').
7881–3 Wisdom 16.20. *deliciousnessis*: 'spiritual delights.' Not recorded by MED in this sense.
7887–8 Matthew 6.11. *abovesubstanciall* is not recorded by MED.
7892 *substancialis*, the reading of B, may have resulted from a faulty scribal expansion of an otiose stroke or tag on final *l*. There are similarly incorrect expansions of final tags in ll. 5653 (*olde*/*oldere*) and 11738 (*thyng*/*thyngis*).
7899–7903 Matthew 20.1–16.
7904 Matthew 6.12.
7910 *acroched or borwed* renders French *acreus*, 'acquired on credit.' MED, s.v. *ącrochen* v., does not record this meaning.
7926–9 Matthew 6.15.
7945–7 Luke 6.32–3.
7952 Luke 6.35, Matthew 5.44.
7955–7 Augustine, *De Civitate Dei*, 14.6 (PL 41, col. 409). Cf. Whiting V30 (To hate the Vice [ill] and not the persons).
7957–61 Romans 12.5, 1 Corinthians 10.17.
7961–2 John 13.34
7962–4 1 John 3.15.
7991–2 Matthew 6.13
7993 Whiting W87 (Whoso is scalded with hot water doubts hot water the more); Hassell E9.
8000 *tempter*: 1 Thessalonians 3.5.
8001 *esprove*: 'make trial of, subject to a deliberate test' (*esprouver*). Not recorded by MED. The earliest citation in OED is 1480 (Caxton). *esprove*/*desprove* (B): for a similar error see ll. 747–63*n*.
8004–6 Bernard, *Sermones super Cantica Canticorum*, 17.3.6 (*Opera* 1, 101).
8008–9 Ephesians 3.17.

8017–19 On the strength, massive size, and materials of the walls constructed by the Muslims, particularly at Constantinople, Nicaea, and Cairo, see Tsangadas, *Fortifications*, 67–8, 153–66; Toy, *Fortifications*, 52–4; Creswell, 'Fortification in Islam,' 112–21; and Foss and Winfield, *Byzantine Fortifications*, 42–60, 70–2. *Myrour* 100/21*n* misunderstands the passage as a reference to Sarsen stones.
8032–3 Ecclesiasticus 34.9–10.
8034 The earliest citation in MED to *heryngseye* is c. 1500.
8045 *And whan ... into theyme* departs from the French *Et quant il nous fault nous y entrons* and loses the contrast between *il nous fault* and *il nous ayde* (*he helpeth us* in line 8046).
8048–9 Matthew 6.13.
8050–3 Augustine, *De Natura et Gratia*, 27.31 (PL 44, col. 262).
8084–97 Isaias 11, 61.10. *mariages* translates *nopces* construed as a plural. *brasyng* and *enbraser* 'fire' translate *brasier*; neither is recorded by MED. *In writynge* is clearly mistaken, *escrit* having been read for *esprit*.
8106–6 John 1.14, 16. *doþe* mistakes French *fu* 'was.'
8116–19 1 Corinthians 12.11.
8121–2 Psalm 110.10.
8123 The Gifts were deemed 'spiritual virtues' according to the prevailing opinion of medieval theologians. Cf. William of Auxerre, *Summa Aurea*, 30.1.2, 586–90, who reviews the issue, deciding finally '*nobis videtur omnia dona esse virtutes*.' Gifts are first called virtues by Ambrose, *De Sacramentis*, 3.2 (PL 16, col. 434) and *De Spiritu Sancto*, 16.178 (PL 16, col. 740).
8132–4 James 1.17.
8139 *mystakyng*: 'being taken back' (*reprendre*). Cf. *Ayen* 120/9–10 *wyþnymynge*, *VV* 118/24 *aȝentakynge*. See AND, s.v. *reprendre* v. The meaning is not recorded by MED.
8147–52 Seneca, *De Beneficiis*, 1.1.9–10, 1.7, 2.3, 6.1. *prophete*, but French *philosophe*. Cf. l. 4289*n*.
8163–4 Pseudo-Dionysius, *De Divinis Nominibus*, 4.1 (PG 3, col. 694).
8165–8 Romans 5.5.
8177–9 *for to conferme oure louff ... fynally and veryly and clenly* translates the French: *confermer nostre amour a la sienne si quelle sont confermee fermement et fine et vraie et nette*. The adjectives (rendered as adverbs) refer to *nostre amour*. *fynally* misconstrues *fine* 'excellent.' *conferme*: 'join, unite, make fast.' Not recorded by MED in this sense.

8183–5 *The ȝifte of fere ... the grete manace of the sentence of Godde.* B's garbled translation stems from a defective French text: *le don de paour est luissier [*sic*]* (D *le sergent*) *a la grant mace cest a dire a* (D *de*) *la grant menace de la sentence de dieu. luissier* should read *huissier. manace* for *masse* 'mace' was undoubtedly an eyeskip. The usher with his mace is similarly interpreted as the fear of judgment and the pains of Hell in *Othea* 61/5–13.
8197–9 Pseudo-Dionysius, *De Caelesti Hierarchia*, 6.2 (PG 3, col. 203).
8201 *in God,* that is, in the presence of God. The French reads *avecques dieu.*
8209–10 Romans 8.14.
8216–17 *but they have soo myche more,* that is, they have so much more spiritual worth. This observation has been added to the French in order to emphasize the difference between the two orders. The French reads *Les secons sont en lestat moien qui gouvernent bien et eulx et autri et vivent selon les commandemens de levangile* (so CPR; other MSS *conseils*) *et non mie sans plus les commandemens. les commandemens* (*conseils*) *de levangile* refers to the injunction to love God and neighbor (Matthew 22.36–40).
8221–4 Hebrews 2.4, 1 Corinthians 12.11.
8241 *descende*: cf. l. 3042*n*.
8246 1 Corinthians 13.13.
8248–54 Augustine, *De Agone Christiano*, 13 (PL 40, col. 299); *Soliloquiae*, 1.1.3 (PL 32, col. 870); *De Moribus Ecclesiae*, 1.12 (PL 32, col. 1320). Cf. Peraldus 1.2.1.3.
8254–5 Colossians 2.2.
8269–72 Wisdom 8.7.
8272–4 Cf. *Summa Virtutum*, 1.34–40. Ambrose was the first to call the four virtues 'cardinal.' See his *Expositio Evangelii secundum Lucam*, 5.62 (PL 15, col. 1653), and *De Paradiso*, 1.3 (PL 14, cols 279–83).
8278 *be no shrewe* is closer to the reading of V (*par nulle mauvaistie*) than of the other MSS (*par nulle mauvaise amour*).
8280–2 Cicero, *De Inventione*, 2.53; *De Natura Deorum*, 3.15.38. *weye*, but French *estat* (as on l. 8280).
8282–4 Nelson (*Myrour* 88/21*n*) attributes the origin of this metaphor to Gregory, *Moralia*, 2.49 (PL 75, col. 592).
8292 *Platon*: so all MSS. *Ayen* 124/28 has *Platoun*, *VV* 123/2 *Ploteus, Plotens*. Francis cites a *Somme* MS reading *Plotin*. Although Plato wrote on the virtues (*Republic* 4), the reference is actually to Macrobius

(1.8.5), from whose *Commentarii in Somnium Scipionis* much of the discussion that follows is taken. The source of the confusion in the *Somme* and *Miroir* traditions stems from Macrobius's attribution of the classification of the virtues to Plotinus as a disciple of Plato. Modern scholars are generally agreed that his observations owe more to Porphyry, *Sententiae*, 22 than to the *Enneads*, 1.2. On the subject of Macrobius's sources see Stahl, *Dream of Scipio*, 32–6, 121 n5.

8294–8 Macrobius 1.8.7. B has lost the second of the three offices: *Ne rien il ne veult faire fors droite raison.* Cf. Vincent of Beauvais, *Speculum Doctrinale*, 5.9. *lyne of reson*: the metaphor is reintroduced at l. 9152.

8302–5 Macrobius 1.8.7. Cf. *Summa Virtutum*, 1.141–6. *refuseth*: 'rejects, shuns' (P *refuse*, C *deboute*, ANS *dante*, V *doubte*, QU *doute*, D *dompte*, R om).

8305–9 1 John 2.15–16.

8311–15 Macrobius 1.8.7. Cf. Ambrose, *De Officiis Ministrorum*, 1.39 (PL 16, col. 80).

8323 Cicero, *De Inventione*, 2.53; *De Natura Deorum*, 3.38.

8323–7 *Summa Virtutum*, 1.111–19, which, however, lacks the attribution to Plato. The statement expands on Cicero's definition of justice and may actually derive from Bernard, *In Adventu Domini*, Sermo 3.4 (*Opera* 4, 178): *Iustitia virtus est quod suum est unicuique tribuens. Redde superiori, redde inferiori, redde aequali cuique quod debes.*

8339 *with strengthe be theyre owne vertu*, that is, strengthened by their own virtue. Cf. *Ayen* 126/12 and *n*.

8340–4 Aelian 5.45; Pliny, *Historia Naturalis*, 8.77. *toille vs*: 'roll in the mud' (ACNQSUV *nous nous toillons*, P *nous nous soullons*, D *voistrons*, R om). *toille* does not appear in MED in this sense.

8345–7 Romans 2.12–29.

8354–68 Augustine, *De Moribus Ecclesiae*, 1.15 (PL 32, col. 1322). *desyreth* (l. 8366) translates *ahert* 'devotes (himself) to.' AND *aerdre* v. Not recorded by MED in this precise sense.

8375–9 Wisdom 10.10. *conceyve*: 'bring about.' MED, s.v. *conceiven* v., 2a.

8406–9 Luke 15.11–32.

8409–10 *Also as Salamon seithe* introduces in *Ayen* 128/16–18 and *VV* 126/25–8 a quotation from Proverbs 23.34–5, which has been lost from the texts of the *Miroir*.

8410–16 Acts 12.4–11. The translator read *grace* as *guerre*.

8418–20 Proverbs 23.34–5.
8425–9 A paraphrase of Hélinand of Froidmont, *Les Vers de la Mort*, 15.10–12: *Laissiez voz chiflois et voz gas! / Teus me cueve desoz ses dras / Qui cuide estre haitiez et sains*. The *Miroir* confuses the poet's name: APQS *elimans*, UV *eliment*, C *elimant*, N *Helimans*, D *Elinas*, R om. The translator failed to recognize the name, or misread it, and gave it a spurious if recognizable identity as the papal saint. Cf. *Ayen* 128/34 and *VV* 127/11.
8435–43 Psalm 141.5, Genesis 3.8–9, 16.7–8. *spredeth hym* mistranslates *espoente* ('frightens'), confusing it with *epandre* or *espandre*. *Ayen* 129/5 has *wiþnimþ* ?'reproves,' *VV* 127/20 *makeþ hem aferd*. *wiff* translates *chamberiere* (D *baisse ou servante*) 'handmaid,' here a euphemism for 'concubine' or 'mistress.' The reference is to Agar.
8480–3 Zacharias 1.18–21. The translator was evidently unfamiliar with the biblical text, and the paraphrase of it in the *Miroir* – itself defective – baffled him. The French reads *Ce sont les quatres cornes et* (D *cestadire*) *les quatre cornadises qui honissent le pays que dieu monstra a zacharie le prophete. Mais les quatre fevres qui lui monstra sont les quatres pensees devant touchees lesquels vindrent apres pour ces quatre cornes abatre*. *pes* – the reading of the text – misconstrues French *pays*, confusing it with *pais* or *peis*, and *corneres* misconstrues *cornadises* 'follies' and was probably intended to mean 'blowers' or 'trumpeters' as in *VV* 129/1 (*blowers*). It is not recorded by MED in this sense, but a single instance of the verb *cornen* 'to blow a horn' is cited c. 1400. The noun *cornes* 'horns' is not recorded by MED, but *corne* 'horn' appears as an adjective (*trumpe corne*) in a single instance from Rolle's *Psalter* (c. 1340). *cestadire*, uniquely present in MS D, clearly preserves the correct reading (cf. *Ayen* 130/22, *VV* 129/1). A clumsy attempt to conflate the two sentences accounts for the lacuna, the translator failing to realize that *these* (l. 8480) refers to the *rootes of pride* (l. 8478) and *fevers* (l. 8482) to the *thoughtes* (l. 8477; French *pensees*). Led astray by a defective French text which had *et* for *cestadire*, he associated the *corneres* with the *fevers*.
8494 *exile*: 'the world as a vale of tears' (*essil*). MED, s.v. *exile* n. 2.
8508 *peines* restores the proper reading of the French. The absurd *frogges* comes from a misreading of *paines* as *raines*.
8524 This chapter is based on Alexander of Canterbury, *Dicta Anselmi*, 1, *De monte humilitatis et septem gradibus eius et duabus eiusdem montis custodibus* (Southern and Schmitt, 110–13). The treatise was attributed to Anselm himself.

8528–30 Bernard, *De Gradibus Humilitatis et Superbiae*, 1.2 (*Opera* 3, 17).
8545 *dispitable* is unrecorded by MED.
8552–4 Bernard, *Sermones super Cantica Canticorum*, 16.10 (*Opera* 1, 95).
8554–9 2 Kings 16.5–10, 19.16–23.
8568 *veryly veraye poore* translates *vray poure adcertes*.
8573–4 Luke 22.15.
8578–81 Matthew 5.3.
8581–3 Matthew 11.29
8587–9 Apocalypse 2.7.
8590 The table of contents reads *Branches* for *Tree*.
8594–5 *holly to truste in the ȝifte of Godde* follows the reading of V: *par lui du don du tout fier*. All other MSS except R (which lacks the line) have what is probably the correct reading: *du tout en dieu fier*.
8603–5 Titus 3.8.
8607 For a similar confusion of *verite* and *merite*, see l. 6843.
8611 *veray*, but French *vive*, which is rendered accurately in ll. 8612, 8618.
8621–4 Matthew 12.36, 16.27.
8626 *bounte*: cf. l. 3250*n*.
8634–7 Bernard, *Sermones super Cantica Canticorum*, 13.3 (*Opera* 1, 70).
8646 *gebet* possibly mistranslates *hart* 'rope.' AND, however, gives as one meaning of *hart* the 'evil rope' or 'gallows.'
8658–61 *litil flye*, that is, bee (*la petite mouchette*). McCulloch, *Medieval Latin*, 95–6; White, *Bestiary*, 153–4.
8665–7 The Psalter reference is to Psalm 80.17, but the text itself actually comes from Deuteronomy 32.13.
8699–8701 *He farith ... fruit and donge*: this statement is made of the lamb in Bartholomaeus Anglicus, *De Proprietatibus*, 18.4.
8702–3 Genesis 18.27.
8703–8 Job 7.5–7, 8.9, 13.25, 14.2, 17.14, 20.7, 25.6, 30.19.
8711–14 Pseudo-Jerome, *Regula Monachorum*, 30 (PL 30, col. 417).
8727 Whiting Y17 (Yield or hang); Hassell R24; Morawski 1571. Cf. l. 4826.
8747–52 Psalms 13.6, 67.10–11, 68.33, 101.18.
8753–4 Job 29.16, 36.6. Job actually describes himself as *fader to pore pepill*.
8754–6 Matthew 5.3, Luke 6.20, 24.

8760–3 Matthew 11.25, Luke 10.21.
8769–70 *For naturelly ... grete cheepe*: *Car naturelement les aigniaulx s'entreaiment et fuient les grans et leur compaignie.* The translator took *les grans* to refer to sheep.
8772–5 *For he seketh ... in festes ne in feleshippes* clumsily conflates two French sentences: *Car il ne quiert ne precieuses viandes ne oultrageuses robes. Nul boban il ne quiert ne en robes ne en chevaucheures ne en maisine ne en feste ne en compaignies. outragious* is made to modify *metes* rather than *robes* as in the French. The failure to translate *en* before *robes* and *chevaucheures* results in a further dislocation of the sense. *grete araye* mistakes the meaning of *chevaucheures* 'cavalcades' or 'fine mounts.' It is not so defined in MED (*arrai* n.). Godefroy, s.v. *chevalcheure* n.; Tobler-Lommatsch, s.v. *chevaucheure* n.; AND, s.v. *chevauchure* n. The term is rendered as *ridinges* in *Ayen* 139/16 and *noble horsynge* in *VV* 137/33.
8791–4 Matthew 3.12, 13.30, Luke 3.17.
8800–1 John 13.5.
8814–15 *a whistle of þe gouuernour*: 'the captain's whistle' (*le tint au gouverneur*). The translator evidently confused *gouverneur* with *gouvernail* 'rudder' and possibly *tint* with *trait* 'stroke.'
8816 *hye sette* follows the defective reading of the French MSS: *le hault assis*. The correct reading of the *Somme* tradition, *hassasis* 'assassin,' a reference to the legend of the Old Man of the Mountain, is found in both *Ayen* 140/25 and *VV* 139/6.
8820–2 Psalm 118.72.
8834–8 *liche as the sterre ... in his owne cours*. Gradon (*Ayen* 141/9–13*n*) translates as follows: 'As the star which is called Saturn does, which traverses as much, within the firmament, in a single day, when propelled by the firmament, as it does in thirty years, in its own circuit, and on its own course.'
8842–3 Isaias 40.29.
8847–9 Aelian 2.25; Pliny, *Historia Naturalis*, 11.36; Thomas Cantimpratensis, 9.21.13–14; Albert the Great, *De Animalibus*, 26.16.
8853–6 Matthew 14.23.
8856–61 Isaias 32.2.
8861–3 1 Corinthians 10.4. *refuge of the garson*: *fuiement et la garison.* Cf. ll. 804, 1505, 4083, 4778.
8863–5 Psalm 103.18. Cf. Pliny, *Historia Naturalis*, 8.53; McCulloch, *Medieval Latin*, 124.
8865–7 Jeremias 48.28.

8875–6 B's original reading, *The worlde is to theym a chartre only of paradise*, misconstrues the French: *Le monde leur est chartre, solitude paradis*. *Chartre* meaning 'prison' was probably unfamiliar to the translator, and *solitude* may have been read as *sole de*. Cf. l. 8888, where *solitude* is translated as *soulness*. The source of the statement is Jerome, *Epistolae*, 125.8 (PL 22, col. 1076).
8876–80 Cicero, *De Officiis*, 3.1.1.
8882 *dyviseth*: 'communicates, discusses' (*devise*). MED, s.v. *devisen* v., 7b.
8883–5 Psalm 24.14.
8890–4 *evyn as a ientilwoman ... God hatthe sent hym*: *Car tout aussi que une damoiselle qui par amours aime a grant vergonde quand elle est aperceue et elle oit que on en parle. Aussi a celle quant elle oit que on parle delle* (CDPU; other MSS *lui*) *et des biens que dieu lui a envoies*. The French exemplar read *lui* rather than *elle*. *sessith* – the reading of B – misrenders the first *oit*, confusing *oir* 'hears' with *oissir* (a variant of *eissir*) 'leaves.'
8895–8 2 Corinthians 12.2.
8903 Isaias 51.6.
8908–24 The subject of this passage is the soul irrespective of the inconsistent use of masculine and feminine pronouns. The confusion (which is also to be found in *Ayen* 143/14–32) goes back to the French, as Gradon notes.
8910–11 Ecclesiasticus 34.1–5.
8911–15 Romans 6.11, Galatians 2.19–20, Acts 2.1–4.
8917 Whiting N186 (Not give a nut); Hassell N27.
8920–4 Matthew 17.19.
8924–5 Bartholomaeus Anglicus, *De Proprietatibus*, 17.155 describes mustard as hot and dry to the fourth degree – an observation that may come, according to Seymour et al. from the medical text *Circa Instans* composed by the Salernitan Platearius (Johannes or Matthaeus) c. 1150 (*Bartholomaeus Anglicus*, 204).
8926–8 Bernard, *Epistolae*, 11.8 (*Opera* 7, 58–9); *De Diligendo Deo*, 8.23–9.29 (*Opera* 3, 138–44).
8935 *voided*: 'treated as nothing, humbled.' Cf. MED, s.v. *voiden* v., 14b.
8940–1 Matthew 5.3.
8964–6 Ephesians 4.3–6.
8970 *comunally*: 'alike.' MED cites this meaning only in the adjectival form *commun(e)*.

8970–4 John 17.20–6.
8974–5 Ecclesiasticus 13.19. Whiting B129 (Every beast loves its like); Hassell P34.
8979 *with on only moneye* renders the French *dune mesmes monnoie*. For the emphatic numeral see OED, s.v. *one* num, II.7.b. The earliest citation is to Caxton (1483). MED does not record the idiom.
8984–5 Romans 13.9.
8990 Two short sentences have been lost or omitted after *comunly*: *Tous il a fais communement. A tous pourvoit communement. Tous iugera communement et guerdonnera a tous largement*, and so forth.
9003–9 Ephesians 5.23, 29–30, John 6.54–7.
9009–11 John 15.13 (here misattributed to Paul).
9021–5 Matthew 7.12. Whiting D274 (Do as you would be done to).
9035–8 1 Peter 1.22, 4.8.
9046–9 2 Peter 1.3–7.
9049–54 Cicero, *De Officiis*, 1.7.22.
9054–62 1 Corinthians 12.12–26.
9072–4 Seneca, *De Clementia*, 1.17.
9076 After *therto* the translator omits the fourfold method of correction from sweet inducement to harsh, outright excommunication: *et a grant paour y doit on la main mettre les oignemens et les emplastres de douces admonicions. Apres se ce ne vault les paroles aspres et poignantes de dures reprehensions. Apres le fer de discipline et sil ne fait se empirer non adoncques doit venir lespee pour le dessevrer ou par excommuniement pour le banir hors du pays ou lui eslongier de lui.*
9077–8 1 Corinthians 12.25–6, Colossians 3.13.
9087 Whiting F634 (A friend in need); Hassell A100.
9090–2 John 15.13.
9092–6 1 Peter 2.21, 1 John 3.16.
9100–3 Matthew 5.4.
9105–12 *This is to vnderstande in iii maneres ... in possession and in heritage* contains two lacunae that make the passage difficult to comprehend without reference to the French text: *Cest entendu en trois manieres. Premierement de la terre des vivans cest dieu mesmes qui est heritage des vivans cest de sains et de saintes et des prodommes aussi comme la terre est habitacion des hommes et des bestes. Et pource que dieu qui est la terre des vivans a les debonnaires en sa main et en sa possession. Car ilz ne font rien fors ce quil lui plait pource est ce droit quilz aient dieu en pocession sicomme dit le psaultier. Les debonnaires*

auront dit il la terre en possession et en heritage. The biblical references are to Psalms 36.11, 141.6 and Matthew 5.5. The passage is based on Augustine, *Enarrationes in Psalmos*, 36.11 (PL 36, col. 390), 141.12 (PL 37, col. 1840), and 145.11 (PL 37, col. 1891).
9113–14 Augustine, *De Salutaribus Documentis*, 10 (PL 40, col. 1050). *in hymselfe*, that is, in possession of himself (*en la sienne*).
9118–19 Proverbs 16.32.
9143–5 Apocalypse 4.6.
9145–7 Zacharias 3.9.
9153 *lityl ligne*: 'level' (French *oeil*). Not recorded by MED.
9153–6 Ecclesiasticus 7.40. Whiting E84 (Look at the end); Hassell F88.
9158 *snake*: ACNPQSU *goupil*, DV *renart*, R om.
9159 *egal*: 'even' (French *egal*). MED cites this meaning only in the adverbial form *'egalli.'*
9197–200 Seneca, *Epistolae*, 3.4. *ne to euerythynge ne too nothynge*: properly 'to everyone and to no one' (*et omnibus credere et nulli*).
9207–9 *And thyngys that men ... to the goode partye* follows the text of ANPQS: *Les choses que on peut tourner a dextre et a senestre que on les entende tousiours en la bonne partie.* However, CDRUV, which, like *Ayen* 152/11–13 and *VV* 151/8–10, have a negative particle, appear to preserve a better reading: *Les choses que on ne peut tourner* (D *deviser*) *a dextre et a senestre*, and so on. The point is that one should take a favorable view of matters that cannot be thoroughly examined. *too the goode partye*, that is, in a favorable light. Not recorded by MED. The earliest citation to the phrase in OED is 1559.
9216–18 John 14.26.
9618–22 Martin of Braga, *Formula Vitae Honestae*, 2 (Barlow, 240). *philosophre*: the reference is probably to Seneca who was credited with the composition of the *Formula* in the Middle Ages. Cf. Augustine, *De Diversis Quaestionibus*, 31 (PL 40, col. 20).
9226 *wisily* 'discreetly, prudently,' but French *envis* ('reluctantly'). Cf. MED, s.v. *aviseli* adv. 2a. *envis* is similarly mistranslated in ll. 1832, 4136, 6478.
9226–8 Ecclesiasticus 21.28.
9234–5 Matthew 7.6. Whiting P89 (Cast not pearls before swine); Hassell P134.
9249 *humoures* is perhaps the result of an eyeskip. The French reads *meurs*.
9253 *than is man sette in hymselfe* renders the French: *Adoncques est homme ordene par dedans lui.*

9256–7 *that the whiche men doothe ... not to softe ne too rude* translates the French somewhat inaccurately: *ce que on fait par iugement droit et loial ne trop mol ne trop roide.*
9258–9 Whiting L296 (as aright as a lyne); Hassell L57. *qwickly* (B *qwcky*): ACDNPQS *vivement*, UV *vraiement*, R om. Cf. *Ayen* 153/22 *onlepiliche*, ?'with singleness of purpose,' and *n.*, *VV* 152/21 *evenliche* 'in a straightforward manner'.
9260 *equalite*: 'fairness, impartiality, equity' (*equalite*). OED, s.v. *equalite* n., 3. MED does not record this meaning.
9269 *to the beholdyng of*: 'with regard to' or 'in accordance with' (*au regart de*). Cf. *Ayen* 153/31 and *VV* 152/30. MED does not record the phrase.
9270–1 Bernard, *De Gratia et Libero Arbitrio*, 2.4 (*Opera* 3, 168–9).
9294–6 For the allegorical motif of the body as a castle protected by the five wits against the assaults of the devil see Cornelius, *Figurative Castle*, 14–23. The metaphor originated with Proverbs 4.13. Cf. also ll. 11,942–6, 12,073–9.
9297 Jeremias 9.21.
9304–5 Job 18.8–9.
9308–10 Seneca, *De Clementia*, 1.6.
9324 *oo grace*: *une mesmes grace.* B's *oo mesure of grace* stems from a misreading of *mesmes* as *mesure.*
9325–7 Cassian, *Collationes*, 11.12 (PL 49, cols 862–6), a reference to Abbot Chaeremon's First Conference on Perfection.
9336–48 Tubach 372. The Aesopian fable of the ass and dog goes back to *Romulus*, 1.16 (Thiele, *Äsop des Romulus*, 64–8) and appears in a large number of story collections. Cf. Jacques de Vitry 15 (Crane, 5 and list of sources on 139–40). *comyng* translates French *venoit*, which may have been read as *venant*. This is the only instance in the text of the use of a participle for a finite verb.
9351–4 Proverbs 23.5.
9361–4 Proverbs 24.30–2.
9365–6 Whiting M170 (A man should be chastised by another); Hassell C101.
9371–2 Augustine, *De Civitate Dei*, 14.6 (PL 41, col. 409). Cf. Whiting V30 (To hate the Vice [ill] and not the persons).
9378 *too weepe* translates *plourer*, the corrupt reading of all French MSS except DN, which properly have *ploier* (*ployer*) 'to bend, incline.' AND, s.v. *ploier*. Gradon (*Ayen* 157/8*n*) suggests the sense is 'to please.' Cf. l. 3971.

9380–2 Gregory, *Moralia*, 3.12 (PL 75, col. 610). The reference to Seneca has not been identified; possibly Martin of Braga, *Exhortatio Humilitatis*, 7 (Barlow, 78): *Haec sola in plano est, et quamvis humilior aliis videatur, caelo tamen est altior, quia in regno eius hominem non ascendendo, sed descendendo perducit.*
9387–90 Although this statement is attributed to Gregory and may ultimately derive from *Moralia*, 32.22 (PL 76, col. 664), it seems closer to Bernard, *In Quadragesima*, Sermo 5.2 (*Opera* 4, 373).
9402–3 The reference is to Job 42.3, although the words are spoken by Job, not God. Gradon (*Ayen* 158/2–3*n*) comments: 'This seems to be a reference to the fact that the Book of Job was thought to contain many allegorical types of the devil and it was to him that Job referred ... on which the *Glossa Ordinaria* [3.81.e] comments: *Absque scientia Leviathan celat consilium quia quamvis contra infirmitatem nostram multis fraudibus occultetur* (iii.414).'
9404–6 Pseudo-Dionysius, *De Celesti Hierarchia*, 3.2 (PG 3, col. 165).
9419–21 Bernard, *Sermones de Diversis*, 23.4 (*Opera* 6^1, 181).
9426–8 1 John 4.1.
9432–3 Ecclesiasticus 34.17.
9433–5 Ecclesiasticus 32.24, Proverbs 19.20. Cf. Whiting C470 (Work all by counsel and you shall not rue); Hassell C277. *after the counselle* possibly misconstrues the French *apres le çop*, but it is more likely an eyeskip. The same statement is rendered accurately in ll. 10,279–81.
9440–2 Matthew 6.22–3, Luke 11.34. *diuers*: 'evil' (*divers*). Not recorded by MED in this sense. Tobler-Lommatsch, s.v. *divers* adj.
9447 *forked*: 'cloven, divided,' that is, equivocal (*forchie*). Not recorded by MED in this sense.
9464–7 Proverbs 8.20.
9467–71 Bernard, *Sermones super Cantica Canticorum*, 85.5 (*Opera* 2, 310).
9475 *bee oo weye* mistakes the French *en vii sens*, *vii* having been read as *un*.
9488–9 Matthew 5.5.
9493 *inequite* is not recorded by MED. It is cited by the OED as from 1566.
9494–5 Psalm 83.7.
9497–9 Ecclesiastes 7.5.
9514–16 Matthew 5.5.
9518 *with strengthe*: 'perforce' (*a force*). Not recorded by MED in this precise sense.

9530–2 Cf. Job 5.7, 7.1, 10.17, 30.12–14.
9539 The earliest citation to *hardenys* meaning 'hardship' in MED is c. 1500.
9561–3 Matthew 5.6.
9563–4 Proverbs 12.26.
9565–8 Bernard, *De Diligendo Deo*, 2.6 (*Opera* 3, 124).
9583–4 Proverbs 6.27.
9593–7 Acts 2.1–11.
9600 Nearly the entire first sentence of this paragraph has been lost: *Les philosophes qui des vertus traictierent deviserent ceste vertu en six manieres qui sont aussi comme six degres par onceste vertu monte et profite mais nostre maistre qui fist les philosophes et la philosophie y met le septime point.* The six-fold division of fortitude into *magnanimite, troste, suerte, pascience, constance,* and *magnificence* derives from the *Summa de bono* of Phillip the Chancellor, as Gauthier demonstrates (*Magnanimité*, 274–7).
9603–5 Matthew 5.6.
9609–60 The discussion of magnanimity combines elements of both classical and medieval views of the topic: the stoic concept of the world; the *rationabilis aggressio* derived from Abelard, *Moralium dogma philosophorum*, and Phillip the Chancellor; and the *magnanimitas fidei*, or pursuit of spiritual perfection, developed by Bernard and later theologians. See Gauthier, *Magnanimité*, 291–4.
9610–2 Cicero, *De Officiis*, 1.20.66.
9612–5 Augustine, *De Libero Arbitrio*, 1.13.27 (PL 32, col. 1235).
9615–7 Seneca, *Epistolae*, 39.4. Cf. also 8.5.
9617–9 *Moralium dogma philosophorum*, 30, l. 4.
9619–20 Isaias 33.17
9624–8 Ecclesiastes 1.1.
9631–2 Psalm 143.4.
9638 *weye of perfeccion*, but French *estat de perfection*: an echo of Psalm 17.33 and Isaias 35.8.
9640–1 *hille of God*: Psalm 23.3.
9641–3 A reference to the Sermon on the Mount (Matthew 5).
9658–9 Whiting H2 (The habit does not make the monk); Hassell H1; Morawski 1053.
9667 *assautis of the worlde, of the flesshe, and of the fende*: on the origin and development of this topos see Wenzel, 'Three Enemies,' and Howard, *Three Temptations*, 61–5. Cf. Hassell M166 (*Le monde, le démon, et la chair*).

9677 *setteth (hym) to*: 'devotes (himself) to' (*se ahert*). MED, s.v. *setten* v., 28a.
9680 Whiting G276 (Where God will help is none helpless); Hassell D95.
9682–4 *Moralium dogma philosophorum*, 30, ll. 6–7.
9690 Whiting L314 (As hardy as a lion); Hassell L70.
9693–6 The statement is taken from Jacobus, *Legenda aurea*, chap. 39 (Graesse, 171).
9699 *tornementis*: 'torments' (*tourmens*), a uncommon variant in *-ne-* of *torment*. MED, *torment* n., and Du Cange, *torneamentum*..
9705–7 Psalm 5.13.
9709–10 Romans 5.3. Whiting F180 (Fire afonds hard iron).
9710–11 Cf. Whiting P61 (Patience vanquishes), S865 (The sufferant overcomes); Hassell P78.
9713–25 Exemplary material drawn from the crafts and nature lore to justify the paradoxical notion of tribulation as a spiritual help is a commonplace of treatises on patience. See Hanna, 'Commonplace,' 76, 85 *nn*32–4.
9718 *scarlet*, that is, a robe of scarlet (*la robe de scarlate*), a cloth of superior quality. 'The woolen scarlet was incontestably the most renowned luxury textile manufactured in medieval Europe ... Scarlets, worn by popes, emperors, kings, and princes, were indeed the medieval European successor to the famed 'royal purple' of the classical and Byzantine world' (Munro, 'Medieval Scarlet,' 14). The cloth-name was eventually transferred to the color with which it was often dyed (kermes). Cf. Walton, 'Textiles,' 338; Douet-D'Arcq, *L'Argenterie*, 372; Zangger, *Contribution*, 50–5; Poerck, *Draperie Médiévale*, vol. 1, 213–14, vol. 2, 70–1.
9721 Whiting I56 (as stronge as iron); Hassell F49. *Soupleth* in the sense of 'softens, makes flexible' appears elsewhere only in *Dicts* 226/13.
9723 *traictable*: 'manageable' (*traictable*). The earliest citation to this sense in OED is 1555. MED (*tractable* adj.) glosses its anatomical meaning only.
9724 Tubach 4156 (Salamander lives in fire). *Physiologus*, 30 (Carmody, 52); Pliny, *Historia Naturalis*, 10.86, 29.23; Bartholomaeus Anglicus, *De Proprietatibus*, 18.82. See also McCulloch, *Medieval Latin*, 161–2; White, *Bestiary*, 182–4; Friedmann, *Bestiary*, 269. An uncommon word in Middle English, *salemandre* was evidently unfamiliar to the translators of both the *Mirroure* and *VV* (168/5).

9725 *baigneth* retains its French spelling.
9734–7 Psalm 90.7. The source of the sentence is Bernard, *In Ramis Palmarum*, Sermo 2.2 (*Opera* 5, 47), as Gradon notes (*Ayen* 168/11–13*n*).
9737–42 Seneca, *De Constantia Sapientis*, 6.1–8.
9744–6 *Moralium dogma philosophorum*, 30, ll. 7–8. Gradon (*Ayen* 168/22*n*) refers to Augustine, *De Diversis Quaestionibus*, 83.21 (PL 40, col. 21). Cf. *Summa Virtutum*, 6.89.
9746–50 Matthew 10.22.
9750–1 1 Corinthians 9.24. *spere*, but French *espee* 'sword,' that is, prize (cf. *Ayen* 168/26–8*n*). *Espie* was read for *espee*.
9735–5 Matthew 10.22, 24.13, Mark 13.13.
9756–7 *But the disciples of oure maister Criste Iesus goothe ferther forthe* renders the French *Mais les disciples nostre maistre Ihesu crist vont plus avant asses*, that is, they far surpassed the pagan philosophers in magnificence.
9757–8 *For whan theye hadde gedered al togyder* mistakes the French *Car quant ilz ont tout assomme*, that is, 'when they had entirely accomplished their task.' *assomme* was clearly confused with, or misread as, *assemble* 'assembled.' D ascribes the statement to Solomon, as do *Ayen* 168/33–5 and *VV* 169/15–16. Gradon cites Ecclesiastes 1.9.
9767–9 Anselm, *Liber Meditationum et Orationum*, 11 (PL 158, cols 768–9). *redeveable* is not recorded by MED.
9776–7 Matthew 5.6.
9781 The table of contents reads *Branches* for *Tree*.
9785–7 Apocalypse 2–3.
9787–9 Bernard, *Sermones super Cantica Canticorum*, 13.4 (*Opera* 1, 72). Part of the subordinate clause has been lost: *Car sicomme dit saint bernard moult est celui fol et oultrecuide qui sans victoire atend a avoir couronne et qui sans bataille cuide avoir victoire.*
9790 2 Timothy 2.5. The relative clause has been lost after *coroune*: *qui loialment ne se combatra.*
9796–9 The English follows the imperfect French text: *Le maistre de nostre champ qui espreuve les nouveaulx chevaliers si comme il est escript ou livre de Roys ce maistre est tres loial si comme dit saint pol et scet bien le povair de chascun. VV* 170/21–2 is based on a more accurate text: *þe maister of oure feld is Ihesu Criste þat assaieth his newe knyȝtes*, and so forth. For the association of David and Christ with the ceremony of knighthood see Gradon's comment to *Ayen* 170/

1–3. The biblical references are to 1 Corinthians 10.13, 2 Corinthians 12.9–10, and 1 Paralipomenon 12.
9799–807 1 Corinthians 10.13, Apocalypse 2–3 (repeating the substance of ll. 9785–7).
9814–15 Apocalypse 3.15–16.
9821 *maske*: 'net.' MED glosses the noun 'mesh of a net.' The meaning is closer to the verb *masken* 'snare in a net, enmesh.'
9826–8 Ephesians 6.13, Romans 13.12, 2 Corinthians 6.7.
9832–3 *the thirde is sufficiant satisfaccion in the worlde* mistranslates the French: *La tierce est satisfacion et suffisante amende.* The translator apparently read *amende* as *a monde.*
9834 *determined*: 'made perfectly' (*enterine*). Not recorded by MED in this sense.
9840–1 Psalm 6.7.
9849 *goddes*: 'goods' (*biens*).
9862–4 Psalm 76.7, Isaias 14.23.
9870–2 Augustine, *In Iohannis Evangelium Tractatus*, 49.2 (PL 35, col. 1747).
9875–80 Pseudo-Augustine, *De Vera et Falsa Paenitentia*, 10 (PL 40, col. 1122). *too Goddewarde*: for this construction see Mustanoja, *Middle English Syntax*, 423.
9885–6 Isaias 38.15.
9888–9 *as a ioglour ... than his owne*: the statement also appears in *Othea*, 110/26–8, where it is attributed to Gregory, but it cannot be found among his works.
9895 *the beynge* mistakes the French *l'estre* 'the stirrup.' Cf. *VV* 171/11 *stirop. Ayen* 173/3 *writ* follows a variant reading, *lescripte*, found in MSS of *Somme le Roi.*
9898 This heading does not appear in the table of contents.
9905 Psalm 118.62. *kynge*, that is, David.
9907–9 Ecclesiasticus 5.8–9.
9918–21 Cf. Whiting D96 (Death is certain, but not the time); Tilley N311. Augustine, *De Contritione Cordis*, 1 (PL 40, col. 943), and Bernard, *Sermo Ad Clericos De Conversione*, 8.16 (*Opera* 4, 90).
9923–5 Apocalypse 13.2.
9931–2 Apocalypse 3.20. *torne azene* (*after*) translates *recouvrer* 'come back (to), return (to).' OED, s.v. *turn* v., 66b.
9936–7 Psalm 7.13.
9944 This heading does not appear in the Table of Contents.

9950–1 Whiting L173 (A leech may not heal a wound unless the sick man show it to him).
9951–4 Boethius, *De Consolatione Philosophiae,* 1, pr. 4.
9960 This heading does not appear in the table of contents.
9968–71 Psalm 31.5.
9974–6 Matthew 7.3–5. Whiting M710 (Mote and beam); Hassell B198.
9976–9 Luke 18.10–13. *bette his blame,* that is, confessed his fault, rendering *batoit sa coulpe.*
9996 *or in a womman of religion*: the French reads *ou en homme ou en femme de religion.*
10,019–20 *men maketh often to grete besynesse and too grete coste,* that is, men often expend too much pain and effort.
10,037–8 *touchynge hymselfe or any ooþer* delicately interprets the French *en soy ou en femme delicter.*
10,044 This heading does not appear in the table of contents.
10,050–2 Psalm 31.5, 38.17–18.
10,070 This heading does not appear in the table of contents.
10,077 *pvmped*: not recorded by MED as a verb.
10,080–1 Whiting U8 (Usage makes mastery); Hassell U3.
10,084 *this*: 'thus, so' (*si*). Cf. ll. 3363–4*n*. *recouere*: 'do again, repeat' (*recouvrer*). Godefroy, s.v. *recovrer* v.; MED, *recoveren* v., 6d.
10,087–9 The source of this story has not been identified.
10,099–10,102 Tubach 836.
10,104 *fere,* but French *honte,* thereby losing the contrast between *lytel* and *grete shame.*
10,111 Whiting S177 (To be aghast of one's shadow); Hassell O59; Tilley S261.
10,117–18 Whiting S539 (To slumber like a sow in a slough).
10,123–5 Gregory, *Homiliarum in Evangelia,* 1.12 (PL 76, col. 1122).
10,125–8 Tubach 892 (Cat playing with mouse comparable to devil). Cf. Whiting C80 (As a cat plays with a mouse); Hassell C89; McCulloch, *Medieval Latin,* 102.
10,144–6 Apocalypse 2.11.
10,156–7 Luke 8.13.
10,157–8 Cf. Whiting W277 (Will he, nill he), citing only *VV* 184/25.
10,159–60 Whiting W160, 161 (To be like a weathercock, To be like a weathervane).
10,162–4 Apocalypse 3.12.
10,171–2 Proverbs 9.13–18.

10,173–80 Judges 16.4–21. Whiting S52 (As strong as Samson); Hassell S34. Cf. ll. 5305–7, 11,305–8.
10,182–4 Apocalypse 3.5, 7.13–14.
10,189–91 Cf. ll. 9734–7*n*.
10,198–9 Apocalypse 3.21.
10,212–19 This statement is based on an amalgam of biblical texts, among them, 1 John 2.18, 4.3; 2 Thessalonians 2.1–12; 1 Timothy 4.1–3; and 2 Peter 2.1.
10,219–20 Apocalypse 13.1–4. On the identification of Antichrist with the Beast of the Apocalypse see Emmerson, *Antichrist*, 21–4.
10,223 *revith*: 'ravage, despoil' (*foullent*).
10,224–7 Apocalypse 2.26.
10,239 Cf. Whiting S96 (The scorpion flatters with its head when it will sting with its tail). White, *Bestiary*, 192.
10,255–9 Apocalypse 2.7.
10,261–4 Matthew 5.6.
10,268 This heading does not appear in the table of contents.
10,276–8 Cicero, *De Officiis*, 1.22.77.
10,279–81 Ecclesiasticus 32.24, Proverbs 19.20. Whiting C470 (Work all by counsel and you shall not rue); Hassell C277. Cf. ll. 9433–5.
10,282–4 Tobias 4.19.
10,284–6 Proverbs 11.14.
10,287–9 Cicero, *De Officiis*, 1.22.76.
10,289–90 Ecclesiasticus 37.9.
10,290 Ecclesiasticus 8.20. Whiting C465 (Take no counsel of a fool).
10,292–3 Job 12.12.
10,294–6 *besinesses necessarie*: 'necessary tasks, affairs, or business occupations' (*besongnes*). *necessarie thyngys*, expressed merely by *choses* in the French, has the same meaning. MED glosses *besoignes* n., b in this sense, citing a Parliamentary Roll dating from 1472–5. Cf. also *nede* n., 4a, *necessity* n., a, and *necessarie* n. The precise phrases do not appear in MED.
10,296–8 3 Kings 12–14, 2 Paralipomenon 10–12.
10,300 This heading does not appear in the table of contents.
10,306–7 Seneca, *Epistolae*, 16.2.
10,310 This heading does not appear in the table of contents.
10,313–16 Proverbs 12.15, Ecclesiasticus 21.18. Between *counsell* and *the whiche* the French has an explanatory clause: *cest a dire que la sage obeist au bon conseil*.
10,316–28 Isaias 11.2, Matthew 19.21. The original reading, *the*

which he brought us from hevyn, is possibly an eyeskip. *the whiche* destroys the syntax of the sentence and receives no support from the French MSS, which read *nous aporta du ciel. tonge of the counsell* (l. 10320) and *the tonge of counselle* (l. 10,325) follow a corrupt reading found only in Q: *langue de conseil*. The other MSS correctly read *lange de conseil* 'the angel of counsel,' as do *Ayen* 185/4–5, 10–11 and *VV* 190/8–9, 13.

10,343 This heading does not appear in the table of contents.

10,344 *vii*: the correct reading uniquely preserved in DQ. B follows the other MSS: *ii degrees*.

10,348–9 Augustine, *De Civitate Dei*, 19.12 (PL 41, col. 639). Whiting F575 (No fowl eats another of its kind). The reference has not been found in the bestiary.

10,350–1 Aristotle, *Historia animalium*, 611a; Aelian, 3.8; Pliny, *Historia Naturalis*, 8.65; Bartholomaeus Anglicus, *De Proprietatibus*, 18.40. The reference has not been found in the bestiary.

10,351–3 Bartholomaeus Anglicus, *De Proprietatibus*, 18.69.

10,369–70 Whiting F634 (A friend in need); Hassell A100.

10,370–3 Matthew 25.34–6.

10,373–4 Ecclesiastes 9.8.

10,380–6 1 John 3.17.

10,387–90 Tobias 4.7–9.

10,390–2 Matthew 19.21.

10,393–4 Psalm 83.12.

10,394–5 Osee 6.6, Matthew 9.13, 12.7.

10,395–7 Augustine, *De Civitate Dei*, 4.23 (PL 41, col. 130) and *Contra Adimantum*, 11 (PL 42, col. 142), quoting Cicero, *Pro Q Ligario*, 12.38.

10,399 *dulle*: 'niggardly' (*merde*: so all MSS except D which has *rudes*). Not recorded by MED with this meaning.

10,402–3 *forfetis*: 'misdeeds,' ACNQRUV *forfais*, but P *oultrages* and DS *sourfais*, meaning 'excesses,' which may be, in fact, the better reading.

10,404 Whiting A40 (As hard as adamant).

10,404–7 *Glossa Ordinaria* 3.101.a, commenting on Psalm 9.15.

10,407–9 *botirflie*, but ACNPQSU *boterel*, V *crapout ou botereau*, R *boute*, D *crapault*. *boterel* 'toad' was unfamiliar to the translator. Cf. l. 3410. The observation is made of the toad by Pliny, *Historia Naturalis*, 8.110 and Bartholomaeus Anglicus, *De Proprietatibus*, 18.17.

10,409–12 John 12.3–6. *thynge loste*, that is, a waste of precious balm. *hym thought*: on the use of the oblique case for the nominative in

Middle-English, see Mustanoja, *Middle English Syntax*, 129–30. Cf. l. 11,070 (*hym oughte*).

10,413–16 A reference to the legend of the three devils recounted in Iohannes Herolt's *Promptuarium exemplorum*, s.v. *Confessio*, Exemplum 15, A5[b]: *Demones impediunt confessionem et restitutionem*. The function of *clobourse* (*claudens bursam*) is to close the purse of penitents to almsgiving. On the origin of the legend and its later appearance in the sermons of Guillaume de Mailly, a popular thirteenth-century Parisian preacher, see Hauréau, 'Sermonnaires,' 452–4, and *Notices*, vol. 4, 144, 159. *Ayen* 187/35 and *VV* 193/7 translate *Clobourse* as 'shut-purse,' the form under which it appears in MED and OED.

10,416–21 James 1.5, Matthew 5.45. *he*, that is, Christ.

10,423–5 Luke 6.36.

10,425–6 Cf. 1 Peter 1.13–21.

10,427–9 Ecclesiasticus 4.10. A portion of the biblical text has been omitted after *theyme*: *et a leur meres soies pour mary.*

10,430–1 Proverbs 14.31.

10,432–5 Matthew 25.40.

10,439–43 Tubach 3192. Its source is Jacobus, *Legenda aurea*, chap. 166 (Graesse, 742).

10,444–6 James 2.13.

10,446–9 Matthew 25.41–6.

10,449–63 Luke 16.19–26. Whiting E14 (To make a deaf ear); Hassell O75. *voided*: 'dismissed, sent away' (*escondist*).

10,465 Hebrews 7.1–3. Cf. 1 Peter 2.17, 25.

10,470–4 Matthew 25.41.

10,482–3 Matthew 5.7.

10,483–5 Matthew 6.14.

10,486–8 Romans 8.28.

10,488–91 Proverbs 3.9–10.

10,495–6 Whiting T217 (To take broad thongs of unbought (other men's) leather).

10,499–500 Matthew 19.21.

10,503–15 Tubach 1462. The story is from Constantius, *Vita Sancti Germani*, 2.2 (*Acta Sanctorum* 31 July, vol. 7, 229–30). After *pore pepill* a sentence has been lost in which Germanus orders the deacon to bestow the remaining three pence on the poor. *vs*, but French *leur*. *cc li, ccc li*: CNPQ *deux cens livres, trois cens livres*, ARUV *cinq cens livres, quinze cens livres*, S *cc livres, xvc livres*, D *dix livres, quinze*

livres. In the *Miroir* and *Somme* the story of Germanus is followed by the story of John the Almoner, which is here omitted.
10,515–25 Gregory, *Dialogae*, 1.9 (PL 77, col. 197).
10,525–37 A variant of Tubach 4089. *taried*: 'remained unfulfilled' (*demouroit*). MED does not record *tarry* in this precise sense.
10,537–46 Tubach 4089 with a reference to Matthew 19.29. Sisam, *Verse & Prose*, 213, suggests that this exemplum is the source of the French fabliau *Brunain*.
10,548 *and euerlastyng goodes* are the closing words of a sentence: *Apres elle empetre vers dieu lez biens expirituelz et les biens perdurables*.
10,549–50 Romans 8.28; Ephesians 2.8–9, 3.7–8. *in present*, that is, in the present life. Cf. l. 11,211.
10,551–2 Psalm 83.12.
10,590–1 Whiting S262 (A shoe holds its first form).
10,592–3 Cf. Whiting C375 (All that a young colt is taught he will hold); Hassell P242. The proverb preserves the rhyme, but renders the sense of the French clumsily: *Quaprent poullain en endenture/Veult tenir tous les jours quil dure*. *for too endente*, translating *en endenteure* 'in training,' should be construed as 'to be tame.' Cf. AND, s.v. *adanter, endenter* v., 'to tame,' Godefroy, s.v. *adenter* v., and MED, s.v. *endaunten* v. The proverb is repeated in ll. 11,739–41.
10,602 *remedy*, but French *conseil*.
10,604 Whiting L455 (Such lord such meiny); Hassell S56; Morawski 165.
10,609–10 Whiting V30 (To hate the Vice [ill] and not the persons); Tilley P238, F710.
10,618 *poore pepil*, but French *malades*.
10,620–1 1 Thessalonians 5.14.
10,622–3 Proverbs 12.25.
10,623–6 Proverbs 27.9.
10,627–8 Whiting F634 (A friend in need); Hassell A100.
10,633–5 Cf. Augustine, *Enarrationes in Psalmos*, 25.2.7 (PL 36, col. 192). The passage appears to be based on Psalm 38.10–11. Defensor, *Liber Scintillarum*, 50.4–5 (CC 117, 170) attributes other statements of a similar nature to Augustine, but they cannot be found among his works.
10,637 *euerlastyng liff*, B's reading, is emended to *euerlastyngly* on the authority of the French MSS.
10,640–1 Hebrews 12.6, Proverbs 3.12, Apocalypse 3.19.
10,650–1 Gregory, *Moralia*, 8.8 (PL 75, cols 810–11).

10,654–9 Exodus 15.23–5.
10,666–7 *tribulacion provith Goddes knyght*: James 1.12. Cf. Whiting K95 (A manly knight's prowess is proved most in mischief).
10,668 *empressed*: 'engaged in a chivalric enterprise' (*empresse*). MED does not record this meaning of the verb. The noun *emprise* (2a), however, is cited in the sense of 'chivalric enterprise.'
10,668–9 Romans 5.4.
10,669–71 Tobias 12.13.
10,672–4 Gregory, *Moralia*, 7.18, 19 (PL 75, col. 777).
10,674–5 Ecclesiasticus 31.2.
10,676–8 Gregory, *Moralia*, 7.19 (PL 75, col. 777).
10,682–5 Gregory, *Moralia*, 12.51 (PL 75, col. 1013), 19.23 (PL 76, cols 122–3), 21.19 (PL 76, cols 207–8).
10,686–8 Matthew 6.15, Mark 11.26.
10,691 After *evil wille* an exemplary story of the Emperor Theodosius, who preferred to rule by love rather than by fear, is omitted: *On dit de lempereur theodose quil tenoit a tres grant honte que on lui faisoit quant on lui prioit quil pardonnast et comme plus estoit courouce adoncques pardonnoit it plus tost. Car il vouloit mieulx a traire ses gens par debonnairetee et par amour que par paour.*
10,695–6 2 Corinthians 11.29.
10,696–8 Gregory, *Moralia*, 22.21 (PL 76, col. 246).
10,699–702 Matthew 5.44–5.
10,714–15 Tobias 4.17.
10,715–17 Proverbs 25.21 (where the injunction relates to any enemy rather than a friend).
10,717–21 Luke 14.13–14.
10,723–33 Luke 16.19–31.
10,736–8 Psalm 40.2.
10,739–43 Matthew 25.34–5, 40.
10,745–6 Tobias 4.17.
10,746–8 Isaias 58.7. After *hym* the *Miroir* adds a brief reference to the charitable ministrations of St Peter.
10,755–60 Deuteronomy 15.7–8.
10,761–3 Luke 6.35, Proverbs 19.17.
10,763–5 Cf. ll. 4599–4603. Cf. Deuteronomy 23.19–20.
10,765–7 Deuteronomy 24.10–14.
10,767–70 Matthew 6.15. After *vs* the *Miroir* adds: *Et de ce met dieu exemple du felon sergant a qui son seigneur avoit pardonne sa debte. Et pource quil ne voulut perdonner a cellui qui le devoit le seigneur*

rappella la bonte quil lui avoit faicte et le fist destraindre et detordre tant quil lui eust rendu ce quil lui devoit. Ainsi fera nostre seigneur sicomme il dit se nous ne pardonnons lun a lautre.
10,773–80 Tubach 1989. Its direct source is *Vitae Patrum*, 5.18 (PL 73, col. 976).
10,780 Job 5.24.
10,784–5 James 1.27.
10,786–94 Tubach 5210 (Water, for washing feet, drunk). The story is taken verbatim from Etienne de Bourbon, 1.155 and is also recounted by Caesarius of Heisterbach, 4.6.
10,795–8 Ecclesiasticus 7.39.
10,798 Proverbs 14.21, Isaias 58.7–8.
10,799 The reference to saints' lives (*scriptures*) is meaningless in the context of the English translation. The *Miroir* follows this statement with an account of the legend of St Mary d'Oignies.
10,799–801 Luke 17.12–14.
10,804–5 Philippians 2.7.
10,809–11 Genesis 18.2–10.
10,812–14 Genesis 19.1–23.
10,814–17 Hebrews 13.2.
10,818–19 Matthew 10.40, John 13.20.
10,820–1 Matthew 25.40.
10,821–9 The story is actually told of Gregory himself. Its source is Jacobus, *Legenda aurea*, chap. 46 (Graesse, 194).
10,831–41 *Vitae Patrum* 5.615 (PL 73, col. 945).
10,844–7 Hebrews 13.3.
10,849–51 Tobias 1.15.
10,851–3 Proverbs 24.11.
10,853–4 Daniel 13.45–64.
10,854–6 John 8.3–11.
10,862–3 Job 29.16.
10,863–6 John 8.6.
10,868 *flit*: 'bend, deviate from justice' (*flexisce*).
10,869–70 John 8.7.
10,871–3 Matthew 7.2
10,873–7 Romans 2.1.
10,877–9 John 8.7.
10,881–8 James 2.13.
10,889–91 Pseudo-Chrysostom, *Opus Imperfectum In Matthaeum*, Homilia 43 (PG 56, col. 878).

10,891–3 James 2.13.
10,893–4 John 8.8–11.
10,900–1 A reference to the 'Harrowing of Hell' recounted in the *Gospel of Nicodemus*, 2.18 (Tischendorf, *Evangelia Apocrypha*, 370–1).
10,902–4 Tobias 1.20, 2.3–7. After *mete* the *Miroir* cites other examples of respect for the dead: *Et nostre seigneur loe las magdalaine de longnement quelle espandi sur son chief dont il dit quelle lavoit fait en signifiance de sa sepulture. Dont Joseph demanda le corps de nostre seigneur et quant il lot il lenseveli diligemment. Les anciens estoient moult curieux de leurs sepultures sicomme dit le scripture et avoient grant regart a la saintete de leurs peres. Et pource vouloient ilz estre ensevelis avec eulx. Dont Iacob dit a son filz ioseph ne mensevelis mie en egipte mais avecques mes peres. Et pource fait il bon gesir entre les prodommes religieux pour avoir leurs prieres. A celle oeure doit esmouvoir nature.*
10,904–7 The same observation appears in *Speculum Humanae Salvationis* 27.31: *Delphini dicuntur mortuis suis compati et eos sepilire*. The *Myrour* (156/20) ascribes the practice to *a manere of fisshe*. There is no reference to it in the bestiary. In Aristotle, *Historia animalium*, 631a; Aelian 12.6; and Pliny, *Historia Naturalis*, 9.10, dolphins are said to carry off a dead comrade and deposit it on shore in order to prevent its corpse from being devoured by sea-monsters. Cf. also Thomas Cantimpratensis 6.16.31–3.
10,928–30 Deuteronomy 17.1.
10,931–3 Ecclesiasticus 34.24.
10,933–5 This statement is attributed to Augustine by Defensor, *Liber Scintillarum*, 49.26 (CC 117, 167), as Nelson (*Myrour* 157/13–15*n*) notes, but it cannot be found among his works. Its source is Seneca, *De Beneficiis*, 1.7.
10,939–40 Ecclesiasticus 12.1.
10,960–3 For the sources of this tale see ll. 735–40*n*.
10,971–2 2 Corinthians 9.7.
10,973–4 *Ayen* (193/26–8) attributes this statement to Gregory. Gradon identifies its source as *In Septem Psalmos Penitentiales*, 4 (PL 79, col. 595). Cf. also *Moralia*, 22.14 (PL 76, col. 229).
10,974–9 Mark 12.42–4, Luke 21.2–4. *peitevines*: deniers poitevins or pictavensis (of Poitou) (Spufford, *Medieval Exchange*, 182, 196). MED, s.v. *poitevin* n. Elsewhere the *Mirroure* converts French to English coinage.
10,984–5 Ecclesiasticus 35.11.

10,985–7 2 Corinthians 9.7.
10,987 A clause has been omitted or lost after *poore men*: *quant ilz leur demandent amosne.*
10,990 *fellenesses* does not appear in MED with the meaning of 'abusive words.'
10,992–4 Ecclesiasticus 4.8.
10,996–8 Proverbs 3.28.
10,998–9 Ecclesiasticus 4.3.
11,005–6 Seneca, *De Beneficiis,* 2.4.
11,007–8 Whiting B636 (He buys dearly who bids).
11,009–15 Ecclesiasticus 14.11–13.
11,017–19 Matthew 25.40.
11,019–23 Tubach 180, citing its appearance only in a late thirteenth century Dominican miscellany extant in British Library, London, MS Royal 7.D.i (Herbert, *Catalogue,* vol. 3, 489, *n*118).
11,023–5 Galatians 6.10. After *vs* the *Miroir* exemplifies St Paul's counsel as follows: *Quant un riche homme doit venir en une ville ou en une cite il envoie ses messages devant pour prendre bon hostel. Autrement il pourroit bien faillir a bon hostel. Les bons fourriers qui prennent le bon hostel et qui appareillent lostel de paradis aux riches hommes sont les amosnes qui font en leur vivant. Les amosnes qui sont faictes apres la mort sont aussi comme les sergans recreans qui viennent tard a lostel sique le seigneur est aucune fois mal herbergie.*
11,027–8 Ecclesiasticus 35.12.
11,028–31 Tobias 4.7–9.
11,032–4 Seneca, *De Beneficiis,* 2.17
11,034–8 The story of Alexander's gift (Tubach 100), although it is taken from Peraldus 1.5.13, ultimately goes back to Seneca, *De Beneficiis,* 2.16.
11,044–7 Ecclesiasticus 29.15.
11,046–7 Gregory, *Homiliarum in Evangelia,* 11.1 (PL 76, col. 1115).
11,048–52 Matthew 6.3–4.
11,058–61 Matthew 5.16.
11,063–5 Mark 8.38.
11,067–9 Gregory, *Homiliarum in Evangelia,* 11.1 (PL 76, col. 1115).
11,071–2 Isaias 58.7.
11,076–9 Job 31.19–20.
11,088 After *myche harme* the French adds *par leurs mauvais conseulx.*
11,094–6 Ecclesiasticus 30.24, Proverbs 11.17.
11,096–8 Ecclesiasticus 14.5.

11,102–4 Psalm 40.2.
11,108–11 Psalm 40.2–3.
11,114–7 Matthew 25.41–3.
11,124–8 Matthew 25.34, 40.
11,131–2 Matthew 5.7.
11,138 A subordinate clause has been lost or omitted after *mercy*: *et quil les delivre de toute adversite et de toute misere. where*: ADNQSV *ou*, CPRU *et*.
11,153–6 1 Thessalonians 4.16.
11,157–8 *maketh theyme solitarie*, B's reading, misconstrues *se alosent*, that is, 'achieve renown,' confusing *aloser* with *assoler*. D explicates the text: *et se alosent cestadire acquierent honneur*.
11,161–5 Luke 10.38–42. Patristic and medieval commentators interpreted Martha and Mary as prototypes of the active and contemplative lives, respectively. See Constable, 'Moderation and Restraint,' 14–22.
11,165 *weye*: *voie* which was evidently misread as *vie*.
11,166–7 Gregory, *Moralia*, 6.37 (PL 75, cols 760–1).
11,182 *is qwik and reysed* appears only as *est elleve* in the French MSS.
11,202–3 *be veray feithe the whiche purgeth the herte*: Acts 15.9.
11,209–12 Matthew 5.8. *veraye* misconstrues *voire* 'truly.' *in presente*, that is, now, in the present life. Cf. l. 10,550.
11,212–13 1 Corinthians 13.12.
11,221–3 Wisdom 2.23. Cf. also Genesis 1.26. The attribution to the Psalter is erroneous.
11,236–7 Matthew 5.8.
11,245–51 Medieval theologians commonly distinguished between desire and consent on the issue of chastity. Cf. Blomme, 'Doctrine du peché,' 46–50, 117–28, 270–1, 306–8.
11,253–5 John 15.3. *metres* or *metraies* was evidently read for *netaies*.
11,256–61 *The secounde thynge ... from al synnes* reduces four sentences from the *Miroir* to one: *La seconde chose est vraie confession qui est le lavouer ou on se doit souvent laver. Le scripture dit en livre des rois que helisee le prophete commanda a naaman qui estoit mesel qui se lavast sept fois ou fleuve Jourdan pour estre netaie de la maladie. Et quant il fu illec lave il fu tout sain et tout net. Le fleuve Jourdan qui vault autant a dire comme russel de iugement segnifie confession ou len se doit iugier a grant doleur de cuer et a grant repentance sique un russel de larmes lui coure par le conduit des yeulx. Aussi sera le mesel gavi et netaie. Cest le pecheur sil se lave sept fois cest a dire de tous peches.*

11,261–3 Bernard, *Epistolae*, 113.4 (*Opera* 7, 289).
11,268–72 Numbers 21.8–9.
11,286–7 Ecclesiasticus 9.10–11.
11,287–8 1 Corinthians 15.33.
11,291–5 Whiting V10 (There may not go out of the vat but what is therein).
11,294–5 Luke 6.45, Matthew 12.34.
11,301–3 Jeremias 9.21.
11,306–7 Whiting S52 (As strong as Samson), D26 (As holy as David), S460 (As wise as Solomon); Hassell S34, S24. Cf. ll. 5306, 10176.
11,310–12 Jerome, *Adversus Jovinianum*, 2.8 (PL 23, col. 310). St Jerome's observation is reinforced in the *Miroir* by reference to the practices of ancient philosophers: *Dont les anciens philosophes senfuirent es lieux lointains et desers pource quilz ne peussent veoir ne oir ne sentir chose qui fust delectable par quoy la force de leurs cuers samoliast ne par quoy ilz perdissent leur chastete. Les autres parce quilz ne fussent empechies de penser a philosophie se creverent les yeulx adcequilz ne veissent chose qui les peust retraire de leur contemplacion. Doncques les sens corporelz sont aussi comme les chevaulz qui courent sans frain siquilz trebuchent leur seigneur mais le cuer chaste les tient au frain de raison.*
11,312–16 Whiting C125, s.v. 1484 (For overmoche mete and drynke alyghteth the fyre of lecherye). *kyndelynge*: 'material for lighting fire' (*alumailles*). Not recorded by MED in this sense. The earliest citation in OED is 1513. The English conflates three sentences of the *Miroir*, omitting the Pauline reference: *Le quart degree est aspresce de vie cest mettre la char soubz pie qui est rebelle a lesprit si comme dit saint pol. Qui veut oster le feu de luxure il convient oster la buche et les alumailles qui nourricent ce feu. Ce sont les delices et les aises du corps qui embrasent et alument le feu de luxure et corrompent chastete.*
11,316–17 Bernard, *Sermo ad Clericos de Conversione*, 21.37 (*Opera* 4, 113). Cf. *Summa Virtutum*, 9.226. Cf. ll. 11,915–6. In the French Bernard's statement is followed by a reference to Jeremias 13: *Le scripture dit que le brayel Iheremie le prophete pourrist deles leaue. Cest chastete qui est significe par le braiel pourrist deles leaue des delices.*
11,320–2 Daniel 1.3–20, 3. *grete mete*, that is, coarse fare (*grosses viandes*).
11,330–1 Whiting A167 (One rotten apple rots the sound).

11,333–4 Psalm 17.26–7.
11,337–9 Proverbs 13.20.
11,343–5 2 Kings 13.1–14. *Aman*, that is, Amnon, is so spelled in the French MSS. After *hirre* the French briefly recounts the story of Joseph and Potiphar's Wife (Genesis 39): *La dame Ioseph quant elle le trouva seul a seul elle le voult faire pecher avec elle mais il sen fui comme sage et la laissa.*
11,345–6 1 Corinthians 6.18.
11,349–51 Genesis 19.15–17.
11,353–5 Whiting P323 (The pot goes so long to the water that at last it comes home broken), B623 (The butterfly and the candle); Hassell P29, P240; Tilley F394 (The fly [moth] that plays too long in the candle singes its wings at last).
11,363–5 Ecclesiasticus 33.29. Cf. Whiting I6 (Idleness is the nurse of the vices), S392, s.v. 1449 (Sloth is the mother [mistress] of vice); Hassell O54; Tilley I13.
11,365–6 Ephesians 4.27.
11,367–70 Jerome, *Epistola ad Rusticum*, 11 (PL 22, col. 1078).
11,370–2 Ezechiel 16.49. Under the influence of this text patristic and medieval commentators often associated *the synne of Sodom* with gluttony and sloth. See Boswell, *Christianity*, 98, citing Augustine, *De Nuptiis et Concupiscentia*, 2.19 (PL 44, col. 456) and Cassian, *De Coenobiorum Institutis*, 5.6 (PL 49, cols 217–18). Cf. also Peter Cantor, *Verbum Abbreviatum*, 138 (PL 205, col. 333).
11,380–3 Job 21.13.
11,386–7 Ambrose, *De Obitu Valentiniani Imperatoris*, 32 (PL 16, col. 1369).
11,388–90 Isidore, *Sententiae*, 3.7.1 (PL 83, cols 671–2).
11,392 *approprid*: 'supported' (*apuiee*). Not recorded by MED in this sense. Cf. *Ayen* 207/19 and *VV* 229/19.
11,393–6 Mark 11.24.
11,396–8 James 1.6.
11,402–4 Psalms 27.7, 36.3.
11,404–5 Psalm 56.2.
11,408 Matthew 7.8. Cf. Whiting S136 (Seek and you shall find); Hassell C116.
11,413 *Fele that thowe aske wisly* misconstrues the French: *Sens, que tu demandes sagement*. The translator took *sens* for a verb rather than a noun, overlooking its repetition from the previous line (*with*).
11,415–17 James 4.3.

11,418 After *theyme* the French continues as follows: *sicomme firent les deux apostres saint Jehan et saint Jaques qui demanderent que lun deulx seist a la dextre de dieu et lautre a la senestre en son roiaume. Il ne demanderent mie sagement mais sembloit estre grant folie et pource respondi nostre seigneur et leur dit vous ne scaues que vous demandes.*
11,419–21 Luke 18.10–12.
11,439–48 Augustine, *Enarrationes in Psalmos*, 37.14 (PL 36, col. 404), 62.6 (PL 36, cols 751–2). The attribution to Ambrose of ll. 11,445–8 is erroneous, as Gradon points out (*Ayen* 209/9–12*n*).
11,448–51 John 15.16, 16.23.
11,453–6 Matthew 6.33.
11,456–7 Cf. ODEP, 273 (He that hopes to go before Follows the lord).
11,472–3 Psalm 33.10.
11,474–5 Cf. Whiting G305 (The more Gold a man has the more he covets).
11,475–6 *moste pepill*, that is, the largest household (*qui plus a de maisine plus lui fault de viande*). Cf. Whiting M790 (They need much that have much); Hassell P208. Its source is Boethius, *De Consolatione Philosophiae*, 2, pr. 5.
11,477–8 Jerome, *Epistolae*, 53.10 (PL 22, col. 549).
11,484–8 Matthew 6.6.
11,488–93 Cyprian, *Liber de Oratione Dominica*, 31 (PL 4, col. 539). *putte, depart, from his herte* translates *departir du cuer*. See above 'Introduction,' 21.
11,493–4 Isidore, *Sententiae*, 3.7.7–8 (PL 83, col. 673).
11,494–6 Augustine, *In Joannis Evangelium Tractatus*, 9.13 (PL 35, col. 1464). *to meve and to bete the lippes*: 'talk' (*mouvoir ne debatre les leures*), expanding on Augustine's *strepitus oris*.
11,496–9 Cf. Whiting C428 (Corn and chaff), F299 (The flour is gone, now sell the bran), S365 (When one looks on the outer skin he knows little what is within).
11,500–1 *Godde cursed ... but levys*: Matthew 21.19.
11,506 *giberisshe* (*patroullas*) does not appear in MED. The earliest occurrence cited in OED is 1554.
11,514–16 John 4.24.
11,517–18 Psalm 140.2.
11,522–3 *goode knowleche*, that is, favorable information.
11,525 *hee doothe evil his erande*, that is, he conducts his affairs poorly (*il fait mauvaisement sa besongne*).

11,525–6 Cf. Whiting F460 (Who sends a fool abides a fool), F410 (A fool's errand may not speed).
11,528–9 Psalm 129.1.
11,529–30 Augustine, *Enarrationes in Psalmos*, 37.14 (PL 36, col. 404). Eyeskip by anticipation accounts for B's unnecessary repetition of the phrase *of the herte*.
11,532–5 Gregory, *Moralia*, 33.22 (PL 76, col. 701). *feted and polisshed woordis* translates *paroles afaities et polies*.
11,538 Two sentences anticipating the biblical allusions in ll. 11,538–43 have been omitted – or possibly lost in the exemplar – after *theefes*: *Aussi devons nous souvent crier a dieu contre le feu de luxure quil nous donne leaue de larmes pour destaindre ce feu quil nembrase nos cuers. Aussi redevons nous crier contre le flos des mauvaises couvetises et des mauvaises pensees qui sourdent souvent on cuer que le cuer ne perisse par consentement*.
11,538–40 Psalm 68.2.
11,540–3 Matthew 8.25.
11,571–2 After *commandement of Godde* a paragraph of hypothetical objections to the preceding statement and the author's response to them is omitted. Cf. *Ayen* 213/31–214/23 and *VV* 236/23–237/9.
11,580–1 Matthew 21.13, Luke 19.46.
11,583–6 Augustine, *In Joannis Evangelium Tractatus*, 7.1 (PL 35, col. 1442).
11,590–2 Matthew 21.12.
11,609–12 Psalm 21.7
11,617–18 Job 1.21.
11,618–19 Pseudo-Bernard, *Meditationes Piisimae De Cognitione Humanae Conditionis*, 3.8 (PL 184, col. 490). Cf. Job 13.28.
11,622–6 Esther 14.2, 16.
11,632–5 1 Timothy 2.9.
11,638 *burgeisesse* is not recorded by MED in this form.
11,638–44 1 Timothy 2.9. On the stag as a symbol of pride, see Hassig, *Bestiaries*, 40 and *n*3. *forhede set vppe ne popped* translates *effrontees ne arbelestres*.
11,644–7 1 Corinthians 11.5–15. *evil sette*: 'disedified' (*mal edifie*). Not recorded by MED in this sense.
11,647–9 1 Timothy 2.10.
11,649–55 Ambrose, *In Epistolam B Pauli ad Timotheum Primam*, 2 (PL 17, cols 467–8).
11,656–61 Augustine, *Sermo CCCLVIII*, 6 (PL 39, col. 1589) based on

Tobias 12.8. The faulty expansion of a tag on final g may account for the reading of *thyngys* in B. The error is repeated in l. 11,738.
11,661–3 Ambrose, *Expositio in Psalmum CXVIII*, 22.5 (PL 15, col. 1513).
11,663–6 Isidore, *Sententiae*, 3.7.12 (PL 83, col. 674).
11,666–70 Pseudo-Bernard, *Liber de modo bene vivendi*, 49 (PL 184, col. 1271).
11,670–2 Lamentations 3.41.
11,674–6 Cf. Isaias 1.15.
11,676 After *synne* the French reads: *Dont il dit par le prophete Quant vous multiplieres vos oroisons je nen oiray nulles. Car vos mains sont toutes plaines de sang. Qui sont ceulx qui ont les mains plaines de sang fors ceulx qui escorchent les poures gens qui sont desoubs eulx et leur tolent le leur a force. Ilz ont les mains toutes plaines du sang aux poures gens. Car ils leur tolent leur vie et leur soustenance par leur couvoitise et par leur rappine et en font les grans oultrages et mengnent les lais morseaulx tous senglans dont ilz paieront dur escot en lautre siecle se le scripture ne ment qui dit que dieu requerra le sang aux poures de leurs mains. Doncques il convient quilz rendent ou quilz pendent. Car sicomme on dit Ou rendre ou pendre. Et pource ne oit pas dieu teles gens. Car ilz nen sont mie dignes qui veult doncques estre oy ne viengne pas devant dieu lespee traicte ne mains senglantes ne mains uuides. Cest a dire en volente de pecher ne en tache de desloiaute ne uuit de bonnes oeures. Car ainsi le dit nostre seigneur en le scripture et dit tu ne tapperas pas devant moy mains uuides. Celui vient mains uuides devant nostre seigneur qui le vient requerre sans lui faire present de bonnes oeures.*
11,676–9 Matthew 25.1–13.
11,684–8 Matthew 21.22.
11,688–93 James 5.14–16.
11,693–5 Exodus 17.8–13.
11,695–7 *Glossa Ordinaria* 1.318.e, a gloss on James 5.16.
11,697–8 Ecclesiasticus 35.21.
11,699 *A goode persone*, but French *une bonne vieille* (D *une bonne femme ancienne*).
11,704–6 A paraphrase of Proverbs 15.29.
11,706–10 The statement of the *hooly man* is attributed to Ambrose in V and in fact derives from his *Commentaria in Epistolam ad Romanos*, 15.108 (PL 17, col. 177).
11,712–14 Matthew 18.19.

11,736–8 Proverbs 22.6. Whiting M308 (What a man learned in his youth will keep best in his eld); Tilley Y42. *thyng*: cf. ll. 11,656–61*n*.
11,739–41 Whiting C375 (All that a young colt is taught he will hold); Hassell P242. The proverb rhymes in French. Cf. l. 10,952–3*n*.
11,741–2 Whiting S262 (A shoe holds its first form).
11,757–94 A summary of the traditional teaching of the *bona matrimonii*, that is, *fides* (ll. 11,757–75), *sacramentum* (ll. 11,775–91), and *proles* (ll. 11,791–4).
11,762–3 Genesis 2.24.
11,769–71 Titus 2.4–5.
11,772–3 Whiting C125, s.v. 1484: *For overmoche mete and drynke alyghteth the fyre of lecherye*. Cf. ll. 11,312–6 and *n*.
11,780 *that was* should obviously read 'that is' or 'that is to say,' the translator's customary translation of French *cest*. Possibly the error is of scribal origin.
11,791–813 On the legitimate reasons for marital relations – chiefly offspring, avoidance of incontinence, and the payment of marital debt – enunciated in medieval theology see Payer, *Bridling of Desire*, 84–97; Makowski, 'Conjugal Debt'; Brundage, 'Sexual Equality,' 69–70; and Cadden, *Sex Difference*, 246.
11,793 The end of one sentence and the beginning of the next have been lost here: *Et dois scavoir que en trois cas puet on faire loevre de mariage sans pechie et y puet on avoir grant merite quant a lame. Le premier cas est quant on fait celle oevre en entencion davoir ligne a dieu servir, et en tele intencion fu mariage premierement establi.*
11,814–31 Ecclesiastical and canonistic attitudes toward marital intercourse to satisfy lust or for the sake of pleasure are discussed by Brundage, 'Carnal Delight'; Payer, *Bridling of Desire*, 118–29; and Cadden, *Sex Difference*, 247.
11,821–5 Cf. Jerome, *Adversus Jovinianum*, 1.49 (PL 23, cols 293–4). See Noonan, *Contraception*, 47–8, and Brundage, 'Sexual Equality,' 67 and *n*14, for the Stoic origins of the views of the Church Fathers and the canonists on this matter.
11,827–30 Cf. Augustine, *De Bono Coniugali*, 10 and 11 (PL 40, cols 381–2); Noonan, *Contraception*, 119–39, 161–2, 172–5; Payer, 'Medieval Regulations,' 359–60, and *Bridling of Desire*, 76–9.
11,833–6 For ecclesiastical prohibitions against intercourse during menstrual periods see Caesarius of Arles, *Sermones*, 44.7 (CC 103, 199); Noonan, *Contraception*, 35, 93, 165; Payer, 'Medieval Regulations,' 368, *Sex and Penitentials*, 25–6, and *Bridling of Desire*, 106–9;

Makowski, 'Conjugal Debt,' 109; Flandrin, *Temps pour Embraser*, 46–54; and Cadden, *Sex Difference*, 268. The prohibition goes back to Leviticus 18.19, 29, and Ezechiel 18.6, 9.
11,843–52 For predetermined periods when sexual intercouse was to be avoided see Caesarius of Arles, *Sermones*, 44.3, 7 (CC 103, 196–7, 199); Payer, 'Medieval Regulations,' 362–7, and *Bridling of Desire*, 98–101, 102–5; Flandrin, *Temps pour Embraser*, 10–33; Cadden, *Sex Difference*, 267. The statement attributed to Augustine is actually a paraphrase of Caesarius, whose sermon was attributed to Augustine in the Middle Ages.
11,852–5 Cf. Caesarius of Arles, *Sermones*, 44.7 (CC 103, 199); Payer, 'Medieval Regulations,' 368–9; Cadden, *Sex Difference*, 268–9.
11,855–7 This observation cannot be found in *Physiologus*. It goes back to Aristotle, *Historia animalium*, 546b, and is found in Thomas Cantimpratensis, 4.33.116–17, and Bartholomaeus Anglicus, *De Proprietatibus*, 18.43. *with her birdeyn*, that is, with child (*prains*).
11,862–7 For ecclesiastical views on marital relations in consecrated places see Payer, *Bridling of Desire*, 101–2.
11,872–6 1 Timothy 5.3, 1 Corinthians 7.8–9. Whiting W162 (It is better to wed than to burn).
11,877–8 *synne of lecherie* loses the Pauline metaphor embodied in the French *feu de luxure* 'fire of lechery.' Cf. *Ayen* 225/19 *uere* and *VV* 226/24 *fier*.
11,889 *profession*: DNPV *profession* (P is corrected from *confession*), ACQRSU *confession*.
11,893–7 Tubach 5008. The reference is to *Physiologus*, 28 (Carmody, 49–50). See also Bartholomaeus Anglicus, *De Proprietatibus*, 12.35; White, *Bestiary*, 145–6; Rowland, *Animals*, 46; Curley, *Physiologus*, 57–8; McCulloch, *Medieval Latin*, 178. The tradition appears to originate with Aristotle, *Historia animalium*, 613a.
11,900–3 Judith 8.5.
11,903–7 1 Timothy 5.11–14. *to miche spekeres* translates *trop parlantes*.
11,909–12 Luke 2.36–7.
11,913–15 1 Timothy 5.6.
11,915–17 Bernard, *Sermo ad Clericos de Conversione*, 21.37 (*Opera* 4, 113). Cf. ll. 11,316–7.
11,921–3 B's reading, *To this state alsoo longeth meke cloothynge and state and not prowde ne besye*, results from an eyeskip. The French reads *A cest estate aussi appartient humble habit et non pas orgueilleux ne curieux*, and so forth.

11,923–5 Judith 8.6–8.
11,937 Although *virginite* is the reading of the *Miroir* MSS, it is probably erroneous. *Ayen* 227/13 *dignite* and *VV* 252/2 *worþinesse* appear to reflect a sounder *Somme* tradition.
11,938–9 Pseudo-Jerome, *Epistola ad Paulum et Eustochium*, 5 (PL 30, cols 126–7). Its author is actually Paschasius Radbertus. Cf. *Summa Virtutum*, 9.464–5. The simile derives from Matthew 22.30.
11,946–8 Matthew 13.44.
11,951–6 Matthew 22.30, Luke 20.35–6, Mark 12.25.
11,958–60 Wisdom 4.1. French readings vary: NSU *clarte*, CPR *charite*, V *chaste*, AQ *quand elle est clere*, D *charite ou clarte*. On *clerenes* meaning 'glory' see MED, s.v. *clernesse* n., 2b.
11,965–7 Cf. Jerome, *Epistolae*, 125.20 (PL 22, col. 1084). A similar statement is attributed to Gregory in *Summa Virtutum*, 9.441–2.
11,968–70 Matthew 23.27.
11,977–9 Gregory, *Homiliarum in Evangelia*, 1.1 (PL 76, col. 1079), quoting James 4.4. The *Myrour* 190/7–8 attributes the statement to Jerome.
11,979–81 1 John 2.15.
11,981–2 Galatians 1.10.
11,985 *curiosite*, that is, elegance of workmanship. The earliest reference to clothes in MED is 1450.
11,988–12,000 Bernard, *Epistolae*, 113.3 (*Opera* 7, 289). *porple*, that is, purple robes. *caroyne*, but French *conscience*, correctly following the Latin (*conscientia*).
12,001–3 Psalm 44.14. A reference to David has been omitted after *blisse: si comme dit David.*
12,006–10 Jerome, *Adversus Jovinianum*, 1.13 (PL 23, cols 241–2).
12,016–18 1 Corinthians 15.33. Whiting S602 (Evil speeches (words) destroy (corrupt) good thews).
12,018–21 Martin of Braga, *Formula Honestae Vitae*, 3 (Barlow, 243).
12,026 Whiting C100 (The tame cat burns oft its skin but not the wild cat).
12,027–30 Canticle of Canticles 2.2. *Myrour* 192/25–6*n* observes: 'This becomes the structural metaphor for the rest of the material on Virgins. The source for such an exposition is presumably Bernard's exposition of this verse in *Sermones in Cantica Canticorum*, 48.1–2' (*Opera* 2, 67–8).
12,033–40 John 13.23, 21.7. For John's virginity Gradon (*Ayen* 230/19*n*) cites Mombrizio, *Sanctuarium*, vol. 2, 60–1. The more likely source is Jacobus, *Legenda aurea*, chap. 9 (Graesse, 56).

12,050–1 Cf. Augustine, *De Mendacio*, 1.7, 19 (PL 40, cols 495, 514); Ambrose, *De Lapsu Virginum*, 4.11 (PL 16, col. 370).
12,052–4 St Lucy's retort to the tyrant (Paschasius) – *Si invitam me feceris violari, castistas michi duplicabitur ad coronam* – is taken either directly from the *Passio Sanctae Luciae* (Gradon, *Ayen* 230/33–5*n*) or its derivative in Jacobus, *Legenda aurea*, chap. 4 (Graesse, 31). It was frequently cited to underscore the voluntary nature of virginity, which was not necessarily destroyed by rape (ll. 12,050–1). Cf. Gratian, *Decretum*, C.32.5.1 (Freidberg 1, col. 1132). For the *corone of blisse*, see l. 12,177 and the note to ll. 12,147–78.
12,054–6 Jerome, *De Perpetua Virginitate Beatae Mariae*, 20 (PL 23, col. 214). The statement is attributed to Isidore in *Summa Virtutum*, 9.516–17.
12,060–6 Bernard, *Sermones in Laudibus Virginis Matris*, 1.5 (*Opera* 4, 17–18).
12,069–71 Luke 1.29.
12,081–4 Genesis 34.1–2.
12,088–90 Matthew 25.1–13.
12,108–11 Augustine, *De Sancta Virginitate*, 29 (PL 40, col. 412).
12,115–16 Bernard, *Epistolae*, 322.2 (*Opera* 8, 258), 109.2 (*Opera* 7, 281).
12,120 The subject of the sentence has been lost: *Dont les foles vierges pource quelles ne implirent mie leurs lampes de ceste oyle furent forcloses des nopces.*
12,123–7 Peter Lombard, *Sententiae*, 3.27.5–6 (PL 192, col. 815). The attribution to Augustine is erroneous. Cf. ll. 4040–6*n*.
12,135–7 Bernard, *Sermones super Cantica Canticorum*, 20.4 (*Opera* 1, 115–16). Cf. *Dives* 3.20.
12,145–6 1 Timothy 1.5.
12,147–78 The account of the rewards of the blest in terms of fruits and crowns is taken from Matthew 13.8, 23, and Apocalypse 2.10, 4.10. The application of the numbers thirty, sixty, and one hundred – originally a method of counting by the fingers – to the estates of marriage, widowhood, and virginity was first made by Jerome, *Adversus Jovinianum*, 1.3 (PL 23, cols 223–4). Virginity was regarded as the perfection of chastity and deserving of a special reward. Hence the reference in l. 12,176 to a *speciall coroune*, the so-called *aureola* or coronet, bestowed on virgins in addition to the ordinary crown of the blest. Payer, *Bridling of Desire*, 195, 256 *n*81, cites Alexander of Hales and Thomas Aquinas in support of this view. For a comprehensive study of exegetical interpretations of the Matthew text see Quacquarelli, *Il Triplice frutto*, especially 43–97. *a figure bon gire,*

rounde (l. 12,166): *une figure ronde*. So all MSS except V, which reads *une figure longue*, a corrupt reading that must have been in the French exemplar. In V the word is split, *lon* appearing at the end of one line and *gue* at the beginning of the next. The translator failed to realize this, and, trying to make sense of what he thought were two words, he converted *lon* to *bon* and *gue* to *gire* 'well-turned,' hence 'round.' Cf. MED, s.v. *giren* v. *above opon* (l. 12,176), a curious tautology noted above in the 'Introduction,' 21, translates the French *pardesus*.

12,181–7 Apocalypse 19.8, 5.9, 14.4.

12,207–8 Leviticus 11.44.

12,208 Whiting L455 (Such lord such meiny); Hassell S56; Morawski 165.

12,210 *dedified or dedicat* renders French *dedie*.

12,222–5 1 Timothy 3.2, 8–10.

12,225–33 Exodus 12.11, 28.39–43. The French reads *Ceste chastete fu signifiee en la vieille loy la ou dieu commanda a ceulx qui devoient mengier de laigniel qui signifioit le corps ihesu crist quilz chaindissent bien leurs rains. La cainture dont les menistres de sainte eglise doivent bien caindre les rains est chastete qui restraint la lecherie de la char. rains* (*reynes*) was evidently read as *mains* (B *handis*).

12,262–3 *And whan ... that is þerin*: *Et quant le mirouer est ort on voit bien la tache de l'ordure qui est dedens*.

12,270–2 Gregory, *Cura Pastoralis*, 2.2 (PL 77, col. 27).

12,272–3 Ecclesiasticus 34.4.

12,274–80 Paschasius Radbertus, *De Corpore et Sanguine Domini*, 12 (PL 120, col. 1310).

12,282 *edifie þe bounte be example of goode liffyng*, that is, the good priest can uplift communicants by his virtuous example. The French reads *et la bonte edifier par exemple de bonne vie*.

12,311–51 A version of Tubach 1663 (Devils Render Accounts) deriving from *Vitae Patrum*, 5.5 (PL 73, cols 885–6). Cf. also Jacobus, *Legenda aurea*, chap. 37 (Graesse, 610).

12,355–7 Matthew 4.1.

12,362–6 Cf. *Fasciculus Morum*, 7.19.58–9.

12,370 *famined*: the aphetic form is not recorded by MED.

12,376–7 Galatians 2.19.

12,381–4 Galatians 6.14.

12,385 There is a long, possibly deliberate, omission after *abhominable*: *Il vouloit dire: tout aussi comme le monde le tenoit pour vil et pour*

abhominable sicomme on fait le prisonnier aussi avoit il le monde pour vil et pour abhominable si comme on a celui qui est cruxefie pour son mal fait.
12,388–9 *be dede ne be desire,* but French *par amour et par desir.* Perhaps an eyeskip with the preceding line.
12,389–1 Philippians 3.20.
12,394–6 Matthew 19.21.
12,396–9 Tubach 4009. Its source is *Vitae Patrum,* 5.583 (PL 73, col. 891).
12,399–401 Matthew 5.3.
12,405 *assende in the hylle of perfeccion: monter en la montaigne de perfection.*
12,405–8 Genesis 19.17.
12,413–15 Genesis 19.26.
12,416 *þat* is superfluous and comes from a slavish rendition of the French: *La femme loth signifie ceulx qui puisquilz sont issus du siecle et sont entres en religion par volente et par desirier qui leurs corp ont en cloistre et leurs cuers sont ou siecle.*
12,420 Whiting S758 (as cold as stone), S763 (as hard as stone); Hassell P176, P174.
12,422 *withoute moisture of pytee and devocion*: ACNPQSU *sans humeur* (CD *humeurs*) *de pitee et devocion,* V *sans pite et sans humeur et sans devocion,* and R (which possibly preserves the correct reading) *sans lamour de pite et de devocion.*
12,429–31 Luke 17.32.
12,435–8 Luke 9.62.
12,450–1 Whiting S873 (To set the sullow before the oxen).
12,456–8 Philippians 3.13.
12,460 *Montioye*: *montioye,* the so-called Mons Gaudii, Hill of Rama, which affords pilgrims the first sight of Jerusalem. The word does not appear in MED with this meaning.
12,471 *fallyng,* that is, lapsing into sin (*cheoir*).
12,474 Matthew 5.8.
12,475–8 John 20.29.
12,478–81 1 Corinthians 13.12.
12,482 *that they shalle see*: a meaningless clause without MSS support that should perhaps be deleted. Possibly an eyeskip by anticipation (*shalle see*).
12,485–6 *fulle of the behaldyng of hym,* that is, filled with satisfaction at the sight of Him.

12,488–91 Isaias 64.4.
12,491–501 Anselm, *Proslogion*, 24–5 (PL 158, cols 239–40). *feture*: 'likeness, semblance.' Not recorded by MED in this sense. Cf. Godefroy, *faiture* n., translated by *VV* 271/44 as *likenesse* and *Ayen* 244/29 as *feture*. Anselm's original Latin reads *homuncio* 'manikin.'
12,518–19 *the whiche with sauoure and with grete swetnes of hert tasteth it* misconstrues the French: *qui est avecques saveur et avec grant douceur de cuer*.
12,521 *scriptures*: a defective reading in both the *Somme* and *Miroir* traditions. Cf. *Ayen* 245/31 and *VV* 245/31 *writinge*. Gradon notes a variant, 'creatures,' in the *Somme* tradition, which, as she rightly observes, 'makes better sense.' All the *Miroir* MSS read *scriptures*.
12,522 *be feithe*, but French, correctly, *par raison*. *worthinesses* renders French *poste* 'power.'
12,529 *vnordinat* (*desordonne*): 'in an abnormal condition, not functioning in a healthy manner,' that is, morally corrupted. *be syn* 'as the result of sin' has been added by the translator for the sake of clarity.
12,537–48 Genesis 28.12. Commenting on these lines in the *Somme le Roi*, Carruthers, 'L'Echelle de Jacob,' draws attention to the structural correspondence between the allegory of Jacob's ladder and the gifts of the Holy Ghost and the virtues. *obeying*: 'submissive, humble' (*humiliant*). MED, s.v. *obeien* v., 1g.
12,548–50 Tilley N195 (The more noble the more humble).
12,553–9 A literal translation of the French which also lacks a main verb: *Car les prodommes qui mainent vie dange en terre par leur saintete quant ilz sont montes au souverain degre de contemplacion ou le don de sapience maine celui qui doit estre joint a dieu quil en a oublie quanque est desoubz dieu pour la grant douceur que le cuer sent qui est ainsi ravi en dieu quil passe tous autres delis*.
12,567 *that it dredith the evil sperit* mistranslates *quil trait lesperit aval* (D adds *a soy*), that is, 'that it depresses the spirit.' *mal* may have been read for *aval*.
12,572–8 Psalm 35.9. The French reads *Mais quant ce venra a celle grant taverne ou le tavernier est si abandonne cest en la vie pardurable ou le dieu damour, de paix, de joie et de soulas sera si abandonne a chascun que tous en seront saoules si comme dit le psaultier car tous le desirs du cuer seront la acomplis*. B's addition of *haboundant* to *tauerner* is without MSS support; it is undoubtedly an eyeskip and should perhaps be deleted. *habaundoned* (l. 12,574) anglicizes the French verb *abandoner* meaning 'to lavish, be prodigal,' confusing it

with *abonder*. Godefroy, s.v. *abondoner, abonder*; AND, s.v. *abanduner, abunder*. MED *abounden* does not convey the meaning of the French verb. For a similar confusion see *Othea* 36/17–18.
12,578–80 Isaias 48.18, 66.12.
12,580–2 Psalm 35.9–10.
12,588–90 Augustine, *In Ioannis Evangelium Tractatus*, 17.8 (PL 35, col. 1915).
12,594–5 Wisdom 8.7.
12,598–9 Proverbs 3.18, 11.30.
12,609 A sentence has been lost or omitted after *wyne*: *Et quant il cuide boire le vin le vin le boit*.
12,612–13 Philippians 3.19.
12,630–2 Matthew 4.3.
12632–5 Genesis 3.1–6.
12,640 *kepeth the liff of holy pepill* misconstrues *regardent les vies des sains*. The translator's exemplar may have read *gardent*.
12,640–2 Wisdom 11.21.
12,646 *oftesythe*: *moult de fois*. Probably a scribal error, although it is possible that the translator, ignoring *moult* and reading *de fois* as *de sois*, rendered it as *of þe selfe*.
12,648–50 Augustine, *De Musica*, 6.16.51 (PL 32, col. 1189).
12,654–6 John 16.33.
12,657 *easeth* misconstrues French *assiet* 'seats,' confusing *asseoir* with *aisier* 'make comfortable.'
12,658–60 John 16.33. *empressed*: 'oppressed' (*empresses*). Cf. MED, s.v. *impressen* v., 2d.
12,660–2 Augustine, *Confessiones*, 1.1 (PL 32, col. 661).
12,662–5 1 Corinthians 10.4. *sur* was misread as, or confused with, *sus* in ll. 12,664, 12,665, and 12,676.
12,672–5 John 4.6.
12,679–80 *That welle feleth not the myre ne the erthe ne þe mares of this world* translates *celle fontaine ne sent mie le fanc ne la terre ne les mares de cestui monde. sanc* was evidently read for *fanc. ne the erthe* may be a scribal omission. Gradon (*Ayen* 250/36*n*) glosses *mares* as 'waters.'
12,704 *tormentis*: 'tournaments' (*tournoiement*) which preserves the metaphor of the previous lines. For the form see l. 1698 and *n*.
12,705–6 *stedfasteth*, translating French *conferme*, is not recorded by MED in the sense of 'restores, refreshes.' Cf. *Ayen* 252/16 and *VV* 279/31 *conforteþ*.

12,723 *reeson* is doubtless an eyeskip (l. 12,722) rather than a deliberate alteration of the text. The French reads correctly *droite foy*.
12,724–7 Romans 12.3.
12,727–8 Proverbs 3.21.
12,729 *self-willed* is first recorded by MED in 1471.
12,730 *flette*: 'be deflected' (*flexisses*). Cf. *Ayen* 253/3 *flechchi*.
12,731 *leve thyn owne witte*: Proverbs 23.4.
12,732–5 Romans 16.26. *remeve*: 'set aside' (*flexir*).
12,737–9 *thoo þat seketh þe molle in mollehilles or too hym þat seketh þe skyn in the egge or to hym þat seketh þe cloude in the resshe*. This passage is corrupt in the French MSS of the *Somme* and the *Miroir*, and has been misconstrued by the translators of B, *Ayen* (253/10–12), and *VV* (280/30–2). The comparisons should appear as 'the meal in the cakes,' 'the chicken in the egg,' and 'the knot in the bullrush.' B's *cloude* seems to show confusion between *neu* and *nue*. In her note to these lines (*Ayen* 253/10–12) Gradon observes that the 'illustrations are designed to characterize the officious or over-anxious person who is concerned to find what is only potentially present.' Whiting F113 (to seek the fell [straw, hair] in the egg), K98 (to seek the knot in the rush), and M812 (to seek mussels among froshes: Caxton's version of *moulle* as *ruissoles*). See also *VV* 280/30–2*n* for a suggested reconstruction of the French original.
12,744–56 Ecclesiasticus 18.30–1. *set the vppon goode reeson* translates *rend bonne raison*.
12,749–50 *whan he feleth hym overcomyn to hym* mistranslates the French *quant il se rend a lui vaincu*. *send* was evidently read for *rend*.
12,751–4 1 Peter 2.11.
12,762–7 Hebrews 11.8–16.
12,770 *costeth*: 'afflicts, troubles' (*grieve*). Not recorded by MED as a verb in this sense.
12,786–8 Martin of Braga, *Formula Honestae Vitae*, 3 (Barlow, 242). Cf. Seneca, *Epistolae*, 18.3–4.
12,794–5 Proverbs 10.19, 17.27.
12,796–7 *In fewe woordes* reproduces the defective reading of the French MSS *en peu de paroles*. The aphorism which is taken from Peraldus, as Craun, *Lies, Slander*, 50–1, notes, reads '*In pondere verborum probatio existit humane vitae*.' The interpretation of this dictum in ll. 12,797–9 depends upon the metaphor of weight. The attribution to Jerome is apparently incorrect. The *Somme* tradition is similarly corrupt. Cf. *Ayen* 254/35 and *VV* 286/20–7 and notes.
12,799 *the crie of the tonge* attempts to make sense of the defective

reading of the French MSS *a la lengue* (D *langue*). Originally the *Miroir* must have read *a lengle* 'at an angle.' Bartholomaeus Anglicus, *De Proprietatibus*, 18.87, observes that *swyne ... holden here heed asyde when they ben seke*. His source is Pliny, *Historia Naturalis*, 7.26–7.

12,799–801 Ecclesiasticus 28.29.

12,804–5 Whiting M555 (To be like a mill without a sluice).

12,809–14 Proverbs 17.14.

12,816–20 Ecclesiasticus 28.29–30.

12,825–7 Psalm 38.2.

12,834 The end of the sentence has been lost here: *car verite acorde lentencion du cuer et la parole de la bouche si que la bouche ne dit fors verite si comme elle est on cuer*.

12,847–8 Cf. *Fasciculus Morum*, Book 3, chap. 3. ll. 18–19 (Wenzel, 160) and the *Treatise on the Ten Commandments* (Royster, 'Treatise,' 26), where the statement is attributed to Augustine. It is found in Peraldus 2.9.2.6 without attribution to Augustine. *Mysseherer* does not appear in MED with this meaning. See, however, *misheren* v., 1a. OED cites *mishearing* 'sinful hearing or listening' from 1483.

12,855–6 Seneca, *De Beneficiis*, 6.30.3.

12,859–61 Ecclesiasticus 28.28.

12,883–7 Luke 16.19. *actaignyauntly*: 'forcibly' (*ataignamment*). Godefroy, s.v. *ataignamment*. Not recorded by MED (*atteinauntli*) in this sense.

12,891 *arayed*: 'covered with a pall' (*paree*). The precise meaning is not recorded by MED.

12,894–5 Cf. ll. 2318–9 on the peacock's tail. For the cock's pride in his comb see Bartholomaeus Anglicus, *De Proprietatibus*, 12.17.

12,900–1 Ecclesiasticus 11.4.

12,901–2 1 Timothy 2.9.

12,916–17 Martin of Braga, *Formula Honestae Vitae*, 4 (Barlow, 245).

12,919 *enfantesied*: 'childish' (*enfantis*). Not recorded by MED.

12925–8 1 Corinthians 13.11.

12,929–30 1 Corinthians 14.20.

12,940–3 Luke 21.34. After *drinke* the French adds *et de mengier*.

12,952 *is mesured amonge*, that is, sets bounds to (the other virtues), translating the French *est mesure entre*. Cf. *Ayen* 260/20 and *VV* 288/20. Not recorded by MED in this precise sense.

12,971–2 Matthew 5.9.

12,972–4 Augustine, *De Sermone Domini in Monte*, 1.2 (PL 34, col. 1233); *De Genesi contra Manichaeos*, 1.20 (PL 34, col. 188).

12,975–7 2 Corinthians 13.11.
12,986 Luke 2.14.
12,997–9 Philippians 4.7.
13,000–1 1 Corinthians 2.9.
13,006–9 On the dates and authorships of the *Miroir* and *Somme*, see above, the 'Introduction,' 7–8. The date 1289 for 1279 is an error common to the Y redaction.

Glossary

The glossary is drawn from a complete, computerized index of some 9,500 different words and forms of words in the edited text. It is therefore selective only and presupposes some knowledge of Middle English. Its aim is to explain only the more unfamiliar words and senses and to record unusual forms and spellings that may check the reader or be of philological interest. Latin words and phrases are not included. A plus sign is added to line references of words, forms, or phrases occurring more than three times. Emendations from MS B are indicated by an asterisk. An *n* is placed after a citation to draw attention to a comment in the explanatory notes. All abbreviations are conventional. In the alphabetical arrangement, *ȝ* follows *g* and *þ* follows *t*. When *y* and *v* represent vowels, they are treated as *i* and *u*, respectively; as consonants, they occupy their usual places.

a *prep.* of 7167

a, an *weakened form of* **have** 345, 380, 1508+

aage *see* **age** *n.*

aageth *see* **age** *v.*

abaieth, abayeth *pr. 3 sg.* barks at 3876, 6083

abasshed, basshed *pp.* dismayed, perplexed 953, ashamed 3047, 8334, afraid 3363

abateth *pr. 3 sg.* strikes down, destroys 1472

abaundoneth, habandoneth, baundon *pr. 3 sg.* indulges in fornication, yields to opposite sex 5195, yields or surrenders 12,790, gives (himself) freely 12,020; *pr. 3 pl.* **abaundoneth, bandoune** permit (themselves), give (themselves) freely 5803, devote (themselves) to 9648, yield (their bodies) to the opposite sex 11,774; *pa. t. 2 sg.* **abaundoned** 2695; *pp.* **abaundoned** freely given 2701, **habaundoned** lavish, prodigal 12,574*n*

abeye *v.* pay dearly 3507
abhominable *adj.* detestable 2926–7, 2927–8, 3792+
abhominacion *n.* abhorrence, detestation 10,069, 10,930, 11,628+; disgust 10788
abide, abyde, bide *v.* remain, stay, dwell 1189, 2843, 9890+, await, wait for 1897, 5385, 5409+, endure 8727, 8918, 9699+, wait 11,000, continue 11,886; *imp.* **abide** 3972; *pr. 2 sg.* **abidest** 1900; *pr. 3 sg.* **abide, abideth, abydeth, abiteth** 2916, 3457, 7638+, delays, hesitates 4152; *pr. 1 pl.* **abide** 594, 2092, 4259+; *pr. 3 pl.* **abide, abyde, abideth** 5423, 6612, 9748+; *pa. t.* **abode, aboode** 1007, 4923, 9906; *pp.* **abiden** 10,531; ~ **faste** stand fast, remain firm 8017
abidyng(e), abydynge *vbl. n.* delay 9910, continuance 5029, 10,014
abovesubstancial(l) *adj.* transcending material substance, spiritual 7888*n*, 7892, 7898
abstene *pr. 3 sg.* abstain, refrain (from) 2557
abstinence *n.* forbearance, self-denial 5264, 6287, 6335+
abstinent *adj.* abstemious in eating or drinking 2556
abusage *n.* sexual misconduct 957*n*
abusion *n.* outrage, wrong 4954
acciduell *adj.* slothful 4257*n*
accorde *v.* be in harmony or agreement 9173; *pr. 3 sg.* **accordeth, acordeth** agrees 5908, reconciles, brings into harmony 9236, 12,833; *pr. 3 pl.* **acordeth** 9169; *pp.* **acorded** 9252; ~ **togyder** mutually agree 11,713
acommpt(e), acompt(e), commpt(e), compt(e) *n.* account, reckoning 571, 5813, 5815+
acorde *n.* harmony 6161, 6066; **at oon** ~ in complete agreement 9270, **drawe (theyme) too theyre** ~ win (them) over, bring under (their) influence 5832
acostomed *pp.* wont, used 10,823
acroched *pp.* acquired on credit 7910*n*
actaignyauntly *adv.* forcibly 12885*n*
actiue *adj.* given to worldly activity 11,145, 11,167, 11,169
acursed *see* **curse**
adamant stone *phr.* diamond 10,404*
adopcion *n.* adoption 7520, 7524, 7530+
aduertised *pp.* informed officially 5239
adulacion *n.* false praise, flattery 1073
aduocat, advocat *n.* advocate, pleader 2352, intercessor 7403, 7456, 8389; *pl.* **advoccates, aduocattys, avocatis** 2129, 5878, attorneys 4667
aduoutery, avoutery, avoutre, avoutre(e), avoutry *n.* adultery 835, 907, 5079+; *pl.* **avouteries** 2702
advisement *see* **avisement**

advises *n. pl.* material benefits, goods 1671*n*
affeccion *n.* (carnal) love 7692, feeling, passion 9168, 9171
afferme *v.* assert, declare 9203; *pr. 3 pl.* **affermeth** strengthens 10,161
afoore, afore *prep.* before 4543, 5509, 5814+
afoore, afore *adv.* before 2974, 5218, 7419+, beforehand 824, 4636, 5225, in front 9149, 12,443
afore or (that) *conj.* before 5006–7. *See* **before or (that)**
aforethought *n.* premeditation 830–1*n*
after, aftir, aftyr *prep.* after 664, 1184, 1192+, according to, in keeping with, like 1143, 1279, 5230+, after the manner of, in imitation of 9637, 10,604, for 1714, 9931
after, aftir, aftyr *adv.* after, behind, afterwards 1174, 1637, 2704+; ~ **here** hereafter 7799
after, aftir, aftyr (*that*) *conj.* after 10,055, 10,441, in proportion to, to the degree (that) 217, 280, 693+; ~ **that theye (the persoones) be** according to their (the persons') estate 5226, 10,418–9
age, aage *n.* old age 742, 747, 3983+, period or stage of life 4409, period of human history 4407, 4411, age of discretion 1130, life, years 6508; **goode** ~ long life 3957, **man of** ~ adult 5409, ~ **of man** adulthood 12,927
age *v.* grow old 1056, 7373; *pr. 3 sg.* **aageth, ageth** 4406, 4427, 4428+; *pp.* **aged** old 5450
ageyn(e), ayein(e), ayen, ayeyn(e), aȝein(e), aȝen(e), aȝeyin, aȝeyn(e) *adv.* again 2585, 3350, 4243+, back, in return 9454, 10,170, 10,491+; **by(e)** ~ redeem, deliver, ransom 1539–40, 7324–5, 10,899+, **bought** ~ 801, 8979
ageyne, ageyns, ageynste, ayeins, ayeinst(e), ayens, ayenst, aȝeins, aȝens, aȝeyns, aȝeynst *prep.* against 57, 3524, 3525+, for 2691, in preparation for 2618, in the midst of 7850, toward 1963, before 6257
ageinge, agyng *vbl. n.* growing older 3957, 7309
agreyng *vbl. n.* consent 7001
ayel *n.* grandfather 756, 762
alegge *v.* alleviate, relieve 6255; *pr. 3 sg.* **alleggeth** 10,651
aleggeth *pr. 3 pl.* affirm 4670
aliance, aliaunce *n.* bond 4689, 4712, 4717
alyed *pp.* ~ **togeder** in alliance or association 4685
alles *n. pl.* quills 6079
almander *n.* almond tree 6307
almes(se) *n.* alms, almsgiving 214, 1478, 2297+, kindness, charity 3450, almsgiving, charitable event 1112*n*
alon(e), aloon(e), alloone *adj.* alone, by itself (myself, yourself, herself, himself) 1689, 1690, 1691+
alonly, aloonly, alloonly, alleoonly *adv.* only 355, 360, 370+

aloweth *pr. 3 sg.* praises, extolls 8674; *pp.* **alowed, lowed** 155, 11,158*
amble *v.* move at an easy pace 3970, 11,740
amend(e) *v.* turn away from sin, mend one's ways, reform 1439, 1901, 3151+, rectify, correct 1452, 1632, 10,598+, make amends for 5728; *pr. 3 sg.* **amendith, mendeth** improves 4141, 12,280; *pa. t.* **amended** 801; *pp.* **amendid** remedied 6918
amendement, mendement *n.* remedy 6917, penance, atonement for sin 10,136; **come to ~** make amends 1136
amendes, amendis *n. pl.* fines 4533*n*, 5718, penance, atonement for sin 7916, 10,103, 10,134
amendyng *vbl. n.* moral improvement, progress 3771, 3774
amerous *adj.* satisfying 12,678
amiable *adj.* lovable 8961, 10,396
amisse *v.* do wrong 5705*n*
amisse, amys(se) *adv.* amiss, wrongly 1069, 6196, 7283+
amonesteth, amonestith, monestith *pr. 3 sg.* admonishes, enjoins, instructs 293, 726, 7511+
an *conj.* and 1352, 2759, 3446+
anamely, anamly, an namly, namly *adv.* especially, in particular 875, 1759, 1989+, even 4599, 8567
ancient *see* **auncient**
and *indef. art.* an 5795, 5796
and *conj.* if 468, 3276, 11,752+
anenst(e) *prep.* in the judgment of 11,654, before 3793, 11,392, 11,568+, with respect to, as regards 8280, 8281
anguisshous *adj.* arousing anxiety or distress 2924
anoyed *pp.* vexed 4197, 7443. *See* **noye**
anoynte *pr. 3 sg.* smear 5884; *pa. t.* **anoynted** anointed 10,410; *pp.* **anoynted** 7249, 7251, 7253
answere *v.* answer 6103, be accountable for 2150*, 5072; *imp.* **answere** 10,994; *pr. 1 sg.* **answer** 366; *pr. 2 sg.* **answerest** 3467; *pr. 3 sg.* **answere, answereth, answerith** 1954, 3482, 3702+, corresponds (to) 6408, 6423, 6462; *pr. 3 pl.* **answer, answereth, answerith** 2848, 3972, 6328+; *pa. t.* **answerd, answered, answerid** 386, 494, 1840+
aparte *adv.* on the side 2737, 2741
ape *n.* ape 2287, 2460, fool 2004, dupe 5342; *poss.* **apes** 6136*bis*; *pl.* **apes** 2788
apon(e) *see* **vpon**
apetite, appetite *n.* strong desire, longing 249, 12,742
appropre *v.* appropriate, make one's own 989

appropred, approprid *pp.* in possession of the endowment or income of a parish church 4577*n*, attributed or assigned as proper to 8161, dedicated or devoted 11,864, 12,199, 12,216, supported 11,392*n*

aquitance *n.* forgiveness 7923

araie, araye *n.* clothing, dress 2492, 2497, 5064+, adornment 1501, 2337; *pl.* **araies, arayes** 2282, 2327, 5355+, adornments, jewels 10,021, 11,623, 11,626+; **grete** ~ *mistranslation, see notes* 8774

araye *v.* prepare 1440, 6661, dress, clothe 2036, 11,633, 12,902+, adorn 10,030, 11,643; *pr. 3 sg.* **arayeth** 6792, 8114, 8751; *pr. 3 pl.* **araieth, araye, arayeth** 1683, 2033, 5037+, equip 8317; *pa. t.* **araied** 1577, 2618; *pp.* **araied, arayed** 4575, 5662, 9037+, covered with a pall 12,891*n*

araynge, arayyng *vbl. n.* clothing 9287, 12,899

arase *v.* uproot, tear away 9589; *pr. 3 sg.* **araseth, arasseth** 8393, 9138

arbetrore *n.* arbitrator 9281

arbiterment *n.* decision 10,135

ardentnesse *n.* fervor, zeal 75*n*

argue *v.* find fault with, reprove 8716; *pr. 3 sg.* **argueth** 6295

aright *adv.* straight 1385*bis*, 5696

arlotries *see* **harlotrie**

armes, armys *n. pl.* arms 2497, 2499, 4156+, weapons or armor 2034, 4377, 9659+, heraldic devices 2865, fighting, warfare 9539, 9588; **men of** ~ armed men, soldiers 668

armoure, armure *n.* armor 9825, 9826, 9835+

article *n.* clause of the Apostles' Creed 1152, 1153, 1156+; *pl.* **articles, articlis** 6, 1139, 1140+

as *conj.* to the extent that 11191, 12694; ~ **who seye** as if to say 412, 506, 2058–9+, ~ **howe that** by means of which 6452

asautis, assautis, assauttis *n. pl.* assaults 6946, 8044, 9667+

ascape, escape *v.* escape 2859*bis*, 3969+, elude, avoid 5673, 8508, 10,636, fail 11,465; *pr. 3 sg.* **ascapeth, eschapeth** 2136, 2860, 10,737

ascryethe *pr. 3 sg.* cries out, gives the alarm 2860

ascuse, excuse *v.* serve as an exculpation 526, 10,612; *pr. 3 sg.* **ascuseth, excuseth** seeks to exculpate 2161, 8676, alleges reasons for an exemption 4173; *pr. 3 pl.* **ascuse, ascuseth, excuse** 2299, 5911, 6179; ~ **hym** beg off 7442

aseethe *n.* satisfaction, payment 7972

asoile *v.* absolve from sin 9879

assay *v.* try by tasting 5653; *pp.* **asaied** experienced 8874

assauteth *pr. 3 sg.* assaults, assails 1481, 2557

asse *n.* birthright, blessing 5580, 5581, 5583

assembleth *pr. 3 sg.* brings together 2892; *pp.* **assemblid** 11,703, 11,711
assigned *pp.* transferred (the rights in an estate) 4870
assotteth *pr. 3 sg.* besots, makes a fool of 4442
assured *pp.* secured, safe 9296
astate, state *n.* state, condition 584, 2192, 5186+, social standing, status 9540, 12,000, 12921; *pl.* **astates, astatis, statis, states** 2720, 8209, 9540+, orders (of angels) 8198; **grete** ~ high position 755
attaigneyng, atteignyng *adj.* persuasive 5564, appropriate 7406
attaignyngly *adv.* appropriately 7599**n*
atteigne, atteyn(e) *v.* reach, attain to 7094, 7366, 9776, achieve, obtain 9350, 9354; *pr. 3 sg.* **attaigneth, atteyneth** 4601, extends, reaches 6474; *pa. t.* **atteigned** 12,538; *pp.* **atteyned** 7641
attyce *v.* induce 4263; *see* **tisseth**
aube *n.* alb 12,249
auctorite *n.* authority, power 9044, worth, importance 11,776; *pl.* **auctoriteis** authoritative statements 13,007; **be the ~ of God** by power delegated from God 10,731
auncient, ancient, avncient *adj.* old 749, 10,295, 10,297+; ~ **time** the past 476, of old, ancient 8267
aunciently *adv.* formerly 9792
austerite *n.* extreme self-restraint 6463**n*
autoriȝed *pp.* given validity, endowed with authority 4288*n*
availe, avayle *n.* benefit, profit, advantage 1426, 1943, 2159+, monetary gain, profit 3510
availe, avayle *v.* help, benefit, profit 7128, 7133, 9867+; *pr. 3 sg.* **availeth, avayleth, aveyleth** 1938, 7167, 11,495, is successful 9328; *pr. 3 pl.* **avayleth** 6496. *See* **vaileth**
avaunce *v.* further, promote 754, 1994; *pr. 3 pl.* **avaunseth** 6130; *pp.* **avaunsed** raised in rank or position 3237
avaunt *pr. 3 pl.* boast 5855, 7098; *pr. 3 pl.* **avaunteth** 6773
avauntyng(e) *vbl. n.* boasting 2123, 5799, 5839+
aventure *n.* chance 3610, 7958, fortune, lot 9731, adultery 4561
avice *n.* **with** ~ deliberately 6199
avice, avise *v.* examine 1451; ~ **the on** consider 2719
avisement, advisement *n.* forethought, prudent consideration 10,274, 10,303, 10,862
avocatis *see* **aduocat**
avoued *pa. t.* pledged 1564, 1586; *pp.* **avowed** vowed 4423
avowe *n.* vow 4579
avowed *pp.* acknowledged 7525

avoutery, avoutre(e), avoutry *see* **aduoutery**
avowerie, avowery *n.* adoption, avowal as one's own 7521, 7524, 9000
aweyte *n.* ambush 9388
aworthe *adv.* **takith** ~ accept (cheerfully) 5531
ayeinward, ayenward, aȝeinward, aȝeynward(e) *adv.* back, in return 1771, 1782, 8115, conversely, on the other hand 1657, 3960, in (its, their) place 1609, 10,340

bacheler *n.* a household knight 2603*n*, 2605, 2617+
backebityng, backebytynge, bakbityng, bakbytyng, bakkebytynge *vbl. n.* slander, defamation 106, 3585, 5917+; *pl.* **bakbitynggys** 6246
baigneth *pr. 3 sg.* bathes, washes 9725*n*
bailie, baily, balie, bayly *n.* bailiff 1541, 1546, 1830+
bailiship(p) *n.* bailiwick 1595, 1910
bakbite *pr. 3 pl.* defame, slander 705
baliage *n.* bailiwick 1581
bandoune *see* **abaundoneth**
banysshed *pp.* exiled 2057, 5116
barat *n.* deception, fraudulent dealing 981
baret *v.* quarrel, brawl 5705
baretor, barettour *n.* trickster, fraudulent dealer 1544, 1606; *pl.* **baraturs, barettoures** 975*, 1562
bareygne, barhaigne, barhayne *adj.* barren, childless 880, 4128, fruitless 6324
barke *n.* shell, rind 7433
baronage *n.* angels, hierarchy of heaven 1992*n*, 1999
barowe *n.* barrow, cart 2079
basshed *see* **abasshed**
baundon *see* **abaundoneth**
bawdes *n. pl.* procurers 4995
bawme *n.* balm 4385
be(e), by *prep.* by, by means of 171, 174, 178+, under 1179, for, on account of 402, 404, 3774+, in 2178, because of 2299, at 3014, near, next to 2180, in accordance with, 11,254; ~ **oo weye** in one respect 9475, ~ **oon and oon** one by one 4992–3, ~ **too and too** two by two 4993, ~ **malice** with malice 1070, ~ **condicion** under terms 976, ~ **reson** with good reason 893, within reason 1124, ~ **siche (a) covenaunt (covenant)** by (in accordance with) an agreement 5580, 5585–6
be(e), ben *v.* be 3572, 5030, 7490+; *imp.* **bee** 5310; *pr. 1 sg.* **am** 1014, 1015, 1500+; *pr. 2 sg.* **art(e), be, was, wer(e)** 543, 1709, 2681+; *pr. 3 sg.* **be(e), beeth, is, ys** 5311, 5590, 12,607+; *pr. 1 pl.* **bee** 3003, 6302, 7057+; *pr. 2 pl.* **be**

7342; *pr. 3 pl.* **ar, arn, be(e)** 1403, 4223, 5158+; *pa. t.* **was, whas, were, weere, where** 290, 752, 1194+; *pp.* **ben, been** 322, 954, 2385+

because, beecause *conj.* because 274, 326, 488+, in order that 871, 972, 1329+; ~ **to** in order to 1013

beeke, beeque *n.* beak 2168*n*, 4748, 4751

beely, bely(e) *n.* belly 439, 4157, 5380+; *pl.* **belies** 2296*

beere *n.* bear 4452; *pl.* **beeres** 3236

beestely, bestely, bestly *adj.* wicked, debased 3188, 6879; **maketh, made, torneth, is tourned** ~ subvert(s)(ed), corrupt(s)(ed), debase(s)(ed) 1611, 3191, 8682, turn upside down 5457–8

before or (that) *conj.* before 869

behaveyng, behavyng(e) *vbl. n.* conduct, behavior 251, 2118, 12,915+, deportment, manners 5064*n*

behest *phr.* **lande of** ~ land of promise 6113

beholde *v.* regard, consider 401, 7362, 9890+, see, observe 1455, 9267, 11197+; *imp.* **beholde** 794, 1800, 5558+; *pr. 1 sg.* **beholde** 1828; *pr. 3 sg.* **beholdeth, behooldeth, beholdith** 3618, 8255*, 8903+; *pr. 1 pl.* **beholde** 2214; *pr. 3 pl.* **beholde, beholdeth** 3317, 5333, 6725+; *pa. t.* **behelde** 932, 11,272, 12,413; *part.* **beholdyng** 1453, 5168

beholdyng(e), behaldyng *vbl. n.* seeing 9292, 10,058, gazing 11,639, vision 12,485, 12,516, 12,525, taking heed to 3055; *pl.* **beholdynges, beholdyngys** sights 9147, looks 8471; **to the** ~ **of** with reference or regard to 9269*n*

behovely *adj.* good 5550

beyng(e) *vbl. n.* divine essence 1158*n*, 7589, nature 1616, existence, life 4315, *mistranslation, see notes* 9895; **ofte** ~ frequent intercourse 880*n*

beite *n.* bait 12,604

belewes *n.* bellows 11,284

benefices, beneficis *n. pl.* ecclesiastical livings 4469, good deeds 7339

benignes(se) *n.* benevolence, love of one's fellow man, benignity 166*n*, 8948

benignite *n.* benignity, benevolence, love of one's fellow man 8959

bere *v.* give 1027, carry 1889, 1892, 1898+, produce 2804, 3750, receive 7525, endure 4181, 8844, give birth to 8092, 8095, bear, support 4153, 5695; *pr. 2 sg.* **beryst** 3074; *pr. 3 sg.* **bereth, berith** 545, 1439, 3071+, impels 8833, ~ **aweye** carries away 4894, 8707, 11617, ~ **oppen (on)** assails 3386, 3446; *pr. 3 pl.* **bere, bereth, berith** 3172, 4374, 6038+; *pa. t.* **bare** 381, 952, 2872+; *part.* **berynge** 7337; *pp.* **borne** 4154, 6944, 11,021

beree, beere *n.* bier, coffin 10,730, 12891

beriell *n.* burial, interment 10,730

beryng *vbl. n.* **in the** ~ in carrying the child 867–8

berke *n.* bark of tree 7330

besantis *n. pl.* spiritual gifts, talents 1581, 1585
beset(te) *pp.* **evil** ~ ill bestowed 1712, **wel** ~ well bestowed 1645
besyd *prep.* near, around 1789
besy(e), beesy *adj.* solicitous, attentive 2633, diligent 4006, 4010, 4019+, elaborate 11,923, 11,984, 12,884, intent 4970, 5082, inquisitive 12,736; *comp.* **besyer** busier 8878
besye *v.* occupy (himself) 12,410
besily, bisily, besyly *adv.* diligently, carefully 2500, 2600, intently 5656*n*, elaborately 10,021, curiously 12,082, with forethought 6023*n*
besines(se), besynes(se), bisinesse *n.* care, concern 1796, 2467, 12,086+, enterprise 9745, effort 2332, 10,020, occupation 4230, undue interest in worldly matters 9632, eagerness, ardor 5656, 5659, 12,078+, required task, business 1992, need 2001*n*; *pl.* **besinesses, besyinesses, besyneses, besynesses, besynessis** 553, 4294, 9633+, transactions 981*n*, troubles, misfortunes 4843, worldly cares 7695; ~ **of the worlde** worldly affairs 9306, ~ **necessarie** necessary tasks, affairs, or business occupations 10,294*n*; **grete** ~ matter of great importance or concern 4306, **temporell** ~ worldly occupation 5446
besom *n.* broom 9863
bestee *n.* beast 1257
betakith *pr. 3 pl.* give 1959; *pa. t.* **betoke, betooke** 734, 811
bete *v.* destroy 3512; *pr. 3 sg.* **beteth** beats, pummels 3446, 7482, chastises 1433, 6181; *pr. 3 pl.* **beteth** 579, 3369; *pa. t.* **beete, bette** 808, 9346, 10,517; *part.* **betyng** 2931; *pp.* **beten, betyn, bette** 1738, 3498, 12,332+; ~ **the lippes** talk 11,495–6, ~ **his blame** confessed his fault 9978*n*
betyme(s) *adv.* early 5466, 5477*bis*+; **al** ~ in good time 10121
betynges *vbl. n. pl.* blows 4454
betokeneth, betokenyd *pr. 3 sg.* betokens 1260, 11,273, 12,227+; *pr. 3 pl.* **betokeneth, betokened** 1280, 12,095, 12,234+; *pp.* **betokenyd** 12,249
biddeth, bideth *pr. 3 sg.* commands, orders 3841, 3944, 4041+; *pr. 3 pl.* **biddeth** 8208; *pa. t.* **bade** 494, 1117, 10,658
bide *see* **abide**
birdeyn *n.* burden 871; **with hir** ~ with child 11,857
biscuit *n.* ship's biscuit 7862
bise *n.* keen north wind 2524, 2526, 2531*n*
bitternesse, bittirnes *n.* ill will 3250; *pl.* **bitternesses** 1262, 8777
blame *n.* blasphemy 471, 5131, blame, censure, criticism 3470, 3953, 4856, fault 9978*n*; *pl.* **blames** blasphemies 449; **reyse, reyseth** ~ demean, belittle by false accusation 2219–20, 5145, 5944
blame *v.* reprove, censure, reproach 39, 2886, 3012+; *pr. 3 sg.* **blame,**

blameth 3096, 3840; *pr. 3 pl.* **blame, blameth** 1506, 2298, 3433+; *pa. t.* **blamed** 537; *pp.* **blamed** 2464
blameyng, blamynge *vbl. n.* blasphemy 112, 5801
blandeshed *pp.* deceived, betrayed 4690
blandesshinge, blaundesshyng, blandshyng *vbl. n.* deceit, deception, betrayal 4684*n*, 4690, 4692+; *pl.* **blandeshynges** 4729
bledderis *n. pl.* bladders 6684
blered *adj.* bleary 11,197
blessyng *n.* supreme bliss, blessedness 10,262, 11,235; *pl.* **blessingys, blessyngis, blessyngys** spiritual joys, beatitudes 7382, 7412, 7652
blustrynge *adj.* tempestuous, turbulent 3361*n*
bobans of the worlde *phr.* worldly pride 2725
bocherye *n.* slaughterhouse 6034
bodily, bodyly(e) *adj.* corporeal, physical 1036, 7021, 10,277+, ?deadly 4201, physical, material 7852, 8133, 11,198+; ~ **goodes** material or worldly property 1785, 1790, ~ **wittes** the senses 12,378
bodily, bodyly *adv.* corporally, physically 581, 2931, 12,378+, with their eyes 12477
body(e), boody(e) body 27, 173, 372+, person 1422, 1499; *pl.* **bodyes, bodies** 2333, 3094, 5537+; ~ **of hooly chirche** the church taken collectively 9065–6, 10,359, **oo** ~ spiritual communion 3313, 7960, **torned the** ~ spurned 2610
boffet *n.* blow with fist 2053
bolde *adj.* shameless 12,021
bolned *pp.* swollen, puffed up 3410
boltel *n.* a garment of loosely woven cloth 752*n*
bon gire *Fr. phr.* round 12,166*n*
bonde *n.* bond of marriage 230
bondes *n. pl.* shackles 1,0851
booke *n.* book of accounts 2501
boole *n.* bull 1676
boorde, borde *n.* dining table 1976, 12,218, 12,219+; *pl.* **bordes** 2476
boost, boste *n.* arrogant self-esteem 1502, ostentatious splendor 5063, 6497, 8773; *pl.* **bostes** shows, parades 1697; **with his** ~ in his deceptive manner, perfidiously 3251–2*n*
booþe *n.* merchant's shop, stall 11,590
bordeler, bordolere *n.* brothel-keeper 2706, 5112
bordelles *n. pl.* brothels 569, 4998
borris *n. pl.* boars 6177
borweth *pr. 3 sg.* acquires on credit 978, 4624; *pp.* **borwed** 7910

bostosly *adv.* rudely, harshly 11,076
bostous *adj.* arrogant 7590
boterel *n.* toad 3410*n*
botonettis *n. pl.* small buttons 2486*n*
botte *n.* dung beetle 5941*n*
bottelleris *n. pl.* wine stewards 2345
boule *v.* trick, deceive 5705*n*
bounde, bounden, bonde, boonde *pp.* tied fast, bound 3670, 3967, 4092+, joined in marriage 231, 870, 5178+, obliged, under obligation 772, 1130, 4512+, fettered as a prisoner 10,847, 10,849, enslaved 1537, 1570, 5520+; ~ **men** serfs 4558
boundes *n. pl.* restraints, moral rules 11,818, 11,824
bounte(e), bonte *n.* goodness in general, excellence, virtue 1572, 7273, 11,649+, munificence, liberality, generosity 1572, 1758, 1761+, act of generosity 8165, good turn 1663, profit, benefit 4602, 8146, 11,004+, honor 12,133, efficacy 12,280, worldly pleasures or goods 250, ?endowments 8110; *pl.* **bountees, bounteis, bounteys, bountez** divine favors or gifts 1622, 1670, 1733+
bountewousnes *n.* beneficence, generosity 1640
bourdes *n. pl.* jests, idle tales 2358, 5979
bourdoures *n. pl.* jesters 1647
bowe *v.* bow in reverence, make obeisance 11,652, bend 10,838, incline the body 9382; *pr. 3 sg.* **boweth** bends 4149, 4161, 12,551, submits 5128; *pr. 3 pl.* **bowe, boweth** bend (the knee) 387, turn, incline 9328; *pa. t.* **bowed** 383, 10,840, 10,893; *part.* **bowyng(e)** 4150, 9257, yielding 8314; ~ **(his, thyn) ere (eerys)** give ear, listen 3886–7*n*, 10,992–3
bowellys *n. pl.* bowels, entrails 4178*n*
boye *n.* serf 1536, 1537, servant 3442; *pl.* **boyes** 1493, 7883
braieth *pr. 3 sg.* cries out 2580; *part.* **brayinge** creaking 4187*n*
bran, bren *n.* bran, husk 7241, 11,497
branchet *n.* small branch 77; *pl.* **branchettis** 49*n*, 58, 76+
braser *n.* fire 7328*n*
brasyng *vbl. n.* fire 8094*n*
breeke, breke *v.* violate, fail to keep 1284, 2293, 5437, shatter, crush 5566; *pr. 3 sg.* **breke, breketh** 714, 910, 3516+, breaks 3448, 4882; *pr. 3 pl.* **breeke, breeketh, breke, breketh, brekith** 4495, 4546, 5140+, destroy 1410, 3652, 11,094+; *pa. t.* **brake** 1407; *part.* **brekyng** 12,471; *pp.* **broken, brokyn** 937, 1133, 1397+, wrecked 12,329
brekyng(e) *vbl. n.* violation, failure to keep 1280, 4579, 12,970
bremston(e) *n.* brimstone 423, 603, 929+

brenne, bryn *v.* burn 602, 3568, 3895+; *pr. 3 sg.* **brenne, brenneth** 4426, 6017, 9584+; *pr. 3 pl.* **brenne, breneth, brenneth, brynneth** 1717, 3652, 4504+; *pa. t.* **brent(e)** 5269, 5616, 12,413+; *part.* **brennynge** 11,318, 11,358; *pp.* **brent** 539, 11,876

brennyng(e) *adj.* burning 422, 6309, 6321+

brere *n.* briar, thorn 1438*; *pl.* **breris, brerys** 1375, 1440

breste *n.* breast 4157

breste *v.* burst 5671, 5672; *pa. t.* 5368

brethirhoode, brotherheed, brotherhoode, brothirhode, brothirhoode *n.* parish confraternity, fraternal organization 1112*n*, 1118, 1122, fellowship, communion 7815–6, 7818, 9001

brewe *pr. 3 sg.* brews 4610

briberie *n.* fraud, deception, betrayal 84*n*, robbery 10,927

bridde *n.* bird 4015

brigge *n.* bridge 3909

bryn, brynneth *see* **brenne**

brisse *v.* break into pieces 6032; *pr. 3 sg.* **brisseth** breaks, shatters 6323

brondes, brondis *n. pl.* brands 1380, 5095

brule *v.* burn, char with fire 12,024; *imp.* **brule** 10,634; *pr. 3 sg.* **bruleth** 12,014, singes 12,026

bulle *n.* papal bull, official seal 5963

bulteth *pr. 3 sg.* sifts 7240

burgeis *n.* burgess, citizen of a town 9532, 9534; *pl.* **burgeses** merchants 3224

burgeisesse *n.* female of the burgess class 11,638*n*

but, butte, bot, bvt, put *prep., adv., conj.* but 324, 370, 5538+, nothing but, merely 120, 594, 1502+, only 367, 892, 2016+, except 354, 1039, 1689+, and 1512, 2501, however 1513; **not ellys** ~ nothing other than 1031, **not (nought)** ~ nothing but 591, 802, **and** ~ however 512, ~ **alonly** other than 360, ~ **that** that ... not 892, 1273, 1291+, ~ **if** unless 6601, 6815, 7782+, without (his gown burning) 9584, **alonly** ~ **for** for any other reason except 360, ~ **that** so that 3413, 11,722, that 6058, rather 331, 344, 734, but rather 985

cacche *see* **kacche**

caityf, caytif(e), caytiff, caytyf(e) *n.* wretch, villain 951, 5054, 5068+; *pl.* **caitiffes** 1769

caitif, caityf, caytif *adj.* wretched, basely wicked 2508, 4526, 5028+

caytifous, caytivouse, caytyvous *adj.* miserable, poor 3099, basely wicked 1649, 2443

caliones *n. pl.* pebbles, flints 8666

called aȝein *pp.* annulled, revoked 10,643
calvys *n. pl.* calves 1624
camelyn *see* **sause camelyn**
can, canste, con, conne, covnne, cowde, cunne *see* **konne**
capital *adj.* capital (sins) 9461
carayne, caroyne *n.* carcass 1637, 5578, 5589+, *in contempt* the living human body 6884, 11,995
cardinal(l) *adj.* cardinal (virtues) 143, 3411, 8267+; *pl.* **cardinales** 8244, 8272
carles *see* **karle**
carye *v.* draw (water) 7421*n*
carterris *n. pl.* carters 4506
caste *n.* drain water 3891*n*
caste *v.* throw, cast 3234, 5258, 5263+, fell, throw down 6324, produce, send forth 6328, utter 7448, proclaim 10,464, cast out, expel, purge 7756, 7935, 7937+; *pr. 3 sg.* **casteth, castith** 1379, 1519, 3768+, tosses 3361, extends 3404, 3505, spreads 8522, gets rid of 9863, puts 5573; *pr. 3 pl.* **casten** 1713; *pa. t.* **keste** 343, 3105, 8558+, cast off, removed 2529; *pp.* **caste, casten, castyn** 4204, 7760, 10,101+, liberated 6114; ~ **vnder foote** despise 3436
castyng *vbl. n.* ray, beam of light 6452*n*
catell(e) *n.* capital 4603*n*, property, possessions 4552, 10,932
cause *n.* reason 506, 507, 510+, situation, circumstances 1815, 1816, affairs, business 1994, reason why 2910, cause, source 3597, 5070, 6252, aim, purpose, intent 7461, 10,004; *pl.* **causes, causys** 787, 848, 5253+, matters 512, 9430, legal actions, cases 4669, 4672; **for ~ of** because of 6310–11
cawght *see* **kacche**
celleris *n. pl.* cellars 10,491
cene *n.* Last Supper 8574
certeyn(e), certoine *adj.* sure 1190, 2921, 2988+, some particular number of 4507*n*
certeynly *adv.* with certainty 6015
chalange, chalenge *n.* false claim or accusation 83, 4648; *pl.* **chalengys** 4678
chalangeth *pr. 3 pl.* make false claims or accusations 4655
chamberer, chamberier *n.* handmaid, chambermaid 1978, 9862; *pl.* **chambereris** servants 1493
chames *n. pl.* shames, disgrace 6901. *See* **shame**
champion *n.* stout fighter 3787, 5370; *pl.* **championes** 4762
chanones *n. pl.* canons (clerics) 7871; ~ **of helle** devils 2413–4
chapelet *n.* garland (of flowers) 4764; *pl.* **chapelettis** coronals (of gold or gems) 2496, 6502

chapiter, chapitre *n.* division of a book 5, chapter-house 4535; *pl.* **chapitres** 1
charge, charche *n.* duty, responsibility 769, 771, 1574+, importance, moment 5434, weight, significance of the sin 9948; *pl.* **charches, charges, chargis** 767, worldly cares, burdens, concerns 3891*, 7260, 7696+
charge, chargeth *pr. 3 sg.* orders 3517, 4172; *pr. 3 pl.* **charcith** burden 7375; *pp.* **charched, charged** loaded, burdened, weighed down 948, 4186, 4778+, ordered, directed 5533
chargynge *vbl. n.* burdening, weighing down 4352
charmours *n. pl.* enchanters 405
charmys *n. pl.* charms, spells 1945
chartre *n.* prison 8876*n*
chase *see* **chese**
chastenes *n.* chastity 6335
chastice, chastie, chastyce, chastye *v.* chastise, reprove, punish, correct 1432, 3441, 3601+, mortify, subdue 3880; *pr. 1 sg.* **chastie** 10,640; *pr. 3 sg.* **chastiseth, chastisseth, chastissith** 1681, 7482, 9043; *pr. 3 pl.* **chastie, chastice, chastiseth** 1506, 2155, 6176; *pp.* **chastyed** 9366*bis*
chasticement, chastisement, chastisment *n.* reproof, chastisement 1505, 6164, 10,636
chastite(e) *n.* chastity 118, 220, 221+
chaufour *n.* kettle for heating water 3424
chaunchyng *vbl. n.* change, alteration 7610
chaunge *n.* change 10,728
chaungeth *pr. 3 sg.* alters his appearance 5971, transforms 8433, converts 8243; *pa. t.* **chaunched** changed, turned (into) 676; *pp.* **chanched, chaunched, changed** 933, 5613, 12,415
chawfeth *pr. 3 sg.* becomes angry 7749; *pr. 3 pl.* **chaufeth** inflame, excite 2509; *pp.* **chawfed** warmed 7292
cheef, chef(e), cheffe, chief *adj.* capital (sins) 1271, 1387, 3944+, main 5797, foremost 5776, 12,685
cheepe *form of* **sheep** 8770
cheffare, geffare *n.* sales-price 7164*n*, ware, merchandise 7159*n*
cheyne *n.* chain 3688*bis*
chekynys *n. pl.* chicks, offspring of the crane 738
chepe *n.* plenty, abundance *in adv. and adj. phr.* **greet (grete)** ~ numerous 12,851, in great numbers 12,856
chere *n.* disposition, mood *in phr.* **make feire** ~ look cheerful 10,984–5
cheressheth *pr. 3 sg.* takes good care of 8805–6
cherte *n.* affection 9008
chese, cheese *v.* choose 1329, 6997, 7523+; *pr. 3 sg.* **chesith** 8358; *pr. 3 pl.*

chase 9644; *pa. t.* **chase** 6703; *pp.* **chosen, chosyn** 1318, 1734, 4468, *as n.* the elect 6138, 7340, 7414

cheuysshans *n.* profit, gain 2279

chide *v.* quarrel 6063; *pr. 3 sg.* **chideth** 3465; *pa. t.* **chydde** 483

chidyng(e), chydyng(e) *vbl. n.* quarreling 50, 3459, 6070+; *pl.* **chidyngis** quarrels 5707

child(e) *n.* child 487, 760, 1573+; *pl.* **childe, childer, childir, childre, childryn, shilder** 479, 502, 579+

childehoode *n.* childhood, infancy 1605–6, 1864, 5475, childishness 6863, 6874–5, 12,927–8

childyng *vbl. n.* child-bearing, delivery 868; **in** ~ with child, 872

cygoigne *n.* stork 10,961

cyment *n.* cement 8017

circumstances, circumstanses, circumstaunses *n. pl.* attendant conditions 9963, 9986, 10,005–6

clayme *v.* proclaim 10,218

clarrie *n.* spiced and sweetened wine 2345

cleered *pp.* calmed, soothed 3506*n*

cleys *n. pl.* claws 2168, 5922

cleme *pr. 3 sg.* climbs 1430

clene *n.* moral purity 221*n*, 222

clene, cleene, clenne *adj.* chaste, morally and spiritually pure 1582, 1988, 3950+, clean 3870, 6447, 12,266, untainted 12,799; *comp.* **clenner** 2560, 7064, 12,217+; *superl.* **clenest** 6733

clenly(e) *adv.* purely, innocently, chastely 223, 232, 11,768+

clennes(se) *n.* purity, innocence 6439, 6450, 6647+

clense *v.* cleanse, purify, purge 1447, 7064, 7756+; *pr. 3 sg.* **clenseth, clensith** 7689, 7689–90, 9862+; *pr. 3 pl.* **clense, clensith** 6560, 12,270, 12,283+; *pp.* **clensed, clensid** 7708, 8539, 11,196+

clere *adv.* brightly 3014, clearly 9318, 9357, 9384

clere, cleere *adj.* bright 1582, 9441, 9446+, clear 12,266, 12,669, 12,672+, perspicacious 6757, open, frank 9944; *comp.* **clerer** brighter 9723

clerely *adv.* clearly 171*, 6542, 7074+, openly, frankly 9947

clerenes(se) *n.* purity 3160, glory 11,960*n*, radiance, light, splendor 3161, 8193, 11,960+, serenity 7762

clere-seeyng *adj.* clear-sighted 9135

clere seerris *n. pl.* clear-sighted persons 6513*n*

clergie, clergye *n.* clergy 2255, learned language, that is, Latin, language of the clergy 6421, knowledge, learning 5649, 7119, 7143+; **hye** ~ wisdom 6857

clerke *n.* scholar 4537, 4630; *pl.* **clerkes, clerkis, clerkys** 4471, 4704, 6710+, clerics 240, 1925, 2406+, law clerks 4669
clymyng *vbl. n.* progressing 5176
cloister *n.* monastery 9165, 12,418
cloyster monk *n.* a monk secluded in a monastery 2459
cloisteris *n. pl.* monks 6124–5
cloystererys *n. pl.* monks 3883
cloosepurse *n.* miser, pinchpurse 10,414*n*
close *v.* close 10,098, 10,415; *imp.* **cloose** 11,486; *pp.* **cloos, closed, closid, cloosid, clos** closed 11,677, 12,858, concealed 12,103, enclosed 7288, 12,075, shut, secluded 11,903, 11,906
closeris *n. pl.* enclosures 7288
cloude *n. mistranslation, see notes* 12,739
clovyn *pp.* divided 9451
cofferis *see* **coofer**
coiffes *n. pl.* headdresses 2495
coygne *n.* species 985
colys *n.* broth 6881
colrique *adj.* choleric 9394
come after *imp.* follow 10,322; *part. as pa. t.* **comyng aȝeins** came up to 9338
comyng(e) downe *vbl. n.* descent 2204; ~ **oute** departure 10,505
cometh *pr. 3 sg.* becomes 1912
comfort(e), confort(e) *n.* spiritual joy, gratification 3677–8, 3679–80, 6535+; *pl.* **confortis** 8884
comfort, confort(e) *v.* strengthen spiritually, comfort 9487, 10,618, 10,843; *imp.* **conforte** 10,621, 10,848; *pr. 3 sg.* **conforteth** 9484–5, 9516, 10,649, strengthens, fortifies 7844–5, 7853; *pr. 3 pl.* **conforteth** 10,629, 10,680; *pa. t.* **conforted** 11,137; *pp.* **conforted** 9489, 9515–16, 10,849+
comly *adj.* pretty, pleasing 6305, 12,180
commandeoure *n.* commander 7769
commaunderesse *n.* female commander 5514*n*
compiled *pp.* composed 13,006
compleyntes *n. pl.* laments 7448
complexion *n.* temperament 9392
complised *pp.* fulfilled, satisfied 12,995
commpt(e), compt(e) *see* **acommpt(e)**
commpt(e), compt(e) *v.* render an account 1631, 1655, 1810+, give account of 7100; *pr. 3 sg.* **compteth** 8723; *pa. t.* **commpted** 1619
compunciones *n. pl.* remorse 11,534*
comunaltee *n.* commonwealth, universal body 7553

commune, comune, comvne *adj.* promiscuous 879, common, shared 980, 990, 1670+, common, ordinary 9160, of inferior quality 5631; ~ **woman (women)** prostitute(s) 881, 2694, 5179, ~ **pepille** community 4452, ~ **profit** common good 9053–4, **in** ~ together 7535–6, 7552, in union 8160

communes *n. pl.* the common people, the lower orders 6123

communion of seintes *phr.* fellowship of the faithful 1224

comunly, comunally, communly *adv.* alike 8970*n*, 8990, commonly 258, 269

concent *v.* consent 6580

conceve, conceyve, conseyve *v.* feel, experience 6615, bring about 8376*n*, conceive 10,881; *pr. 3 sg.* **conceyvith, conseyvith** 7841, 8664, absorbs 8955; *pp.* **conceyved, conseyved, conseyvyd** 1171, 8102, 8486+, devised 5833*n*

concorde *n.* amity 3539–40, 6100

condescend(e) *v.* make allowance for the frailty (of) 4337; ~ **after** lower (myself) to 9378

condicion *n.* nature 788, 1053, 9911, quality, characteristic 9904, 9958, 9962+, stipulation 1688, 4626, terms 976, circumstances 9994; *pl.* **condiciones, condicions** habits, practices, manners 4097, 6759, 6792+

condit(e), conduit *n.* conduit, channel 7185, 10,455, 11,260

condit(e), conduite *v.* conduct, guide 9141, 9289, 11,140; *pr. 3 sg.* **conditeth, condith, counditeth** 8847, 10,336, 10,456+; *pr. 3 pl.* **conditeth** 9465, 9469, 12,254+

conferme *v.* confirm, establish 6020, join, unite, make fast 8177*n*, strengthen 11,566; *pr. 3 sg.* **confermeth, confermith, confermyth** 7664, 7785*, 8234, makes secure 7704; *pp.* **confermed, confermyd** 4825, 7659, 7671+, steadfast 10,462

conforme *pr. 3 pl.* act conformably, show compliance 2730

confounde *v.* harm, destroy 3744, revile 10,063; *pp.* **confounded, confunded** destroyed 889–90, 2935

confusion *n.* humiliation, shame 340, 12,890, damnation 11,992, 11,993

conyng *adj. see* **konnyng**

connyng(e), conyng *n. see* **konnyng(e)**

coniure *pr. 1 sg.* charge, call upon 12,752

conquere *v.* overcome, conquer 1258, 6927, achieve 8586, win, secure 9676, 9794; *pr. 2 sg.* **conqueridest** 4704; *pa. t.* **conquered** 5001; *pp.* **conquerid** 1904, 2106, 6509+

consacrat *pp.* consecrated 374

conseil, consel(l), councell, counseile, counsell(e) *n.* counsel, advice 488, 1023, 3596+, one of the gifts of the Holy Ghost 7783, 7794, 10,273+, advisable course of action 5262, body of advisors 8204*, 10,297, 10,298, secret purpose 9194; *pl.* **counsellez, counsellis** 10,307, 10,319, 10,625, secrets, divine mysteries 7121, 8760, 9642; **is in** ~ advises 827, **sette** ~ advise 5728

consell, counsel(l), counselle *v.* advise 2115, 4715, 9878–9+; *imp.* **counsell** 10,290; *pr. 1 sg.* **counseile, counsell** 1304, 1904, 7621; *pr. 3 sg.* **conseilleth, consellith, counsell, counsellith** 1035, 9042, 10,303–4+; *pr. 3 pl.* **councelleth, counseille, counsellith** 4587, 6170, 10,578; *pa. t.* **counselled** 10,283

consent(e), concent *v.* yield, submit to, acquiesce in 1080, 6580, 9811; *pr. 3 sg.* **consente, consenteth, consentith** 5716, 11,247, 11,248+; *pr. 3 pl.* **consent** 8042, 12,778; *pa. t.* **consented** 12,634–5

consentyng(e) *vbl. n.* consent, agreement, acquiescence 830, 1081, 1087+

consider, considre, consyder, consydre *v.* consider, think about, reflect on 3065, 3082, 3088+

consolacion *n.* satisfaction, pleasure 4387, 4389, 4390

constabil *n.* warden of a castle 806

constance *n.* constancy, steadfastness 9603, 9726, 9727

constreynynge *part.* compelling 4532

contec *n.* strife, contention 6069

contemplacion *n.* devout meditation 3395, 4078–9, 12,513+

contemplatif(f), contemplatiue *adj.* given to religious contemplation, the 'contemplative life' 11,148, 11,166, 11,171+

contenance, contenaunce, countenance, countenaunce *n.* appearance, pretence 2609, 2619, 2731+, demeanor, behavior, conduct 251, 12,914, 12,933+; *pl.* **contenaunces** 4741; **make (maketh)** ~ make a show 2731, 12,873

contenyd, conteyned, contynned *pp.* contained 766, 1149–50, 1171+

conterpeise *n.* counterweight 12,566

contirfete *pr. 3 pl.* pretend to be 2790; *pp.* **contirfet, contirfetid, contrefete** monstrous, deformed 1259, false, deceptive 2762, *mistranslation, see notes* 5065

contrarie *v.* oppose, resist 412

contrarie, contrarye *n.* opposite 596, 1240, 2847+

contrarie, contrary(e) *adj.* opposed 4830, 7558, 8238+; ~ **aȝens** opposed 462–3

contrarious, contrarius *adj.* hostile, rebellious 5340, 5504, 6156

contrariously *adv.* in a contrary manner 5869

contrevith *pr. 3 sg.* fabricates, invents 8731; *pr. 3 pl.* **contreve, contryve** 5943, plot 5953, design 2338; *pp.* **contrevith thynges** fabrications 1945–6*n*

conuersacion *n.* behavior, way of life 3080, 4363, 5301+, dwelling, true home 6534, 8220, 12,389+

conuersant *adj.* living, dwelling 290, 6965
conuersid *pp.* lived, dwelled 6549
conuersyng *part. mistranslation, see notes* 7563
conuerte *v.* turn (to) 5880, convert 7129; *pr. 3 sg.* **conuertith** 7785; *pp.* **conuertid** 7087
coofer *n.* alms box 7163; *pl.* **cofferis** chests 2471
coole *n.* coal 11,332; *pl.* **colys, cooles** 4903, 11,332
coorde *n.* cord 4252
copable, coupeable, coulpable, culpable, culpaple *adj.* culpable 1957, 9967, 9974+
corage *n.* heart, spirit, disposition 3180, 3208, 3412+
coragyous *adj.* brave 3184
coriouste, curiosite *n.* elaborateness of dress 2485, elegance of workmanship 11985*n*, fastidiousness 5645**n*, 5661*
cormeraunt *n.* cormorant 5483
corne *n.* wheat, grain 5966, 8719, 8791+; *pl.* **cornes, cornys** 1723, 3574, 5547
corneres *n. pl.* blowers, trumpeters 8481*n*
corone, coroune *n.* celestial crown of the blessed 2429**n*, 3861, 12,172+, the aureole of the virgin 12,054, 12,170, 12,176, meritorious wreath of laurel 4148, 9752, 9790; *pl.* **corounes, crounes** 8006, 9786, 9805; crowns of Beasts of Apocalypse 1257, 1283
corparax *n.* altar cloth 12,201
correccion *n.* punishment 9065, 9074
corrompyng *vbl. n.* violation of chastity 914*n*
corrumpe *v.* corrupt spiritually, defile 1946, 2783; *pr. 2 sg.* **corrompe** 12,052; *pr. 3 sg.* **corrompeth, corrumpeth** 2236, 6330, 11,330, ferments 11,329; *pr. 3 pl.* **corromped, corrompeth** 11,288, 11,316, 12,018; *pa. t.* **corromped** 11345; *pp.* **corromped, corrumped, corumped** 229, 917, 3189, perverted, debased 6878, vitiated, contaminated 8425
corrupcion *n.* corruption, moral disintegration 6256, 8362, 11,936+
corues *n. pl.* labor services 4531*n*
cosyn, coosyn *n.* kinsman 3493, 3568, 5184; *pl.* **cosines, cosynes** 3544, 4614, 5220+
coste *n.* cost, outlay, expenditure 4552, 6920, labor, effort 1516, 4592, 10,020+; **didde grete** ~ incurred great expense 2624, **of litel** ~ of small cost, inexpensive 5632, **of dere** ~ of great cost, very expensive 5639
coste *n.* **of** ~ indirectly, on the side 4511*n*
costelewe *adj.* costly 5811
costeth *pr. 3 sg.* costs 2420, 3931, 4549+, afflicts, troubles 12,770*n*; *pp.* **coste** 1742

costome, costum(e), coustume *n.* custom, practice 522, 2699, 5414+; *pl.* **costomes, costumes, custumes** 1348, 1442, 3968+, customary dues 4533*n*
couche *n.* bedroom, inner chamber 11,485, bed 9842
couetice, couetise, coveitice, covetice, covetise, covetyce, covetyse, covitice *n.* avarice, greed 76, 87, 88+, craving, desire 1105, 1106, 1123+; *pl.* **covetices, covetises** 4901, inordinate material or worldly desires 5782, 8305, 9315+
couetous(e), covetous(e) *adj.* greedy, avaricious 4902, 4903–4, 4981+, eager to eat or drink 5515, *as n.* greedy persons 440, 6424
counselloures *n. pl.* councilors 10,289–90
counterpeysed *pp.* counterbalanced 12,146
cours *n.* course 8838, 12,805
cours(e) *n.* sentence of damnation 10,464, 10,467
courteise *n.* kind-hearted person 4860
courteyoures *n. pl.* ?courtiers 4761*n*
coustometh *pr. 3 sg.* is wont 4021–2
couvir *v.* cover, conceal 12890; *imp.* **covere** 10,746, 10,747; *pr. 3 sg.* **coueryth, couereth** 2782–3, 6340, 8429, shields, protects 9706; *pr. 3 pl.* **couere, couerith** 5911, 5913; *pp.* **couered** 11,645
coveite, coveyt *v.* strongly desire or crave 1078, 1101, 2192+; *pr. 2 sg.* **coveitest** 2911; *pr. 3 sg.* **coueyteth, coveiteth, coveitethe, coveitith, coveyteth** 1092, 1110, 2222+; *pr. 3 pl.* **coueitith, coveitith** 5752, 7204; *pa. t.* **coveited** 1122
covenable *adj.* suitable 7298
covenant, covenaunt, covenaunte *n.* agreement, contract 3516, 4638, 5580+; *pl.* **covenantes, covenantys** 4547, provisions, stipulations 4629, pledges 5328
covent *n.* covenant, agreement 976
covent *n.* community, fellowship 7820, monastic community 11,709; *pl.* **coventis** 1763, 11,702
covert *adj.* crafty, deceitful 975, 4557
covetously *adv.* avariciously, greedily 1017
crafte *n.* trickery 2325, 2344, 3466+, trade, occupation 8001, cleverness, skill 7143; *pl.* **craftes, craftys** 86, 4582, 4759+
crede *n.* Apostles' Creed 1150, 1156, 1861
creme *n.* chrism, consecrated oil used in anointing 7252*bis*
cresceth *pr. 3 sg.* increases, grows in intensity 4133
cresset *n.* lamp 2180
cristened, cristined, cristyned *pp.* baptized 4304, 7950, made Christian 1839, 8976, 10,218

crokyd *adj.* crippled, deformed 1792; *as n.* **the crookyd** crippled (persons) 5691

crompyng *vbl. n.* genuflecting, bending the knees 2458

crucified *pp.* crucified 1181, 12,835; *pa. t.* **crucified** 2660, 7941; **is ~ to** is despised by 12,383

cruel(l), cruelle *adj.* fierce, ferocious 1257, 3355, 4448+, harsh 2778, 4189, 8464+, merciless 4397, 6386, mad, insane 3378; *comp.* **crueller** 2505; *superl.* **cruellest** 4862

cruelly *adv.* fiercely, ferociously 1296, 2853, sorely 9933, harshly 2707, 2934, 6245+

cruelnes *n.* fierceness, ferocity 1270, mercilessness 3514

cruelt(e) *n.* cruel deed, crime 4519, tyranny 10,886, excessive severity, sternness, intemperate behavior 6333, 6334

curat *n.* parish priest 1023, 10,530, 10,532

curse *v.* speak ill of 4883, damn, consign to hell 10,470; *pr. 3 sg.* **corseth, curseth, cursith** 729, 3206, 6084+, rail profanely at, speak impiously against 2875; *pr. 3 pl.* **curse** blaspheme 3376, excommunicate 4566; *pa. t.* **cursed** 5793, 11,500; *pp.* **acursed, cursed, cursid, corsed** 1013, 2874, 2877+, excommunicated 420, 2054, 2056+

cursyng *vbl. n.* cursing 6084, 7378

curteice, curteis(e), curteys *adj.* courteous, polite 1725, given to proper behavior 1833, refined, noble 1626, 7885, generous, kind, liberal 1535, 1648, 7497+

curteisely, curteisly, curteysly *adv.* graciously 10,986, 11,031, benevolently, mercifully, kindly 9487, 9576, respectfully 7669, 7851, moderately 5531, truthfully 8090–1

curtesi(e), curtesye, cortesye *n.* kindness, generosity 1597, beneficence 1828, 3217, 7393+, virtue, moral purity 1633, 5495*n*, 6627, act of courtesy, noble behavior 8081; *pl.* **courtesies, curtesies** favors 1620, 1632, 1657+, salutations 2369*n*

custumabilly *adv.* habitually, usually 6002

daunger *n.* hesitation or reservation 9039

daunte *v.* subdue 3880

dawe *n.* ?hypocrite, ?fool 3959*n*

debates *n. pl.* conflicts 12,335

debbith *pr. 3 sg.* equips, invests 6909

debonair(e), debonayre, deboneir(e), deboneyre *adj.* meek 7353, 9102, 9103–4+, merciful 4028, 6394, 8951+, gentle 3525–6, 6381, 7479+, sweet 2518; *as n.* **debonayre** merciful person 6398

debonairenes, deboneirnes(se), debonerrenes *n.* mildness, mercy, gentleness, kindness 2563, 6386, 6394+

debonairly, deboneirly, deboneyrly *adv.* graciously, meekly, courteously 3698, 6390, 10,994

debonairte, debonartee, deboneirte, deboneyrte, debonnairte *n.* mildness, gentleness, kindness, mercy 2014, 3407, 6044, gentility, courtesy 6756–7, humility 1597

deceit(e), deceyte, disceit(e), disseit *n.* fraud, deception 4451, 4690, 6632+; *pl.* **deceitis, disceites, disceytes, disseitis** 4583, 4650, 4658+, tricks, wiles 1264, 4852; **withowte** ~ assuredly 6044

dedely, dedly, deedly *adj.* deadly, mortal 1170, 2987, 3340+

dedely, dedly, deedly *adv.* mortally 235, 1021, 3592+

dedicat *pp.* dedicated 7686, 12,210*n*

dedifieth *pr. 3 sg.* dedicates 7694**n*; *pp.* **dedified** dedicated 7697*, 12,210**n*

deele *n.* **a grete** ~ by far 4494

deez *see* **dis**

defamed *pp.* dishonored, disgraced 10,606

default(e), defaut(e) *n.* lack, absence 993, want, deprivation 597, 10,383, fault 2614, flaw, defect 5955, 6094, misdeed 3520, wickedness 6256, 8528, failure in duty 71; *pl.* **defaultes, defaultis, defautes, defautis** sins 3720, 6748, 7738+, disfigurements 11,427; ~ **of herte** pusillanimity 6348. *See* **fault**

defauteth *pr. 3 sg.* fails to fulfill an obligation 4144*n*

defence, defens *n.* defense 2051, prohibition 893

defend(e) *v.* defend, protect 181, 1769, 3095+, forbid, prohibit 5351; *pr. 3 sg.* **defendeth, defendith** 508, 1474, 1507+; *pr. 3 pl.* **defendeth, defendith** 5319, 5351, 5910+; *pa. t.* **defended** 385; *part.* **defendyng** 9967; *pp.* **defended** 821, 1028, 1325+

defoule, defolle, defule, fyle *v.* trample under foot, crush, destroy 1267, 4790, subdue, mortify 4338, 11,754; *pp.* **defouled** 2728, 3475, 9718

defouleth *pr. 3 pl.* befoul, soil 11,973; *pr. 3 sg.* **fouleth, foulleth** 10,075, 12,614; *pp.* **defiled, filed, fyled, fouled** 955, 2682, 4906*, defiled 4346, ill-favored, ugly 876

defuse *adj.* hard to understand, obscure 9206

degysee *see* **disgesy**

degouted *pa. t.* ~ **of** ran from 7333*n*

degree *n.* stage, level 186, 5031, 8527+, step, *fig.* gift of the Holy Ghost 12,537; *pl.* **degrees, degreeys, degreis, degreys, degrez** 43, 151, 185+, states, conditions 2723

delayeth *pr. 3 pl.* postpone or hinder the probate of 4525, keep (them) waiting 11,002; *pp.* **delaied** delayed 9512

delayinglye *adv.* hesitantly, with procrastination 3997*n*
delectable, delictable *adj.* delightful, pleasant 7821, 12,493–4
delectacion *n.* delight, pleasure 1097
deliberacion *n.* careful consideration 518, 10,275, 10,302+
deliceously, deliciously, delyciously *adv.* sumptuously 97, 5408, 10,726
delicious *adj.* delightful, pleasurable 1373, 4390, rich, choice 2173, 4386–7, 4388+, luxurious 5148; ~ **man** a person given to sensual pleasure 6818
deliciousnessis *n. pl.* spiritual delights 7882*n*
delyng *vbl. n.* having intimate relations 883
delitable, delitabil *adj.* delightful, pleasurable 134, 6820, 9423–4+
delyuerance *n.* release, freedom 7024, delivery, bringing forth of an offspring 11,853
deliuere, delyuere *v.* release, deliver 1185, 1191, 4866, save, save from 4977, 4982, 8056+; *imp.* **delyuere** 428, 7801, 8417+; *pr. 3 sg.* **delyuereth** 10,558, 10,559, 12,610; *pa. t.* **deliuered, delyuered, delyvered** saved 1748*bis*, 8416+, handed over, gave 1586, 7122, 7323; *pp.* **delyuered** 4875, 5270, 7452+
delve *v.* dig, cultivate 5319, 7751; *pr. 3 pl.* **delve** 4633
demande *n.* request 11,449; *pl.* **demandis, demaundis** questions 8441, 8444
deme *v.* judge 2705, 6671, 10,883+; *pr. 3 sg.* **deemeth** judges 3554*
demenyth *pr. 3 pl.* conduct (themselves) 10,613
depart(e) *v.* remove 11,490, distribute, share with 4812; *imp.* **depart** separate, sever 6521; *pr. 3 sg.* **depart, departeth, departith** 3401, 8118, 9045+, departs 6836; *pa. t.* **departed hym** *mistranslation, see notes* 664, left 11,911; *pp.* **departed, departet** 7031, 7679*, 11,154+, parted, spread out 1652, divided 2231*; *see* **parteth**
departyng *vbl. n.* separation, severance 10,477
depenes, depnesse *n.* depth, profundity 9195, 11,527, 11,529+
der, derre *pr. 1 sg.* dare, presume 2989, 12,064; *pr. 3 sg.* **derre, therre** 796, 2811, 2875+; *pr. 1 pl.* **derre** 2849; *pr. 3 pl.* **derre, ther** 2307, 3904, 3907+; *pa. t.* **dorste** 690, 2842, 9596; ~ **vndirtake** declare 390
dere *adj.* dear, beloved 285, 7323, precious 6794, 12,959, expensive, costly 5639; **holde** ~ hold in high esteem 5540
dere, derely, derly *adv.* expensively, at a high cost 803, 1431, 2798+, dearly, fondly 1460; *comp.* **derer, derrer** 2482, 4619, 11,006
derision *n.* scorn, mockery 22, 2132, 2133
derthe *n.* scarcity 6147, 12,852
descende, discende *v.* descend 1193, 10,900, 12,560+, proceed (to consideration of) 3042*n*, 8240, derive, be descended from 3299; *pr. 3 sg.* **descendeth, descendith, dessendeth, discendeth, dissendith** 1097, 2210, 4134+; *pr. 1 pl.*

descende 8241; *pr. 3 pl.* **descende, descendeth** 43, 710, 1277+; *pa. t.* **discendid, descended** 675, 1009, 6109+; *pp.* **descended** 3297
descendyng *part. adv.* in descending order 8124–5
descendynge *vbl. n.* descent 12,562
descrye *v.* describe 7891
desert(e) *n.* merit 7526, 7946; *pl.* **dessertes** rewards 292
deserte *adj.* desolate 1375
deserve *v.* deserve, merit 1584, 1773–4, 11,812; *pr. 3 sg.* **deserueth, deservith** 5544–5, 11,804, serves to the end 4146*n*; *pr. 3 pl.* **deserue, deserve** 280, 1650, 4541+; *pp.* **deserved, deservid** 2678, 2981, 3663+
desflourryng *vbl. n.* depriving a woman of virginity 913
desgysynesses *n. pl.* eccentric or extraordinary behavior 6414*n*
desioine, disioine *v.* sever, separate 7705, disunite, divide 7718
desire *v.* devote himself to, give himself up (to) 4010*n*; *pr. 3 sg.* **desyreth** 8366*n*
desirous, desyrous *adj.* avaricious, covetous 4770, 4902, 4904, eager 4078
desirously, desyrously *adv.* eagerly 2554, 3233
despice, despise, despyse, dispice, dispise, dispyse *v.* despise, scorn, look down on 2073, 2078, 7238+; *imp.* **dispise** 11,072; *pr. 3 sg.* **despiseth, dispiceth, dispise, dispiseth** 855, 2440, 9613+; *pr. 3 pl.* **dispiseth, dispiceth** 6774, 9529, 10,316+, **dispice, dispise** speak ill of, belittle 5666, 5866; *pa. t.* **dispiced, dispised** 6712, 8331, 9977; *pp.* **dispised** 5345, 6943, 9636; ~ **his harme** scorns injury 9564
despit(e), despyte, dispit(e), dispyt(e) *n.* disdain, scorn, contempt 17, 1476, 1855+, contemptuous speech 2930, 8559
determined *pp.* produced, made perfectly 9834*n*
detraccion *n.* slander, calumny 2219, 5950; *pl.* **detraccions** 2908
dette *n.* debt, obligation 8146, 8149, 8634+, the marital debt 11,795, 11,811; *pl.* **dettis** 7908, 7909, 7975
deuocion, devocion *n.* devotion, reverence, piety 2407, 3396, 8664+
deuoire, devoir(e) *n.* utmost 1369, 1635, 1845+
devided *pp.* separate, apart 12,212
devine *adj.* theological (virtues) 142*n*, 8244, 8247+
devynite *n.* theology 1925
devinours *n. pl.* soothsayers, augurs 390, 411
devise *v.* describe 6575, 8946, 12181+, distinguish 6672, 6811, imagine 6556, 6558, 7481; *pr. 3 sg.* **deviseth, dyviseth** discusses, communicates 4469, 8882**n*, divides 5405, 8355; *pa. t.* **devised** planned 8292; *pp.* **devised** 5015, 5075, 9804+
dewed *pp.* dewy 8659

dewith *pr. 3 sg.* bedews 7294
dyggys *n. pl.* clamps, shackles 4087*n*
dignite(e) *n.* high estate, rank, position 1708, 2071, 3624+; *pl.* **dignitees, digniteis** 4468, 4474, 4742+, functions, offices 12,129
diligens *n.* persistent effort 4949, 5661, 11,412+
dymme *adj.* dark 9442
dymnes *n.* dullness of vision 11,198
dis, diz, deez *n. pl.* game of dice 2004, 4320, dice 4763
disceuith *pr. 3 sg.* destroys 1488
discharcheth *pr. 3 sg.* disburdens 7375
discipline *n.* mortification of the flesh by penance 12,239, 12,366; **take goode** ~ exert self-control, that is, mortify the flesh 6163–4
discipline *v.* regulate, govern 4003, 4014, 9280; *pr. 3 pl.* **discipline** 5537
discomfit, disconfit *v.* defeat 1338, 5003; *pp.* **discounfit** overcome, ruined 10,285–6
discorde *n.* dissension, strife 3389, 3542, 3547+; *pl.* **discordis** 6098
discouere *v.* disclose, reveal 2710, 9949, 9957
discrecion *n.* prudence, moderation 4339, 4349–50, 4350+
discrese *v.* diminish, abate 1057; *pr. 3 sg.* **discreesceth** suffers reverses 3227
discrieth *pr. 3 sg.* announces, proclaims 2126
discrye *v.* describe 4631; *pr. 3 pl.* **discrie** 9745
discryveth *pr. 3 sg.* describes 6304
disdeyne, dysdeyne *n.* scorn, disdain 6074–5, 8558–9, 10,801
disease, disese, disesse *n.* distress, hardship 1797, 4802, 5822+, illness 9951; *pl.* **diseasses, diseassis, diseses, disseses** 5766, 10,224, 10,698
diseassed *pp.* in distress, hardship 10,713, 10,824, 10,956
disfigured, disfygured *pp.* disfigured, ugly 876, monstrous 3130
disfiguryngys *vbl. n. pl.* alterations of appearance 2328**n*
disgesy, degysee *adj.* strange, extraordinary 2120, distinct, different (from) 7373
disgyse *v.* dress in elaborate or fashionable clothing 2281; *pr. 3 sg.* **disgyseth** disguises 9403; *pp.* **disgyssed** disfigured, monstrous 1254
disgysyngys, disguysynges *vbl. n. pl.* elaborate or fashionable attire 2327, 2485
disheretyng, dysseherytinge *vbl. n.* disinheritance 3664, 5197
disheryteth, disseheriteth *pr. 3 sg.* disinherits 4562, 5400–1; *pr. 3 pl.* **disseheryte** 4660; *pp.* **disheretid, disseheryted** 1825, 3654
dishonest, disonest, dyssehonest *adj.* dishonorable 8025, unchaste, lewd, shameful 11,729, 12,869
dishoneste *n.* sexual indulgence 11,284

dishonestly, disonestly *adv.* lewdly, immodestly 5038, 5354, 10,037
dismesureth *pr. 3 sg.* abuses, uses excessively 4113*n*
disnaturel *adj.* unnatural, brutish 3527
disordeyned *pp.* forbidden, prohibited 5200*n*
disordenat, disordonat, disseordenat, disseordonat *adj.* immoderate, excessive, inordinate 1422, 4916, 6374+, dissolute 5064, irregular, disordered 1378, 1390, 1403+
disordenatly, dissordonatly *adv.* excessively, immoderately 1391, 4430
dispende *v.* spend 4432, 4792, waste, squander 2444; *pr. 2 sg.* **dispende, dispendest** 2082–3, 2699, 5518; *pr. 3 sg.* **dispendeth, despendeth, dispendith** 2445, 5623, 9183+; *pr. 3 pl.* **dispende, dispendeth, despendeth** 4488, 4819, 10,402+; *pa. t.* **dispended, dispent** 2630, 5621; *pp.* **dispended, dispent** 584, 1896, 8407+
dispens *n.* expenditure 1502; *pl.* **dispenses** 5635, 9894
dispensatoures *n. pl.* stewards 4816
dispitable *adj.* wretched, despicable, lowly 8545*n*, 8556, 8799
dispiteth *pr. 3 sg.* scorns, looks down on 8906; *pp.* **dispited** belittled, disparaged 874
dispiteful, dispitful *adj.* wretched, despicable 2640, 11,614
dyspoyle *v.* undress, strip 3868; *pr. 3 pl.* **dispoyleth** rob, plunder 4520; *pa. t.* **dispoiled** 2529
disporte *n.* amusement, entertainment 11,381; *pl.* **disportes, disportis, disportys** diversions, entertainments 1694, 2664, 6502+
disporte *v.* amuse, enjoy (himself) 5305; *pr. 3 sg.* **disporteth** 2350, 2355
disposeth *pr. 3 pl.* conduct, govern (themselves) 10,605
disprayse, disprise *v.* think or speak depreciatingly of 157, 6345*, 8593*+; *pr. 3 sg.* **disprayseth** 8692, 8710–1, 8906; *pa. t.* **dispreysed** 6523
disputacion *n.* debate 3937, 5516
disputed *pa. t.* discussed, engaged in philosophic disputation 6797, 9626
dysseyveable *adj.* deceitful, scheming 3928
disseuerance *n.* separation 4886
disseuere *v.* separate, part, sever 7705; *imp.* **disseuere, desseure** 6552, 6624; *pr. 3 sg.* **deseuereth, desceuereth** 4891, 7241; *pp.* **disseuered, deseueryd, desevred, desseuered, desseueryd** 814, 3327–8, 7679+
disseueryng, disceueryng *vbl. n.* separation, severance 6519, 6529
distemperaunce *n.* improper proportion 9248, 9250–1
distinge *v.* distinguish 9211, 9420
distorbeth, distorbith *pr. 3 pl.* hinder, impede, obstruct 4671, 6099; *pp.* **distorbed** prevented (from) 4267
distribucion *n.* portion, share 7870

disworshipeth, disworshippeth *pr. 3 sg.* dishonors 727–8, treats with contempt 2949–50; *pr. 3 pl.* **disworshipeth** 580

disworshippe *n.* dishonor 5323

diuers(e), dyuers(e) *adj.* different 1263, 3345, 4246+, adverse, hostile 4843, vicious 1259, cruel 279, 6574, perverse 6156, 6187, evil 9442*n*

dyuerse *pr. 3 pl.* differ 8290

dyviseth *see* **devise**

do(o) *v.* do, act 75, 122, 273; *imp.* **doo** 1635, 3538, 3956+; *pr. 1 sg.* **do(o)** 1507, 1510, 1512; *pr. 2 sg.* **doest, doo, dooest(e), doost(e)** 553, 762, 2068+; *pr. 3 sg.* **do(o), doeth, dooeth, dooth(e), dooþe, doth(e), doþe** 3312, 3825+; *pr. 1 pl.* **doo** 2232, 2491; *pr. 2 pl.* **do(o)** 385, 2847; *pr. 3 pl.* **do(o), doeth, don, doon, dooth** 454, 540, 1948+; *pa. t. 1 sg. and pl.* **dide, dedde** 3483, 6598; *pa. t. 2 sg.* **didest** 2692, 5121; *pa. t. 3 sg.* **did(e), didde, dydde, ded(e), dedde** 663, 3277, 3613+; *pa. t. 3 pl.* **did, didde** 347, 745, 969+; *pp.* **don(e), doon(e)** 14, 585, 1508+; ~ **after** imitate 9330, ~ **evil his erande** conducts his affairs poorly 11,525*n*

doctrinis *n. pl.* beliefs, teachings 4831

doyng(e), dooyng *vbl. n.* doing, acting, performing 5487, 5856, bestowing 2793

dome, doome *n.* divine judgment 3555, The Judgment 3952; *pl.* **domes, doomes** opinions 3195, 3667; **day(e) of** ~ Judgment Day 797, 1210, 1243+

dominacioунes *mistranslation, see notes* 4414

donne mouse *mistranslation, see notes* 3161

doome, domme, doomme, doumbe *adj.* dumb, without critical faculties 1615, 3751, 5413+, silent 11,496; **the** ~ dumb persons 5692

dotardes *n. pl.* fools, simpletons 2332

double *adv.* twice over 1064, 2162, 2769+; ~ **foolde** 5894

doubt(e), doulte, dowte *n.* doubt, uncertainty 2746, 7642, 8577+

doubt(e), doute, dowte *v.* fear 4386, 6745, 7633+, doubt 2244; *imp.* **doute, dowte** 5980, 6058, 7137; *pr. 3 sg.* **doubteth, douteth, dowteth, dowthet** 4202, 4856, 8313+; *pr. 1 pl.* **dowte** 4259; *pr. 3 pl.* **doubte, doubteth, doute, dowte, douteth** 2333, 6933, 7018+; *pa. t.* **doubted** 3571; *pp.* **doute, douted** 1554, 10477

doubtyng, doutyng(e) *vbl. n.* doubt, doubting 11,398*bis*, 11,400+

dragon *n.* serpent 3256, 3258, the Devil 9925

draughtis *n. pl.* drinks 4507

drawe *v.* lead, attract 277, 291, 1547+, keep back, restrain 798, 811, draw away 1432, lead out 1185, eradicate 1372, 1443, 7410, be drawn 2193, bear (witness) 6021, pull 10,642, elicit 8668, bring back 9670, ~ **abakke** put back, detract 2220, ~ **aright** follow the right path 1385; *pr. 3 sg.*

draweth 1272*, 5435, 10,347+, refrains (from) 5419, withdraws 10,079, lures, entices 11,828, draws, bends (bow) 9939, causes 11,329; *pr. 3 pl.* **drawe, draweth** 5253, 6440, 7650+, drag, pull 704, 2287; *pa. t.* **drewe, drowe, drue** 850, 1012, 1195+; *part.* **drawyng aȝeyns** opposing, reversing 2698; *pp.* **drawen** 2642, 2863, 9937, drawn (sword) 3912

dresse *v.* care for, tend to 4015, address (one's) attention, apply (oneself) to 9219; *pr. 3 sg.* **dresseth** 8805, arms 3181; ~ **his saille** direct his course, proceed 10,241, ~ **his peyne** directs his efforts 2257

drinkes *n. pl.* drinking bouts 5643*n*

dropyngys *n. pl.* sap 7332

droughte, drouthe *n.* drought 3440, 6147

drye *adj.* paid in cash 4643*n*

due *adj.* appropriate, proper 273, 5530

dulle *adj.* listless, disinclined 4218, 8834, niggardly 10,399*n*

duresse *n.* harm,injury 9598

dureth *pr. 3 sg.* lives, endures 10,593

dwelle *v.* remain, stay 284, 859, 5676+, live, dwell, reside 1888, 3116, 7768+; *pr. 3 sg.* **dwelleth, dwellith** 3231, 5028, 5733+; *pr. 3 pl.* **dwellith** 7058; *pa. t.* **dwelled** 931; *pp.* **dwelled, dwelte** 9902, 10,000

dwelleres *see* **nere dwelleres**

dwellyng *adj.* ~ **place** home, residence 3240

dyee *v.* dye 7704

ease *n.* **(welle, wel) at** ~ easy of mind, relaxed 4311, 5393, undisturbed 7262, 12,702, free from want or care 4801; *pl.* **eases, easses** pleasures 5076, 11,314

ease *v.* mitigate 9980, free from anxiety, relieve (the burden of) 1037; *pr. 3 sg.* **easeth, eeseth** alleviates 10,653, rests 12,657*n*, deprives 3703

easy *adj.* easy, not difficult 10,664, gentle, not oppressive 12,571

eddir *n.* adder 2511

edifie *v.* improve, strengthen spiritually 11,085, 12,282

eegre *adj.* angry 3368

eevyn, evyn *n.* evening 578, 3885, 8574+

egal *adj.* equal (to), on a par (with) 1162, even 9159*n*

egirly, egrely *adv.* harshly 2675, 6369

eyen *see* **iye**

eyre ere(e), erre *v.* plough 4633, 5318, 11,950

eyre *n.* heir 7524. *See* **heire**

either, eyther *see* **oother**

elles *n. pl.* measures 3955

embelissheth, enbelesshith *pr. 3 sg.* endows or adorns with beauty 7315*, 12,064; *pr. 3 pl.* **embelesshith** 12,116
empeched *pp.* hindered, impeded 4343
empechement *n.* impediment 11,887
emperoures *n. pl. mistranslation, see notes* 4414
emploie, employe, enploie *v.* utilize, use, make use of 2478, 4006, spend 4644, devote, apply (himself) to 570, 11,574; *pr. 2 sg.* **emploiest** 2665; *pr. 3 sg.* **employeth** 6262; *pr. 3 pl.* **emploieth** 11,375; *pp.* **employed** 1871, 1895, 7537+
empressed *pp.* called to service, engaged in a chivalric enterprise 10,668*n*
empressed *pp.* oppressed with adversity 12,659*n*
emprice, emprise *n.* enterprise 6919, 6925, 6929+; *pl.* **emprises** 6362, 6921, 10,276
enbrace, enbrase *v.* enkindle, inflame 5021, 6068; *pr. 3 sg.* **embrasceth** 4270; *pr. 3 pl.* **enbraceth** 11,315; *pp.* **enbrased** 8497
enbraceth, enbraseth, enbrasith *pr. 3 sg.* embraces, grasps 1268, 3179, 7084–5; *pp.* **enbrassed** 1269; **enbrasid togeder** in each other's grasp 4930
enbraser *n.* fire 8097*n*
enchaunteth *pr. 3 sg.* bewitches, beguiles 4847; *pr. 3 pl.* **enchant, enchanteth** 2510, 5900; *pa. t.* **enchaunted** 1612; *pp.* **enchaunted** 2827, 3188*
enchantour *n.* magician, sorcerer, conjuror 378, 384, 2510; *pl.* **enchantours, enchantures** 410, 1921, 5900+
enchauntementis *n. pl.* magic spells 4503
enclineth *pr. 3 sg.* is inclined 9288; *pp.* **enclined** 9392
encloseth *pr. 3 sg.* contains, comprehends 5192, 7450; *pp.* **enclosed** 7364, 7370
encrece *n.* profit, growth, augmentation 4601
encrese, encresse *v.* grow 6313, become more numerous 1056, magnify, worsen 10,006; *pr. 3 sg. encrese,* **encresceth, encresseth, encressith** 5226, 11,239, 12,714, prospers 3227, increases 3252, 4859, 9803; *pr. 3 pl.* **encrese, encreseth, encressith** 4130, 5893, 6179+; *pp.* **encressed** 8576–7
ende *n.* death 4169, 4223
endente *v.* be tame 10,593*n*
endeted, endetted *pp.* obligated 9567, in debt (to) 7975, 8642
endure *v.* last 4207, 6575, 9066+, endure, suffer 6557; *pr. 3 sg.* **endureth** lives 11,741; *pr. 3 pl.* **endureth** 576, 9748; *part.* **enduryng** 6951; *pp.* **endured** 6945
enduryng *vbl. n.* endurance 9587
enfamine *v.* starve 12,369; *pp.* **famined** 12,370*n*, 12,373
enfantesied *pp.* childish 12,919*n*

enflamed *pp.* aroused 3364
enforce *v.* constrain, compel 7000; *pr. 3 pl.* **enforceth** try, make an effort 2765; *pp.* **enforced** ravished, raped 3661, ~ **ayein** with added force 2869–70
enforme *v.* train, instruct 10,591
engin, engyne *n.* intelligence, skill 7143, catapult 4138, 8019; *pl.* **enginis** tricks, snares 9389
engloute, englotte *v.* swallow 5754; *pr. 3 pl.* **englotte** gulp down 4508*n*
enhaunseth, enhuanseth *pr. 3 sg.* exalts, elevates spiritually 8938*bis*, exalts itself 2947; *pa. t.* **enhuansed** 2972; *part.* **enhaunsynge** increasing 4531–2; *pp.* **enhansed** raised, advanced 2018
enlaced *pp.* bound 10,115
ennoy *n.* weariness 3742*
enpeire, enpeyre *v.* impair, harm 1067, 12,281; *pr. 3 sg.* **enpeirith** 12,279; *part.* **empeyryng** deteriorating, growing worse 4120–1, 4123; *pp.* **enpeired, enpeyred** damaged 939, 940
enpride, enpryde *v.* pride (oneself) 3070, 3075; *pr. 3 pl.* **enprideth** 6773
ensample *n.* model 364, illustration, example 10,800, 11,622; *pl.* **ensamples** 10502
enserchyng *part.* act of examining or enquiring into 9195*
entechid *pp.* infected 5777
entenciones *n. pl.* purposes, intentions 3193, 9206–7
entent(e) *n.* purpose, intention 280, 813, 1032+
ententively *adv.* purposefully 11,480
entirmellid *pa. t.* intermixed 1561
entremete *v.* concern (himself) 9205
entrete *v.* deal with 9074; *pp.* **vilensly entreted** mistreated, abused 8555
envenymeth, envenemed *pr. 3 sg.* infects with poison 5957, 12,863*; *pp.* **envenimed, envenymed** 3173, 11,277
envenimoures *n. pl.* poisoners 421*n*
envenimous(e) *adj.* malevolent, pernicious 3220, 5565
equalite *n.* equity, impartiality, fairness 9260*n*
equite(e), equity *n.* equity, impartiality, fairness 170, 174, 178+, moderation, prudence, reasonableness 9286, 9290, 9322+, temperance, sobriety 12,936
er *prep.* before 3980; *see* **or**
eraigne *n.* spider 9624
erande *n.* affairs 11,525*n*
ernest *n.* intense desire 3122
erres *n. pl.* paths 4194*
erthely *adj.* worldly 430, 699, 7691+; ~ **paradis** Garden of Eden 5584, 7305, 11,776–7

escape *see* **ascape**
eschapeth *see* **ascape**
eschaufed *pp.* warm 3684–5
eschewe *adj.* easily frightened 10,110
eschewe *v.* avoid, shun, escape 841, 1276, 2050+; *pr. 3 sg.* **escheweth** 10,148; *pr. 3 pl.* **eschewe** 983, 3797; *pa. t.* **eschewed** 6739
esyly, eesyly *adj.* meekly, gently 3699, 8556, easily 6899
esprove *v.* make trial of, subject to deliberate test 8001**n*
estamme *Fr. n.* a garment or covering of coarse light cotton or woolen cloth 751**n*
every *pron.* everyone 8177, 9966, 10,365+
evildooerris *n. pl.* wicked people 10,857
evilseierris, evilseiers *n. pl.* detractors 5918, 5930
evil taught *phr.* ill mannered 6003
evil(le) wil (will, wille) *phr.* hatred, ill will, malevolence 2904, 7985–6, 11,666+; *pl.* ~ **willes** 6098, 7754
evinly, evynly *adv.* on a par 3589, equal in rank 8327
evyn *adj.* straight along 6473; ~ **as** on a par with, equal to 398
evynsonge *n.* vespers 5346
example *n.* model, pattern 5232, 10,356, 12,268+, exemplary tale 34, 481, 1534+, illustrative example 733, 2524, 3274+, bad example 2734, 2784, 12,282; *pl.* **examples, examplis** 177, 3767, 4262+
excite *v.* rouse 4014
executoures *n. pl.* executors (of wills) 4524
exhersisist *pr. 2 sg.* devote (yourself) to 1864
exile *n.* the world as a 'vale of tears' 8494*n*, 11,616*
exilleth *pr. 3 sg.* ruins, destroys 1488; *pp.* **exiled, exyled** exiled, banished 3654, in exile 1736
exortacion *n.* urging 4846

fabille, fable *n.* fable 9336, idle talk 2002, 4753; *pl.* **fables, fablis** 4753, 9348, falsehoods 4321
fade *adj.* tasteless, insipid 7693
fade *v.* weaken 7692
faile *n.* **withowten** ~ doubtless, for certain 2331
fail(e), fayle *v.* fail (to perform) 273, 6806*bis*+, diminish, fade 6841; *pr. 3 sg.* **faile, faille, faileth, fayleth** is lacking 3789, 3790*, 9834+, makes default of 9895, 9896, 9897, fades 6834; *pr. 3 pl.* **faile, failleth** 6503, 11,465, 11,469+; *pp.* **failled** 10,387
fayre, feyre *n.* fair 2242, 4008, 6682

faire, fayre, feyr(e), feir(e), ferre *adj.* morally good, honorable 764, 2252, 7406+, bright, shining 1721, 11,960, pleasant, attractive, beautiful 2327, 2467, 6831+, clean, pure 11,961, flattering 2612; *comp.* **feirer** 4846, 9010; *superl.* **feirest, feyrest** 2326, 6281, 6732+

falle *v.* happen, befall 3651, 11328; *pr. 3 sg.* **falleth** 1953, 3579, 4650+; *pa. t.* **fel, felle** 381, 536, 10,788+; *pp.* **falle** 10,968

fallyng *vbl. n.* transgression, lapsing into sin 7997, 12471*n*

fals *n.* falsehood 515, 6038

falseire *n.* falsifier, counterfeiter 5965*

falsenes, falsnes *n.* falsehood 1074, 4650, 12838+; *pl.* **falsnesses** 4678, 5983

falseth, falsed *pr. 3 sg.* falsifies 5962*bis*

familiar, famylyer *adj.* intimate 12,035, belonging to the household 3233

familiarite *n.* intimacy, close acquaintanceship 10,607, 12,033, 12,036

famined *see* **enfamine**

fane *n.* weathervane 10,159

fanne *v.* winnow 8792

fantesie *n.* hypocrisy, deception 2807

fantesieth *pr. 3 sg.* imagines, conjures 9421

fanteth *pr. 3 sg.* declines, grows weak 4142

fardel *n.* bundle, contents 2468

fastynggys *vbl. n. pl.* fasts 11,754

fastynggoyng *n.* Shrovetide 1112

fatnesse *n.* fat 11,325

fat(te) *adj.* rich 10,501, 11,324

fault, faute *n.* lack, absence 6571; ~ **of herte** pusillanimity 4067, **for ~ of seyng of gremercy** for want of thanking 1827

favcon *n.* falcon 4080; *pl.* **faucons** 2281

favcouner *n.* falconer 4015

fauoryng *part.* mitigating guilt 9967

fauoure *n.* sympathetic regard, goodwill 10,577

febil(l), feble, feeble *adj.* faint 8706, fragile 12,069, weak 3089, 8043, 11,943+; *comp.* **febiler** 6873; *superl.* **febilest** 9080, 9398

febleth, feebleth *pr. 3 sg.* weakens 2891, 2893, 3783+

feend(e), fende *n.* devil 1260, 1264, 1268+; *pl.* **fendes, fendis, feendes, feendis, feendys** 2081, 2709, 3254+

feerse *adj.* proud, haughty 2439, fierce 4648

feyne *adj.* glad 8408

feintise, feyntise *n.* deceit, guile, pretence 4692, 8562, 8739

feirnes(se) *n.* beauty 6306, 6851

feith(e), feythe *n.* religious faith 1138, 1853, 11,211+, pledged word 911, 1587, 1936+, loyalty 2253, 2620, 4685+

felawe *n.* friend, companion, associate 952, 3628, person, fellow 3785, 4177, counterpart, match 4541, 5234, 12,844, fellow man 4586, peer 7558, ally 9422, opponent 5370; *pl.* **felawes** 537, 538, 2138+, partners 3304, 4626, 4999, spouses 6436, members 8393

felawly *adj.* friendly 1545

feleship(p), feleshippe, feleshypp, felechipp *n.* fellowship, companionship 1408, 1410, 1696+, companions 1693, 11,726–7, friendship 4586–7, partnership 4625, company 944, sexual intercourse 1082; *pl.* **feleshippes, feleshipes, felishippes** 1706, 2357, 4896+, entertainments 1698, bands of companions 8775

feleshipp(e) *v.* associate 3058, 4902, mate 11,896, have sexual intercourse with 11,839; *pr. 2 sg.* **feleshipest** 7514; *pr. 3 sg.* **feleshippeth** 3059, 3061; *pr. 1 pl.* **feleshipp** 7530; *pr. 3 pl.* **feleshipeth, feleshippeth** 2878*, 4904, 4906+; *pa. t.* **feleshipid** 1548; *pp.* **feleshiped** 7543

felle *adj.* harsh, cruel, sharp 756, 3596, 6076+, angry, irate 3360, 3703, 3707+, wicked 9130, fierce 6080, 6082

fellenes *n. pl.* villains 3355

fellenes(se), felnes(se) *n.* harshness, severity 6382, ill will 6129, 10,685, ire, wrath 3354*n*, 3703, 9462–3+; *pl.* **fellenesses** abusive words 10,990*n*

felleth *pr. 3 pl.* fill 2471

felly *adv.* harshly, cruelly, sharply 2934, 6076

felonye, felounye *n.* ill will, malice 3735, 7930; *pl.* **felonyes** 8953

fendely *adj.* fiendlike, diabolical 3005

fendesse *n.* female devil 395*n*

ferde *pp.* afraid 6932

ferde evil *phr.* ill treated 12,326

fere *adj.* distant, far away 4656, far 12,359

fere, ferre *adv.* afar, far 8565, 9620, 10,078+; **oo** ~ far off, from afar 7191

fere *conj.* **as** ~ **as** as far as, to the extent (that) 12,244

ferme *adj.* secure 9295, 10,163, 10,461+

fermyth *pr. 3 sg.* makes firm 7677

ferre *adj.* fair 5132*n*

feruent, fervent *adj.* zealous 4123, 6470, ardent, fervid 1396, 7842, 7861+, **fervent** *mistranslation, see notes* 5973, 5977; *comp.* **ferventlier** 2560

feruently(e), fervently *adv.* eagerly 1427, 4431, *with reference to food implying gluttony* 96*n*, 1716, 5576+, ardently, fervidly 1755, 3782, 7067+, hotly, passionately 5995, 8894, vehemently 6641

feruentnes(se), ferventnes(se) *n.* fervor, ardor, zeal 75*n*, 4336, 4342+, eagerness 4571, 5034, 9688, *with reference to food implying gluttony* 4387, 4395, 5590+, heat 6322

feruour *n.* ardor, passion 6329

fesantes *n. pl.* pheasants 5432

feste, feeste *n.* religious festival, holy day, feast day 591, 594, 596+, banquet, festivity, revel, entertainment 2086, 2292, 2452+; *pl.* **feestis, festes, festis, festys** 566, 581, 4495+, rejoicing 7263

festful *adj.* ~ **dayes** feast days 707, 2041, 9992

feted *pp.* elegant, polished 11,533

fetis *adj.* elegant, fashionable 2330

fetisly *adv.* elegantly 2487

feture *n.* semblance, likeness 12,498*n*

fevers *n. pl.* smiths 8482

figure *n.* form, appearance 6850, figure 12,166, 12,168, prefigurement 591; *pl.* **figures** 12,167, images, likenesses 5026, 9412

fygureth *pr. 3 pl.* imagine 7194*n*; *pp.* **figured** prefigured 10,655

fikilneses *n. pl.* deception 5983

filde, felde *n.* field 11,948, field of battle 6359, 8497

fyle *see* **defoule**

filed *see* **defouleth**

fyled *see* **defouleth**

filthe, filþe, fylthe *n.* (moral) filth, sinfulness, evil 5245, 5246, 5288+, dirt, filth 12,272, excrement 12,616, trash 6639, 6867, 6895+, baseness, abjectness 11,613, impurity, defilement (of sin) 11,967

fynde *v.* acquire, receive 273*n*, 7357, 9929, contrive 6886

fyndyng *vbl. n.* acquisition 9160

fyne *v.* refine, purify 6593; *pr. 3 sg.* **fynyth** 7690; *pp.* **fyned** 6592, 7708

fine, fyne *adj.* pure, virtuous 4051, 6656, excellent 2480*n*, sheer 2498, utter 3858

firste fader *phr.* Adam 8438

first modir *phr.* Eve 394

flaile *n.* leper's rattle 2372*n*

flambe, flaumbe, flaume, flavmbe *n.* flame 3259, 5160, 6071+

fle(e) *v.* avoid, shun 39, 121, 11,348+, flee, run away 2542, 2858; *imp.* **flee** 5166*bis*, 5278+; *pr. 3 sg.* **fleeth, fleith** 5362, 6571, 6651+, passes 9632; *pr. 3 pl.* **fleeth, fleith** 2134, 2725, 8770+; *pa. t.* **fledde** 2723, 6711; *pp.* **fled** 8852

flee *v.* fly 4078, 4081, 4099+; *pr. 3 sg.* **fleeth** 11,355, 12,779; *pr. 3 pl.* **fleeth, fleith** 5928, 8866; *part.* **fleyng(e)** 6078, 6498

flee *v.* flay 4537*; *pr. 3 sg.* **fleith** 5720 *n*; *pr. 3 pl.* **flee, fleeth(e)** 4530*, 5720*n*, 10,223

fleyng(e) *vbl. n.* fleeing 5165, 5282, 8181
fleeynge *adj.* fleeting 4052
fleeys *n. pl.* flies 3095, 3097
fleer *n.* flayer 2516
fleyngys *vbl. n.* evasive flights 9909
flematique *adj.* phlegmatic person 9395
flesshe *n.* human nature, physical or sensual nature 202, 224, 846+, human body 5756, meat 1112, 2557, 5632+, kindred, family 924; **mevying of the ~** sexual arousal 840, **lightnes of the ~** promiscuity 850*n*, **delit of the ~** sensual pleasure 1423
flesshely *adv.* carnally 923, 11,762
flesshely(e) *adj.* sensual, carnal 837, 854, 8308+, human, natural 2714, 5725, 7051, earthly, worldly 3008, 3011, 10,012+; ~ **dede** sexual intercourse 869–70, ~ **delites** sensual pleasures 7210, ~ **felechipp (feleship)** sexual intercourse 836, 1082
flit, flytte *v.* deviate from justice 10,868*n*, change (his) behavior 3151*n*; *pr. 2 sg.* **flette** be deflected 12,730**n*; *pr. 3 sg.* **fliteth** passes away, departs 6834
flode, floode *n.* the Deluge 665, 4412, flood 12,578, 12,583, 12,586, water (of the sea) 11,399; *pl.* **flodis, floodes** rivers 673, floods 11,546
floorisshe *v.* grow vigorously 7302–3; *pr. 3 sg.* **florissheth, florisshet** 6307, 6319, 10,409; *pr. 3 pl.* **florissheth** 7317; **florisshed woordis** rhetorical language 11,531–2
flore *n.* floor 7741
flossoye *Fr. n.* a garment or covering of coarse woolen or cotton cloth 751*n*
flour(e) de liz (lis) *n.* lily 12,027, 12,030, 12,040+
floure *n.* flour 7241, 7857, 11,497
floured *pp.* flowery 8659
floureth, flowreth *pr. 3 sg.* blossoms 545, thrives 546
foilde *pr. 3 sg.* ~ **aȝein** returns 9447
foilde, folde, foolde *n.* times 2443, 2491, 6641+; **double** ~ 5894
fole, foly(e), fooly *adj.* foolish 37*bis*, 75+, lewd, lascivious 2411, 6599, 10,033+
foliche *adj.* foolish 5841, 5844
folily(e), folyly *adv.* foolishly 578, 5621, 10,402+, lewdly, lasciviously 10,037
folisshe, folysshe, foolysshe *adj.* foolish 748*, 4336, 6331+, lewd, lascivious 440, 10,025
follying *part.* acting foolishly 12,499
fonde *pa. t.* invented, devised 5969; *pp.* **founde, founded** 393, built, erected 8009, 9729, 12664
fonned, fonnyd *pp.* foolish 5050, 5054, 6373

foole *n.* foal 10350

for *prep.* because of 280, 283, 451+, for the sake of 361, 362, 663+, as, as being 493, 942, 1116+, with regard to 466, 467, 807, in 985*bis*, with 1470, in exchange for 1291, 1293*bis*+, from 3326, 8859, 8860, in return for 1596*bis*, 1597+

forbedyng *vbl. n.* prohibition 892

forbedith *pr. 3 sg.* forbids 1086, 1087, 1102+; *pa. t.* **forbade** 396, 891; *pp.* **forbedyn, forboden, forbodyn** 837, 846, 866+

forbere *v.* show forbearance 3721, 3722, have a care for 9077, 9079, 9081, restrain (himself) 11,842, 11,843, refrain from, forgo 11,846, 11,849, 11,850+, spare 8027; *pr. 3 sg.* **forberith** 9019, 9933; *pr. 3 pl.* **forberith** 9077; *pp.* **forborne** 9080

forby, forthby *adv.* nearby 381, 2594, 8649+

fordoo *v.* destroy 6385; *pr. 3 pl.* **fordothe** 1411

forein(e), foreyn *adj.* external 9306, 9313, acquired rather than native 6771

forfete *v.* transgress, violate 1428

forfetis *n. pl.* misdeeds 10,402–3*n*

forgeth *pr. 3 sg.* makes, forges 5970, 8006; *pa. t.* **forged** 5969

forȝete, forgete *v.* forget 3348, 11,602, 12,457; *imp.* **forȝete** 6568; *pr. 3 sg.* **forgeteth, forgetheth, forȝethet, forȝeth, forȝeteth, forȝetith, foryeteth** 1714*n*, 10,082, 12,959+; *pr. 3 pl.* **forȝete, forȝetith, foryeteth** 432, 6654, 7207+; *pa. t.* **forgate, forȝat, forȝate** 734, 1549, 1615+; *pp.* **forȝetin, forȝetyn** 1823, 5749, 7977+

forȝetynge, foryetyng *vbl. n.* forgetting 4045, 12,127

forȝif(f), forȝefe, foryeve *v.* forgive 2563, 2662, 7925+; *imp.* **forȝif** 7801, 7975, 7982+; *pr. 1 sg.* **forȝif** 7932; *pr. 3 sg.* **forȝefeth, forȝiffeth, forȝiff** 6393, 10,130, 10,683+; *pr. 1 pl.* **forȝif** 7906, 7924, 7989; *pa. t.* **forȝaf** 7940; *pp.* **foryeven, foryoven, forȝovyn** 1812, 6209, 6211+

forked *adj.* cloven, divided, *fig.* ambiguous, equivocal 9447*n*

forme *n.* semblance, likeness 373, 3257, 6847+, image 9416, model, pattern 5231, 10,356, shape, form 9230, 10,590, 11,741+; *pl.* **formes, fourmes** images 9407, 9410, 9412, appearances, guises 5970

forme *v.* make 7404; *pr. 3 sg.* **formeth** 7403; *pr. 3 pl.* **forme** 11,414; *pa. t.* **formed, formyd** 1568, 7049, 7405

forsake *v.* repudiate, disavow 1516, refuse, reject 5113; *pr. 3 sg.* **forsaketh** 5941–2; *pr. 3 pl.* **forsaketh** renounce 9650; *pa. t.* **forsooke** 5330, 8331; *part.* **forsakyng** 854; *pp.* **forsakyn** 419, 2866

forse *n.* matter, concern 895

forsighte *n.* prudence 9365

forswere *v.* commit perjury 536, 1029, 4662+; *pr. 1 sg.* **forswere** repudiate, renounce 1848; *pr. 3 sg.* **forswere, forswereth, forswerith** 515, 528, 5139+; *pr. 3 pl.* **forswereth** 504; *pp.* **forsworne** 2276

forswererris *n. pl.* perjurers 1919

forsweryng(e) *vbl. n.* perjury 108, 5800, 5993

fort *adj.* strong, powerful 10,176

forthby *see* **forby**

forthynketh, forthynkith *pr. 3 sg. with personal object* I regret *or* repent 1513, 2848, 5956

fortuned *pa. t.* happened 2602

foryetefull *adj.* forgetful 3928

foryetill *adj.* forgetful 4040

foryetilnes, foryetylnes, forȝetilnesse *n.* forgetfulness as a branch of sloth 68, 4034, 4035+, disregard, neglect 4526*n*; *see* **putteth**

foule, fowle *adj.* foul, heinous 1576, 2123, 2127+, wicked 1378, 3435, 3542+, mean, base, wretched 2640, 2682, 2683+, disgraceful, ignominious 1362, 10,175, corrupt 2574, 12,614, ugly 3134, 8905, coarse, common 5579, unchaste 6441, 11,487, 12,917+, offensive, obscene 11,292, dirty, filthy 12,263*bis*, 12,265+, clouded 9441; *comp.* **fouler, fouller** 11,971, 12,257, 12,259+; *superl.* **foulest, fowlest** 3067, 5132, 7213+; ~ **feende** devil 5022

fouled *see* **defouleth**

fouler *n.* fowler 12,782

fouleth, foulleth *see* **defouleth**

foulnes *n.* ugliness, hideousness 812

freelnes *n.* frailty, weakness 8485

freely, frely *adv.* with freedom of will 6997, unreservedly 6998

freendly *adj.* loving 4522

freller *comp. adj.* frailer, weaker 6874

frendeship(p), frendshipp *n.* benignity, benevolence, love of one's fellow man 166*n*, 167, 9013+, favor, goodwill 2875, friendship, affection 116, 6373–4, 8326+, love 9462

frenesse *n.* liberality, grace of God 1553

frensye *n.* madness 3425

frere *n.* friar 4256, 13,006

fresshely *adv.* gaily 2618

freteth *pr. 3 sg.* gnaws, champs 4192

friture *n.* fritter 2180; *pl.* **fritures** 2172

froo *adv.* **too and** ~ back and forth 3361–2, 11,399–400

fro(o) *conj.* from the time that 1046; ~ **that** 3705, 4099

frosshe *n.* frog 10,099, 10,100

froward *adj.* willful, perverse 901, 1712
fructifie *v.* bear fruit 7300, prosper, flourish 7303; *pr. 3 sg.* **fructifieth** grows 10500; *pr. 3 pl.* **fructifieth** 7317; *pa. t.* **fructified** 12,153
fruite *n.* offspring 878
fulfille, fullefille *v.* obey, follow 349, 1131, 9646+, fill to the full 1756, sate, satisfy 6990, 7199, 7220, bring to completion 1199; *pr. 2 sg.* **fulfille** 12746; *pr. 3 sg.* **fulfilleth** 557, 7078, 7223+; *part.* **fulfillyng** 333; *pp.* **fulfilled, fulfylled** 2017, 2870, 2907+
fulfillynge *vbl. n.* fulfillment 12,967
full(e), ful *adj.* complete 1094, 1107, full (of) 1261, 1371, 1375+; *comp.* **fuller** 4732; ~ **wexen** abounding, laden (with) 3278, **dranke** ~ **his throte** drank his fill 10,790
full(e) *adv.* very, exceedingly 308, 399, 5804+
fullers *poss. n.* cloth worker 9718
fully *adv.* completely 6583, 9573
funte *n.* font, basin 6587

game *n.* wild animal 9334, prize of victory 2231, 3776, 4147+; *pl.* **games** amusing behavior 2461. *See also* **paume**
garner *n.* granary 8794; *pl.* **gerneres, gernerys** 4698, 10,491, 10,520+
garson *n.* defence, garrison 8862
gate, gatis, gatys *see* **yeate**
gawdis, gawdys *n. pl.* jests, scoffs 5830; **make** ~ **and iapes** make (them) objects of scorn and mockery 5144–5
gaye *adj.* fine, splendid 8774
gebet *see* **gybet**
gedder, geder, gedir (togeder, togedir) *v.* gather 1878, 3964, 6263+, assemble, bring together 2178, 4852, amass (wealth) 4917, 9535; *pr. 3 sg.* **gederith** 2082; *pr. 3 pl.* **gader, gedreth** 4590, 10,906; *pp.* **geder, gedered** 9758, 10,521
geete, gete *v.* get, acquire, win 1480, 4453, 4917+; *pr. 3 sg.* **geeteth, geteth, geth, getheth, getith** 2078, 10,480, 10,794+; *pr. 2 pl.* **gete** 11,417; *pr. 3 pl.* **geeteth, geteth** 5187, 5760, 11,700+, bring, cause 5760; *pa. t.* **gate** 1004; *pp.* **geetyn, geten, getyn** 1002, 5511, 8053+
geffare *see* **cheffare**
geyneseyinge, geyneseynge, geyneseyyng, geynseyng, geynseyyng *vbl. n.* **withoute** ~ without question or contradiction 5539, 7790, 12,127+
genepre *n.* juniper tree 6314
general(l) *adj.* universal 1223**n*, 1236, in general 9*n*, 1377, 3052+
generally *adv.* commonly 838, 10,393, universally 8810, 8838, in general 7272

gentil, gentyl, ientil(le), ientyl *adj.* noble, well born 7100, 7102, 7110+, well bred 4097, 4098, 6655, excellent, noble in character 1626, 6656, 12,180+

gentillesse, ientilles(se) *n.* noble birth, nobility 7041, 7093, 7099, kindnesses, favors 1557*n*

gerdouned *see* **guerdon**

germayne, germain, germeines *adj.* natural, related by blood 2089, 2094, 9000

gesyne *n.* childbed 11,853

gesses *n. pl.* jesses 12,779, 12,780

geten *pp.* begotten 4561

getyng *vbl. n.* acquiring or amassing (wealth) 4431

giberisshe *n.* gibberish, unintelligible speech 11,506*n*

gybet, gebet *n.* gibbet, gallows 8413, 8740, 9847, rope, noose 8646*n*

girdel(l), girdle *n.* belt 12,228, 12,233, 12,236+

gyse *n.* manner 2037; *pl.* **gyses, guyses, gwyses** styles, fashions in dress 2338, 5065, ways, manners 5971, 9403, dishes 5664*n*

glaiue *n.* sword 971

glene *n.* acorn 1821*n*

glorifyeth, gloryfieth, gloryfyeth *pr. 3 sg.* takes pride (in), exults (in) 2956, 3006, 4372–3; *pp.* **glorified** 2968, praised, glorified 11,061

glorious(e) *adj.* vainglorious 2965, illustrious 6628, 7344

glose *n.* gloss, commentary 6240, 10406

glosyngys *vbl. n.* flatteries 8856

glotyth *pr. 3 pl.* swallow 5483*n*; *see* **engloute**

go(o) *v.* go 592, 698, 1384+; *imp.* **go(o)** 701, 1702, 10,471+; *pr. 1 sg.* **goo** 8028, 8824; *pr. 2 sg.* **goest** 1696, 1697, 1698+; *pr. 3 sg.* **gooeth, goeth, gooth(e), gothe, goo** 3785, 4187, 5257+; *pr. 1 pl.* **goo** 2086, 4187; *pr. 2 sg.* **goo** 5543; *pr. 3 pl.* **go(o), goeth, goothe, gothe** 712, 2200, 2361; *pa. t.* **went(e)** 476, 1006, 2622+; *pp.* **gon, goon** 1751, 1807, 3417+

godhed, godheede *n.* divine essence 1158, 1163, 7834

goyng *vbl. n.* going 5170

gomme *n.* sap 7331

goodedoer *n.* benefactor 1594; *pl.* **goodedoerris** 8630, 11,704

good(e) *n.* property, goods, wealth 347, 487, 496+; *pl.* **goddes, goodes, goodez, goodis, goodys** 433, 492, 499+, good things, benefactions, divine favors 148, 585, 1802+, virtues 7, good deeds 3815, 5893; **lytyll (litil)** ~ goods of fortune 124, 6689, 6690+, ~ **naturel(l)** goods of nature 2649, 7143, **mene** ~ goods of nature 125, 6681, 6754+

goodenes(se), goodnes(se) *n.* (divine) favor(s), benefaction(s), gift(s) 1219, 1603,

3136+, prosperity, good fortune 3292, 7462, 10422+, good deeds, benefaction 3036, 5844, 7132+, grace 5117, benefit 8080, good in general, spiritual virtue, piety 1316, 1477, 2236+, kindness, generosity, bounty 1654, 5599, 11,575+, worth, excellence 6858, 7896, honor, praise 2020, good things 2349, 2952, 12,997+; *pl.* **goodenesses, goodenessis, goodnesses, goodnessis** 1657, 3268, 8385+

goost(e), goste *n.* spirit, soul 3002, 8098, 8099

goostely(e), goostly, gostely, gostly *adj.* spiritual 1802, 2522, 3008+; ~ **fader** confessor 10,141, ~ **faderis** 766–7

goostely(e), gostely(e) *adv.* spiritually 790, 3301, 3329+

goouernance, gouernaunce *n.* rule, control 10,285, 10,286–7

gossep, gossop *n.* baptismal sponsor 5212, familiar acquaintance 3465; *pl.* **gossepis** 2355

gote *n.* goat 11,499

gouerne *v.* govern, rule, control 1777, 4022, 4370+; *pr. 3 sg.* **gouernyth, gouerneth** 6980, 8210, 8222+; *pr. 3 pl.* **gouerneth, governeth** 8203, 9526, 12095; *pa. t.* **gouerned** 8299; *pp.* **gouerned** 3225, 8275

gouernour(e), gouuernour *n.* master 7474, 8329, 9468, ruler 7769, captain 8815**n*

goupil *Fr. n.* she-fox 5915

grace *n.* boon, benefaction, favor 380, 4877, good name or reputation 1067, material favor, prosperity, good fortune 1104, 1106, divine grace, spiritual help 1219, 1278, 1279+, natural favor or endowment 2225, beauty, charm 2377, mercy, pardon 11430; *pl.* **graces** gifts of the Holy Ghost 139, 8101, 8109+, thanks 1465, 1658, 8761

graunte *v.* give 11,714; *pr. 3 sg.* **graunte, graunteth, grauntith, granteth** 5130, 5733, 12,501, accedes to 5129, allows 11,830; *pp.* **graunted, granted, grantid** 887, 894, 5322

graunges *n. pl.* farms 3653

graunte *n.* privilege, right 7817

greable *adj.* pleasing 741

gredy *adj.* greedy 10,729

gree *v.* show satisfaction 1623

grees, grese, gresse *n.* lard, fat 2177, 7242, 11,326

greeys *n. pl.* steps 3865

greyne *n.* **dyed in** ~ dyed crimson 7713*n*

greynes *n. pl.* seeds 12,048, 12,118, 12,124+

gremercy *n.* thanks 1721, 1725, 1726+

grenesse *n.* verdure 7286

gresse *n.* grass 3265, 3268, 10,642; **evil** ~ weeds 1380

grete mercy *phr.* thanks 1641
grete mete *n.* coarse food 11,321
gretnes(se) *n.* magnitude, greatness 908*, 915, 9609
greuously, grevously *adv.* gravely 527, 772–3, 1997+
greve *v.* burden, weigh down 1037, offend, make angry 2290, 2608, 3507+, harm, injure 3210, 3507; *imp.* **greve** 3734; *pr. 3 sg.* **grefeth, greve, greveth, grevith** 5474, 6648, grieves, annoys, vexes 2443, 3536, 4050; *pr. 3 pl.* **greveth** 3359, 3856, 4047; *pa. t.* **grevid** 2604, 2628, 2744+; *pp.* **grevid, greved, grevyd** 3346, 4865, 9838+
grevous(e) *adj.* hard, difficult to observe 314, 7937, grave 10,674, harsh 2877, heinous 922, 5192, 5449+, harmful, injurious 4808, 5829, 10,175+; *comp.* **grefouser, grevouser** 4814, 5449, 6778
grypeth *pr. 3 sg.* seizes 5049
groos *adj.* coarse, inferior 7243
grounde *n.* foundation 1147
grucche *v.* grumble, complain 6104, 6154; *pr. 3 sg.* **gruccheth** 3216, 6135, 6149+; *pr. 3 pl.* **grucche** 3441, 6144
grucchyng(e) *vbl. n.* grumbling, complaint 110, 4170, 6126+; *pl.* **grucchyngis** 6246
guerdon *n.* payment 1516
guerdon *v.* repay 2454; *pp.* **gerdouned** rewarded 10,911
guyle, gyle *n.* deception 85, 981, 4734
gurmantis *n. pl.* gluttons 577

ȝaraȝineis *adj.* of Saracen manufacture 8018
ȝeere, ȝere, ȝeres, ȝeris *see* **yere**
ȝefe, ȝeif, ȝif(e), ȝiffe, etc. *see* **yeve**
ȝefing *see* **yefyng**
ȝeynweyeth *pr. 3 sg.* reconsiders 8718
ȝelde, ȝeldeth, ȝoldeth, ȝalde, ȝolden, ȝoldyn *see* **yelde**
ȝerde *n.* yard 6833
ȝerde *n.* rod 10,636
ȝerely *adv.* yearly 2060, 4821
ȝifer, ȝiffer *n.* giver 8144, 8176, 10,986
ȝift(e), ȝiftes, ȝiftis *see* **yifte**
ȝisterevyn, ȝistirevyn *n.* last evening 5390, 5392
ȝone *adj.* that 10,837
ȝonge, yonge *adj.* young 2288, 2460, 5004+
ȝougethes *n.* youthful folly 6175
ȝough, ȝougthe, ȝouthe, yough, yougthe *n.* youth 742, 4103, 10,293+

habandoneth *see* **abaundoneth**
habaundoned *see* **abaundoneth**
haberion, haubergion *n.* coat of mail 9833, 10,142
habit(e) *n.* clothing 9658, 12,423, 12,456
habondantly, habundantly *adv.* plentifully 3085, 7660
haboundance, haboundaunce *n.* abundance 3247–8, 11,294, 12,996
haboundant *adj.* bountiful, generous 12,573, 12,576
habounde *v.* be full or complete 8383; *pr. 3 sg.* **haboundeth** abounds 11,146; *pr. 3 pl.* **haboundeth** abound 6630
haire, hayre *n.* hair-shirt 2793, 6415, 7151+
halowe *pr. 2 sg.* observe solemnly 551; *pr. 3 sg.* **haloweth** hallows 7688; *pp.* **halowed, halwed** 7671, 7706, 7727+, consecrated 12,201, 12,216
haloweth *pr. 3 sg.* cries out against, denounces 4782
halsse *pr. 3 pl.* embrace 2288; *pa. t.* **halsed** 12346
halsyngis *vbl. n.* embraces 2369
halte *adj.* the lame, the crippled 10,719
halteth *pr. 3 sg.* limps, walks unsteadily 9088
halydaye *n.* holy day 11,572; *pl.* **halidayes, halydayes** 227, 2040, 11,571
handel *v.* handle 12,200
happe *v.* chance, happen 522, 5787, 10,724; *pr. 3 sg.* **happeth, happith** 745, 862, 1273+
happy *adj.* blessed 12,968
hardde, harde *adj.* hard, difficult 3350, 3969, 4979+, harsh, severe, cruel 495, 746, 748; *comp.* **harder** 3968, 10,758; *superl.* **hardest** 4787; **of** ~ with difficulty 2116
harde *v.* harden 10,884; *pr. 3 sg.* **hardeth** 3150
hardely, hardily, hardyly *adv.* boldly 5574, 5880, 8918+, surely 5324
hardenes, hardnes(se) *n.* obstinacy, obduracy 3149, 4164, rigor, severity 10,169, 10,885
hardenys, hardinesse, hardynes *n.* boldness, bravery 6910, 9561, hardship 9539*n*
hardy(e) *adj.* bold, courageous, fearless 2515, 3469, 6359+
harlot *n.* rogue, rascal 3498, 3520, 3798 (*here* a fly); *pl.* **harlotes** base fellows 7884
harlotrie, harlotry(e), harlottrye *n.* wickedness, corruption, sin 2771*n*, 4164, 11,293+, ribaldry, obscenity 5827, 6258, filth, excrement 3071*n*, 3073, 12,616+; *pl.* **arlotries, harlotries, harlotryes** 7708–9, 7757, 9863+
harre *adj.* bitterly cold 2531*n*
harrowe *interj.* help! 4542
hasty *adj.* rash, hurried 10,276

haunteth *pr. 3 sg.* frequents 5396; *pr. 2 sg.* **hauntist** busy (yourself) with 1867; *pr. 3 pl.* **haunteth** 568
havyn *n.* port, harbor 6539, 7023, 10,239+
hazarde *n.* risk of loss 9851
hecche *n.* hedge 12,100, 12,360
hecchehogges *n. pl.* hedgehogs 8863
hede, heede *adj.* chief, capital (sin) 3338, 3740
heere *n.* hair 10,024
heerein *adv.* in this matter 5729
height(e), heighthe, heyghte, hight *n.* height 4134, 6305, 7640; **on** ~ aloft, on high 6474, 8963, 9457+, at their height 2803
heire, heyre *n.* heir 493, 890, 3629; *pl.* **heires, heyres, heyris, heyrys** 1326, 2539, 7541+
heyueth, hyveth *pr. 3 sg.* rises 2209, exalts itself 2947, is more heinous 5216*n*, 5229
helpe *n.* **in** ~ in collusion 827
helpes *n. pl.* assistants, helpers 3617
helthe, helþe *n.* bodily health 5555, 5556, 9873+, prosperity 11,020, salvation, spiritual health or well-being 1460, 2911, 6788+
herbe *n.* plant 9245; *pl.* **herbes, herbis** 3750, **evil** ~ weeds 1371, 8189
herbergh(e) *v.* lodge 10,806, 11,140–1; *pr. 3 sg.* **herboroweth** 3230; *pp.* **herberghed, herborghed, herborwed** 5267, 8486, 10834
herdis *n. pl.* hards 2398, 5284
here, hire, hiere *v.* listen to, hear 471, 1765, 5692+; *imp.* **here, hiere** 5103, 11,528; *pr. 1 sg.* **here, hiere** 2409, 5131; *pr. 2 sg.* **herist, hirest** 1462, 2026, 11,493; *pr. 3 sg.* **heeyrith, hereth, herith, hiere, hiereth, hireth, hirith, hyrith** 3244, 4196, 5933+; *pr. 3 pl.* **here, hereth, herith, hireth, hirith** 4320, 4321, 5093+; *pa. t.* **herde** 473, 475, 689+; *pp.* **herde** 497, 1072, 5678+
hereafter *adv.* at a future time 5805
herefore, herfore *adv.* for this reason, therefore 5624, 9774
hereof *adv.* of this 604, 1863, 3784+
herer *n.* hearer 5981; *pl.* **hererris** 5826
hereto *adv.* to this matter 2257
heryng(e), hirynge, hyryng(e) *vbl. n.* hearing 2025, 5355, 12,379+
heryngseye *n.* hearsay, report 8034*n*
heritage, herytage *n.* inherited or inheritable property, a legal inheritance 753, 1007, 4562+; *pl.* **heritages, herytages** 889, 4557, 5400; **feendis** ~ hell 1470
hert(e) *n.* **with** ~ with sincerity 8566, **aȝeins his** ~ unwillingly 10,789
herte *n.* hart 11,642

hertely *adv.* abundantly, much 2627, 8586, 8630, cheerfully 10,973
hertely *adj.* true, heartfelt 12,577
herthe *n.* earth 12,552
hevy(e) *adj.* of great importance 1839, 2719, sad, doleful 2584, 2732, 2743+, heavy 4377, 12,567, sluggish 3839, *mistranslation, see notes* 5974, 5977; *comp.* **hevyer** 8794, 8795
hevines(se), hevynes(se) *n.* sluggishness 3742, 3838, 8279+, sadness 2585, 10,983, 10,993+
hyder *adv.* hither 4213
hydyng *part.* concealing or withholding (the truth) 9967*
hie, hye *adj.* exalted in rank, station, dignity 1645, 2252, 2303+, strong, violent 2536, loud 4054, weighty, important 4291, deep 10,241; *comp.* **hier, heyer, hyer, heier** 3649, 7060, 11,418+; *superl.* **heyest, hyest** 2192, 3625, 8127+; **an** ~ above, aloft 2972
hyenes(se), hynes(se), heynesse *n.* high rank, estate 1391, 5230, 8698+, haughtiness, pride 2291, dignity, majesty 7095, 7364, 8256+, height 2192, 9196
hight *see* **height**
hight(e) *pr. 3 sg.* is called 8584; *pr. 3 pl.* **highte** 6117; *pa. t.* **hight** 6311, 8441, 11,910+
hille *v.* ~ **with** cover 752–3; *pr. 3 pl.* **hilleth** 2470–1
hily, hyly *adv.* nobly 1347, richly 6561
hynder(e) *v.* harm, injure 6886, 6889, 6891; *pr. 3 pl.* **hynder** spoil (wine) 4508*n*
hyndryng *vbl. n.* detriment 1416
hynge *v.* lean, incline 12,834; *pr. 3 sg.* **hange, hangeth, hyngeth, hongeth** 9162, hangs 3428, 10,778, droops 3524, is suspended 4841; *pr. 3 pl.* **hynge, hange** 4673, 5399; *pa. t.* **hange** 10,661, 11,274; *pp.* **hanged, hongen, hungen** 3661, 4826, 11,273+
hinginge *adj.* leaning 4152
hire, hyre *n.* payment, wages 328, 4146, 7902+, prize, reward 4254, 9753; *pl.* **hyres, hirres** wages 4540, rewards 9786*, 9806; **to** ~ under the terms of metayage 4628*n*
hired *pp. mistranslation, see notes* 1903
hirne *n.* den 4585; *pl.* **hirnes** 8896
his *pr. 3 sg.* is 2258*n*
his *pron.* its 94, 670, 1239+
ho(o) *pron.* he 2105, 9392, 9946
holde, hoolde *v.* follow, observe, obey 304, 310, 5541+, regard as, consider 2851, 5872, 5875+, maintain, support 2279, keep 6046, 11,734, abide

12,409, restrain 11,789, contain, keep in 12,808, endure 6697, hold 4748; *imp.* **holde** 4837, 7623, 11,439+; *pr. 1 sg.* **holde** 1940; *pr. 3 sg.* **holdeth, holdith, hooldeth** 942, 1930, 2109+; *pr. 1 pl.* **holde, hoolde** 8983, have, possess 8250; *pr. 3 pl.* **holde, holdeth, hooldeth** 2277, 3920, 5499+, behave 2729; *pa. t.* **helde** 4440, 4444, 12,384, agreed, sided (with) 400; *part.* **holdyng** withholding, retaining, greedy 4771*bis*; *pp.* **holde, holden, holdyn, hoolden** 493, 2782, 3959+, obligated 1818, 4680; ~ **feleshipp(e), feleshippes** keep company 4908, 5502, 5558, ~ **dere** esteem, prize 5540, ~ **toged(d)er, togedir** are joined, cohere 56, 3687

hole, holle, hoole, hoolle *adj.* whole, complete, entire 1173, 1929, 4061+, healthy, sound 1791, 11,967, 12,049+, morally pure 9549; **made** ~ repaired 12106

hole, holly, holy(e), hoole, hooly(e) *adj.* holy 228, 6609, 10,368+; *comp.* **hollyer, holyer, hoolyer** 5305, 11,306, 12,298+; *superl.* **holyest** 5564

holely, holly, hooly, holy, hoolly *adv.* completely, entirely, wholly 1475, 1487, 3038+

holly, hollyly, holyly, hoolyly(e) *adv.* devoutly, piously, in a holy manner 232, 9311, 11,785+

holnes *n.* health, soundness 12,048

homelylye *adv.* intimately, familiarly 4297

homly *adv.* privately 7348

homlynesse *n.* intimacy, familiarity 8901

homly, hoomly *adj.* familiar, intimate 10,305, domestic, of the household 4574, at home (with) 4312, *mistranslation, see notes* 2134

honest(e), onest *adj.* honorable, decent, respectable 512, 3825, 6644+, proper, seemly 2397, 12,020, modest 11,634, comely 7336

honeste, oneste *n.* honor, virtue 5476, 6657, moral purity 5529, 11,233, 11,246, propriety 11,854

honestly *adv.* properly, modestly 11,577

hoope *pr. 3 pl.* think, believe 2424*n*

hoosyn, hosyn *n. pl.* hose 1299, 2487, 10,039

horibilnes *n.* repulsiveness, hideousness 812

horible, horrible *adj.* hideous, repulsive 813, dreadful, horrible 921, 1950, 3283+, shocking, shameful 6204; *comp.* **horribler** 2505

hornes *n. pl.* arrangement of a woman's hair in rolls 10,024

horribly *adv.* in a horrible manner 524

hothe *see* **oothe**

hotte *n. mistranslation, see notes* 2078

hounte *n.* shame 2828*bis*n*

howest *see* **owe**

howeth *see* **owe**
howghe *conj.* how 7620
howleth *pr. 3 pl.* wail, lament 6495
howte *v.* shout, howl 2045
howteyng *vbl. n.* clamor 2856
hullour *n.* debauchee 5398
humaine *Fr. adj.* humane 8960
humanite *n.* human nature 8088
humeres, humeris, humores, humoures *n.* harmful bodily fluids 8425, 8433, 8456+

iangle *v.* chatter, gossip 11,579
iangleresses *n. pl.* female gossips 11,905
iape *v.* mock, scorn 9371, 11,511; *pr. 3 pl.* **iape, iapeth, iapith** 6171, 11,510, joke 2287
iape *n.* jest 1647; *pl.* **iapes, iaapes** 2384, 5472, 5665+, pranks 2789, tricks 4545, idle pastimes, entertainments 2376, 8882, objects of scorn or mockery 5145
iaperris *n. pl.* jesters 5978
iapyngly *adv.* in mockery, scornfully 2374
iche *adj.* each 490, 863, 1018+
idiot *n.* fool 947
ydoilles, ydoles *n. pl.* idols 2046, 12,314
ientille, ientyl *see* **gentil**
ientilles(se) *see* **gentilesse**
ientilly *adv.* tenderly, kindly 10,352
illusions *n. pl.* deceptive appearances 1957
ymage, image *n.* likeness, figure 814, 2075, 7058+, statue 933, 4155, 12,415+; *pl.* **ymages** 359; **fals** ~ idols 358
ymaginacion *n.* fancy 9414
ymbir dayes *n. pl.* ember days 2293
ympes *n. pl.* shoots, saplings 1372, 1444, 7293+
in *prep.* of 10,293; ~ **alle** completely 841, ~ **the face** face to face 12,483, ~ **thy lifyng** during your life 6568, ~ **thy dyynge** at your death 6569
incontinence *n.* sexual impurity 957
indignacion *n.* anger, wrath 829
indiscrete *adj.* imprudent 4337, 4368
indulgence *n.* remission of sin 10,481
inequite *n.* injustice 9493*n*
iniquite *n.* evil, wickedness 9633

inne *n.* house 12,702
innocence, innocens *n.* innocence, moral purity 1576, 2647, 3945
innocencie, innocency *n.* innocence, moral purity 10,184, prelapsarian state of innocence 11,777, freedom from wrongdoing 9021
inoghe, inough(e), inowe *n.* enough, a sufficiency 5485, 7824, 11,100+, plenty, an abundance 1892, 3223, 5505
inoghe, inoughe, ynoughe *adj.* sufficient, enough 6620, 7893, 8015+, many 10,224
inoughe, inowe, ynoughe, ynowe *adv.* enough, sufficiently 456, 7843, 12,946+, much 3199; **wel(le)** ~ very well 759, 5385, 9674
inreuerence *n.* scorn 1476
into(o) *prep.* to, unto 1410, 1894
iobbardis *n. pl.* hypocrites 2851*n*
ioglour *n.* minstrel, itinerant entertainer 9888*n*
ioye *v.* take pleasure in 11,608; *pr. 3 sg.* **ioieth, ioyeth** 2173, 6839, 12,304+; *pr. 3 pl.* **ioyeth** 2448, 11,629, 12,307+
ioyneth *pr. 3 sg.* unites, joins 5294, 6793, 7088+; *pr. 3 pl.* **ioyne** make 976; *pa. t.* **ioyned** 682; *pp.* **ioyned** 6978, 11,762, 12,556+
ioly(e) *adj.* handsome 5355, finely dressed 2331
iolylye *adv.* wantonly 5038
iolines, iolynes(se) *n.* wantonness 4408, 9395, merriment 1605, 1610, 2398+
iorney(e) *n.* day's work 3964, 4645, 7901+, journey 12,763; *pl.* **iorneys, iorneyes** 3748, 4115
ioyouse *adj.* happy, glad 2745
iren *n.* sword 11,668
ireous, irous *adj.* angry, wrathful 45, 1392, 3357+
irreguler *adj.* not in strict accordance with the rules of law 3605*n*, 3609
irrogularite *n.* a violation of the provisions of canon law 3612*
is *pron.* his 1055, 8665, 9844
isce *n.* ice 3910
isse *v.* issue (from) 3707; *imp.* **isse oute of** leave 6551*bis*; *pr. 3 sg.* **isseth** grows 2118
issue *n.* offspring 11,793
issues *n. pl.* revenues, profits 1561, 5717
iuge *n.* judge 1060, 1062, 1179+; *pl.* **iuges** 4655, 4656, 4673+
iuge *v.* judge 1211, 4721, 6347+; *pr. 2 sg.* **iugest** 10,875, 10,876; *pr. 3 sg.* **iugeth** 3258, 6612, 8298+; *pr. 3 pl.* **iuge** 3196; *pa. t.* **iuged** 498***n*; *pp.* **iuged** 1180, 5965, 6245+, sentenced 1738, awarded 10,546
iugement *n.* legal judgment, sentence, decision 500, 1932, 3552+, trial 510–11, 511–12, 1029+, opinion 2306, 3024, 3221, Last Judgment 6612, 8463,

8714+; *pl.* **iugementis** 9196; **(of, be) right** ~ (with) good reason 745–6, 1813, 1957–8, **daye of** ~ Judgment Day 6614

iustice *n.* judge 489; *pl.* **iustices** 4590

iusticer *n.* one who disciplines or punishes for sins or faults 6401, governor, ruler 1593, 2517; *pl.* **iusticeris** judges 4998*n*

iustifye, iustyfye *v.* judge 2989–90, 2993; *pr. 3 sg.* **iustifieth** governs 6977; *pp.* **iustified** exculpated 6231

iye, ye(e) *n.* eye 2194, 3312, 4273*+, *mistranslation, see notes* 1093; *pl.* **iyen, yeien, yen, yeyen, oyen, eyen** 1615, 3317, 6279+

kacche, cacche *v.* grab 3449, lay hold of 3506, 3514, take possession of 4896; *pa. t.* **cawght** 4752

kan *see* **konne**

karle *n.* bondman 1310; *pl.* **carles** fellows 1861, common men (of non gentle birth) 7884

karol(le) *v.* dance 1855, 2046, 5317+; *pr. 3 pl.* **karoleth, karolle** 5101*, 5325, 5352

karol *n.* dance 2015; *pl.* **karoles, karolles** 5083, 5331, 5349+, songs used in a carol 5094, 5346, 6502

kechyn *n.* kitchen 9861

keepe, kepe *v.* take care of, look after 735, 770, 4530+, guard, protect 804, 807, 3940+, observe 18, 227, 304+, preserve 3944, refrain 777, 3034; *imp.* **kepe** 6248, 10,289; *pr. 2 sg.* **kepest** 7236; *pr. 3 sg.* **kepeth, kepith** 558, 1341, 1465+; *pr. 3 pl.* **kepeth, kepyn** 3370, 3615, 4720+; *pa. t.* **kepte** 10,510, 10,813, 10,816+, **kept after** followed, imitated 1016; *part.* **kepyng, kepynge** 333, 2793, 12,110, grasping 4780; **kept, kepte** 228, 608, 609+

kele *v.* cool, refresh by cooling 604, 10,732; *pp.* **keelid, kelyd** 5615, 10,734

kemb, keme *v.* comb 4011, 10,030; *part.* **kemyng** combing 10,027

keper *n.* guardian 809, 1536, 2163; *pl.* **keperes, keperris** 4272, 4816, 5011+

kepyng(e) *vbl. n.* care, protection 5172, 9279, 11,743, power, control, jurisdiction 1702, 1884, looking after, rearing 868

keste *see* **caste**

kevirchefes *n. pl.* kerchiefs, headscarves 2495–6

kyen *n. pl.* cows 10,542

kynde *n.* nature 3295, 4724, 9850+

kyndelynge *vbl. n.* kindling 11,313*n*, 11,773, 12,364; *pl.* **kyndelynges** 11,319

kyndil *v.* kindle, inflame, set afire 2398; *pr. 3 sg.* **kyndeleth** 3478; *pr. 3 pl.* **kyndelith** 4903, 6070, 11,315+; *pp.* **kyndelid, kyndelyd** 5095, 11,285

kynnes *n. pl. mistranslation, see notes* 4087

kynrede *n.* kindred, lineage, descent 7100, 7102, 7110
kitte aweye, kutte *v.* cut, cut away, remove, 1115, 12,365–6; *imp. kt aweye* 12,785–6
klatereth *pr. 3 pl.* chatter about 9084
knackes *n. pl.* ~ **and mowes** jeers and grimaces 2460
knaweth *pr. 3 pl. mistranslation, see notes* 5934
knytte *pp.* joined 3669
knotte *n.* field of battle, midst of battle 4147*n*
knoweleche, knowlech(e) *n.* knowledge, perception 7674, 11,175, 11,176+, information 11,523*n*
knoweleche, knowleche *v.* acknowledge 1463, 1631, 2166; *pr. 1 sg.* **knowleche** 1819, 1829; *pr. 2 sg.* **knowelechest, knowelechist, knowlechist** 1787, 7470, 7476; *pr. 3 sq.* **knowelecheth** 2957, 8632; *pr. 3 pl.* **knowelecheth** 1653–4; *pa. t.* **knowleched** 11,612–3, 11,624
knowelechyng *vbl. n.* legal cognizance, formal acknowledgment 4667
knyghthode, knyghthoode *n.* order of knighthood, chivalry 26, 2251, 2252+, military service, knighthood 2272, 2272–3, 2299+, warfare 9532
konne, kunne, can, cunne, con, covnne *v.* have mastery of 7428, know, know how to, be able to 1452, 2101, 6479+; *pr. 1 sg.* **can, con** 1623, 3230; *pr. 2 sg.* **canste, conne, can** 2063, 4709, 8069+; *pr. 3 sg.* **kan, kanneth, can, con** 1764, 3292, 5861+; *pr. 2 pl.* **can** 11,417; *pr. 3 pl.* **can, con** 3436, 3818, 3822+; *pa. t. 1 sg.* **cowde** 1596, 7119; *pa. t. 2 sg.* **kowdest** 4750; *pa. t. 3 sg.* **cowde, koude** 7647, 8559, 9877; *pa. t. 1 pl.* **cowde** 7405; *pa. t. 3 pl.* **cowde** 9755; ~ **thanke** express thanks 1747
konnyng, conyng *adj.* knowing, wise 7969, 9137; *comp.* **konnynger** cleverer 2103
konnyng(e), konyng, kunnyng, connyng(e), conyng *n.* intelligence, wisdom 170, 6517, 8100+, knowledge, understanding 1331, 6347, 7130+, cleverness, cunning 1366, 4581, branch of learning, erudition 4651

laboreth *pr. 3 sg.* treads 5546*n*
laced *pp.* ensnared, entrapped 9305
lache *adj.* dilatory, remiss 3928, 4120, 4171+
lachely *adv.* dilatorily 2421*n*; *comp.* **lachelyer** more slackly or tardily 4137
lachesse *n.* slackness, remissness, negligence 70, 10,886
lampreis, lampreys *n. pl.* lampreys 5431, 5634
lande *n.* clearing 11,642
langache, langage *n.* language 7800, 11,505, 11,509, speech 2340; *pl.* **langaches, langachis, langagis** 7120, 7130, 8885-6+; **lewde** ~ obscene speech 2358

langour(e) *n.* apathy, inertia 3742, 4111, 4170+, infirmity 5573, depression 4197, sorrow, anguish 4205, 7259
lappe *n.* fold of a garment 9584
lapped *pp.* wrapped 10,442
large *adj.* liberal 327, 1535, 1594+, at liberty, free 1896, large, ample 5509, 5522, 10,495, prodigal 6426; *as n.* liberal person 6428
largely *adv.* liberally 216, 2043, 6708+
largenesse *n.* liberality 5512
largesse *n.* liberality 2561, 3216, 7532+, magnitude 7639, 8904, prodigality, waste 4323; *pl.* **largesses** liberal expenditures 2449; **fooly** ~ prodigality, waste 6333–4, 6422, 6424
laser, laserur, laȝar, lazar *n.* leper 4809*n*, 4813, 10,451+
laste *v.* last, endure, continue 266, 4691; *pr. 3 sg.* **lasteth, lesteth** 426, 2016, 6924; *pr. 3 pl.* **lasteth** 11,446
laton *n.* latten, brass 4157, 4162, 6683
laudes *n.* Lauds, one of the canonical hours 5389
lauoure *n.* wash basin 11,257
lawde *n.* praise 12,063
laye *adj.* not a cleric 4472, 6124, 12,260+
leche, leeche *n.* physician 3715, 8432, 8536
leche fried *phr. mistranslation, see notes* 1717
lecherie, lechery(e), legerie *n.* lechery 91, 92, 93+; *pl.* **lecheries** 2701, 3811–2
lecherous(e) *adj.* lecherous 439, 1055, 1395+; ~ **bodye** ?debauchee 1421–2*n*
lechoures *n. pl.* lechers 1805
ledder, leder *n.* ladder 4364, 12,537, 12,540
ledder *n.* leather 10,496
lede, leede *n.* plummet 9153, 9161
leen, lene *v.* lend 2876, 3504, 4612+; *imp.* **lene** 1115, 4835, 10,761; *pr. 3 sg.* **lene, leneth** 4600, 4623, 4860; *pr. 3 pl.* **lene** 6385; *pp.* **lent(e)** 432, 984, 4613+
leenynge *vbl. n.* lending 4601–2, 4619
leese, lese *v.* lose 496, 3511, 3573+; *pr. 2 sg.* **lesest** 2082; *pr. 3 sg.* **lese, leseth, lesith, lesseth, leese, leeseth, leesith** 1109, 3326, 3502+; *pr. 1 pl.* **leese** 3092; *pr. 2 pl.* **lese** 2797, 12,114; *pr. 3 pl.* **leese, lese, leseth, lesith** 2130, 5761, 9474+; *part* **leesyng** 4627
leff *v.* live 6291
left *pa. t.* bequeathed 487
leide *pp.* brought 10,978, 10,979
leyser *n.* leisure 5171; **be** ~ in a leisurely manner 5381–2, **be grete** ~ very slowly 2209

lekys *n. pl.* leeks 1859
lene *adj.* thin 5507, 5526, poor 10,501
lengthet *pr. 3 sg.* prolongs 6289; *pp.* **lengthed** 11,132
lengtheyngis *n. pl.* extensions of life 9909
lenten, lentyn *n.* lent 3972, 3975, 3983+
lentilles *n. pl.* lentils 5579*n*
lerne *v.* learn 176, 1331, 1631+, teach 3970; *imp.* **lerne** 6478, 6481, 6521+; *pr. 1 sg.* **lerne** 9365; *pr. 3 sg.* **lerneth, lereth** 258, 2187, 4760+; *pr. 3 pl.* **lerne, lerneth, lernyth** 121, 4097, 5760+; *part.* **lernyng** 9184; *pp.* **lerned** 1331, 4302, 5654+
lesyng(e) *vbl. n.* losing 1491, 3306, 8139
lesyng *vbl. n.* lie, falsehood, lying 5969; *pl.* **lesynges, lesyngis, lesyngys** 2005*n*, 5895, 8911+
lessyn *v.* decrease, decline in numbers 882; *pr. 3 sg.* **leeseth, lesseth** disparages 3251, 3326, extenuates, diminishes 8677; *pp.* **lessed** diminished 3040
let(e), lette *v.* leave 4239, 4707, cease, desist from 12,837, *in impers. and hortative expressions* allow, permit, grant 4095, 4208, 4880+; *pr. 2 sg.* **letest** 2672; *pr. 3 sg.* **lete, leteth, letteth** 3895, 12,742, 12,812+; *pr. 3 pl.* **lete, letith** 5775, 5809, give the use of (for a time) 4627; *pa. t.* **lete,** 10,177; *pp.* **letyn** 1751
let, lette *v.* prevent, hinder, obstruct 468, 10,608, 11,748; *pr. 3 sg.* **letteth, lettith** 888, 11,663; *pr. 3 pl.* **leteth, letteth** 3097, 8051, 10,095+; *pp.* **leted, letted** 2151, 11,664
lettere, lettre *n.* surface meaning 7434, scripture, gospel 10,483; *pl.* **letteres, letteris, letters** legal documents 4656, 4666, 10,481+; **settith to** ~ educates 7426
lettyng *vbl. n.* impediment 198; *pl.* **lettynggys, lettyngis** 6174, 10,093
leue, leve *v.* forgo, abstain from 3888, 5672, desert 875, divorce 5221, 5490, cease, desist from 669, 1290, 2839+, leave behind 4946, disregard, pass over 8720, bequeath 7866, give up, reject, renounce 6752, 10,060, 10,067+; *imp.* **leve** 3732, 10,815; *pr. 3 sg.* **leueth, leve, leveth, levith** 911, 3671, 3784+; *pr. 3 pl.* **leve, levith** 432, 1959, 2840+
leuer, lever, levyr *adv.* more gladly, willingly, rather 496, 3501, 3852+
levain *n.* leaven 11,328
leve *n.* leave, permission 3808, 5238, 5366+
leveth, levith *pr. 3 sg.* believes 2156, 4209; *pp.* **leved** 12,477
levours *n. pl.* rods, clubs 9345
lewde *adj.* lascivious, unchaste 864, 5064*bis*+, lewd, obscene 2358, 11,297, 11,376+, vile, base 6445, ignorant 6145, foolish 2817, 6374, 6445 common 7883, dumb 11,226

lewke *adj.* lukewarm 3790, 3795, 3798, indifferent, slothful, indolent 3792, 3799, 6388*n*
lewkenes *n.* lukewarmness, tepidity 59*n*, 3780, 3792
libertee *n.* privilege, prerogative 4496
licoures *n. pl.* liquids 10,377
lye (with) *v.* have sexual intercourse (with) 5205
lye *v. mistranslation, see notes* 6345; *pr. 3 sg.* **lieth, lyeth** belies 911, 1936, contradicts, gives the lie to 6073*n*; *pp.* **lied** belied 1936, 1940
liein *n.* bond, fetter 11,748*n*; *pl.* **lyeinys** 4082, **liaines** snares 6715*n*
life(e), liff(e), lyf(e), live *n.* life 263, 1237, 1290+; *pl.* **liffes** 9308, 10,558, 11,132
lif(e), liff(e), lyff(e), leff, leve, lyve *v.* live 2261, 2830, 5610+; *pr. 2 sg.* **liffest** 11.012; *pr. 3 sg.* **lifeth, liff, liffed, liffeth, lyfeth, lyffeth, lyveth** 4786, 4884, 5607+; *pr. 1 pl.* **liffe** 8998*bis*; *pr. 3 pl.* **leveth, lif, lifeth, liff, liffeth, lyf(e), lyven** 3329, 5421, 5532+; *pa. t. 2 sg.* **lifed** 1780; *pa. t. 3 sg.* **levid, lifed, lyfed** 1244*bis*, 5612+; *part.* **liffyng** 1814, 8016; *pp.* **lifed, liffed** 1618, 1621, 8489
liferris, lifferres, lifferris *n. pl.* livers 5493, 9108, 9110+
lyffetyme *n.* lifetime 11,701
liffyng, lyffyng, lyveinge, lyvynge *vbl. n.* living, life 6577, 12,269, 12,282+, livelihood 3587, 3756, 4101
light(e), lyght *adj.* promiscuous 2699, mild 1123, 3091*bis*; *comp.* **lyghter** easier 6751
lightely, lightly, lyghte, lyghtely, lyghtly(e) *adv.* easily 2563, 3290, 4825+, quickly 829, 3348, 3724+, indifferently, not seriously 521, 5999, 10,308, lightly 4905, readily 3932, 4263; *comp.* **lightlyer, lightlyere, lyghtlyer** 2432, 3034, 12,022
ligne(e), lignie, linee, lyne *n.* offspring, family, lineal descent 885, 889, 5586+; **grete** ~ high birth 3498, **gentil** ~ noble birth 7100
ligne, lyne *n.* line, cord 2863, 9259, 9444+, plumb line 9157, accord 1548, line of demarcation 9277, rule, principle 8296*n*; **lityl** ~, **litil** ~ level 9153*n*, 9161, **be** ~ justly, fairly 9487, **oute of the** ~ off course, amiss 10,426–7
likerous, lykerous, likorouse *adj.* gluttonous, greedy 5431, 5439, *as n.* the glutton 1421
likerousnes(se) *n.* gluttony 98, 5410, 5638+, intense desire 5998
likly *adj.* like, akin (to) 10,354
likenyth *pr. 3 pl.* compares 7284; *pp.* **likenyd, likned** 459, 3005, 3007+
lyme *n.* rasp, file 9227*
linage, lynage *n.* lineage 924, noble family or ancestry 5309, 10,467; **humaine** ~ human race 882

lyne *see* **ligne**

liste *n.* wish, desire 2295, 6149, 10,248+; **at his** ~ freely 12,813

list(e), lyste, luste *pr. 3 sg.* deem worthy, deign 1641, 1766, 1768+, *impers.* wish, desire 3220, 3402, 6135+; *pr. 3 pl.* **list(e), lyste, luste** 2052, 4612, 8616+

lithe *pr. 3 sg.* lies 11,852

litil flye *phr.* bee 8658*n*

lokke *n.* lock 1132

lollerie *n.* heresy 1923*n*

lolleris, lollerris *n. pl.* heretics 1917*n*, 1948, 12,720+, Lollards 5992*n*

longaigne *n.* excrement, filth 3686*

longe *v.* belong 499; *pr. 3 sg.* **longeth** belongs, is a part or attribute 4538, 4649, 5878+, is related to 3507, is the responsibility (of) 884, 3613, pertains 1145, 1162, 1177+, *personal and impersonal* befits, is fitting, proper 2779, 9203, 11,034+; *pr. 3 pl.* **longe, longen, longeth** 86, 4817, 12,155+; *pa. t.* **longed, longyd** 2686, was of concern 6391; *part.* **longeyng, longynge** 1213, 11,193

loos, los(e), losse *n.* renown, fame 6923, praise, commendation 162, 2363, 8859, reputation 2831

lordeshipp(e), lordship(p), lordshippe *n.* lordship 1543, 1708, 2942+, dominion, rule 3114; *pl.* **lordshipis** 1798

losenge, losengeries, losengery *n.* deceitful flattery 105*n*, 1073*, 2218+

losengeres, losengeris, losengiers *n. pl.* deceistful flatterers 32*n*, 2129, 2344+

lot *n.* whole 2476

loue, louf(e), louffe(e), love, luf(e), luff(e) *n.* love 794, 799, 3301+; *pl.* **louffes, lofes, loffes** 1424, 1433, 8356+

loue, louf(e), loffe, louff(e), love, luff(e) *v.* love 246, 1414, 1629+; *imp.* **louf, louff(e)** 5110, 11,261, 12,500+; *pr. 1 sg.* **louf(f)** 5955, 10,641; *pr. 2 sg.* **loufest, louff, louffest, lovest, luff** 1460, 2024, 2663+; *pr. 3 sg.* **lofeth, loofeth, loueth, loufeth, louffeth, louffith, loveth, lovith, luffeth** 2638, 2812, 7067+; *pr. 3 pl.* **loueth, louf, loufeth, louff(e), louffeth, love, loveth, luf, luff, luffeth** 2146, 3500, 3845+; *pa. t.* **loufed, louffed, loved, luffed** 2625, 2689, 3632+; *pp.* **loued, lofed, louffed, luffed** 1750, 2356, 3948+

louffyng *vbl. n.* loving 7043, 8961

lowed *see* **aloweth**

loweth *pr. 3 sg.* is less heinous 5216, 5226, 5229, extenuates, makes light of 8677; *pr. 3 pl.* **loweth** belittle 8680

lowlynes *n.* (feigned) meekness, humility 4741

lowsy *adv.* lice ridden 3869

lucys *n. pl.* pike 5634

lufferes *n. pl.* lovers 6656
luste *see* **list(e)**

madde *adj.* mad, insane 5691, 7005
magnanimite *n.* noble-mindedness lending to great enterprises 186, 9601, 9609+
magnificath *n.* Magnificat 2970
magnificence, magnificience *n.* perseverance as a subdivision of prowess and fortitude 191, 9603, 9745
mayden, maydyn *n.* unmarried girl 2591, 8894–95, 9996; *pl.* **maydenis, maydenys** handmaidens, servant girls 7420, 11,903
maiest, maist(e) *pr. 2 sg.* may 2666, 3538, 8849+, can 1704, 1781, 10,997+; *pr. 3 sg.* **may(e)** 283, 376, 2196+; *pr. 3 pl.* **maye** 233, 470, 522+; *pa. t.* **might, myght(e)** 1676, 10,409, 11,085+
maymed *adj.* crippled 8647, 8652
maymes *n. pl.* injuries, wounds 8648
mayny(e), meny(e), meni, moneye *n.* household, retinue, attendants 47, 2854, 4883+
maister *n.* ~ **of werkys** master mason 9150
maistras, mastres *n.* lady, mistress 4418, 4421, 5489+
maistri *n.* control 12,628
maistrieth *pr. 3 sg.* governs, controls 9118; *pr. 3 pl.* **maistreth** 9116, 9117
make *v.* bear away 5863*n*
maker *n.* creator, God 367, 1154, 2958+
malice, malyce *n.* malice, hatred, ill will 2805, 3139, 3150+, wickedness, evil 3006, 3281, 4444+; *pl.* **malices, malyses, malyseys** 3225, 3812, ruses 4669; **of** ~, **be** ~ maliciously 729, 1070, **to doo (no)** ~ to do (no) evil 4215, **to fynde** ~ to contrive evil 6886
malignite(e) *n.* malice, wickedness 79, 4499
manace *n.* threat, menace 8185; *pl.* **manaces, manasses** 2676, 6095
manace *v.* threaten, menace 6064, 6948, 9561; *pr. 3 sg.* **manceth** 2704; *pr. 3 pl.* **manasseth** 7376
maner(e) *n.* moderation, measure 12,914, character, nature 9391, way 308, 513, 851+, *collectively* kinds 448, 846, 1028+; *pl.* **maneres, maneris, maners, manerys, manerz** 1915, 2099, 2566+, moral conduct, behavior 12,018, 12,920
mankyndely, mankendely *adj.* human 3005–6, 3007, humane 8960
mankynde *n.* men 10,913
mankyndelynes *n.* manhood 1169
manslaught(e), manslauwght *n.* murder, destruction of life 54, 811–12, 816+; *pl.* **manslaughtys** 3581

manslaughter, manslaughtir *n.* murder, destruction of human life 798, 5707

mansleer *n.* manslayer, homicide 824, 3503, 3583+; *pl.* **mansleers, mansleeris, mansleerres, mansleerrys, mansleers** 420–21, 3614, 4381+

mansuetude *n.* benevolence, love of one's fellow man 166*n*, 8948, 8959

marchande, marchant, marchaunde, marchaunt *n.* merchant 2553, 7157–58, 10,547+; *pl.* **marchandes, marchandis, marchandys, marchaundes, marchaundis, marchaundys** 983, 4450, 4625+, secondhand clothes dealers 2480*n*

marchandis, marchandys(e), marchaundis(e), marchaundys(e) *n.* salable commodity 977, 4621, 4622, bargain, agreement 4635, transaction 8145; *pl.* **marchaundyses, merchandises** trades, businesses 4582, transactions 981–82

marchandyse *v.* trade with (me) 2875

marches, marchis *n. pl.* surrounding lands or territories 11,351, 11,352–53

mareis, mares *n. pl.* waters 12,663, 12,680

martir *n.* martyrdom 7324

mary *n.* marrow, pith 7435

maske *n.* mesh of a net, *here* the net itself 9821*n*

masse *n.* mace, scepter of office 8184**n*

mate *v.* subdue, overcome 12,098, *pp.* **mate** 10,286

matines, matins *n. pl.* Matins, one of the canonical hours 2284, 5386, 5389+, Little office of the Blessed Virgin Mary 2063*n*

mattok *n.* mattock 8019

maugre *prep.* despite, in spite of 6180, 6181*bis*

mawmentrie *n.* idolatry 3390

me *n. pl. weakened form of* **men** 1028, 7703

mede, meede *n.* merit. worth 6843*n*, 7152, 8600+. reward, recompense 11,791 11,804, 11,812+

medil *v.* ~ **togeder** have sexual intercourse 5214; *pp.* **medelid** combined, blended 5427, mixed 11,054

medle(e) *n.* fighting, brawling 52, 3457, 3523; *pl.* **medleis** 5707

meeke, meke *adj.* humble 2934, 2972, 3074+, *with reference to clothing* modest 2845*n*, 11,922; *comp.* **meker** 2315–16, 7995, 8030+; *superl.* **mekest** 2575

meeke, meke *v.* humble oneself 3101, 10,049, 10,086+; *pr. 3 pl.* **meke** 6746; *pa. t.* **meked** 11,624; *pp.* **meked** 8935

meekenes, mekenes(se) *n.* humility 3057, 3073, 3076+

meete, mete *n.* food 5390, 5579, 5589+; *pl.* **meetes, meetys, metes, metis, metys** 2173, 2683, 5602+; **grete** ~ coarse food 11,321*n*

mekely *adv.* humbly 216, 2729, 3092+

mele *n.* meal, flour 7240

melleis *n. pl.* strifes, combats 6095

melte *v.* dissolve (into tears) 9845

membir, membre *n.* body limb, organ, or part 3330, 7957, 9019+, ~ **of Godde** Christian 3324; *pl.* **membres, membris** 450, 3308, 3310+, ~ **ill of Criste Iesus, hooly chirche, oo bodye ... of hooly chirche, the bodye ... of Criste** fellow Christians, *fig.* members of the body of Christ 3319, 3328, 9003–4+, ~ **of Antecriste** adversaries of Christianity 10,213, 10,217, 10,219, **veleins** ~ private parts 1986*n*

memorial *n.* reminder 10,748–49

mendement *see* **amendement**

mendeth *see* **amend(e)**

mene, meene *adj.* ignoble 4450, middle, moderate 6428, inferior, of little value 6681, 6784, mediocre, middling 8677, 8681; ~ **goodes** goods of nature 125, 6754, 6755+

menistrellis, ministerell, ministrelles, ministrellis, mynystrelles *n. pl.* minstrels 2376, 2477, 5978+

menys *n. pl.* means 10,330

men of the worlde *phr.* laymen 5228

mere *n.* mare 10,350

meremaidynes, meremaydynes, meremeidynes *n. pl.* sirens 5921*n*, serpents sirena 5927*n*, sirens and serpents 5919

merite *n.* meritorious character, excellence 12,274; *pl.* **merites** spiritual credits, merits 11,468

meruelious, mervelouse *adj.* monstrous 4434, wonderful 7224

merveile, merveille, mervel(l), merveyle *n.* marvel, wonder 2388, 2486, 5651+ *pl.* **merveilles** 2237

merveileth, mervelle *pr. 3 pl.* marvel, wonder 4063, 12,484; *pa. t.* **merveyled** 953, 10,826; *part.* **merveylyng** 11,958–59

merveliously *adv.* in a marvellous degree, astonishingly 1254

mese *n.* but 5954

meselle *n.* leper 3532; *n. pl.* **meselles** 10,800

mesellerye *n.* leprosy 3867

meses, mesys *n. pl.* dishes 5641, 5663, 5664

messages *n. pl.* messengers, *here* angels 7053

messages *n. pl.* errands 8207

messe *n.* mass 1760, 1765, 2002+; *pl.* **messys** 3852

mesurable *adj.* moderate 7299

mesure *n.* moderation, restraint 248, 5482, 5486+, measurement 982, 5618, 5642, vessel for measurement 5521, 5522, 5524; *pl.* **mesures** 5503, 5508, 5521; **oute of** ~ immoderately 1437, **withowte** ~ immoderately 5407, without limit 5501, 6931, **be** ~ moderately, with restraint 9225, 12,902

mesure *v.* temper, moderate, restrain 3414, 12,723, *pr. 3 sg.* **mesureth** 12,795; *pp.* **mesured** 12,693, 12,922; **is ~ amonge** sets bounds to 12,952*n*
meteȝeifer *n.* hospitable person 5619
meve, move *v.* extend 4775, move, beat (wings) 3873, prompt, impel 3890, 9917, 10,370+, **~ hymselfe (hym)** be moved, inclined 10,884, 10,895, **~ the lippes** chatter 11,495–96; *pr. 3 sg.* **meveth, mevith** 4137, 11,511, 11,805, urges, exhorts 306, 8965; *pr. 3 pl.* **meve, meven, mevith** 3316, 8022, 10,907, stir up, provoke 6098, 7965, rouse sexually 5274; *pa. t.* **mevid** 10,004; *part.* **mevyng** 5353; *pp.* **meved, mevid** 1463, 3146, 12,320+
meveable *adj.* transient 3392, 3393, 3399+, changeable 7635, 8134
mevyng *vbl. n.* sexual excitement, arousal 840, inclination, impulse 1124, 4137, emotion 9032, alteration, change 7610*n*; *pl.* **mevyngis, mevyngys** 5357, 9027, 12,044+
mich(e), mych(e), moche, mooche *adv. and adj.* much 1171, 1174, 2845+; **in so(o) ~ (that)** to such an extent (that) 749, 948, 5223+, **in as ~ as** to such an extent (that) 6360, 6361–62, 7519, since, because 2614, 2845, 4958+, **in soo ~** to that extent 5181, **in as ~** to the same extent 9768
myddaye *n.* south 8286
middes, myddes *n.* midst 379, 2404, 10,259+
mynde, myende, mende *n.* memory 3416, 7656, 7659+, remembrance 360, 4047, 7874+
myned *pp.* dug out 7759
ministre *v.* dispense, distribute 9048; *pr. 3 pl.* **ministre** 12,284; *pp.* **ministred** 12,275
mire, myre *n.* mud 1568, 3068, 10,118+
mirri, myyry *adj.* muddy 12,271, made of clay 4177*n*
mysbeleve, mysbelyve *n.* disbelief, lack of faith 1195, 1959; *pl.* **mysbelevis, mysbelevys** heresies 6190, 8615
mysbeleverris, myssebeleverris *n. pl.* heretics 6199, infidels 10,908
mysbelevyng *part. adj.* **~ pepil** heretics 12,721
myschevis *n. pl.* wrongs 10,224
mysdo(o) *v.* do wrong 497, 7988; *pr. 3 sg.* **missedoothe, myssedooth** 3496, 10,967; *pr. 3 pl.* **mysdoothe** 7907; *pp.* **mysdon, mysdone, mysdoon, myssedoon** 3480, 6183, 7926+
mysdrawe *v.* go astray 1385
myshappe, myssehappe *n.* misfortune 3598, 3609, 7019; *pl.* **myshapes, myshappes** 1434, 6947
myssebeleve *pr. 3 pl.* disbelieve, lack faith 10,157
missedede, mysdede, myssedede *n.* misdeed, wrong 1463, 9377, 10,136+; *pl.* **mysdedes, mysdedis, mysdedys, myssedeedes** 3482, 5718, 7906+

myssedooer *n.* wrongdoer, malefactor 3567
missehandelith *pr. 3 pl. mistranslation, see notes* 5934
missehappe *pr. 3 sg.* suffers misfortune 10,967; *pr. 3 pl.* **myshappe** 3433; *pp.* **myshapped** 1868
mysseherer *n.* one who listens to slanders 12,848*n*
myssey(e) *v.* slander, speak wrongly, insult 469, 470, 1066+; *pr. 3 sg.* **mysseth** 3932; *pr. 3 pl.* **mysseye, musseiethe, mysseieth** 457, 3933, 7940+, blaspheme 6203
mysseyer *n.* slanderer, vilifier 12,848; *pl.* **mysseierris, mysseyerres, mysseyerris** 8680, 9084, 12,868+
mysseyinges *vbl. n. pl.* slanders 3565
myssewordes *n. pl.* curses 449
mystake *v.* transgress, err 5596; *pr. 3 pl.* **missetaketh, missetakith** 6917, 9483; *pa. t.* **myssetoke** gave offense or was guilty of a transgression 2310
mistakynge, myssetakyng, mystakyng *vbl. n.* misunderstanding 9179–80, wrongdoing, error 9292; **withoute (withowte)** ~ without question 7790, without any doubt 6893, without being taken back 8139*n*
mysterman, mystirman *n.* kind of man 1566, 3218
mystes *n. pl.* mists 7736
mystorneth *pr. 3 sg.* perverts, changes for the worse 3191
moche, mooche *see* **mich(e)**
moyen *adj.* of mean quality 3263
moiste *adj.* moist, damp, watery 5362, 9247
moiste *v.* water 7421; *pr. 3 sg.* **moisteth** 7388, 7392, 8013+; *pp.* **moisted** 8515
moistenesse, moistnesse *n.* moisture 7298–99, 7330, 8952–53
mokke *v.* deride, jeer 5554
mokkes *n. pl.* derision, mockery 8731
molle *n.* mole 12,737*n*
mollehilles *n. pl.* molehills 12,738*n*
monestith *see* **amonesteth**
moneye *see* **mayny**
moneye-makerys *n. pl.* **fals** ~ conterfeiters 4763
monoy *n.* money 2796
monstres *n. pl.* monsters 5926
moornyng *adj.* troubled 4193
morfewe *n.* morphea, scurvy eruption 4088*n*
morthre *n.* murder 3283
mosel *n.* snout 5546
moste *pr. 1 sg.* must 5384, 9415; *pr. 2 sg.* **moste** 1774, 1974, 5553+; *pr. 3 sg.*

moste(e), mooste, muste 259, 4946, 5253+; *pr. 1 pl.* **moste** 2300, 8623; *pr. 3 pl.* **moste** 571, 1325, 1882+
mouled *pp.* mouldy 12,012
moules *n. pl. mistranslation, see notes* 4088
mounted *pp.* esteemed 5649*n*
mouthe, mouþe, moothe *n.* mouth 222, 12,605, 12,631+; *pl.* **mouthes** 2382, 2487, 6088+
mowes *n. pl.* grimaces 2460
mvet *adj.* mute 10,101
multiplie, multiplye *v.* increase by procreation 878, multiply 1437, 4004, 6314+; *pr. 3 sg.* **multiplieth, multiplyeth** 10,502, 10,547; *pp.* **multiplied** 1490
multiplyinge *vbl. n.* growth of profit 4604*n*
musart *n.* fool 1558; *pl.* **musardis** 5039, 6693*
muse *v.* gape 5039; *pr. 2 sg.* **muse** meditate, ponder 7621; *pp.* **mused** idled away (time) 1902; *part.* **musyng** looking 12,081–82

namly *see* **anamely, anamly**
nater *n.* nature 3297*
navies *n. pl.* ships 2238
neantyssheth *pr. 3 sg.* destroys, brings to nought 3783–4; *pp.* **neyntysshed** 8936
necessarie *adj.* ~ **thyngys** necessary tasks, affairs, or business occupations 10,294*n*. *See also* **besines(se)**
necessite(e), nesessite *n.* compelling need 718, 5454, constraining circumstances 3598, 3605, hardship 10,383; **of** ~ because of the constraint of circumstances 10,953
necke *n.* **in his** ~ completely 2530, **that lyeth in his** ~ that are his responsibility 3658
negard(e) *n.* miser, avaricious person 1420, 11,477; *pl.* **negardis** 1710
negardshipp *n.* niggardliness 4984
neghboroughshipp *n.* neighborliness 3540*n*
neither, nethir, neyther, neythir, neythyr, neþer, noþer, mouther *conj. with* **ne** neither 783, 1298, 1356+
nere *adj.* close, hand to hand 5280, 5289
nere-dwelleres *n. pl.* neighbors 3543*n*
nerehand(e) *adv.* nearly, almost entirely 1272, 3173, 6679
nerre *comp. adj.* nearer 8201
nese, nesse, noose *n.* nose 950, 9293, 10,036+
nesethrilles *n. pl.* nostrils 10,779

newe *adv.* anew 9759
nice, nyce *adj.* foolish, senseless 1547, 5847, 6450+
nysete *n.* folly 12,139
no *conj.* nor 4489
nobil, noble, noobil *adj.* noble in rank or character 2571*, 2818, 9559+, rich, elegant 5357, sumptuous 7880, *comp.* **nobiler** 7060; *superl.* **noblest** 7215
nobilly *adv.* sumptuously 97*n*, 5609, 5611+, splendidly 7061, richly, elegantly 12,179
noblesse, nooblesse *n.* nobility of rank or character 132, 3016, 3859+; *pl.* **noblesses** 8907
noyance, noyaunce *n.* annoyance, vexation 3679, 4204, 4380+
noye *v.* harm, injure 828, 829, 1030+, vex, annoy, trouble 9500, 12,859; *imp.* **noye** 6565, 10,796; *pr. 3 sg.* **noye, noyeth** 3537, 4086, 4196+; *pr. 3 pl.* **noyeth** 6770, 6772, 8886; *pa. t.* **noyed** 2632; *pp.* **noyed** 348, 9547
noynge *adj.* harmful, injurious 5981
noyous(e) *adj.* harmful, injurious 3419, 4333, 5974+, troublesome 9813, *mistranslation, see notes* 6692
noise, noyse *n.* clamor 3877, 9344, 11,593, sound 2406, 11,531, roar 3362, uproar, disturbance 3388, 6070; *pl.* **noyses** 5706
noyseth *pr. 3 pl.* hold, believe 2266
nones, nonnes *n. pl.* nuns 2864, 5332
noon *adj.* null, invalid 11,891
noone *n.* noon 2536
noose *see* **nese**
nootes, notes, notis *n. pl.* words 8066, notes 7647, 7648
norice *n.* nursemaid, governess 1474, 9516; *pl.* **norices, norsces** 3614, 5882
norisshe, norysshe *v.* encourage 843, nourish, feed 5540, 5598, 5600–1+, nurture, bring up 870, 7411; *pr. 3 sg.* **norissheth, norisshith** 1475, 6898, 7097+; *pr. 3 pl.* **norissheth** 10,350, 11,325; *pa. t.* **norisshed** 2687, 7338; *part.* **norisshyng** 7298, 7894; *pp.* **nooriched, norisshed, norryshed, norysshed** 1795, 3823, 6116+
norisshyng(e) *vbl. n.* upbringing 884, nourishment 7894, 7896
noteth *pr. 3 sg.* makes note of 2490
notte *n.* nut 8917
notwithstandyng *adv.* yet, nevertheless 519
notwithstandyng *conj.* although 753
nouches *n. pl.* jeweled clasps, brooches 2496
noughty *adj.* worthless 9634
novelryes *n. pl.* novelties 9160–1

novice *n.* probationer 6337; *pl.* **novices** 6450

o(o) *interj.* oh 1341, 2351, 2699+
o(o) *card. num.* one 342, 367, 369+
o(o) *indef. art.* a 901, 1113, 2247+
o(o) *prep.* out of 456, in 2295, 3912, of 5895, 10,706, 11,271, 11,332+
obeissance *n.* obedience 7505
obeying *part. adj.* submissive, humble 12,548*n*
oblie *n.* consecrated host, wafer 1929; *pl.* **obleys** offerings 5879**n*
obliged *pp.* bound, under obligation 7913
occupacion *n.* task, work, activity 5754, 11,368; *pl.* **occupacions, ocupaciones** 3984, 11,360, 11,362
occupie, occupye *v.* engage, occupy (himself) 5750, 8812; *pp.* **ocupied** 11,359, 11,369
odure *n.* odor, fragrance 10,407
of(f), oof *prep.* for 756, 1071, 6092+, because of 858, from 701*bis*, 969+, by 393, 3948, 9143+, to 10,857, over 11,941, 12,178, on 204, 917, 998+, above and beyond 928, out of 800, 1568*bis*, for the sake of 783, some of 2624, 2649, 8084+, in 3007, 12,930, against 6345, 9971; ~ **malice** maliciously 729, ~ **nature** by nature 3163, 4133, ~ **louff** nobly, in a courtly manner 8891
office *n.* duty, task, function 2392, 9291, 9325+; *pl.* **offices, officis** 8207, 8290, 8302+
officeris *n. pl.* monastic officials 6125, servants 8206
offrande *vbl. n.* sacrifice, offering 12,007
oftesythe *adv.* often 12,646**n*
of that *conj.* because 2464
oyen *see* **iye**
oignement, oygnement, oynement *n.* ointment, balm 2646, 12,632, medicinal salve 11,667; *pl.* **oignementis** 10,792
on *indef. art.* an 3576
on, oon *prep.* in 438, 1132, about 1834, 2718, by 2719, 6303; ~ **a tyme** once 483, 537, 1062
ondiscrecion *n.* imprudence, lack of moral discernment 6330
ondue *adj.* illicit, unlawful 914
ones onys *adv.* **at(te)** ~ at once 4968, 6752, ~ **of (on) the daye** once a day 1765, 6567–8
onest *see* **honest**
oneste *see* **honesty**
onlynesse *n.* solitude 8876**n*

oo-lyve *adv.* alive 11,871
oopinly, oopynly, openly, opinly, opynly, oopin *adv.* clearly, manifestly 4214, 4456, 9946+, publicly, in full view 2785, 11,066, 12,481+
ooste, oste *n.* army, host 670, 5004, 5008+
oothe, othe, hothe *n.* oath 4547, 5140, 6014+; *pl.* **oothis** 5995, 6013, 6019
oother, othir, outher, outhir, ovther, owther, either, eyther *conj. with* **or** either 1066, 1762, 3264+
oouther *conj.* or 3819
open, opon, oppon *see* **vpon**
opinion *n.* belief, doctrine 5992; *pl.* **opiniones** 6190
or *prep.* ~ **tyme** too early, prematurely 95
or (that) *conj.* before 5929, 9719
ordenatly *adv.* properly, in an orderly or regulated manner 8323, 9186
ordeyn(e) *v.* put in order, govern, regulate 1454, 7279, 9268+; *pr. 3 sg.* **ordeyneth** 9236, prepares 12,490, 13,001; *pr. 3 pl.* **ordeyneth** put in a proper relationship to 1128; *pa. t.* **ordeyned** created 556, appointed 609, applied himself to 4294; *pp.* **ordeyned** 279, 805, 1241+
ordenaunce, ordinance, ordounance *n.* will, decree, command 3709, 4374, 8297, order 1319; *pl.* **ordenaunsys** 276; **foule** ~ disorder, corruption 12,918
ordenour *n.* ruler, commander 7474
ordre *n.* order 988, 9165, 9178+, religious order 322, 2252, 2864+, sacrament, rite of marriage 1228, 5201, Holy Orders 1228, 5341, 11,890, fraternity, society 1408, 1412, status, rank 8125, 8126, 9997, battle rank 6411, proper relationship or disposition 8281, moral or spiritual order 5535; *pl.* **oordres** Holy Orders 4466; **be** ~ in order 50
ordred *pp.* in religious orders, ordained 241, 5225, 12,193
ordure excrement 5941
orison, oryson *n.* prayer 1656, 2009; *pl.* **orisones** 8782, 8855–6
orrour *n.* horribleness, repugnance 815
or *conj.* as 1425*n*, 10,048
ostries *n. pl.* hostelries 4999
ou *Fr. conj.* or 751
ouer, over, ovir *prep.* over 1284, 2912, 2942+, over and above, beyond 4874, 7898, 9800, across 9650, 10,786
oueral(le), overalle *adv.* everywhere 1485–6, 4876, 8838+
ouercome, ouercomme, ouercomen, overcome, overcommen *v.* overcome, vanquish 1365, 5164, 6929+, destroy, eradicate 3879, win 10,150, 10,201; *pr. 3 sg.* **ouercometh, ouercommeth, overcommeth** 3374, 5575, 9703+; *pr. 1 pl.* **overcometh** 8047; *pr. 3 pl.* **ouercometh** 10,209; *pa. t.* **ouercome** 4415–6, 11,693, 12,633 *pp.* **ouercomen, ouercomme, ouercommen, ouercomyn,**

overcome, overcomme, overcommen, overcomyn 1482, 5569, 6416+, convicted 1063
ouergilt(e), overgilte *pp.* overlaid with gold 2752, 2757, 2760
ouerhoope, overhoope, overhope *n.* arrogance, presumption 19, 1524, 2096
ouerhopeyng, overhoopeyng *vbl. n.* arrogance, presumption 2098, 5862
ouerledeth, overledeth *pr. 3 sg.* overcomes 4110, 4194
ouerleyeth *pr. 3 sg.* overcomes 3426; *pp.* **ouerleyde** 4053
ouerselle *pr. 3 pl.* overcharge 4642*n*
ouertaken, ouertakn *pp.* overcome 12,509, 12,607
ouerthrow(e), overthrowe *v.* destroy 1238, 1348, 8483+, cast down, bring to ruin 343, 12,303, 12,308+, fall, fall over 2549, 4150, vanquish 6467; *pr. 3 sg.* **ouerthroweth, overthroweth** 1268, 2185, 3260+; *pr. 3 pl.* **overthroweth** 2202, 2547, 3184; *pp.* **ouerthrowen, overthrowen** 1269, 2202, 5370+
ouerthrowe *n.* instrument of destruction 2184–5
ouerwenyng *part, adj.* arrogant, presumptuous 2110
oultrage *see* **outerage**
oute, owte *prep.* ~ **of his (theyre) witte** mad 1766, 3368, 3450+, ~ **of hirre mynde** 10,523, ~ **of the weye** astray 1384, 2680–1, 6471–2+, ~ **of the ligne** astray 10,426–7, ~ **of tyme** other than at appointed times 5407
outecaste *n.* a forlorn person, an abject 2683
outerage, oultrage, outrage *n.* excess, excessive indulgence, extravagance 843, 11,636, 12,594+, flagrant wrongdoing 5622; *pl.* **outerages, outeragis, outrages, outragis, owterages** 2279–80, 5768, 10,038+, flagrant sins 10,474
outeragious(e), outragious *adj.* excessive 5759, 8773, excessively indulgent 12,612, intemperate 12,808, enormous, extraordinary 7322
outeragiously, outeragyously *adv.* excessively, immoderately, 95*n*, 5480, 5481
outeragiousnes, outragiousnes *n.* excessive indulgence 12,600, flagrant wrongdoing 2271
outetaken *pp.* except 10,469
owe *v.* owe 7504; *pr. 1 sg.* **owe** 7983; *pr. 2 sg.* **owest(e), howest** 1672, 1742, 1778+; *pr. 3 sg.* **owe, oweth, owith, howeth** 7915, 7972, 8986+, ought to, should 2253, owns 965; *pr. 3 pl.* **owe** 576*bis, pa. t. 1, 3 sg and pl.* **ought(e)** 1492, 2923, 7541+; *pa. t. 2 sg.* **oughtest** 1704

page *n.* boy 1972; *pl.* **pagis, pagys** servants 5727, grooms 6799
paiement, payement *n.* wages 7022, payment of debt 7982
paienyme, payenyme *n.* pagan, heathen 1179, 1573; *pl.* **paienes, paienymes, payenymes, paynemys** 4282, 7948, 8335+; *poss.* **payenymes** 12,313
palaice *n* palate, throat 5664; *pl.* **places** 5646*n*

paleyses *n. pl.* palaces 3231
papelard, papelart *n* sycophant, hypocrite 2301, 2781, 3960+; *pl.* **papilardes** 2776
pappe *n.* pap, nipple 1796
paramours *adv.* nobly, in a courtly manner 5101, 5102, 5108–9+
parelleth *pr. 3 sg.* dresses, arrays 7758*
parfit(e), parfyt(e) *adj.* perfect, flawless 7037, 7155, 7245+, complete, absolute 830, 1094, *comp.* **parfiter** 10,697, 12,547
parfitely, paritly, parfytly *adv.* completely 1447, 2885, 6343+, perfectly 6706, 6761, 8945+
parfiteth *pr. 3 sg.* completes 11,204
paryshones *n. pl.* parishioners 5334*n*
parlement *n.* discussion, conference 4307
part(e), partee *n.* part, section, division 421, 2476, 9984+, matter, case 1642, 6030, side 2201, 5605, 5606+, allotted portion, share 2232, 7816, 7818+, share of an inheritance 1470, 3333, 10,703, person or group of persons involved in a lawsuit 4677; *pl.* **partees, partes** parts 1526, 3168, 4700+; **what** ~ where 8505, **eville** ~ pudendum, private part 4450*n*, **hatthe** ~ **of** has sexual intercourse with 5218, 5222, 5224, **haue** ~ **of, therof** participate in, partake of, share 3334–5, 5114, 5334, **beste** ~ **of the game** upper hand, victory 2080, **as of theire** ~ as far as concerns them 11,194–5, **to his** ~ on his part 1134–5
partenere, partoner *n.* associate, companion, accomplice 3307, 12,844; *pl.* **parteneres, parteners, partoneris** 3305, 4999, 5723+, partakers, shares 3003
parteth *pr. 3 sg.* departs 2914; *pp.* **parted** separated 7032; *see* **depart(e)**
partie, party(e) *n.* part, section, division 1193, 9236, 10,298, side 5958, 8679, matter, case, affair 9286, person or group of persons involved in a lawsuit 4674*bis*, division of an inheritance 4893*n*; *pl.* **partes, parties, partyes, partis** 195, 1526, 5887+; **in** ~ partly 7007, **too the goode** ~ favorably 9209*n*, **in** ~ little by little 7839, **be smale** ~ bit by bit 1656*n*
pase *n.* Passover 8574
passage *n.* journey 6484, 6488, 6505+
passe *v.* cross over 3909, 7863, surpass 4750, pass through 6506, get through 7809, 7812, pass 8507, *pr. 3 sg.* **passeth, passith** 829, 1396, 3509+; *pr. 3 pl.* **passe, passeth** 1425, 2324, 3938+, pass away 7198; *pa. t.* **passed** 381, 668, 2594+; *part.* **passyng** 1764, 5353, 9888, transient 8134; *pp.* **passed, paste** 2713, 6486, 6527+, out of him 815
passion, passyon *n.* the Passion 361, 693, 1177+, suffering, affliction 362, 1178

passyng *vbl. n.* passing of time, transience 7617–8, passage 6487, passing away, death 8575
paste *n.* dough 7856, 11,329
paththe, patthe *n.* path 3913, 10,328*bis*+
patrimonie *n.* property, estate 2450
paume *n.* **game of the** ~ game in which ball is struck with the hand 6728*n*
pece, peece *n.* piece 1115, 1120, 4748+
peerys *n. pl.* pears 4565
peese *v.* appease, assuage 3350, 3352; *pp.* **pesid** at peace, tranquil 7263
peesyble, pesibble, pesible *adj.* tranquil, peaceful 3387, 12,992; *ellip. n.* the peaceful, the peacemakers 7359, 12,971, 12,972+
peesse *n.* drinking vessel, cup 9714
peintures, peyntures *n. pl.* bites, stings 11,272, 11,277
peitevines *n. pl.* small coins used in Poitou 10,977*n*
peyse *n.* weight 7173
peysed *pp.* weighed (in the mind), pondered 9228, 12,801, 12,831
pelir *n.* pillar 10,163; *pl.* **peleris** 11,685
penance, penaunce *n.* sacrament of penance 195, 1228, penance (for sin) 597, 946–7, 8740+, misery, pain, suffering 3757, 4742, 5562+; *pl.* **penaunces** 2786, 4371, 6413
pensifnesse *n.* vexation 7755
pensyon *n.* payment 3123
perauenture, peraventur(e) *adv.* perhaps 579, 3512, 6213+
perceyve, perseyve *v.* comprehend, understand 2666, 8500; *pr. 3 sg.* **perceyvith, perseyvith** 544, 2575, sees, observes 6337–8; *pr. 3 pl.* **perseyve** 5804; *pa. t.* **perceivid** 2605; *pp.* **perceyved** 8890
perche *n.* bar, perch 4080, pole 11,271, 11,273; *pl.* **perchis** 2471
perdicion *n.* damnation 3992**n*, road to damnation 9361–2
peresshyng *vbl. n.* spiritual destruction, suffering death of the soul 849
perfeccion *n.* spiritual perfection achieved through contemplation 245, 2195, 3277+
performe *v.* bring to completion, finish, achieve 4354, 6914, 9665
perid *pa. t.* appeared 12,071
perlious(e), perlyous *adj.* perilous, dangerous 522, 832, 1096+; *superl.* **perliouseste** 1503
perliously, perlyously *adv.* perilously, dangerously 1367, 12,781
persith *pr. 3 sg.* pierces 11,698
peruersion *n.* corruption 988
pervert *n.* pervert, corrupt 4653; *pr. 3 sg.* **peruerteth, perverteth** 3253, 5958; *pr. 3 pl.* **perverteth** 8681

pese, peese, peesyn *n. pl.* peas 1859, 5430, 8131+
pestilence *n.* iniquity, evil 6335
petiful *adj.* compassionate, merciful 10,428
petouse, piteouse, pitouce, pitous(e) *adj.* compassionate, merciful 8951, 9135, 10,364+; charitable to poor 10,516, 10,822, 11,029+; indulgent 6387
pharaseye, phareseye *n.* Pharisee 9976, 11,421
phisike *n.* medical science 5495, 5524
phisissian, phizisien *n.* physician 9950*bis*, 10,139+; *pl.* **phisissienes** 8925
piement *n.* wine sweetened with honey and spiced with herbs 2346
pike *n.* pickax 8019; *pl.* **pikkes** 7750
pylche *n.* furred garment 3970
pirle *n.* pupil (of the eye) 9416
pismere, pissemere, pyssemer *n.* ant 1880, 3752, 8849; *pl.* **pyssemyres** 4129
pytousely *adv.* with compassion 3317
placebo *phr.* **synge** ~ play the sycophant, flatter 5904
places *see* **palaice**
playe, pleye *v.* engage in a game 2003, 2372, imitate, make pretence of 2301, 4860, 5611, *mistranslation, see notes* 2058; *imp.* **pleye** enjoy (yourself) 10,120; *pr. 3 sg.* **pleyeth** toys with, trifles with 4202, 19,126; *pr. 3 pl.* **pleye, pleyeth** 704, 2781, 4320; *pa. t.* **pleied, pleyed** 474, 10,128
plainly, pleinly, pleynelye *adv.* fully, completely 1454, 4045, 8123+, clearly 1456, expressly, unambiguously 9100
plant(e) *n.* branch, shoot 1523*n*, 2118, 2153; *pl.* **plantes** 1608
plate *adj.* smooth 2353
plee *n.* (false) allegation 3435, 3565, litigation 4650, 6887, strife, contention 7376, 11,593, 12,813; *pl.* **plees** 9306, *mistranslation, see notes* 1561
plege, plegge *n.* surety 8610, 8613, 8618; **to ~, as a ~, too the ~** as a surety 1587, 2274, 7545–6+
pleye *n.* game 476, 8908
pleye (hym) *v. mistranslation, see notes* 2058
pleyer *n.* gambler 5397; *pl.* **pleyerris** gamblers, *possibly* actors 6202
pleyne *adj.* level 9159
pleyne *adv.* completely 10,525
pleyne *v.* complain 3641, bewail, lament 8534; *pr. 2 sg.* **pleyne** 3470; *pr. 3 sg.* **pleyneth** 3316, 8399, 8401+; *pr. 3 pl.* **pleyneth** 3640
pleyneres *n. pl.* complainants 4654
plenteuously *adv.* abundantly 10,726
plesance, plesans *n.* pleasure, delight 2224, 10,062, pleasantness 6850
pleser *n.* pleasure, delight 2309
plete *v.* plead 7459

pletyngis *n. pl.* disputations 9586
pletoures *n. pl.* pleaders, advocates 4509
plite, plyte *n.* state, condition 563, 3121, 7610+
poigniant *adj.* pungent, spicy 5275
point(e), poynt(e) *n.* reason, cause 404, respect 2990, principle 4725, 4727, consideration 5112, constituent part, branch, or division 9600, 9601, stylus 9152, 9153, short space of time, instant 11,383; *pl.* **pointes, pointis** 4168, 4200, 4223+, ?dots on dice 3777*n*, basic tenets or articles of faith 321, 12,717, regulations, rules 323, cases 4477, degrees 9491; **at the ~ of** at the moment of 11,383, **a ~** about 5671
pointeth, poynteth *pr. 3 sg.* points out 4782*n*, assails, attacks 6075*n*
polayle *n.* poultry 4564
polissed, polisshed *pp.* polished, refined 5792, 7446, 7448+
pompe *n.* **~ of the world** worldly vanity 10,722–3
poore, pore, poere *adj.* poor 1570, 2934, 3119+, insufficient, inadequate, scanty 3486, 4645*bis*, mean, paltry, despicable 4956, 11,615, 11,996+, inferior 8790, weak 3094, 8833, 10,951+, lowly, humble 2927, 7096, 8512+; *superl.* **poorest** 7213; **~ dayes** misery, poverty 5142–3
popped *pp.* painted with cosmetics 11,641*n*
pore *adv.* utterly, completely 2653
porple *n.* garment or gown made of rich cloth 2465; *pl.* **porple, pourple** 11,995, 12,887
pors(e) *n.* money-bag, purse 5515, 5518, 5523+
portespine *n.* porcupine 6078
pose *n.* mucus 950
potente *n.* crutch 3786
pouder(e), powder, powdre *n.* dust 3099, 6448, 7739+; *pl.* **powderes** 6456
pouerte(e) *n.* sinfulness of heart or soul 2762*n*, 7396, 8405+; *pl.* **pouertees** hardships 4957
power(e) *n.* **to (too, vnto) my (thye, his, theyre) ~** to the utmost or full extent of my (your, his, their) power 558, 1490, 3262+
praye *n.* prey 5511
prayes *n. pl.* reward, gifts 3232
prais(e), prayse, preise, preyse *v.* praise, extoll, glorify 1465, 1834, 2045+, *used passively* 3012, 11,937, 11,956+, flatter 1547, prize, esteem, put a value on 163, 1603, 6737+; *pr. 2 sg.* **praysest** 1301; *pr. 3 sg.* **prayse, prayseth, praysith** 2129, 2955, 3042+; *pr. 3 pl.* **prayse, praysen, prayseth** 1071, 3046, 3851+; *pa. t.* **praysed** 4291; *pp.* **praysed** 155, 1412, 1499+
praise, prayse, preise *n.* praise, renown, fame 2243, 2265, 2267+, honor, glory 2234

praysyng *vbl. n.* praise, praising 1729, 2225, 2231+, flattery 2535, *mistranslation, see notes* 2698; *pl.* **praysyngis, praysyngys** 2347, 8856
prebendis *n. pl.* prebends, stipends 4475
preciousnes, prescyousnes *n.* great spiritual worth 6270, 6278, 6287+, value 6866
preynte, prynte *n.* form, shape 6844, 6849; *pl.* **prentes** 9407
prelasies *n. pl.* dignities 5014
prelat, prelet *n.* high ecclesiastical dignitary 8832, 10,599, 11,889+; *pl.* **prelates, prelatis, prelattis** 768, 4711, 5013+
prese, pris(e), prys(e) *n.* price 5620, 10,361, value, worth 4962, esteem 3232; **of** ~ of great value 11,643
present(e) *phr.* **in** ~ in the present life 10,550*n*, 11,211*n*
presume *v.* confidently expect 11,043
preuyly, prevely, previly, prevyly(e) *adv.* privately 1656, 4305, secretly 2786, 12,315, alone 11,341, 11,899, intimately 4297, 11,340
preve *n.* proof 8608
previlage *n.* ~ **of grace** divine favor, benefit of grace 1278
prevy, prive *adj.* intimate 7347, hidden, secluded 8860, 12,316*, domestic 12,026*
pryckes *n. pl.* quills 6081
prycketh *pr. 3 sg.* pricks 9154; *pr. 3 pl.* **pricketh, priketh, prikketh** 2217–8, 12,044, 12,871; *part.* **prikkyng, prikyng** 2212, 2217
pride *n.* wicked show or spectacle (of the devil) 5331, ostentatious splendor, magnificence 5063, 8774, 10,403, exalted position 3013; *pl.* **prides** 5331*n*
prideth, prydeth *pr. 3 sg.* prides (himself) 12,888, 12,894; *pa. t.* **prided** 1933
procured *pp.* obtained unlawfully 959
prodigalite *n.* wastefulness 6334, 6424
professid *pp.* **be** ~ have taken vows of religion 12,294
profession *n.* act of entering a religious order 11,889**n*
profit(e), profyt(e), prophit *n.* benefit, gain, advantage 113, 306, 332+; **comune** ~ common good 9053–4
profit *phr.* ~ **of the tonge** advantage of eloquence 113, 6228
profit(e), profyte *v.* profit, benefit 6217, 7128, 8342, grow, increase 6313, 7296, 7300+; *pr. 3 sg.* **profiteth, profyteth, propheteth** 2028, 3269, 6318+; *pr. 3 pl.* **profit, profiteth** 7145, 7317, 7387+; *part.* **profityng** progressing 12,544
profitabilly *adv.* advantageously, beneficially 8850
profitable *adj.* advantageous, beneficial 133, 512, 897+
profre *pr. 3 pl.* offer 460

prononcit *pr. 3 sg.* utters 375; *pp.* **pronunsed** declared aloud, proclaimed 2049

proper, propre *adj.* own 802, 903, 8837+, of his (their) own 886, 905, 906+, exact, true 6685, correct, appropriate 7584, self 7786, 8805, rightful 8172, 12,656

properly, propirly, proprely *adv.* actually 2378, 2413, 2415+, solely 3551, 8147, completely, thoroughly 7661, in strict or proper time 4767, correctly, appropriately 7599

prouoste, provoost, provoste *n.* chief magistrate 3599, 5715, 9892, prison warden 8413

prove *v.* try, test 1955, 10,671, 12,697, prove (themselves) worthy 9791; *pr. 1 sg.* **preve** prove, demonstrate 1695; *pr. 3 sg.* **provith** 9161, 9796, 10,666+; *pr. 3 pl.* **provith** 9586; *pa. t.* **proved** 1200; *pp.* **proved, provid** 2699, 8032, 8316+, experienced 9428, 10,294, 10,295+, evinced 12,796*n*

provendre *n.* prebend, stipend 7875*; *pl.* **prouendres** 3123

prudens of the flesshe *phr.* worldly wisdom 5648

pvmped *pp.* freed from bilge water by means of a pump 10,077*n*

purchace *v.* obtain, procure 3680, 5657; *pr. 3 sg.* **purchaceth, purchaseth, purchasith** causes, brings about, perpetrates 826, 1282, 3655+; *pr. 3 pl.* **purchace, purchaseth, purchasseth** 4509, 7649, 12,988–9; *pp.* **purchased** 12,320

purchasyng *vbl. n.* (sinful) behavior 10,004

pure *adj.* absolute 824, sheer, utter, complete 1039, 9090, 10,022, pure, unadulterated 7242, true, genuine 8633, sincere 8829; *comp.* **purer** more refined 8794, 9723

purely *adv.* solely, exclusively, only 5136, 8143, 8147+, truly 12,067

purgacion *n.* purification of sin 11,204

purge, porge *v.* purify, cleanse, rid of sin or impurity 1447, 6600, 7766; *pr. 3 sg.* **purgeth, purgith, porgeth, porgith, pourgith** 6596, 7077, 7689+; *pp.* **purged, porged** 6584, 8439*, 11,196+

purpose *v.* have a resolve 10,158; *pr. 3 pl.* **purposeth** 11,935; *pa. t.* **purposed** 3706

purveyance, purviance *n.* foresight 6914–15, 8285

purveye, purvoye *v.* provide, make provision (for) 873*bis*, 1889+; *pr. 3 sg.* **purveieth, purveith, purveyeth** 1880, 2083, 8296+; *pr. 3 pl.* **purveieth** 1879, 1886

purveyour *n.* provider 7474

pusillanimite(e) *n.* timidity, cowardice 64, 3902, 6332+

put *see* **but**

put *pr. 3 pl.* butt, push 2287

putok, puttokke *n.* kite 3875, 5483
put, putte *v.* put, place 355, 1858, 4799+, give, sacrifice 9092, bring 5705, use, employ 5157; *imp.* **put, putte** 5171, ~ **oute,** ~ **from** banish, put aside 8428, 11,489–90; *pr. 2 sg.* **putte** say, offer (prayers) 7552; *pr. 3 sg.* **putteth, puttith, puttyth** 2195, 3391, 4798+; *pr. 3 pl.* **put, putte, putteth** 356, 2303, 5773+, make 2275, 9654, engage (in), perform 2415, add 5894; *pa. t.* **put** 7856, 8570, 9093, entered 10,787; *pp.* **put, putte** 733, 4903, 11,332+; *phrases* ~ **grete (more) peyne (besines, besynesse)** exert great effort 2331–2, 10,029, 12,296, ~ **in myende** brings to mind 5089, ~ **hym therto** performs 8800, ~ **in foryetilnes** leave unnoticed, negect, disregard 4525–6*n*, ~ **to the dethe** execute(d) 2140, 2593–4, 3341, ~ **in sepulchre** buried 1181, ~ **to gresse** put to pasture 10,642, ~ **in Cristen beriell** given a Christian burial 10,730, ~ **vnder foote** overcome, subdue 1337–8, 10,338, 12,099, ~ **intoo an evil weye** lead amiss, cause to go astray 6458, ~ **to (intoo) thraldom** bring (brought) to bondage or subjection 4787, 12,734–5, ~ **mesure** exercise moderation 12,741, ~ **in possession** given possession 11,122, ~ **in mysbelyve** cause to lose faith 1958–9, ~ **in velenye** corrupted 1831, ~ **in writyng** records 1982, ~ **owte (his, their, this) yee** blind(s) 2188–9, 2195, 3891–2*n*, ~ **owte of the grace** puts out of (divine) favor 6049, *with adverbs* ~ **oute (owte, aweye, froo)** exclude, banish, remove, expel, cast aside 697, 7010, 7556+, eradicate 1371, put out, quench, 11,312, 11,318, ~ **forthe,** ~ **hym forthe** further 8656, extends, stretches out 9089, puts himself out (for) 9086

qhoso *form of* **whoso** whoever 1288
qualitees *n. pl.* bodily humors 9248
quarell *n.* plee, litigation, suit 4676, 7164, 9306; *pl.* **quarellis, quarellys** matters of concern 4294, 4307, 6361, disputes 6916
queynte, qweynte *adj.* proud, haughty 7096, fashionable, elegant 5355
queintises *n. pl.* fineries, *here* elaborate ornaments 12,899
quencheth, quenchith *pr. 3 sg.* repels 11,391, destroys 5946; *pp.* **quenched, qwenched** stifled, brought to an end 11,323, extinguished 10,735
quicke, quycke, quykke, qwik(e), qwycke, qwyk *adj.* live, burning 4903, 8351, 11,331, alive, living 3911, 5720, 6109+, flowing 7421, lively, energetic 4070, alert, keen 11,182, immediately intelligible 8612, 8618; *comp.* **qwyker** 9010; *ellip. n. pl.* **quycke** the living 1211
qwickly *adv.* vigorously 9259**n*
quikned *pp.* inspired 3767
quit(e), quyte, quytte *adj.* free, free of, clear 3999, 4036, 4488+
quyte, qwyte *v.* pay for, reward 1679, absolve (of debt) 8644; *imp.* **quite** 7908; *pr. 1 pl.* **quite** 7908; *pp.* **quytte** 8726, 9367

qweyntly *adv.* elegantly 5353
qwiknesse *n.* life, vitality 7391
qwom *form of* **whom** 1306

raceth, raseth, rasith *pr. 3 sg.* uproots, tears out, plucks 8188, 8236, 10,339+; *pr. 3 pl.* **raseth, rasith** 7650, 8477; *pp.* **rased** 4849
rage *n.* tempest, tumult 8860
rancoure, rancure, rankoure *n.* bitter animosity, malignant hatred 3463, 7930, 7935+
raveyn(e), ravyne *n.* rapine, robbery 80, 856, 973+; **birdys of ~** birds of prey 8867–8
raveyneth *pr. 3 sg.* robs 6424
ravisshed *pp.* transported 689, 4929, 6801+, filled with ecstasy 11,154, 12,558, violated 12,083, seized, taken away 8913
rebaude, rebaute, rybawde *n.* rascal 1567, 5398, wastrel 8396; *pl.* **rebawdes, ribaudes, ribautis** 862, 1804, 4845+
rebaudie, ribaudy, rybaudye *n.* obscenity 11,729, debauchery 8407, 11,284
recche *v.* care, be concerned 9678; *pr. 2 sg.* **rekyst** 1893; *pr. 3 sg.* **reckith, rekkyth** 1043, 2105, 2538+; *pr. 3 pl.* **recke, recketh, rekke** 2021, 2292, 4526+
receitis *n. pl.* monies received 9894
recomendyng *part.* praising 712
recouer(e), recover *v.* recover, regain possession of 3815, 3981, 5581+, repeat 10,085*n*; *pp.* **recouered, recoueryd** 5586, 12,114
recreant *adj.* cowardly, afraid 4211
recreauntis *n. pl.* cowards 10,156
reculeth *pr. 3 sg.* retreats 5571
redelid *adj.* pleated, gathered 2486
redeveable *adj.* indebted, beholden 9768*n*
redily, redyly *adv.* quickly, soon 2381, 8811, 8812
redresse *v.* straighten 6476; *pr. 3 sg.* **redresseth** corrects, reforms 9044; *pp.* **redressid** cured, restored 5691
refeit *pp.* nourished, refreshed 8665*
reformeth *pr. 3 sg.* remakes, restores to a former state 6843; *pp.* **reformed, reformyd** 7057, 7082
refressh(e) *v.* restore (oneself), regain 7302, 7390; *pr. 3 sg.* **refresseth, refresshith** 5464, 7315; *pp.* **refresshed** 8014
refreyne *v.* restrain 842, 4401, abstain 2293
refuseth *pr. 3 sg.* rejects 8305*n*, 8358, denies 11,799
regard(e) *n.* **to (too, unto) ~ of** in comparison with 594, 6491, 6852+, **as to ~ of** with respect to 1302
regratories *n. pl.* market commodities (especially victuals) 4852*n*

reherce, reherse *v.* expound 1464, record 2500, tell 5850, remember 10,007; *pr. 3 sg.* **reherseth** makes mention of 8088; *pr. 3 pl.* **rehersith** reveal 9055; *pp.* **reherced, rehersed, rehersid** 5730, 6211, 6244+

reigne *v.* rule, govern, prevail 4591, 5734; *pr. 3 sg.* **regneth, reigneth** 4404, holds sway 6120*n*; *pr. 3 pl.* **reigneth** 4408, 4409, 5734; *pa. t.* **reigned** 4413

reynes *n. pl.* loins 12,228*, 12,229*; **delit(e) of the** ~ sexual gratification 1395, 3685

reynes *n. pl.* rains 8288

reyseth, reysith *pr. 3 sg.* uplifts 7084, 12,533; *pr. 3 pl.* **reyseth** exalt 8680; *pp.* **reysed** raised, elevated 11,182

reysyng *vbl. n.* instigation 3055–6

releve *v.* rise from sin 7397*n*

religion *n.* monastic rule 323, 5178, monastic order 1006, 1011, 4469+

religious(e) *adj.* belonging to a religious order, bound by a monastic or other religious vow 242, 321, 4576+

religious *n.* member of a religious order 12,393; *pl.* **religious, religiouses** 2255, 3023, 12,289+

remembrance, remembrans *n.* memory 934, 7087, 11,263+

remeueth *pr. 3 pl.* set free 4558

remeve *v.* ?sweep, clean 6454*n*, set aside 12,734*n*

remission *n.* forgiveness of sins 1232

reneying, renoyinge, renoyng(e) *vbl. n.* act of abjuring or renouncing 16, 1911, 1935+

rengeid *pp.* set in battle rank 6410

renne, ryn, rynne *v.* run, hasten 317, 5262, 5577+, flow 11,259, ~ **on (oppon)** assail, attack 2851, 3916–17, 4648, resort (to) 11,457, slacken 12,743, ~ **be** report 10,007, ~ **to** consider, examine 10,032; *pr. 3 sg.* **renneth, rynneth** 3203, 5411, 8536+, traverses 8835, follows its course 6952, passes 6403, ~ **after (aftir)** pursues 3209, 9331, 9670+; *pr. 3 pl.* **renneth, rennyth, ryn, rynne** 2136, 2291, 2425+, compete 9751; *pa. t.* **ran, ranne** 9343, 9345, 9913+; *part.* **rynnyng** 3747; *pp.* **ronne be the waye** followed the path 316

renogat *n.* apostate 4214

renoie *pr. 1 sg.* abjure, renounce 1848; *pr. 2 sg.* **reneye** 5125; *pr. 3 sg.* **reneyeth** 1915; *pr. 3 pl.* **renoyeth** 3376, 3437; *pp.* **reneyed** 1953; **man** ~ apostate 1915, 1916

rentes, rentis, rentys *n. pl.* income, revenues 1561, 1797, 2260+, payments in money or service due to a lord 4532*n*, rents 5717, (1) tithes 4492, (2) dues 4492*n*, treasury of merit or grace 4704

repaire *v.* go 588

repent(e) *v. mistranslation, see notes* 1702, 3516
repreve, reprove *v.* reprove, blame 4179, 9068, 10,594+; *pr. 2 sg.* **reprovist** 2675; *pr. 3 sg.* **repreveth, reprevith, reproveth, reprovith** 2493, 6295, 8718+; *pr. 3 pl.* **repreve, reprove, reproveth, reprovith** 2154, 6093, 6177+; *pa. t.* **reprevyd, reproved** 537, 11,117–18; *part.* **reprevyng** 712
reproche *v.* revile, abuse 6064; *pr. 3 sg.* **reprocheth** 6091
reproche *n.* blame, censure 3701; *pl.* **reproches** 6091, 10,989
require *v.* ask, request 587, 4073, 5224+; *pr. 3 sg.* **requireth** 5127, 7810, 7814+, requires, demands, 5496, 11,636, 11,761+, seeks 11,811; *pr. 3 pl.* **require, requireth** 5496, 5532–3, 6437+; *pa. t.* **required** 11,810; *pp.* **required** 8055
rerewarde *n.* rearguard 8058, 10,238
resoigne *pr. 3 sg.* fears 4500*n*
reson, reeson *n.* reason, judgment 736, 1130, 1142+, ground, cause 3074, 5284, 5308+, equity, justice 5536, knowledge, understanding 9177, 4351, 4353, account 1899, 5815, 9891, justification 9010; *pl.* **resones** 2884, 3030, 5282+; **is** ~ is reasonable 3308, 11,137–8
resonable *adj.* discreet, prudent 4349, 6285, 9618+, rational 4355, sound, reasonable 5412, 6008, 9765–6+
resoneth *pr. 3 sg.* addresses 4205, 5105
resouneth, resowneth *pr. 3 sg.* resounds 4163, echoes 5908
respite, respyte *n.* delay, extension of time of life 3987, 3989, 4951
resshe *n.* rush 12,739*n*
rest(e), reeste *n.* rest, repose 560, 992, 3743+, tranquility of mind or soul 7761, 8583*bis*+, temporary interruption or cessation 11,148, refreshment 3423; **in** ~ at peace, tranquil 4317, **haue** ~ be at peace 3505, **in grete hertis** ~ in great tranquility of soul 7027
restore *v.* make amends for 4512, 5073, 5190; *pp.* **restored** 4682
restrayne, restreyn(e) *v.* restrain 281, 841, restrict, withhold 4853; *pr. 3 sg.* **restreyneth, restreynyth** 2533, 5755, 5778–9+; *pp.* **restreyned** 12,243
revel *n.* revelry 2045; *pl.* **revellis** festivities, entertainments 2280
revith *pr. 3 pl.* ravage 10,223*n*
rewle *n.* rule, level 9153, 9158, rule, regulation 4824, 5541, 9480; *pl.* **rewlis** rules of conduct 7367; **in** ~ in order and discipline 5476
rewlith *pr. 3 sg.* rules, governs 8295
riche *adj.* splendid, elegant 2084, 3869, 11,924
right(e) *n.* justice, righteousness, equity 1340, 4548, 4653+, right 7478, 7503, just claim, due 5222, 11,797, 11,801, rights 7816, 7819, 9283, legal title 7918; *pl.* **ryghtes** 4652; **o** ~ by rights 498, 2076, **o good** ~, **veray** ~ with good reason 258–9, 6050

right(e), ryght *adv.* very 127, 133, 134+, at all 6176, rightly 12,974, directly 12,768, strictly 9277, truly 1881; ~ **a(n) (evil, gret vntrouthe, grete herte, etc.)** a very *(intensifier)* 4572, 5790, 6395+

right(e) *adj.* right 204, 1207, 2188+, straight 493, 5694, 9259+, proper, appropriate, due 295, 988, 5409+, rightful, legitimate 493, 890, 4562+, strict 7918, true 1937, 7880, 8348+, authoritative 6040, ?pure 7841, just, righteous 9277; *superl.* **rightest** straightest 491; **o (be)** ~ **iugement** with good reason 745–6, 1813, ~ **iugement** reasonable 1957–8

rightfully *adv.* rightly, properly, correctly 7177, 8175, 10,335+, accurately, precisely 9210, legitimately 4808

rightly *adv.* directly 295, 10,336, properly 2258

rightwis(se), rightwys, ryghtwys(se) *adj.* righteous 2548, 3714*n*, 4027+, equitable, just 4893, rightful 6785

rightwisnes(se), rightwysnes, rightvissnesse *n.* justice, righteousness, equity 1341, 8272, 11,796+

rightwosly *adv.* rightly, truly 502

rigorous *adj.* severe, harsh 6397**n*

rigoure *n.* harshness, severity 3180

rynne *see* **renne**

riott *n.* rigmarole 7446

ripe, rype *adj.* mature 3266, 3279

roile *n.* charger 3970

romaunses *n. pl.* fictitious narratives 4321

roset *see* **sugre roset**

roveres, rovers *n. pl.* robbers 1546*n*, 1604

rowe *mistranslation, see notes* 2119

rowtes *n. pl.* throngs 2179

rude *adj.* ignorant, uncouth 7590, harsh 9257

sabat, sabbat *n.* Sabbath 560, 694, 11,557

sacrament, sacrement *n.* ~ **of the auter** Eucharist 371, 1228–9, 7825–6+

sacreth *pr. 3 sg.* consecrates 376; *pr. 3 pl.* **sacreth** 12,203; *pp.* **sacred** 709, 12,201, bound by vow (to God) 920

sacrileged *adj.* guilty of sacrilege 4578

sadde *adj.* prudent, wise 7968

sadly *adv.* prudently 9311

saf *adv.* in safety 4866

safe, saffe, save *adj.* saved, brought to salvation 4980, 9754, safe, secure 10,286

safe, save *prep.* except (for) 1163, 4958, 7613+

safe, saue, save *v.* guard 9283, save, preserve 1036, 8753, achieve salvation 4240, 9545, 9546+, bring to salvation 7395, save from damnation 11,091; *imp.* **saue, save** 11,539, 11,542, 12,408; *pr. 3 sg.* **saueth** 1846; *pr. 3 pl.* **savith** 7467; *pp.* **saued, saved, savid, savyd, sauyd** 1145, 1752, 5732+, spared 11,322

saye, sey(e), seie *v.* say, state 1206, 1641, 10,999+; *imp.* **seye** 1708, 7577; *pr. 1 sg.* **seye** 331, 344*bis*+; *pr. 2 sg.* **seist, seyist, seyst(e), seiest** 2010*bis*, 7506+; *pr. 3 sg.* **seye, seeyth, seyeth, seyth(e), seith(e), seiþe, setthe** 1500, 3956*, 8578+; *pr. 1 pl.* **seye** 1758, 2232, 4073+; *pr. 2 pl.* **seye** 5877, 8548; *pr. 3 pl.* **seye, seyen, seieth, seith(e), seyth(e), seyeth** 258, 269, 370+; *pa. t.* **seid(e), seyde** 302, 386, 397+; *part.* **seying(e), seyng, seyyng** 458, 508, 1012+; *pp.* **seid(e)** 466, 467, 471+

saileth *pr. 3 sg.* assails 11,390

saille *n.* sail 10,241

sallaryes *n. pl.* fees 4672

sanguyn *adj.* sanguine 9395

sanke *pa. t.* perished 932; ~ **intoo the grounde** 5243

saoule *v.* fill, satisfy 7220, 7232; *pp.* **saouled** 7356, 11,161

sarplere *n.* canvas sack 2087, 2467

satisfaccion *n.* act of reparation, atonement for sin 199, 3860, 9832+

saunec *prep.* except for 11,758

sause *n.* sauce 10,646; *pl.* **sauses** 5275; ~ **camelyn** spicy sauce 5425–6*n*, **vinegre** ~ sauce with a vinegar base 10,647

sauely *adv.* safely 510

savyng *prep.* except 1293, 8152

sauory, sauoury *adj.* delicious 2402, 5426, 12,955, spiritually delightful 6903, 12,681, characterized by spiritual understanding 12,517

sauour *v.* experience 7202, have an offensive odor 11,329; *pr. 3 sg.* **sauoreth, sauoureth** 12,570, 12,684, tastes 5428, 5632, 12,519; *pr. 3 pl.* **sauour** 7202; *pp.* **sauoured** 7237

sauour(e), savoure *n.* pleasure, delight 1715, 1718, 3397+, taste, flavor 7841, 8752, 10,054+, spiritual understanding 12,518, 12,683, *mistranslation, see notes* 4095; *pl.* **sauoures** 7882

savouryly *adv.* with spiritual understanding 7680*n*

savourisly *adv.* with spiritual understanding 7681*n*

scalte *pp.* scalded 7993

scapeth *aphetic form of* **escapeth** 9671

scarcely *adv.* stingily 4432

scarlet *n.* woolen cloth 9718*n*

scarse *adj.* parsimonious 5523, 10,399, abstemious 5508

scarsnesse *n.* abstemiousness 5508
scluse *n.* sluice 12,805, 12,807, 12,811
scorne, skorne *v.* mock, deride 705, 2375, 9371+; *pp.* **scorned** 1738, 8558
scornes *n. pl.* mockeries, derisions 4410, 8777
scornynggys *n. pl.* mocks, jibes 5830
scripture *n.* the Bible 822, 908, 2700+, God's book of accounts 2490, book of canon law, *here* the *Decretum* 6040, writings of the Fathers 6676; *pl.* **scriptures** 1199, 7053, 12,272+, written accounts of saints' lives 10,799, writings 12,521*n*
scusacions *n. pl.* justifications, excuses 572
secret(e) *adj.* private, hidden 2767, 8762, 8896+
secretely(e), secretly *adv.* in secret 3036, 3037, 3039+
secretenesse, secretnesse *n.* **in** ~ in secret 11,050–1, 11,051
secretes, secretis *n. pl.* secrets (of God) 690, 7121, 8202+
seculer, seculier *adj.* worldly 11,490, 11,593, *as n.* secular priest 9989; ~ **man** publican 9977
see *v.* see 2004, 2008, 2009+; *imp.* **see** 1633, 2268, 2269+; *pr. 1 sg.* **see** 2178, 3358, 9369+; *pr. 2 sg.* **seeist, seest, seeyst, seist, seyste** 1678, 1754, 1786+; *pr. 3 sg.* **seeith, seeithe, seeth, seeyth, seyth** 2584, 2988, 3125+; *pr. 1 pl.* **see** 278, 881, 1498+; *pr. 3 pl.* **se, see, seeith, seeth, seeyth** 708, 709, 1106+; *pa. t. 1 sg.* **saw(e)** 1612, 3364, 3367+; *pa. t. 3 sg. and pl.* **saw(e), saugh** 867, 1113, 11,541+; *part.* **seeyng, seyng** 538, 8334; *pp.* **seen, seeyn, seyn(e)** 1072, 3611, 5313+
seege *n.* seat 2971
seese *v.* seize 3512
seyer *n.* speaker 5981
seying(e), seyng *vbl. n.* saying 525, 1827, 2012+, opinion, observation 9222, 11,179; *pl.* **seynggys** 12,922; **of the** ~ from saying it 468–9
seyng(e) *vbl. n.* seeing 5355, 7184, 12,379
seisine *n.* possession 8942
seldom *adv. mistranslation, see notes* 1832
selfe-wille *n.* pursuit of one's own desires or opinions 7786
selfe-willed *adj.* obstinate 12,729*n*
selfe, selve *adj.* very, same 5846, *as n.* the same person 8902, 12,276, 12,781
selle, sille, sylle *v.* sell 4619, 5400, 8758; *pr. 2 sg.* **sellist** 2011; *pr. 3 sg.* **sellith** 4996, 5397, 7008; *pr. 3 pl.* **selle, selleth** 4465, 5856*; *pa. t.* **soolde, sould, soilde** 996, 5580, 11,592+; *pp.* **solde, soolde** 980, 1118, 1738; **to** ~ for sale 2033, ~ **(hym) the asse** treat as a fool 2011*n*
selve-wit(te) *n.* self-wisdom, pride 6330*n*, 6333, 8804
sen *conj.* since 1699, 1741, 5319+. *See* **sithen**

senguler, singuler *adj.* individual, personal 1671*bis*, 1783
sent *imp.* send 3752; *pa. t.* **sende** sent 5542
sentence, sentense *n.* judgment 1089, order 495, 6157, 10,879+, meaning 2410, 7436, sentence of excommunication, anathema 2869, 2876; *pl.* **sentensis** 6188
septentrion *n.* the north 8287
serche *n.* inquiry, investigation 9202
serche *v.* inquire into, investigate 9175, 9191, 10,614+, examine, probe 9882
serchyng(e) *vbl. n.* investigating 7622, 7834–5, 8609
sercle, serkle *n.* circuit 8837, circle 9448, 9454, band of a crown 1637
seriant *n.* officer of a court 5715
sertein *adj.* sure 1107
sertes, sertis *adv.* for a certainty 1646, 5954, 12,965
seruage, servage *n.* bondage 1576, 7014, 7579+
serueth *pr. 3 sg.* undertakes a task 4146*n*
seruice *v.* serve 2424*n*
set, sette *v.* set down 2032, 3325, 12,953+, plant 1444, govern, regulate 9311, establish, set up 755, place (in) 4795; *imp.* **set, sette** sit, be seated 5311, place 9409; *pr. 3 sg.* **set, sette, setteth, settith** 308, 8409, 9336+, puts, places 4806, 4861, 5633+, lays down 275, attributes 2957, sets about, applies himself to 3680, arranges 8124, unites 7088, devotes himself to 9302, 9677*n*, 10,160+, makes 7076, 7696, employs 4691, applies, administers 10,602*n*; *pr. 1 pl.* **set, sette** 3088, 6105; *pr. 3 pl.* **set, sette, setteth, settith** 431, 1128, 2271+, direct 719, 1128, bestow 1646; *pa. t.* **set, sette** 910, 1151, 1156+, took up a position, that is, entered the field of battle 9794, bestowed 2630, located 6799; *pp.* **set, sette** 489, 1935, 2390+, noble, gentle 6656*n*, ordained 9996, arranged 8126, fixed, firmly set 7027, 11,154, 12,728, appointed 11,557, 11,558, bestowed on 11,604, disposed, ordered 12,959, regulated 9252, 9253, 12,130; *phrases* ~ **vppon** follow 12,746*n*, ~ **in the weye** instruct 1662, ~ **in the right weye** direct(s) aright, put(s) on the right path 8281, 8377–8, ~ **(my) yen in the erthe** cast (my) eyes downward 1614–15, ~ **(it) behynde hym** put (it) behind him, *fig.* forget (it) 12,457–8, ~ **(oure) peyne** endeavor, expend (our) efforts 7055, ~ **al (his) labour and (his) entent** endeavors and resolves to the utmost 2402–3, ~ **alle his stodye** expends all his efforts 3564–5, ~ **a (goode) bridill(e)** curb, restrain 12,787, ~ **in balance** weigh 12,817, ~ **vnder (vndir) foote** subdue, overcome 223–4, 8368, ~ **the worlde vnder his fete** despises 6964*n*, ~ **my face aȝeyns** opposed 411–12*n*, ~ **on werke, awerke** put(s) to work 3810, 4638, ~ **(hym) in his occupacions** puts (him) about his (the devil's) work 11,362, ~ **in oure mynde** bear in mind, remember 3695, ~ **at hazarde** put at

risk 9851, ~ **(theym) writyn** write (them) down 4731, ~ **lowe** humbles 8743–4, ~ **o fyre** ignites 11,332, ~ **to lettre** teaches to read 7426, ~ **hym ayein to his werke** resumed his work 4243, ~ **vppe** raised 11,640*n*, ~ **to compte** call to account 11,604, ~ **his soule** die(d) 9096, 9096–7, ~ **alle atte alle** ?set aside completely, give up completely 4207, ~ **mesure** exercise(s) moderation 248, 12,716, 12,937+, set bounds 12,641, 12,728, ~ **not a straw be,** ~ **not by a notte** have (has) no regard for 7017–18, 8917, ~ **prise be** value 4962–3, ~ **in disease (vnease)** disturb(s), distress(es) 5822, 12,652, ~ **in ordre** establishes a proper relationship with 8281, ~ **atte noght** destroy 5945–6*n*, ~ **(no(o)) st(o)ore,** ~ **(not) be,** ~ **at nought, nothynge, nought be** set (no) store by, have (no) care or regard for 2284, 6404, 10,926+, ~ **hert(e) (hertis)** set (his, her, their) heart(s) upon 436, 2622, direct the mind 8247, devote themselves (himself) (to) 9313, succumbs (to) 11,877*n*, give their hearts (to) 6937, 7062–3, ~ **his love (in)** desire 3288, ~ **wele thyn herte** be firmly resolved 1461, ~ **theyre hertis from** withdraw from 8217–18, ~ **counselle** decide on a course of action 5728, ~ **theym to plegge** make them give a pledge 2274, **wel (welle, weele)** ~ disciplined, ordered, regulated 1315, 1373, 3198, **evil** ~ disedified 11,646*n*, **hye** ~ seated high 8816*n*

shadowe (hym) *v.* shade (himself) 7362

shakyng *part. mistranslation, see notes* 5354

shal, shall(e) *pr. 1 sg.* shall, will 1662, 1728, 1835+; *pr. 2 sg.* **shall(e), shalt(e)** 319, 6554, 10,782+; *pr. 3 sg.* **shal, shall(e)** 1245, 1729, 1772+; *pr. 1 pl.* **shal, shall(e)** 273, 607, 11,059+; *pr. 2 pl.* **shal, shall(e)** 398, 2984, 10,873+; *pr. 3 pl.* **shall(e)** 9129, 12,286, 12,587+; *pa. t. 1 sg.* **sholde** ought to, should 1569, 1587, 1609+; *pa. t. 2 sg.* **sholdest(e), sholdist** 304, 3727, 6580+; *pa. t. 3 sg.* **scholde, shholde, shold(e), shulde** 173, 2992, 11,758+; *pa. t. 1 pl.* **shold(e), shoolde** 3697, 3698, 11,567+; *pa. t. 3 pl.* **shold(e), shoolde, shulde** 18, 1423, 3139+

shame *n.* shame 37, 2817, 2846+, disgrace, dishonor 324, 2303, 11,993+, blasphemy 2021, 3435, decency, modesty 5864, shameful death 8575, injurious conduct or language 5724; *pl.* **shames** shameful deeds 6395, 6404; **have** ~ feel ashamed 778, 3828, 10,064+, **doest, doo, dothe or purchasith** ~ dishonor(s) 826, 2032, 2047+

shamefast(e) *adj.* ashamed 1985, 12,068, modest 11,640, bashful, shy 11,798, 11,808, virtuous in behavior and character 10,955

shameful(l), shamefulle, shamful *adj.* disgraceful, ignominious 2832, 3830, 4781+, demeaning 4179; *superl.* **shamefulest** 1739, 5132

shamefully, shamfully *adv.* disgracefully, ignominiously 2707, 5575

shapyn *pp.* shaped, cut 2487

sharpe *adj.* austere, rigorous 946, 9639, 10,109+, keen 2531, acute 3425, harsh, severe 6697, 9401, 10,631+, pungent 8924; *comp.* **sharper** 2354, 6077

sharpenes(se) *n.* hardship 6703, austerity 9657, 11,913, 12,097+; *pl.* **sharpenesses** mortifications 8865, 9656

sheefes, shevys *n. pl.* sheaves 4565, 4694

shelde, shilde *n.* shield 9705, 11,387

shende *v.* destroy, ruin, injure 3271, 5286, 9067; *pr. 3 sg.* **shendeth** 5401, 12,004; *pr. 3 pl.* **shendeth** 8307, 11,727; *pa. t.* **shent** 2593, 8481; *pp.* **shent, shente** 955, 4841

shenshippe *n.* disgrace 4696*n*

sherewe, sherewes *see* **shrewe**

shette *v.* shut 10,383; *pp.* **shette** 682, 12,120

shewed *pp.* viewed with favor 2374*n*

sheweth *pr. 3 sg.* avoids, shuns 4148*n*

shewyng *vbl. adj.* apparent 6673, 11,971, 12,300

shewyngys *vbl. n.* displays 2369

shilder *see* **child(e)**

shoo *n.* shoe 10,591, 11,741; *pl.* **shone, shoon, shoone** 1299, 2487, 10,039

shrede *pr. 3 pl.* fleece, strip of wealth 4531*n*

shrewde *adj.* wicked, malicious 1526

shrewdely *adv.* dishonestly 1004, 4918, wickedly, sinfully 2320, 2430

shrewdenes(se), shrewedenes, shrewdnes *n.* wickedness, evil, depravity 1804, 3741–2, 3855+

shrewe, sherewe *n.* wicked person, sinner 6141, 6354, 8547, wretch 3863, devil 8056, 8059, 8063, vice 8278; *pl.* **shrewes, shrewis, shrewys, sherewes** 179, 1071, 11,334+

shrewed *adj.* wicked, sinful 3064

shrewys *n. pl.* sheriffs 8202

shrifte *n.* confession 9985

sich(e), syche, sige *adj.* such 6706, 7220, 12,264+

sige *see* **sich(e)**

signifyng *vbl. n.* prefigurement, signification 591, 1032

sille *see* **selle**

sylle *see* **selle**

simonye, symonie, symonye *n.* simony 77, 4464, 4470

simpilly, simply, symplye *adv.* humbly 8822, honestly, sincerely 6043, absolutely 9193

sympilnes *n.* innocence 8825

simple, sympel, symple *adj.* lacking other factors 847, 891, lacking additional legal stipulations 11,880, 11,884, 11,925, blameless, innocent 4580,

5140, 9443+, sound, healthy 9440, modest 11,638, 11,639, plain, clear 8603, 8606, 8614, direct 12,515, 12,525; ~ **man** ordinary person 9990

symplesse *n.* innocence 6040

singulerteis *n. pl.* singular behavior 6414

sithen, sithyn (that) *conj.* since 341, 906, 10,421+; *see* **sen**

sithen, sitthyn *adv.* afterwards 5586, 9597

slaundred *pp.* disgraced, shamed 3322

slavaine, slavyne *n.* coarse woolen mantle 758*n*, 2467

sloggy, sluggy *adj.* indolent, slothful 3928, 4083, 4085+

sloggynes, slokkenesse, slokynes *n.* slothfulness, indolence 4066, 4111, 4112+

sloggyng *vbl. n.* sloth 3943

sloughe, slowe *pa. t.* slew 818, 2139

slouth(e), slowthe, slowe *n.* sloth 58, 65, 3678+

slowe *adj.* slothful, indolent 1416, 3752, 5751+; *as n.* **the** ~ slothful person 1393

slowefull(e) *adj.* slothful 4276, 6355

slowly *adv.* slothfully 2421, 4187**n*

slutty *adj.* dirty 11,229

sobirly *adv.* temperately, with restraint 12,590

sobirnes(se), soobirnes *n.* temperance, sobriety, moderation 248, 2555, 12,902+

sobre, soobre *adj.* moderate, temperate 2556, 11,772, 12,692+

sodeyn *adj.* hasty 12,603

sodenly *adv.* swiftly 2207

softe *adj.* gentle 2522, 2525, 2528+, easy (to bear) 10,664, lenient 2517, 9257; *comp.* **softer** 12,682

softely, softly, softe *adv.* gently 3317, 9072, 9366+, meekly 9026, tenderly 2019, 7839, quietly, silently 10,880; ~ **norryshed** of a weak or delicate constitution 3823

soget *n.* subject 9069; *pl.* **sogettis, soiettis, soiettys, subgettis, subgettys** 4712, 4714, 10,223+

soget, sogget *adj.* subject 2943, 3672, 11,819

soilde *see* **selle**

sokere *imp.* help 3537

solace, solas, soolas *v.* comfort 1768, 2396, please 6695, divert, amuse 5979

solas, soolas *n.* joy, pleasure 3683, 7722, comfort 3676, 4299, 4318+; *pl.* **solaces** entertainments, amusements 598

solempne *adj.* sacred 715, 11,844

solempned *pp.* solemnized 11,888

solempnitee *n.* celebration, sacred festival 592

sonne-goynge-adowne *n.* sunset 5463–4
soo that *conj.* so long as 3611, 4394, 4965+, in order that 4393, 8758
soole *adj.* sole, exclusive 886
soophyme *n.* sophistry, specious argument 6039
soore, sore *adv.* much, sorely 1997, 2629, 3910, dearly 6919; *comp.* **soorer** 9936; **ful** ~ very much 1692
sootenes *n.* sweetness 3396*
soothe, sothe *adj.* true 1890, 6678, 9553+
soothe, sothe *n.* truth 2247, 5417, 5877; *pl.* **soothes** 5895
soothenes *n.* truth 12,853
soothyn, sothyn *pp.* boiled, 7858*bis*
soppe *n.* sop, piece of toasted bread dipped in wine 7702
sorceres, sorceris, sorciers, sorseris, sorsers *n. pl.* those who practice sorcery, wizards, magicians 389, 405, 1948+
sot *n.* fool 2004, one who eats to excess 5484*n*
soteth *pr. 3 sg.* deceives, deludes 1487; *pp.* **sotted** demented 2520
sothefastnes *n.* veracity, truth 4832
sotheseyerris *n. pl.* truth-tellers, candid advisors 12,856
sotil(e), soutil, sottyle, subtil(e) *adj.* cunning, crafty, deceptive 4580, 4780, 8499+, difficult 7437, 9420; *superl.* **sotillest** 2778
sotilly, sotylly, sootelly, sootilly, soutilly *adv.* cunningly, deceitfully 4580, 6341, subtly, cleverly 4630, 5826, 8293+
sotilte(e), subtilte *n.* guile, treachery 3281, 5628, 8036+; *pl.* **subtelteis** dishes or courses of a meal 4852–3
soudoier *n.* soldier 2258; *pl.* **soudeoures** 8994
souerayne, souereigne, souerein, souereyn(e) *adj.* highest, supreme 6021, 6802–3, 12,555+
souereyne *n.* lord, master 2940, 2941, 2962–3+
souereinly, souereynly *adv.* supremely 1987, 2885, 3031
sought after *pa. t.* informed himself concerning 1560
souke *v.* suck 8666; *pr. 3 sg.* **ȝifeth sowke** nurses 5882–3
souleheele, soulehele *n.* salvation 6170, 11,183, 12,858
soulnesse *n.* solitude 8888**n*
sounde *adj.* healthy 1792
soupleth *pr. 3 sg.* softens (metal) 9721*n*
sourmounteth, surmounteth, surmounth *pr. 3 sg.* surpasses 7889, 10,377, 12,999+
sowdes *n. pl.* wages 2260
spare *v.* refrain from 4853, 11,843; *pr. 2 sg.* **spare** hoard 5519; *pr. 3 sg.* **spareth** spares 9400; *pr. 3 pl.* **spareth** 11,837
spekeres *n. pl.* **to miche** ~ chatterers 11,906*n*

spekyngys *n. pl.* talk 2351
spence *n.* expense, expenditure 4676
spere *n.* spear, *here* prize 9751*n*
sperid *pp.* secured, fastened with a buckle 2487
spice *n.* appearance, likeness 6341
spyre *n.* spire, shoot 3269
spyreth *pr. 3 sg.* sprouts, germinates 3266
sporrynge *part.* spurring 6301*
spot(te) *n.* stain, blemish, moral defect or flaw 1636, 11,215, 11,967, disease of the eye 12,257; *pl.* **spotes, spotis, spottes, spottis, spottys, spotys** 1451, 1634, 1962+
spoted, spotted *pp.* morally blemished, tainted, flawed 3999, 11,216, 12,008
sprede, spreede *v.* diffuse, disseminate 8164, spread 5096, ~ **into** widely practice 850; *pr. 3 sg.* **spredeth, spredith** grows 1518, spreads, extends 2399, 8522, ~ **hym** *mistranslation, see notes* 8436; *pr. 3 pl.* **sprede** 1436; *pa. t.* **spredde** 451; *pp.* **spredde** widely practiced 4620
springe *n.* shoot, offshoot 20, 21, 22+; *pl.* **spryngis, spryngys** 1327, 1383, 1519+
sprynge *adj.* living 8103
springlyngis *n. pl.* shoots 1446*n*
spute *aphetic form of* **dispute** 12,735
stabill(e), stable *adj.* steadfast, constant 6914, 8021, 10,163+
stabilly *adv.* firmly, steadfastly 7614
stabilmentis *n. pl.* ordinances 276, 287
stabilnes *n.* stability 7609
stablid *pa. t.* ordained, established 11,779; *pp.* **stabled** 11,579
stablissheth *pr. 3 sg.* settles an inheritance upon 912*n*; *pa. t.* **stablisshed** established, founded 11,776; *pp.* **stablisshed** 715, 11,565
stamyne *n.* a garment or covering of coarse light woolen or cotton cloth 752*n*
stanche *v.* extinguish, put out 12,363; *pr. 3 sg.* **stancheth** allays 7822; *pp.* **stanched, staunched** 3366, 6573, 9912+
standyng(e) *conj.* since, considering (that), inasmuch as 996, 1142, 1711+
stang *n.* pool 422
state, statis *see* **astate**
stately *adj.* royal 2215*n*
stavys *n. pl.* staves 9346
stedde *pp.* **evil** ~ beset with troubles 7802
stedefast(e), stedfast *adj.* steadfast, constant, firm 6913, 8021, 9677+, devoted (to) 7724*n*
stedefastly, stedfastly *adv.* firmly, steadfastly 1141, 8178, 12,110+

stedefastnes, stedfastnes(se) *n.* steadfastness, constancy 190, 6910, 7609+, bond 7718
stedfast *v.* make resolute 1349; *pr. 3 sg.* **stedfasteth** fixes firmly 8015–16, refreshes, restores 12,705–6*n*; *pp.* **stedfasted** firm 2659
steyne *v. mistranslation, see notes* 2148, 3272
steplis *n. pl.* steeples 2239
steryngys *n. pl.* sexual stirrings, arousals 5349
sterre *n.* star 8834, 9621; *pl.* **sterres, sterris, sterrys** 1680, 1723, 3746
sterveth *pr. 3 pl.* die of hunger 3884*
stey, styed *pa. t.* rose 1205, 11,563
styed *see* **stey**
stille, stylle *adj.* silent 1038, 6385, 7965+
stobill *n.* stubble 8707
stocke, stokke *n.* branch 3280, 3284, 3549+
stockys, stookes *n. pl.* stocks 4775, 8411
stored *pp.* provided, supplied 4840
storme *n.* strong wind 2525
stormy *adj.* strong, violent 2530
straunge *adj.* foreign 12,755
strecche *v.* extend, stretch out 2561, 3860, reach, *fig.* comprehend 7601*n*, strain, strive for 9350; *pr. 3 sg.* **strecche, streccheth, strecchith** 7190*n*, 9156, 9819, *mistranslation, see notes* 3192; *pp.* **strecched, streccheth** 1652*n*, 11,641
streynyd *pa. t.* bound tightly, clasped 2527
streyningly *adv.* tightly 4431*n
streit(e), streyte, strette *adj.* narrow 2486, 5525, 6748, rigorous 6445, strict 8464, 8507, parsimonious, niggardly 10,399, 10,454; *comp.* **streitlyer** 6778; *as n.* ~ **pepill** misers 10,449
streitly, streytly *adv.* strictly 608, 5813, 6242+
strenght, strenghth(e), strength(e) *n.* fortitude 146, 3412, 8278+, strength 1267, 4362, 3789+, merit 3052, force 4357, 4359, 4361, power, authority 4467, fortress 5714; **with** ~ perforce 9518*n*, strengthened 8339*n*
strengthe *v.* strengthen 1339; *pr. 3 sg.* **strengheth, strengtheith** 2892, 7845
strete *n.* village, town 676*n*
stuffe *n.* stores, provisions 1346, 4641
stuffe *v.* supply, store with provisions 1340, 1350; *pr. 3 sg.* **stuffeth** 7862, arms 8285; *pp.* **stuffed** 4840
sue *v.* pursue, follow 11,900
suerte(e), suretee, surte *n.* security 1334, 8917, 8940, confidence 188, 9602, 9683+
sufficed *pr. 3 sg.* (it) is sufficient 9544, 9644

suffrance *n.* patient endurance 2014
suffre, soffre *v.* allow, permit 469, 471, 479+, tolerate, abide 2146, 3091, endure affliction or hardship 3698*bis*, 3709+; *imp.* **soffre, suffre** 3537, 5304; *pr. 2 sg.* **suffrest** 6390, 10,677; *pr. 3 sg.* **suffreth, suffrith, soffreth** 3878, 4854, 5765+; *pr. 1 pl.* **suffre** 4958; *pr. 3 pl.* **suffreth, suffrith, soffreth** 467, 2174*, 3755+, delay (action), leave (unproven) 4525; *pa. t.* **suffred, suffrede, soffred** 361, 362, 3697+; *pp.* **suffred, suffrid, soffred** 1757, 3758, 6945
suffryng *vbl. n.* endurance 9587
sugre roset *phr.* sugar flavored with rose water 2401
suying *vbl. n.* pursuing 10,058
supporte *imp.* sustain, look after 765
sure *adj.* safe, secure 2240, 5362, 8284+, certain 12,994, confident 9690, 9699
surely(e) *adv.* safely, securely 295, 10,240, 10,336+, confidently 1898, 6612, 7268
surenesse *n.* confidence 9682
surfet *n.* excess 12,907
suspecious(e), suspicious *adj.* of questionable character 11,348, 11,900, 12,079, giving rise to suspicion 11,341
sustenaunce *n.* sustenance 4393, 6968, 8776
sustene, sustien, sustine *v.* maintain, support, sustain 502, 2446, 12,564+; *pr. 3 sg.* **sussteyneth, susteyneth** 3534, 6898, 7853; *pr. 3 pl.* **sustene, susteyneth, susteynyth** 4615, 4995, 6097–8+; *pa. t.* **susteyned, sustenyd** 7608, 11,137; *pp.* **sustened, susteyned** 12,636, 12,906
suterys *n. pl.* petitioners, plaintiffs 4657
sware *pa. t.* swore 531
swerde *n.* sword 3912, 5205; *pl.* **swerdys** 4503
swete, swote *n.* sweat 1515, 3807, 3852*n*
swette *v.* sweat, toil 3020
swolweth *pr. 3 sg.* swallows 7837
swote *n. see* **swete**

tables, tablis *n. pl.* **at(te) (the)** ~ backgammon 474, 2003, 4320+
taboures *n. pl.* drums 5095
tacche *n.* fault, vice 4066; *pl.* **tachis, tecches** 66, 3925
taile, tale, tayle *n.* tail 2318, 5053, 5914+; *pl.* **tailles** 5912
take, taake *v.* assume 935, receive, accept 1042, 7174, 11,037+, capture, seize, catch, ensnare 964, 4534, 11,945+, follow 4193, eat, consume 4392, 7830, 7875+, bear 9827, exact (satisfaction) 2978, take away, deprive of, remove 3216, 8053, 11,313+, use (idly) 446; *imp.* **take** 1701, 3977, 9408;

pr. 2 sg. **takest** 7825; *pr. 3 sg.* **take, taketh, takith, takyth** 1288, 2234, 5423+, bears, endures 3713, takes in marriage 5221, has intercourse with 5220, takes up, considers 4300; *pr. 1 pl.* **take** 4701, 8107; *pr. 3 pl.* **take, taketh, takith** 3422, 4490, 4511+, engage in 7210, take by force, seize 971*n*, give, betake themselves (to) 4576; *pa. t.* **toke, tooke** 6699, 10,539, 10,804+, gave 490, 1116, assumed 8087; *pp.* **take, taken, takyn** 3659, 4379, 5042+, entrusted 807, 9855, found guilty (of) 8645, overcome 8895, 8931, undertaken 1401; *part.* **takyng(e)** 2932, 4770, 5949; ~ **vppon hym,** ~ **on hande** undertake 4174, 8252, 9556+, ~ **his owne wille** follow his own inclination 6411, ~ **good discipline** practice strong self-control 5263–4, ~ **a pensifnes** becomes anxious 7755, ~ **a worthe** accept (cheerfully) 5531, ~ **ayeins (aȝeyns, ageyns)** attack(s), assail(s) (attacked, assailed) 3496–7, 3566–7, 6149+, ~ **with thefte** found stealing 1538

talent *n.* desire, inclination 2811, 3398, 5424+

tarye *imp.* delay, postpone 9908; *pr. 3 sg.* **taryeth** 9938, waits 11,012; *pp.* **taried** remained unfulfilled 10,531*n*

tauerne, taverne *n.* inn, hostel 100, 5685, 8397+; *pl.* **tauernes, tavernes** 455, 468, 569+

tauerner *n.* innkeeper 12,574; *pl.* **taverneris, tavernerys** 5711, 5712

techyng(e) *vbl. n.* reprimand, correction, discipline 1505, 6165; *pl.* **techynges, techyngys** instruction 4262, 11,736, precepts, doctrines 1849

temperal, temperell, temporel, temporell(e) *adj.* material, worldly 1424, 1434–5, 1583+, fleeting, transitory 1786, 2650, 6690+

temperance *n.* temperance, one of the cardinal virtues 145, 246, 3413–14+

temperat *adj.* moderate, temperate 8956, 9245, 9246+

tempereth *pr. 3 sg.* measures, governs 12,795

tempred *pp.* characterized by a proper proportion of humors 9244

temmps *n.* time 5852

tender, tendre *adj.* weak 6697, 9081

tendernes, tendirnesse *n.* physical softness or delicacy 60, 3802, 4108+

tente *v.* incline 2193, pay heed, attend (to) 4234, 10,593, devote (himself) to 11,147, 11,575, 11,593+; *pr. 3 sg.* **tenteth** strives, aims 3232, devotes (himself) to 8677, 11,159, 11,160, ministers (to) 11,104, 11,109, gives thought (to) 11,149, 11,150; *pr. 1 pl.* **tente** 592, 3303; *pr. 3 pl.* **tenteth** 9530, 11,121

tentif *adj.* attentive, diligent 4022

tentifly *adj.* with close attention 2600

terme *n.* end 295, 296, duration 3988, appointed time of service 4145, time of life 7639, appointed time 8837; *pl.* **termes** limits 11,818; **to a** ~ for a prescribed period 977

terreboles *n. pl.* fire stones 5156**n*
tha *weakened form of* **that** 2524*n*, 2795, 8089+
than, thanne, þan *adv.* then 369, 380, 382+
that *pron.* those 1773
thath *form of* **that** 9489
the *pron.* they 4531, 4544, 4591+, them 3890*n*
thedder, theder, thedir, thyder *adv.* thither, there 4073, 5697, 6569+
thee *form of def. art.* the 1706, 4428, 4815+
thentente *phr.* **to** ~ for the purpose 280
therafter *adv.* afterwards, that is, to follow it 8347, 10,313
theraȝeins *adv.* in their place 8237
therat *adv.* at it 6171
therby(e), þerbye *adv.* thus, by this means 478, 10,797, 10,798, by this statement 5109
thereof, therof, þerof *adv.* of it, of that 298, 311, 374+, from that, out of that, from it 44, 3212, 9501+
therethorugh *adv.* through it 3248
thereto, therto(o), þertoo *adv.* also 701, 3243, to it 2452, 2490, 8042+
therevppon, theropon, þervppon, thervppon *adv.* on it (them) 5794, 9302–3, 12,233+
therfro(o), þerfroo *adv.* from it 842, 2915, 3034+, thence 5698
therin, þerin, therinne, therein, thereinne *adv.* in that matter or place 234, 980, 1372+
ther(re) *see* **der**
theron, theroon *adv.* about it 1893, 5027, 8702
therst, thirst(e), thrist(e) *n.* 192, 403, 6573+
therwith, therewith *adv.* thereby 754, 828, 2428+, with it (them) 4055, 5427, 10,128+
therwithal *adv.* therewith 9762–3
therytage *phr.* the inheritance 4562
theymwarde *adv.* toward them 11,428
thyes *n. pl.* thighs 4157
thikke, thykke *adj. mistranslation, see notes* 3197, 3222, 6215
thyne *adj.* thin 2498
thynkeyng, thynkynge *vbl. n.* occupying the mind (with business) 583, turning one's thoughts 11,484
this *adj.* these 1856
this *adv.* thus 3363*n*, 10,084*n*
tho(o), þoo *adj.* those 139, 2621, 6455+
tho(o), þo(o) *pron.* those 229, 231, 355+

tholde *phr.* the old 2029
thorne *n.* thorn-bush 3381*n; *mistranslation, see notes* 6079
thorogh, thorough(e), thorugh, thorw, thurgh, thourgh *prep.* through 1649, 3276, 3671+
thother *see* **toother**
though(e), thowe, þowe, thugh *conj.* if, even if 2021, 3491, 3576+, although, even though 800, 1044, 2077+; **than** ~ as if 1706–7, 1754, **as** ~ as if 1685, 10,428
thought(e) *n.* meditation 4078, 6532, 6552+, anxiety 4778, erotic thought 5030, 5031, 12,008, care, concern 6661, fancy, imagination 9414; *pl.* **thoughtes, thoughtis, thoughtys, thoghtis, þouȝthis** 5026, 5660, 11,247+
thought afore *pp.* premeditated 824*n*
thraldom(e) *n.* servitude 4787, 6115, 10,175+
threteth *pr. 3 sg.* reviles 2928, harms, molests 2930
thrist(e) *see* **therst**
thwarte *v.* oppose, hinder 6063
tigneuse *Fr. adj.* scabby 6388*n*
tysyng *vbl. n.* enticement, inducement 3055
tisseth, tysceth *pr. 3 sg.* induces, incites 3942, 5245; *see* **attyce**
to(o) *adv.* too 96, 97*bis*+
to(o) *card. num.* one 384, 2838, 9452+
to(o), tweyn(e), two(o) *card. num.* two 7, 335, 4485+
to(o) *conj.* until 761, 2644, 3505+
to(o) *prep.* until 3982, 5098, 10,125+, in comparison with 5867, against 45, 46, 47+, for 406, 898, 1232+, directed toward 1976, 1977, 1978+, upon 709, of 1114, 2788, 3107+, in 2074, 4795, 7050+, with 5294, into 8355, among 9983
tofoore, tofore, toofore *prep.* before 797, 5247, 11,060+
tohewe *imp.* cut to pieces 10,634
toille *pr. 1 pl.* roll in the mud 8343*n
token, tokyn, tooken, tookyn *n.* characteristic mark 2918, token, sign, evidence 2921, 11,626, 12,891+; *pl.* **tokenes** reasons 659; **in** ~ as a sign 4702, 5365, **for a** ~ as a sign 1116–7, **maketh a** ~ indicates 10,858
ton(e), toon(e) *pron.* (the) one 335, 943, 947+
too *ord. num.* second 17*n*
toofore *conj.* before 9881
toother, tooþer, tother, toþer, tothir, thother *pron.* (the) other 3130, 3138, 4142+, (the) others 1128
torment, tourment, tourrment *n.* affliction, torment 1012, 2182, 2505+,

tempest 7023; *pl.* **tormentes, tormentis, tourmentis, turmentis, tornementis** 422, 1661, 9699*n*+

torne, tourne *v.* turn 3892, 3900, bring 336, 337, become 522, 3730, deviate 9207; *imp.* **torne** deflect 12,745; *pr. 2 sg.* **tornest** 2320; *pr. 3 sg.* **torneth, tornyth, tournyth** 333, 1504, 2159+, revolves 10,160, 12,805, has recourse to 11,389; *pr. 3 pl.* **torn(e), torneth, tornyth, turneth** 2158, 2519, 5337+; *pa. t.* **torned, tourned** 10,825, returned 383*n*; *pp.* **torned, tourned** 2434, 6403, 6501; ~ **his erre therfroo** refuses to listen 11,503, ~ **from** diverts 2856–7, ~ **the body from** turned away from, ~ **hym thy backe, the bakke to hym, hirre backe to hirre lorde, the backe to my right lord** turns away from 1550, 1613, 2012+, ~ **(theyme) to confusion** confound (them) 11,922–3, ~ **too (into) evyl (evylle)** corrupt(s), pervert(s) 3253–4, 9425, ~ **ageyne** revolves 9454, ~ **aȝein (aȝene, aȝeyn)** return(s)(ed) 9931*n*, 10,536, 12,168+, ~ **to the wers partye** corrupts 5958, ~ **vp (vppe) soo downne (doun)** considered and reconsidered 9625, overthrows, demolishes 6692, throws over, throws on its back 3448

torneye *n.* tournament 3788

tortille *n.* turtledove 11,893, 11,895

toscorkelid *pa. t.* completely parched with heat 6310

touche *v.* examine by a sense of touch 2158; *pr. 3 sg.* **touchith** touches 1096, 4905; *part.* **touchynge** 10,037; *pp.* **touched, touchid** discussed 6643, 11,174, 12,956

touchyng *prep.* with respect to 1802

touchyngis, touchyngys, tochyngis *n. pl.* sexual contacts (with hands) 958, 1084, 5152+

tounne *n.* tun 9717; *pl.* **tunnes** 4507

toure *n.* fortress 2104*

tournement *n.* tournament 7509, 8028, 12,701; *pl.* **tormentis, tornementis, tournementis** 1698*n*, 9692–3, 10,249+

towaile, towelle *n.* towel 10,073, 12,237

toward(e) *prep.* to 383, 4169, with respect to 909, 12,631, 12,633

traictable *adj.* pliant, manageable 9723*n*

trayson(e) *n.* treachery, breach of faith 3283, 3585, 5103+; *pl.* **traysones** 5106

trauaile, trauaille, trauayle, trauaylle, travaile *n.* torment, suffering 1795, exertion, labor, toil 10,651, 10,772, 12,673+; *pl.* **trauailles** 12,707

travayle *v.* work, toil 3763; *pr. 3 sg.* **travayleth** fatigues, overworks 4113; *pr. 3 pl.* **trauayleth, travayle, trauailleth** torment, vex 3422, cause distress 4654–5, expend effort 8909, resort (to) 405–6*n*; *pa. t.* **trauailed, trauailled, travailled** 9841, 10,775, 10,778

trauaillyng, trauaylyng *part. adj.* travelling 10,806, 10,832
trauaylyng *vbl. n.* giving birth 6589
trauerse *n.* **o** ~ sideways, askance 11,642
treedeth *pr. 3 pl.* trample 3436–7
treeson, treson *n.* treachery, betrayal 3272, 4997, 5085
trespasseth *pr. 3 sg.* violates, transgresses, does wrong to 1918; *pr. 3 pl.* **trespasse, trespassith** 430, 442–3, 6052; *pa. t.* **trespassed** 341–2, 3447; *pp.* **trespassed** 1296, 6055
trespassyng *vbl. n.* violation, transgression 5195
treste, troste *n.* trust, confidence 187, 8919, 9602+
tretable *adj.* receptive 7291
trete, tretie *n.* treatise 9643, 12,946
trete *v.* treat 5210, expound 9756; *pr. 3 sg.* **treteth, treeteth, tretith** conducts, deals with 4306, expounds 9327; *pa. t.* **treted, treteed** 4293, 8880; *pp.* **treted, tretid** 757, 11,195, drawn 3594*n*; ~ **vilaynously** violates 4482, **veleynsly** ~, **velensly** ~, **evil** ~ abused, mistreated 757, 8563, 8573
tretice, tretyce, tretys *n.* treatise 8685, 11,731, 12,815, words, speech, discourse 3594
tretyng *vbl. n.* discussion 11,230
triacle, tryacle *n.* medicament 1504, 5929, 8953+
tricheries *n. pl.* treacheries 4649*
tryeth *pr. 3 sg.* examines 8717
triffle *v.* jest, talk idly 11,580; *pr. 3 pl.* **trifelith** 1998
triffles, trifflis, tryffles *n. pl.* idle jests or tales 5665, 6258, 6599+
trippe *pr. 3 pl.* caper 5098
trone *n.* throne 10,198, 12,318
troste *see* **treste**
trost(e), truste *v.* have faith or confidence in 5302, 5309, 8594, presume 4400; *imp.* **truste** 5303; *pr. 2 sg.* **trost** give credence to 5104; *pr. 3 sg.* **tristeth, trusteth** 5379, 8675, 11,405+
trouble *v.* disturb, distress 1350, 9707; *pr. 3 sg.* **trobeleth, troubleth** 8435, 9139, 12,651; *pr. 3 pl.* **troubleth** 3359; *pp.* **troubled** 3026, 9122
trouble *n.* ?unrest, disturbance 7611
trouble *adj.* turbid 12,654
trouthe, trouþe, trowthe *n.* truth 511, 519, 1038+, righteousness 1556, 8106, 9763+, faith, loyalty 1488, 1963, 4685+
trowantis, trowauntis *n. pl.* beggars 9954, 10,989
trueseyrres *n. pl.* truth-tellers 1059*n*
twelle *n.* pipe, tube 9710
twyned *pa. t.* twisted 4242

þeraboute *adv.* about it 12,322, 12,338
þowe *see* thurgh

vmbethynke *v.* remember 9941; *imp.* **vmbethinke, vmbethynke** bethink, consider 2772, 3732, 10,846+; *pr. 3 sg.* **vmbethynke, vmbethynketh** 11,279, 12,535–6; *pr. 3 pl.* **vmbethynke** 4534, 4630
vnccion *n.* **holy** ~ extreme unction 1229*n*
vnclennes *n.* impurity 12,206
vnderstandyng *vbl. n.* intention 274*n*
vndertake, vndirtake *v.* engage in, undertake 8375; *pr. 3 sg.* **vndertaketh** 10,275, takes unawares 9920; *pp.* **vndertake, vndertakyn** 9663, 9750; **derre** ~ declare 390, set about, venture 6927, 8919–20
vndiscrecion *n.* imprudence 4110, 6332
vndiscrete *adv.* imprudent 4341
vnease *n.* **at** ~ disturbed 7262*n*, **setteth in** ~ disturbs 12,652
vnethe, vniþe, vnnethe *adv.* scarcely, hardly, with difficulty 469, 1042, 1273+
vnnethes *adv.* scarcely 3157
vngoodly *adj.* evil, sinful 12,917
vnhappy(e) *adj.* wretched, miserable 1015, 3127, 3238
vnhylle *pr. 3 pl.* uncover 5809
vnite *n.* mystical union, spiritual concord 6794, 8254, integrity 9260
vnknowynge *vbl. n.* ignorance 4673
vnknowynge *part.* *is.* ~ fails to recognize 9325
vnkonnyng(e) *adj.* ignorant 4656, 5871, untrained 9333
vnmeveable *adj.* immutable, permanent 3392–3, 3402
vnordinat *adj.* disordered, morally corrupt 12,529
vnshamefaste *adj.* shameless 12,021
vnto *conj. phr.* ~ **the tyme (that)** until 531, 739, 2802–3+
vnto *prep.* until 3080, 3972, 3983+, to 1378, 1464, 2969+, for 3985*tres*, into 11,540, into the hands of 8463; ~ **þe regard of** compared with 6590, ~ **(my, his, theire) power** to the best of (my, his, their) ability 1490, 6224, 9779–80+
vntrewe, vntrue, vntrwe *adj.* faithless, disloyal 2636, 2680, 3927+, false, dishonest 1919, 5960
vntrouth(e), vntrowth(e) *n.* faithlessness, disloyalty, dishonesty 12, 15, 1523+, evil, wickedness, wrong 2817, 2954, 4216*n*+; *pl.* **vntrouthes, vntrowthes** 1517, marital infidelities 2705, 2712
vntruly *adv.* dishonestly 4822, 4836
vpon, vppon, apon(e), open, opon, oppon *prep.* upon 709, 929, 2920+, in 8067, over and above 4603, directed toward 3827, to 2271, 9313, on the pledge of 7910, according to, in accordance with 897, 936, 1089+, con-

formably to 5494*bis*, 5495+; **hatthe** ~ inflicts, imposes on 4224, ~ **a tyme** once 10,788, **cryed** ~ denounced 2300, **rynneth** ~ attack, assail 2874, 3182

vsage *n.* habit, practice, custom 4083, 5414, use 6968, 7005, 12,888; *pl.* **vsages** 4489, 4819, 7458

vse *n.* use 2062, 3550, 4702+

vse *v.* employ, make use of 6738, 8138, habituate, accustom 10,587, 11,738, practice 12,698, uphold 7918, consume 5658, 11,321; *imp.* **vse** 3978; *pr. 2 sg.* **vsest** 2320; *pr. 3 sg.* **vse, vseth, vsith** 3051, 6706, 6777+; *pr. 3 pl.* **vse, vseth, vsith** 527, 2429, 5594+; *pa. t.* **vsed** 951; *pp.* **vsed, vsid** 11,390, 11,606, expended 1902, 2502, **evil** ~ wasted, misused 7980; *part. vsyng* 5636

usher *n.* usher 8184*

vsynge *vbl. n.* use, practice 11,390

vsure *n.* usury 82, 979, 988+, interest 10,767

vsurer, vsurrere *n.* usurer 991, 4597, 4598+; *pl.* **vsureres, vsureris, vsurers, vsurerys, vsurreris** 4451, 4603, 4605+; *poss. pl.* **vserers, vsureris** 2275, 8643

vaileth, vaylith, vayleth, vailleth *pr. 3 sg.* avails, profits, helps, is of use 6915, 7166, 8734+; *pr. 3 pl.* **vaileth, vailith, vailleth** 4247*bis*, 11,251+; *pa. t.* **vailed** 2609, 6525, 7125. *See* **availe**

vaine, vayne, veyne, veine *adj.* foolish 4053, 5818, 12,085+, worthless 6023, 6895, 6924+; **in** ~ idly, to no purpose 447

vainly *adv.* in a vain or futile manner 6819

valewe, valu, value, valve, valwe *n.* value, worth 4629, 7273, 7891+

vaunce *v.* advance, promote 6888

vaunt *v.* boast 4001; *pr. 3 sg.* **vanteth, vaunteth** 2127, 5842; *pr. 3 pl.* **vaunteth** 5858; *pa. t.* **vaunted** 11,421; *part.* **vauntyng** 2929

vauntagis *n. pl.* benefits, advantages 6813

vauntour *n.* braggart, boaster 2124

vauntyng, wantyng *vbl. n.* boasting 104, 2121, 4162+; *pl.* **vauntynggis, vauntyngis** 2909, 5848

velain, velein(e) *n.* mean spirited, ungrateful person 1640, 1760, 1781+, baseborn person 1923; *pl.* **veleins** gluttons 5588*n*

velains, veleins, veleyns, veleynsce, velins, vileins, vilens *adj.* vile, scurrilous, blasphemous 458, 466, 6245+, wicked, evil, sinful 1699, 1985, 5077+, discourteous 10,987, mean spirited, ungrateful 1627, 1639, 1641+, low born 1790; ~ **membris** private parts 1986*n*

velenis, veleynyes *adj.* evil, wicked, sinful 6234, 11,488

velany, veleni, veleny(e), velonye, veleyny, vileny, vilonye, vylonie, vylonye

n. villainy, wickedness, wrongdoing 1532, 1551, 1639+, ill usage, wrong, injury 1737, 3494, base ingratitude 1597*bis*, 1598+, dishonor 340, blasphemy, insulting or reproachful words 471, 2929, 3701, sin 7498; *pl.* **velanies, velenies, velenyes, velonyes** 449, 1632, 2676+, ?erotic thoughts, ?sexual misconduct 3811

velansly, veleinsly, velensly, veleynsly, vilensly *adv.* blasphemously 450, 2023, 6029+; severely, harshly 10,988; ~ **treted, entreted** mistreated, abused 8555, 8563, 8573

velenisly, veleynisly, vilaynously *adv.* wickedly, grievously 6035, blasphemously 6203; **treteth** ~ violates 4482

veleynly *adv.* ignominiously 451, blasphemously 6202

velyes *n. pl.* valleys 5863

venge *v.* avenge 828, 928, 1393+; *pr. 3 sg.* **venge, vengeth** 3412, 3564, 9030+; *pr. 3 pl.* **vengeith, vengeth** 6558, 6559, 7959; *pp.* **venged** 3558, 6597

venial(l), veniel *adj.* pardonable 1126, 1429, 2591+

venially, venyally *adv.* pardonably 235, 11,814, 11,817+

venymeth *pr. 3 sg.* poisons 1047

venimous, venymous *adj.* poisonous 3172, 3249, 11,277

veraly, verely, verily, veryly *adv.* truly, really 372, 7032, 7602+, honestly 6613; *comp.* **verilier** 7066

veray(e), verey(e), verray(e), verrey(e), verry *adj.* true 1639, 1661, 1956+, indisputable 8611, ?wise 7368; **of** ~ **right** rightly, justly 6050

verite *n.* truth 7078*, 7640*

verre *n.* glass 12,521

vers(e) *n.* verse 1647, a verse from the Psalms 4048*n*, 11,110; *pl.* **verses** 8427

vertu(e) *n.* virtue, merit, moral excellence 4, 127, 133+, power, efficacy 374, 1172, 1233+, property, quality 3176*bis*, 3180+, vigor, might 3413, 8193; *pl.* **vertues, vertuez, vertuis, vertus, vertuz** 1884, 3174, 3189+

vesyly, visily *adv.* deliberately, intentionally 518*n*, 5982

viage *n.* journey 1891

vice *adv. mistranslation, see notes* 4136; **in** ~ *mistranslation, see notes* 6478

vigile *n.* vigil, the eve of holy days 593, 595, 597+; *pl.* **vigiles** 2293

vigne, vyne *n.* vine 1374, 9363; *pl.* **vignes, vygnes, vynes** 3574, 4529, 4633

vigneȝerde *n.* vineyard 327

vigorous(e), vygorous *adj.* hardy, strong 3183, 4131*, 7496+, vigorous, energetic 4219, 9812

vigorously, vigerously *adj.* actively and strongly 8810, 8845, valiantly 8364

vigorousnesse *n.* moral strength 4142*n*, 8321

vigour(e) *n.* moral strength 8318, 10,269, energy 8193
vigoure *v.* invigorate, strengthen 7635
vil(e), vyle *adj.* cheap in price 4618*n, of little worth 6688, 6894, 11,431+; **the moste** ~ most ignominious 4787*, **holden (holde) for** ~ scorned, despised 8545, 8553, 8562
viled *pp.* abused 874
vyne *see* **vigne**
violens *v.* force, rape 920*n*
voide, wide *adj.* empty, devoid (of) 2030, 8503, 11,678, worthless 4694, 6830, 6834+, destitute 8905
voydeth *pr. 3 pl.* empty 4329, 5811; *pa. t.* **voided** dismissed, sent away 10,451*n*; *pp.* **voided, voyded** treated as nothing, humbled 8935*n*, expelled from 4217
vowe *n.* vow 11,881, 11,882, 11,883+; *pl.* **vowez** 1837; *see* **avowe**
vowe *pr. 1 sg.* vow 1843; *pr. 3 sg.* **voweth** 12,057; *pp.* **vowed** 12,057, 12,111, 12,291; *see* **avoued**

wacche, wachche *n.* watchman 2859, 8187, vigil (as a devotional practice) 954, 4338
wacche *v.* remain awake 5455; *pr. 3 pl.* **waccheth** keep vigil (as a devotional practice) 6414
wacchyngis *vbl. n.* wakeful states, ?religions vigils 5471
wages, wagis, wagiz, wagys *n. pl.* reward(s) 292, 1774*n*, 2234+
waies, wayes *n. pl.* woes 2677, 9699
waiknes of herte *phr.* faintheartedness 6332
waiour *n.* wager 2525
waisse, waisshe, weisshe, wesshe *v.* cleanse (from sin) 1635, 6610, 11,258+, wash 8801, 9842, 10,076+; *pa. t.* **wasshed, waysshed** 1575, 2645, 2684+; *pp.* **waisshyn, wasshen, wesshyn** 7713, 7886, 8977+
waysshyng(e), wesshyng *vbl. n.* washing 10,027, 10,074, cleansing from sin 8977
wayten *v.* watch 3233; *pr. 3 sg.* **wayteth** 3234; *pr. 3 pl.* **waiteth** 11,536, 12,756, 12,823
walweth *pr. 3 sg.* surges 4269
wanhoope, wannehope, whanhoope, whannehoope *n.* despair 3147, 4170, 4879+
wanhooped *adj.* desperate 4214–15
wantyng *see* **vauntyng**
wardes, wardis *n. pl.* prisons 8411; ridges projecting from inside plate of a lock 1132, 1133

ware, warre *adj.* on guard, wary 11,585, 11,994
wars, wers(e), wors *comp. adj.* worse 452, 1510, 3055+; *superl.* **werst(e)** 927, 5667, 6097+
waste *v.* destroy 3366; *pr. 3 sg.* **wasteth** dispels 7736, 7737, wastes, squanders 5473, 5623; *pr. 3 pl.* **waste, wasteth** 573, 1885, 5473+; *pa. t.* **wasted** 1562, 1903, 5621; *pp.* **wasted** 5069, 8407, 8452, decayed, rotted 1374, 1438
wawe *n.* wave (of the sea) 4269
wax(e) *v.* grow 7296, 7390, 9471+, become 3061, 3064; *pr. 3 sg.* **waxeth** 3455, 5290, 6318+; *pr. 3 pl.* *waxe,* **waxeth** 1436, 3643, 4885; *pa. t.* **wexe** 1544, 2529, 2627; *pp.* **waxen, wexen** 2803, 3278
waxyng *vbl. n.* growing 2207
webbe *n.* spider's web 9624; *pl.* **webbis** growths in the conjunctiva symptomatic of disease 11,198
webbed *pp. adj.* opaque, exhibiting a growth in the conjunctiva 11,197
wed(de) *n.* pledge, security 7911; *mistranslation, see notes* 4611
wedehoke *n.* weedhook 8188.
weery, wery(e) *adj.* weary 2627, 5099, 9335+
weeteth *pr. 3 sg.* softens 7291*n*
weye *aphetic form of* **aweye** away 2823
weye *v.* weigh, be of value or account 7175; *pr. 3 sg.* **weyeth** weighs, considers, assesses the value of 8717, 10,686, 12,820; *pa. t.* **weyed** 5619
weykly *adv.* weakly 3781*
weyle *v.* wail, lament 9844
weymentacion *n.* lamentation 9837; *pl.* **weymentaciones** 9841, 11,534
wel-avised *adj.* prudent 7497, wary, cautious 10,237
wel-beseyen *adj.* well arrayed 12,179
weldede, weledede *n.* good deeds, virtue in general 364–5, 2151, 5436+
well-taughte *adj.* sober, prudent 12,795
welle-beryng *adj.* productive 8957
welle-smellyng *adj.* fragrant 10,792
welle-tempered *pp. adj.* temperate 12,876
wellys *n. pl.* sources 6826
wene *v.* think, judge, consider 2989, 5151; *pr. 2 sg.* **wenest, wenyst** 2028, 2489, 11,492+; *pr. 3 sg.* **weeneth, wene, weneth, wenyth** 1925, 2986, 3472+; *pr. 3 pl.* **weene, wene, weneth, wenyth** 2240, 5039, 5851+; *pa. t.* **wende** 1508, 5375, 9347+; *part.* **weenyng, wenynge** 4063, expecting 10,530
were *v.* wear 1660; *pr. 3 sg.* **were** wears 9719; *pr. 3 pl.* **werith** 2865, 6415; *pa. t.* **werid** 11,928; *part.* **weryng** 2793
were *conj.* where 10,655

werre *n.* strife, war, contention 45, 46, 47+; *pl.* **werres, werris** 3380, 3643, 5707+

werre, werrey(e), werry(e) *v.* engage in strife, contention, war 5714, 10,217, 10,220+; *pr. 2 sg.* **werreyeste** 2322; *pr. 3 sg.* **werreieth, werreyeth, werrieth** 1471, 2855, 3143+; *pr. 3 pl.* **werreth, werreþ, werreye, werreyeth, werrieth, werrye** 461, 2147, 3649+; *pa. t.* **werreyed, werried** 1565, 2604; *part.* **weryng** 2793; *pp.* **werreyed** 2368

werstyl *v.* wrestle 5285

wetyngly, wittyngly, wityngly, wyttyngly(e), wytyngly *adv.* knowingly, intentionally 504, 3155, 3591+

wham *pron.* whom 10,937

whas *pa. t.* was 8570

what(e), whatte *adv.* how 1514, 1860, 1896+

whe *pron.* we 9527

wheder that euer *conj.* whatever 5986

whelpes *n. pl.* cubs 4126

whens(e), wens(e) *conj.* whence 7, 8, 1286+

wherby(e), whereby(e), werbye *adv.* by which, by means of which 2254, 3599–600, 9456+, through which 9297, 11,301, 11,302, in order that 3693, 4940, 11,223+

where *form of* **were** 6364, 8122

whereas *adv.* where 2437

wherefoore, wherefor(e), wherfor(e), werfore *adv.* therefore 348, 472, 7287+, why 2872, 2884

wherein, wherin *adv.* in which 281, 345, 2005+, in 1244, in which manner 8153

whereof, wherof, wereof *adv.* why 3908, of which 1034, 1468, 4445+, for what 1448, the means 2278, 2453, 4878+, with what 214, 10,916, 10,923+

whereon *adv.* in which 2899

whereopon, wherevppon *adv.* on which 2047, 10,019, 10,661

wherethorough, wherethorugh, wherethurgh, wherthurgh *adv.* whereby 576, 7185, 10737+

whereto, weretoo *adv.* to what 2114*n*, 3730

wherewhith, wherewith, wherwith *adv.* with which 2241, 3670, 12,865+, the means 11,011

wherfore *adv.* where 12,225

wherfro *adv.* from which 426

whidirward *conj.* whither 2086

whiffes *n. pl. see* **wiff**

whyle, whiles, whilest (that) *conj.* while 3761, 3832, 3946+

whistle *v.* hiss 3918
wicche *n.* hag, crone 1924*n*; *pl.* **wicches, wycches** magicians, sorcerers 405, 1920, sorceresses 1946
wide *adj. see* **voide**
wiff *n.* concubine, mistress 8441*n*; *pl.* **whiffes** wives 11,837
wil *v.* wish, desire 8544, 8561; *pr. 1 sg.* **wil, wille, wyl** 989, 1327, 3484+; *pr. 2 sg.* **wilt(e)** 303, 307, 1299+; *pr. 3 sg.* **wil(l), wille, wyl, wylle** 942, 1039, 1290+; *pr. 1 pl.* **wil(le), wyl(le)** 3032, 4900, 5738+; *pr. 2 pl.* **wil** 1632; *pr. 3 pl.* **wil(le), wyl(le)** 770, 1292, 1643+; *pa. t. 1 sg.* **wolde** 1510, 1600, 9099; *pa. t. 2 sg.* **woldest, wooldest** 1297, 1300, 1655+; *pa. t. 3 sg.* **wolde, woolde** 346, 380, 398+; *pa. t. 1 pl.* **wolde** 4731; *pa. t. 2 pl.* **wolde** 1635, 10,848; *pa. t. 3 pl.* **wold(e), woolde** 859, 2422, 3868+; *part.* **willyng** 2781; *pp.* **wolde** 1675
wildirnesse *n.* desert 946
wyle *n.* wile, trick 8277; *pl.* **whiles, whyles, wiles, wyles, wylys** 182, 1264, 4575+
willyngly *adv.* deliberately, intentionally 727, 728, 5996+
wyly *adj.* crafty, deceitful 974
wilne, willne *v.* desire, will 7089, 7781, 9372+; *pr. 3 sg.* **willneth** 10,253
wymplis *n. pl.* veils 2495
wyn(ne) *v.* gain, profit 1585, 2876, 4760+, gain a place in 3898, earn 4016, 12,172, 12,589, gain the favor of 6731, win over, convert 9379; *pr. 2 sg.* **wynyst** 987; *pr. 3 sg.* **wyneth, wynneth** 2081, 7158, 7164+; *pr. 3 pl.* **wyn, wynneth** 4741, 8909; *pa. t.* **wan, wanne, whan** 2142, 4607, 4609; *part.* **wynyng** 326; *pp.* **wonne** 336, 338, 574
wynnyng(e), wynynge *vbl. n.* gain, profit 989, 4623, 4662+
wise, wisse, wyse, whise *n.* way, manner 439, 979, 1133+; *pl.* **wises, wyses** 8031, 9330, 11,814
wisily *adv. mistranslation, see notes* 9226
wit, with, witt(e), wytte *n.* wit, wisdom 2156, 5462, 11,412+, mind, intellect, intellectual ability 988, 1409, 8109+; *pl* **wites, wittes, wittis, wittys** 1979, 6878, 8616+, (five) senses 7193, 7211, 11,296+
wit(e), wete *v.* know 319, 5452, 6993+; *imp.* **wit** 1655; *pr. 1 sg.* **woote** 11,679; *pr. 2 sg.* **wootest, wotest** 1665, 1890, 2639+; *pr. 3 sg.* **wyt, woote, wote** 3370, 3934, 4546+; *pr. 3 pl.* **woote, wote** 3908, 6045, 6721+; *pa. t.* **wist(e)** 488, 1006, 4922+
with *prep.* by, by means of 462, 1349, 2078+, by 1745, 1746, 2650+, at 2789, to 870, 3307, 3485+, through 865, against 1258, 2595, 3530+, in 2034, 3219, 4801+
withal(le) *adv.* therewith 1585, 2279, 7258+

withdrawe *v.* withhold, 2948, withdraw, remove 4382–3, 5258, refrain (from) 4983, 5767, draw away, divert 5832–3, 6458–9, restrain 5415; *imp.* **withdrawe** 12,787; *pr. 2 sg.* **withdrawest** 5835; *pr. 3 sg.* **withdraweth** 1434, 1980, 5951+; *pr. 3 pl.* **withdrawe, withdraweth** 4491, 5773; *pp.* **withdrawen** 3990

withdraweyngly *adv.* hesitantly 3930–1

withholde *v.* retain, keep back 964, 3926, 7239, withhold, hold back 10,055, hold, keep 6187; *imp.* **withholde** restrain, hold back 12,811 *pr. 1 sg.* **withhoold** 2982; *pr. 3 sg.* **withholdeth** 1020, 12,821; *pr. 3 pl.* **withholdeth** 1002, 4491, 4819+; *pp.* **withholden** 3550, 12,780

withholdyng *vbl. n.* retaining 4431, restraint 9027

withholdynge *part. adj.* withholding payment or satisfaction 4605

withlettyng *vbl. n.* impediment, obstacle 2896*n*

witnes(se), withnesse, wittenesse, wyttenes *n.* testimony 1027, 1030, 1936+, witness 7545, attestation 6005; *pl.* **witnesses, witnessis, wittenesses, wittenessez** 1075, 4657, 5896+; **berith ~, yeveth ~** attest(s), give(s) evidence 3002, 6038, 7745–6

withoute, withowte *conj.* ~ **that** unless 5747, ~ **þat** without its being the case that 11,746–7, ~ **this** *legal phrase denoting* exception to the general rule 11,752

withoute(n), withowte(n), withoutyn, withowtyn *prep.* outside of 229, 959, 8346+; ~ **more (moo, moore, any more)** only, merely 2199, 2412, 7897+, alone 2539, at once 3887

withstande *v.* resist 3090, 6945, 8043; *pr. 1 pl.* **withstande** 8046

withsterte *v.* resist 8506

wode, woode *adj.* mad 459, 578, 1019+

wodenes, woodenes(se), woodnesse *n.* madness 15, 1532, 1564+

woke, wooke *n.* week 695*bis*, 10,775+; *poss.* **wokys** 574

wombe *n.* belly 7859, 8086, 12,611+

woorde, worde, wourd *n.* statement 302, 497, 4210+, command 5013, saying, maxim 268, 5428, divine message (particularly as conveyed through scripture) 3882, 5606, 5740+; *pl.* **woordes, woordis, woordys, wordys, wordes, wordis** 3249, 3419, 4179+; **white** ~ deceitful words 4744

woorthe, worthe, worþe *adj.* of value or merit 1673*bis*, 1674+

woorthy(e), worthy(e) *adj.* hardy, brave 4219, 6911, 6921+, worthy, deserving 1823, 7767, estimable 4292, fit 7292; *comp.* **worthier** 8031; *superl.* **worthyest** 3625

woorthines(se), worthines(se), worthenes, worthynes(se) *n.* hardiness, prowess 185, 186, 6910+, act of prowess 9733, power 12,523*n*; *pl.* **worthinessis** acts of chivalry 5850*n*; **foly (fooly)** ~ foolhardiness 117, 6407, 6409+

woortis, woortys, wortys *n. pl.* herbs, vegetables 5256, 5431*, 5631
wordly *adj.* worldly 599
worship(p), worshippe *n.* honor 339, 1588, 2435+; *pl.* **worshipes, worshippes, worshippis** 1619–20, 2198, 3010+
worship(p), worshippe *v.* honor, venerate 153, 1554, 1630+; *imp.* **worshipp** 724–5, 10,489; *pr. 3 sg.* **worshipeth, worshippeth, worshiped** 1912, 8595, 8598+; *pr. 1 pl.* **worship, worshipp** 359, 365, 367+; *pr. 3 pl.* **worshipeth, worshipp** 357, 6414, 9077+; *pa. t.* **worshiped, worshipped** 7104, bowed down (to) 12,327, 12,340; *pp.* **worship, worshiped, worshipped** 154, 1554, 3948+
worshipful(l) *adj.* reputable, worthy of honor or respect 127, 6812, 6816+
worshipfully, worshippfully *adv.* honorably 2690, 5530
wrecche *n.* wretch 8530
wrecchednes, wrecchidnesse *n.* meanness, despicableness 3089, misery, grief 7034
wreke *v.* avenge 3375; *pr. 3 pl.* **wreke** 3375
wretthe *n.* wrath 1389
writyng(e), wrytynge *vbl. n.* writing 4249, treatise 2668, *mistranslation, see notes* 8085; **putteth in** ~ records in a book of accounts 1982

yeate, gate, ȝeate *n.* gate 3395, 4813, 8647+; *pl.* **ȝatis, ȝeates, ȝeatis, gatis, gatys** 682, 9296, 11,311+
yefyng, ȝefyng *vbl. n.* giving 215, 7167, 7168
ye(e), yeien, yen, yeyen *see* **iye**
yelde, ȝelde *v.* give, bestow 1757, 1899, 3085+, yield, surrender 5122, pay 9569, 9576, 9578+, ~ **aȝein (aȝeyn)** give back, repay, restore 4826, 4869, 5055+; *imp.* **ȝelde** 744, 1465; *pr. 3 sg.* **ȝelde, ȝeldeth, ȝoldeth** 741, 1021, 12,750+; *pr. 3 pl.* **yelde, ȝeldeth** 1644, 1654, 4475; *pa. t.* **ȝalde** 1596, 1820, 1909+; *pp.* **yolden, ȝolden, ȝoldyn** 1022, 1363, 4880+
yere, ȝeere, ȝere *n.* year 4061, 4123*bis*+; *poss.* **yeris** 3982; *pl.* **ȝeres, ȝeris** 606, 9886
yeve, ȝefe, ȝeif, ȝif, ȝiff(e) *v.* give 2899, 2976, 2980+, sell 978; *pr. 2 sg.* **yevest, gevist, ȝefest, ȝifest** 1294, 1306, 4697+; *pr. 3 sg.* **yefeth, yeve, yeveth, ȝeefeth, ȝefe, ȝefeth, ȝeffeth, ȝefith, ȝeveth, ȝiefeth, ȝifeth, ȝiffeth, ȝife, ȝif** 252, 275, 330+; *pr. 3 pl.* **yeve, yeven, ȝefeth, ȝeifeth, ȝiefeth, ȝifeth, ȝiffeth, ȝif** 735, 977, 1856+; *pa. t.* **yaf, yafe, ȝaf, ȝafe, ȝeaf, ȝeafe, ȝeaff** 286, 1050, 1120+; *part.* **yevyng, ȝifyng** 331, 4248; *pp.* **yoven, ȝifen, ȝovyn, ȝofyn** 264, 2969, 6775+; ~ **ageyne** return, make restitution 10,497, ~ **occasion to** caused, gave rise to 1050
yeynes *n. pl.* chains 8410

yifte, ȝift(e) *n.* gift 219, 244, 4476+; *pl.* **yftes, yiftis, yeftes, yeftys, ȝiftes, ȝiftis** 138, 2428, 4466+, bribes 4478, 4616, 4676+
ynoughe *adj. see* **inoghe**
ynoughe, ynowe *adv. see* **inoughe**
yongeth *pr. 3 sg.* is rejuvenated 4429
yough, yougthe *see* **ȝough**

Bibliography

PRIMARY SOURCES

Manuscripts

Arras: Bibliothèque Municipale 183 (1057)
Chantilly: Musée Condé 136
London: British Library Harley 4172; Additional 28206, 28208, 28209, 28212, 38692; Sloane 4
Oxford: Bodleian Library Bodley 283; Magdalen College Fastolf Papers
Paris: Bibliothèque de l'Arsenal 2124; Bibliothèque Nationale Fonds Français 459, 952, 22934, 22935
Soissons: Bibliothèque Municipale 221
Tours: Bibliothèque Municipale 401
Vatican City: Biblioteca Apostolica Vaticana Fondo Reginense Latino 1448, 2055

Printed Sources

Aelian, Claudius. *On the Characteristics of Animals.* Trans. A.F. Scholfield. 3 vols. Loeb Classical Library. Cambridge, Mass.: Harvard University Press; London: Heinemann, 1958–59.

Aesop. *The Complete Fables.* Trans. Olivia and Robert Temple. London: Penguin Books, 1998.

[Albert the Great] Albertus Magnus. *De Animalibus XXVI Nach der Cölner Urschrift.* Ed. H. Stadler. 3 vols. Beiträge zur Geschichte der Philosophie des Mittelalters. Vols 15(1916), 16:1(1920), 16:2(1921). Münster: Aschendorffsche Verlagsbuchhandlung.

– *Opera Omnia.* Ed. A. Borgnet. 38 vols. Paris: Vivès, 1890–99.

Alexander of Canterbury. *Dicta Anselmi.* In *Memorials of St Anselm*, ed. R.W. Southern and F.S. Schmitt. Auctores Britannici Medii Aevi 1. London: Oxford University Press, 1969.

Amyot, T. 'A Transcript of two Rolls, containing an Inventory of Effects formerly belonging to Sir John Fastolfe.' *Archaeologia* 21(1827): 232–80.

Aristotle. *Historia animalium.* Trans. D.W. Thompson. Oxford: Clarendon Press, 1910.

– *The Nicomachean Ethics.* Trans. H. Rackham. Loeb Classical Library. Cambridge, Mass. Harvard University Press; London: Heinemann, 1945.

[Avianus]. *The Fables of Avianus.* Ed. R. Ellis. Oxford: Clarendon, 1887.

[*Ayen*]. *See* Michel, Dan.

Babrius and Phaedrus. Ed. and trans. by B.E. Perry. Loeb Classical Library. Cambridge, Mass. Harvard University Press; London: Heinemann, 1965.

[Bartholomaeus Anglicus]. *On the Properties of Things: John Trevisa's Translation of Bartholomaeus Anglicus De Proprietatibus Rerum.* Ed. M.C. Seymour et al. 3 vols. Oxford: Clarendon, 1975–88.

Bec, P., ed. *La Lyrique Française au Moyen-Âge (XIIe-XIIIe siècles).* 2 vols. Paris: Picard, 1977–78.

[Benet, John]. 'John Benet's Chronicle for the years 1400 to 1462.' Ed. G.L. Harriss and M.A. Harriss. Camden Miscellany 24. Camden Society. 4th ser., vol. 9. London: Royal Historical Society, 1972.

Bernard de Clairvaux, Saint. *Opera*, Ed. J. Leclercq, H.M. Rochais, and C.H. Talbot. 8 vols. Rome: Editiones Cistercienses, 1957–77.

Biblia Sacra: iuxta vulgatam versionem. Ed. R. Weber. 2d ed. 2 vols. Stuttgart: Württembergische Bibelanstalt, 1975.

Boethius. *Philosophiae Consolatio.* Ed. L. Bieler. Corpus Christianorum. Series Latina 94. Turnhout: Brepols, 1957.

Bokenham, Osbern. *Legendys of holy wummen.* Ed. M.S. Serjeantson. EETS O.S. 206. London and Oxford: Oxford University Press, 1938.

Bollandus, J. *Acta Sanctorum quotquot toto orbe coluntur.* New ed. Ed. J. Canandet. Vol. 7. Paris: Palmé, 1868.

[Bonaventure]. *Collationes De Decem Praeceptis.* In *Opera Omnia*, vol. 5. Quaracchi: Collegium Sanctae Bonaventurae, 1891.

The Book of Vices and Virtues. Ed. W.N. Francis. EETS O.S. 217. London: Oxford University Press, 1942.

Brayer, E. '*La Somme le Roi*, Édition du ms. Mazarine 870.' Unpublished doctoral dissertation, University of Paris, 1940.

The Brut or The Chronicles of England. Ed. F.W.D. Brie. Part 2. EETS O.S. 136. London: Published for the Early English Text Society by Kegan Paul Trench Trübner and by Henry Frowde, Oxford University Press, 1908.

Bullarium Danicum. Ed. A. Krarup. 2 vols. Copenhagen: Kommission hos G.E.C.D. Gad, 1931–32.

Caesarius of Arles. *Sermones.* Ed. G. Morin. 2d ed. *Corpus Christianorum.* Series Latina 103–4. Turnhout: Brepols, 1953.

Caesarius of Heisterbach. *Dialogus Miraculorum.* Ed. J. Strange. 2 vols. Cologne: Haberle, 1851–57. Reprint. Ridgewood: Gregg, 1966.

Campbell, B.R. 'A Partial Edition of The Book of Good Condicions: A Middle English Translation of Le Livre Des Bonnes Moeurs of Jacques Legrand. Edited from University of Glasgow Library Hunter MS. 78.' Unpublished doctoral dissertation, University of Ottawa, 1978.

Caxton, W. *The Ryal Book.* Westminster: Caxton, ?1488. STC 21429.

Chaucer, Geoffrey. *The Riverside Chaucer.* 3d ed. Ed. L.D. Benson. Boston: Houghton Mifflin, 1987.

Chroniques de Jean Molinet. Ed. G. Doutrepont and O. Jodogne. 3 vols. Brussels: Palais des Académies, 1935–1937.

[Cicero]. *M. Tullii Ciceronis Scripta Quae Manserunt Omnia.* Ed. R. Klotz. 5 Pts. Leipzig: Teubner, 1868–72.

Corpus Christianorum. Series Latina. Turnhout: Brepols, 1953–.

Curley, M.J., trans. *Physiologus.* Austin: University of Texas Press, 1979.

Curye on Inglysch. Ed. C.B. Hieatt and S. Butler. EETS S.S. 8. London: Oxford University Press, 1985.

[Decretum] Gratian. *Decretum.* In *Corpus Iuris Canonici,* ed. D. Friedberg. 2 vols. Leipzig: Tauchnitz, 1879–81. Reprint. Graz: Druck und Verlagsanstalt, 1959. [Cited by Pars, Causa, Quaestio, and caput.]

Defensor. *Liber scintillarum.* Ed. H.M. Rochais. Corpus Christianorum. Series Latina 117. Turnhout: Brepols, 1957.

[*Dicts*]. *See* Scrope, S.

Dives and Pauper. Ed. P.H. Barnum. EETS O.S. 275, 280. Oxford: Oxford University Press, 1976–80.

The Doctrinal of Sapience. Ed. J. Gallagher. Middle English Texts 26. Heidelberg: Winter, 1993.

Douet-D'Arcq, L., ed. *Comptes de l'argenterie: des rois de france au XIVe siécle.* Paris: Jules Renouard, 1851.

Eliot, Thomas. *The Castell of Helthe.* London: Berthelet, 1539.

An English Chronicle of the reigns of Richard II, Henry IV, Henry V, and Henry VI. Ed. J.S. Davies. Camden Society 64. London: Royal Historical Society, 1856.

Étienne de Bourbon. *Anecdotes historiques, Légendes et apologues.* Ed. Lecoy de La Marche. Paris: Renouard, 1877.

Fasciculus Morum: A Fourteenth-Century Preacher's Handbook. Ed. and trans. S. Wenzel. University Park and London: Pennsylvania State University Press, 1989.

Fisher, J.H., M. Richardson, and J.L. Fisher. *An Anthology of Chancery English.* Knoxville: University of Tennessee Press, 1984.

Gairdner, J., ed. *Historical Collections of a Citizen of London.* Camden Society, n.s. 17. London: Royal Historical Society, 1876.

– *Three Fifteenth Century English Chronicles.* Camden Society, n.s. 28. London: Royal Historical Society, 1880.

Galen, *Selected Works.* Trans. P.N. Singer. Oxford: Oxford University Press, 1997.

Garin le Loherenc. Ed. A. Iker-Gittleman. 3 vols. Paris: H. Champion, 1996–7.

Gesta Henrici Quinti: The Deeds of Henry the Fifth. Trans. F. Taylor and J.S. Roskell. Oxford: Clarendon Press, 1975.

Gesta Romanorum. Ed. H. Oesterley. Berlin: Weidmann, 1872.

Glossa Ordinaria. In *Textus biblie cum glossa ordinaria; Nicolai de Lyra postilla Moralitatibus eiusdem; Pauli Burgensis additionibus Matthie Thoring replicis.* 6 vols in 5 pts. Basel: Johannes Froben & Johannes Petri für Johann Amenbach, 1506–8. [Cited by volume, folio, and section.]

Gough, H., ed. *The Register of the Fraternity or Guild of the Holy and Undivided Trinity and the Blessed Virgin Mary in the Parish Church of Luton in the County of Bedford, from a.d. MCCCCLXXV to MDCXLVI.* London: Chiswick Press, 1906.

Grosseteste, Robert. *De Decem Mandatis.* Ed. R.C. Dales and E.B. King. Auctores Britannici Medii Aevi X. Oxford: Oxford University Press, 1987.

Guillaume Le Clerc. *Le Bestiaire.* Ed. R. Reinsch. Wiesbaden: Martin Sändig, 1967.

Guy de Chauliac. *The Cyrurgie.* Ed. M.S. Ogden. EETS O.S. 265. London: Oxford University Press, 1971.

Hélinant de Froidmont. *Les Vers de la Mort.* Ed. F. Wulf and E. Walberg. Société des Anciens Textes Français 53. Paris: Didot, 1905.

Herolt, Iohannes. *Sermones discipuli de tempore et sanctis cum promptuario exemplorum et miraculis beate Marie virginis.* London: Julyan Notary, 1510. [STC 13226]

Hugh of Strassburg. *Compendium Theologicae Veritatis.* In *Albertus Magnus: Opera Omnia*, ed. A. Borgnet. Vol. 24. Paris: Vivès, 1895.

Innocentius IV. *Apparatus super quinque libros Decretalium.* Strassburg: Eggestein, 1478 (Goff I95).

Jacobus a Voragine. *Legenda aurea.* Ed. T. Graesse. 3d. ed. Breslau: Koebner, 1890. Reprint. Osnabrück: Zeller, 1969.

[Jacques de Vitry]. *The Exempla or Illustrative Stories From the Sermones Vulgares of Jacques de Vitry.* Ed. T.F. Crane. Publications of the Folk-lore Society 26. London: Published for the Folk-lore Society by D. Nutt, 1890.

Knyghthode and Bataile. Ed. R. Dyboski and Z.M. Arend. EETS O.S. 201. London: Published for the Early English Text Society by Humphrey Milford, Oxford University Press, 1935.

Lavynham, Richard. *A Litil Tretys on the Seven Dedly Sins.* Ed. J.P.W.M. van Zutphen. Rome: Institutum Carmelitanum, 1956.

Liber Exemplorum ad usum praedicantium. Ed. A.G. Little. British Society of Franciscan Studies 1. Aberdeen: Aberdeen University Press, 1908.

Lydgate, John. 'A Balade in Commendation of Our Lady.' In *Poems*, ed. J. Norton-Smith. Oxford: Clarendon, 1966.

Macrobius. *Ambrosii Theodosii Macrobii Commentarii In Somnium Scipionis.* Vol. 2. Leipzig: Teubner, 1963. Trans. W.H. Stahl under the title *Commentary on the Dream of Scipio.* New York: Columbia University Press, 1952.

Mannyng, Robert, of Brunne. *Handlyng Synne.* Ed. I. Sullens. Binghamton, NY: Medieval and Renaissance Texts and Studies, 1983.

Martin of Braga. *Opera Omnia.* Ed. C.W. Barlow. Papers and Monographs of the American Academy in Rome 12. New Haven: Yale University Press, 1950.

Maskell, W. *Monumenta Ritualia Ecclesiae Anglicanae.* 3 vols. 2d ed. Oxford: Clarendon Press, 1882.

Michel, Dan. *Dan Michel's Ayenbite of Inwyt or Remorse of Conscience.* Ed. R. Morris. EETS O.S. 23. London: N. Trübner, 1866; Reprint, 1965 (with corrections to the text). Vol. 2, with Introduction, Notes, and Glossary by Pamela Gradon, was issued by EETS O.S. 278. London: Oxford University Press, 1965.

Midrash Rabbah. Esther. Ed. and trans. H. Freedman and M. Simon. London and New York: Soncino Press, 1983.

Migne, J.-P., ed. *Patrologia cursus completus. Series graeca.* 166 vols. Paris: J.-P. Migne et al., 1857–66.

– *Patrologia cursus completus. Series latina.* 221 vols. Paris: J.-P. Migne et al., 1844–64.

Le Mireour du monde. Ed. F. Chavannes. Mémoires et documents publiés par la Société d'histoire de la Suisse romande 4. Lausanne: G. Bridel, 1845.

Mombrizio, B. *Sanctuarium; seu, Vitae sanctorum.* New ed. by monks of Solesmes. 2 vols. Paris: Fontemoing, 1910.

Das Moralium dogma philosophorum des Guillaume de Conches. Ed. J. Holmberg. Uppsala: Almquist and Wiksell, 1929.

A Myrour To Lewde Men And Wymmen. A Prose Version of the Speculum Vitae. Ed. V. Nelson. Middle English Texts 14. Heidelberg: Winter, 1981.

Novus Physiologus Nach Hs. Darmstadt 2780. Ed. A.P. Orbán. Leiden: Brill, 1989.

O'Keefe, J.G. 'Cain Downaig.' *Ériu: Journal of the School of Irish Learning,* 2(1905): 189–214.

[*Othea*]. *See* Scrope, S.

Paston Letters and Papers of the Fifteenth Century. Ed. N. Davis. 2 vols. Oxford: Clarendon Press, 1971, 1976.

Pecock, R. *The Repressor Of Over Much Blaming Of The Clergy.* Ed. C. Babington. 2 vols. Rolls Series 19. London: Longmans Green, Longman, and Roberts, 1860.

[Peraldus]. Perault, G. *Summarium Summae Virtutum et Vitiorum per figuras.* Lyons: Nicolaus de Benedictis, 1500 [Hain 12392, Goff P88]. [Cited by book, tract, part, and chapter.]

Petrus Alfonsi. *Disciplina clericalis.* Ed. A. Hilka and W. Söderhjelm. Heidelberg: Winter, 1911.

Physiologus latinus. Éditions préliminaires, versio B. Ed. F.J. Carmody. Paris: Droz, 1939.

The Pilgrimage of the Lyfe of the Manhode. Ed. A. Henry. 2 vols. EETS O.S. 288, 292. London: Oxford University Press, 1985–88.

Pliny [the Elder]. *Natural History.* Trans. H. Rackham. Loeb Classical Library. 10 vols. Cambridge, Mass. Harvard University Press; London: Heinemann, 1938–63.

[Porphyrius]. *Porphyrii Sententiae Ad Intelligibilia Ducentes.* Ed. E. Lamberz. Leipzig: Teubner, 1975.

Raimundus de Pennaforte. *Libellus Pastoralis De Cura et Officio Archidiaconi.* Ed. L. Delisle. *Catalogue Général* 1(1849): 592–649.

– *Summa de Paenitentia.* Ed. X. Ochoa and A. Diaz. Universa bibliotheca iuris 1. Rome: Commentarium pro religiosis, 1976.

Robbins, R. H., ed. *Historical Poems of the XIVth and XVth Centuries.* New York: Columbia University Press, 1959.

Robert of Flamborough. *Liber Poenitentialis.* Ed. J.J.F. Firth. Toronto: Pontifical Institute of Mediaeval Studies, 1971.

[*Rosarium Theologie*]. *The Middle English Translation of the Rosarium Theologie.* Ed. C. Van Nolcken. Middle English Texts 10. Heidelberg: Carl Winter, 1979.

Royster, J.F. 'A Treatise on the Ten Commandments.' *Modern Philology* 6(1910): 3–39.

Sajavaara, K., ed. *The Middle English Translations of Robert Grosseteste's 'Chateau d'Amour.'* Mémoires de la Société Néophilologique de Helsinki, 32. Helsinki: Société néophilologique, 1967.

Scrope, S., trans. *The Dicts and Sayings of the Philosophers.* Ed. C.F. Bühler. EETS O.S. 211. Oxford: Oxford University Press, 1941. (The Helmingham Hall MS version of the *Dicts* is published on facing pages, the Abbreviated Version on pp. 297–320).

– *The Dicts and Sayings of the Philosophers.* Ed. Margaret F. Schofield. Philadelphia: Published by the editor, 1936.

– *The Epistle of Othea.* Christine de Pisan. Ed. C.F. Bühler. EETS O.S. 264. London and New York: Oxford University Press, 1970.

– *The Epistle of Othea to Hector.* Christine de Pisan. Ed. Sir G.F. Warner. London: J.B. Nichols, 1904.

L. Annaeus Seneca. *Opera quae supersunt.* Ed. F. Haase. 3 vols. Leipzig: Teubner, 1862–1902.

Sisam, K., ed. *Fourteenth Century Verse & Prose.* Oxford: Clarendon Press, 1921.

Smeltz, J.W. '*Speculum Vitae: An Edition of British Museum Manuscript Royal 17.C.viii.*' Unpublished doctoral dissertation, Duquesne University, 1977.

Speculum Humanae Salvationis. Ed. J. Lutz and P. Perdrizet. Leipzig: Hiersemann, 1907–09.

Le Speculum Laicorum. Ed. J.T. Welter. Paris: A. Picard, 1914.

Stahl, W.H., trans. *Commentary on the Dream of Scipio.* New York: Columbia University Press, 1952.

Summa Virtutum de Remediis Anime. Ed. S. Wenzel. Athens: University of Georgia Press, 1984.

La Tabula Exemplorum secundum Ordinem Alphabeti: Recueil d'exempla compilé en France à la fin du XIIIe siècle. Ed. J.T. Welter. Paris: Guitard, 1926.

Tanner, N.P., ed. *Decrees of the Ecumenical Councils.* Vol. 1, *Nicaea I to Lateran V.* London: Sheed and Ward; Washington D.C.: Georgetown University Press, 1990.

[Thibaut d'Amiens]. 'La Prière de Thibaut d'Amiens.' Ed. A. Langfórs. In *Studies in Romance Philology and French Literature Presented to John Orr by Pupils, Colleagues and Friends.* Manchester: Manchester University Press, 1953.

Thiele, G., ed. *Der lateinische Äsop des Romulus und die prosa-fassungen des Phädrus.* Heidelberg: Winter, 1910.

Thomas Cantimpratensis. *Liber de Natura Rerum.* Vol. 1. Ed. H. Boese. Berlin: De Gruyter, 1973.

Thomas, A.H., and I.D. Thornley, eds. *The Great Chronicle of London.* London: G.W. Jones, 1938.

Tischendorf, L.F.C. von, ed. *Evangelia Apocrypha.* Leipzig: Avenarius & Mendelssohn, 1853.

Vegetius Renatus, Flavius. *Epitoma Rei Militaris.* Ed. C. Lang. Bibliotheca Teubneriana. Stuttgart: Teubner, 1967.

[Vincent of Beauvais]. Vincentius Bellovacensis. *Speculum Doctrinale.* Strassburg: Rusch, ?1477.

Whitaker, E.E. 'A Critical Edition of *The Mirroure of the Worlde.*' 4 vols. Unpublished doctoral dissertation, New York University, 1971.

White, T.H., trans. and ed. *The Bestiary: A Book of Beasts.* New York: Putnam, 1954.

[William of Auxerre]. Guillelmus Altissiodorensis. *Summa Aurea.* Ed. J. Ribaillier. 7 vols. Paris: Éditions du Centre national de la recherche scientifique, 1980–87.

[Worcester, W.] *The Boke of Noblesse Addressed To King Edward the Fourth On His Invasion of France in 1475.* Ed. J.G. Nichols. London: Roxburghe Club, 1860.

– *Itineraries.* Ed. J.H. Harvey. Oxford: Clarendon Press, 1969.

SECONDARY SOURCES

Acworth, M.W. 'A Misleading Brass.' *Bedfordshire Magazine,* 4(1954): 203–4.

Adams, J.N. *The Latin Sexual Vocabulary.* London: Duckworth, 1982.

Alexander, J.J.G. *Medieval Illuminators and Their Methods of Work.* New Haven and London: Yale University Press, 1992.

Allen, E.A. 'Never Less Alone Than When Alone.' *Modern Language Notes* 24(1909): 123.

Anciaux, P. *La Théologie du sacrement de pénitence au XIIe siècle.* Louvain: E. Nauwelaerts, 1949.

Anglo-Norman Dictionary. Ed. L.W. Stone and W. Rothwell. 7 vols. London: Modern Humanities Research Association, 1977–92.

Arnould, A., and J.M. Massing. *Splendours of Flanders.* Cambridge: Cambridge University Press, 1993.

Arnould, E.J. *Le Manuel des péchés: Etude de littérature religieuse anglo-normande (XIIIme siècle).* Paris: Droz, 1940.

Aston, M. *Lollards and Reformers: Images and Literacy in Late Medieval Religion.* London: Hambledon Press, 1984.

L'Aveu: Antiquité et Moyen-Âge: Actes de la table ronde organisée par l'École Française de Rome avec le concours du CNRS et de l'Université de Trieste, Rome, 28–30 mars 1984. Collection de l'École Française de Rome. Rome: École Française de Rome, 1986.

Bacchiocchi, S. *From Sabbath to Sunday.* Rome: Pontifical Gregorian University Press, 1977.

Backhouse, J. 'Founders of the Royal Library: Edward IV and Henry VII as Collectors of Illuminated Manuscripts.' In *England in the Fifteenth Century,* ed. D. Williams. Woodbridge: Boydell, 1987.

– Review of *The Caxton Master and his Patrons. Medium Aevum* 47(1978): 201–5.

Bailey, D.S. *Homosexuality and the Western Christian Tradition.* London, New York: Longmans, Green, 1955. Reprint. Hamden: Archon, 1975.

Baldwin, F.E. *Sumptuary Legislation and Personal Regulation in England.* Johns Hopkins University Studies in Historical and Political Science, series 44, no. 1. Baltimore: Johns Hopkins University Press, 1926.

Baldwin, J.W. *The Medieval Theories of the Just Price.* Transactions of the American Philosophical Society, n.s., 49, pt 4. Philadelphia: American Philosophical Society, 1959.

Baukham, R.J. 'Sabbath and Sunday in the Medieval Church in the West.' In *From Sabbath to Lord's Day,* ed. D.A. Carson. Grand Rapids: Zondervan, 1982.

Beadle, H.R.L. 'The Medieval Drama of East Anglia.' 2 vols. Unpublished doctoral dissertation, University of York, 1977.

Bean, J.M.W. *From Lord to Patron: Lordship in Late Medieval England.* Philadelphia: University of Pennsylvania Press, 1989.

Bennett, J. 'The Language and the Home of the *Ludus Coventriae.*' *Orbis* 22(1973): 43–63.

Bense, J. F. *A Dictionary of the Low-Dutch Element in the English Vocabulary.* 5 pts. London: Milford; The Hague: Nijhoff, 1926–39.

Benskin, M. 'Local Archives and Middle English Dialects.' *Journal of the Society of Archivists* 5(1977): 500–14.

Benskin, M., and M.L. Samuels. *So meny people longages and tonges: Philological Essays in Scots and Mediaeval English Presented to Angus McIntosh.* Edinburgh: Benskin & Samuels, 1981.

Bergmans, P. 'Marguerite d'York et les pauvres Claires de Gand.' *Bulletin de la Société d'Histoire et d'Archéologie de Gand* 18(1910): 271–84.

Bériou, N. 'La confession dans les écrits théologiques et pastoraux du XIIIe siécle: médication de l'âme ou démarche judiciaire?' In *L'Aveu: Antiquité et Moyen-Âge*, Rome: École Français de Rome, 1986.

Bertoni, G. 'Ricerche sulla *Somme le roi* di Frère Laurent.' *Archiv für das Studium der neueren Sprachen und Literaturen* 112(1904): 344–65.

Bibliothèque Impériale. Départment des Manuscrits. *Catalogue des Manuscrits Français*. vol. 1, *Ancien Fonds*. Paris: Didot, 1868.

Bibliothèque Nationale. *Catalogue Général des Manuscrits Français par H. Omont, Anciens Petits Fonds Français II.* Paris: Leroux, 1902.

Blake, N.F., ed. *The Cambridge History of the English Language*. Vol. 2, *1066–1476*. Cambridge: Cambridge University Press, 1992.

Blomme, R. *La doctrine du péché dans les écoles théologiques de la première moitié du XIIe siècle.* Louvain: Publications Universitaires, 1958.

Bloomfield, M.W. 'Piers Plowman and the Three Grades of Chastity.' *Anglia* 76(1958): 227–53.

– *The Seven Deadly Sins: An Introduction to the History of a Religious Concept, with Special Reference to Medieval English Literature.* 1952 Reprint. East Lansing: Michigan State University Press, 1967.

Bloomfield, M.W., et al. *Incipits of Latin Works on the Virtues and Vices, 1100–1500 A.D.* Cambridge, Mass. Medieval Academy of America, 1979.

Bohman, H. *Studies in the Middle English Dialects of Devon and London.* Göteborg: Aktiebolaget Pehrssons Förlag, 1944.

Boser, C. 'Le Remaniement provençal de la *Somme le roi* et ses dérivés.' *Romania* 24(1895): 56–85.

Bossuat, R. *Manuel Bibliographique de la Littérature Française du Moyen Âge.* Melun: Librairie d'Argences, 1951.

Boswell, J. *Christianity, Social Tolerance, and Homosexuality.* Chicago and London: University of Chicago Press, 1980.

Bourgain, L. *La Chaire Française au XIIe Siècle.* Paris: Palmé, 1879.

Boyle, L.E. 'Aspects of Clerical Education in Fourteenth-Century England.' In *Acta IV: The Fourteenth Century*, ed. P.E. Szarmach and B.S. Levy. Binghamton: Center for Medieval and Early Renaissance Studies, 1977.

– 'The Fourth Lateran Council and Manuals of Popular Theology.' In *The Popular Literature of Medieval England*, ed. T.J. Heffernan. Tennessee Studies in Literature 28 (1985).

– 'The Inter-Conciliar Period, 1179–1215, and the Beginnings of Pastoral Manuals.' In *Miscellanea Rolando Bandinelli Papa Alessandro III*, ed. F. Liotta. Siena: Accademia senese degli intronati, 1986.

– 'A Study of the Works Attributed to William of Pagula with Special Reference to the *Oculus sacerdotis* and *Summa Summarum*.' 2 vols. Unpublished doctoral dissertation, Oxford University, 1956.

Bradley, R., Sr. 'Backgrounds of the Title "Speculum" in Medieval Literature.' *Speculum* 29(1954): 110–15.

– 'The Speculum Image in Medieval Mystical Writers.' In *The Medieval Mystical Tradition in England*, ed. M. Glasscoe. Cambridge: Brewer, 1984.

Brayer, E. 'Contenu, structure et combinaisons du *Miroir du Monde* et du *Somme le Roi*.' *Romania* 79(1958): 1–38, 433–70.

– 'Livres d'heures contenant des textes en français.' *Bulletin d'Information de l'Institut de Recherche et d'Histoire des Textes* 12(1963): 31–102.

Brewer, W.F. 'Never Less Alone Than When Alone.' *Modern Language Notes* 24(1909): 226.

Brown, M.P. *A Guide to Western Historical Scripts from Antiquity to 1600*. London: British Library, 1993.

Brundage, J.A. 'Carnal Delight: Canonistic Theories of Sexuality.' In *Proceedings of the Fifth International Congress of Medieval Canon Law*, ed. S. Kuttner and K. Pennington. Monumenta Iuris Canonici, Subsidia, vol. 6. Vatican City: Vatican Library, 1980.

– *Law, Sex, and Christian Society in Medieval Europe*. Chicago: University of Chicago Press, 1987.

– 'Sexual Equality in Medieval Canon Law.' In *Medieval Women and the Sources of Medieval History*, ed. J.T. Rosenthal. Athens: University of Georgia, 1990.

Bugge, J. *Virginitas: An Essay in the History of a Medieval Ideal*. The Hague: Nijhoff, 1975.

Bühler, C.F. 'The Apostles and the Creed.' *Speculum* 28(1953): 335–59.

– 'The Revisions And Dedications of *The Epistle of Othea*.' *Anglia* 76(1958): 266–70.

– 'Sir John Fastolf's Manuscripts of the *Epître d'Othéa* and Stephen Scrope's Translation of the Text.' *Scriptorium* 3(1949): 123–8.

Bullough, V.L. 'The Sin against Nature and Homosexuality.' In *Sexual Practices and the Medieval Church*, ed. V.L. Bullough and J. Brundage. Buffalo: Prometheus Books, 1982.

Burnley, J.D. 'Late Medieval English Translation: Types and Reflections.' In *The Medieval Translator: The Theory and Practice of Translation in the Middle Ages*, ed. R. Ellis. Woodbridge: Brewer, 1989.

– 'Lexis and Semantics.' In *The Cambridge History of the English Language*. Vol. 2, *1066–1496*. Cambridge: Cambridge University Press, 1992.

Burrow, J.A. *The Ages of Man: A Study in Medieval Writing and Thought.* Oxford: Clarendon Press, 1986.

Buzza, D.T. 'English Female Costume 1400 to 1485 as Represented on Monumental Brasses and Brass Rubbings.' 2 vols. Unpublished University of Minnesota doctoral dissertation, 1986.

Cadden, J. *Meanings of Sex Difference in the Middle Ages.* Cambridge: Cambridge University Press, 1993.

Campbell, B.R. 'A Partial Edition of the Book of Good Condicions. A Middle English Translation of *Le Livre des Bonnes Moeurs* of Jacques Legrand, Edited from University of Glasgow Library Hunter MS. 78.' Unpublished doctoral dissertation, University of Ottawa, 1978.

Carpenter, C. 'The Religion of the Gentry of Fifteenth-Century England.' In *England in the Fifteenth Century*, ed. D. Williams. Woodbridge: Boydell, 1987.

Carruthers, L.M. 'L'Echelle de Jacob ou le Bonheur Celeste dans La Somme Le Roi.' In *L'Idee de Bonheur au moyen âge. Actes du Colloque d'Amiens de Mars 1984.* Göppinger Arbeiten zur Germanistik 414. Göppingen: Kümmerle, 1990.

– 'Lorens of Orléans and the *Somme le Roi or The Book of Vices and Virtues.*' *Vox Benedictina* 5(1988): 190–200.

– *La Somme le Roi et ses traductions anglaises: étude comparée.* Paris: Association des médievistes anglicistes de l'enseignement supérieur, 1986.

Carus-Wilson, E.M. 'Evidences of Industrial Growth on Some Fifteenth-Century Manors.' *Economic History Review*, 2d ser. 12 (1959): 190–205.

Casagrande, C., and S. Vecchio. *I Peccati Della Lingua.* Rome: Istituto Enciclopedia Italiana, 1987.

Catalogue of Additions to the Manuscripts in the British Museum in the Years 1854–1875. Vol. 2. London: British Museum, 1877.

Catalogue Général des Manuscrits des Bibliothèques Publiques des Départements. Vols 1, 4. Paris: Plon, 1849, 1872. Vol. 37. Paris: Plon, 1900.

Catalogue Général des Manuscrits des Bibliothèques Publiques de France. Catalogue des Manuscrits de la Bibliothèque de l'Arsenal. Paris: Plon, 1885.

Catalogue Général des Manuscrits des Bibliothèques Publiques de France. Bibliothèque de l'Institut. Musée Condé à Chantilly. Bibliothèque Thiers. Musées Jacquemart-André à Paris et à Chaalis. Paris: Plon, 1928.

Catto, J. 'Religious Change under Henry V.' In *Henry V: The Practice of Kingship*, ed. G.L. Harriss. Oxford: Oxford University Press, 1985.

Catto, J.I., and R. Evans, eds. *The History of the University of Oxford*. Vol. 2, *Late Medieval Oxford*. Oxford: Clarendon Press, 1992.

Cavanaugh, S.K. *Books Privately Owned in England, 1300–1450*. Cambridge: D.S. Brewer, 1988.

Chantilly. *Le Cabinet des Livres. Manuscrits*. Vol. 1. Paris: Plon, 1900.

Chew, S.C. *The Virtues Reconciled: An Iconographic Study*. Toronto: University of Toronto Press, 1947.

Clayton, M. *A Catalogue of Rubbings of Brasses and Incised Slabs*. London: Victoria and Albert Museum, 1929.

Cobb, P.J. 'The History of the Christian Year.' In *The Study of Liturgy*, ed. C. Jones, G. Wainwright, and E. Yarnold. London: SPCK, 1980.

Cobban, A.B. *The King's Hall Within the University of Cambridge in the Later Middle Ages*. Cambridge: Cambridge University Press, 1969.

Codices Manuscripti in Bibliotheca Sancti Vedasti Apud Atrebatiam. Paris: Pihan de la forest, 1828.

Collins, A.H. *Symbolism of Animals and Birds Represented in English Church Architecture*. London: Pitman, 1913.

Constable, G. 'Moderation and Restraint in Ascetic Practices in the Middle Ages.' In *From Athens to Chartres: Neoplatonism and Medieval Thought. Studies in Honour of Edouard Jeauneau*, ed. H.J. Westra. Leiden, New York, Cologne: Brill, 1992.

– *Three Studies in Medieval Religious and Social Thought*. Cambridge: Cambridge University Press, 1995.

Cook, A.S. 'Never Less Alone Than When Alone.' *Modern Language Notes* 24(1909): 54–5.

Cooper, L. 'Never Less Alone Than When Alone.' *Modern Language Notes* 26(1911): 232.

Cornelius, R.D. *The Figurative Castle: A Study in the Medieval Allegory of the Edifice with Especial Reference to Religious Writing*. Bryn Mawr, Pa.: Bryn Mawr University Press, 1930.

Corstanje, C. van, Y. Cazaux, J. Decavele, and A. Derolez, eds. *Vita Sanctae Coletae*. Leiden: Brill, 1982.

Coss, P.R. 'Literature and Social Terminology: The Vavasour in England.' In *Social Relations and Ideas: Essays in Honour of R.H. Hilton*, ed. T.H. Ashton, P.R. Coss, C. Dyer, and J. Thirsk. Cambridge: Cambridge University Press, 1983.

Cotgrave, R. *A Dictionarie of the French and English Tongues. Reproduced from the First Edition, London, 1611*. Introduction by W.S. Woods. Columbia: University of South Carolina Press, 1950.

Cramer, P. *Baptism and Change in the Early Middle Ages, c. 200 – c. 1150.* Cambridge: Cambridge University Press, 1993.

Craun, E.D. *Lies, Slander, and Obscenity in Medieval English Literature.* Cambridge: Cambridge University Press, 1997.

Creswell, K.A.C. 'Fortification in Islam before A.D. 1250.' *Proceedings of the British Academy* 38(1952): 89–125.

Cunnington, C.W., and P. Cunnington. *Handbook of English Mediaeval Costume.* 2d ed. London: Faber & Faber, 1969.

Daniel, N. *Heroes and Saracens.* Edinburgh: Edinburgh University Press, 1984.

Davenport, M., E. Hansen, and H.-F. Nielsen, eds. *Current Topics in English Historical Linguistics.* Odense: Odense University Press, 1983.

Davis, N. 'The Epistolary Usages of William Worcester.' In *Medieval Literature and Civilization: Studies in Memory of G.N. Garmonsway*, ed. D.A. Pearsall and R.A. Waldron. London: Athlone, 1969.

– 'Language in Letters from Sir John Fastolf's Household.' In *Medieval Studies for J.A.W. Bennett*, ed. P.L. Heyworth. Oxford: Clarendon Press, 1981.

– 'The Language of the Pastons.' *Proceedings of the British Academy* 40(1955): 119–44.

– 'Scribal Variation in Late Fifteenth-Century English.' *Mélanges de linguistique et de philologie Fernand Mossé in memoriam.* Paris: Didier, 1959.

– 'Styles in English Prose of the Late Middle and Early Modern Period.' In *Langue et littérature: Actes du VIIIe Congrès de la Fédération Internationale des Langues et Littératures Modernes.* Paris: Société d'Édition 'Les Belles lettres,' 1961.

Dawson, W.B. 'The Lore of the Hoopoe.' *The Bridle of Pegasus: Studies in Magic, Mythology, and Folklore.* London: Methuen, 1930.

Deanesly, M. *The Lollard Bible.* Cambridge: Cambridge University Press, 1920; reprint, 1966.

Degli Innocenti, M. 'Una *Confessione* del XIII secolo.' *Cristianesimo nella storia* 5(1984): 245–302.

Delaissé, L.M.J. *A Century of Dutch Manuscript Illustration.* Berkeley: University of California Press, 1968.

Delumeau, J. *Sin and Fear: The Emergence of a Western Guilt Culture, 13–18 Centuries.* Trans. E. Nicholson. New York: St Martin's Press, 1990.

De Roover, R. *Money, Banking and Credit in Mediaeval Bruges.* Cambridge: Mediaeval Academy of America, 1948.

Derrett, J.D.M. 'The History of "Palladius on the Races of India and the Brahmans."' *Classica et Mediaevalia* 21(1960): 64–135.

Dictionary of National Biography. Ed. L. Stephen and S. Lee. 21 vols. Reprint. Oxford: Oxford University Press, 1921–22.

Diekstra, F.N.M. 'Some Fifteenth-Century Borrowings from the *Ancrene Wisse*.' *English Studies* 77(1990): 81–104.

Di Stefano, G. *Dictionnaire des Locutions en Moyen Français*. Montreal: Ceres, 1991.

Dobson, E.J. *English Pronunciation, 1500–1700*. 2 vols. 2d ed. Oxford: Clarendon Press, 1968.

Dobson, R.B. *The Peasants' Revolt of 1381*. 2d ed. London: Macmillan, 1983.

Dondaine, A. 'Guillaume Peyraut, vie et oeuvres.' *Archivum Fratrum Praedicatorum* 18(1948): 162–236.

Donnelly, J.S. *The Decline of the Medieval Cistercian Laybrotherhood*. New York: Fordham University Press, 1949.

Douie, D. *Archbishop Pecham*. Oxford: Clarendon Press, 1952.

Doyle, A.I. '*Lectulus noster floridus*: An Allegory of the Penitent Soul.' In *Literature and Religion In the Later Middle Ages: Philological Studies in Honor of Siegfried Wenzel*, ed. R.G. Newhauser and J.A. Alford. Binghamton, NY: Medieval and Renaissance Texts and Studies, 1995.

Driver, M.W. 'Mirrors of a Collective Past: Reconsidering Images of Medieval Women.' In *Women and the Book: British Library Studies in Medieval Culture*. London: British Library, 1996.

Duby, G. *Rural Economy and Country Life in the Medieval West*. Columbia: University of South Carolina Press, 1968.

Du Cange, C. du Fresne. *Glossarium Mediae et Infimae Latinitatis*. 5 vols. Graz: Akademische Druck-U. Verlagsanstalt, 1954.

Duffy, E. *The Stripping of the Altars: Traditional Religion in England c. 1400 – c. 1580*. New Haven and London: Yale University Press, 1992.

Dugmore, C.W. *The Influence of the Synagogue upon the Divine Office*. London: Oxford University Press, 1944.

Dyer, C. *Standards of Living in the Later Middle Ages: Social Change in England, c. 1200–1520*. Cambridge: Cambridge University Press, 1989.

Eberly, S.S., and D. Chamberlain. '"Under the Schaddow of the Hawthorne Greene": The Hawthorn in Medieval Love Poetry.' In *New Readings of Late Medieval Love Poems*, ed. D. Chamberlain. Lantham: University Press of America, 1993.

Einenkel, E. *Geschichte der englischen Sprache*. Vol. 2, *Historische Grammatik*. Strassburg: Trübner, 1916.

Ellis, R. 'The Choices of the Translator in the Late Middle English Period.' In *The Medieval Mystical Tradition in England*, ed. M. Glasscoe. Exeter: University of Exeter, 1982.

Emden, A.B. *A Biographical Register of the University of Cambridge to 1500.* Cambridge: Cambridge University Press, 1963.

– *A Biographical Register of the University of Oxford to A.D. 1500.* Vol. 3, *P to Z.* Oxford: Clarendon Press, 1959.

Emmerson, R.K. *Antichrist in the Middle Ages.* Seattle: University of Washington Press, 1981.

Faire Croire: Modalités de la diffusion et de la réception des messages religieux du XIIe au XVe siècle. Table Ronde organisée par l'École Française de Rome, en collaboration avec l'Institut d'histoire médiévale de l'Université de Padoue (Rome, 22–23 juin 1979). Collection de l'École Française de Rome 51. Rome: École Française de Rome, 1981.

Faral, E. 'La queue de poisson des sirènes.' *Romania* 74(1953): 433–506.

Fischer, N. 'Handlist of Animal References in Middle English Religious Prose.' *Leeds Studies in English,* n.s., 4(1970): 49–100.

Fischer, O. 'Syntax.' *In The Cambridge History of the English Language.* Vol. 2, *1066–1476.* Cambridge: Cambridge University Press, 1992.

Fischer, S.K. *Econolingua.* Newark: University of Delaware Press, 1985.

Flandrin, J.-L. *Un Temps Pour Embraser.* Paris: Éditions du Seuil, 1983.

Foss, C., and D. Winfield. *Byzantine Fortifications: An Introduction.* Pretoria: University of South Africa Press, 1986.

Foulet, L. 'L'effacement des Adverbs de Lieu.' *Romania* 69(1946–47): 1–79.

Fox, D. 'Stephen Scrope, Jacques Legrand, and the Word "Mankyndely."' *Notes and Queries,* n.s., 29 (1982): 400.

Friedmann, H. *A Bestiary for Saint Jerome: Animal Symbolism in European Religious Art.* Washington, D.C.: Smithsonian Institution, 1980.

Fryde, E.B. 'Peasant Rebellion and Peasant Discontents.' In *The Agrarian History of England and Wales,* ed. E. Miller. Vol. 3, *1348–1500.* Cambridge: Cambridge University Press, 1991.

Ganshof, F.L., and A. Verhulst. 'Medieval Agrarian Society in its Prime. 1: France, The Low Countries, and Western Germany.' In *The Cambridge Economic History of Europe,* ed. M.M. Postan. Vol. 1, *The Agrarian Life of the Middle Ages.* 2d ed. Cambridge: Cambridge University Press, 1966.

Gaspar, C., and F. Lyna. *Philippe le Bon et ses Beaux Livres.* Brussels: Éditions du Cercle d'Art, 1944.

Gauthier, R.A. *Magnanimité: L'Idéal de la Grandeur dans la Philosophie Païenne et dans la Théologie Chrétienne.* Paris: Vrin, 1951.

Gheyn, J. Van Den. *Histoire de Charles Martel: Reproduction des 102 Miniatures de Loyset Liédet (1470).* Bruxelles: Vromant, 1910.

Gibbs, M., and J. Lang. *Bishops and Reform, 1215–1272: With Special Refer-*

ence to the Lateran Council of 1215. London: Oxford University Press, 1934; reprint, 1962.

Gibson, G.M. *The Theatre of Devotion.* Chicago and London: University of Chicago Press, 1989.

Gillespie, V. 'Thy Will Be Done: *Piers Plowman* and the Pater Noster.' In *Late-Medieval Religious Texts and Their Transmission: Essays in Honour of A.I. Doyle.* ed. A.J. Minnis. Woodbridge: Brewer, 1994.

– 'Vernacular Books of Religion.' In *Book Production and Publishing in Britain, 1375–1475*, ed. J. Griffiths and D. Pearsall. Cambridge: Cambridge University Press, 1989.

Glausser, B. *The Scottish-English Linguistic Border: Lexical Aspects.* Bern: Francke, 1974.

Godefroy, F. *Dictionnaire de l'Ancienne Langue Française.* 10 vols. Paris: Vieweg, 1881–1902.

Goering, J. *William de Montibus (c. 1140–1213): The Schools and the Literature of Pastoral Care.* Toronto: Pontifical Institute of Mediaeval Studies, 1992.

Goff, F.R. *Incunabula in American Libraries.* New York: Bibliographical Society of America, 1964.

Goodich, M. *The Unmentionable Vice: Homosexuality in the Later Medieval Period.* Santa Barbara, Calif., and Oxford: ABC-Clio, 1979.

Gordon, J.B. 'The Articles of the Creed and the Apostles.' *Speculum* 40(1965): 634–40.

Grabes, H. *The Mutable Glass: Mirror-Imagery in Titles and Texts of the Middle Ages and English Renaissance.* Trans. G. Collier. Cambridge: Cambridge University Press, 1982.

Gransden, A. *Historical Writing in England.* Vol. 2, *c. 1307 to the Early Sixteenth Century.* Ithaca: Cornell University Press, 1982.

Gray, D. '"A Fulle Wyse Gentyl-Woman of Fraunce": *The Epistle of Othea* and Later Medieval English Literary Culture.' In *Medieval Women: Texts and Contexts in Late Medieval Britain.* Ed. J. Wogan-Browne, R. Voaden, A. Diamond, A. Hutchison, C.M. Meale, L. Johnson. Turnhout: Brepols, 2000.

Green, V.H.H. *Bishop Reginald Pecock.* Cambridge: Cambridge University Library, 1945.

Gregg, J.Y. *Devils, Women, and Jews.* Albany: State University of New York Press, 1997.

Griffiths, J. Review of *The Mirroure of the Worlde. Book Collector* 32(1983): 235–8.

Griffiths, J., and D. Pearsall. *Book Production and Publishing in Britain, 1375–1475.* Cambridge: Cambridge University Press, 1989.

Griffiths, R.A. *The Reign of King Henry VI.* Berkeley and Los Angeles: University of California Press, 1981.

Grunwald, K. 'Lombards, Cahorsins and Jews.' *Journal of European Economic History* 4(1975): 393–8.

Gy, P.-M. 'Les définitions de la confession après le quatrième concile du Latran.' In *L'Aveu: Antiquité et Moyen-Âge.* Rome: École Française de Rome, 1986.

Hackett, M.B. *The Original Statutes of Cambridge University: The Text and Its History.* Cambridge: Cambridge University Press, 1970.

Hain, L.F.T. *Repertorium Bibliographicum.* 2 vols. Stuttgart: Cotta, 1826–38.

Halliwell, J.O. *A Dictionary of Archaic and Provincial Words.* 2 vols. London: Smith, 1881.

Handover, P.M. *Printing in London.* London: George Allen & Unwin, 1960.

Hanna, R., III. 'Some Commonplaces of Late Medieval Patience Discussions: An Introduction.' In *The Triumph of Patience,* ed. G. J. Schiffhorst. Orlando: University Presses of Florida, 1978.

Harvey, I.M.W. *Jack Cade's Rebellion of 1450.* Oxford: Clarendon Press, 1991.

Hasler, C. *The Royal Arms: Its Graphic and Decorative Development.* London: Jupiter, 1980.

Hassall, A.G., and W.O. Hassall. *Treasures from the Bodleian Library.* New York: Columbia University Press, 1976.

Hassell, J.W., Jr. *Middle French Proverbs, Sentences, and Proverbial Phrases.* Subsidia Mediaevalia 12. Toronto: Pontifical Institute of Mediaeval Studies, 1982.

Hassig, D. *Medieval Bestiaries: Text, Image, Ideology.* Cambridge: Cambridge University Press, 1995.

Hauréau, B. 'Les Filles du Diable.' *Journal des Savants* (1884): 225–8.

– *Notices et Extraits de Quelques Manuscrits Latins de La Bibliothèque Nationale.* 6 vols. Paris: Klincksieck, 1890–3.

– 'Sermonnaires.' *Histoire Littéraire de la France* 26(1873): 387–468.

Heath, P. *Church and Realm, 1272–1461.* London: Fontana, 1988.

Henkel, N. *Studien zum Physiologus im Mittelalter.* Tübingen: Niemeyer, 1976.

Herbert, J.A., ed. *Catalogue of Romances in the Department of Manuscripts in the British Museum.* Vol. 3. London: British Museum, 1910.

Hobson, A.R.A. *Great Libraries.* London: Weidenfeld and Nicolson, 1970.

Holdsworth, W.S. *A History of English Law.* Vol. 4. London, Methuen, 1924.

Horrox, R., ed. *Fifteenth-Century Attitudes: Perceptions of Society in Late Medieval England.* Cambridge: Cambridge University Press, 1994.

Howard, D.R. *The Three Temptations: Medieval Man in Search of the World.* Princeton: Princeton University Press, 1966.

Huber, H. *Geist und Buchstabe der Sonntagsruhe.* Salzburg: Müller, 1957.

Hudson, A. *Lollards and their Books.* London and Ronceverte: Hambledon Press, 1985.

– *The Premature Reformation: Wycliffite Texts and Lollard History.* Oxford: Clarendon Press, 1988.

Hughes, G. *Swearing.* Oxford: Blackwell, 1991.

Hughes, J. *Pastors and Visionaries: Religion and Secular Life in Late Medieval Yorkshire.* Woodbridge: Boydell Press, 1988.

– 'Stephen Scrope and the Circle of Sir John Fastolf: Moral and Intellectual Outlooks.' In *The Ideals and Practice of Medieval Knighthood IV.* Woodbridge: Boydell Press, 1992.

Huguet, E. *Dictionnaire de la Langue Française du Seizième Siècle.* 7 vols. Paris: Didier, 1925–66.

Hunt, T. '"The Four Daughters of God": A Textual Contribution.' *Archives d'Histoire Doctrinale et Littéraire du Moyen Âge* 48(1981): 287–316.

Ibanès, J. *La Doctrine de l'Église et les Réalités Économiques au XIIIe Siècle.* Paris: Presses Universitaires de France, 1967.

Immaculate, M., Sr. 'The Four Daughters of God in the *Gesta Romanorum* and the *Court of Sapience.*' *Publications of the Modern Language Association of America* 57(1942): 951–65.

Jacob, E.F. *The Fifteenth Century, 1399–1485.* Oxford: Clarendon Press, 1961; reprint, 1993.

Johnson, A.H. *The History of the Worshipful Company of the Drapers of London.* 5 vols. Oxford: Clarendon Press, 1914–22.

Jolliffe, P.S. *A Check-List of Middle English Prose Writings of Guidance.* Toronto: Pontifical Institute of Mediaeval Studies, 1974.

Jones, C.M. 'The Conventional Saracen of the Songs of Geste.' *Speculum* 17(1942): 201–25.

Jones, P.M. 'British Library MS Sloane 76: A Translator's Holograph.' In *Medieval Book Production: Assessing the Evidence*, ed. L.L. Brownrigg. Los Altos Hills, Calif.: Anderson-Lovelace, 1990.

Jordan, R. *Handbuch der Mittelenglischen Grammatik.* Heidelberg: Winter, 1925.

Kaeppeli, T. *Scriptores Ordinis Praedicatorum Medii Aevi.* Vol. 3. Rome: ad S. Sabinae, 1980.

Kaiser, R. *Zur Geographie des mittelenglischen Wortschatzes.* Palaestra 205. Leipzig: Mayer & Müller, 1937.

Katzenellenbogen, A. *Allegories of the Virtues and Vices in Mediaeval Art, from Early Christian Times to the Thirteenth Century.* Trans. A.J.P. Orick. Studies of the Warburg Institute 10. London: Warburg Institute, 1939. Reprint. New York: Norton, 1964.

Keen, M. 'The End of the Hundred Years War: Lancastrian France and Lancastrian England.' In *England and Her Neighbors, 1066–1453. Essays in Honour of Pierre Chaplais*, ed. M. Jones and M. Vale. London: Hambledon, 1989.

– Review of *The Mirroure of the Worlde. Burlington Magazine* 124(1982): 311.

Kelly, F.M., and R. Schwabe. *A Short History of Costume & Armour.* Vol. 1, *1066–1485.* New York: B. Blom, 1968.

Kelly, J.N.D. *Early Christian Creeds.* 3d ed. London: Longman, 1972.

Kendrick, T.D. *British Antiquity.* London: Methuen, 1950.

Kihlbom, A. *A Contribution to the Study of Fifteenth Century English.* Uppsala: A.-B. Lundequistka Bokhandela, 1926.

Knowles, D. *The Religious Orders in England.* 3 vols. Cambridge: Cambridge University Press, 1950–59.

Knowles, R.B. 'The Manuscripts of the Most Honourable the Marquis of Bute, at Eccleston Square.' *Third Report of the Royal Commission on Historical Manuscripts.* Appendix. London: Published for Her Majesty's Stationery Office by Eyre & Spottiswoode, 1872.

Kosmer, E.V. 'Gardens of Virtue in the Middle Ages.' *Journal of the Warburg and Courtauld Institute* 41(1978): 302–7.

– 'The "noyous humoure of lecherie."' *Art Bulletin* 57(1975): 1–8.

– 'A Study of the Style and Iconography of a Thirteenth-Century *Somme le Roi* (British Museum MS Add. 54180) with a Consideration of Other Illustrated Somme MSS of the Thirteenth, Fourteenth and Fifteenth Centuries.' 2 pts. Unpublished doctoral dissertation, Yale University, 1973.

Kren, T., ed. *Renaissance Paintings in Manuscripts: Treasures from the British Library.* New York: Hudson Hills, 1983.

Kretzenbacher, L. *Die Seelenwaage.* Klagenfurt: Verlag des Landesmuseums für Kärnten, 1958.

Kristensson, G. *A Survey of Middle English Dialects, 1290–1350: The Six Northern Counties and Lincolnshire.* Lund, 1967.

Kuntsmann, J.G. 'The Bird That Fouls Its Nest.' *Southern Folklore Quarterly* 3(1939): 75–91.

Kurze, D. 'Die festländischen Lollarden.' *Archiv für Kulturgeschichte* 47(1965): 48–76.

Laing, M. 'Studies in the Dialect Material of Mediaeval Lincolnshire.' 2 vols. Unpublished doctoral dissertation, University of Edinburgh, 1978.

Långfors, M.A. *Les Incipits de poèmes français antérieurs au XVIe siècle.* Paris: Champion, 1941.

– 'Notice sur les manuscrits 535 de la Bibliothèque Municipale de Metz et 10047 des nouvelles acquisitions du fonds français de la Bibliothèque Nationale.' *Notices et Extraits des Manuscrits de la Bibliothèque Nationale* 42(1933): 139–291.

Langlois, C.V. *La Vie en France au moyen âge de la fin du XIIe au milieu du XIVe siècle.* Vol. 4, *La Vie spirituelle: Enseignements, méditations et controverses d'après des écrits en français à l'usage des laïcs.* Paris: Hachette, 1928.

Langlois, E. 'Notices des manuscrits français et provençaux de Rome antérieurs au XVIe siècle.' *Notices et Extraits des Manuscrits de la Bibliothèque Nationale et Autres Bibliothèques* 33:2(1890): 1–347.

Lass, R. 'Phonology and Morphology.' In *The Cambridge History of the English Language.* Vol. 2, *1066–1476.* Cambridge: Cambridge University Press, 1992.

Leader, D.R. *A History of the University of Cambridge.* Vol. 1, *The University to 1546.* Cambridge: Cambridge University Press, 1988.

Le Goff, J. 'Métier et Profession d'après les manuels de confesseurs au Moyen Âge.' *Miscellanea Mediaevalia* 3(1964): 44–60.

Lekai, L.J. *The Cistercians: Ideals and Reality.* Kent, Ohio: Kent State University Press, 1977.

Lerner, R.E. *The Heresy of the Free Spirit in the Later Middle Ages.* Berkeley: University of California Press, 1972.

Leroquais, V. *Les livres d'heures manuscrits de la Bibliothèque Nationale.* 3 vols. Paris: Imprimerie Nationale, 1927; Supplément, 1943.

Lescher, B. 'Laybrothers: Questions Then, Questions Now.' *Cistercian Studies* 23(1988): 63–85.

Lester, G.A. *Sir John Paston's 'Grete Boke.'* Woodbridge: Brewer, 1984.

Lindström, B. 'Four Middle English Passages.' *Studia Neophilologica* 46(1974): 151–8.

Logan, F.D. *Excommunication and the Secular Arm in Medieval England: A Study in Legal Procedure from the Thirteenth to the Sixteenth Century.* Toronto: Pontifical Institute of Mediaeval Studies, 1968.

Lottin, O. 'Les premières définitions et classifications des vertus au moyen âge.' *Revue des sciences philosophiques et théologiques* 18(1929): 369–407.

Lowes, J.L. 'Never Less Alone Than When Alone.' *Modern Language Notes* 25(1910): 96.

Luchaire, A. *Innocent III: Le Concile de Latran et la réforme de l'église.* 6 pts in 3 vols. Paris: Hachette, 1908. Reprint. Westmead: Gregg, 1969.

Lundquist, E.R. *La Mode et son Vocabulaire.* Göteborg: Wettergren und Kerber, 1950.

Lynch, J.H. *Godparents and Kinship in Early Medieval Europe.* Princeton: Princeton University Press, 1986.

MacCracken, H.N. 'Never Less Alone Than When Alone.' *Modern Language Notes* 25(1910): 28–9.

McCulloch, F. *Medieval Latin and French Bestiaries.* University of North Carolina Studies in Romance Languages and Literatures, 33. Rev. ed. Chapel Hill: University of North Carolina Press, 1962.

McCutchan, J.W. '"A Solempne And A Greet Fraternitee."' *Publications of the Modern Language Association of America* 74(1959): 313–17.

McFarlane, K.B. 'William Worcester: A Preliminary Survey.' In *Studies Presented to Sir Hilary Jenkinson*, ed. J.C. Conway. London: Oxford University Press, 1957.

McIntosh, A. 'The Analysis of Written Middle English.' *Transactions of the Philological Society* (1956):26–55.

– 'A New Approach to Middle English Dialectology.' *English Studies* 44(1963): 1–11.

– 'Present Indicative Plural Forms in the Later Middle English of the Northern Midlands.' In *Middle English Studies Presented to Norman Davis*, ed. D. Gray and E.G. Stanley. Oxford: Oxford University Press, 1983.

– 'Word Geography in the Lexicography of Medieval English.' *New York Academy of Sciences Annals* 211(1973): 55–66.

McIntosh, A., M.L. Samuels, and M. Benskin, eds. *A Linguistic Atlas of Late Mediaeval English.* 4 vols. Aberdeen: Aberdeen University Press, 1986.

McIntosh, A., M.L. Samuels, and Margaret Laing. *Middle English Dialectology.* Aberdeen: Aberdeen University Press, 1989.

McKenna, J.W. 'Popular Canonization As Political Propaganda: The Cult of Archbishop Scrope.' *Speculum* 45(1970): 608–23.

McLaughlin, T.P. 'The Teaching of the Canonists on Usury (XII, XIII, and XIV Centuries).' *Mediaeval Studies* 1(1939): 81–147; 2(1940): 1–22.

Madan, F., and H.H.E. Craster. *A Summary Catalogue of Western Manuscripts in the Bodleian Library at Oxford.* Vol. 2, pt i. Oxford: Clarendon Press, 1922.

Makowski, E.M. 'The Conjugal Debt and Medieval Canon Law.' *Journal of Medieval History* 3(1977): 99–114.

Mandonnet, P. 'Laurent d'Orléans, auteur de la Somme-le-Roi.' *Revue des langues romanes*, 6th ser., 6(1913): 20–3.

Les Manuscrits de la Reine de Suède au Vatican. Réédition du Catalogue de Montfaucon et Cotes Actuelles. Studi e Testi 238. Vatican City: Biblioteca Apostolica Vaticana, 1964.

Martin, H. *Catalogue des Manuscrits de la Bibliothèque de l'Arsenal.* Vol. 2. Paris: Plon, 1886.

Matthews, W. 'South Western Dialect in the Early Modern Period.' *Neophilologus* 24(1939): 193–209.

Meale, C. 'Patrons, Buyers and Owners: Book Production and Social Status.' In *Book Production and Publishing in Britain, 1375–1475*, ed. J. Griffiths and D. Pearsall. Cambridge: Cambridge University Press, 1989.

Meyer, P. 'Notice sur le manuscrit 27 de la Bibliothèque d'Alençon (Somme le Roi: Vie des saints, en prose).' *Bulletin de la Société des Anciens Textes Français* 18(1892): 68–93.

Meyer-Lübke, W. *Romanisches Etymologische Wörterbuch.* 5th ed. Heidelberg: Winter, 1972.

Michaud-Quantin, P. *Sommes de casuistique et manuels de confession au moyen âge (XII–XVI siècles).* Analeccta Mediaevalia Namurcensia 13. Louvain: Nauwelaerts, 1962.

Middle English Dictionary. Ed. H. Kurath, S.M. Kuhn, and R.E. Lewis. Ann Arbor: University of Michigan Press, 1956–.

Milroy, J. 'Middle English Dialectology.' In *The Cambridge History of the English Language.* Vol. 2, *1066–1476*, ed. N. Blake. Cambridge: Cambridge University Press, 1992.

– 'On the sociolinguistic history of /h/-dropping in English.' In *Current Topics in English Historical Linguistics*, ed. M. Davenport, E. Hansen, and H.-F. Nielsen. Chicago: University of Chicago Press, 1987.

Minnis, A.J. 'Late-Medieval Discussions of *Compilatio* and the Role of the Compilator.' *Beiträge zur Geschichte der deutschen Sprache und Literature* 101(1979): 385–421.

– *Medieval Theory of Authorship.* 2d ed. Philadelphia: University of Pennsylvania Press, 1988.

Moore, S. 'Patrons of Letters in Norfolk and Suffolk, c. 1450.' *Publications of the Modern Language Association of America* 27(1912): 188–207.

Moore, S., S.B. Meech, and H. Whitehall. 'Middle English Dialect Characteristics and Dialect Boundaries.' In *Essays and Studies in English and Comparative Literature* University of Michigan Publications: Language and Literature 13. Ann Arbor: University of Michigan Press, 1935.

Morawski, J. de. *Proverbes français antérieurs au XVe siècle.* Paris: Champion, 1925.

Mosher, J.A. *The Exemplum in the Early Religious and Didactic Literature of England.* New York: Columbia University Press, 1911.

Möske, B. *Caritas: Ihre figurative Darstellung in der englischen Literatur des 14. bis 16. Jahrhunderts.* Bonn: Bouvier Verlag, 1977.

Mt., A. 'Early Missal: Abp. Richard Scrope.' *Notes and Queries*, 2d ser., 1(1856): 489.

Mueller, J. *The Native Tongue and the Word: Developments in English Prose Style, 1380–1580.* Chicago and London: University of Chicago Press, 1984.

Munro, J.H. 'The Medieval Scarlet and the Economics of Sartorial Splendour.' In *Cloth and Clothing in Medieval Europe: Essays in Memory of Professor E.M. Carus-Wilson*, ed. N.B. Harte and K.G. Ponting. London: Heinemann, 1983.

Mustanoja, T.F. *A Middle English Syntax: Part I. Parts of Speech.* Mémoires de la Société Néophilologique de Helsinki 23. Helsinki: Société Néophilologique, 1960.

– 'Some Features of Syntax in Middle English Main Clauses.' In *Historical and Editorial Studies in Medieval and Early Modern English for Johan Gerritsen*, ed. M.-J. Arn and H. Wirtjes. Groningen: Wolters-Noordhoff, 1985.

Naetebus, G. *Die Nicht-Lyrischen Strofenformen des Altfranzösischen.* Leipzig: Hirzel, 1891.

Nelson, A. '"Chateaux en Espagne" dans le latin médiévale.' *Eranos* 49(1951): 159–69.

Nelson, B. *The Idea of Usury from Tribal Brotherhood to Universal Otherhood.* 2d ed. Chicago: Univerity of Chicago Press, 1969.

Nevanlinna, S. 'Background and History of the Parenthetic *As Who Say/ Saith* in Old and Middle English Literature.' *Neuphilologische Mitteilungen* 75(1974): 568–601.

Newhauser, R. *The Treatise on Vices and Virtues In Latin and the Vernacular.* Turnhout: Brepols, 1993.

Nichols, A.E. *Seeable Signs: The Iconography of the Seven Sacraments, 1350–1544.* Woodbridge: Boydell, 1994.

Noonan, J.T., Jr. *Contraception.* Cambridge, Mass.: Belknap Press, 1965.

– *The Scholastic Analysis of Usury.* Cambridge, Mass.: Harvard University Press, 1957.

O'Connor, M.C. *The Art of Dying Well: The Development of the Ars Moriendi.* New York: Columbia University Press, 1942.

O'Reilly, J. *Studies in the Iconography of the Virtues and Vices in the Middle Ages.* New York: Garland, 1988.

The Oxford Dictionary of English Proverbs. 3d ed. Rev. F.P. Wilson. Oxford: Clarendon Press, 1970.

Oxford English Dictionary. 2d ed. 20 vols. Oxford: Clarendon Press, 1989.

Owst, G.R. *Literature and Pulpit in Medieval Engand.* Cambridge: Cambridge University Press, 1933. Reprint. New York: Barnes and Noble, 1961.

– '*Sortilegium* in English Homiletic Literature of the Fourteenth Century.' In *Studies Presented to Sir Hilary Jenkinson,* ed. J.C. Conway. London: Oxford University Press, 1957.

Pächt, O. *Die Illuminierten Handschriften und Incubabeln der Österreischen Nationalbibliothek: Flämische Schule I.* Vienna: Verlag der Österreichischen Akademie der Wissenschaften, 1983.

Pächt, O., and J.J.G. Alexander. *Illuminated Manuscripts in the Bodleian Library, Oxford.* Vol. 1, *German, Dutch, Flemish, French, and Spanish Schools.* Oxford: Clarendon Press, 1966.

– *Illuminated Manuscripts in the Bodleian Library, Oxford.* Vol. 3, *British, Irish, and Icelandic Schools.* Oxford: Clarendon Press, 1973.

Pächt, O., and D. Thoss. *Die Illuminierten Handschriften und Incubabeln der Österreischen Nationalbibliothek: Flämische Schule II.* 2 pts. Vienna: Verlag der Österreichischen Akademie der Wissenschaften, 1990.

Pantin, W.A. *The English Church in the Fourteenth Century.* London: Cambridge University Press, 1955. Reprint. Notre Dame, Ind.: University of Notre Dame Press, 1962.

Parker, K.L. *The English Sabbath.* Cambridge: Cambridge University Press, 1988.

Parkes, M.B. *English Cursive Book Hands, 1250–1500.* Oxford Palaeographical Handbooks. Oxford: Clarendon Press, 1969. Reprint. Berkeley: University of California Press, 1980.

– 'The Influence of the Concepts of *Ordinatio* and *Compilatio* on the Development of the Book.' In *Medieval Learning and Literature: Essays Presented to Richard William Hunt,* ed. J.J.G. Alexander and M.T. Gibson. Oxford and New York: Clarendon Press, 1976.

– *Pause and Effect: An Introduction to the History of Punctuation in the West.* Aldershot, U.K.: Scolar Press, 1992.

Patrouch, J.F. *Reginald Pecock.* New York: Twayne, 1970.

Payen, J.C. 'La Pénitence dans le Contexte Culturel des XIIe et XIIIe Siècles.' *Revue des Sciences Philosophiques et Théologiques* 61(1977): 399–428.

Payer, P.J. *The Bridling of Desire: Views of Sex in the Later Middle Ages.* Toronto: University of Toronto Press, 1993.

– 'Early Medieval Regulations Concerning Marital Sexual Relations.' *Journal of Medieval History* 6(1980): 353–76.

– *Sex and the Penitentials.* Toronto: University of Toronto Press, 1984.
Pearsall, D., ed. *Manuscripts and Texts: Editorial Problems in Later Middle English Literature.* Cambridge: Brewer, 1987.
Pfander, H.G. 'Some Medieval Manuals of Religious Instruction in England.' *Journal of English and Germanic Philology* 35(1936): 243–58.
Piccard, G. *Wasserzeichen Fabeltiere Greif-Drache-Einhorn.* Findbuch 10. Stuttgart: Kohlhammer, 1980.
Pirenne, H. *Economic and Social History of Europe.* New York: Harcourt, Brace and World, 1937.
Plomer, R. 'The King's Printing House under the Stuarts.' *The Library,* n.s. 2(1901): 353–75.
Poerck, G. *La Draperie Médiévale en Flandre et en Artois.* 3 vols. Bruges: De Tempel, 1951.
Pollard, G. 'The Names of Some English Fifteenth-Century Binders.' *The Library,* 5th ser. 25(1970): 193–218.
Quacquarelli, A. *Il Triplice frutto della vita cristiana: 100, 60 e 30 (Matteo XIII-8, nelle diverse interpretazioni).* Rome: Coletti, 1953.
Quetif, J., and J. Echard. *Scriptores Ordinis Praedicatorum.* Vol. 1. Paris: Ballard & Smart, 1719.
Rachewitz, S. de. *De Serenibus.* New York and London: Garland, 1987.
Raymo, R.R. 'Works of Religious and Philosophical Instruction.' In *A Manual of the Writings in Middle English, 1050–1500,* ed. A.E. Hartung. New Haven: Connecticut Academy of Arts and Sciences, 1986.
Réau, L. *Iconographie de l'Art Chrétien.* 3 vols. Paris: Presses universitaires de France, 1955–58.
Reuter, O. 'Some Notes on the Origin of the Relative Combination *the which.*' *Neuphilologische Mitteilungen* 38(1937): 146–88.
Rézeau, P. *Répertoire d'Incipit des Prières Françaises à la Fin du Moyen Âge.* Paris: Droz, 1986.
Richardson, M. 'Henry V, the English Chancery, and Chancery English.' *Speculum* 55(1980): 726–50.
Richmond, C. *The Paston Family in the Fifteenth Century.* 2 vols. Cambridge: Cambridge University Press, 1990, 1996.
Rissanen, M. 'The Use of *One* and the Indefinite Article with Plural Names in English.' *Neuphilologische Mitteilungen* 73(1972): 340–52.
Rivière, J. *The Doctrine of the Atonement.* Trans. L. Cappadelta. 2 vols. London: Kegan Paul, Trench, Trübner, 1909.
Rojdestvensky, O. *Le culte de saint Michel et le moyen âge latin.* Paris: Picard, 1922.

Rordorf, W. *Sunday.* Philadelphia: Westminster Press, 1968.

Rosenthal, J.T. 'The Universities and the Medieval English Nobility.' *History of Education Quarterly* 9(1969): 415–37.

– *The Purchase of Paradise.* London: Routledge & Kegan Paul, 1972.

– *Patriarchy and Families of Privilege in Fifteenth-Century England.* Philadelphia: University of Pennsylvania Press, 1991.

Rouse, M.A., and R.H. Rouse. *Authentic Witnesses: Approaches to Medieval Texts and Manuscripts.* Notre Dame: University of Notre Dame Press, 1991.

Rowland, B. *Animals with Human Faces.* Knoxville: University of Tennessee Press, 1973.

– *Birds with Human Souls.* Knoxville: University of Tennessee Press, 1978.

Rowley, H.H. *Darius the Mede and the Four World Empires in the Book of Daniel.* Cardiff: University of Wales Press Board, 1964.

Rubin, M. *Corpus Christi: The Eucharist in Late Medieval Culture.* Cambridge: Cambridge University Press, 1991.

Rusconi, R. 'La confessione dei peccatori nelle "summae de casibus" e nei manuali per i confessori (metà XII – inizi XIV secolo).' In *L'Aveu: Antiquité et Moyen-Âge.* Rome: École Française de Rome, 1986.

– 'De la Prédication à la Confession: Transmission et Contrôle de Modèles de Comportement au XIIIe Siècle.' In *Faire Croire.* Rome: École Française de Rome, 1981.

Russell, H.G. 'Lollard Opposition to Oaths by Creature.' *American Historical Review* 51(1946): 668–84.

Samuels, M.L. *Linguistic Evolution.* Cambridge: Cambridge University Press, 1972.

– 'Some Applications of Middle English Dialectology.' *English Studies* 44(1963): 81–94.

Scattergood, [V.]J. 'Fashion and Morality in the Late Middle Ages.' In *England in the Fifteenth Century*, ed. D. Williams. Woodbridge: Boydell, 1987.

– *Politics and Poetry in the Fifteenth Century.* New York: Barnes and Noble, 1972.

Schmidt, M. 'Miroir.' In *Dictionnaire de Spiritualité.* Paris, 1980.

Scott, K.L. *The Caxton Master and His Patrons.* Cambridge Bibliographic Society Monograph 8. Cambridge: Cambridge Bibliographic Society, 1976.

– *Later Gothic Manuscripts, 1390–1490.* 2 vols. London: Harvey Miller, 1996.

– 'A Mid-Fifteenth-Century English Illuminating Shop and Its Customers.' *Journal of the Warburg and Courtauld Institutes* 31(1968): 170–96.

– *The Mirroure of the Worlde: MS Bodley 283 (England c.1470–1480). The Physical Composition Decoration and Illustration.* Oxford: Roxburghe Club, 1980.
– 'The Illustration and Decoration of the Register of the Fraternity of the Holy Trinity at Luton Church, 1475–1546. In *The English Medieval Book*, ed. A.S.G. Edwards, V. Gillespie, and R. Hanna. London: British Library, 2000.
Scott, K.L., gen. ed. An Index of Images in English Manuscripts from the Time of Chancer to Henry VIII c. 1380 – c. 1509. Bodleian Library, Oxford I. MSS Additional-Digby by A.E. Nichols, M.T. Orr, K.L. Scott, and L. Denrison. Turnhout: Harvey Miller, 2000.
[Scott], K.L. Smith. 'An Archaeological Analysis of MS Bodley 283, *The Mirroure of the Worlde*, Produced by a Publishing House of Vernacular Literature in Mid-Fifteenth Century England.' Unpublished doctoral dissertation, University of California, Berkeley, 1966.
Scott, M. *Late Gothic Europe, 1400–1500.* London: Mills & Boon; Atlantic Highlands, NJ: Humanities Press, 1980.
The Scottish National Dictionary. Ed. W. Grant and D.D. Murison. 10 vols. Edinburgh: Scottish National Dictionary Association, 1941–76.
Scrope, G.N.D.P. *History of the Manor and Ancient Barony of Castle Combe in the County of Wilts.* London: Printed by G.P. Scrope for private circulation, 1852.
Serra, F. 'Frère Lorens et Remigio Girolami.' *Atti dei Reale Accademia delle Scienze di Torino* 70(1934–35): 305–13.
Seymour, M.C., and colleagues. *Bartholomaeus Anglicus and His Encyclopedia.* Aldershot, U.K.: Variorum, 1992.
Sharpe, R.R., ed. *Calendar of Letter-Books of the City of London. Letter-Book L: Temp Edward IV – Henry VII.* London: Francis, 1912.
Shepard, O. *The Lore of the Unicorn.* London: George Allen & Unwin, 1930.
A Short-Title Catalogue of Books Printed in England, Scotland, and Ireland and of English Books Printed Abroad, 1475–1640. 2d ed. First compiled by A.W. Pollard and G.R. Redgrave. Rev. and enl. W.A. Jackson, F.S. Ferguson, and K.F. Pantzer. 3 vols. London: Bibliographical Society, 1976–91.
Sicard, G. 'L'usure en milieu rural: notes sur le bail à cheptel dans la doctrine de la fin du Moyen Âge.' In *Études d'Histoire du Droit Canonique Dédiées à Gabriel le Bras.* Vol. 2. Paris: Sirey, 1965.
Le Siècle d'Or de la Miniature Flamande le Mecenat de Philippe le Bon. Exposition Organisée à l'Occasion du 400e Anniversaire de la Fondation de la Bibliothèque Royale De Philippe II à Bruxelles, le 12 Avril 1559. Bruxelles: Palais des Beaux-Arts, 1959.

Sinclair, K.V. *Prières en ancien français*. Hamden: Greenwood, 1978. *Supplément*. Townsville, Australia: James Cook University of North Queensland, 1987.

Skidmore, M. *The Moral Traits of Christian and Saracen as Portrayed by the Chansons de Geste*. Colorado Springs: Dentan, 1935.

Smith, A. 'Aspects of the Career of Sir John Fastolf, 1380–1459.' Unpublished DPhil dissertation, Oxford University, 1982.

– 'Litigation and Politics: Sir John Fastolf's Defence of His English Property.' In *Property and Politics in Later Medieval English History*, ed. T. Pollard. Gloucester and New York: Sutton and St Martin's Press, 1984.

Smith, R.M. 'Three Obscure English Proverbs.' *Modern Language Notes* 65(1950): 441–7.

Sonet, J. *Répertoire d'Incipit de Prières en anciens français*. Société de Publications Romanes et Françaises 54. Geneva: Droz, 1956.

Sotheby Parke Bernet. Auction Catalogue. *Catalogue of the Bute Collection of Forty-Two Illuminated Manuscripts and Miniatures*. London: Sotheby Parke Bernet, 13 June 1983.

Spector, S., ed. *Essays in Paper Analysis*. Washington, D.C.: Folger Shakespeare Library, 1987.

Spufford, P. *Handbook of Medieval Exchange*. London: Royal Historical Society, 1986.

Stechow, W. 'Shooting at Father's Corpse.' *Art Bulletin* 24(1942): 213–15.

Stevens, M. 'The Towneley Plays Manuscript (HM1): *Compilatio* and *Ordinatio*.' *Text* 5(1991): 157–73.

Stevenson, A. 'Paper as Bibliographical Evidence.' *Library*, 5th ser. 17(1962): 197–212.

Stone, H. 'Cushioned Loan Words.' *Word* 9(1953): 12–15.

– 'Learned By-Forms in Middle-French Medical Terminology.' *Lingua* 4(1954): 81–8.

– 'Puzzling Translations in the Thirteenth Century: Multiple Equivalents in Early French Medical Terminology.' *Romance Notes* 10(1968): 174–9.

Storey, R.L. *The End of the House of Lancaster*. London: Barrie and Rockliff, 1966.

A Summary Catalogue of Western Manuscripts in the Bodleian Library at Oxford. Ed. F. Madan, H.H.E. Craster, and N. Denholm-Young. Oxford: Clarendon Press, 1922; reprint, 1937.

Sutton, A. 'Dress and Fashions c. 1470.' In *Daily Life in the Late Middle Ages*. Ed. R. Britnell Stroud, U.K.: Sutton, 1998.

Sutton, A.F., and L. Visser-Fuchs. 'Richard III's Books: XII. William Worcester's *Boke of Noblesse* and his Collection of Documents on the War in Normandy.' *Ricardian* 9(1991): 154–65.

Swain, J.W. 'The Theory of the Four Monarchies Opposition History under the Roman Empire.' *Classical Philology* 35(1940): 1–16.

Swanson, R.N., ed. *A Calendar of the Register of Richard Scrope, Archbishop of York, 1398–1405.* 2 pts. York: Borthwick Institute, 1981, 1985.

Tanner, N.P. *The Church in Late Medieval Norwich, 1370–1532.* vols. Toronto: Pontifical Institute of Mediaeval Studies, 1984.

Tatlock, J.S.P. 'Never Less Alone Than When Alone.' *Modern Language Notes* 34(1919): 441.

Tawney, R.H. *Religion and the Rise of Capitalism.* London: Murray, 1929.

Thomas, W. *Der Sonntag im frühen Mittelalter.* Göttingen: Bandenhoeck and Ruprecht, 1929.

Thompson, S. *Motif Index of Folk Literature.* Rev. and enl. 6 vols. Bloomington: Indiana University Press, 1955–58.

Thomson, J.A.F. *The Later Lollards, 1414–1520.* Oxford: Oxford University Press, 1965.

Tilley, M.P. *A Dictionary of the Proverbs in England in the Sixteenth and Seventeenth Centuries.* Ann Arbor: University of Michigan Press, 1950.

Tobler, A., and E. Lommatsch. *Altfranzösisches Wörterbuch.* Berlin: Weidmann, 1925–.

Torti, A. *The Glass of Form.* Cambridge: Brewer, 1991.

Toy, S. *A History of Fortification from 3000 B.C. to A.D. 1700.* London: Heinemann, 1955.

Traver, H. *The Four Daughters of God.* Bryn Mawr College Monographs 6. Bryn Mawr, Pa.: Bryn Mawr College, 1907.

Tsangadas, B.C.P. *The Fortifications and Defense of Constantinople.* East European Monographs 71. New York: Columbia University Press, 1980.

Tubach, F.C. *Index Exemplorum: A Handbook of Medieval Religious Tales.* Folklore Fellows Communications 204. Helsinki: Akademia Scientiarum Fennica, 1969.

Tudor-Craig, P. *Richard III.* National Portrait Gallery Exhibition Catalogue. No. 17 (entry by K.L. Scott). London: National Portrait Gallery, 1973.

Tuve, R. *Allegorical Imagery: Some Medieval Books and Their Posterity.* Princeton: Princeton University Press, 1966.

– 'Notes on the Virtues and Vices. Part I: Two Fifteenth-Century Lines of Dependence on the Thirteenth and Twelfth Centuries.' *Journal of the Warburg and Courtauld Institutes* 26(1963): 264–303.

– 'Notes on the Virtues and Vices, Part II: "Hely": Two Missing Notes in the Somme le Roi Illuminator; the Unicorn; "Sevens" in the Belleville Breviary and Some Psalters and Horae.' *Journal of the Warburg and Courtauld Institutes* 27(1964): 42–72.

Unwin, G. *The Guilds and Companies of London.* London: Methuen, 1908.

Vale, B.M. 'The Scropes of Bolton and of Masham, c. 1300–1450. A Study of a Northern Noble Family with a Calendar of the Scrope of Bolton Cartulary.' Unpublished doctoral dissertation, University of York, 1987.

Venn, J., and J.A. Venn. *Alumni Cantabrigienses*, pt 1, vol. 4. Cambridge: Cambridge University Press, 1927.

Vickers, K.H. *Humphrey Duke of Gloucester.* London: A. Constable, 1907.

Virgoe, R. 'Some Ancient Indictments on the King's Bench Referring to Kent, 1450–1452.' *Kent Records* 18(1964): 214–65.

Visser, F.T. *An Historical Syntax of the English Language.* 3 vols. Leiden: Brill, 1963–9.

Vodola, E. *Excommunication in the Middle Ages.* Berkeley: University of California Press, 1987.

Voigts, L.E. Review of *The Mirroure of the Worlde. Speculum* 59(1984): 413–16.

Wagner, A., N. Barker, and A. Payne. *Medieval Pageant Writhe's Garter Book: The Ceremony of the Bath and the Earldom of Salisbury Roll.* London: Roxburghe Club, 1993.

Waldron, R. 'The Manuscripts of Trevisa's Translation of the *Polychronicon*: Towards a New Edition.' *Modern Language Quarterly* 51(1990): 281–317.

Walker, S. 'Political Saints in Later Medieval England.' In *The McFarlane Legacy*, ed. R.H. Britnell and A.J. Pollard. New York: St Martin's Press, 1995.

Wallner, B. 'On the .i. Periphrasis in the N.Y. Chauliac.' *Neuphilologische Mitteilungen* 88(1987): 286–94.

Walther, H. *Proverbia sententiaeque Latinitatis medii aevi.* 6 vols. Göttingen: Vandenhoeck & Ruprecht, 1963–7.

Walton, P. 'Textiles.' In *English Medieval Industries: Craftsmen, Techniques, Products*, ed. J. Blair and N. Ramsey. London: Hambledon Press, 1991.

Wartburg, W.V. *Französische Etymologisches Wörterbuch.* Basel: Zbinden, 1944–57.

Watkins, O.D. *A History of Penance.* 2 vols. London and New York: Longmans, Green, 1920. Reprint. New York: B. Franklin, 1961.

Welter, J.T. *L'Exemplum dans la littérature religieuse et didactique du moyen âge.* Bibliothèque d'histoire ecclésiastique de France. Paris: Guitard, 1927.

Wenzel, S. 'The Continuing Life of William Peraldus's *Summa vitiorum.*' In *Ad Litteram: Authoritative Texts and Their Medieval Readers*, ed. M.D.

Jordan and K. Emery, Jr. Notre Dame Ind., and London: University of Notre Dame Press, 1992.

– 'The Seven Deadly Sins: Some Problems of Research.' *Speculum* 43(1968): 1–22.

– *The Sin of Sloth: Acedia in Medieval Thought and Literature.* Chapel Hill: University of North Carolina Press, 1967.

– 'Sloth in Middle English Devotional Literature.' *Anglia* 79(1961): 287–318.

– 'The Three Enemies of Man.' *Mediaeval Studies* 29(1967): 47–66.

Werner, J. *Lateinische Sprichwörter und Sinnspruche des Mittelalters.* Heidelberg: Carl Winter's Universitätsbuchhandlung, 1912.

Whitaker, E.E. 'Lacunae and the *Id Est* Brevigraph in Oxford, Bodleian Library, MS Bodley 283.' *Manuscripta* 36(1992): 191–9.

– 'Soissons MS 221: An Acephalous Somme le Roi / Miroir du Monde Containing Two Unrecorded Illustrations.' *Medium Aevum* 61(1991): 83–6.

Whiting, B.J., with H.W. Whiting. *Proverbs, Sentences, and Proverbial Phrases from English Writings Mainly before 1500.* Cambridge, Mass.: Harvard University Press, 1968.

Wieck, R.S. *Time Sanctified.* New York: Braziller, 1988.

Williams, D., ed. *England in the Fifteenth Century: Proceedings of the 1986 Harlaxton Symposium.* Woodbridge: Boydell, 1987.

Wolffe, B. *Henry VI.* London: Eyre Methuen, 1981.

Woodforde, C. 'A Medieval Campaign against Blasphemy.' *Downside Review* 55(1937): 357–62.

Workman, H.B. *John Wyclif.* 2 vols. Oxford: Clarendon Press, 1926.

Workman, S.K. *Fifteenth Century Translation as an Influence on English Prose.* Princeton Studies in English 18. Princeton: Princeton University Press, 1940. Reprint. New York: Octagon Books, 1972.

Wright, J.D., ed. *The English Dialect Dictionary.* 6 vols. London: Henry Frowde, 1898–1905.

Wylie, J.H. *Henry of England under Henry the Fourth.* Vol. 2, 1405–1406. London: Longmans, Green, 1894.

– *The Reign of Henry the Fifth.* 3 vols. Cambridge: Cambridge University Press, 1914–29.

Zangger, K. *Contribution à la terminologie des tissus en ancien français.* Bienne: Schüler, 1945.

Index of Names

The list is inclusive of all names with the exception of familiar and recurrent names of the deity (God, Criste, Iesus, Holy Goste) and Latin forms of names that are subsequently rendered in English (Augustinus/Austyn, Mare Rubeum/ Rede See, etc.). Emendations from MS B are indicated by an asterisk.

www.ingramcontent.com/pod-product-compliance
Lightning Source LLC
LaVergne TN
LVHW090756070826
844660LV00022B/1000

9781442657366